THE PILLARS OF GLOBAL LAW

In an increasingly interconnected world, progress in the areas of development, security and human rights must go hand in hand. There will be no development without security and no security without development. And both development and security also depend on respect for human rights and the rule of law. (Report of the Secretary-General, UN Doc. A/59/2005 (21 March 2005), Annex, para. 2)

This research project has been financed by the Italian Ministry of University and Research.

The Pillars of Global Law

GIULIANA ZICCARDI CAPALDO

Routledge
Taylor & Francis Group
LONDON AND NEW YORK

First published 2008 by Ashgate Publishing

2 Park Square, Milton Park, Abingdon, Oxfordshire OX14 4RN
711 Third Avenue, New York, NY 10017

Routledge is an imprint of the Taylor & Francis Group, an informa business

First issued in hardback 2018

British Library Cataloguing in Publication Data
Ziccardi Capaldo, Giuliana
The pillars of global law
1. International law 2. Globalization 3. International organization 4. Intervention (International law)
5. International cooperation
I. Title
341'.01

Library of Congress Cataloging-in-Publication Data
Ziccardi Capaldo, Giuliana.
The pillars of global law / by Giuliana Ziccardi Capaldo.
p. cm.
Includes bibliographical references and index.
ISBN 978-0-7546-7345-3
1. International law. 2. Globalization. 3. International organization. 4. Intervention (International law) 5. International cooperation. I. Title.

KZ1318.Z53 2008
341--dc22

2008004393

ISBN 13: 978-0-7546-7345-3 (hbk)
ISBN 13: 978-1-138-37649-6 (pbk)

To those who will play a role in shaping tomorrow's global world.

To my grandchildren, Federico Karol and Giuliana

Contents

Preface

This book aims to meet the pressing need – among international scholars, political scientists, legal practitioners, and students – for a systematic assessment of the changes taking place under the impact of globalization on the international community and its legal order; it describes how different constitutive processes of globalization transform key aspects of international society, its institutions and legal norms.

Fundamental shifts in the rules and structure of the classical international community highlight the 'public' dimension of international law, which is developing rules increasingly oriented towards a structuring process for a universal human society (i.e., global community), and the protection of common values and goods (such as world peace and security, fundamental rights of individuals and peoples, collective management of common human beings, etc.) accompanied by objective safeguard mechanisms and procedures. These changes raise the question of whether the evolution of the classical international legal system has produced a corpus of rules autonomous enough from inter-state law to be called 'Global Law'. This, in turn, raises the question of the distinctive features of this new body of laws.

These questions are not merely theoretical. For several years I have studied the evolution of the international order, starting from its origins and moving through a wide analysis of the relevant practices of states, international organizations, and other new actors, including an analysis of the case law of international courts and tribunals. This analysis addresses important key legal issues from the Westphalian period to the post-war period, and from the establishment of the UN to the present, in order to provide an overview of the new world order. The basic goal is to identify, from the great variety of international practices in political and jurisprudential contexts, a uniform set of legal rules and procedures designed to manage global interests and goods, established for the purpose of institutionalizing governance mechanisms and procedures, defining and allocating powers to the global level, and creating authorities or bodies exercising functions of a public nature.

Attention on international institutions (and their activities) undoubtedly predominates in my book and my selection of them as referentially appropriate was with a view to identifying those changes in international law which are indicators to the birth of global law. This is the result of a methodological choice that I believe provides a useful approach to problems that are intrinsically linked to the scope of my work, which is to focus particularly on 'structural' changes and key features brought about by the impact of the globalization on 'inter-state' international law. The aim of my research is made even more evident by the book's title which employs the word 'pillars' in its most denotative sense, referring to the fact that this investigation is directed at the 'structural' aspects of emerging global law, rather than to substantive ones.

Interest in the structural profile derives from the fact that most internationalists have made important contributions to changes that have occurred through the effect of globalization in various areas of substantive international law (human rights, world peace, world health, commons protection, etc.). Conversely, the structural profile and features of the growing global community and new world legal order has barely been touched on and no specific, systematic study exists.

My investigation is especially based on the decisions of international bodies with a supranational nature (Security Council, General Assembly, WTO panels, International Court of Justice and other international courts, etc.). Certainly, I am well aware that there are other centers of international power apart from international institutions: many important international and transnational normative regimes are not found in international institutions, but in more informal law-making promulgated by international arbitral panels, networks of regulatory entities, or non-state accreditation and standard-setting bodies; just as it is true that various forces of globalism also contribute to mechanisms of global governance. It makes today's international legal framework more complex because there are many centers of international power and influence, and powerful new forces; that is why my analysis focuses on new integrated procedures and mechanisms of shared governance between States, international organizations and the global NGO community acting jointly with a supranational authority. Already the substantial international community has developed mechanisms of integration with the organized international community and, above all, the United Nations, and other forces of globalism in the areas of human rights, international criminal law and international environmental law.

These new forces of international power, however, do not yet have a well established role at a general level and on the decision-making processes which the present book examines (i.e., global constitutive processes and basic constitutional principles). I myself complain in my book about their exclusion and marginalization within international world bodies and hope that more weight will be given to them in those forums where nowadays the power of world decision-making resides.

The changes I detail (summarized in the annexed Tables) have been considered with reference to three phases that characterise the evolution of the international order towards a law for a global community: (1) the Westphalian phase (see Table 1 *infra*); (2) the post-Westphalian phase (see Table 2 *infra*); and (3) the post-UN Charter phase, characterised by globalization (see Table 3 *infra*).

In considering these three periods, changes in the international legal order may be said to have taken place as a result of the interplay of five variables in the international community:

1. the enhancement of international functions;
2. the expansion of the social base;
3. the legality of norms depending on their substantive content and their role in structuring the principles and practices of a public nature;
4. the development of interaction between legal systems regional, national, and international; and
5. the promotion of collective guarantees.

On the basis of these variables, today's international legal order presents the following distinctive features compared to prior phases of the international order (see Tables 4, 5, 6 *infra*).

1. *A (re)organization of power structures and authority*. The classical, unorganized international community is progressively moving towards becoming a more organized entity, vertically structured, due to the increasing institutionalization of law-making, law enforcement, and judicial processes; the proliferation of international courts and tribunals; the increasing authority of international bodies, and the development of democratic forms of participation in the decision-making process for various new actors. A wide range of new law-making processes and enforcement mechanisms results in integrated procedures more rapid as compared to customary procedure and more informal as regards UN Chapter VII enforcement system, working to overturn the veto rule.
2. *An expansion of the social base and the development of constitutional principles*. The transformation of international law from mere inter-state law to the law of universal human society, in which the range of legal subjects increasingly includes not only states but also individuals and new players. Constitutional norms and legal principles protecting public values and goods have been established at an international level, together with the fundamental rights of individuals and of peoples; these supreme principles, which are 'public' in character, complement the 'private' norms that protect the interests of individual states and relations between them.
3. *A development of integration processes between legal systems*. Domestic law is increasingly adapting to international law through regional integration, the harmonization of legislation, and by means of standard conventions.
4. *A consolidation of collective guarantees*. New mechanisms, inspired by the principle of collective enforcement, have been established for the objective enforcement of the above-mentioned supreme constitutional principles, by setting up new international tribunals and forms of judicial control and introducing new sanctions regimes, suitable to function against states, entities, groups and individuals.

It follows that globalization has changed not only the law but also international decision-making processes, enforcement strategies and the interactions between the international legal system and legal systems at other levels (regional and domestic). On the basis of these findings, I have identified the key elements of the global legal system which I have termed the 'pillars' of global law, i.e., verticality of decision-making processes; legality and safeguarding of common values and goods; integration between legal systems and processes; development of forms of collective guarantees. What I am arguing for is also that States have agreed on a set of legal rules and procedures and an operating organization which is based on that set of rules to collectively deal with public needs. Thus, this book aims to explicate the existence of an autonomous legal system: using a systemic approach, it strives to present the foundations of this emerging law for the global community – what I will call 'Global Law'.

The book is organized into four Parts, reflecting the four pillars outlined above, dealing with the ways in which the decision-making processes of the global legal system and fundamental functions of the global community are carried out/performed (law-making; law-enforcement; judicial functions); the features peculiar to the system, both the fairness/legality and the law-integration; and the construction of an embryonic system of collective guarantees.

Accordingly, the global legal system is described by examining:

Part I – Verticality and sharing of the decisional processes
Part II – Legality principles and common global values
Part III – Integration of legal systems in the direction of global law
Part IV – Collective guarantees: an embryonic new system.

Therefore, the first part deals with constitutive processes of social organization such as hierarchy, authority, allocation of powers, and functions, through an analysis of the mechanisms of joint governance and processes of multilateral authoritative decision-making; it is devoted to the three above-mentioned functions, in which more and more international institutions are taking part, thus fostering the development of a supranational system of governance and the verticalization of international power (Part I, Chapters 1–3).

There then follow two parts describing the main characteristics of the emerging global law system. One of them describes the increasing legality of a system which overturns the 'private' nature of inter-state law by shifting the centre of gravity from the State towards Humanity and to future generations, and safeguarding the basic right of Man as well as universal values, to the detriment of the sovereignty of the States that are restricted through principles of legality. Legality, a cornerstone of the new global law, is compared with the principle of effectivity, a cornerstone of the classical international system that has been eroded by the rise of legality, yet remains ready to re-emerge (Part II, Chapter 4). The other part addresses the growing harmonization between domestic and international legal systems, describing the process of integration between legal systems, achieved through the subordination of national law to norms laid down by international organizations, regional and universal. The emphasis here is on the rules and principles that ensure an effective and uniform application of international law in state legal systems in the move towards the construction of a global law. I describe an integrated structure of global legal order and its organization into concentric circles within which the various legal systems (national, sub-regional, regional, international), ordered hierarchically and subordinated between themselves, are dominated by the system of the UN Charter; all of which, in turn, is subject to the supreme principles of global law (*jus cogens*). The verticality of the global system poses problems of coordination between various different legal systems and this leads to the necessity to focus on the relationship between them (Part III, Chapter 5).

The final part underlines the passage from self-protection to heteronomous processes for the protection of global fundamental values and contains a reconstruction of a new collective guarantee system: procedures and integrated mechanisms of safeguard which seek to adapt to the needs and characteristics of the non-state actors following the broadening of the social base to accommodate the new actors (Part IV, Chapters 6–9).

In conclusion, I argue that today's international legal order is developing into a truly global system of law. I certainly do not mean to say that it has already been structured, much less disavow the importance that 'inter-state' international law has had and will continue to have. In my vision of a world law system, the sphere of legal relationships established between states comes within the field of what in internal law is 'private' law, whilst emerging 'global law' represents the 'public' dimension of the world legal system, establishing a new juridical organization of the world.

The book is complemented by six Tables in the annex that provide an overview of the development of international law in the three stages of development from the Congress of Westphalia in 1648 to the present. Two tables supplement the text and facilitate reading; the other four summarize in systematic form the topics under discussion and the features of a global legal system.

This book draws on more than 25 years of analysis of the transformation of the international community and its legal system. It arises from the thesis of the 'verticalization' of the international community, which I first outlined in 1977[1] and developed further in a number of later studies. This thesis, moreover, has been largely confirmed by recent developments in international practice and the rise of globalization. International integrated processes of decision making based upon this concept have become concrete and formal.

Some of the chapters in this book, previously published as articles, have been carefully updated and further developed to produce this volume (Oceana Publications and Harvard International Law Journal granted the permission to their use); the date and the place of publication are identified in a note. However, the present book attempts a new and difficult task: to outline the general framework of the new body of norms regulating global society and the world order. Therefore, in addition, previously unpublished essays are included here in line with the basic goals of this study. Because the ideas contained in these papers have been developed and refined over time, the reader might encounter some of them more than once. I apologize, in advance, for this occurrence.

Among those who supported the project, I am extremely grateful to M. Cherif Bassiouni, Professor of Law at the DePaul University College of Law in Chicago. Steven Becker and Gilbert Lenz, also of the DePaul University College of Law, made helpful comments and editorial revisions. For that I would like to express my appreciation. A group of researchers in the Ph.D. program at the University of Salerno, including Anna Oriolo and Michele Nino, also contributed to the production of this book by providing editorial assistance in preparing the manuscript for publication, and I shall always be grateful to them for their support. Finally, special thanks to my son Antonio, who provided support and encouragement for

1 Giuliana Ziccardi Capaldo, Le Situazioni Territoriali Illegittime nel Diritto Internazionale/Unlawful Territorial Situations in International Law (1977) (Summary in English).

this project and with whom I discussed the processes and dynamics of globalization in a more comprehensive, socio-economical perspective. Remaining errors are my responsibility.

Giuliana Ziccardi Capaldo

List of Abbreviations

CFIEC	Court of First Instance of the European Communities
CSCE	Conference on Security and Cooperation in Europe
ECHR	European Court of Human Rights
ECJ	Court of Justice of the European Communities
ECOWAS	Economic Community of Western African States
ICJ	International Court of Justice
ICSID	International Centre for Settlement of Investment Disputes
ICTY	International Criminal Tribunal for the former Yugoslavia
ILC	International Law Commission
KFOR	Kosovo Forces (NATO)
OACI	Organisation de l'Aviation Civile Internationale
OAS	Organization of African States
OCHCR	Office of the High Commissioner for Human Rights
OMPI	Organisation des Modjahedines du Peuple d'Iran
OSCE	Organization for Security and Cooperation in Europe
PCIJ	Permanent Court of International Justice
UNAT	United Nations Administrative Tribunal
UNCLOS	United Nations Convention on the Law of the Sea
UNIFIL	United Nations Interim Force in Lebanon
UNITA	União Nacional para a Indepência Total de Angola
UNMIK	United Nations Interim Administration Mission in Kosovo
WEU	Western European Union
WTO	World Trade Organization

International Law Journals

AM. J. INT'L.L.	American Journal of International Law
ANN. FR. D.I.	Annuaire Français de Droit International
BYIL	British Yearbook of International Law
CASE W. RES. J. INT'L L .	Case Western Reserve Journal of International Law
DENVER J. INT'L L. & POL'Y	The Denver Journal of International Law & Policy
EMORY INT'L L. REV.	Emory International Law Review
EUR. J. INT'L L.	European Journal of International Law
FORDHAM INT'L L.J.	Fordham International Law Journal
GCYILJ	The Global Community. Yearbook of International Law and Jurisprudence (G. Ziccardi Capaldo ed., Oceana Publications/ Oxford University Press, New York)
HARV. ENV. L . REV.	The Harvard Environmental Law Review
HARV. INT'L L.J.	Harvard International Law Journal
IND. J. GLOBAL LEGAL STUD.	Indiana Journal of Global Legal Studies
INT'L & COMP. L.Q.	International & Comparative Law Quarterly
INT'L LEGAL MAT.	International Legal Materials
LJIL	Leiden Journal of International Law
N.Y.U. J. INT'L L. & POL.	New York University Journal of International Law & Politics
NETH. INT'L L. REV.	Netherlands International Law Review
OR. L. REV.	Oregon Law Review
REV. BELGE D.I.	Revue Belge de Droit International
REV. GEN. D.I.P.	Revue Générale de Droit International Public
REV. HELL. D.I.	Revue Hellénique de Droit International
ST. LOUIS U. L. J.	Saint Louis University Law Journal
TEX. INT'L L .J	Texas International Law Journal
U. COLO. L. REV.	University of Colorado Law Review
U. KAN. L. REV.	University of Kansas Law Review
VA. J. INT'L L.	Virginia Journal of International Law
VAND. J. TRANSNAT'L L.	Vanderbilt Journal of Transnational Law
Y. INT'L L. COMM.	Yearbook of International Law Commission

Introduction

The Four Pillars of Global Law: Verticality, Legality, Integration, and Collective Guarantees*

Since the end of World War II, with the creation of the United Nations, the rules and structure of the traditional inter-state community have been changing. International law is increasingly shifting its focus from the state to the individual. It gradually lost the features of the classical era, placing greater emphasis on individuals, peoples, human beings as a whole, humanity, and future generations.[1] State sovereignty has been redefined by developments in the field of the safeguard of human rights, peoples' law, the 'human' environment, the common heritage of mankind, the cultural heritage, sustainable development and international trade. New norms protect the universal community's interests.[2] New actors, other than states, are emerging on the international scene.[3] New international norms allow individuals, groups of individuals, corporations, and non-governmental organizations to bring claims before international jurisdictions.[4]

---

* This chapter is based on the paper by Giuliana Ziccardi Capaldo, *A New Dimension of International Law: The Global Law*, Editor's Introduction, Forum: The Case for Global Law: Is Global Law True Law?, 5 The Global Community Yearbook of International Law and Jurisprudence [hereinafter GCYILJ], xvi (2005–I). That early text has been updated and modified. The changes to international law I detail therein have been summarized in Table 3.

1 Giuliana Ziccardi Capaldo, *Editorial*, 1 GCYILJ xix (2001).

2 Dissenting opinion of Judge Jessup, South West Africa, Second Phase, 1966 ICJ Reports 6 (July 18, 1966); Giuliana Ziccardi Capaldo, Le Situazioni Territoriali Illegittime nel Diritto Internazionale/Unlawful Territorial Situations in International Law (1977); Prosper Weil, *Towards Relative Normativity in International Law*?, 77 American Journal of International Law 413 (1983) [hereinafter Am. J. Int'l. L.]; Oscar Schachter, *Philip Jessup's Life and Ideas*, 80 Am. J. Int. L. 878 (1986); Bruno Simma, *From Bilateralism to Community Interest in International Law*, 250 Recueil des Cours 221, 233 (1994–VI); Mohamed Shahabuddeen, *The Evolution of the Global Legal Framework*, *in* 1 Boutros Boutros-Ghali Amicorum Discipulorumque Liber 701 (1998).

3 Rainer Hofmann, Non-State Actors as New Subjects of International Law, International Law – From the Traditional State Order Towards the Law of the Global Community. Proceedings of an International Symposium of the Kiel Walther-Schücking-Institute of International Law, March 25 to 28, 1998 (1999).

4 See generally Francisco Orrego Vicuña, *International Dispute Settlement in an Evolving Global Society, Constitutionalization, Accessibility, Privatisation*, Hersch Lauterpacht Memorial Lectures 23 (2004). For the individual access to regional Courts of human rights see Antônio Augusto Cançado Trindade, *El Nuevo Reglamento de la Corte Interamericana de*

Structurally, we are witnessing an ongoing and gradual 'verticalization' of power.[5] The international society has been creating objective rules and procedures to safeguard interests and values of humanity as a whole. Judicial organs and institutionalized procedures to monitor states' activities have been established. In recent years, there has been a proliferation of international courts and tribunals[6]

Derechos Humanos (2001), 30/31 INTER-AMERICAN INSTITUTE OF HUMAN RIGHTS: REVISTA IIDH 45 (2001); for the Iran–United States Claims Tribunal, see Charles N. Brower, *The Iran–United States Claims Tribunal*, 224 RECUEIL DES COURS 123 (1990–V); David D. Caron, *The Nature of the Iran–US Claims Tribunal and the Evolving Structure of International Dispute Resolution*, 84 AM. J. INT.'L. L. 104 (1990) and, for the activities of the Tribunal in the years 2001–2004, see Mirta Fava, *Iran–U.S. Claims Tribunal, Introductory Note*, 1 GCYILJ 2001, 741 (2001); Mohsen Aghahosseini & Hossein Piran, *Iran–U.S. Claims Tribunal, Introductory Note*, GCYILJ 1597 (2006–II); *Id.*, 1435 (2006–II); *Id.* 1787 (2007–II). For the Convention on the Settlement of Investment Disputes between States and Nationals of Other States, 18 March 1965 (575 UNTS 159; 4 INTERNATIONAL LEGAL MATERIALS 532 (1965)) [hereinafter INT'L LEGAL MAT.], see, among others, Aron Broches, *The Convention on the Settlement of Investment Disputes between States and Nationals of Other States*, 136 RECUEIL DES COURS 331 (1972–II); Andrea Giardina, *The International Center for Settlement of Investment Disputes between States and Nationals of Other States*, *in* ESSAYS ON INTERNATIONAL COMMERCIAL ARBITRATION 214 (Petar Šarčević ed., 1989); for the activity of the International Centre for Settlement of Investment Disputes (ICSID), see August Reinisch, *ICSID, Introductory Note,* GCYILJ 1653 (2005–II); *Id.*, 1449 (2006–II); *Id.*, 1779 (2007–II). On the debate dealing with *locus standi in judicio* of international organizations, see INTERNATIONAL ORGANIZATIONS AND INTERNATIONAL DISPUTE SETTLEMENT (Laurence Boisson de Chazournes, Cesare Romano & Ruth Mackenzie eds, 2002); Mohammed Bedjaoui, *Les Organizations Internationales Devant la Cour Internationale de Justice*: *Bilan et Perspectives*, GAOR 49th sess. (Oct. 24, 1994). See also David Weissbrodt, *The Contribution of International Nongovernmental Organizations to the Protection of Human Rights*, *in* HUMAN RIGHTS IN INTERNATIONAL LAW: LEGAL AND POLICY ISSUES 403 (Theodor Meron ed., 1984).

5 See *infra*, note 39 *et seq*. and corresponding text.

6 See JOHN MERRILLS, INTERNATIONAL DISPUTE SETTLEMENT (2nd ed., 1991); Sir Robert Jennings, *The Proliferation of Adjudicatory Bodies: Dangers and Possible Answers*, *in* IMPLICATIONS OF THE PROLIFERATION OF INTERNATIONAL ADJUDICATORY BODIES FOR DISPUTE RESOLUTION, AMERICAN SOCIETY OF INTERNATIONAL LAW BULLETIN No. 9, 2 (Laurence Boisson de Charzournes ed., 1995); Hugh Thirlway, *The Proliferation of International Judicial Organ: Institutional and Substantive Questions – The International Court of Justice and Other International Courts*, *in* PROLIFERATION OF INTERNATIONAL ORGANIZATIONS: LEGAL ISSUES 251 (Niels M. Blokker & Henry G. Schermers eds, 2001) [hereinafter PROLIFERATION OF INTERNATIONAL ORGANIZATIONS]; Gilbert Guillaume, *The Future of International Judicial Institutions*, 44 INTERNATIONAL & COMPARATIVE LAW QUARTERLY 848 (1995) [hereinafter INT'L & COMP. L.Q.]; ERNST-ULRICH PETERSMANN, THE GATT/WTO DISPUTE SETTLEMENT SYSTEM: INTERNATIONAL LAW, INTERNATIONAL ORGANIZATION AND DISPUTE SETTLEMENT (1997); MANUAL ON INTERNATIONAL COURTS AND TRIBUNALS (Philippe Sands, Ruth Mackenzie & Yuval Shany eds, 1999); TULLIO TREVES, LE CONTROVERSIE INTERNAZIONALI. NUOVE TENDENZE, NUOVI TRIBUNALI (1999); Florentino Feliciano & Peter L.H. Van den Bossche, *The Dispute Settlement System of the World Trade Organization: Institutions, Processes and Practice*, *in* PROLIFERATION OF INTERNATIONAL ORGANIZATIONS, *supra* at 207; Antonio Tizzano, *La Cour de Justice après Nice:*

and, in general, of mechanisms and compliance control procedures[7] which, from their position of authority, ensure respect of norms (customary and treaty-based).[8] International organizations – in particular those of a universal character – partake in the management of international power by carrying out 'some' general functions in several areas of law. The erosion of states' sovereignty is giving way to the global community and a new international power structure[9] based on multilateral decisional processes aimed at protecting fundamental interests and global values.

These changes raise the question of whether the birth of the universal community gave rise to a new set of international norms, and whether these norms amount to a system coherent enough to be called 'Global Law'. This begs the question of whether this new body of laws is different and distinguishable from traditional international law (inter-state law), and what its distinctive features are.

Our analysis takes place within the context of the fundamental doctrinal and political debate of our days: the question of the extent to which the world has been reshaped by globalization, to use David Held and Anthony McGrew's expression.[10] Accordingly, we aim to analyse the impact of global forces and processes on international law.

It is this book's thesis that globalization caused changes not only to the law but also to the international decisional processes and the way the global legal system interacts with other systems at different levels (inter-state, regional, and domestic). Scholars studied the impact of globalization in some specific fields: human rights,[11] the

---

Le Transfert de Compétences au Tribunal de Première Instance, 4 Revue du Droit de l'Union Européenne 665 (2002), at 670.

7 See, for instance, Manfred Nowak, *Human Rights in EU and EEA Law, in* International Human Rights Monitoring Mechanisms: Essays in Honour of Jakob Th. Möller (Gudmundur Alfredsson, Jonas Grimheden, Bertram G. Ramcharan & Alfred de Zayas eds, 2001).

8 Lori Fisler Damrosch, *The Permanent Five as Enforcers of Controls on Weapons of Mass Destruction*, 13 European Journal of International Law 305 (2002) [hereinafter Eur. J. Int'l L.].

9 Philip Alston, *The Myopia of the Handmaidens: International Lawyers and Globalization*, 8 Eur. J. Int'l L. 435 (1997).

10 David Held & Anthony McGrew, Globalization/Anti-Globalization 7 (2002).

11 See Christian Tomuschat, *Human Rights in a World-Wide Framework. Some Current Issues*, 45 Zeitschrift für Auslandisches Offentliches Recht und Völkerrecht 547 (1985); Human Rights in the World Community: Issues and Action (Richard P. Claude & Burns H. Weston eds, 1992); Paul Tavernier, Nouvel Ordre Mondial et Droits de l'Homme. La Guerre du Golfe (1993); René Foqué, *Global Governance and the Rule of Law, Human Rights and General Principles of Good Global Governance, in* International Law: Theory and Practice. Essays in Honour of Eric Suy, 691, 702 (Karel Wellens ed., 1998); Ramesh C. Thakur, *Global Norms and International Humanitarian Law, an Asian Perspective*, 83 Revue Internationale de la Croix Rouge 19 (2001); Tom Hadden & Colin Harvey, Local Conflict, Global Intervention, a Handbook of Human Rights, Armed Conflict and Refugee Law (2003); Theodor Meron, The Humanization of International Law (2006).

'worldwide/cosmopolitan' democracy,[12] economy,[13] trade,[14] health,[15] environment,[16] social rights,[17] etc. They expounded in detail several of the underlying themes of

---

12 RICHARD FALK, ON HUMANE GOVERNANCE: TOWARD A NEW GLOBAL POLITICS; THE WORLD ORDER MODELS PROJECT REPORT OF THE GLOBAL CIVILIZATION INITIATIVE (1995); DAVID HELD, DEMOCRACY AND THE GLOBAL ORDER: FROM THE MODERN STATE TO COSMOPOLITAN GOVERNANCE (1995); David Beetham, *Human Rights as a Model for Cosmopolitan Democracy*, *in* RE-IMAGINING POLITICAL COMMUNITY: STUDIES IN COSMOPOLITAN DEMOCRACY 58 (Daniele Archibugi, David Held & Martin Köhler eds, 1998) [hereinafter RE-IMAGINING POLITICAL COMMUNITY]; Giuliana Ziccardi Capaldo, *Democratizzazione all'Est e Diritto Internazionale Generale, in* DEMOCRATIZZAZIONE ALL'EST E DIRITTO INTERNAZIONALE 27 (Giuliana Ziccardi Capaldo ed., 1998).

13 Daniel K. Tarullo, *Law and Governance in a Global Economy*, 93 PROCEEDINGS OF THE ANNUAL MEETING OF THE AMERICAN SOCIETY OF INTERNATIONAL LAW 105 (1999); THOMAS COTTIER, STUDIES IN GLOBAL ECONOMIC LAW/STUDIEN ZUM GLOBALEN WIRTSCHAFTSRECHT/ETUDES EN DROIT ECONOMIQUE MONDIAL (1999); JOHN H. DUNNING, MULTINATIONAL ENTERPRISES AND THE GLOBAL ECONOMY (1993); CLAIRE A. CUTLER, PRIVATE POWER AND GLOBAL AUTHORITY: TRANSNATIONAL MERCHANT LAW IN THE GLOBAL POLITICAL ECONOMY (2003); BENJAMIN J. COHEN, THE FUTURE OF MONEY (2004).

14 Alicia Morris Groos, *International Trade and Development: Exploring the Impact of Fair Trade Organizations in the Global Economy and the Law*, 34 TEXAS INTERNATIONAL LAW JOURNAL 379 (1999) [hereinafter TEX. INT'L L.J.]; RAMON J. JEFFERY, THE IMPACT OF STATE SOVEREIGNTY ON GLOBAL TRADE AND INTERNATIONAL TAXATION (1999); John H. Jackson, *The Perils of Globalization and the World Trading System*, 24 FORDHAM INTERNATIONAL LAW JOURNAL 371 (2000) [hereinafter FORDHAM INT'L L.J.]; STEVE CHARNOVITZ, TRADE LAW AND GLOBAL GOVERNANCE (2002); Olu Fasan, *Global Trade Law: Challenges and Options for Africa*, 47 JOURNAL OF AFRICAN LAW 143 (2003).

15 John D. Blum, *The Role of Law in Global E-Health, a Tool for Development and Equity in a Digitally Divided World*, 46 SAINT LOUIS UNIVERSITY LAW JOURNAL 85 (2002) [hereinafter ST. LOUIS U. L.J.]; David P. Fidler, *International Law and Global Health*, 48 UNIVERSITY OF KANSAS LAW REVIEW 1 (1999) [hereinafter U. KAN. L. REV.]; RAJENDRA KUMAR NAYAK, GLOBAL HEALTH LAW (1998); Allyn L. Taylor, *Global Governance, International Health Law and WHO, Looking Towards the Future*, 80 BULLETIN OF THE WORLD HEALTH ORGANIZATION 975 (2002).

16 CHRISTOPHER D. STONE, THE GNAT IS OLDER THAN MAN: GLOBAL ENVIRONMENT AND HUMAN AGENDA (1993); GREENING INTERNATIONAL LAW (Philippe Sands ed., 1993); Jeffrey L. Dunoff, *From Green to Global, Toward the Transformation of International Environmental Law*, 19 THE HARVARD ENVIRONMENTAL LAW REVIEW 241 (1995) [hereinafter HARV. ENV. L. REV.]; Roberta M. Fay, *Citizen's Arrest: International Environmental Law and Global Climate Change*, 14 GLENDALE LAW REVIEW 73 (1995); Malgosia A. Fitzmaurice, *Liability for Environmental Damage Caused to the Global Commons*, 5 REVIEW OF EUROPEAN COMMUNITY & INTERNATIONAL ENVIRONMENTAL LAW 305 (1996); Richard J. Mac Laughlin, *Sovereignty, Utility, and Fairness: Using U.S. Takings Law to Guide the Evolving Utilitarian Balancing Approach to Global Environmental Disputes in the WTO*, 78 OREGON LAW REVIEW 855 (1999) [hereinafter OR. L. REV.].

17 SILVANA SCIARRA, HOW 'GLOBAL' IS LABOUR LAW?, THE PERSPECTIVE OF SOCIAL RIGHTS IN THE EUROPEAN UNION (1996); Harry W. Arthurs, *The Collective Labour Law of a Global Economy*, *in* LABOUR LAW AND INDUSTRIAL RELATIONS AT THE TURN OF THE CENTURY. LIBER AMICORUM IN HONOUR OF ROGER BLANPAIN 143 (Chris Engels ed., 1998); Adelle Blackett, *Global Governance, Legal Pluralism and the Decentered State: A Labor Law Critique of Codes of*

this book, focusing on the differences between traditional international law and the new principles and processes along which the universal society and world power are (re)organized,[18] and how this is related to domestic power.[19] Examples are Richard Falk's analysis[20] of the interconnections between the Westphalian vision

---

Corporate Conduct, 8 INDIANA JOURNAL OF GLOBAL LEGAL STUDIES 401 (2001) [hereinafter IND. J. GLOBAL LEGAL STUD.].

18 Piero Ziccardi, *Les Caractères de l'Ordre Juridique International*, 95 RECUEIL DES COURS 266 (1958–III); Gerald Fitzmaurice, *The Future of Public International Law and of the International Legal System in the Circumstances of Today*, *in* LIVRE DU CENTENAIRE 1873–1973. EVOLUTION ET PERSPECTIVES DU DROIT INTERNATIONAL. ANNUAIRE DE L'INSTITUT DE DROIT INTERNATIONAL 196 (1973); PHILIP ALLOTT, EUNOMIA. NEW ORDER FOR A NEW WORLD (1990); Giuliana Ziccardi Capaldo, *Da Yalta ad un Nuovo Ordine Politico Internazionale*, 45 LA COMUNITÀ INTERNAZIONALE 210 (1990); Edith Brown Weiss, *The New International Legal System*, *in* PERSPECTIVES ON INTERNATIONAL LAW 63 (Nandasiri Jasentuliyana ed., 1995); POLITICS, VALUES AND FUNCTIONS. INTERNATIONAL LAW IN THE 21ST CENTURY. ESSAYS IN HONOUR OF PROFESSOR LOUIS HENKIN (Jonathan I. Charney, Donald K. Anton & Mary Ellen O'Connell eds, 1997); William Michael Reisman, *Unilateral Action and the Transformations of the World Constitutive Process: The Special Problem of Humanitarian Intervention*, 11 EUR. J. INT'L L. 3 (2000); Pippa Norris, *Global Governance and Cosmopolitan Citizens*, *in* GOVERNANCE IN A GLOBALIZING WORLD, 155 (Joseph S. Nye & John D. Donahue eds, 2000); EDWARD MACWHINNEY, THE UNITED NATIONS AND THE NEW WORLD ORDER FOR A NEW MILLENIUM. SELF-DETERMINATION, STATE SUCCESSION, AND HUMANITARIAN INTERVENTION (2000); Marcelo Kohen, *Internationalisme et Mondialisation*, *in* LE DROIT SAISI PAR LA MONDIALISATION 107 (Charles-Albert Morand ed., 2001); Charlotte Ku, *Global Governance and the Changing Face of International Law*, Annual Meeting of the Academic Council in the United Nations System, 16–18 June, Puebla, Mexico, 2001, ACUNS REPORTS AND PAPERS No. 2 (2001); DAVID HELD & ANTHONY G. MCGREW, GOVERNING GLOBALIZATION. POWER, AUTHORITY AND GLOBAL GOVERNANCE (2002); GLOBAL TRENDS AND GLOBAL GOVERNANCE (Paul Kennedy, Dirk Messner & Franz Nuscheler eds 2002); Jochen Frowein, *Ist das Völkerrecht tot?*, 23 FRANKFURTER ALLGEMEINE ZEITUNG No. 168, 6 (2003); Martti Koskenniemi, *Global Governance and Public International Law*, 37 KRITISCHE JUSTIZ 241 (2004); Karsten Nowrot, *Legal Consequences of Globalization: The Status of Non-Governmental Organizations Under International Law*, 6 IND. J. GLOBAL LEGAL STUD. 579 (1999); JOHN J. KIRTON AND JUNICHI TAKASE, NEW DIRECTIONS IN GLOBAL POLITICAL GOVERNANCE: THE G8 AND INTERNATIONAL ORDER IN THE TWENTY-FIRST CENTURY (2002); EDWARD MACWHINNEY, THE SEPTEMBER 11 TERRORIST ATTACKS AND THE INVASION OF IRAQ IN CONTEMPORARY INTERNATIONAL LAW (2004).

19 Brigitte Stern, *Etats et Souverainetés: La Souveraineté de l'Etat Face à la Mondialisation*, *in* 3 UNIVERSITÉ DE TOUS LES SAVOIRS, QU'EST-CE QUE LA SOCIÉTÉ? 829 (Yves Michaud ed., 2000); GLOBAL LAW WITHOUT A STATE (Gunther Teubner ed., 1997); ROBERT COOPER, THE POST-MODERN STATE AND THE WORLD ORDER (1996); William Michael Reisman, *Designing and Managing the Future of the State*, 8 EUR. J. INT'L L. 409 (1997); Serge Sur, *The State between Fragmentation and Globalization*, *id.*, at 421; Stephan Hobe, *Global Challenges to Statehood: The Increasingly Important Role of Nongovernmental Organizations*, 5 IND. J. GLOBAL LEGAL STUD. 191 (1997); RAMON J. JEFFERY, THE IMPACT OF STATE SOVEREIGNTY ON GLOBAL TRADE AND INTERNATIONAL TAXATION (1999); Kanishka Jayasuriya, *Globalization, Law, and the Transformation of Sovereignty – The Emergence of Global Regulatory Governance*, 6 IND. J. GLOBAL LEGAL STUD. 425 (1999).

20 Richard Falk, *The Interplay of Westphalia and Charter Conceptions of the International Legal Order*, *in* THE FUTURE OF THE INTERNATIONAL LEGAL ORDER. RETROSPECT AND PROSPECT 32

and the Onusian vision of international legal order; Steven Ratner's study[21] about 'new realities' and 'new ideas' in global norms and their impact on international law; Paul Stephan's analysis[22] of the definition of some characteristics of the new global legal system; Mireille Delmas-Marty's 'global illusion' and her 'three challenges' to overcome to build the common law of humanity;[23] and, finally, the new and very extensive work by Christopher Joyner[24] on the system of rules of global governance.

To answer the fundamental questions raised in this book, it is necessary to inquire whether the stated aim of the UN General Assembly (i.e., building a universal legal system that recognizes mankind in all its diversity, grants and guarantees 'every' individual and 'every' people 'all' human rights, and 'every' human person the right to a just and democratic international order, a healthy environment, and the benefits of a common heritage of mankind[25]) has been attained.

Since the 1970s, we have been tracking the development of international principles and norms for the progress of the universal human society.[26] These norms safeguard the interests and needs of the whole of humanity, and create decision-making centers and processes to ensure implementation of these principles by way of objective ascertainment of violations and, eventually, coerce implementation. Their aim is to protect the supreme interest of humanity. They cannot be derogated (*jus cogens*)[27] and must override the interest of individual states (and, in general, individual actors of the global community) because global interests and goods have value greater than those of single entities (states/individuals/groups/etc.). They are

(Richard A. Falk & Cyril E. Black eds, 1982–I); *Id.*, LAW IN AN EMERGING GLOBAL VILLAGE. A POST-WESTPHALIAN PERSPECTIVE (1998).

21 Steven R. Ratner, *International Law: The Trials of Global Norms*, 110 FOREIGN POLICY 65 (1998).

22 Paul B. Stephan, *The New International Law, Legitimacy, Accountability, Authority, and Freedom in the New Global Order*, 70 UNIVERSITY OF COLORADO LAW REVIEW 1555 (1999) [hereinafter U. COLO. L. REV.].

23 MIREILLE DELMAS-MARTY, TROIS DÉFIS POUR UN DROIT MONDIAL (1998); *Id.*, GLOBAL LAW: A TRIPLE CHALLENGE V–VIII (Naomi Norberg transl., 2003).

24 CHRISTOPHER C. JOYNER, INTERNATIONAL LAW IN THE 21ST CENTURY. RULES FOR GLOBAL GOVERNANCE (2005).

25 See especially, *A Promotion of a Democratic and Equitable International Order*, GA Res. 56/151 (Feb. 8, 2002); and recently, *Globalization and its Impact on the Full Enjoyment of all Human Rights,* GA Res. 59/184 (March 8, 2005). On this concept see Héctor Gros Espiell, *The Common Heritage of Mankind and the Human Genome, in* INTERNATIONAL LAW. THEORY AND PRACTICE. ESSAYS IN HONOUR OF ERIC SUY 519 (Karel Wellens ed., 1998); Christopher C. Joyner, *The Concept of the Common Heritage of Mankind in International Law*, 13 EMORY INTERNATIONAL LAW REVIEW 615 (1999) [hereinafter EMORY INT'L L. REV.].

26 ZICCARDI CAPALDO, *supra* note 2. For a 'quasi-legislative' function performed by the ICJ, see *Id.*, *Il Parere Consultivo della Corte Internazionale di Giustizia sul Sahara Occidentale: Un'Occasione per un Riesame della Natura e degli Effetti della Funzione Consultiva*, 15 COMUNICAZIONI E STUDI 532 (1978), at 556.

27 ROBERT KOLB, THÉORIE DU *JUS COGENS* INTERNATIONAL, ESSAI DE RELECTURE DU CONCEPT (2001).

guaranteed by an international responsibility regime more burdensome than the one ordinarily applicable to the other norms.

The UN Charter started, and largely fuelled, this evolutionary process.[28] The foundations laid in Article 1 ('Purposes and principles') were subsequently developed through the practice of the World Organization on the basis of the principles of legality, aimed to safeguard interests and universal fundamental values. The Charter, although hinged on the principle of states' sovereignty (Article 2 (1) and (7)), is concerned with the rights of individuals and peoples. The protection of self-determination, civil and political rights, fundamental freedoms, as stated in the UN Charter, necessitates limitations to states' domestic jurisdiction (e.g., the prohibition of colonial domination, genocide, apartheid, torture, dictatorships, etc.). The principles of legality contained in the General Assembly's declarations – accepted by states – have become peremptory norms of general international law; the practice of UN organs of declaring 'illegal' territorial situations arising in violation of these principles pitted the principle *ex injuria jus non oritur* against the classical principle of effectivity (*ex factis oritur jus*), thus reducing the scope of the latter.[29] This gave the impetus to the increasing 'legality' of the international legal system which, starting from the second half of the twentieth century, has developed a marked 'public' character. According to Thomas M. Franck, the legality of the system is thus strengthened.[30]

Furthermore, the UN has made available its organized structure to the international community – which does not have one – for the objective implementation of such principles and created enforcement mechanisms. The international legal order, which is fundamentally anorganic, has relied on the organic apparatus of international organizations, principally the UN and the WTO, to manage global values and interests, and the implementation of the institutional principles safeguarding them. The law-making and law-enforcement processes are changing.[31] Structures and procedures to punish those (e.g., states, individuals, and entities) who jeopardize such goods and values are being established. The safeguard of shared values is enshrined in international norms and is ensured, even beyond the Charter framework, through multilateral processes involving states, the UN, international regional and universal organizations, governmental and non-governmental, and new powers.[32] World governance is legitimized by pronouncements of the International Court of Justice, where it affirms its authority and power of control on states' organs and on those international organs endowed with the world's decision-making power.[33]

---

28 Giuliana Ziccardi Capaldo, *Nazioni Unite ed Evoluzione dell'Ordinamento Internazionale*, paper presented at the conference on 'Nazioni Unite e Diritto Internazionale', Napoli 20–21 Novembre 1995, *in* Democratizzazione all'Est e Diritto Internazionale, *supra* note 12, at 299.

29 Ziccardi Capaldo, *supra* note 2.

30 Thomas M. Franck, *Fairness in the International Legal and Institutional System*, 240 Recueil des Cours 13 (1993–III).

31 See *infra* chapters 1 and 2 of this book and authors cited therein.

32 See *infra* notes 39–47 and corresponding text.

33 Giuliana Ziccardi Capaldo, *Global Trends and Global Court: The Legitimacy of World Governance*, 4 GCYILJ 127 (2004–I); see *infra* chapter 3 of this book, under the headings

The building of the legal system of the universal community has begun. There are signs of the emergence of a Global Constitution,[34] that is to say, a legal order where force is outlawed, and where legality is embodied in principles aimed at protecting human life and individuals as a whole from war, terrorism and tyrannical and bloody governments, hunger and ecological disasters, and where cultural and environmental goods and natural resources, the high seas, and air space and outer space, are for all humanity to enjoy.[35] On a structural level, new centers of power are being created, that is to say, new authorities to which states and new international actors are subject. Social functions are increasingly no longer subject to the will of states or entrusted to states only (think, for instance, to individual self-defence, arbitration, or custom as a source of general international law). This marks the transition from an inter-state legal system of a 'private' nature, as it was in classical international law, to a world constitutional system of a 'public' character.

This distinction is similar to the one usually made in domestic legal systems between 'private' and 'public' law. Global law has the value and carries out the functions of constitutional law in the domestic system. It is made of the founding principles of the global community, the procedures and institutions that regulate public functions. The result of this Copernican revolution of the international legal system, from states' law to law of all humanity, from inter-state law to global law, is the hatching of an embryonic universal constitution. Thus the international legal system, as the domestic system, has two branches: one regulating the relationships between states taken individually, and the other regulating the supreme values and interests of the universal society in its entirety, including the fundamental rights of individuals and peoples. At the universal level, as well as in domestic law, it is difficult to draw a clear distinction between private and public.

As stated, acts of the General Assembly and the general and special international agreements on human rights, the environment, etc., contain detailed lists of civil, political, economic, social, and cultural rights guaranteed to each individual and people. Relying on a distinction made by legal scholars with regard to domestic systems, we can say that the constitutional principles and rights listed in these international instruments are the 'formal' constitution. The effective constitution (the 'material constitution'), which is supported by the prevailing forces acting in the global community, is only a part of the formal constitution. It rests on a body of rules that aim to safeguard goods and interests of mankind considered as a whole, of

---

'The Court's "Authority" Over State Organs' and 'Judicial Control Over the Acts of UN Political Organs'.

34 Richard A. Falk, Robert C. Johansen & Samuel S. Kim, *Global Constitutionalism and World Order*, *in* The Constitutional Foundations of World Peace 3 (Richard A. Falk, Robert C. Johansen & Samuel S. Kim eds, 1993); Richard A. Falk, *The Pathways of Global Constitutionalism*, *id.*, at 13 *et seq.*

35 See the Millennium project presented by the General Assembly in January 2005; its final report, entitled *Investing in Development: A Practical Plan to Achieve the Millennium Development Goals* to the Secretary-General, available at <http://www.unmillenniumproject.org/reports/index.htm>; after the tsunami see *UN Flash Appeal Indian Ocean Earthquake – Tsunami 2005*, available at <http://www.unisdr.org/ppew/tsunami/pdf/un–tsunamiflashappeal.pdf>.

people, of human beings, of human life. These rules guarantee a limited number of individual human rights, prohibiting states to commit *gross violations* – serious and generalized violations of human rights committed on a large scale, like genocide, torture, atrocities, etc. – and providing individuals a few instruments to invoke the responsibility of the offender (state and/or other individuals) and ensure redress.[36] It is only in some regional contexts that states can be subject to sanctions triggered by individual's actions.[37] Likewise, the determination of the responsibility of individuals for international crimes and the creation of international judicial bodies to prosecute such violations is still an exception.[38] We are still far from the objectives set by the General Assembly for global law.

Current global law purports general interests: it reveals its essential goals through constitutional principles collectively guaranteed; it disciplines the organization of centers of power for the world's governance, as well as the relationships with other legal systems and the underlying community, which is no longer a community of states but of mankind as a whole (common humanity). On the basis of these considerations, we can identify the four pillars of global law. These are the pivots of the global legal system: *verticality, legality, integration, and collective guarantees.*

Verticality

Global law organizes the fundamental public/social functions. It creates the structures and regulates the decisional processes of ascertainment and implementation of norms aimed at safeguarding global interests. The creation of global power centers is the result of the empowerment and the broadening of the institutional powers of UN organs and other international organizations. They thus operate both as organs of their respective institutions and as organs of the global community.[39] The international

---

36 M. Cherif Bassiouni, *Accountability for Violations of International Humanitarian Law and Other Serious Violations of Human Rights*, 1 GCYILJ 3 (2001); Steven Ratner & Jason Abrams, Accountability for Human Rights Atrocities in International Law (1997).

37 Thomas Buergenthal, *The Inter-American Court of Human Rights*, 76 Am. J. Int.'l. L. 231 (1982); *Id., The Advisory Practice of the Inter American Human Rights Court*, 79 Am. J. Int.'l. L. 1 (1985); Héctor Gros Espiell, *La Convention Américaine et la Convention Européenne des Droits de l'Homme: Analyse Comparative*, 218 Recueil de Cours 167 (1989–IV); Nico Krisch, *The Establishment of an African Court on Human and Peoples Rights*, 58 Zeitschrift für Ausländisches Offentliches Recht und Völkerrecht 713 (1998); Antônio Augusto Cançado Trindade, *supra* note 4 and, for the activities of the regional Courts of human rights in the years 1999–2004, see *Id., Inter-American Court of Human Rights, Introductory Note, Developments in the Case-Law of the Inter-American Court of Human Rights*, GCYILJ 1203 (2002–II); *Id.*, 1111 (2003–II); *Id.*, 1441 (2004–II); *Id.*, 1483 (2005–II); *Id.*, 1357 (2006–II); *Id.*, 1675 (2007–II); Vincenzo Starace, *European Court of Human Rights, Introductory Note*, GCYILJ 659 (2001); *Id.*, 983 (2003–II); *Id.*, 1285 (2005–II).

38 For a background analysis, see Marc Weller, *Undoing the Global Constitution: UN Security Council Action on the International Criminal Court*, 78 International Affairs 693 (2002).

39 Giuliana Ziccardi Capaldo, *Verticalità della Comunità Internazionale e Nazioni Unite. Un Riesame del Caso Lockerbie*, *in* Interventi delle Nazioni Unite e Diritto Internazionale

judicial function is considerably strengthened by the creation of specialized international courts and tribunals,[40] the broadening of their competences,[41] and the reduction of the importance of arbitration, as contrasted to the classical period,[42] which was hinged upon the principle of the sovereignty of states (*superiorem non recognoscentes*).

The global legal system introduces multilateral democratic decisional processes[43] and the sharing of responsibilities for managing social and economic development, health and global environment, and threats to peace and the world's security. It establishes systems of *shared governance* under UN control involving the forces of the global community (UN organs, states, non-state actors, international governmental organizations, together with the civil society, non-governmental international organizations, and private sectors). It creates the norms that institutionalize procedures and mechanisms of integration between the international community and international organizations.

The verticalization of international power has taken place on the basis of the Charter, and even beyond the Charter. Indeed, because of the inadequacy of the Charter and international institutions, this emerging system is developing outside the UN system by way of an ample practice of co-management of goals and global interests leading to general international norms, substantive and procedural, and integrated mechanisms. We dubbed 'integrated system' the set of procedures and rules redefining and organizing multilateral decisional processes. The 'integrated

---

61 (1995); *Id.*, *Il Disconoscimento delle Credenziali del Sud Africa come Sanzione contro l'Apartheid*, 68 Rivista di Diritto Internazionale 299 (1985).

40 Jonathan I. Charney, *The Impact on the International Legal System of the Growth of International Courts and Tribunals*, 31 New York University Journal of International Law & Politics 697 (1999) [hereinafter N.Y.U. J. Int'l L. & Pol.]; Angela Del Vecchio, Giurisdizione Internazionale e Globalizzazione. I Tribunali Internazionali tra Globalizzazione e Frammentazione (2003). See also *supra* note 6.

41 See, for instance, Dinah Shelton, *The Environmental Jurisprudence of the European Court of Human Rights, 2003–2004*, 4 GCYILJ 293 (2004–I).

42 Lucius Caflish, *Cent Ans de Règlement Pacifiques de Différends Interétatiques*, 288 Recueil des Cours 285 (2001).

43 Thomas M. Franck, *The Emerging Right to Democratic Governance*, 86 Am. J. Int.'l L. 46 (1992); in general see Peter Spiro, *New Global Communities: Non-Governmental Organizations in International Decision-Making Institutions*, 18 Washington Quarterly 45 (1995); Christine M. Chinkin, *Global Summits: Democratising International Law-Making?*, 7 Public Law Review 208 (1996); Robert W. Cox, *Globalization, Multilateralism and Democracy*, *in* Approaches to World Order 530 (Robert W. Cox & Timothy J. Sinclair eds, 1996); John O. MacGinnis, *The Appropriate Hierarchy of Global Multilateralism and Customary International Law, The Example of the WTO*, 44 Virginia Journal of International Law 229 (2003) [hereinafter Va. J. Int'l L.]. For critical remarks, see James Crawford & Susan Marks, *The Global Democracy Deficit: An Essay on International Law and its Limits*, *in* Re-Imagining Political Community, *supra* note 12, at 72 *et seq.*; Eric Stein, *International Integration and Democracy: No Love at First Sight*, 95 Am. J. Int.'l L. 489 (2001); Multilateralism v. Unilateralism, Policy Choices in a Global Society (John. B. Attanasio ed., 2004).

system' directs the organization of global power, regulates fundamental social functions, and guarantees the world's governance.[44]

In the 1990s, we foretold the 'vertical' evolution of international power evidenced by the

> '… tendency on the part of the United Nations, both to perform on behalf of the community of states, some general functions of organization of the international order (production, ascertainment and guaranteeing of primary norms that safeguard fundamental interests of the international society as a whole) and to develop mechanisms for the joint exercise of those functions … thereby indicating a progressive integration and a superposition of an organized international community to a mere inter-state society.'[45]

We called this the '*cogestione pubblicistica*/public co-management'[46] of interests and emerging global values, and we hailed the development. Since then, the process has taken roots. The terms employed to describe the phenomenon (e.g., co-management; integrated systems; shared governance) have appeared in UN acts that indicate integrated processes as the instrument for world's governance, fine-tune increasingly numerous and articulated mechanisms, and lead to their expansion.[47]

Legality

The global legal system is based on the principle of legality and on constitutional principles that address the supreme values of mankind and set obligations *erga omnes* for states, individuals, entities, and groups. The principle of international legality (i.e., *ex injuria jus non oritur*) is increasingly overtaking that of effectivity (i.e., *ex factis oritur jus*).[48] Contemporary international law requires governments to be legitimate: control of legitimacy is entrusted to international bodies that use universal standards;[49] measures taken to sanction illegitimate governments are beginning to be increasingly invasive of sovereignty.

---

44 See *infra* chapter 2 of this book.

45 Giuliana Ziccardi Capaldo, *Foreword*, Repertory of Decisions of the International Court of Justice/Répertoire de la Jurisprudence de la Cour internationale de Justice (1947–1992), 2 vols (1995), at lix, lxi.

46 Giuliana Ziccardi Capaldo, Terrorismo Internazionale e Garanzie Collettive/International Terrorism and Collective Guarantees 128 (1990).

47 GA Res. 59/193 (March 18, 2005), para. 4 (o); see also UN resolutions, *infra* note 76.

48 See Giuliana Ziccardi Capaldo, Le Situazioni Territoriali Illegittime nel Diritto Internazionale/Unlawful Territorial Situations in International Law (1977), at 27 *et seq.*; see *infra* chapter 4 of this book.

49 Thomas M. Franck, The Power of Legitimacy Among Nations (1990); Mohamed Shahabuddeen, *Does the Principle of Legality Stand in the Way of Progressive Development of Law?*, 2 Journal of International Criminal Justice 1007 (2004).

In recent years, the International Court of Justice has postured as the ultimate guardian of the universal constitutional values[50] and the legitimacy of *global governance*.[51] By widening its powers and functions, the Court protects human rights, human life, and peace; it consolidates its authority *vis-à-vis* state and international organs – executive and judicial – by striving to exercising judicial control.[52]

Integration

Global law supports the integration of legal systems within regional international organizations (especially the EU treaties and the 2007 Treaty of Lisbon),[53] universal organizations, and between the two.[54] At the same time it develops the general

---

50 See Edward MacWhinney, *The International Court as Constitutional Court and the Blurring of the Arbitral/Judicial Processes*, 6 Leiden Journal of International Law 279 (1993); Shigeru Oda, *The International Court of Justice Viewed from the Bench (1976–1993)*, 244 Recueil des Cours 9 (1993–VII); Shabtai Rosenne, The World Court 37 (5th ed., 1995); Giuliana Ziccardi Capaldo, *Tendenze Evolutive della Politica Giudiziaria della Corte internazionale di Giustizia, in* Il Ruolo del Giudice Internazionale nell'Evoluzione del Diritto Internazionale e Comunitario, Atti del Convegno di Studi in Memoria di Gaetano Morelli, 257 (Francesco Salerno ed., 1995); Georges Abi-Saab, *The International Court as a World Court, in* Fifty Years of the International Court of Justice. Essays in Honour of Sir Robert Jennings (Vaughan Lowe & Malgosia A. Fitzmaurice eds, 1996); Gilbert Guillaume, *La Mondialisation et la Cour Internationale de Justice*, 2 International Law Forum du Droit International 242 (2000); *Id.*, La Cour Internationale de Justice à l'Aube du XXIème Siècle. Le Regard d'un Juge (2003).

51 David D. Caron, *The Legitimacy of the Collective Authority of the Security Council*, 87 Am. J. Int.'l L. 552 (1993); Geoffrey R. Watson, *Constitutionalism, Judicial Review, and the World Court*, 34 Harvard International Law Journal 1 (1993) [hereinafter Harv. Int'l L.J.]; Mohammed Bedjaoui, The New World Order and the Security Council (1994); William Michael Reisman, *The Supervisory Jurisdiction of the International Court of Justice: International Arbitration and International Adjudication,* 258 Recueil des Cours 9 (1996); Daniel M. Bodansky, *The Legitimacy of International Governance*, 93 Am. J. Int.'l L. 596 (1999); Giuliana Ziccardi Capaldo, *Global Trends and Global Court: The Legitimacy of World Governance*, 4 GCYILJ 127 (2004–I).

52 See *infra* chapter 3 of this book.

53 L' Integration du Droit International et Communautaire dans l'ordre Juridique National. Etude de la Pratique en Europe/The Integration of International and European Community Law into the National Legal Order (Pierre M. Eisemann ed., 1996).

54 Antônio Augusto Cançado Trindade, *Co-Existence and Co-Ordination of Mechanisms of International Protection of Human Rights (At Global and Regional Levels)*, 202 Recueil des Cours 9 (1987–II); Regional Integration and the Global Trading System (Kim Anderson & Richard Blackhurst eds, 1993); Paolo Mengozzi, *Les Valeurs de l'Intégration Face à la Globalisation des Marchés*, 1 Revue du Marché Unique Européen 5 (1998); Paolo Mengozzi, *Private International Law and the WTO Law*, 292 Recueil des Cours 249 (2001); Thomas Cottier, *A Theory of Direct Effect in* Global Law, European Integration and International Co-Ordination. Studies in Transnational Economic Law in Honour of Claus-Dieter Ehlermann 99 (Armin von Bogdandy, Petros C. Mavroidis & Yves Mény eds, 2002); Ernest Ulrich Petersmann, *Time for a United Nations* 'Global *Compact' for Integrating Human*

principles of harmonization between the international legal system and the states' systems. Both international and domestic courts and tribunals have developed international standards that discipline the relationships between domestic and international legal systems, and that place limits on states and their freedom on how to implement international law. The evolution of the international society into a global community requires greater observance and adherence to international law by domestic law.[55] As the international legal system continues to expand, increasingly regulating economic processes and significant sectors of social life, it requires states to comply with certain minimum international standards for internal implementation of obligations undertaken. These standards, namely, good faith, direct applicability, and the primacy of treaties and customs, are held by international courts to be established general principles of international law. The standards foster the creation of a legal global system and the adherence to its values and principles.[56]

For what concerns the relationship between the various international legal regimes, international courts, including those belonging to specific treaty-regimes, regard themselves as subject to the rule of general international law ('*sous l'empire du droit international general*'[57]), thus contributing to the harmonization of the international system.[58] Recently the ECHR, in a general statement of principle, declared that the European Convention on Human Rights 'should be interpreted as far as possible in harmony with other principles of international law of which it forms part'.[59] The WTO's Appellate Body adopted a similar orientation.[60] Likewise, and before the ECHR, the European Court of Justice had stated that '... the rules

---

Rights into the Law *of Worldwide Organizations, Lessons from European Integration*, 13 Eur. J. Int'l L. 621 (2002); George P. Fletcher & Steve Sheppard, American Law in a Global Context. The Basics (2005).

55 Detlev F. Vagts, *Hegemonic International Law*, 95 Am. J. Int.'l L. 843 (2001); José Alvarez, *Editorial Comment: Hegemonic International Law Revisited*, 97 Am. J. Int.'l L. 873 (2003).

56 See *infra* chapter 5 of this book.

57 Hervé Ascensio, *Existe-T-Il des Organes du Droit International?*, Studi di Diritto Internazionale in Onore di Gaetano Arangio Ruiz 3 (2004–I), at 23.

58 In general on this topic, see Pierre-Marie Dupuy, *L'Unité de l'Ordre Juridique International*, 297 Recueil des Cours 9 (2002); Rosalin Higgins, *The ICJ, the ECJ, and the Integrity of International Law*, 52 Int'l & Comp. L.Q. 1 (2003); Antonio Tizzano, *Ancora sui Rapporti tra Corti europee. Principi comunitari e c.d. Controlimiti Costituzionali*, Il Diritto dell'Unione Europea 734 (2007).

59 Vlastimir and Borka Bankovic, Zivana Stojanovic, Mirjana Stoimenovski, Dragana Joksimovic and Dragan Sukovic v. Belgium, the Czech Republic, Denmark, France, Germany, Greece, Hungary, Iceland, Italy, Luxembourg, the Netherlands, Norway, Poland, Portugal, Spain, Turkey and the United Kingdom, Application No. 52207/99, Decision on Admissibility (Dec. 12, 2001), 2001–XII Reports of Judgments and Decisions, para. 57. See Stefania Negri, *Interpreting the European Convention on Human Rights in Harmony with International Law and Jurisprudence: What Lessons from* Ocalan v. Turkey*?*, 4 GCYILJ 243 (2004–I).

60 Appellate Body Report, United States-Standards for Conventional and Reformulated Gasoline, 29 April 1996, WT/DS2/AB/R, para. 182. See Gabrielle Marceau, *A Call for Coherence in International Law, Praises for the Prohibition Against 'Clinical Isolation' in WTO Dispute Settlement*, 33 Journal of World Trade 87 (1999).

of customary international law ... are binding upon the Community institutions and form part of the Community legal order'.[61] Recently, in overseeing an increasingly globalized international community, the Court has declared that it 'is empowered to check, indirectly, the lawfulness of the resolutions of the Security Council ... with regard to *jus cogens*.' Those principles are binding on all subjects of international law, including the bodies of the UN. In the Court's opinion, 'there exists one limit to the principle that resolutions of the Security Council have binding effect: namely, that they must observe the fundamental peremptory provisions of *jus cogens*'.[62]

Collective Guarantees

The global legal system has tools and mechanisms to implement the values of the universal community and to counteract threats against them. A system of co-management of the safeguards of Global Law is emerging. This system provides for multilateral management of sanctioning and enforcement functions, which complements the one of the UN. Yet, it operates beyond the Charter, on the basis of norms of general international law. Such a *shared governance* system relies on systematic integrated mechanisms of monitoring, ascertainment, and coercive implementation measures taken not only by the UN, but also by governments, international organizations, both regional and global, both governmental and non-governmental, and various civil society actors. The Security Council plays a pivotal role in the system. The developments of the integrated system of safeguards – whose structure we analysed and outlined in the different phases of its implementation[63] – resulted in:

1. decisional co-managed processes with regard to measures involving the use of force and economic sanctions against states and against individuals, entities and movements of national liberation (i.e., *smart sanctions*);
2. an integrated system for the monitoring of the enforcement of sanctions enacted by the Security Council (e.g., the monitoring system of *smart sanctions* against terrorism[64]) and the respect of human rights in domestic and international armed conflicts (for instance, the protection of children affected by armed conflicts[65]);

61 Racke GmbH& Co. v. Hauptzollamt Mainz, Case C–162/96, Judgment of 16 June 1998, 1998 ECR I–3655, para. 46.

62 Ahmed Ali Yusuf and Al Barakaat International Foundation v. Council of the European Union and Commission of the European Communities, Case T–306/01, Judgment of 21 September 2005, paras 277, 280, 281.

63 See *infra* chapters 2, 4 and 6 of this book.

64 See *infra* chapter 8 of this book.

65 See the Reports of the Secretary-General to the Security Council on Children and Armed Conflict (UN Docs. S/2000/712 (July 19, 2000); S/2001/852 (Sept. 7, 2001); S/2002/1299 (Nov. 26, 2002); S/2003/1053–A/58/546 (Oct. 30, 2003); S/2005/72 (Feb. 9, 2005)).

3. integrated diplomatic systems to settle conflicts (e.g., the Road Map[66]), or mixed systems to reconstruct countries ravaged by civil war (e.g., Kosovo[67]);
4. judicial initiatives such as the creation of international criminal courts (*ad hoc* criminal courts,[68] mixed courts in Cambodia, Sierra Leone, etc.,[69] and the International Criminal Court itself[70]) carried out by states and international organs according to the competencies given by the various Statutes to punish those responsible for major violations of human rights and to provide redress to victims;[71] and
5. systems of co-management of the environment[72] (e.g., the Amazon forest), cultural heritage, the use of natural resources (e.g., the system established in the Montego Bay Convention[73]), and the use of marine, polar (Antarctica), cosmic spaces, and the atmosphere (i.e., global commons[74]).

---

66 SC Res. 1515 (Nov. 19, 2003).

67 See *infra* chapter 2 of this book, under the heading 'Mechanisms to Co-Manage Measures Involving the Use of Force', and chapter 4 under the heading 'Processes of Multilateral Authoritative Decision-Making'.

68 Alain Pellet, *Le Tribunal Criminel International pour l'Ex-Yougoslavie. Poudre aux Yeux ou Avancée Décisive?*, 98 Revue Générale de Droit International Public 7 (1994); Sean D. Murphy, *Developments in Criminal Law. Progress and Jurisprudence of the International Criminal Tribunal for the Former Yugoslavia*, 93 Am. J. Int.'l L. 57 (1999), and, for the activities of the two Tribunals in the years 1999–2004, see Reinhold Gallmetzer & Kazuna Inomata, *International Criminal Tribunal for the Former Yugoslavia, Introductory Note*, 1 GCYILJ 493 (2001); Rafael Nieto–Navia, *International Criminal Tribunal for the Former Yugoslavia, Introductory Note*, GCYILJ 663 (2002–II); *Id.*, 593 (2003–I); *Id.*, 623 (2004–I); *Id.*, 623 (2005–I); *Id.*, 393 (2006–I); *Id.*, 367 (2007–I); William A. Schabas, *International Criminal Tribunal for Rwanda, Introductory Note*, GCYILJ 591 (2001); *Id.*, 1027 (2002–II); *Id.*, 705 (2003–I); *Id.*, 977 (2004–II); *Id.*, 935 (2005–II); *Id.*, 641 (2006–II); *Id.*, 617 (2007–II).

69 See Cesare Romano, *Mixed Jurisdictions for East Timor, Kosovo, Sierra Leone and Cambodia: The Coming of Age of Internationalized Criminal Bodies?*, 2 GCYILJ 97 (2002–I).

70 William A. Schabas, An Introduction to the International Criminal Court (2nd ed., 2004); The International Criminal Court and the Crime of Aggression (Mauro Politi & Giuseppe Nesi eds, 2004); M. Cherif Bassiouni, The Legislative History of the International Criminal Court: Introduction, Analysis, and Integrated Text (2005).

71 See mainly Bassiouni, *supra* note 36, at 32 and Richard A. Falk, *World Tribunal on Iraq: Truth, Law, and Justice*, 6 GCYILJ 15 (2006-I).

72 Malgosia A. Fitzmaurice & Catherine Redgwell, *Environmental Non-Compliance Procedures and International Law*, 31 Netherlands Yearbook of International Law 35 (2000); Randall S. Abate, *Dawn of a New Era in the Extraterritorial Application of U.S. Environmental Statutes: A Proposal for an Integrated Judicial Standard Based on the Continuum of Context,* 31 Columbia Journal of Environmental Law 87 (2006).

73 Bernard H. Oxman, *The Rule of Law and the United Nations Convention on the Law of the Sea*, 7 Eur. J. Int'l L. 353 (1996).

74 Global Public Goods: International Cooperation in the Twenty-First Century (Inge Kaul, Isabelle Grunberg & Marc Stern eds, 1999); John Vogler, The Global Commons: Environmental and Technological Governance (2nd ed., 2000); Patrick J. O'Keefe,

In sum, how global law develops is clear: it grows vertically. This is the basic understanding of the phenomenon amongst scholars, regardless of differences between underlying theories.[75] States' practice and international acts support the idea of verticalization towards the integration of global forces. Both necessitate multilateral actions for managing worldwide economic and social development, as well as threats to international peace and security, 'in accordance with the UN Charter and the international legal order'[76] and highlight the UN's central role, thus attesting to the urgency of institutionalization of integrated processes for the implementation of global law.

SHIPWRECKED HERITAGE: A COMMENTARY ON THE UNESCO CONVENTION ON UNDERWATER CULTURAL HERITAGE (2002); ALEX G. OUDE ELFERINK & DONALD R. ROTHWELL, OCEANS MANAGEMENT IN THE 21ST CENTURY: INSTITUTIONAL FRAMEWORKS AND RESPONSES (2004); Roger O'Keefe, *World Cultural Heritage: Obligations to the International Community as a Whole?*, 53 INT'L & COMP. L.Q. 189 (2004).

75 See mainly ROLANDO QUADRI, DIRITTO INTERNAZIONALE PUBBLICO 27 *et seq*., 87 *et seq*. (5th ed., 1968); Piero Ziccardi, *Règles d'Organisation et Règles de Conduite en Droit International. Le Droit Commun et les Ordres Juridiques*, 152 RECUEIL DES COURS 119, 275 (1976–IV); ALFRED VERDROSS & BRUNO SIMMA, UNIVERSELLES VÖLKERRECHT. THEORIE UND PRAXIS (1984); Bardo Fassenbender, *The United Nations Charter as Constitution of the International Community*, 36 COLUMBIA JOURNAL OF TRANSNATIONAL LAW 529 (1998).

76 See CHR Res. 2003/63 (April 24, 2003); GA Res. 56/151 *supra* note 25, reiterated in GA Res. 58/317, *Reaffirming the Central Role of the United Nations in the Maintenance of International Peace and Security and the Promotion of International Cooperation* (Aug. 5, 2004), preamble. See Vera Gowlland-Debbas, *Panel on the EU, the Threats of Globalisation and the Role of International Law, Présentation Donnée lors du 7e ECSA World Conference,* THE EUROPEAN UNION AND EMERGING WORLD ORDERS: PERCEPTIONS AND STRATEGIES, Bruxelles 30 Novembre – 1er Décembre 2004, available at <http://hei.unige.ch/sections/dr/nouveau%20site%20section/publicat/Contribution%20Gowlland.pdf>.

PART I
Verticality and Sharing of the Decisional Processes

SECTION I
Global Law-Making

Chapter 1

Dynamics of Global Rule-Formation Processes*

Introduction

Since the 1990s, several new rules of general international law have been added to international human rights law.[1] The fact that many of them came into being *directly* and *instantaneously*, by way of the immediate transformation of the will of the international community into law, without the need for custom (i.e., *omisso medio*), raises critical questions as to their ultimate nature. In particular, this begs reconsideration of the widespread notion that rules of general international law are almost exclusively customary international law norms. Both the International Court of Justice (ICJ)[2] and the overwhelming majority of scholars hold rules of general international law to be customary norms. 'General principles of law recognized by

---

* This chapter does not deal with 'quasi-legislative' activity performed by the International Court of Justice; on this topic and for the attention paid by the Court to human rights, see *infra* chapter 3 of this book. The changes to international law I detail therein have been summarized in Table 4.

1 In the contemporary human rights literature see e.g.: HUMAN RIGHTS: THIRTY YEARS AFTER THE UNIVERSAL DECLARATION. COMMEMORATIVE VOLUME ON THE OCCASION OF THE 13TH ANNIVERSARY OF THE UNIVERSAL DECLARATION OF HUMAN RIGHTS (Bertrand G. Ramcharan ed., 1979); THE INTERNATIONAL DIMENSION OF HUMAN RIGHTS (Karel Vasak & Philip Alston eds, 1982); Philip Alston, *A Third Generation of Solidarity Rights: Progressive Development or Obfuscation of International Human Rights Law?*, 29 NETHERLANDS INTERNATIONAL LAW REVIEW 307 (1982); Christian Tomuschat, *Human Rights in a World-Wide Framework – Some Current Issues*, 45 ZEITSCHRIFT FÜR AUSLÄNDISCHES OFFENTLICHES RECHT UND VÖLKERRECHT 547 (1985); JACK DONNELLY, UNIVERSAL HUMAN RIGHTS IN THEORY AND PRACTICE (1989); Bruno Simma, *International Human Rights and General International Law: A Comparative Analysis*, IV COLLECTED COURSES OF THE ACADEMY OF EUROPEAN LAW 153 (1995–II); Nicholas Howen, *International Human Rights Law-Making-Keeping the Spirit Alive*, 6 EUROPEAN HUMAN RIGHTS LAW REVIEW 566 (1997); Giuliana Ziccardi Capaldo, *Democratizzazione all'Est e Diritto Internazionale Generale*, *in* DEMOCRATIZZAZIONE ALL'EST E DIRITTO INTERNAZIONALE 27, 30 (Giuliana Ziccardi Capaldo ed., 1998); *Id.*, *Legittimità Democratica, Tutela dei Diritti Umani e Produzione Giuridica Primaria nell'Ordinamento Internazionale*, XLVI JUS, RIVISTA DI SCIENZE GIURIDICHE 639 (1999); THE FUTURE OF INTERNATIONAL HUMAN RIGHTS (Burns H. Weston & Stephen P. Marks eds, 1999). See also *infra* note 28 and accompanying text.

2 On the relevant Court jurisprudence, see GIULIANA ZICCARDI CAPALDO, REPERTORY OF DECISIONS OF THE INTERNATIONAL COURT OF JUSTICE/RÉPERTOIRE DE LA JURISPRUDENCE DE LA COUR INTERNATIONALE DE JUSTICE (1947–1992), 2 vols, (1995) [hereinafter REPERTORY], vol. I, Nos 1001–1003, at 5; Nos 1005–1007, at 9, 11; No. 1009, at 11.

civilized nations' (Article 38 (1)(c) of the ICJ Statute) are also regarded by some authors as a sort of *sui generis* custom.[3] Yet, what is more relevant here is that rules of general international law, which have emerged immediately, are subsumed under the so-called 'instant custom' rubric.[4]

The epochal events in the East at the end of the 1980s are at the basis of the current development of international human rights law. They swept away the previous anorganic structure of the international community based on antagonizing blocs, to give way to a process of 'verticalization' of the international legal order driven by the rekindling of the UN.

As will be illustrated in this chapter,[5] the development of international human rights law experienced in the last two decades can be largely attributed to this process of verticalization. It was brought about by the ever-increasing role the UN and other international organizations play in the management of world power, including the creation, ascertainment, and enforcement of general international law. The development of substantive and procedural norms to guarantee the fundamental interests of the international community as a whole is the result of the increasing integration between the 'organized community' (i.e., the UN and other inter-governmental organizations) and the 'substantive community' (i.e., the states and other new international actors). This marks the dawn of the global governance era, which is characterized by deep changes to international law-making processes. This phenomenon started in the second half of the twentieth century and was accelerated by the demise of the bloc-based international structure, the reduction of the hegemony of superpowers, and the emergence of new dominant global agents.[6]

The Principle of Democratic Legitimacy: Changes During the 1990s

In the second half of the 1980s, the Soviet Union formally recognized the principle of democratic legitimacy, the first steps being the Geneva summit of November 1985 between Reagan and Gorbachev and the subsequent meetings between the two leaders (i.e., Washington summit of 7 December 1987; Moscow summit of 29 May 1988; and Malta summit of 2 December 1989). These events marked the onset of the profound transformation of the regimes of Eastern Europe.[7]

The end of the Cold War was the result of the radical transformation of the communist and socialist countries into liberal and market-based democracies, where individuals' civil and political rights are constitutionally guaranteed.

---

3 See, for example, BENEDETTO CONFORTI, DIRITTO INTERNAZIONALE 43 *et seq.* (6th ed., 2002).

4 Bin Cheng, *UN Resolutions on Outer Space: 'Instant' International Customary Law?*, 5 INDIAN JOURNAL OF INTERNATIONAL LAW 23 (1965).

5 See *infra* this chapter under the heading 'The "Quasi-Organic" Nature of New Global Principles'.

6 Giuliana Ziccardi Capaldo, *Da Yalta ad un Nuovo Ordine Politico Internazionale*, 45 LA COMUNITÀ INTERNAZIONALE 210 (1990).

7 LE MONDE, Nov. 19, 1985; Dec. 8, 1987; May 31, 1988; Dec. 3–4, 1989.

The change of attitude of the former Soviet Union had an *immediate* impact on the content of international human rights law, substantially widening it. As it is known, during the Cold War, because of the opposition of the communist bloc, certain civil and political rights could not acquire the status of customary international law. Despite the attempts of Western countries within the UN and other international organizations (e.g., NATO, OAS, and CSCE), during that period the only rules in the field of international human rights law that could claim customary status were those banning gross violations, like torture, apartheid, and genocide.[8]

At the behest of Western countries, as of the early 1950s, the UN and certain regional organizations secured the conclusion of international agreements providing for the international guarantee of those human rights that were guaranteed by the promoters' own constitutions (e.g., the 1966 International Covenants on Civil and Political Rights and on Economic, Social and Cultural Rights; the 1950 European Convention for the Protection of Human Rights and Fundamental Freedoms; and the 1969 American Convention on Human Rights). However, until the early 1990s,

---

8 On UN activities in the field of human rights, see generally HERSCH LAUTERPACHT, INTERNATIONAL LAW AND HUMAN RIGHTS (1950); NEHAMIAH ROBINSON, THE UNIVERSAL DECLARATION OF HUMAN RIGHTS. ITS ORIGIN, SIGNIFICANCE, APPLICATION AND INTERPRETATION (1958); Marc Schreiber, *La Pratique Récente des Nations Unies dans le Domaine de la Protection des Droits de l'Homme*, 145 RECUEIL DES COURS 297 (1975–II); Egon Schwelb, *Entry into Force of the International Covenants on Human Rights and the Optional Protocol to the International Covenant on Civil and Political Rights*, 70 AMERICAN JOURNAL OF INTERNATIONAL LAW [hereinafter AM. J. INT. L.] 511 (1976); Giōrgos Ténékides, *L'Action des Nations Unies contre la Discrimination Raciale*, 168 RECUEIL DES COURS 269 (1980–III); Jack Donnelly, *Recent Trends in UN Human Rights Activity: Description and Polemic*, 35 INTERNATIONAL ORGANIZATION 633 (1981); Dana D. Fisher, *Reporting under the Covenant on Civil and Political Rights: The First Five Years of the Human Rights Committee*, 76 AM. J. INT. L. 142 (1982); Theodor Meron, *Norm Making and Supervision in International Human Rights: Reflections on Institutional Order*, *id.*, at 754 *et seq.*; Thomas M. Franck, *Of Gnats and Camels: Is there a Double Standard at the United Nations?*, 78 AM. J. INT'L.L. 811 (1984); JOHN P. HUMPHREY, HUMAN RIGHTS AND THE UNITED NATIONS: A GREAT ADVENTURE (1984); THEODOR MERON, HUMAN RIGHTS LAW-MAKING IN THE UNITED NATIONS: A CRITIQUE OF INSTRUMENTS AND PROCESS (1986); Antônio Augusto Cançado Trindade, *Co-Existence and Co-Ordination of Mechanisms of International Protection of Human Rights*, 202 RECUEIL DES COURS 9 (1987–II); AGNÈS DORMENVAL, PROCÉDURES ONUSIENNES DE MISE EN OEUVRE DES DROITS DE L'HOMME: LIMITES OU DÉFAUTS? (1991); DOMINIC MCGOLDRICK, THE HUMAN RIGHTS COMMITTEE. ITS ROLE IN THE DEVELOPMENT OF THE INTERNATIONAL COVENANT ON CIVIL AND POLITICAL RIGHTS (1991); PHILIP ALSTON, THE UNITED NATIONS AND HUMAN RIGHTS: A CRITICAL APPRAISAL (1992); LES NATIONS UNIES ET LE DROIT INTERNATIONAL HUMANITAIRE/THE UNITED NATIONS AND INTERNATIONAL HUMANITARIAN LAW (Luigi Condorelli, Anne-Marie La Rosa & Sylvie Scherrer eds, 1996); Emmanuel Decaux, *Coordination et Suivi dans le Système de Protection des Droits de l'Homme des Nations Unies*, *in* L'EFFECTIVITÉ DES ORGANISATIONS INTERNATIONALES. MÉCANISMES DE SUIVI ET DE CONTRÔLE; JOURNÉES FRANCO-HELLÉNIQUE, 7–8 MAI 1999 229 (Hélène Ruiz-Fabri ed., Paris, 2000); Sara E. Allgood, *United Nations Human Rights 'Entitlements'*, 31 GEORGIA JOURNAL OF INTERNATIONAL & COMPARATIVE LAW 321 (2003); Barbara Wilson, *L'Efficacité des Mécanismes de Protection des Droits de l'Homme Mis en Place par les Nations Unies*, 13 AKTUELLE JURISTISCHE PRAXIS 1355 (2004).

this remarkable array of international agreements fell short of producing an equally remarkable guarantee of human rights at a general level. The opposition of the Eastern bloc, sternly defending domestic jurisdiction and sovereignty, prevented the enlargement of the notion of gross violations of human rights to include serious and systematic violations of civil and political rights, as proposed by the Western bloc.[9]

It is only with the acceptance by the Soviet Union of the principle of democracy, at the above-mentioned summits, that general international human rights law suddenly changed.

The Conference on Security and Cooperation in Europe, known today as the Organization for Security and Cooperation in Europe (OSCE), was the arena where the démarche taken by the two superpowers in Geneva was taken to the next level. Once ideological barriers between the two powers had been broken down, the Conference received a spur to place high on the agenda the promotion of human rights. The meetings of the CSCE held in Vienna from 1986 to 1989 paid much greater attention to human rights than the previous meetings held in Belgrade and Madrid (1980 and 1983). The subject of human rights, which from the beginning had been considered one of the essential areas covered in the Helsinki agreements, was prominent in the three meetings of the Conference on the Human Dimension (Paris in June 1989, Copenhagen in June 1990, and Moscow in September 1991). In a new climate of understanding and cooperation, the multitude of proposals, presented both by individual states or collectively, was gradually integrated, leading to fewer and more homogeneous submissions. The ideological division gradually disappeared as consensus grew over proposals underwritten by states of both blocs, with the exception of Rumania, which eventually remained completely isolated. The Copenhagen document (1990) not only restated basic freedoms and rights, such as the freedom of expression, the right of assembly and of association, freedom of thought, of conscience, of religion, and the right of every individual to leave his or her country. It also ensured their implementation by introducing control mechanisms and procedures (i.e., the Human Dimension Mechanism), and by acknowledging that they are the 'foundations of the rule of law and of the principle of pluralistic democracy'.[10]

Once the basic rules aimed at the creation of a 'European public order' had been agreed upon, the CSCE states, during the Moscow meeting of 1991, made wider and bolder statements of principle. The remarkable acceleration of the process of democratization of Central and Eastern Europe evidently gave the impetus. Hence, in the Moscow meeting's final document, participating states emphasized that 'issues relating to human rights, fundamental freedoms, democracy and the rule of law are

9 The US opposition to dictatorial regimes was articulated in the Wilson doctrine first and then in the Reagan doctrine (Charles Rousseau, *Elaboration d'une Nouvelle Doctrine sur les Rapports des Etats-Unis avec les Régimes Dictatoriaux (Message du Président Reagan au Congrès, 14 mars 1986)*, *Chronique des Faits Internationaux*, 90 Revue Générale de Droit International Public 646 (1986)). On the Reagan Doctrine, see *infra* chapter 4 of this book under the heading 'A New Concept of Worldwide Democracy'.

10 29 International Legal Materials 1305 (1990) [hereinafter Int'l Legal Mat.].

of international concern, as respect for these rights and freedoms constitutes one of the *foundations of the international order*'.[11]

Parallel to the CSCE's work, coordinated action was being taken by the then 12 members of the European Communities[12] and by the members of NATO.[13] Links were established between the promotion of the human dimension of the CSCE and the protection of human rights in the Council of Europe.[14] Meanwhile, at the UN, the idea of democracy based on human rights and fundamental freedoms was being discussed in depth.[15]

---

11 30 INT'L LEGAL MAT. 1670 (1991) (emphasis added).

12 The Twelve's cooperation in the field of human rights led, in 1986, to a ministerial statement (EC BULLETIN 7/8–1986, para. 2.4.4) and, in 1987, to the creation of a specialized working group, in accordance with the express request of the European Parliament. This cooperation developed in 1989 with the adoption by the European Parliament of a resolution entailing the adoption of the Declaration of Fundamental Rights and Freedoms (see text in EC BULLETIN 4–1989, para. 3.2.1). In particular, on East–West relations and on cooperation, in the 1980s, between the EC and the Council of Europe and the CSCE, see European Parliament resolutions (29 OFFICIAL JOURNAL No. C283 66–67 (1986)); the positions of the European Council in Hannover, 27–28 June 1988 (EC BULLETIN 6–1988, at 166), in Madrid, 26–27 June 1989 (EC BULLETIN 6–1989, para. 1.1.16), in Strasbourg, 8–9 December 1989 (EC BULLETIN 12–1989, para. 1.1.20); and the statements at the economic Summits of Tokyo of 4–6 May 1986 (EC BULLETIN 5–1986, para. 3.4.4), of Venice of 8–10 June 1987 (EC BULLETIN 6–1987, para. 3.7.37), and of Paris of 14–16 July 1989 (EC BULLETIN 7/8–1989, paras 3.2.3; 3.2.5). Finally, one should mention the statements made by the Twelve during those years in international fora, especially in the UN General Assembly on 22 September 1987 (EC BULLETIN 9–1987, para. 3.4.1) and on 27 September 1988 (EC BULLETIN 9–1988, para. 3.4.1).

13 See, e.g., the Madrid meeting of 9 June 1988 of the foreign ministers of the Alliance to discuss the result of the Moscow summit between Reagan and Gorbachev and the CSCE reactions in light of the summit. See KEESING'S RECORDS OF WORLD EVENTS 36000, 36059 (1988).

14 Helsinki 2 (1992) defined procedures through which cooperation between the CSCE and the Council of Europe would be established (31 INT'L LEGAL MAT. 1385 (1992)).

15 Réné-Jean Dupuy, *Concept de Démocratie et Action des Nations Unies*, 7–8 BULLETIN DU CENTRE D'INFORMATION DES NATIONS UNIES 61 (Dec. 1993); Mohammed Bennouna, *L'Obligation Juridique dans le Monde de l'Après-Guerre Froide*, 39 ANNUAIRE FRANÇAIS DE DROIT INTERNATIONAL 41 (1993) [hereinafter ANN. FR. D.I.], at 45. Beginning in the 1980s, the UN Human Rights Committee (now Council), which overseed application of the 1966 Civil and Political Rights Covenant, also intensified its activity, discussing, in specific cases, the democratic quality of the regime of a state and whether or not it reflected the will of the people. See, among the cases in which this topic was dealt with, those concerning Spain (UN Doc. A/34/40 (1979), para. 208; UN Doc. A/40/40 (1985), paras 478–479); the Soviet Union (UN Doc. A/40/40 (1985), para. 260); Korea (UN Doc. A/43/40 (1988), para. 428); Panama (UN Doc. A/46/40 (1991), paras 422–423); Madagascar (*id.*, at paras 531–533); Colombia (UN Doc. A/47/40 (1992), paras 352, 377, 391); Nepal (UN Doc. A/50/40 (1995), para. 64); Morocco (*id.*, at para. 104); Argentina (*id.*, at para. 147); Paraguay (*id.*, at para. 196); Haiti (*id.*, at para. 226 *et seq.*); the Ukraine (*id.*, at para. 310); the Russian Federation (*id.*, at para. 379). On this issue, see Giuseppe Palmisano, *L'Autodeterminazione Interna nel Sistema dei Patti sui Diritti dell'Uomo*, 76 RIVISTA DI DIRITTO INTERNAZIONALE 365 (1996).

In hindsight, those landmark events are the source of the principle of democracy as a norm of general international law.[16] It should be stressed that, currently, states conceive 'democracy' as fundamentally unique in its guiding principles.[17] In actuality, the template is the Western democracy model, where both political freedoms (e.g., free and secret elections, multi-party systems) and civil liberties (e.g., expressions of the individual personality, such as freedom of thought, of speech, and of association) are guaranteed.

At the international level, the instantaneous creation of the principle of democratic legitimacy was limited to certain political freedoms like the exercise of free and secret universal suffrage, and the freedom to form political parties. Evidence of this can be found, besides the statements of political leaders throughout the world, in the adoption of multi-party systems and the incorporation of the principle of pluralistic democracy in the constitutions of former socialist countries, as well as in the strengthening of democratic regimes between 1989 and 1990 in many Latin American countries. Moreover, all the most developed countries of Africa, Asia, and the Pacific have since adopted, or are in the process of adopting, constitutional systems based on the democratic paradigm. Since 1991, free elections with universal suffrage have taken place in the great majority of states.

Scholars consider the global democratic revolution as the most significant development of the end of the twentieth century.[18] This is also the opinion of the UN General Assembly, which regards democracy as a universally recognized value to be protected by the UN, with assistance aimed at supporting and strengthening new or restored democracies.[19] Internationally, respect for political freedoms is assured by

---

16 On the principle of democratic governance, see generally William Michael Reisman, *Sovereignty and Human Rights in Contemporary International Law*, 84 Am. J. Int. L. 866 (1990); Oscar Schachter, *Is There a Right to Overthrow an Illegitimate Regime*, Le Droit Interne au Service de la Paix, de la Justice et du Développement. Mélanges Michel Virally 423 (1991); Thomas M. Franck, *The Emerging Right to Democratic Governance*, 86 Am. J. Int. L. 46 (1992); Thomas Franck, *Legitimacy and the Democratic Entitlement*, *in* Democratic Governance and International Law 25 (Gregory H. Fox & Brad R. Roth eds, 2000).

17 Paolo Biscaretti di Ruffia, Costituzioni Straniere Contemporanee (1996–I).

18 Thomas M. Franck, *Fairness in the International Legal and Institutional System. General Course on Public International Law*, 240 Recueil des Cours 9, 100 (1993–III).

19 GA Res. 51/31 (Jan. 10, 1997); GA Res. 51/96 (March 3, 1997). See also the resolutions of the UN General Assembly '*Enhancing the Effectiveness of the Principle of Periodic and Genuine Elections*' (GA Res. 44/146 (Dec. 15, 1990); GA Res. 45/150 (Dec. 18, 1990); GA Res. 46/137 (Dec. 17, 1991); GA Res. 47/131 (Dec 18, 1992); GA Res. 49/190 (Dec. 23, 1994)). On the role of the UN in elections and various processes of democratization, see The UN Role in Promoting Democracy: Between Ideals and Reality (Edward Newman & Roland Rich eds, 2004), available at <http://www.unu.edu/unupress/new/ab–UNrole.html>.

direct UN supervision of elections,[20] by pressuring non-democratic states,[21] and by

---

20 See the well-known cases of Namibia, SC Res. 632 (Feb. 16, 1989), for the setting up of the United Nations Transition Assistance Group (UNTAG); Haiti, GA Res. 45/2 (Oct. 10, 1990), on the sending of observers to oversee elections (ONUVEH); El Salvador, SC Res. 693 (May 20, 1991), on the setting up of observation forces for the peace process, including elections (ONUSAL) and SC Res. 729 (May 14, 1992), for extending the mandate; Cambodia, SC Res. 718 (Oct. 31, 1991), for the setting up of a United Nations Advance Mission in Cambodia (UNAMIC), and SC Res. 745 (Feb. 29, 1992), for the setting up of the United Nations Transitional Authority in Cambodia (UNTAC); Angola, SC Res. 747 (March 24, 1992), for the extension of the mandate of the United Nations Angola Verification Mission II (UNAVEM II) and SC Res. 1087 (Dec. 11, 1996), for the United Nations Angola Verification Mission III (UNAVEM III); Republic of Croatia, SC Res. 1037 (Jan. 15, 1996) for the setting up of United Nations Transitional Administration for Eastern Slavonia, Baranja and Western Sirmium (UNTAES) with mandate to organize elections, to assist in their conduct, and to certify the results; Western Sahara, GA Res. 51/2 (Oct. 29, 1996), for the Referendum; Tajikistan, SC Res. 1138 (Nov. 14, 1997), on the dispatch of an expert team to monitor the 1997 parliamentary elections (UNMOT); East Timor, SC Res. 1272 (Oct. 25, 1999), on the organization and holding of elections by the United Nations Transitional Administration (UNTAES); Fiji, GA Res. 55/280 (July 25, 2001), on the creation of the United Nations Fijian Electoral Observation Mission in East Timor (UNFEOM). For further details on the activities of the United Nations Electoral Assistance Division see <http://www.un.org/Depts/dpa/ead/assistance_by_country/ea_d_g.htm>. Other missions/sending of observers to oversee elections are carried out also by regional organizations and, in particular, by the Organization for Security and Co-operation in Europe. These operations include the European Union election-observing missions (EU-EOM) in South Africa and Palestine. See the EU's Human Rights & Democratisation Policy, available at <http://europa.eu.int/comm/external_relations/human_rights/eu_election_ass_observ/index.htm>, and the OSCE Mission in Bosnia-Herzegovina available at <http://www.oscebih.org/democratization/?d=3>.

21 One should mention the UN condemnation of the violent and brutal interruption of the democratic process in Haiti (GA Res. 46/7 (Oct. 11, 1991); GA Res. 46/138 (Dec. 17, 1991)), which was followed by the UN authorization to intervene in the country to safeguard democracy and the citizens' right to free elections (SC Res. 940 (Jul. 31, 1994)); the urgent request made by the General Assembly to the Nigerian Government to take concrete measures to restore democracy in the country after the Commonwealth's decision to suspend Nigeria as a member (GA Res. 50/199 (Dec. 22, 1995)); the request that the Government of Myanmar take measures for the establishment of a democratic state and allow all citizens to participate freely in the political process (GA Res. 46/132 (Dec. 17, 1991)); the request that Iran guarantee respect for the human rights and the political rights of all Iranian citizens in accordance with the international human rights Covenants, in particular, the Covenant on Civil and Political Rights (GA Res. 49/202 (Dec. 23, 1994)); the UN intervention in the national reconciliation process in Mozambique and the repeated requests of the Security Council to observe democratic principles in the Country (SC Res. 957 (Nov. 15, 1994) and SC Res. 960 (Nov. 21, 1994)); the request that democracy be restored in Liberia (SC Res. 866 (Sept. 22, 1993); SC Res. 1014 (Sept. 15, 1995); SC Res. 1020 (Nov. 10, 1995); SC Res. 1041 (Jan. 29, 1996)); the human rights situation in Cuba (GA Res. 47/139 (Dec. 18, 1992); GA Res. 51/113 (1997)); and the request that the military junta in Sierra Leone take immediate steps to relinquish power and make way for the restoration of the democratically-elected government and a return to constitutional order (SC Res. 1132 (Oct. 8, 1997)).

firmly demanding respect for the freely expressed popular will.[22]

However, the definition and guarantee of civil freedoms, which is a constituent element of contemporary democratic governments, took longer to turn into a norm of general international law, although the constitutions of some Eastern European states referred to the rights listed in the 1948 Universal Declaration of Human Rights or in the 1966 UN Covenants.[23]

Although most modern constitutions contain lists of fundamental civil rights, they are of varying length and detail, changing from country to country. There is not yet a universally accepted catalogue of such rights.[24] The problems experienced by the Human Rights Committee (now Council), which monitored compliance with the 1966 Covenant on Civil and Political Rights, are particularly significant in this regard.[25] Although the Committee stepped up its activities as of the 1980s, states have proven to be reluctant to modify their domestic laws to conform to the provisions of the Covenant and to set up mechanisms, at a national level, that would make the rights recognized in the Covenant justiciable.[26]

In Europe, at least between EU member states, the goal of establishing a minimum common standard of inalienable fundamental freedoms has been achieved with the adoption of the 2007 Treaty of Lisbon.[27]

To summarize, the democratization of Eastern Europe has fostered the emergence, on a general level, of an international principle mandating governments to let their citizens freely choose, consistently with democratic methods, their own form of government and representatives (a principle set forth in Article 21 of the Universal Declaration of Human Rights and in Article 1 of the 1966 International Covenant on Civil and Political Rights).

We believe that this principle came into being *immediately* at the end of the twentieth century, on the 'initiative' of the dominant political/social forces within the international community in the given period. This principle is meant to come into effect immediately and to be legally binding on all, regardless of the constant

---

22 Besides the cases of Angola and Haiti see *supra* note 21 and the corresponding text. See also the international pressure exerted on the Republic of Yugoslavia (Serbia and Montenegro) for respecting the electoral results of 17 November 1996 (SC Res. 1074 (Oct. 1, 1996), para. 5).

23 Russian Constitution, Art. 55 (1); Rumanian Constitution, Art. 20.

24 An example in this sense is the issue of the death penalty (see UN Commission on Human Rights Resolution 1997/12, UN Doc. E/CN.4/1997/12 (April 3, 1997), which was the background issue in three recent cases before the ICJ (see *infra* chapter 3 of this book, under the heading 'Judicial Protection of Human Rights Beyond the ICJ Statute').

25 See José Antonio Pastor Ridruejo, *Les Procédures Publiques Spéciales de la Commission des Droits de l'Homme des Nations Unies*, 228 Recueil des Cours 182 (1991–III).

26 See Jean Dhommeaux, *Monismes et Dualismes en Droit International des Droits de l'Homme*, 41 Ann. Fr. D.I. 447 (1995); *Id.*, *Jurisprudence du Comité des Droits de l'Homme des Nations Unies (novembre 1993–juillet 1996)*, 42 Ann. Fr. D.I. 679 (1996); *Id.*, *Jurisprudence du Comité des Droits de l'Homme des Nations Unies (novembre 1996–novembre 1998)*, 44 Ann. Fr. D.I. 613 (1998).

27 See <http://europa.eu/lisbon_treaty/full_text/index_en.htm>.

repetition of a given behaviour over time, which is the typical requirement of the formation of customary international law.[28]

New Principles in the Field of Human Rights

Several international crises of the 1990s (e.g., the Gulf War, Yugoslavia, Somalia, Rwanda, Serbia, the Great Lakes Region, and Albania) caused the instant creation of rules and principles of general international law. In many cases, this led to the modification of current customary international rules, both procedural and substantive.

To illustrate, on the occasion of those crises, at the behest of the hegemonic powers, there emerged a substantive and procedural principle allowing states to use force in order to re-establish peace and protect fundamental global interests, provided that the force is used on behalf of the international community and with the 'authorization' of the Security Council.[29]

The principle that force can be lawfully used if 'authorized' by the Security Council emerged for the first time during the Persian Gulf crisis and was promptly accepted by the majority of states and social forces. It expands the scope of Article 51 of the Charter, a peremptory norm of general international law, according to the International Court of Justice[30] and scholars. It adds a further exception, besides the one already included in Article 51 (self-defence), to the overall prohibition of the use of force by states; it derogates from the spirit of the system of collective security provided by Chapter VII of the Charter, which gives the Security Council, and not

---

28 On the debate over the nature and sources of international human rights law, see especially Theodor Meron, Human Rights and Humanitarian Norms as Customary Law (1989); Isabelle Gunning, *Modernizing Customary International Law: The Challenge of Human Rights*, 31 Virginia Journal of International Law 211 (1991); Bruno Simma & Philip Alston, *The Sources of Human Rights Law: Custom, Ius Cogens, and General Principles*, 12 Australian Yearbook of International Law 82, (1992), at 213 *et seq*.

29 Noteworthy is the Council practice of 'authorizing' coalitions of states and/or regional organizations to use force to oppose the occupation or annexation of territories or to affirm the principle of democracy or to end serious breaches of humanitarian law. See, e.g., the resolutions in which the Security Council authorized the states to oppose the Iraqi occupation of Kuwait (SC Res. 678 (Nov. 29, 1990)), to guarantee observance of no-fly zones in the air space above the Republic of Bosnia-Herzegovina (SC Res. 816 (March 31, 1993)), to support the UN protection force (UNPROFOR) operating there (SC Res. 836 (June 4, 1993)), to set up the multinational force for protecting human rights in Somalia (SC Res. 794 (Dec. 3, 1992)), and to assure restoration of democracy in Haiti (SC Res. 940, *supra* note 21) and humanitarian assistance in the Great Lakes region (SC Res. 1080 (Nov. 5, 1996)) and in Albania (SC Res. 1101 (March 28, 1997)).

On NATO intervention in the former Yugoslavia and on the authorization to the states to intervene individually or through international organizations, see SC Res. 816, *supra*, para. 4; SC Res. 836, *supra*, para. 10; SC Res. 908 (March 31, 1994), para. 8; SC Res. 958 (Nov. 19, 1994), para. 1; SC Res. 981 (March 31, 1995), para. 6. These resolutions are extensively dealt with in chapter 2 of this book.

30 Repertory, *supra* note 2, Vol. I, Nos 1050–1051, at 48.

the states, decision-making power regarding the use of force for maintenance of peace.

This principle came from the will of dominant powers and was supported by nearly unanimous consensus, within regional organizations, amongst states and other social forces. The UN has embraced it.[31]

On a strictly humanitarian level, in the 1990s, the need to urgently safeguard minorities and, more generally, uphold human rights in those war zones, led, very rapidly, to very broad consensus amongst the Western powers and also with Russia, on the need to allow humanitarian intervention (i.e., armed intervention in another state) by states acting collectively and with UN authorization. To safeguard human dignity and the protection of fundamental freedoms, sovereignty of the territorial state could be limited. This principle allows for the creation by the Security Council of protected areas (no-fly zones and humanitarian corridors)[32] to facilitate the delivery of aid to populations of states *unwilling or unable* to guarantee the protection of fundamental human rights in their own territory.[33]

The principle of collective humanitarian intervention emerged at the behest of powerful states with the help of UN organs, regional international organizations, and civil society, which supported its authority. During those crises, the Security Council authorized states and humanitarian organizations to provide assistance to suffering populations (e.g., the Kurds and Shiites in Iraq, the Croatians and Bosnians in the former Yugoslavia, and the people of Somalia and Rwanda), at times even against the will of the territorial state.[34]

---

31 With regard to the Gulf crisis, worthy of note is the strong solidarity of the West, shown in NATO and in the European Community, and the new relationship that was established between the Soviet Union, Europe and the US, and the convergence of the Arab Countries with the international Community, as shown in regional organizations and in the UN. One should mention the Joint Statement of the US and Soviet foreign ministers of 3 August 1990, the day after the Iraqi invasion of Kuwait, followed by the joint Bush–Gorbachev statement of 9 September 1990. These understandings were sealed by the resolutions passed in the UN and in other regional fora, including those in Africa (see Documents on the Gulf crisis, *in* The Kuwait Crisis: Basic Documents (Elihu Lauterpacht, Christopher Greenwood, Marc Weller & Daniel Betlehem eds, 1991)); see generally Les Aspects Juridique de la Crise et de la Guerre du Golfe (Brigitte Stern ed., 1991); Ugo Villani, Lezioni su l'ONU e la Crisi del Golfo (2nd ed., 1995). Without strong agreement between the US and the Soviet Union, the decision to authorize an anti-Iraq multinational force would not have been adopted.

32 SC Res. 688 (Apr. 5, 1991), paras 3, 4; SC Res. 816, *supra* note 29, paras 1–6.

33 See Giuliana Ziccardi Capaldo, Terrorismo Internazionale e Garanzie Collettive/International Terrorism and Collective Guarantees 75–102 (1990) [hereinafter Ziccardi Capaldo, Terrorismo Internazionale]. See also Mario Bettati, Le Droit d'Ingerence, Mutation de l'Ordre International (1996). For further information and discussion, see *infra* chapter 2 of this book.

34 The Security Council Resolution 678 (Nov. 29, 1990), para. 2, constituted the basis for an unprecedented humanitarian action in Iraqi territory, led by the member states of the anti-Iraq coalition (mainly France, the UK and the US) which, with the support of military forces, installed 'humanitarian centers' in northern Iraq in order to promote the return of displaced persons, and carried out policing and administrative activities there. See *also* UN resolutions on humanitarian intervention in Rwanda, the former Yugoslavia, Somalia, Angola, Haiti, the

It is clear that, on those occasions, the Security Council acted well beyond the UN system, for the Charter does not give it any powers regarding the protection of human rights. And the fact that, to justify those steps, the Security Council framed those crises as a 'breach of the peace (Article 39 UN Charter)' cannot allow it to overcome the statutory limits to its powers.[35]

We believe that in those instances international organizations and, in particular the UN Security Council, integrated general rule-formation and rule-enforcement processes; they did this to protect fundamental interests of the global community. Clearly, the Council contributed to the creation of new rules of international law and integrated general law-making and law-enforcement functions; it did so with the support of the General Assembly, which did not censure the Council's actions. Moreover, consistently with a now established practice, the relevant Security Council resolutions were addressed to *all* states, not only UN member states.[36]

Finally, one should also mention the Security Council resolutions creating *ad hoc* tribunals for punishment of the perpetrators of international crimes in the former Yugoslavia and in Rwanda.[37] The UN took this step to fill in the impunity gap created by deficiencies of the then-existing international legal order, which made it impossible to uphold internationally the criminal responsibility of the individual, as distinct from that of the state of which he/she is/was an organ.[38] This is relevant here because it shows how the Security Council heeded the international community's

---

Great Lakes area, Albania. See also 2005 World Summit Outcome, A/60/L.1 (20 Sept. 2005), paras. 138–139.

35 In legal literature, the debate over the powers of the Security Council has intensified, especially after the end of the Cold War. See *infra* chapter 2 of this book under the heading 'Innovative Trends in the Practice of UN Bodies'.

36 See, e.g., SC Res. 661 (Aug. 6, 1990), paras 3, 5, 6(b), 7, 9; SC Res. 748 (March 31, 1992), paras 4, 5, 6, 7, 8, 9(b), 10; SC Res. 1087, *supra* note 20, para. 15; SC Res. 1097 (Feb. 18, 1997), para. 2.

37 The creation of the Tribunal for the former Yugoslavia, provided by SC Res. 808 (Feb. 22, 1993), and then examined by the Secretary-General in a detailed Report (UN Doc. S/25704, paras 18–30 (May 3, 1993)) was decided on with Security Council resolution SC Res. 827 (May 25, 1993). For Rwanda, see SC Res. 955 (Nov. 8, 1994). On the creation of a permanent international criminal jurisdiction to try individuals responsible for *crimina juris gentium*, see *infra* note 43.

38 It is well known that the distinction between state responsibility and responsibility of individual criminals is at the heart of the Draft Code on Crimes Against the Peace and the Security of Mankind (Art. 5 of the Draft Articles of the Draft Code of Crimes against the Peace and Security of Mankind, UN Doc. A/46/10, Yearbook of the International Law Commission (1991) Vol. II, (Part Two), at 94, 100), which, at its 43rd session, in 1991, the Commission, provisionally adopted on first reading. At its 48th session, in 1996, the Commission adopted the final text of a set of 20 draft articles constituting the code of crimes against the peace and security of mankind (UN Doc. A/48/10, Yearbook of the International Law Commission (1996) Vol. II, (Part Two) (available at <http://www.un.org/law/ilc/texts/dcodefra.htm>). See also Commentary to Part Two, Chap. III *of the Draft Articles on Responsibility of States for Internationally Wrongful Acts* adopted by the International Law Commission at its 53rd session in 2001 (UN Doc. A/56/10), available at <http://www.un.org/law/ilc/texts/State_responsibility/responsibility_commentaries(e).pdf#pagemode=bookmarks>).

call for justice, seeking to fill a legal and institutional gap.[39] The Security Council did the same with the resolutions adopted in the *Lockerbie* and *Sudanese* cases for the 'effective' punishment of alleged Libyan and Egyptian terrorists.

The rationale of UN actions for the punishment of the crimes perpetrated in Bosnia and Rwanda is that of limiting state jurisdiction for reasons of objectivity in the protection of collective interests, where the state's exercise or the failure to exercise sovereign rights jeopardizes the protection of fundamental interests of the global community. The same *ratio* inspired SC Resolutions 731 and 748 in the *Lockerbie* case; however, in this case, the Security Council, rather than establishing an *ad hoc* tribunal and instead taking the direct management of the protection of the general collective interest upon the UN, 'authorized' the holding of the trial of the presumed Libyan terrorists in the courts of the UK and the US. It thus confirmed both the request of these countries that Libya extradite the presumed guilty persons and their intention to act *uti universi*. In so doing, the Council, acting outside the powers given to it by the Charter, filled an institutional gap in the international legal system, which lacked the mechanisms for the punishment of the authors of crimes against humanity.[40]

These resolutions support and enforce the authority of a rule of general international law, both substantive and procedural, which establishes the individual's responsibility for the perpetration of war crimes and other serious breaches of humanitarian law, such as international terrorism.[41] It gives the Security Council the power to mete out effective punishment to those responsible for those acts, removing them, when necessary, from national tribunals that *normally* would have competence and subjecting them to a fair trial before *ad hoc* international jurisdictions.[42] This rule of general international law, which gives the Security Council the power to create *ad hoc* criminal tribunals and which is nowhere found in the UN Charter, arose *immediately*. It is the expression of the present structural changes in the international community in an organic way, evidencing the progress being made towards the establishment of procedures for the institutionalization of international law-making and law-enforcement functions.

It is well known that the individual's international criminal responsibility principle was the focus of the work of the International Law Commission on the creation of an international criminal tribunal.[43] Pending the establishment of such tribunal, the Security Council heeded the call of the international community and took over

---

39 UN Doc. S/PV. 3063 (March 30, 1992), at 83.

40 On the *Lockerbie* case, see SC Res. 731 (Jan. 21, 1992), para. 3, and SC Res. 748, *supra* note 36 (See also *infra* chapter 2 of this book and bibliographic references therein. On the *Sudanese* case, see SC Res. 1054 (April 26, 1996), para. 1; SC Res. 1070 (Aug. 16, 1996), para. 1).

41 SC Res. 859 (Aug. 24, 1993), para. 7; SC Res. 935 (July 1, 1994), preamble.

42 UN Doc. S/PV. 3033 (Jan. 21, 1992), at 98; UN Doc. S/PV. 3063, supra note 39.

43 In 1989, the UN requested the International Law Commission to study how a permanent international criminal tribunal could be created. The request was reiterated several times in the following years (GA Res. 44/39 (Dec. 4, 1989), para. 1; GA Res. 45/41 (Nov. 28, 1990), para. 3; GA Res. 46/54 (Dec. 9, 1991), para. 3). The Statute of the International Criminal Court was adopted in Rome on 17 July 1998, and entered into force on 1 July 2002.

the management of law-making and law-enforcement functions in the international legal system. This new direction is consistent with the universalistic core of the UN Charter and always pursued by the UN. The demise of communism and socialism in Eastern Europe and, consequently, of the division of the world in antagonized blocs, made it possible for the permanent members to take over the public management of world affairs, thus strengthening the role of the UN as overseer of the global community and accelerating the ongoing process of 'verticalization'.

A Theory of Global Rule-Formation Processes

What are the theoretical consequences of the statement at the beginning of this essay that at the end of the 1980s international human rights expanded '*immediately*' and that general principles discussed above emerged '*instantly*'? Generally speaking, we draw inspiration from the thesis – propounded by Rolando Quadri – which holds that principles of international law (hereinafter 'principles'), being the 'immediate' and 'direct' expression of the will of the international community, are rules of general international law. As such, they are different from the general principles of law recognized by civilized nations, as mentioned in Article 38 (1)(c) of the Statute of the International Court of Justice (hereinafter 'general principles of law').[44] We claim that, consistent with the most recent reassessments of that thesis, principles are a source of general international law, together with custom.[45]

Many international legal scholars do not regard principles as a source of general international law different and autonomous from custom[46] (we obviously do not refer to the 'general principles of law' to which we will return later). The International Court of Justice also gives the 'principles' a customary nature, pointing out that 'the association of terms "rules" and "principles" is no more than use of a dual expression

---

The decision of the Security Council to refer the situation in Darfur to the Court has marked the beginning of operations (SC Res. 1593 (March 31, 2005)).

44 Rolando Quadri, Diritto Internazionale Pubblico 109–110, 119–120 (5th ed., 1968). See also, even if with different implications, Charles De Visscher, Théories et Réalités en Droit International Public 184 (3rd ed., 1960); Paul Guggenheim, Traité de Droit International Public 306–07 (2nd ed., 1967).

45 Rather to the contrary, Quadri placed principles, as primary rules, above custom and treaties, which he construed as secondary rules.

46 In international law doctrine, many works deal with the making of rules of general international law; see the classic works by Alfred Verdross, Die Verfassung Der Völkerrechtsgemeinschaft (1926); *Id.*, Völkerrecht 136 (5th ed., 1964); Piero Ziccardi, La Costituzione dell'ordinamento Internazionale (1943); Wilhelm Wengler, 1 Völkerrecht 171 (1964), and writings in L'Élaboration du Droit International Public, Société Francaise pour le Droit International, Colloque de Toulouse (1975); Bin Cheng, *On the Nature and Sources of International Law*, *in* International Law: Teaching and Practice 203 (Bin Cheng ed., 1982); Prosper Weil, *Towards Relative Normativity in International Law?*, 77 Am. J. Int. L. 413 (1983); Change and Stability in International Law-Making (Antonio Cassese & Prosper Weil eds, 1988); Benedetto Conforti, *Cours Général de Droit International Public*, 212 Recueil des Cours 9 (1988–V); Edward MacWhinney, *New International Law and International Law Making*, 16 Chinese Yearbook of International Law 33 (1997–1998).

to convey one and the same idea': they can be distinguished from 'rules' of general or customary international law 'because of their more general and more fundamental character'.[47] Yet, a very large majority of international legal scholars considers custom a primary source of general international law. This is also the holding of the International Court of Justice which, on numerous occasions, in confirming custom as a primary source, stressed that the formation of a customary norm requires the concurrent presence of both classic requirements of *opinio iuris sive necessitatis* and *diuturnitas*, that is to say, the repetition of a given state practice overtime.[48]

The mandatory requirement of *diuturnitas* – an essential constituent element of international custom according to a vast literature[49] – is incompatible with the idea of 'instant custom', which has been put forward by a minority of scholars.[50] More crucially, this excludes that principles, which instantly emerged in the field of human rights, as described below, could be construed as 'customary' norms.

Undoubtedly, the 'instant custom' idea, despite its inherent contradictions,[51] stems from the practical need of accounting for the *instant* formation of primary rules of general international law; a phenomenon that is undeniably taking place

47 Delimitation of the Maritime Boundary in the Gulf of Maine Area (Canada v. United States of America), Judgment, 1984 ICJ Reports 246 (Oct. 12, 1984), para. 79, at 288; See also Repertory, *supra* note 2, Vol. I, Nos 1027–1028, at 27.

48 For the relative references, see Repertory, *supra* note 2, Vol. I, Nos 1001, 1006, 1013, 1019, 1029, 1040, at 4, 8, 14, 20, 28, 38, respectively.

49 Extensive legal literature exists on custom and its constitutive elements. See especially Hans Kelsen, *Théorie du Droit International Coutumier*, 1 Revue International de la Théorie du Droit 253 (1939); Paul Guggenheim, *Les Deux Eléments de la Coutume en Droit International*, La Technique et les Principes du Droit Public. Études en l'Honneur de George Scelle 275 (1950); Piero Ziccardi, *La Consuetudine Internazionale nella Teoria delle Fonti Giuridiche*, 10 Comunicazioni e Studi 190 (1958/59); René-Jean Dupuy, *Coutume Sage et Coutume Sauvage*, La Communauté Internationale. Mélanges Offerts à Charles Rousseau 75 (1974); Bin Cheng, *Custom: The Future of General State Practice in a Divided World*, *in* The Structure and Process of International Law: Essays in Legal Philosophy Doctrine and Theory 496 (Ronald St. John Macdonald & Douglas M. Johnston eds, 1983); Luigi Ferrari Bravo, *Méthodes de Recherche de la Coutume Internationale dans la Pratique des Etats*, 192 Recueil des Cours 233 (1985–III); Luigi Condorelli, *Custom*, *in* International Law: Achievements and Prospects 179 (Mohammed Bedjaoui ed., 1991). More recently, see Ian Brownlie, *Some Problems in the Evaluation of the Practice of States as an Element of Custom*, Studi di Diritto Internazionale in Onore di Gaetano Arangio-Ruiz 313 (2004–I); Bin Cheng, *Hazards in International Law Sharing Legal Terms and Concepts with Municipal Law Without Sufficiently Taking into Account the Differences in Structure Between the Two Systems – Prime Examples: Custom and Opinio Juris*, *id.*, at 469 *et seq.*, [hereinafter Cheng, *Hazards*]. See also *supra* note 46.

50 See Cheng, *supra* note 4. See also Richard R. Baxter, *Treaties and Custom*, 129 Recueil des Cours 25, 44–67 (1970–I); George Abi Saab, *La Coutume dans Tous Ses Etats ou le Dilemme du Developpement du Droit International General dans un Monde Eclaté*, Il Diritto Internazionale al Tempo della sua Codificazione. Studi in Onore di Roberto Ago 53 (1987–I); Anthony A. D'Amato, Identifying Rules of Customary Law 107 (1997).

51 Mark E. Villiger, Customary International Law and Treaties 4 (1985); Condorelli, *supra* note 49, at 201.

in the contemporary international legal order. However, one should realistically consider that this phenomenon is, after all, the result of the propulsive will of the great powers. This is consistent with the view according to which, when it comes to the instant formation of general international norms, preponderant consideration is given to the will of powerful states acting in the name of interpreting and expressing the will of the entire international social body/community as a whole, instead of each state's acceptance that a given rule is part of general law, as is required for the creation of a norm of customary international law (which, it goes without saying, includes instant custom).

This is no place to test theories about custom as a source of general international law. It is rather more apposite to consider custom as the expression of the will of 'the large majority of states' meaning a majority where all essential components and political groupings of the international society at any given time are represented (e.g., during the Cold War this would have required an adequate representation of states belonging to the West, East, and non-Aligned blocs). It is the product, if not of unanimous determinations, of stratification, over time, of the will of this majority of states, as made manifest by repeated and uniform behaviours rooted in the social fabric. It is, in sum, a process whose basis is the acknowledged need of new legal rules applicable to all members of the international community (*opinio juris*), translating into an acceptance by uniform and constant behaviour of each individual state (*diuturnitas*), so that the will of 'each' state remains distinct and distinguishable.

In synthesis, in our opinion, custom necessitates the actual participation of states (*diuturnitas* and *opinio juris*), in their own capacity (*uti singuli*), to the formation of the general norm. In this regard, we agree with Bin Cheng who wrote, 'Each state's acceptance constitutes its own *opinio individualis juris generalis*, its own *opinio juris* of what is the rule of the general law applicable to all on the subject'.[52]

The Dynamic Process Behind the Formation of New Principles: 'Proposals' by the Dominant Powers and Consensus Reached in International Fora

Conversely, principles of international law, according to the theory of Quadri, are the 'direct' expression of the will of the social body as a whole. They are the result of the determination of the prevailing forces within the international community (i.e., the so-called superpowers) that authoritatively state the values and goals of the entire community. They are, in short, following this line of thought, norms *imposed* on all states by the forces dominating politically the international scene at any given time.[53]

Quadri's theory of principles should be reconsidered. Though conceding that prevailing forces play a specific role in the formation of principles, we would like to stress that in the current era, characterized by substantial changes in the structure of the international society, there are sound reasons for doubting the continuing validity of the traditional approach that considers principles as norms that are not only

52 Cheng, *Hazards*, *supra* note 49, at 488.

53 See *supra* note 44 and accompanying text.

wanted but also *imposed* on 'all' by the dominant political forces of the international community.

Truly, the idea that principles emerge because they are imposed is increasingly questionable in light of the rapidly changing political and economic structure of the international community and because of the trend in the international community towards institutionalization[54] and the emergence of various dominant forces (economic, cultural, religious, and mediatic) and different forms of power (i.e. new powers).[55]

The foregoing explains why the traditional theory of principles no longer seems suitable to explain the present process of creation of principles of international law, although the powerful states will still continue to guide general political and economic policy. We rather believe that the will of dominant forces of the global community (that is to say, the dominant forces driving globalization, which include not only major states but also NGOs, multinational corporations, religious movements, media, etc.) does not turn into law (principles) because it is imposed. It becomes law only as insofar as it is supported by a wide consensus expressed in institutional fora. Principles are created by way of an integrated process. The will of major states provides only the spark, while consensus reached in international fora provides the fuel.

In this integrated and complex process, dominant social forces simply put forward what is believed to be the general will of the international society. They act '*uti universi*'; that is to say, in the common interest, as an expression of the international social body. This will eventually turns into legal materiality by way of agreements reached within institutional regional, inter-regional and universal fora, like international organizations, clearly the most suitable arena to engender consensus. The will of dominant political forces, mitigated by the dialectic influences of other acting social forces becomes 'law' binding on 'all' because (and provided that) it (the rule) represents the intersection and the acme of equilibrium achieved in international fora between the interest of prevailing powers and public interest.

Starting from the 'proposal' of dominant powers, through diplomatic consultations, consensus increasingly spreads to an increasing number of international actors as it is discussed, examined, combined, and patched together. As consensus expands to various international fora at different levels, the original proposal becomes the will of the global social body. This view of the 'quasi-organic' character of principles is different, evidently, not only from Quadri's proposal but also from Anglo-American doctrine, which attributes to international organizations – especially the UN – the power to issue norms endowed with general compulsory force.[56] In our opinion,

54 See, e.g., Piero Ziccardi, *Règles d'Organisation et Règles de Conduite en Droit International*, 152 Recueil des Cours 119 (1976–IV).

55 Mireille Delmas-Marty, Global Law. A Triple Challenge 99–111 (2003); Kenichi Ohmae, The End of the Nation-State: The Rise of Regional Economies (1995).

56 For a critical analysis of this doctrine, with bibliographic references, see Gaetano Arangio Ruiz, *The Normative Role of the General Assembly of the United Nations and the Declaration of Principles of Friendly Relations*, 137 Recueil des Cours 419, 434, 460, 629 (1972–III).

organic acts of international organizations are different stages of the process of generalization of the proposal. They are the 'moments' of the dynamic process of formation of principles.

The Mechanisms Developed by the G8 and the Security Council's Open Debates

Since its founding in 1975, the Group of Eight leading industrialized countries (G8) has played a decisive role in the actual direction of world affairs, influencing such issues as finance, trade policy, security, human rights, environment, sustainable development, famine, health, water, etc. Today, the statements emanating from the annual G8 summit represent the 'proposals' of the prevailing forces of the contemporary global community, around which consensus may form in world institutions for the creation of principles of international law. The power of G8 members to initiate new basic international rules is being strengthened because the annual institutionalization of the meetings and because of the enlarged participation (i.e., of the EU) and dialogue with countries, groups of countries, and institutions outside their group, especially the emerging countries and civil society (NGOs). The Group of 20 (G20) is a forum for cooperation and discussion on financial globalization. The mechanism of regularly meeting and consulting developed by the G8 largely contributes to the progressive institutionalization of the formation process of principles of international law.

The interactive mechanisms play a similar role in the management of major global issues developed from the end of the last century, in UN procedures and in efforts to reform Security Council working methods, aimed at increasing the involvement of states not members of the Security Council in its work and at developing more general connections with groups of NGOs and representatives of non-state actors.[57]

The growing number of activities undertaken by the Council, closely related to the widening interpretation of its competence, has fostered the emergence of the category of thematic open debates. Since the late 1990s, various thematic debates on certain issues of current global relevance (such as peace and security, protection of civilians in armed conflict, children and armed conflict, women, HIV/AIDS, climate change) have become frequent events and continue to be held regularly. Meetings such as these allow for an exchange of ideas between members of the Council and outsiders, whenever the Council is about to consider an important issue. On 16 December 1994, the Council adopted a presidential statement in which it declared that "...there should be an increased recourse to open meetings, in particular at an

---

57 See Open Debates in the UN on the Question of SECURITY COUNCIL TRANSPARENCY, LEGITIMACY AND EFFECTIVENESS: Efforts To Reform Council Working Methods 1993-2007 available at www.securitycouncilreport.org. For detailed information on G8-activities, see G8 Information Centre, available at <http://www.g7.utoronto.ca/>; JOHN J. KIRTON & JUNICHI TAKASE, NEW DIRECTIONS IN GLOBAL POLITICAL GOVERNANCE: THE G8 AND INTERNATIONAL ORDER IN THE TWENTY-FIRST CENTURY (2002); *Id., NEW DIRECTIONS IN GLOBAL ECONOMIC GOVERNANCE: MANAGING GLOBALIZATION IN THE TWENTY-FIRST CENTURY* (2002); MICHELE FRATIANNI, PAOLO SAVONA & JOHN J. KIRTON, SUSTAINING GROWTH AND GLOBAL DEVELOPMENT: G7 AND IMF GOVERNANCE (2003).

early stage in its consideration of a subject" (S/PRST/1994/81). Another important mechanism for Council interaction with outsiders has been the availability of draft decisions before they are adopted, as well as the practice of meeting with local NGOs during Council travel and inviting NGOs and other actors to Arria formula briefings. By means of these instruments and all these forms of interaction the Council seeks to reach consensus on its proposals by setting up a legal framework of agreed general international regulations (soft law) in key sectors of the life of the global community, as a basis on which to continue the search for consensus and the achievement of general principles of law.

The 'Quasi-Organic' Nature of New Global Principles

New principles of international law should not be confused with 'general principles of law' recognized by civilized nations (Article 38 (1)(c) of the Statute of the International Court of Justice (ICJ).[58] Unlike the former, the latter do not express directly the will of the international social body. The principles here discussed are 'general' international norms (described in various ways in literature) whose formation is filtered by the acceptance by 'each' state of certain core legal principles (e.g., rules of legal logic, such as *nemo judex in re sua*, *ne bis in idem*, etc., and principles of natural law, such as the outlawry of genocide, apartheid, torture, etc.). States place them at the core of their own legal system because they recognize them as universal. For the same reason, they are also taken in at the core of the international level. States recognize them as basic principles of any legal order, thus of the international order, too. The process of generalization is achieved at the international level, mainly through the enunciation of those principles in general acts of international organs (e.g., Declarations of Principles of the UN General Assembly) and their application by international judges and arbitrators.

Our thesis on the 'quasi-organic' nature of the principles of international law develops and complements the vision, put forward and discussed in previous works, of the current tendency of the international society to verticalization, towards the global community.[59]

Indeed, the present international community is in search of a new political and institutional order. The international community moulded in Westphalia, anarchic and horizontal in structure, was put in question after the Second World War by the growing need to safeguard fundamental values and interests of the world community. The weakening of the hegemonic function of the superpowers has further put strains on this weakened structure.

We are witnessing profound changes in the way international power is managed, and a new era has dawned. It began in the second half of the twentieth century,

58 Bin Cheng calls 'general principles' 'the basic tenets of the concept of law' (BIN CHENG, GENERAL PRINCIPLES OF LAW AS APPLIED BY INTERNATIONAL COURTS AND TRIBUNALS (1953)); *Id.*, *Hazards*, *supra* note 49, at 469 *et seq.*

59 See GIULIANA ZICCARDI CAPALDO, *Verticalità della Comunità Internazionale e Nazioni Unite. Un Riesame del Caso Lockerbie*, *in* INTERVENTI DELLE NAZIONI UNITE E DIRITTO INTERNAZIONALE 337 (1995), at 61 *et seq.*, *passim*, especially at 79 *et seq.*

around the 1960s, and is characterized by the progressive integration of initiatives of states acting collectively (i.e., *uti universi*) with general activities of the organized community.[60]

In the current age, these transformations concern the protection of fundamental interests of the international community as a whole (e.g., peace and security, self-determination, human rights, the fight against terrorism, democracy). Effectively protecting these public interests necessitates objectivity. An unorganized community, as is the inter-state community, could not guarantee this and has therefore necessitated the development of institutionalized processes of global governance. International organizations actively participate in the management of international power.[61]

By using the term 'verticality' with reference to changes in the structure of the international community we describe an ongoing evolutionary process. From the structural decentralization (which still characterizes the international community), it is gradually moving toward a centralized system, along the lines of the state system, where law-making, law-enforcement, and law-ascertainment functions are centralized and organized, opened to the participation of all social forces.

The 'verticalization' of the international community is manifested by the increasing international governance activities carried out by international organizations, mainly the UN, whose pre-eminence over other organizations is sanctioned by Chapter VIII of the Charter. The UN has put its organized structure 'at the service' of the community of states[62] in order to integrate – by authorizing, endorsing, or condemning – non-organized activities of a public law nature that the

---

60 We should mention the development, beginning in the 1960s, of the practice of 'countermeasures' (unilateral economic, political or diplomatic coercive measures) adopted mainly by the Western countries but also by socialist countries. They are justified as reaction to occupation, aggression, international terrorism or serious violations of human rights and of the principle of self-determination. States have often justified sanctions by pointing to decisions of the UN ascertaining violations of obligations *erga omnes*. The fact that the UN made the determination gives their actions the clout of objectivity they would otherwise lack. However, UN organs have reaffirmed and retained the power of control over the legitimacy of their implementation. In some cases, the General Assembly has condemned unilateral trade embargoes adopted by some states and demanded their termination (see, e.g., GA Res. 40/188 (Dec. 17, 1985); GA Res. 47/19 (Nov. 24, 1992)). See generally GA Res. 51/17 (Nov. 21, 1996); GA Res. 51/22 (Nov. 27, 1996). One should also mention the usual practice by which the Security Council examines states' use of force to ascertain whether it falls within Art. 51 of the Charter and the practice of the Council of authorizing the use of force by states acting collectively and to exercise control on it (see *supra* note 29).

61 In this sense, albeit from a different perspective, see Simma & Alston, *supra* note 28, at 102; See also Roda Mushkat, *Public Participation in Environmental Law Making*, 1 Chinese Journal of International Law 185 (2002); Gerhard Loibl, *The Role of International Organisations in International Law-Making International Environmental Negotiations*, 1 Non-State Actors and International Law 41 (2001).

62 See Giuliana Ziccardi Capaldo, *Il Disconoscimento delle Credenziali del Sud Africa come Sanzione contro l'Apartheid*, 68 Rivista di Diritto Internazionale 299 (1985), at 306; *Id.*, Terrorismo Internazionale, *supra* note 33, at 127–130. With regard to the Security Council practice of acting beyond the limits set by the Charter, see *infra* chapter 2 of this book and bibliographic and documentary references therein.

states claim for themselves. Consequently, the international institutions, mainly the UN organs, sometimes carry out functions (i.e., of supervision and endorsement) that are '*integrative*' of the public activities of the states. At other times, they take over the role of states, directly acting on behalf of the international community and carrying out its general functions. After all, from its inception, the UN has been seeking to make up for the structural deficiencies of the international society and, from time to time, has acted to protect global interests through its organs.

Granted, there are several fundamental problems: the General Assembly lacks law-making authority under the Charter; decision powers are allocated exclusively to the Security Council, an organ with limited membership and whose competence is restricted to maintenance of the peace. In addition, the legal definition and the lack of enforcement mechanisms for the other fundamental principles laid down in the Charter (Article 1) and at the global level, with the exception of non-use of armed force, the only one guaranteed by Chapter VII, are problematic; so is the freezing of activities under Chapter VII caused by the use of the right of veto. Be that as it may, the UN, because of its universal character and because it undertakes to protect the interests of the whole community of states, is perhaps the kernel of an ideal organization for the international society as a whole. It provides an institutional framework suitable for general purposes. It is thus clear why, in the period following the Second World War, the international community met the need to establish mechanisms for implementation and enforcement caused by the growth of norms protecting the collective fundamental interests, which were being expressed in practice, by using the institutional framework of the UN, the most suitable vehicle for guaranteeing the objectivity required by a public law function. It is also clear why, in the face of the already-mentioned inadequacy of the system of collective security provided under the Charter, reserved solely for maintenance of the peace, the tendency to develop binding powers of ascertainment of the General Assembly, as well as Security Council powers, going beyond the Charter system took hold.

Therefore, despite the well-known structural deficiencies affecting the World organization, it can be said that during the last fifty years the UN organs have been given functions different from (and complementary to) those written in the Charter.

For these reasons, even if, at the present time, the replacement *in toto* of the international community, based on the principle of equality of states, with the organized community is not conceivable, there are nonetheless recognizable processes of verticalization of international power taking place. These processes are growing in quantity and importance, and need to be regulated.

In previous works, we noted that the verticalization of the international community is embodied in the public general functions that the UN carries out with regard to the *ascertainment* of violations and the *guarantee* of fundamental international social values, beyond the Charter system.[63] It is possible to add that in regard to the *formation* of principles protecting these values, too, the integration between substantial community and the organized community is taking place. Also

---

63 Giuliana Ziccardi Capaldo, Le Situazioni Territoriali Illegittime nel Diritto Internazionale/Unlawful territorial situations in International law (1977) especially at 110 *et seq*. See also *infra* chapter 2 of this book.

with regard to the creation of principles of international law, the UN and other international organizations put their apparatus and their institutions at the service of the global community to complement general law-making processes. This way, the international society is moving toward more advanced forms of international governance. It gradually relinquishes anorganic law-making processes like those of the classic inter-state community (e.g., custom), which cannot adequately satisfy the increasing need of objectivity and legality in the safeguard of public interest of the contemporary world society. All this takes place by eroding and constraining state sovereignty.

Concluding Remarks: The Intersection of Prevailing Forces and the Public Interest in Global Rule-Formation Processes

In conclusion, principles of international law are a source of law better fitting the drive of the international community towards the institutionalization of social functions, based on the model of national systems. In the case of principles, the dominant forces have the power to initiate new norms, a function typical of executive powers, while it is up to the international institutions to exercise control and to create a broad consensus of other forces acting in the global community around the 'proposal' of the dominant powers; thus, proposal and consent represent the basic elements of a dynamic, democratic/integrated process for the adoption of general international norms.

It is obvious that evidence of new/global constitutional principles of international law cannot be found in the practice of the 'individual' states (as is usually done in the case of customary norms) but must be found in acts, declarations, and joint statements of the major powers and, at the same time, in the decisions of the highest UN organs, often reiterated by other international organizations, approving or disapproving acts of states and of other actors of the international community. In the ascertainment of the principles, the pronouncements of international organizations, which might declare and/or sanction their violations, carry great weight. The same is valid in the case of the express endorsement by, or the lack of reaction of, the organized community to the unilateral adoption of sanctions by states acting *uti universi.*

One should add that these stages of the 'organic' principles-making process are not yet formalized. The process is still only in embryonic stages. However, in the contemporary changing political and social context, where new rules and new governance processes are emerging,[64] the creation of principles by way of the search for convergences, reached within international institutions, between the interest of great powers and public interest heralds the new course of international law; a course where custom, as a source of primary (constitutional) law, is in decline.[65]

64 Christine M. Chinkin, *Global Summits: Democratizing International Law-Making?*, 7 Public Law Review 208 (1996); Edward MacWhinney, *Separation or Complementarity of Constitutional Law-Making Powers of United Nations Security Council, General Assembly and International Court of Justice*, Studi di Diritto Internazionale in Onore di Gaetano Arangio-Ruiz 339 (2004–I) .

65 On the identity crisis of customary law, see Simma & Alston, *supra* note 28, at 88.

It is important to pay attention to the system promoted by the UN for the protection of human rights, which is aimed at creating institutionalized cooperation between the UN and the UN human rights treaty bodies, on the one hand, and, on the other, regional organizations and institutions, including the Council of Europe, the Organization for Security and Cooperation in Europe, the League of Arab States, the Inter-American Commission on Human Rights, and the African Commission on Human and Peoples' Rights. Recently, the General Assembly has urged 'all actors on the international scene' to build a democratic and equitable international order, and has requested the Secretary-General 'to bring its determination to the attention of states, UN organs, bodies and components, intergovernmental organizations, in particular the Bretton Woods Institution, and non-governmental organizations, and to disseminate it on the widest possible basis'.[66]

In conclusion, at present, 'principles' are sources of general international law just like general principles of law (ICJ Statute, Article 38 (1)(c)) and custom; these three categories of sources represent different law-making processes of basic rules of the global legal system; but not all principles (nor customs) are non-derogable norms.[67] The move is from an anorganic society to an institutionalized society. Even when current organized structures are resorted to, especially those of the UN, this process of formation of primary norms takes place outside the Charter system, for the Charter does not give UN organs general law-making powers.

---

66 See *Promotion of a Democratic and Equitable International Order*, GA Res. 59/193, (March 18, 2005), paras 7, 14. See also Vienna Declaration and Programme of Action adopted by the World Conference on Human Rights on 25 June 1993 (UN Doc. A/CONF. 157/24 (Part I), chap. III); GA Res. 59/196 (March 22, 2005).

67 See *infra* Table 4.

SECTION II
Global Law-Enforcement System

Chapter 2

The Integrated System of Law-Enforcement*

Introduction

The international law-enforcement system is currently undergoing a transition away from its bilateral, unorganized character centred on the reaction of the state suffering injury (self-help), exceptionally assisted by other states in the case of armed attack, in compliance with Article 51 of the UN Charter.[1] The international legal order is showing a marked tendency towards increasing institutionalization and the development of a collective system of law enforcement, co-managed by states, inter-governmental and non-governmental organizations, and the UN bodies, outside the Charter system.

These changes correlate with the development of international norms protecting fundamental values and interests of the international community as a whole (i.e., global constitutional principles): norms of a 'public' nature, giving rise to obligations *erga omnes*.[2] The proliferation of these rules means that the international legal order has to face the problem of their 'objective' protection, giving rise to the need for law-enforcement procedures to provide a response to any infringement on the part of the whole international community.

---

* This chapter is based on the paper by Giuliana Ziccardi Capaldo, *The Law of the Global Community: An Integrated System to Enforce 'Public' International Law*, 1 The Global Community. Yearbook of International Law and Jurisprudence [hereinafter GCYILJ], 71 (2001); that early text has been updated and extensively modified. The changes to international law I detail therein have been summarized in Tables 2 and 5.

1 On the general character this Article has acquired through custom, see Military and Paramilitary Activities in and against Nicaragua (Nicaragua v. United States of America), Merits, Judgment, 1986 ICJ Reports 14 (June 27, 1986), para. 193, at 102–103; Ziccardi Capaldo, Repertory (1947–1992), 2 vols, (1995), vol. I, No. 1050, at 49.

2 We attribute the category of obligations *erga omnes* with the value of norms of a public nature; we have thus set out a detailed analysis of the origin, content, and nature of constitutional norms on the basis of which the legitimacy of governments and territorial situations are evaluated, and non-recognition of regimes established. See Giuliana Ziccardi Capaldo, Le Situazioni Territoriali Illegittime nel Diritto Internazionale/Unlawful Territorial Situations in International Law 11–14, 27–49 (1977). See also Jost Delbrück, who defines such norms as 'public interest norms', *in* Comments, Allocation of Law Enforcement Authority in the International System. Proceedings of an International Symposium of the Kiel Institute of International Law, March 23 to 25, 1994, 174, 179 (Jost Delbrück ed., 1995) [hereinafter Delbrück, Allocation of Law Enforcement].

A wide-ranging debate has taken place since the 1980s about the changes to the international system of sanctions relating to these developments, focusing above all on the power of states to act unilaterally to defend the public interests. Contributing to the contemporary debate on emerging tendencies in international law, we argued that the collective international processes for the protection of fundamental community interests and values lies in the progressive integration between the community of states and the organized community, i.e., between state action performed in the common interest and measures supplementing state action taken by international institutions on behalf of the international legal order.[3] From the mid-twentieth century onward, we have witnessed instances of the collective guarantee of the norms referred to, at times outside the UN enforcement system and reflecting the inadequacy of this system, put into effect by states that have not been directly affected, operating in a collective capacity. The supervision of the UN bodies has been imposed in such cases, with these bodies acting on behalf of the international community beyond the powers conferred on them by the Charter. The development and consolidation of this practice (spasmodic and often inconsistent) has led to an evolution in the international enforcement system: alongside self-help, which continues to be the typical form of unilateral implementation for international legal norms of a 'private' nature, international legal processes capable of responding collectively have asserted themselves at a general level for the enforcement of the norms of a public nature referred to above. For the protection of such norms, the principle has prevailed that states that are not directly affected may act to restore the law that has been infringed. This entails acting 'in the common interest' (*uti universi*),[4] with the cooperation of the UN bodies vested with general functions of control by the international legal order. Thus, the control exercised by international bodies gives the action undertaken 'unilaterally' by states or groups of states the objectivity needed to endow it with a 'public' nature and avoid abuses, providing an institutional control of legitimacy.[5] In the practice over the past 30 years, procedures and mechanisms for the collective protection of community values have emerged

3 On the development and scope of such norms and the parallel institutionalization of the international law-enforcement system, see Ziccardi Capaldo, Terrorismo Internazionale, *passim*, especially at 126–130 (1990); *Id.*, *supra* note 2, at 99–128. On changes in the enforcement system see especially Christian Tomuschat, *Obligations Arising for States Without or Against Their Will*, 241 Recueil des Cours 199, 353–369 (1993–IV); Jochen A. Frowein, *Reactions by Not Directly Affected States to Breaches of Public International Law*, 248 Recueil des Cours 355–366 (1994–IV); Bruno Simma, *From Bilateralism to Community Interests in International Law*, 250 Recueil des Cours 256–284 (1994–VI); the contributions *in* The Future of International Law Enforcement, New Scenarios – New Law? Proceedings of an International Symposium of the Kiel Institute of International Law, March 25–27, 1992 (Jost Delbrück ed., 1993); and those in Delbrück, Allocation of Law Enforcement, *supra* note 2. For further doctrinal contributions, see *Symposium: The Changing Structure of International Law Revisited*, 8 Eur. J. Int'l L. (1997); 9 Eur. J. Int'l L. (1998). See also *infra*, *passim*.

4 See Rolando Quadri, Diritto Internazionale Pubblico 277 (1968) (5th ed.).

5 On this concept, see for more details, *infra* section later in this chapter under the heading 'States Acting …', especially at note 41.

that envisage 'integrated' decision processes, since states, international institutions, and other globalization forces all take part in enforcement. The procedures in question are embodied in general norms of the international legal order and, while they envisage the use of the UN institutional structure, they are not carried out within the legal bounds of the Charter and therefore fall outside the collective security system set forth in Chapter VII.

The aim of the present chapter is to identify the mechanisms of 'shared governance' operating between the international community and the organized community – in particular between states, international organizations, and UN bodies – for the 'objective' implementation of global constitutional principles, which have been developed up to now through practice and have become customary procedural rules and general principles of international law; such procedures, however, must be more precisely defined and formalized.

It should be pointed out that our analysis focuses in particular on processes of collective guarantees pertaining to the breach by states of obligations *erga omnes*. These cases concern 'punitive' social action exercised 'against' the state responsible and intervention to repress serious breaches of norms protecting fundamental collective values. Accordingly, we shall not cover another form of collective guarantee here – one which we defined as '*tutelare*' (i.e., tutelary) (as opposed to the punitive action referred to above) in a previous study,[6] where we presented the processes of collective protection of public international values in a broader perspective. We bring within the concept of 'tutelary guarantees' all the limitations that are placed on the sovereign rights of states by the international legal order for the purposes of preventing a material prejudice to public interests that may arise from the exercise (or non-exercise) of such rights. In such cases, as a result of the restriction on the jurisdiction of the state with territorial sovereignty, quite exceptionally, the authoritative intervention of states acting in the common interest and/or of international organizations acting on behalf of the international community becomes lawful. Limitations of this type are not punitive in character, although they compel the sovereign state to tolerate (*pati*) the implementation of the collective will by reason of the greater value accorded to general interests as compared with particular interests of states. This is why we make a distinction between this category of collective guarantees and the category termed 'punitive guarantees' (albeit improperly) concerning the infringement of *erga omnes* obligations, where the guarantee consists of the response by the international community to the state responsible for the wrongdoing.[7]

The survey that follows takes as its starting point the norms that impose obligations *erga omnes* on states; we will then turn our attention to the changes to the international legal order resulting both from action by states on behalf of the international community to protect the basic values embodied in those norms, and the concurrent activity carried out by UN bodies 'outside the institutional framework' to integrate collective state enforcement action, thus granting it legitimacy. In our view,

---

6 This argument is developed *in extenso* in our work TERRORISMO INTERNAZIONALE, quoted *supra* note 3, at 10–11, 71–131. See also the part of the text relating to note 126, *infra*.

7 For more detail see, *infra* chapter 6 of this book.

the mechanisms of shared governance for enforcing 'public' norms are modifying the structure of the international legal order, moving towards the organization and institutionalization of its functions, for these mechanisms impact the international community and its legal order in a 'vertical' direction.

It is not the first time this matter has come to our attention, and in the present work we intend to develop and consider in greater depth the conclusions reached in previous writings, following the same integrated approach, which has found further confirmation in the practice. On the basis of this approach, the analysis of the mechanisms for protecting fundamental global values should not be carried out solely with regard to the procedures of the Charter but needs to take account of the international decision-making process relating to law enforcement, from an unorganized process governed by the hegemonic states to an integrated process (i.e., quasi-organic, incorporating institutional decisions), while taking account of the role assigned to the UN in the present global system, along with the states and the other global forces, to protect global values in the international order.

The Private-Public Approach to Law-Enforcement

In this perspective, the international law-enforcement system is moving towards institutionalization and the development of mechanisms and procedures for the joint protection by states and international institutions of fundamental community values. This perspective requires us to go beyond the traditional positive theory that regards international law as being concerned solely with the protection of 'individual' state interests but incapable of adequately protecting 'collective' interests, which are therefore a matter for the UN Charter system. Our approach highlights the fact that the analysis by international relations scholars of the problems arising from the implementation of the principles considered has been carried out mainly in theoretical terms, while paying scant attention to changes in the international order and the new mechanisms and processes for protecting the global values that go beyond the Charter system.

Our intended perspective will become clearer once we have analysed the practice over the past 30 years of states and UN bodies in sanctioning serious breaches of obligations *erga omnes* (see the following major section of this chapter). Before doing this, it should be noted that in practice there is a well-known tendency by states to react to breaches of obligations *erga omnes* with a degree of enforcement that does not correspond, at least broadly speaking, to the traditional measures of customary international law. The characteristic feature of this practice is that often the response to the wrongdoing cannot be justified in terms of the violation of the rights of the states taking action (as would customarily be the case); rather, the responsive action is taken by states other than those directly affected.

No less significant is the related practice of UN bodies (and international organizations) over the same period (see below under the heading 'Innovative Trends in the Practice of UN Bodies'), aimed at developing enforcement mechanisms that go beyond the limits laid down by the Charter and implementing new procedures and mechanisms for the protection of fundamental community interests, holding themselves out as the guardians of the legality and objectivity of enforcement action carried out by states in the common interest.

The focus of legal scholars has been mainly devoted on certain aspects of the practice referred to, in particular the fact that the reaction to a breach of obligations *erga omnes* does not come only from the state directly affected. The extensive debate arising from this issue has concerned the existence of a 'right' for 'all' states to adopt enforcement measures in protecting a fundamental collective interest that has been violated. Some authors argue that such a right exists, especially at a theoretical level. The collective character of the obligations *erga omnes* laid down by the international norms protecting fundamental values of the community 'as a whole' has been stressed: consequently, it is claimed that such norms are enforced in the case of a breach by special protection; that is to say, the right for all states to take action in response to infringements, in the common interest, on behalf of the international community.[8]

This line of reasoning has been strengthened by the change in the concept of a 'legal right or interest' to react to a wrongful act, apparent in the case law of the International Court of Justice. As early as the 1960s, the Court introduced a change in its previous stance by holding that 'a legal right or interest need not necessarily relate to anything material or "tangible", and can be infringed even though no prejudice of a material kind has been suffered'. As a result, the Court stated that 'States may be entitled to uphold some general principle even though the particular contravention of it alleged has not affected their own material interests … States may have a legal interest in vindicating a principle of international law, even though they have, in the given case, suffered no material prejudice'.[9]

A few years later the Court elaborated on its earlier pronouncement, providing the well-known distinction between two categories of international legal norms: (1) norms having as their object the protection of states' 'own' interests; and (2) norms for the defence of the fundamental values of the international community (e.g., the principles and rules outlawing acts of aggression and genocide, or concerning the basic rights of the human person, including protection from slavery and racial discrimination), for which all states may be deemed holders of a 'legal interest'.[10]

Notably, the Court's distinction between these two categories of international norms was used by the International Law Commission (ILC) as the basis for distinguishing between 'delicts' and 'crimes', recognizing a different regime of

---

8 See the examination of the divergent views in the doctrine by Frowein, *supra* note 3, at 406–410; see especially Roberto Ago, *Obligations* Erga Omnes *and the International Community*, *in* International Crimes of States: A Critical Analysis of the ICL's Draft Article 19 on State Responsibility 237, 238 (Joseph H.H. Weiler ed., 1989).

9 South West Africa, Second Phase (Ethiopia v. South Africa; Liberia v. South Africa), Judgment, 1966 ICJ Reports 6 (July 18, 1966), para. 44, at 32–33; see our Repertory, *supra* note 1, vol. I, No. 1585, at 615–617.

10 Barcelona Traction, Light and Power Company (Belgium v. Spain), Limited, Judgment, 1970 ICJ Reports 3 (Feb. 5, 1970), paras 33–34, at 32; see our Repertory, *supra* note 1, vol. I, No. 1071, 1586, at 71, 617, respectively.

international responsibility for the two classes of wrongful acts.[11] This distinction has led jurists to carry out an in-depth examination of the differences between international norms relating to the sanctions regime, in order to identify the so-called peremptory norms whose infringement would constitute a crime and which would therefore be collectively sanctioned. Following this tendency, various authors have examined the matter of 'collective guarantees' from a perspective giving greater weight to the definition of international crimes and the regime of responsibility, which is more onerous than the ordinary regime in that the reaction against the offending state could or should be carried out by all the other states, even though they are not directly affected.[12]

In subsequent developments, from another perspective, part of the international legal literature has been increasingly active in recognising a gradual shift of the international law-enforcement system towards a public approach. Some authors, emphasizing the individual states' authority to react to a violation of community values, maintain that in these cases states act 'as agents' of the international community 'in the public interest',[13] as constitutional bodies of the international community.

---

11 See the Commission commentary on draft Art. 19, *Report of the International Law Commission, Draft articles on the Responsibility of States for Internationally Wrongful Acts* (UN Doc. A/CN.4/Ser.A/1976/Add.1 (Part 2); UN Doc. A/CN.4/291), YEARBOOK OF INTERNATIONAL LAW COMMISSION (1976) [hereinafter Y. INT'L L. COMM.] LC, Vol. II, (Part Two), at 96 and the proposals made by the Special Rapporteur, Roberto Ago, Fifth Report, Y. INT'L L. COMM. (1976), Vol. II, (Part One), at 3, 24 (UN Doc. A/CN.4/291, *supra*, para. 89, at 828). For the text of the same Article adopted by the Commission see Y. INT'L L. COMM. (1980), Vol. II, (Part Two), at 31 (UN Doc. A/CN.4/1980/Add. 1 (Part 2). See also *id.*, draft Art. 40 (3), UN GAOR, 51st Sess., Supp. No. 10, at 121, 170; UN Doc. A/51/10 (1996)).

12 From a wealth of literature, see Vincenzo Starace, *La Responsabilité Résultant de la Violation des Obligations a l'Egard de la Communauté Internationale*, 153 RECUEIL DES COURS 263 (1976–IV); Pierre-Marie Dupuy, *Action Publique et Crime International de l'Etat: A Propos de l'Art. 19 du Projet de la Commission du Droit International sur la Responsabilité des Etats*, 25 ANN. FR. D.I. 539 (1979); *Id., Observations sur le 'Crime International de l'Etat'*, 84 REVUE GÉNÉRALE DE DROIT INTERNATIONAL PUBLIC [hereinafter REV. GEN. D.I.P.] 449 (1980), at 468; Geoff Gilbert, *The Criminal Responsibility of States*, 39 INT'L & COMP. L.Q. 345 (1990); M. Cherif Bassiouni, *International Crimes:* 'Jus Cogens' *and* 'Obligatio Erga Omnes', 59 LAW & CONTEMPORARY PROBLEMS 63 (1996); *Id., Accountability for Violations of International Humanitarian Law and Other Serious Violations of Human Rights*, 1 GCYILJ 2001, 3; ANDRÉ J.J. DE HOOGH, OBLIGATIONS ERGA OMNES AND INTERNATIONAL CRIMES: A THEORETICAL INQUIRY INTO THE IMPLEMENTATION AND ENFORCEMENT OF THE INTERNATIONAL RESPONSIBILITY OF STATES (1996). See also the contributions in INTERNATIONAL CRIMES OF STATES: A CRITICAL ANALYSIS OF THE ILC'S DRAFT ARTICLE 19 ON STATE RESPONSIBILITY, *supra* note 8; Karl Zemanek, *New Trends in the Enforcement of* Erga Omnes *Obligations*, 4 MAX PLANCK YEARBOOK OF UNITED NATIONS LAW 1 (2000); Christian J. Tams, *Enforcing Obligations* Erga Omnes *in International Law*, CAMBRIDGE STUDIES IN INTERNATIONAL AND COMPARATIVE LAW (No. 43), 2005. For the ILC work on the topic and proposals on the consequences of crimes presented by Special Rapporteurs W. Riphagen and G. Arangio Ruiz, see Simma, *supra* note 3, at 303–308.

13 PHILIP ALLOTT, EUNOMIA. NEW ORDER FOR A NEW WORLD 168, 170–171, 298 (1990); RUDOLF SMEND, STAATSRECHTLICHE ABHANDLUNGEN UND ANDERE AUFSATZE 309–310, 418 (3rd ed., 1994); Jost Delbrück, *The Impact of the Allocation of International Law Enforcement*

Those opposing such a view underline the abstract quality of the theory referred to above, based on the argument that since state action in the common interest lacks the minimum features of a public function (such as objectivity and a certain level of institutional power structures), it is necessary to turn towards the constitutional approach, with particular emphasis on the notion of a written constitution, viewing the UN Charter as the written constitution of the international community as a whole.[14] As a result, it is argued that the 'public' function of enforcement must be implemented pursuant to Chapter VII of the Charter.

An analysis of what happens in international practice leads us to reject both these approaches (while underlining the fact that the term 'practice' is used in the present chapter in a non-technical sense, to refer to events that take place in the context of dynamic phenomena in the formation of international legal norms, and not only as *diuturnitas*, the underlying element of customary law).

We propose an integrated approach to the organization of the functions of the international legal order, in line with the practice based on the development of a more inclusive and complex process of building a constitutional world order, moving beyond both the procedures of the Charter and the unilateral action of an inter-state system.[15]

We therefore wish to draw attention to those manifestations of practice relating to the mechanisms of control over the enforcement action of states in the public interest, to the distinct signs of innovation that have been evident for years now in the activity of the UN bodies and international institutions to 'integrate' public action by states to protect the basic norms of international law, and to the procedures originating from such practice and the resulting changes in the international enforcement system

---

Authority on the International Legal Order, *in* Delbrück, Allocation of Law Enforcement, *supra* note 2, at 135, 154; Torsten Stein, *Decentralized International Law Enforcement Agent*, *id.*, at 107. For the first important contributions in this sense, see also Hans Kelsen, Principles of International Law 25 (1952); Quadri, *supra* note 4. In the Draft Articles adopted on second reading, in 2001, the ILC, too, does not recognize the existence of any distinction between state 'crimes' and 'delicts' (see *Commentaries to the Draft Articles on Responsibility of States for Internationally Wrongful Acts*, at 281, available at <http://www.un.org/law/ilc/texts/State_responsibility/responsibility_commentaries(e).pdf#pagemode=bookmarks>). The Commentary to Art. 48 (Chap. III of Part Two) underlines that this Article deals with the invocation of responsibility by states other than the injured state 'acting in the collective interest'; it emphasizes that 'A State which is entitled to invoke responsibility under article 48 is acting not in its individual capacity … but in its capacity … as a member of the international community as a whole' (*id.*, at 319, para. 1), therefore in a 'public' capacity.

14 For this view and for a survey of scholars who present the UN Charter as the constitution of the international community, see Bardo Fassbender, *The United Nations Charter as Constitution of the International Community*, 36 Colom. J. Transn'l L. 529 (1998), at 538–551. See also the part of the text relating to note 131, *infra*.

15 This argument is developed under the heading 'The Osmotic Relationship…' later in this chapter. On the notion of integration associated with the constitutional process, see generally Allott, *supra* note 13, at 119; for articulation of this notion, see the relevant contributions by Richard A. Falk, *Global Constitutionalism and World Order*; *Id.*, *The Pathways of Global Constitutionalism*, *in* The Constitutional Foundations of World Peace 3, 13 (Richard A. Falk, Robert C. Johansen & Samuel S. Kim eds, 1993).

and legal order. The fact is that legal doctrine is mainly oriented towards bringing within the Charter framework (especially Chapter VII) the practice of UN bodies aimed at sharing with states the law-enforcement function of norms protecting basic values of the international community: this is a practice that obviously goes beyond the powers these bodies were granted institutionally, and even beyond the area of competence *ratione materiae* of the UN itself, although this is a very broad area.

The evident contrast between the practice of UN bodies and the provisions of the Charter confirms the need for analysis and a systematic reconstruction of the collective guarantees in the international legal order. The delays and uncertainties in approaching the subject can be ascribed above all to the diffidence surrounding an international enforcement function of a public nature. In the first place, the unorganized structure of the classic inter-state community and the resulting lack (at a general level) of a framework for international institutional power are hardly ideal conditions for ensuring objectivity in the protection of public interests. On the other hand, the contradictory conduct of states has certainly not helped to shed light on the phenomenon: at once concerned to keep their sovereignty intact, yet at the same time keen to see certain fundamental values given protection of a public character – values they themselves have promoted and turned into norms of a general character, through unequivocal practice.

The marked contrast between the activities of the UN bodies and the provisions of the Charter confirms the need to continue with the construction of an integrated system of collective security as examined in previous studies, utilising the analytical approach proposed in those studies, in order to identify the mechanisms and processes arising from international law as a whole that, going beyond the Charter, provide for the enforcement of norms protecting global interests.[16] We therefore need to reconsider the practice of recent decades to pursue our proposed aim of identifying the procedures asserted by general international law for enforcing norms protecting fundamental public interests (irrespective of the Charter procedures). In so doing, we shall adopt a prudent approach and consider all the signals coming from both the action of states operating in the common interest and the related integrative action of the UN bodies.[17]

The aim is therefore to identify:

1. 'whether' and 'how' individual states or groups of states may lawfully react in a collective capacity (in the common interest, *uti universi*) to the infringement of basic norms of international law, even outside the system provided by the Charter, under the terms of general international law;
2. the role played by the UN bodies for the enforcement of the basic norms of the world community; the powers conferred on them by general international law (over and above the powers they possess under the Charter); the forms

16 Ziccardi Capaldo, Terrorismo Internazionale, *supra* note 3. See recently, Tom J. Farer, *Beyond the Charter Frame: Unilateralism or Condominium?*, 96 Am. J. Int'l. L. 359 (2002).

17 See in this connection the third and fourth sections of this chapter.

of control they exercise over states' reactions in the common interest and the modalities for implementation;

3. the new norms of general international law that are both substantive and procedural, governing mechanisms and procedures for enforcing public norms; and
4. the changes in the law-enforcement system and the consequent repercussions on the current world constitutive structure.[18]

States Acting in the Common Interest and Institutional Control

From the 1970s onwards a practice has developed, primarily through the action of the Western States, which is viewed with some apprehension by international scholars: even outside the UN framework (that is to say, in the absence of a specific mandate from the UN), we have witnessed responses by states not directly affected aimed at sanctioning breaches of norms protecting the fundamental interests of the international community as a whole. The difficulty entailed in protecting the collective values in question within the legal framework existing at the time gave rise to recourse to countermeasures on the part of third-party states operating on behalf of the international community; the difficulty stemmed from the bilateral character of the classic law-enforcement system and the inadequacy of the Charter, with its collective security system under Chapter VII enforcing only the principle of the non-use of force. Countermeasures consist mainly of unilateral recourse to economic sanctions and/or political and diplomatic sanctions, or the boycotting of high-profile international sporting events, and are justified as reactions to an occupation, acts of aggression or serious violations of human rights, or the principle of self-determination.

The use of such measures by states as a reaction against breaches of obligations *erga omnes* escalated in the 1970s and 1980s[19] in a series of well-known cases:

18 See William Michael Reisman, *Unilateral Action and the Transformations of the World Constitutive Process: The Special Problem of Humanitarian Intervention*, 11 Eur. J. Int'l L. 3 (2000), at 7–11, who describes four types of constitutive configurations.

19 The literature on this practice is enormous. See, e.g., Margaret P. Doxey, *International Sanctions in Theory and Practice*, 15 Case Western Reserve Journal of International Law [hereinafter Case W. Res. J. Int'l L.] 273 (1983); *Id.*, International Sanctions in Contemporary Perspective (1987); Domingo E. Acevedo, *The U.S. Measures Against Argentina Resulting from the Malvinas Conflict*, 78 Am. J. Int'l. L. 323 (1984); Elisabeth Zoller, Peacetime Unilateral Remedies: An Analysis of Countermeasures (1984); Jonathan I. Charney, *Third State Remedies in International Law*, 10 Michigan Journal of International Law 57 (1989); Ziccardi Capaldo, Terrorismo Internazionale, *supra* note 3, at 46–67, 109–125; Frowein, *supra* note 3, at 416–422; Torsten Stein, *International Measures against Terrorism and Sanctions by and against Third States*, 30 Archiv des Völkerrechts 38 (1992). See generally Christine M. Chinkin, Third Parties in International Law (1993); Denis Alland, Justice Privée et Ordre Juridique International. Etude Théorique des Contre-Measures en Droit International Public (1994); Edward MacWhinney, Jeffery Atik & Gregory Shaffer, *Extraterritorial Sanctions and Legality under International and Domestic Law*, 94 American Society of International Law: Proceedings of the Annual Meeting 82 (2000); Peter

the Soviet occupation of Afghanistan, the Vietnamese invasion of Cambodia, the hostage-taking of the American diplomats in Iran, the imposition of martial law in Poland, the Falkland/Malvinas war, the Israeli intervention in Lebanon in 1978, the restriction of trade-union freedoms in Chile in 1987, the authoritarian turn of the Noriega government in Panama and of the Sandinista government in Nicaragua, Iraq's use of chemical weapons and genocide against the Kurds, the bloody repression of student protests of 4 June 1989 in Communist China, and other cases.

The tendency to sanction serious breaches of international law unilaterally, irrespective of a specific UN mandate, found further application at that time in the Western States' strategy against state-sponsored terrorism. In fact, the decisive turning-point in Middle-Eastern terrorism in the 1980s set in motion mechanisms for the collective implementation of coercive measures against the sponsoring states, confirming the tendency noted above. This occurred when the 'two-headed' nature of such terrorism became apparent in its configuration as not just individual or group terrorism, but also state-sponsored terrorism.

At the level of the implementation of sanctions, first, the well-known case where American diplomatic staff were taken hostage by the Iranian authorities led to the US's decision of 7 April 1980 and of that of the principal Western governments to adopt economic and diplomatic sanctions against Iran,[20] whose conduct was condemned as 'intolerable' from the humanitarian standpoint. In later initiatives undertaken against Afghanistan, Libya, Syria, and North Korea, the main justification for the sanctions was unequivocally the condemnation of international terrorism.

The Montebello Declaration issued at the Ottawa economic summit of 1981[21] is the first case of the express condemnation of active support lent by states to international terrorism: the enforcement of sanctions against Afghanistan (suspension of incoming and outgoing flights) was expressly taken as a response to that country's support of terrorism and the consequent breach of basic norms of international law. The sanctions passed were proposed for all states, who were invited to comply with them so as to

---

WALLENSTEEN, INTERNATIONAL SANCTIONS BETWEEN WORDS AND WARS IN THE GLOBAL SYSTEM (2005). See also the literature cited *supra* at note 12, *infra* at notes 31, 35.

20 Robert Carswell, *Economic Sanctions and the Iran Experience*, 60 FOREIGN AFFAIRS 247 (1981–1982); Jean-Louis Dewost, *La Communauté, Les Dix, et Les 'Sanctions' Economiques: de la Crise Iranienne à la Crise Malouines*, 28 ANN. FR. D.I. 217 (1982).

21 For the text, see 20 INT'L LEGAL MAT. 956 (1981). This act imposed sanctions (albeit quite modest in scope) against the government of Kabul, denouncing its connivance in the hijacking of an aircraft belonging to Pakistan International Airlines skyjacked by a Pakistani citizen and forced to land in Kabul in March 1981. After ascertaining the breach of basic international norms and of the duties undertaken with the Hague Convention, the states assembled at Montebello, applying the earlier Declaration of Bonn of 17 July 1978, *reprinted in* 17 INT'L LEGAL MAT. 1285 (1978), decided to suspend flights *to* and *from* Afghanistan, until such a time as the 'offending' country should take measures to fulfil its international obligations. France, the Federal Republic of Germany, and the UK rescinded from their respective accords with Afghanistan, as the only states affected by the decision since the other countries did not at the time have air services serving Kabul. See Kevin Chamberlain, *Collective Suspension of Air Services With States Which Harbour Hijackers*, 32 INT'L & COMP. L.Q. 616 (1983).

contribute to civil aviation safety. The action subsequently taken against Libya was wider in scope, from the drastic move by which the US interrupted all economic and diplomatic relations with the country in 1986, to the support by the European Community and other Western countries for the measures.[22] The sanctions against Syria also deserve mention: unlike those against Libya, they were not promoted by the US but were primarily a European initiative.[23] Further economic and diplomatic sanctions against international terrorism were adopted in that period by Washington and Tokyo against North Korea, 'responsible beyond all doubt' for blowing up a South Korean airplane with 115 people on board in November 1987.

The 1986 Tokyo Declaration[24] marked a turning point in the concept of international sanctions, outlining as it does mechanisms for the implementation of obligations *erga omnes*. The seven most industrialized countries asked all states to apply collective measures against Libya in the Declaration, which: (1) viewed the international responsibility of the sponsoring state as responsibility towards the international community as a whole; (2) claimed the public character of action undertaken against sponsoring states: the reference to the international community 'as a whole', on which the task of fighting terrorism falls, evokes the obligations *erga omnes* whose breach all states can (or must) respond to; and (3) aimed at establishing accord between the public character of the obligations breached and the intervention of the community at large, outlining the relevant mechanisms. While expressing the desire that unilateral measures be combined with international cooperation, it indicated the participation of institutions of a universal character, such as the UN and specialised agencies, as the most appropriate means for integrating the unilateral countermeasures against terrorism and the governments supporting it.[25]

A further reason for disquiet compared with the practice of peaceful countermeasures so far referred to was represented by enforcement activity against sponsoring states. It consisted in the attempt on the part of some states (notably Israel, the US, and the UK) to legitimate recourse to armed force – taking the form of either individual self-defence or public action in the form of intervention – against sponsoring states and terrorist targets (logistic or operational bases) 'wherever' they were located.

More specifically, in cases of armed intervention of this sort (and we are clearly referring to the Israeli incursion in October 1985 against the Palestinian Liberation Organization (PLO) bases in Tunisia and the American action against Libya of April 1986, as well as the Israeli incursions in Lebanon in 1978), grounds of individual self-defence went hand-in-hand with arguments based on the objective protection of the law. The principal argument put forward by the intervening states to justify their armed incursions was, without doubt, the need to repress the breach of an

---

22 *Documents Showing the Evolution of Sanctions against Libya*, 25 Int'l Legal Mat. 173–221 (1986). For Security Council sanctions against Libya in the *Lockerbie* case, and against other states sponsoring international terrorism, see *infra* notes 69 and 70 and corresponding text.

23 EC Bulletin 11–1986, at 98.

24 For the text, see 25 Int'l Legal Mat. 1005 (1986).

25 *Id.*, at paras 2, 5.

international *erga omnes* obligation, expressed as a generic appeal to their 'right' to fight terrorism, to underline the public character of their action. At the same time, the states promoting the actions mentioned above also evoked their own 'individual' infringed interests. In particular, they claimed the right to intervene to protect their own nationals falling victim to terrorist violence and the right to act in self-defence under Article 51 of the UN Charter.[26] With this end in mind, state terrorism was represented as unconventional warfare, used in the era of nuclear strategy as a 'surrogate' for classical war.[27]

The prevailing trend during those years towards pursuing unorganized actions against breaches of obligations *erga omnes* saw the Western States themselves deeply divided as to the choice of a common strategy (apart from prevention), which was at the same time lawful and likely to prove effective. The options discussed, especially in relation to the countries responsible for conniving with terrorism, were the military option and economic and political isolation, and, in practice, they came up against obstacles reflecting the basic inadequacy of unorganized social action. The hindrance posed by the fact that international society is fragmented into a plurality of sovereign bodies, each with 'particular' economic interests, and deeply divided on a political and ideological level, makes it extremely difficult to reach agreement on a common strategy. Consequently, with the political and economic burden of the action weighing on a small number of states, its efficacy and prestige risked being weakened.

The military option, however, was supported by a minority of states; taking the form of both individual and collective self-help, it was technically possible but politically and legally risky and full of unknown factors, since there were well-founded objections to the claim to legitimate such actions by extending the notion of armed attack under Article 51 of the UN Charter to embrace terrorist attacks.[28]

---

26 See President Reagan's Message to the Nation, United States Air Strike Against Libya (April 14, 1986), *in* W. Comp. Pres. Docs., Vol. 22 (April 21, 1986), at 491–492; US Congress, House Committee on Foreign Affairs. Subcommittee on Arms Control, International Security and Science, War Powers, Libya, and State-Sponsored Terrorism: Hearings, 99th Cong., 2nd Sess. (April–May 1986); especially Abraham D. Sofaer's report of April 29, *The War Powers Resolution and Antiterrorist Operations*, 86 Dept. State Bul. 68–71 (Aug. 1986). See also the American Ambassador Vernon A. Walters' declaration to the UN Security Council in the sitting of 15 April, UN Doc. S/PV.2674 (1986). For the analogous British position, see Mrs Thatcher's Declaration (HC Debs., Vol. 95, cols. 729–730 (April 15, 1986)) and for the British position at the UN, see UN Doc. S/18016/Rev.1.

27 See US Senate, Committee on Armed Services, To Combat Terrorism and Other Forms of Unconventional Warfare, 99th Cong., 2nd Sess., 1987, U.S. GPO 1987; Robert A. Friedlander, *Retaliation as an Anti-Terrorist Weapon: The Israeli Lebanon Incursion and International Law*, 8 Israel Yearbook of Human Rights 63 (1978), who defines terrorism 'as surrogate warfare' at 77; George Shultz, *Low-Intensity Warfare: The Challenge of Ambiguity*, 738 Department of State, Current Policy 4 (January 1986).

28 Serge Regourd, *Raids 'Anti-Terroristes' et Développements Récents des Atteintes Illicites au Principe de Non-Intervention*, 32 Ann. Fr. D.I. 79 (1986); Richard A. Falk, *Rethinking Counter-Terrorism*, 6 Scandinavian Journal of Development Alternatives 19 (1987). For general aspects on this topic, *cf.* Derek W. Bowett, *Reprisals Involving Recourse to Armed Force*, 66 Am. J. Int'l. L. 1 (1972), at 10; Oscar Schachter, *International Law in*

The attempt to construe the exception to the absolute prohibition on the use of force widely, so as to give legal backing to military actions unrelated to it, failed to win the approval of the international community. The vast majority of states and the UN strongly condemned the unilateral use of force to sanction serious breaches of international law, together with the attempt to construe loosely the right to self-defence envisaged by Article 51 of the Charter.[29]

It appeared clear (even to the Western States) that the actions in the public interest performed by states had to be linked with the 'supra-national' collective powers conferred on the Security Council for the maintenance of peace. Hence, for measures involving the use of force, a further factor working against the unilateral use of force consisted of the divesting of power from states and regional organizations and the centralization of the exercise of such measures in the UN, deriving from the combined effect of Articles 2(4), 51, and 53 of the Charter. However, a different approach appears to emerge from Resolution 1368 (2001), adopted by the Security Council immediately after the devastating terrorist attacks of 11 September 2001, in the US. The nature of these attacks, similar to an act of war and carried out on a large scale, directly on the territory and against the centres of power of the US, represented a significant development in the terror offensive, so that the definition of 'indirect attack', assigned to terrorist attacks in the past, was entirely inappropriate, with the result that they are now covered by Article 51 of the Charter.[30]

Theory and Practice, 178 Recueil des Cours 9 (1982–V); Sean D. Murphy, *Terrorism and the Concept of 'Armed Attack' in Article 51 of the U.N. Charter*, 43 Harv. Int'l L.J. 41 (2002); Carsten Stahn, *Terrorist Acts as 'Armed Attack'. The Right to Self-Defense, Article 51 (1/2) of the UN Charter and International Terrorism*, 27 The Fletcher Forum of World Affairs 35 (2003); Ved P. Nanda, Law in the War on International Terrorism (2005). See also *infra* chapters 4 and 7 of this book.

29 The Security Council expressly condemned Israel's invasion of Lebanon, see SC Res. 425 (March 19, 1978). The Council also condemned the 1985 Israeli raid in Tunisia by a decision not vetoed by the US (SC Res. 573 (Oct. 4, 1985)): the UN did not consider the air raid to be a legitimate response to the act of terrorism at Larnaca in September 1985 and rejected Israel's thesis that armed responses were legitimate against terrorism under Art. 51 of the UN Charter (UN Doc. S/17535). The Security Council condemned with equal vigour Israel's violation of Tunisian sovereignty and territorial integrity with its 'repeated aggression' of April 16, 1988 (SC Res. 611 (April 25, 1988)). The majority of states also stigmatised the US air attack on Libya in 1986, and, in fact, the European Community member states did not support it. See Ian Davidson, *U.S., E.C. Disagree on How to Deal With Terrorism: Reaction to U.S. Raid on Libya Underscores Differences Over the Use of Military Force*, Europe 16 (1986). The states gathered in the UN General Assembly condemned the military operation as 'illegal', ruling out the possibility that it could find a legal basis in Art. 51 of the Charter (GA Res. 41/38 (Nov. 20, 1986)). See David C. Morrison, *The 'Shadow War': The Air Attack on Libya Marks a New Phase in the U.S. Counterterrorism Struggle, An Era in Which the Military Will Likely Play a Much Greater Role*, 18 National Journal 1100 (1986); Richard H. Shultz (Jr.), *Can Democratic Governments Use Military Force in the War Against Terrorism? The U.S. Confrontation with Libya*, 148 World Affairs 205 (1986).

30 See *infra* chapter 4 of this book, under the subheading 'Self-Defence' in the early pages.

Rather, it may be said that in that period, both in terms of global public opinion and initiatives taken by states against governments violating *erga omnes* norms, there was a wave of sentiment supporting the economic and/or politico-diplomatic isolation of states responsible for breaches. However, when it came to their applying them, some governments certainly had reservations about the effectiveness of these enforcement measures (that had proved insufficient on other occasions), while other governments applied checks, fearing they would jeopardize their own national economy.[31] At the general normative level, the trend towards legitimating peaceful 'countermeasures' taken by third-party states grew stronger: the form of collective guarantee known as non-participation was gaining ground within the framework of general international law, along similar lines to the provisions of Article 41 of the Charter. By using isolation to prevent states that violate basic norms of international law from sharing in the benefits that derive from cooperation,[32] non-participation has the aim of inducing them to restore the rule of law. It does not in any case seem capable of inference from the Charter that the UN enjoys an exclusive role in the matter of collective measures not involving the use of force;[33] nor did the UN declare

31 On the effectiveness and use of international economic sanctions, whether on a unilateral basis or by UN action, see, in addition to the works already cited at note 17, Johan Galtung, *On the Effects of International Economic Sanctions, With Examples from the Case of Rhodesia*, 19 World Politics 378 (1967); Donald L. Losman, International Economic Sanctions: The Case of Cuba, Israel, and Rhodesia (1978); Henry Bienen & Robert Gilpin, *Economic Sanctions as a Response to Terrorism*, 3 Journal of Strategic Studies 89 (1980), at 92–95; Margaret P. Doxey, Economic Sanctions and International Enforcement 133 (2nd ed., 1980); John Polakas, *Economic Sanctions: An Effective Alternative to Military Coercion?*, 6 Brooklyn Journal of International Law 289 (1980); Robin Renwick, Economic Sanctions (1981); The Utility of International Economic Sanctions (David Leyton-Brown ed., 1987); Vera Gowlland-Debbas, Collective Responses to Illegal Acts in International Law: United Nations Action in the Question of Southern Rhodesia (1990); William Micheal Reisman & Douglas L. Stevick, *The Applicability of International Law Standards to United Nations Economic Sanctions Programmes*, 9 Eur. J. Int'l L. 86 (1998); August Reinisch, *Developing Human Rights and Humanitarian Law Accountability of the Security Council for the Imposition of Economic Sanctions*, 95 Am. J. Int'l L. 851 (2001); Mohamed Bennouna, *Les Sanctions Economiques des Nations Unies*, 300 Recueil des Cours 9 (2002); John B. Reynolds, *Export Controls and Economic Sanctions*, 37 The International Lawyer 263 (2003); For more detail on their lawfulness see the section headed 'Mechanisms …' later in this chapter.

32 See Charles Leben, Les Sanctions Privatives de Droits ou de Qualité dans les Organisations Internationales Specialisées (1979); Ebere Osieke, *Sanctions in International Law: The Contribution of International Organizations*, 31 Neth. Int'l L. Rev. 183 (1984).

33 The exclusive role of the Security Council had already been invoked to support the incompatibility with the UN Charter of the amendment to the Chicago Convention proposed by the UK and Switzerland in 1973 (LC/ Working Draft N. 829 of 17 February 1973, *reprinted in* 12 Int'l Legal Mat. 383–385 (1973)); this envisaged sanctions of the type indicated by Art. 41 of the Charter, in particular, the interruption of air communications from and to the states party to the amendment that should infringe their treaty obligations (ICAO Doc. 9050–LC/169–1 at 10, 41). It should be stressed that the sanctions were, however, judged compatible with the UN system by the Legal Committee of the ICAO, which, on 27 January

that it had an exclusive role during those years by condemning the states taking sanctions, as it had done, by contrast, in cases of military interventions aimed at protecting fundamental values of the community as a whole (at least according to the declarations of the promoting states) and undertaken outside the UN procedures and in breach of Article 51 of the Charter.[34]

Nonetheless, even the practice of countermeasures not involving the use of force posed the problem of the legal status of unorganized (in the sense of unilateral) action to protect collective interests. The question was extensively debated among jurists, in the presence of spasmodic and often contradictory practice reflecting diverging attitudes, against a background of political exploitation. Appeal was made to the law of the UN and the status of UN members to deny the lawfulness of unilateral actions undertaken in a collective capacity,[35] while the exclusive role of the UN in collective measures was upheld.

The debate among legal scholars was fuelled by the critical stance of the Third World and former Socialist countries. As is widely known, Western countermeasures were challenged by those countries, who were concerned that powerful states would monopolize the function of protecting public values, operating in the common interest on behalf of the collectivity of states, to the clear detriment of the objectivity of such a function. These countries maintained that even measures not involving the use of force should be decided by the UN: by the General Assembly, according to the first group, and by the Security Council, according to the second. In an awareness of the inadequacy of the Charter system and mindful of the signals emerging from the practice of the UN bodies, they proposed new objective guarantee mechanisms: assigning to the General Assembly law-enforcement powers not expressly conferred on it and extending *ratione materiae vis-à-vis* the law-enforcement powers of the Security Council, restricted in the Charter solely to the maintenance of peace.

In fact, despite their sometimes acrimonious protests against the practice of Western States, these countries ended up taking a less rigid stance than suggested by their verbal declarations. During that period both Socialist and Third World States had recourse to unilateral measures clearly bearing the mark of sanctions against

---

1973, recommended the Council to submit the project to the attention of the Assembly in an extraordinary session. See Gilbert Guillaume, *L'Echec de l'Assemblée Extraordinaire de l'Oaci et de la Conférence de Droit Aérien de Rome*, 36 Revue Générale de l'Air et de l'Espace 261 (1973); Claude Emanuelli, Les Moyens de Prévention et de Sanction en Cas d'Action Illicite contre l'Aviation Civile Internationale 132 n. 39 (1974); Chamberlain, *supra* note 21, at 629; Jean Louis Magdelenat, *La Nouvelle Annexe 17. Le Dernier Apport de l'Aviation Civile Internationale pur la Lutte Contre le Terrorisme*, XI Air & Space Law 87 (1986).

34 See *supra* note 28.

35 See the reservations over their lawfulness expressed by Derek W. Bowett, *Economic Coercion and Reprisals by States*, 13 Va. J. Int'l L. 1 (1972), at 2; Charles Leben, *Les Contre-Mesures Inter-Etatiques et les Réactions à l'Illicite dans la Société Internationale*, 28 Ann. Fr. D.I. 9 (1982), at 29; Christian Dominicé, *Observations sur les Droits de l'Etat Victime d'un Fait Internationalement Illicite*, Institut des Hautes Etudes Internationaux, Cours et Travaux, 1981–1982 (1983); Pierre-Marie Dupuy, *Observations sur la Pratique Récente des 'Sanctions' de l'Illicite*, 87 Rev. Gen. D.I.P. 523 (1983), at 533, 541.

occupying states, or those responsible for serious breaches of fundamental human rights. The following instances come especially to mind: the sanctions adopted by the former Socialist States against South Africa, which were not decided by the UN;[36] the oil embargo imposed by the Arab exporting states against the West to protest against the Arab–Israeli War of 1973;[37] the decision of the USSR and the Socialist countries to break off diplomatic and other relations with Israel after the Six Day War of 1967; and the breaking off of diplomatic relations with the Jewish State decided by many African States in 1973 after the Yom Kippur War.[38] Other instances that come to mind are the denunciation of the Warsaw Pact by Albania in 1968 after the invasion of Czechoslovakia;[39] the decision by Islamic countries at the Islamabad Conference of 1980 to break off diplomatic relations with the states that had decided to transfer their embassy to Jerusalem, proclaimed the capital of Israel by the Knesset, contrary to the UN resolutions on that city's Statute;[40] the withdrawal of diplomatic staff from Tel Aviv decided by Egypt – the only Arab country to have re-established 'normal' relations after the events of 1973 – in order to protest against the Israeli invasion of Lebanon in 1978; further, the interruption of diplomatic relations between China and Vietnam after Vietnam occupied Cambodia; the decision of Islamic countries to boycott the Moscow Olympic Games after the Soviet invasion of Afghanistan; and that of the Commonwealth countries to desert the 1986 Edinburgh Games in protest against the British government's policy in favour of South Africa, as well as the sanctions adopted by China against the US.

On close examination, the states did not have irreconcilable differences. The Socialist and Third World countries did not challenge the individual state's authority to react to violations of community values but laid stress on the 'modalities' with which unorganized enforcement in the common interest became operative, with a view to ensuring that the unilateral enforcement should possess the required objectivity. The difference of views that emerged reflected the real weak point of unorganized action: that it cannot be reconciled with the 'public' nature of a function of protecting collective interests. The requisites of 'objectivity' and 'impartiality' needed for the protection of collective interests were put forward forcefully by the Socialist and Third World countries; these states identified the UN bodies as the institutions capable of guaranteeing the objectivity of unilateral state action on behalf of the international community, a function that must therefore not be taken away from UN control. UN supervision was not in principle contested by Western States, either; their choice to use unorganized measures must not be interpreted as

---

36 See Harare Summit (Sept. 2–7, 1986).

37 Hartmut Brosche, *The Arab Oil Embargo and the United States Pressure Against Chile*, 7 Case W. Res. J. Int'l L. 30 (1974), at 32; Economic Coercion and the New International Economic Order (Richard B. Lillich ed., 1976); Roy M. Mersky, Conference on Transnational Economic Boycotts and Coercion (1978).

38 For the sanctions adopted by the Arab League against Israel, see Richard Stuart Olson, *Economic Coercion in World Politics, With a Focus on North–South Relations*, 31 World Politics 471 (1978–1979).

39 Charles Rousseau, *Chronique des Faits Internationaux* [hereinafter Rousseau, Chronique], 89 Rev. Gen. D.I.P. 1004 (1985).

40 Islamabad Conference (Jan. 27–29, 1980), Res. 1/EOS.

a wish to set unilateral enforcement action against UN action, thus substituting the latter, during that period of paralysis. Their enforcement action frequently referred expressly, for the purposes of legitimacy, to the intense activity carried out by the UN bodies also outside the established Charter mechanisms (a fact illustrated by the practice of Western countermeasures for the repression of terrorism).

The disagreement between the two sides did not call into question whether states have the 'right' to react to violations of obligations *erga omnes*; rather, the differing outlooks displayed divergence on aspects that may be called 'procedural' and 'instrumental', pertaining to the way such a right may be exercised and the forms of co-participation of international institutions in the emerging function of protecting public interests of a global, post-Westphalian community. Procedures and mechanisms for such forms of participation were already being outlined in UN practice.

The long travail that witnessed the Western countries on the one hand opposing Socialist and Third World countries on the other, finally brought states and the UN to agree on some essential points: (1) the inadequacy of the Charter's collective security system, guaranteeing only the maintenance of peace (Chapter VII) as against the broader scope of the basic norms of international law; (2) the authority of third-party states to enforce the breach of such norms, outside the UN institutional framework; (3) the need for the role of enforcing such norms not to be entrusted to a few members of the international community (the powerful states); and (4) the necessity for states to coordinate their enforcement action in the common interest with the action of international organizations, and to submit such action to UN control to verify its objectivity/legitimacy, so regaining for unilateral activity the 'public' connotation that it is intended to have. The contrast that is still evident today in individual cases concerns the balancing between the ever-present tendency in the international community towards the anarchical decentralization of state reactions to breaches of obligations *erga omnes* on the one hand, and on the other, the need (now accepted by states) for the 'institutional control of legitimacy'[41] over the reactions themselves, to be carried out by international institutions.

Innovative Trends in the Practice of UN Bodies

Over the past 30 years or so, there have been signs of a move towards a 'vertical' course of development of the international legal order: the UN has put its institutional

---

41 We therefore use this expression in TERRORISMO INTERNAZIONALE, quoted *supra* note 3, at 130. The International Law Commission introduced the notion of countermeasures 'legitimate under international law' in Art. 30 of the Draft Articles on State Responsibility, appealing to an inevitably 'objective' evaluation. For the text of the Draft, see UN Doc. A/CN.4/Ser.A/1980/Add.1(Part 2); Y. INT'L L. COMM. (1980), Vol. II, (Part Two). The same view has prevailed in Art. 54 of the Draft Articles adopted in 2001, that subject states, other than an injured state, take 'lawful measures' against the responsible state, subjecting the lawfulness of the countermeasures to several parameters of legality (see *Commentaries to the Draft Articles on Responsibility of States for Internationally Wrongful Acts*, *supra* note 13, Art. 54, para. 7, at 355).

structure at the service of the international community so as 'to integrate' the activity of states in protecting collective interests, making up for the international community's lack of an organized structure.

The Determination of Serious Breaches of Basic Global Principles

This has been strongly confirmed by innovative trends in the practice of UN bodies since the era of the blocs. During the Cold War years, the paralysis of the Security Council and the inadequacy of the Charter enforcement system for protecting collective interests other than the maintenance of peace reinforced the tendency of the UN political bodies to perform certain sanctioning and verification functions going beyond the UN institutional system and aimed at implementing public norms of the international legal order. Consider, for instance, the Security Council practice, also adopted by the General Assembly, of declaring 'illegal' territorial arrangements arising from oppressive or heinous conduct by governments: colonialism, occupation, apartheid, genocide, etc. According to a key statement by the International Court of Justice:

> 'A determination made by a competent organ of the United Nations to the effect that a territorial situation is illegal cannot remain without consequence ... The declaration of illegality is opposable to all States – even to non-member States – in the sense of barring *erga omnes* the legality of a situation which is maintained in violation of international law ...'[42]

The determination of 'illegality' reached by such bodies with regard to a territorial situation resulting from the breach of basic international norms brings about effects *erga omnes*, in the sense that, by estoppel, it precludes the situation declared illegal from being subsequently considered lawful by the fact of its becoming effective. At the level of general international law it gives rise to the obligation (or the possibility) for 'all' states to abstain from diplomatic and other relations with the governments concerned, to adopt sanctions against them, and to deny any extraterritorial effects to acts issued by them in the name of the territory concerned.

It is important to consider the activity of the General Assembly aimed at ascertaining violations, and in specific cases, censuring the 'coercive policies' of occupying or colonial governments, or those practising apartheid or any other form of racial discrimination. This activity ranges from resolutions declaring such policies 'illegal' and denying those governments the right to represent the people, to the practice of repudiating the credentials of their representatives to the UN and the numerous resolutions with which the General Assembly has pointed out to states the consequences of the breach of 'absolute' or 'objective' obligations, in the form of economic and diplomatic sanctions to be adopted at the national level or within

---

42 Legal Consequences for States of the Continued Presence of South Africa in Namibia (South West Africa) notwithstanding Security Council Resolution 276 (1970), Advisory Opinion, 1971 ICJ Reports 16 (June 21, 1971), paras 117, 126, at 54–56; see also Repertory, *supra* note 1, vol. I, No. 1600, at 631–633. For more detail, see our work quoted *supra* note 2 at 49, 82–88, 102–107.

international organizations. This form of action has taken place in the absence of Security Council decisions and where it has been impossible to implement such measures within the UN institutional framework.[43]

Closely linked to the above, we may also recall the General Assembly's extensive practice of affirming the legitimacy of national liberation movements struggling for the self-determination of peoples subjugated by oppressive governments as mentioned above: the General Assembly's ascertainment that the principle of self-determination applies to a particular territorial situation authorizes 'all' states to sanction the unlawful possession of the territory and, in derogation from classic international law, to assist the movements fighting against the oppressor in any way whatsoever. The General Assembly activity surveyed can now be considered to be accepted by states as a way of putting into effect basic principles of general international law. Indeed, resolutions of the type indicated have produced *erga omnes* effects at a general level, in the sense that the determination of a breach of basic principles contained in the resolutions has been deemed such that all states acquire the right to adopt unilateral enforcement measures against the offending state.[44]

---

43 See the General Assembly's resolutions adopting economic sanctions against South Africa and states' adhesion before SC Res. 569 (July 26, 1985) deliberating 'voluntary' sanctions; especially Rousseau, Chronique, *supra* note 39, 90 Rev. Gen. D.I.P. 173–178, 408–409 (1986). See also the resolutions condemning the occupation of Afghanistan (GA Res. ES–6/2 (Jan. 14, 1980); GA Res. 36/34 (Nov. 18, 1981); GA Res. 37/37 (Nov. 29, 1982); GA Res. 38/29 (Nov. 23, 1983); GA Res. 39/13 (Nov. 15, 1984); GA Res. 40/12 (Nov. 13, 1985); GA Res. 41/33 (Nov. 5, 1986); GA Res. 41/158 (Dec. 4, 1986)); express reference was made to the resolutions mentioned above in succeeding decisions of international bodies and official government declarations, in adopting enforcement measures against the Soviet Union. Making reference to General Assembly Res. ES–6/2, the Islamabad Conference (*supra* note 40) suspended the Afghan government from membership of the Conference and invited member states to withhold recognition from the illegal Afghan regime and to break off diplomatic relations with Afghanistan until the total withdrawal of Soviet troops should ensue. The General Assembly resolutions that condemned the Vietnamese occupation of Cambodia operated in a similar way. See the meeting of the ten EEC members and the five ASEAN Nations of 24 and 25 March 1983 in Bangkok issuing a final statement confirming the condemnation of Vietnam and support for the UN resolutions of July 1981; aid to Vietnam was suspended but only to the extent that the Vietnamese occupation of Cambodia had been favoured. Japan also reacted to the invasion of Cambodia, announcing on 19 January 1979 that it wished to suspend the disbursement of economic aid to Vietnam. See Pierre Fistié, *Le Japon Face aux Crises Cambodgienne et Afghane*, 3 Revue Française de Science Politiques 451 (1982), at 469. Also deserving mention is the GA Res. 50/199 of 22 December 1995, condemning arbitrary executions and other violations of human rights and fundamental freedoms in Nigeria and urging 'immediate and concrete steps to restore democratic rule' (para. 4). On this topic see generally Dupuy, *supra* note 35, at 515–519, 534; Leben, *supra* note 35, at 31 and references *infra* note 58.

44 For detailed treatment of the General Assembly's extensive enforcement function performed 'at the service' of the international legal order, see Giuliana Ziccardi Capaldo, *Il Disconoscimento delle Credenziali del Sud Africa come Sanzione contro l'Apartheid*, 68 Rivista di Diritto Internazionale 299 (1985); *Id.*, *supra* note 3, at 106–109.

Innovative Security Council Policies Regarding Collective Actions

During the Cold War years and the ensuing paralysis, the Security Council also sent signals of a change in the regime of collective measures; endorsing the trend of countermeasures to be adopted by states, it placed the UN 'at the service' of the community of states. Important confirmation of this comes from innovative Security Council policy regarding collective measures, above all starting from the Resolution of 26 July 1985, which recommended 'voluntary' economic sanctions against South Africa to be adopted by individual states.[45] The innovative feature of that resolution with regard to collective measures (reported in the press with the picturesque expression '*sanctions à la carte*')[46] was certainly highlighted by careful examination in the legal literature, which underlined its 'voluntary' and 'selective' nature, far removed from the 'binding force' and 'indivisibility' of the law-enforcement regime institutionally envisaged by Article 41 of the Charter.[47]

In practice after the fall of the Soviet bloc, the Security Council's tendency to perform collective guarantee functions together with states took on more precise shape in terms of the mechanisms. The activism of the Security Council established it as the 'agent' of the world community to implement the basic principles of the international legal order. Extending its own powers beyond those conferred on it by the Charter (which, as we know, only grants the Security Council 'responsibility' for the maintenance of international peace and security), by tracing every matter back to the threat to peace, the Council drew within its powers any matter whatsoever included among the Charter aims, as well as matters falling outside the competence *ratione materiae* of the UN.[48] In so doing, the Council ascertained the breach of any principle considered fundamental by the international legal order: not only breaches of the prohibition of the use of force, but also of the principles of self-determination, democracy, humanitarian law, as well as the interdiction against sponsoring international terrorism, drug trafficking, environmental pollution, and so on.

Based on practice set in motion by the Gulf crisis in 1990, the Security Council has granted 'authorization' to individual states or groups of states and/or regional organizations to use any means, including force,[49] to oppose the occupation or annexation of territory, to affirm the principle of democracy or to end serious violations of humanitarian law and human rights. Referring to Chapter VII, the Council has 'authorized' the use of all necessary means in many cases, namely: to

45 SC Res. 569, *supra* note 43.

46 Le Monde (July 28–29, 1985), at 1, 3.

47 Rousseau, Chronique, *supra* note 39, 90 Rev. Gen. D.I.P. 177 (1986).

48 In this sense, see Giuliana Ziccardi Capaldo, *Verticalità della Comunità Internazionale e Nazioni Unite. Un Riesame del caso Lockerbie*, 61 Interventi Delle Nazioni Unite e Diritto Internazionale (1995), at 79–81.

49 The Council did not make authorization subject to the conditions required by Chapt. VIII of the UN Charter in these resolutions. See Djamchid Momtaz, *La Délégation par le Conseil de Sécurité de l'Execution de ses Actions Coercitives aux Organisations Regionales*, 43 Ann. Fr. D.I. 105 (1997), at 107.

oppose the occupation of Kuwait by Iraq;[50] to protect human rights in Somalia;[51] to ensure the application of the embargo on arms destined for the territory of the former Yugoslavia; to ensure observance of the flight ban in the airspace of Bosnia and Herzegovina, and respect for the safe areas in those countries[52] and support for the United Nations Protection Force (UNPROFOR) operating there;[53] to ensure the restoration of democracy in Haiti and to cooperate with the legitimate government of that country to halt outward, as well as inward, maritime shipping in order to inspect and verify their cargoes and destination;[54] to ensure humanitarian assistance in the Great Lakes zone[55] and in Angola;[56] to restore peace and facilitate humanitarian aid operations in East Timor and protect the United Nations Mission (UNAMET).[57] Going beyond the powers conferred on it by the Charter, in some instances, the Council has asked all states to adopt 'voluntary' measures, both economic and of other kinds, to sanction serious breaches of international law, in this way often endorsing initiatives already undertaken by states;[58] on other occasions, once it has determined serious breaches of international law, the Council has exercised 'general' powers, laying the

50 SC Res. 678 (Nov. 29, 1990), para. 2; THE KUWAIT CRISIS: BASIC DOCUMENTS (Elihu Lauterpacht, Christopher Greenwood, Marc Weller & Daniel Betlehem eds., 1991).

51 SC Res. 794 (Dec. 3, 1992), para. 16.

52 See, e.g., SC Res. 787 (Nov. 16, 1992), para. 14; SC Res. 816 (March 31, 1993), para. 4; SC Res. 958 (Nov. 19, 1994), para. 1; SC Res. 981 (March 31, 1995), para. 6.

53 SC Res. 836 (June 4, 1993), para. 10.

54 SC Res. 940 (July 31, 1994), para. 4; SC Res. 917 (May 6, 1994), para. 10.

55 SC Res. 1080 (Nov. 15, 1996), para. 5.

56 SC Res. 1087 (Dec. 11, 1996), para. 15; SC Res. 1127 (Aug. 28, 1997), para. 4.

57 SC Res. 1264 (Sept. 15, 1999), para. 3.

58 The US has approved over 40 laws and executive decisions to apply unilateral economic sanctions against 75 nations (see '1998 Trade Policy Agenda of the United States') to react against breaches of basic international norms. Cf. ELISABETH ZOLLER, ENFORCING INTERNATIONAL LAW THROUGH U.S. LEGISLATIONS (1985). For an examination of the UK sanctions against Southern Rhodesia see Doxey, *supra* note 19, at 37. The following instances may be highlighted among the many cases where states have adopted economic sanctions or embargoes as members of regional international organizations: the sanctions adopted by the OAS against Haiti, or by ECOWAS against Liberia and Sierra Leone (*infra* note 114). See especially the sanctions decided by the Council of the European Communities against: Iraq (Reg. 2340/90; 3155/90; 3541/92; 2465/96); Yugoslavia (Reg. 3300/91; 3301/91; 3302/91); the Republics of Serbia and Montenegro (Reg. 1432/92); the Federal Republic of Yugoslavia (Reg. 926/98; 2111/1999 and 1999/318/CFSP); Libya (93/614/CFSP; 99/318/CFSP); Haiti (Reg. 1964/94); Angola/UNITA (Reg. 1705/98) and the imposition of embargoes against Sudan (94/165/CFSP); Nigeria (95/515/CFSP); Burma/Myanmar (96/635/CFSP); the Federal Republic of Yugoslavia (96/184/CFSP; 99/273/CFSP; 99/318/CFSP; 99/481/CFSP); Afghanistan (96/746/CFSP); Sierra Leone (98/409/CFSP); Ethiopia and Eritrea (99/206/CFSP); Libya (99/318/CFSP). On this point see generally Dewost, *supra* note 20, at 215; Eckart Klein, *Sanctions by International Organizations and Economic Communities*, 30 ARCHIV DES VÖLKERRECHTS 101 (1992); Claude-Pierre Lucron, *L'Europe devant la Crise Yugoslave. Mesures Restrictives et Mesures Positives*, 354 REVUE DU MARCHÉ COMMUN ET DE L'UNION EUROPÉENNE 7 (1992); Christine M. Chinkin, *The Legality of the Imposition by the EU in International Law*, *in* ASPECTS OF STATEHOOD AND INSTITUTIONALISM IN CONTEMPORARY EUROPE 183 (D. Malcolm Evans ed., 1997).

burden on 'all' states to adopt the specific measures it has decided[59] the measures cannot always be traced back to those envisaged by the Charter.[60]

It emerges quite clearly from the practice just outlined that on many occasions the Security Council has performed 'general functions' of a community body in determining responsibility and law enforcement to protect values considered fundamental by the international community; in so doing, it has governed the enforcement processes of the international legal order jointly with states, especially with the powerful states that are, realistically speaking, the community's guiding force. In this way, it has assisted the international community in protecting public values. In confirmation of this, it is interesting to note in the cases mentioned above how the Security Council has made general reference to Chapter VII, basing its decisions not only on the Charter itself, but also on international law;[61] further, it has often expressly addressed its decisions to 'all' states, even 'to non-Member States'.[62] Further demonstration comes from the Council's orientation directed at generically condemning breaches of general international law or treaty law (such as the prohibition on using child soldiers,[63] the interdiction against deliberately hindering humanitarian assistance destined for civilians in case of armed conflicts,[64] the 'illicit' production of opium,[65] and the proliferation of nuclear arms[66]) where the Security Council has threatened to intervene with coercive measures.

Finally, we should highlight the more-established Council practice of affirming and protecting general principles that are not explicitly contemplated by the Charter and that are difficult to trace back to the principles expressed there, by means of measures that clearly overstep those envisaged by the Charter, which these include the principle of 'individual responsibility' in the perpetration of war crimes and other gross human rights violations and the 'effective punishment' of persons committing these acts. In this regard, mention should be made of the resolutions with which

---

59 See SC Res. 660 (Aug. 2, 1990), para. 3; SC Res. 661 (Aug. 6, 1990), para. 3; SC Res. 687 (April 3, 1991), paras 24, 29; SC Res. 748 (March 31, 1992), paras 3–7; SC Res. 864 (Sept. 15, 1993), para. 20; SC Res. 1087, *supra* note 56, para. 15; SC Res. 1054 (April 26, 1996), para. 3; SC Res. 1070 (Aug. 16, 1996), para. 3; SC Res. 1127, *supra* note 56, para. 4; SC Res. 1160 (March 31, 1998), para. 8; SC Res. 1173 (June 12, 1998), paras 11, 12; SC Res. 1267 (Oct. 15, 1999), paras 4, 7; SC Res. 1306 (July 5, 2000), paras 1, 9, 22. On some occasions the Security Council expressly 'calls upon *all* states, *including States not members of the United Nations* ... to act strictly in accordance with the provisions' decided on the basis of Chap. VII (*emphasis added*). See especially SC Res. 847 (June 30, 1993), para. 7; SC Res. 917, *supra* note 54, para. 12; SC Res. 1054, *supra*, para 5. See also *infra* text at and notes 70–71.

60 For more details see *infra* notes 67–74.

61 See, e.g., SC Res. 687, *supra* note 59, preamble; SC Res. 827 (May 25, 1993), preamble; SC Res. 1214 (Dec. 8, 1998), para. 5; SC Res. 1267, *supra* note 59, preamble.

62 See *supra* note 59.

63 SC Res. 1261 (Aug. 25, 1999), preamble, para. 1.

64 SC Res. 1265 (Sept. 17, 1999), para. 10.

65 SC Res. 1267, *supra* note 59, preamble.

66 SC Res. 1172 (June 6, 1998), paras 1, 10, 11.

the Security Council, having asserted the principle of individual responsibility,[67] established *ad hoc* criminal tribunals for the punishment of those charged with crimes against humanity in the former Yugoslavia and Rwanda.[68] This move was determined by the need to counteract the inadequacy of the international legal order to punish individuals responsible for *crimina juris gentium*. It is linked to analogous initiatives undertaken by the Security Council to ensure the effective punishment of individual terrorists. In the *Lockerbie*, *Sudanese*, and *Afghanistan* affairs, the Security Council compelled those harbouring the suspected terrorists (the Libyan and Sudanese governments and the Taliban militia, respectively), and who were thus suspected of sponsoring terrorism, to extradite the alleged terrorists to states that would provide for their trial and sentencing.[69] In both sets of circumstances we have considered, the Security Council, interpreting a need of the community of states, has set itself up as the 'agent' of the international legal order. This has been the case both in matters in which the Council has provided for the establishment of *ad hoc* tribunals and also where it has 'authorized' the trial of alleged terrorists before courts of states operating in the common interest, which would proceed on to judge those accused 'effectively'. In both these ways, the Security Council has performed international enforcement functions jointly with states: in the first case, taking upon itself the direction of the protection of community values by providing directly for the establishment of tribunals, while contemporaneously requiring 'all' states to cooperate with the tribunals established[70] and reinforcing this request by underlining that a state may not have resort to its own internal law to refuse to absolve 'peremptory obligations of international law';[71] in the second case, allowing states to act on behalf of the entire international community and asking all the other states to contribute to delivering the individuals suspected of the crimes to countries acting for their 'effective' punishment.[72] Moreover, it should moreover be pointed out that neither the establishment of the said Tribunals[73] nor the request for extradition

---

67 SC Res. 859 (Aug. 24, 1993), para. 7; SC Res. 935 (July 1, 1994), preamble, para. 1; SC Res. 1315 (Aug. 14, 2000), preamble.

68 SC Res. 827, *supra* note 61, para. 2; SC Res. 955 (Nov. 8, 1994), para. 1; SC Res. 1315, *supra* note 67, paras 1–8.

69 See SC Res. 731 (Jan. 21, 1992), para. 3; SC Res. 748, *supra* note 59; SC Res. 1070, *supra* note 59; SC Res. 1044 (Jan. 31, 1996), para. 4; SC Res. 1054 (*Sudanese* affair), *supra* note 59; SC Res. 1192 (Aug. 27, 1998) (*Lockerbie* affair); SC Res. 1214, *supra* note 61, para. 13; SC Res. 1267 (*Afghan* affair), *supra* note 59, para. 2.

70 SC Res. 1192, *supra* note 69, para. 4; SC Res. 1265, *supra* note 64, para. 6.

71 SC Res. 1207 (Nov. 17, 1998), para. 2. In the cases referred to, the Council calls upon all states 'to act strictly in accordance' with the measures imposed 'notwithstanding the existence of any rights or obligations conferred or imposed by any international agreement or any contract entered into ... prior to the date of coming into force of the measures imposed'. See SC Res. 1267 and SC Res. 1160, *supra* note 59, paras 7, 10, respectively. See also SC. Res. 687, *supra* note 59, para 25; SC Res. 1199 (Sept. 23, 1998), para. 7.

72 SC Res. 1207, *supra* note 71.

73 The Tribunal for the Former Yugoslavia has indicated Art. 41 of the Charter as the legal basis for its establishment. In the Report of May 3, 1993, the Secretary-General considered this Tribunal to be a subsidiary organ of the Council under Art. 29 of the Charter

of suspected terrorists are manifestations of powers conferred on the Council by the Charter, despite attempts to cast them as such by legal scholars.[74]

The practice thus briefly outlined leads us to see how the powers exercised by the UN bodies when determining and sanctioning breaches of general norms exceed those institutionally granted by the Charter. We are referring to the above-mentioned powers of ascertainment and enforcement binding on all states, which are now internationally accepted. Clearly, we are alluding to: (1) the *erga omnes* opposability attributed to the determination of breach of basic general norms by either the General Assembly or the Security Council; (2) the *erga omnes* force attached to the enforcement powers assumed by the General Assembly in matters of human rights and self-determination; and (3) the general effects connected with the law-enforcement function of the Security Council when, after determining serious breaches of general law, it 'authorizes' or imposes sanctions, in the latter case requiring all states, and not just member states, to implement them.

Next to be considered are the derogations from features characterising the Charter enforcement system (in Chapter VII), which follow from the exercise by the Security Council of the law-enforcement powers noted above: for instance, the authorization granted to states to adopt 'voluntary' measures either at the national level or within international organizations conflicts with the 'binding force' and 'indivisibility' of the regime of collective sanctions envisaged by Chapter VII of the Charter, a point already made; similarly, the Security Council's method of authorizing the use of force contradicts the spirit of the Charter system for the maintenance of peace, which centres entirely on the prohibition of the use of force for states and the concentration of the use of force in the Security Council (apart from self-defence as provided by Article 51). Finally, it should be noted that sometimes the measures decided by the Security Council to sanction breaches of general law are not among those listed in Articles 41 and 42 of the Charter and cannot even be traced back to the 'categories' arising from those provisions.

(UN Doc. S/25704, Add. 1, at 18–30). Doctrine generally finds the legal basis for *ad hoc* criminal tribunals in the Charter. For critical considerations, see Gaetano Arangio Ruiz, *The Establishment of the International Criminal Tribunal for the Former Yugoslavia and the Doctrine of Implied Powers of the United Nations*, *in* Dai Tribunali Penali Internazionali *Ad Hoc* a una Corte Permanente, Atti del Convegno, Roma 15–16 Dicembre 1995, 36 (Flavia Lattanzi & Elena Sciso eds, 1996). For a different approach see Ziccardi Capaldo, *supra* note 48, at 83–85. In our view the establishment of such tribunals falls within the enforcement function performed by the Council as a 'body' of the international community, to implement principles of the international legal order protecting fundamental community values; it is thus in general international law rather than in the Charter that the legal basis for those tribunals is to be found.

74 The question of the legitimacy of extensive enforcement powers implemented by the Council has been a matter of dispute. For prominent voices in this regard, see Christian Dominicé, *Le Conseil de Sécurité et le Droit International*, 43 Jugoslovenska Rewvija Za Medunarodno Pravo 197 (1996), and the contributions *in* Le Développement du Rôle du Conseil de Sécurité/The Development of the Role of the Security Council, Peace-Keeping and Peace-Building, Colloque, La Haye, 21–23 Juillet 1992, (René-Jean Dupuy ed., 1993) [hereinafter Dupuy, Le Développement].

It is for these reasons that debate among jurists over the powers of the Security Council has intensified, a fact that occurred chiefly at the time when the Council discovered activism at the end of the Cold War. Doubts have been expressed about the legality on the basis of the Charter of this activity on the part of the Council: scholars have referred to the extensive use of Chapter VII with regard to humanitarian aid resolutions. There has also been discussion as to whether shipping restraint measures should fall under Article 41 or 42 of the Charter, and similar debate has focused on measures setting up *ad hoc* criminal tribunals.[75] Then again, different articles of the Charter have variously been advanced as the basis for resolutions 'authorizing' states or regional organizations to use force.[76] In the face of the objective difficulty of placing the decisions cited within the Charter framework, it is evidence of uneasiness among legal scholars that some authors have persistently asserted the view that any action of the Council is lawful provided it conforms to the spirit of the Charter and is appropriate to the given situation,[77] even though it was not expressly envisaged by the Charter provisions on the maintenance of peace and cannot be set among the 'specific' powers referred to in Article 24 (2).

In our view, the legal basis for these powers exercised by the Council is not to be found in the Charter; they are plainly not retraceable to it, even appealing to the spirit of the Charter and/or a wide interpretation of its provisions. The reason for this is that the general powers exercised by the UN bodies overstep the limits inherent in the Charter and the collective security system it lays down, which binds member states alone. At times, these powers contradict the logical basis of the Charter maintaining the balance between the political bodies; at other times, they openly clash with the spirit of the collective security system designed by the Charter. As an example of the former, consider the functions of ascertaining responsibility and enforcement in a broad sense exercised by the General Assembly: these functions are deliberately withheld from the Assembly by the Charter and reserved for the Security Council; an example of the latter is provided by the 'decentralization' of the collective law-enforcement function brought about by the practice of 'authorizations' for states to use force, contradicting the idea of a system centralized in the Security Council.

We would also exclude the possibility that new specific rules have been developed through UN practice, assigning to the UN bodies the wider powers that are implemented in practice and modifying the Charter, since such rules could not in any case assign to UN bodies the 'general' powers binding on all states. The rules

75 See, e.g., SC Res. 665 (Aug. 25, 1990); SC Res. 688 (April 5, 1991); SC Res. 770 and SC Res. 771 (Aug. 13, 1991); SC Res. 787, *supra* note 52; SC Res. 794, *supra* note 51; SC Res. 875 (Oct. 16, 1993). See also *supra* notes 68, 74.

76 For a critical analysis of such theories, see Helmut Freudenschuss, *Between Unilateralism and Collective Security: Authorizations of Use of Force by the UN Security Council*, 5 Eur. J. Int'l L. 492 (1994), at 523.

77 See, e.g., Christian Dominicé, *La Sécurité Collective et la Crise du Golfe*, 2 Eur. J. Int'l L. 85 (1991), at 103; Eugene W. Rostow, *'Until What? Enforcement Action or Collective Self-defence'*, 85 Am. J. Int'l. L. 506 (1991); Oscar Schachter, *United Nations Law in the Gulf Conflict*, 85 Am. J. Int'l. L. 452 (1991), at 460; *Id.*, International Law in Theory and Practice 403–404 (1991); Philippe Weckel, *Le Chapitre VII de la Charte et son Application par le Conseil de Sécurité*, 37 Ann. Fr. D.I. 165 (1991), at 192.

that could arise from such a modification would share the conventional nature of the Charter rules thereby modified and would thus share the limit of having a binding effect on member states alone.

In reality, we must take cognizance of the fact that it is impossible to place the aforementioned Security Council resolutions within the provisions of the Charter and, more generally, to find therein the basis for the powers exercised by the UN bodies with *erga omnes* validity. Such an activity must be placed outside the bounds of the Charter, and has its basis in general international norms; these norms retain a separate existence from the Charter norms. It might also be appropriate to appeal to the inspiration of universalism behind the Charter; not to find there the basis for these powers, naturally, but to understand how it is that the UN has been able to put its organized structure 'at the service' of the unorganized world community, with a view to its institutionalization. The assertions we have just made do not mean that we subscribe to the theory that the UN acts in substitution of the community of states: as we will illustrate more fully below, our opinion inclines to the belief that the international community is still largely unorganized, but sporadically avails itself of the UN bodies to perform certain social functions for the entire international community. The solution that we propose views the powers exercised by UN bodies with *erga omnes* validity as powers conferred by rules of general international law.[78] The point we wish to emphasize (while referring the reader to later parts of our survey for in-depth analysis) is this: no one denies that the practice we have examined has brought into being substantive customary rules allowing any state – even though not affected – to react internationally to serious violations of human rights or attacks on the principle of self-determination of peoples and other serious breaches of international law; we believe that, in addition, the objective control mechanisms for the exercise of such a right by states, which practice has contributed to consolidation, can now be deemed to be established through custom and embodied in general norms.

Some Mechanisms of the Joint Governance

We now turn our attention to the recognition of the mechanisms of the integrated system of international law enforcement. No attempt will be made to conceal the difficulty inherent in identifying the procedural rules in question, given the fluidity of practice, which is never at a loss to provide fresh solutions linking the community of states and the organized community. Despite the variety of forms that cooperation takes on, it is nevertheless possible to identify certain principles on which it is based.

In our view, underpinning the system is the general principle by which the right of states to sanction *uti universi* breaches of fundamental rules must be 'integrated' with the general functions conferred on international institutions of 'determining' the breaches themselves and of 'control' over the activity carried out by states;

78 See our works quoted *supra* note 2, at 122; note 3, at 106, 128; note 44, at 307; note 48, at 79, 84.

hence, the enforcement action of states in the common interest is subordinate to both objective determination and to control carried out by UN bodies.

As we noted in the third major section of this chapter, international crises – even in the era of the two competing blocs – have usually given rise to a firm condemnation by the UN bodies and a clear initial determination of the actual breach of essential obligations, although these have often not been followed up by the decision to impose sanctions on the part of the Security Council, paralysed by the veto. The General Assembly's determination has provided the legal basis for peaceful countermeasures adopted by third-party states, which have often referred to such a determination in the absence of express authorization by the Security Council.[79] The determination of breaches referred to above, the practice of verification with an *erga omnes* effect, is now accepted as a way of protecting fundamental values of international law. It represents an integrated activity between states and the UN bodies, with the UN indicating the violation of fundamental principles to the community and permitting states to sanction the breach by means of peaceful countermeasures to be adopted at the national level or within regional organizations. This role has been usefully performed by the General Assembly, mainly in the fields of human rights and self-determination, but also with great vigour in cases of aggression.

The Security Council has also worked intensively at ascertaining responsibility for the breach of basic international norms, especially in the last ten years, and has not restricted itself to the institutional role of determination granted by Article 39 of the Charter. It has extended the powers of verification conferred on it by Article 39, tracing the breach of any basic norm back to a 'threat to the peace'. In an examination of the Council practice referred to – which is accepted by states – the Council may be deemed under general international law to enjoy wide powers of verification *ratione materiae*, in respect of all states. The only limit is compliance with international law:[80] the Council may therefore declare as 'illegal' *erga omnes* only conduct by states that violates interests recognised as fundamental by the global community, which, as such, are protected by general international law. This much is borne out by certain Security Council resolutions that – in specifying that the Council holds the state perpetrating the breach responsible 'under international law'[81] – underscore the general role performed by the Council, rather than the role it has by virtue of

79 See *supra* notes 40, 41 and corresponding text. the Assembly has determined responsibility and condemned 'strongly' and 'in the strongest terms' the 'grave' violations of international humanitarian law in Rwanda (GA Res. 49/206 (Dec. 23, 1994), paras 2, 3) and the same violations perpetrated by the Iraqi government in occupied Kuwait (GA Res. 45/170 (Dec. 18, 1990), para. 1) and in Iraq (GA Res. 46/134 (Dec. 17, 1991), para. 2); by the Federal Republic of Yugoslavia in Kosovo (GA Res. 49/204 (Dec. 23, 1994), para. 1; GA Res. 53/144 (Dec. 17, 1998), para. 8); and by Indonesia in East Timor (GA Res. 54/194 (Dec. 17, 1999), preamble), in each case calling on the government responsible to fulfil specific obligations. The express reference made by the Assembly to the peculiar characteristics of crimes against humanity, such as the gravity, systematic nature, and large-scale occurrence of the violations, highlights the Assembly's intention to envisage the responsibility of the above-named states for international crimes.

80 See *supra* notes 45–48; *infra* note 97 and corresponding text.

81 See *supra* notes 59–67 and corresponding text.

the Charter. In other cases, the Security Council emphasizes most insistently that it is acting on the basis of the Charter, explicitly addressing only member states.[82] Nevertheless, it should be added that no review of the legality of Security Council resolutions has yet been formalized, although the issue has been examined by the International Court of Justice.[83]

Mechanisms to Co-Manage Peaceful Enforcement Measures

In our view, it is well established that, in principle, states may adopt peaceful countermeasures either at the national level or within regional organizations, even in the absence of Security Council authorization. What we would now like to stress is this: the principle of law-enforcement authority being shared between states and the international institutions outlined above allows us to come down in favour of the lawfulness of 'non-authorized' peaceful state countermeasures, provided the measures are adopted in response to a grave and manifest violation of basic norms of general international law and provided there are clear references to pronouncements of the UN political bodies or the International Court of Justice objectively determining serious violations of basic norms by the target state. We are clearly referring to 'non-authorized' state countermeasures (different from measures of retortion) consisting of the breach of an international obligation (failure to fulfil treaty obligations and/or other obligations deriving from general international law). The will of the UN to endorse such measures may be presumed to be absent, due to the fact that no declaration of unlawfulness of the countermeasures adopted has been forthcoming from UN bodies.

This conclusion draws attention to the function of 'control' of the legitimacy of unilateral countermeasures conferred on the UN bodies by international law, which we commented on at the beginning of the third section of this chapter. The General Assembly has laid claim to this role on several occasions, such as when it condemned

---

82 In some cases the Council specifies emphatically that its resolution binds member states, finding 'the legal basis in the Charter of the United Nations'. See, e.g., SC Res. 1168 (May 21, 1998), para. 3; SC Res. 1174 (June 15, 1998), Part III, preamble; SC Res. 1247 (June 18, 1999), Part III, preamble; SC. Res. 1305 (June 21, 2000), Part III, preamble. In other cases, basing its decisions not only on breach of the Charter but also on the violation of international law, it addresses *all* states (*supra* notes 59, 70, 71 and corresponding text).

83 In its advisory opinion on the *Namibia* case, appealing to 'the exercise of its judicial function', the Court examined the validity of the General Assembly and Security Council resolutions involved, before pronouncing on the legal consequences stemming from them; however, it declared that under the Charter: 'the Court does not possess powers of judicial review or appeal in respect of the decisions taken by the United Nations bodies' (see *supra* note 42, para. 89, at 45; see also our Repertory, *supra* note 1, vol. I, No. 2404, at 1011). In favour of a review, see the individual opinion of the *ad hoc* judge Lauterpacht, attached to the Court order of 13 September (Bosnia and Herzegovina v. Yugoslavia), Provisional Measures, Order, 1993 ICJ Reports 325, *id.* Elihu Lauterpacht, *Judicial Review of the Acts of International Organisations*, *in* International Law, The International Court of Justice and Nuclear Weapons (Laurence Boisson de Chazournes ed., Cambridge University Press, Cambridge, 1999). See also *infra* chapter 3 of this book.

ex post facto the unilateral trade embargo and other economic sanctions applied by some states against the dictatorial regime in Nicaragua, requesting their withdrawal.[84] Along similar lines were the General Assembly's resolutions on the need to halt the economic, financial, and trade blockade applied by the US against Cuba.[85] On the other hand, the countermeasures adopted by the US (economic sanctions and certain unilateral measures against Iran) after the seizure of its embassy in Iran on 4 November 1979, were considered by the International Court of Justice to be lawful 'measures taken in response to ... grave and manifest violations of international law by Iran'.[86] The International Court of Justice, 'admitting in principle that some of these actions were not unlawful in themselves' brings to mind the need for the institutional control of legitimacy.[87]

In appraising the lawfulness of measures not involving the use of force adopted in a collective capacity by states, the UN bodies examine both the legal basis for the measures – the actual serious breach of basic norms – and their compliance with the criteria normally set by general international law for their lawful implementation. Such measures must therefore be applied in compliance with international law standards and conform to the criteria of necessity and proportionality in relation to the aim to be achieved, namely, restoring the rule of law; accordingly, they must cease when that aim has been achieved. Further, they must not result in breaches of peremptory international norms (*jus cogens*). In this last regard, the UN's attention towards the modalities with which economic sanctions are applied should be noted, since there is a risk that these may result in the breach of humanitarian law and human rights. This danger has led the UN to pay greater attention to unilateral sanctions of this type.

The General Assembly has issued a generic appeal to states to withdraw all unilateral economic sanctions. Starting from the 1990s, the General Assembly has called on the international community to take urgent and effective initiatives to put an end to coercive economic measures used unilaterally by states as a means of applying political and economic pressure. In so doing, it aims to affirm more incisive UN control over this means of exerting pressure, appealing to the norms of general international law and the purposes and principles of the UN (particularly that of economic cooperation among states), as well as to the inalienable right of every state to freely choose its economic, political, and social system.[88] More incisive action is performed by the Assembly in condemning the continued promulgation and

84 GA Res. 40/188 (Dec. 17, 1985).

85 GA Res. 47/19 (Nov. 24, 1992); GA Res. 48/16 (Nov. 3, 1993); GA Res. 50/10 (Nov. 2, 1995); GA Res. 51/17 (Nov. 12, 1996); GA Res. 52/10 (Nov. 5, 1997); GA Res. 58/171 (Dec. 22, 2004) ; GA Res. 59/188 (March 15, 2005).

86 United States Diplomatic and Consular Staff in Tehran (United States of America v. Iran), Merits, Judgment, 1980 ICJ Reports 3 (May 24, 1980), para. 53, at 27–28; see our Repertory, *supra* note 1, No. 1595, vol. I, at 627, 629.

87 Military and Paramilitary Activities, *supra* note 1, para 245, at 126; see also our Repertory, *supra* note 1, vol. I, No. 1039, at 37.

88 GA Res. 51/22 (Nov. 27, 1996), approved by only 56 votes in favour, with 6 against and 76 abstentions. The GA has 'urged ... all States to refrain from adopting or implementing any unilateral measures not in accordance with international law' and has called on states to

application by states of laws and measures of economic, commercial, and financial embargo 'with extraterritorial effects' that affect the sovereignty of other states, create obstacles to trade relations among states and impede the full realization of all human rights.[89] The resolutions adopted for ending the embargo measures against Cuba imposed by US laws[90] contain statements of a general character. By an overwhelming majority, the Assembly reiterates in these resolutions its call on 'all states' to refrain from laws and measures of this kind and 'urges' states to repeal or invalidate them; in so doing, it has performed functions of control to guarantee obligations laid down not only by the Charter, but also by international law 'which, *inter alia*, reaffirmed the freedom of trade and navigation'– as the Council underlines.[91] However, the poor response to such requests must be highlighted, even where appeals have been expressly made to individual states. This leads one to question the lawfulness of

respect the rights established by the Universal Declaration of Human Rights (GA Res. 53/141 (Dec. 9, 1999)).

89 See *supra* notes 84–85.

90 See especially the Helms-Burton Act (*Cuban Liberty and Democratic Solidarity (Libertad) Act*) and D'Amato-Kennedy Act (*Iran and Libya Sanctions Act*), passed in 1996. Notably the extraterritorial nature of these and other US measures provoked reactions from some states that have adopted domestic laws to protect their trade and investments; further, they have collectively undertaken initiatives as members of international organizations. The European Union countries, after adopting Council Regulation 2271/96 ((22 Nov. 1996), OFFICIAL JOURNAL No. L 309 (Nov. 29, 1996)), asked the WTO to establish a Special Panel against the US, which was approved on 20 November 1996, and later suspended following the agreement reached on 11 April 1997 (see EU–US: Memorandum of Understanding Concerning the Helms-Burton Act and the US Iran and Libya Sanctions Act). On 21 October 1998, the Dispute Settlement Body (DSB) established a panel to examine complaints by the EC and Japan against Massachusetts law disallowing the granting of government procurement contracts to companies doing business in or with Myanmar. They claimed this law violated provisions of the multilateral Agreement on Government Procurement. The issue of the international lawfulness of these US laws has received broad coverage among policy-makers and jurists. See, e.g., Brice M. Clagett, *Title III of the Helms-Burton Act Is Consistent with International Law*, 90 AM. J. INT'L. L. 434 (1996); *Id.*, *The Cuban Liberty and Democratic Solidarity (Libertad) Act, Continued. A Reply to Professor Lowenfeld, id.*, at 641; Andreas F. Lowenfeld, *The Cuban Liberty and Democratic Solidarity (Libertad) Act Congress and Cuba: the Helms-Burton Act, id.*, at 419; Michel Cosnard, *Les Lois Helms-Burton et D'Amato-Kennedy, Interdiction de Commercer avec et d'Investir dans Certains Pays*, 62 ANN. FR. D.I. 33 (1996), at 49; August Reinisch, *Widening the US Embargo Against Cuba Extraterritorially: A Few Public International Law Comments on the Cuban Liberty and Democratic Solidarity (Libertad) Act of 1996*, 7 EUR. J. INT'L L. 545 (1996), at 551; Brigitte Stern, *Vers la Mondialisation Juridique? Les Lois Helms-Burton et D'Amato-Kennedy*, 100 REV. GEN. D.I.P. 979 (1996); Theodor Meron & Detlev F. Vagts, *The Helms-Burton Act: Exercising the Presidential Option*, 91 AM. J. INT'L. L. 83 (1997); Vaughan Lowe, *US Extraterritorial Jurisdiction. The Helms-Burton and D'Amato Acts*, 46 INT'L & COMP. L.Q. 378 (1997); Susan Kaufman Purcell, *La Ley Helms-Burton y el Embargo Estadounidense Contra Cuba*, 43 FORO INTERNACIONAL 704 (2003).

91 GA Res. 52/10, *supra* note 85, para. 2; the resolution was approved by 143 votes in favour, with only three against and 17 abstentions.

sanctions persisting even where the General Assembly has issued a 'specific' appeal for their withdrawal.

Control over state countermeasures is also exercised by the Security Council, which has developed procedures and mechanisms that do, however, need to be improved in order to become really effective: in 'authorizing' the adoption of voluntary sanctions, it places limits on states dictated by humanitarian needs and the requirement for proportionality, and establishes mechanisms for checking that they are correctly applied.[92] Tighter control is ensured in those cases where the Security Council accedes to the appeals made by states or regional organizations, or adopts as its own the initiatives these entities have already undertaken and resolves to sanction serious breaches of fundamental law, imposing the specific measures to be adopted in the specific case and the modalities for applying them on all states. This obviously represents another means of performing enforcement functions jointly with states. The Security Council, taking charge of the action against the state responsible, decides (with a generic reference to Chapter VII of the Charter) on the enforcement measures to restore the law breached, compelling 'all' states to comply with them, and presenting the measures as sanctions imposed by the entire international community. The proper implementation of the measures is ensured, while their intensity is graded in relation to the actual results obtained from time to time, and checks are made that their inevitable incidence on the civilian population is kept within the bounds of humanitarian principles.[93] Control that states implement

92 On the humanitarian impact of economic sanctions, see, e.g., DANIEL L. BETHLEHEM, THE KUWAIT CRISIS: SANCTIONS AND THEIR ECONOMIC CONSEQUENCES (1991); ECONOMIC SANCTIONS: PANACEA OR PEACEBUILDING IN A POST-COLD WAR WORLD? (David Cortright & George A. Lopez eds, 1995); Paul Szasz, *The Law of Economic Sanctions*, *in* THE LAW OF ARMED CONFLICT INTO THE NEXT MILLENIUM 455 (Michael N. Schmitt ed., 1998); Christopher Wall, *Human Rights and Economic Sanctions: The New Imperialisms*, 22 FORDHAM INT'L L.J. 77 (1998); August Reinisch, *Developing Human Rights and Humanitarian Law Accountability of the Security Council for the Imposition of Economic Sanctions*, 96 AM. J. INT'L. L. 851 (2001). For the UN activity, see *Humanitarian Impact of Sanctions*, Statement of the five Permanent Members, UN Doc. S/1995/300 (1995) and *infra* notes 92, 93.

93 Exceptions to UN economic sanctions programmes for humanitarian purposes are contemplated in many Security Council resolutions. See, e.g., SC Res. 253 (May 29, 1968), para. 3(d), against Southern Rhodesia; SC Res. 661, *supra* note 59, paras 3(c) and 4; SC Res. 666 (Sept. 13, 1990), para 8, relating to the Gulf crisis; SC Res. 841 (June 16, 1993), para. 7, against Haiti; SC Res. 760 (June 18, 1992); SC Res. 820 (April 17, 1993), para. 22(a) and (b); SC Res. 943 (Sept. 23, 1994), paras 1, 2, against the Federal Republic of Yugoslavia (Serbia and Montenegro). See also SC Res. 748, *supra* note 59, para. 4, providing for a block on air communications *from* and *to* Libya, although exempting flights from the ban for humanitarian reasons, authorized by a specially constituted Committee. The Council has reaffirmed its readiness, whenever measures are adopted under Art. 41 of the Charter of the UN, to give consideration to their impact on the civilian population, bearing in mind the needs of children, in order to consider appropriate humanitarian exemptions (see SC Res. 1265, *supra* note 64, para. 16. See also SC Res. 1261, *supra* note 63, para. 17(c)). For more detail on this topic, see especially JOHN STREMLAU, SHARPENING INTERNATIONAL SANCTIONS: TOWARD A STRONGER ROLE FOR THE UNITED NATIONS, REPORT TO THE CARNEGIE COMMISSION ON PREVENTING DEADLY CONFLICT (1996).

he measures properly is entrusted to *ad hoc* committees and/or to the Secretary-General, who is requested to report to the Security Council.[94] Although, at present, it is still inadequate to ensure the lawfulness of the sanctions, this last procedure for coercive enforcement of international law is to be preferred on account of the higher level of institutionalization attained, and it is evident that states do show a preference for it. The foregoing holds true both from the standpoint of objectivity and fairness (the Security Council can exercise tighter control over the enforcement action of states and ensure greater observance of necessity, proportionality, discrimination, and compliance with peremptory international law), and from the standpoint of efficacy, which is enhanced by the obligation imposed on all states. In such cases, the Security Council performs a law-enforcement function under the terms of general international law; it accordingly enjoys discretion over the type of measures to adopt, which need not necessarily come within those envisaged by the Charter (Article 41) but must comply with international law standards.

This last point goes to the core of the question widely debated among international legal scholars: whether the Security Council is subject to limits in the exercise of its law-enforcement activity. The issue has been examined mainly from the viewpoint of the limits laid down by the Charter and, as a result the power of ascertainment conferred by Article 39, has been considered '*totalement discretionnaire*',[95] and the Council considered *legibus solutus* when acting under Chapter VII. Above all, proponents of this view rule out the possibility that international law may set limits to the Council's power to determine the existence of a threat to the peace and/or to decide the sanctions envisaged by Chapter VII. In particular, they maintain that the measures not involving the use of armed force, provided by Article 41, may be decided in derogation from international law.[96]

---

94 Sanctions Committees have been set up to monitor economic sanctions against Southern Rhodesia (SC Res. 253, *supra* note 93, para. 20); against Iraq (SC Res. 661, *supra* note 59, para. 6; SC Res. 666, *supra* note 93, paras 5, 6, 8); against Haiti 'for essential humanitarian needs' (SC Res. 841, *supra* note 93; SC Res. 917, *supra* note 54, para. 7); against Libya (SC Res. 748, *supra* note 59, para. 9(b)–(f)). See the greater determination shown in concrete terms by the Council at the humanitarian situation in Iraq, with SC Res. 1284 (Dec. 17, 1999), in which it asks the Secretary-General to enhance the instruments for completing and actually implementing the humanitarian programme, 'drawing as necessary on the advice of specialists, including representatives of international humanitarian organisations' and providing for more direct Council control over the implementation of the programme (*id.* at C, para. 21). See Paul Conlon, *Lessons from Iraq: The Functions of the Iraq Sanctions Committee as a Source of Sanctions Implementation Authority and Practice*, 35 VAND. J. INT'L L. 633 (1995).

95 See Judge WEERAMANTRY, 1992 ICJ REPORTS 160, 176. *Contra*, the opinions expressed in the *Namibia* case by Judges FITZMAURICE and GROS, quoted *supra* note 83, at 293, 340, respectively.

96 Christian Tomuschat, *The Lockerbie Case Before the International Court of Justice*, 48 INTERNATIONAL COMMISSION OF JURISTS. THE REVIEW 38 (1992); Benedetto Conforti, *Le Pouvoir Discrétionnaire du Conseil de Sécurité en Matière de Constatation d'une Menace Contre la Paix, d'Une Rupture de la Paix ou d'Un Acte d'Agression*, *in* DUPUY, LE DÉVELOPPEMENT, *supra* note 74, at 55, 59; Vera Gowlland-Debbas, *Security Council Enforcement Action and Issues of State Responsibility*, 43 INT'L & COMP. L.Q. 55 (1994).

Our own view on the matter is differently inclined, and we hold our conviction not only by reason of the dual role we assign to the Security Council – both as a UN body under the terms of the Charter and also as an 'agent' of the international community under general international law. We believe, in fact, that the Security Council is not empowered to impose sanctions that are inconsistent with the criteria of lawfulness envisaged or inherent in the notion of sanctions accepted by international law (i.e., necessity, proportionality, and compliance with peremptory international law).[97] These assertions are supported by the analysis of legal scholars, as well as by Security Council practice, which is increasingly oriented towards compliance with international standards, particularly due to the fact that the economic sanctions programmes usually provide exceptions for cases where a breach of human rights – and, thus, a breach of a peremptory norm of general international law – arises from their implementation. Furthermore, some resolutions expressly require that the enforcement measures decided must cease once the objective of restoring the law has been achieved. It is the task of the Security Council to verify whether the objectives have been achieved, and the Council has forcefully affirmed as much in its resolutions.[98] The aim of preventing unnecessary suffering on the part of the civilian population gives rise to the notion of 'smart sanctions' that are intended to have an impact on those responsible for illicit actions, terrorist activity, or grave violations of human rights, including rulers, leaders, organizations, and movements.[99] However, we cannot fail to express our agreement with the views of those authors who believe that the Council still pays inadequate consideration to international law standards in implementing mandatory UN economic sanctions and who advocate solutions aimed at effective control over their legality.[100]

97 In this sense, see Ziccardi Capaldo, *supra* note 48, at 94; *Draft Articles on Responsibility of States for Internationally Wrongful Acts, Report of the International Law Commission on the work of its 53rd Session* (23 April–1 June and 2 July–10 August 2001), Arts. 50 (1)(d), 51, UN Doc. A/56/10, chp.IV.E.1, at 56 *et seq.*, available at <http://www.un.org/law/ilc/reports/2001/2001report.htm>; see also *Commentaries to the Draft Articles on Responsibility of States for Internationally Wrongful Acts*, *supra* note 13, Part Three, Chap. II, para. 5, at 327; Art. 50, para. 9, at 336, Art. 51, paras 1–7, at 341–344.

98 SC Res. 1267, *supra* note 59, paras 3, 14; see also *supra* notes 92–94 and corresponding text. In authorizing economic sanctions or adopting sanctions programmes, the Council sets the objectives to be achieved. See, e.g., SC Res. 569, *supra* note 43, preamble, towards South Africa; SC Res. 780 (Oct. 6, 1992) and SC Res. 787, *supra* note 52, relating to the Yugoslavian crisis; SC Res. 794, *supra* note 51, in the Somali conflict. In SC Res. 1192, *supra* note 69, the Council explicitly 'decides' in para. 8 (as it does similarly in para. 16 of Res. 883 (Nov. 11, 1993) and para. 3 of Res. 748, *supra* note 59) that the measures set forth in its resolutions 'shall be suspended immediately' if the obligations imposed have been fulfilled and the objectives set achieved.

99 See *infra* chapter 8 of this book, under the subheading 'The Concept of "Smart Sanctions" ', and chapter 9.

100 See especially the contributions by Reisman & Stevick, *supra* note 31, at 96, 121–141.

Mechanisms to Co-Manage Measures Involving the Use of Force

We shall now analyse the question as to whether international law has established mechanisms and procedures enabling states to use armed force in the common interest outside the legally designated institutions or procedures of the Charter (Chapter VII). This issue has attracted the attention of jurists and policy-makers since the time of the Gulf War, and such attention has increased since the case of NATO intervention in Kosovo.

Authorized Uses of Force

In the Supplement to *An Agenda for Peace* of 1992, the Secretary-General indicated the following as being enforcement instruments involving the use of force other than self-defence: to ensure observance of an embargo or to disarm opposing factions fighting in a civil war; to ensure the protection of humanitarian operations; and to protect civilian populations in designated safe areas.[101] There is no question that any use of force by states outside Article 51 of the Charter, to sanction serious breaches of norms protecting fundamental values of the international order, is subject to prior 'authorization' by the Security Council. States have on various occasions been granted prior authorization to use force at the national level or in the framework of regional agreements, considered in detail below. In our opinion, starting from the Gulf War in 1990 and then in the succeeding international crises (in Yugoslavia, Somalia, Rwanda, the Great Lakes, Albania and Timor), a principle of general international law, which is both substantive and procedural, has become established, according to which Security Council authorization is required for states or groups of states or regional organizations, acting in their collective capacity, to use force to sanction serious breaches of obligations in the interest of the international community as a whole, such as the prohibition of aggression and grave and wide-ranging violations of human rights, as well as violation of the principle of self-determination and other principles protecting fundamental interests.[102] From the substantive point of view, the principle under consideration provides a further exception to the absolute prohibition on the use of force by states; this exception now stands beside that contemplated by Article 51, which has become a norm of general international law.[103] Moreover, it

101 *An Agenda for Peace*, UN Doc. A/47/277–S/24111 (June 17, 1992). UN Doc. A/50/60–S/1995/1 Supp. (Jan. 3, 1995), para. 34.

102 Chapt. III of Part Two of the International Law Commission's Draft includes the notion of 'obligations under peremptory norms of general international law', focusing on the right of all states, entitled to invoke responsibility under Art. 48 (see *supra* note 13), to act in the collective interest, in the interest of the international community as a whole (see *Commentaries to the Draft Articles on Responsibility of States for Internationally Wrongful Acts*, *supra* note 13, Art. 54, at 355); see also *id.*, Part Two, Chapt. III, at 277, 281, 324 *et seq.*). For the practice of Council's authorizations, see *supra* notes 46–54 and corresponding text.

103 See *supra* chapter 1 of this book. In this sense see also Giuliana Ziccardi Capaldo, *Democratizzazione all'Est e Diritto Internazionale Generale*, *in* DEMOCRATIZZAZIONE ALL'EST E DIRITTO INTERNAZIONALE 27 (Giuliana Ziccardi Capaldo ed., 1998), at 52. The illegality of the use of force by states or groups of states where prior Security Council authorization is

confers powers on the Security Council for determining and sanctioning the breach of any internationally protected fundamental value, with the result that when the Council acts at the level of general law its relative competence is wider than its institutional competence as a UN body, restricted, as we well know, by the Charter to any threat to the peace, breach of the peace, or act of aggression (Chapter VII). From the procedural angle, the rule affirms a mechanism for joint implementation by states and the UN of sanctions involving the use of force: the 'authorization' represents a 'condition' for the exercise by states of the right to use force; it is therefore required as a 'prior and express' act of the Council.

Ample debate has arisen among policy-makers and international law scholars as to the modalities for authorization to use force, since events have occurred in practice that seem to contradict the need for a prior explicit authorization by the Security Council and open the way for implied authorization or a subsequent tacit endorsement also to be admissible. Disputes have arisen over the lawfulness of the American and British attack on Iraq of 1998 and the NATO action in Kosovo. In the first of these cases, discussion centred on whether the authorization to use force granted in Security Council Resolution 678[104] and reasserted in Resolution 686,[105] could constitute the legal basis for the Anglo-American attack on Iraq; or whether the 'extended force' of that authorization must be excluded in that its validity ceased with the definite end to hostilities deliberated by subsequent Resolution 687 – by which the legitimacy of the attack also ceased.[106]

The tendency of some Western States to bypass the requirement for explicit authorization should certainly be considered.[107] On the other hand, it should be pointed out that the Russian Federation, too, has had recourse to force on occasion without asking for Security Council authorization, conducting military operations for the maintenance of peace in the territory of the member states of the Commonwealth of Independent States (CIS).[108] Generally speaking, the tendency to use force when not expressly authorized does not appear to be upheld by a sufficient *opinio juris*

---

absent is affirmed by most scholars. See especially SCHACHTER, INTERNATIONAL LAW IN THEORY AND PRACTICE, *supra* note 77, at 126–129, 402; William Michael Reisman, *Coercion and Self-Determination: Construing Charter Article 2(4)*, 78 AM. J. INT'L. L. 642 (1984). For general aspects on this topic, see Thomas M. Franck, *The Use of Force in International Law*, 11 TULANE JOURNAL OF INTERNATIONAL & COMPARATIVE LAW 7 (2003); John D. Becker, *The Continuing Relevance of Article 2(4), A Consideration of the Status of the U.N. Charter's Limitations on the Use of Force*, 32 THE DENVER JOURNAL OF INTERNATIONAL LAW & POLICY [hereinafter DENVER J. INT'L L & POL'Y] 583 (2004). See also the literature quoted *infra* note 118–119. See also *infra* chapter 4 of this book.

104 SC Res. 678, *supra* note 50.

105 SC Res. 686 (March 2, 1991).

106 SC Res. 687, *supra* note 59.

107 Jules Lobel & Michael Ratner, *Bypassing the Security Council: Ambiguous Authorizations to Use Force, Cease-Fires and the Iraqi Inspection Regime*, 93 AM. J. INT'L. L. 124 (1999); *Legal Authority for the Possible use of Force Against Iraq*, 92 AMERICAN SOCIETY OF INTERNATIONAL LAW: PROCEEDINGS OF THE ANNUAL MEETING 136 (1998). See *supra* notes 27–29 and corresponding text. See also *infra* chapter 4 of this book.

108 Momtaz, *supra* note 49, at 112–113.

of states and the UN. The international community has reacted strongly to the use of force not authorized by the Security Council, and the justifications argued by intervening states seem to admit by implication (or not to exclude) the requirement for prior authorization. At the time of the 1998 attack on Iraq, the US and the UK invoked as grounds for the action Iraq's persistent breach of obligations it had been called on to perform by binding decisions of the Council (under the terms of Resolution 687); this supposedly had the effect of 'reviving' the authorization to use force already granted, the suspension of which had been subordinated to performance of the obligations imposed.[109] On other occasions, states maintained that their intervention had been requested by the 'victim' states themselves (as the Russian Federation did in the case mentioned above), tracing their action back to Article 51 of the Charter and in this way overcoming the objection that there was no authorization.[110] As for the grounds put forward by the US and the UK in the Iraqi case referred to above, this case has quite expediently brought to light the need for a clear determination of material breach on the part of the Security Council.[111] We believe this last point receives support from the Council's clear claims to the power to verify whether the state responsible has fulfilled the obligations imposed on it through Council decisions. The Security Council has on many occasions affirmed the need to determine the re-establishment of legality on the part of the target state, before all the other states can consider themselves exonerated from the duty to cooperate in the application of mandatory sanctions.[112] These brief considerations lead us to insist that explicit prior authorization is required for the use of force by a state or states acting in a 'collective' capacity and outside Article 51.

Unauthorized Humanitarian Interventions

It is only in cases of humanitarian intervention that states and the Security Council itself take a different approach. We are referring to the cases of military intervention

109 The bombing of Iraq in December 1998 in response to its defiance of the UN Special Commission was widely disapproved by states. Most members of the Security Council did not even agree with the justification, also advanced by the two states carrying out the armed attack, that Res. 1154 (March 2, 1998) endorsing the memorandum of understanding regarding inspections, signed by Kofi Annan and the Iraqi Deputy Prime Minister, authorized the unilateral use of force.

110 It must be said that Art. 29 (2) of the 1980 Draft Articles on State Responsibility excluded the possibility that an affected state's consent may be invoked as a cause precluding wrongfulness in cases like the one in question, involving breach of a peremptory norm. Y. Int'l L. Comm. (1980), Vol. II, (Part Two), at 32; UN Doc. A/CN.4/Ser.A/ 1980/Add. 1 (Part 2). See also *Commentaries to the Draft Articles on Responsibility of States for Internationally Wrongful Acts*, adopted in 2001, *supra* note 13, Art. 20, para. 7, at 175; Art. 26, para.6, at 208.

111 Lobel & Ratner, *supra* note 107, at 150.

112 See, e.g., *supra* note 59: SC Res. 1054, para. 8; SC Res. 1070, para. 4; SC Res. 1267, para. 3.

in Northern Iraq to protect Iraqi Kurds in 1991,[113] by the ECOWAS states in Liberia and Sierra Leone,[114] or by NATO in Kosovo.[115] In these cases, the intervening states appealed to a 'duty of humanitarian intervention' and there was no substantial reaction from the international community and world public opinion, despite the absence of express prior authorization from the Security Council. The Russian Federation and China's strong protests against NATO's armed intervention in Kosovo should certainly be taken into account, but the fact that the Security Council rejected the draft resolution for the immediate suspension of the NATO bombing should also

---

113 In 1991, the UK, the US, and France used force to provide humanitarian aid to the Kurdish refugees in northern Iraq and to enforce a no-fly zone there. These states maintained that such actions were implicitly authorized by UN resolutions condemning Iraq's acts of repression against the civilian population, and they did not elicit a strong reaction from the other member states. See Jane E. Stromseth, *Iraq's Repression of Its Civilian Population: Collective Responses and Continuing Challenges*, *in* ENFORCING RESTRAINT: COLLECTIVE INTERVENTION IN INTERNAL CONFLICTS 77, 100 (Lori Fisler Damrosch ed., 1993) [hereinafter DAMROSCH, ENFORCING RESTRAINT].

114 During the civil war in Liberia, the Security Council endorsed the military operations (SC Res. 788 (Nov. 19, 1992); SC Res. 813 (March 26, 1993)) not initially authorized by the UN, which were conducted from 1990 to 1992 by the African peace-keeping forces ECOMOG (ECOWAS Cease-fire Monitoring Group) to enforce a cease-fire ordered by the ECOWAS; this was done *ex post facto* and without objections of UN member states. See, e.g., Georg Nolte, *Restoring Peace by Regional Action: International Legal Aspects of the Liberian Conflict*, 53 ZEITSCHRIFT FÜR AUSLÄNDISCHES OFFENTLICHES RECHT UND VÖLKERRECHT 603 (1993), at 627; David Wippman, *Enforcing the Peace: ECOWAS and the Liberian Civil War*, *in* DAMROSCH, ENFORCING RESTRAINT, *supra* note 113, at 157, 182. See also documents reported in REGIONAL PEACE KEEPING AND INTERNATIONAL ENFORCEMENT: THE LIBERIAN CRISIS (Mark Weller ed., 1994). At the Abuja Summit of 28–29 August 1997, the Authority of ECOWAS heads of state and government wholeheartedly condemned the 'violent and anti-constitutional' overthrow of the democratically elected government in Sierra Leone of 25 May 1997; underlining that the objectives set by the Community had received the endorsement of the UN, it decided to include Sierra Leone in the ECOMOG mandate to control the ceasefire and restore peace (21 DOCUMENTS D'ACTUALITÉ INTERNATIONALE 738 (1997)); it also approved a series of sanctions and embargoes as supplementary measures in view of the restoration of the legitimate government of President Tejan Kabbah (*id.*, at 739); see Jeremy Levitt, *Humanitarian Intervention by Regional Actors in International Conflicts, and the Cases of ECOWAS in Liberia and Sierra Leone*, 12 TEMPLE INTERNATIONAL & COMPARATIVE LAW JOURNAL 333 (1998), at 347; Karsten Nowrot & Emily W. Schabacker, *The Use of Force to Restore Democracy: International Legal Implications of the ECOWAS Intervention in Sierra Leone*, 14 AMERICAN UNIVERSITY LAW REVIEW 321 (1998). The Security Council also endorsed the military actions by CIS in Georgia. See SC Res. 1124 (July 31, 1997); SC Res. 1150 (Jan. 30, 1998); SC Res. 1225 (Jan. 28, 1999), preamble, para. 12; SC Res. 1287 (Jan. 31, 2000), preamble, para. 11; SC Res. 1311 (July 28, 2000), preamble; SC Res. 1339 (Jan. 31, 2001), preamble, para. 15. See Stephen N. MacFarlane, *On the Front Lines in the Near Abroad: The CIS and the OSCE in Georgia's Civil Wars*, *in* BEYOND UN SUBCONTRACTING 115 (Thomas G . Weiss ed., 1998).

115 The weak reaction of UN bodies to the intervention should be underlined. On this point see the literature quoted *infra* notes 118–119.

be underlined.[116] It seems decisive that the Council incorporated into Resolution 1244 of 10 June 1999 the principles set by NATO and accepted by Serbia for the re-establishment of peace in the Balkans;[117] this fact leads us to believe that the Council meant to endorse the intervention *ex post facto* and to give legitimacy to NATO's unauthorized action.[118]

These considerations lead us to concur with authors who support the view that unauthorized humanitarian interventions are lawful in the face of Security Council inaction when a number of conditions are met,[119] though we hold the same view

---

116 The draft resolution sponsored by Belarus, India, and the Russian Federation received only three votes in favour and 12 against (UN Doc. S/1999/328).

117 See *infra* notes 121, 122 and corresponding text.

118 Most scholars see NATO's action in Kosovo as unlawful, since Security Council authorization was absent; nevertheless, it has been justified in different ways and considered to be on the borderline between legality and illegality. See, e.g., Thomas M. Franck, *Lessons of Kosovo*, and William Michael Reisman, *Kosovo's Antinomies*, 93 Am. J. Int'l. L. (1999), at 857 and 860, respectively; Bruno Simma, *NATO, The UN and the Use of Force: Legal Aspects*, 10 Eur. J. Int'l L. 1 (1999), at 22; these authors underline the exceptional character of the action. In justification of the NATO's intervention, repeated reference is made to the inaction of the Security Council, paralysed by the exercise of the veto. For Council ratification 'after the fact' see, e.g., Louis Henkin, *Kosovo and the Law of 'Humanitarian Intervention'*, 93 Am. J. Int'l. L. 824 (1999), at 827. It has also been emphasized that the lack of explicit condemnation by the UN bodies could suggest the 'acquiescence' of the UN in the intervention; see Jonathan I. Charney, *Anticipatory Humanitarian Intervention in Kosovo*, *id.*, at 834, 840. 'Implied approval of military action' has also been raised; see, in this sense, Christine M. Chinkin, *Kosovo: A 'Good' or 'Bad' War?*, *id.*, at 843. The theory of implied authorization has been strongly contested. See, e.g., Lobel & Ratner, *supra* note 107, at 130. For general aspects on this topic, Vaughan Lowe, *International Legal Issues Arising in the Kosovo Crisis*, 49 Int'l & Comp. L.Q. 934 (2000); John C. Yoo, *Kosovo, War Powers, and the Multilateral Future*, 148 University of Pennsylvania Law Review 1673 (2000); Jean Allain, *The True Challenge to the United Nations System of the Use of Force. The Failures of Kosovo and Iraq and the Emergence of the African Union*, 8 Max Planck Yearbook of United Nations Law 237 (2004).

119 In favour of unilateral enforcement as a remedy for grave human rights violations 'if the Security Council cannot' intervene, see Reisman, *supra* note 18, at 15. The Kosovo example has led commentators to believe (albeit very cautiously) that a customary rule may be forming, or to look forward to the emergence of a rule on humanitarian intervention falling within well-defined parameters. See Richard A. Falk, *Kosovo, World Order, and the Future of International Law*, 93 Am. J. Int'l. L. 853 (1999), at 856; Ruth Wedgwood, *NATO's Campaign in Jugoslavia*, *id.*, at 828. The development of the norm is viewed in an increasingly favourable light in the international community; in his Annual Report to the General Assembly, the Secretary-General also augured the development of a norm 'in favour of intervention to protect civilians from wholesale slaughter' (see *Secretary-General Presents His Annual Report to General Assembly*, UN Doc. Press Release SG/SM/7136, GA/9596 (Sept. 20, 1999)). On humanitarian intervention and jurists' views on the subject, see Sean D. Murphy, Humanitarian Intervention: The United Nations in an Evolving World Order (1996); Humanitarian Intervention and the United Nations (Richard B. Lillich ed., 1973); Edward MacWhinney, The United Nations and the New World Order for a New Millennium. Self-determination, State Succession, and Humanitarian Intervention (2000);

starting from a different perspective. As we have noted elsewhere, humanitarian intervention has to meet specific requirements (i.e., it needs to be: (1) carried out 'in the common interest'; (2) to put an end to the 'grave and manifest' violation of human rights perpetrated by the territorial state, objectively verified by the UN bodies; (3) multilateral conduct (i.e., not disapproved of by the majority of states and world public opinion), possibly with the involvement of regional organizations; and (4) subsequently approved by the Security Council as respectful of *jus cogens*. In this case, in our opinion, the intervention is to be considered legitimate and of a 'collective' nature, albeit implemented outside the procedures of the Charter, and it is to be placed in the framework of the integrated system of collective guarantees of a 'punitive' nature under the terms of general international law.

It may be argued that a general norm that has the specified prerequisites has developed to enforce the prohibition of gross violations of human rights, derogating from the international principle normally requiring the prior and explicit authorization of the Security Council for non-Article 51 uses of force. Since such a norm is set in the framework of the integrated system of law enforcement co-managed by states and the international institutions, in our view, the lawfulness of the humanitarian intervention remains in any event subject to the general procedural requirements on which this system is based, namely, to the determination on the part of the UN of the serious breach of human rights and the resulting need to bring it to an end, and to the endorsement – albeit subsequent – of the Security Council, which verifies compliance of the action with the humanitarian aims of the intervention and with international standards of legitimacy.[120]

In the case of NATO intervention in Kosovo, the tacit approval that 'legitimates' the intervention *ex post facto* results from 'conclusive' facts (as well as resulting from the lack of explicit censure by the UN bodies): the Security Council incorporated in Resolution 1244 the 'general principles for the solution of the crisis in Kosovo'[121] laid down by the NATO states acting in the common interest for the re-establishment

---

Eric A. Heinze, *Reconciling Approaches to Enquiry in the Humanitarian Intervention Debate*, 8 International Journal of Human Rights 367 (2004).

120 Judith Gardam, Necessity, Proportionality and the Use of Force by States (2004).

121 SC Res. 1244 (June 10, 1999), preamble. The NATO states insistently referred to the repeated determination of the 'grave' violations of human rights in Kosovo (and the resulting need to bring an end to a humanitarian catastrophe) made by the Security Council (SC Res. 1199, *supra* note 71; SC Res. 1203 (Oct. 24, 1998)) and by other international organizations (see the Report transmitted by the Chairman-in-Office of the OSCE to the UN Secretary-General (UN Doc. S/1999/315) and the Secretary-General of NATO's Report of 23 March 1999 transmitted to the Security Council on 25 March (UN Doc. S/1999/338). See also the Secretary-General's Annual Report to the General Assembly, quoted *supra* note 119. The UN did not formally condemn the intervention and neither did the General Assembly. The Security Council approved the military action in a 'concrete way': integrating the activity of the NATO states with later collaborative activity decided in the resolutions for the re-establishment of peace in the region; by so doing, it granted the intervention the required objectivity and legitimacy. See also GA Res. 54/183 (Feb. 29, 2000), paras 1, 2. On the collective character of NATO's intervention, see also Henkin, *supra* note 118, at 826.

of 'legality'. In so doing, the Council recognized this function *de facto* as pertaining to those states and endorsed the NATO intervention as lawful collective action in accordance with its own objective ascertainment determining *erga omnes* the 'serious' violations of human rights in Kosovo, a determination to which express and repeated reference was made in the resolution cited. The Council's decisions are presumed to be valid.[122]

On the basis of its own practice, in registering satisfaction at Yugoslavia's acceptance of NATO's principles, the Council presented the 'Accord' as the expression of the international community's will, to be implemented through its decisions and under the aegis of the UN. It then laid limits on Serbian sovereignty[123] with an unprecedented operation involving co-deployment in Kosovo of an international civilian and security presence (respectively UNMIK and a NATO-led force known as KFOR) to give effect to international administration of the territory until substantial autonomy could be achieved.

We do not see the need for 'authorization,' but, for different reasons from those outlined above, for another category of humanitarian intervention that, in the presence of certain prerequisites, is to be considered legitimate. This matter will be examined in depth in another chapter.[124] We are referring to the case of incursions by a state in the territory of another state, exclusively for the purpose of saving individuals or groups whose lives are in grave peril. In such a case, the intervention is not carried out for punitive purposes as part of a law-enforcement action or as a form of sanction. It is not directed 'against' the territorial state, whose responsibility may be objectively verified. Rather, it has the sole aim of putting an end to the violation of an internationally recognised fundamental interest, for the sake of protecting that interest itself. This type of action is not a substitute for law enforcement, but is intended rather as a form of tutelary protection of public interests, in the sense that it is made possible by the 'exceptional widening of the material and coercive powers of the state engaged in the intervention,' which are exercised outside its own jurisdiction.[125]

---

122 In the advisory opinion on Namibia cited (see *supra* note 42, paras 20–22; also our Repertory, *supra* note 1, vol. I, No. 1507, at 531), the Court reaffirmed a presumption of validity of resolutions of UN bodies: 'A resolution of a properly constituted organ of the United Nations which is passed in accordance with that organ's rules of procedure … must be presumed to have been validly adopted' (*id.*, at para. 20 at 22; Repertory, *supra* note 1, vol. I, No. 1507, at 531), in conformity with its own prior pronouncement (Certain Expenses of the United Nations (Art. 17 (2), of the Charter), Advisory Opinion, 1962 ICJ Reports 151 (July 10, 1962), at 168. See also Repertory, *supra* note 1, vol. I, No. 1506, at 531).

123 SC Res. 1244, *supra* note 121, paras 7–10, imposed a mandatory international regime on the Republic of Yugoslavia, limiting its sovereignty severely; comparable restrictions had been imposed on Iraq with SC Res. 687, *supra* note 59, paras 5, 6, at the end of the military operation authorized by the Security Council in 1990 and conducted by the anti-Iraqi coalition. Such restrictions are not attenuated by the requested 'acceptance' of the states affected (see SC Res. 687, *supra*, para. 33, requesting Iraq's formal acceptance of the peace plan laid down by the same resolution and SC Res. 1244, *supra* note 121, para. 5).

124 See *infra* chapter 6, under the heading 'A Theory Arguing for the 'Tutelary' Intervention of the 'Agent' State.

125 Ziccardi Capaldo, Terrorismo Internazionale, *supra* note 3, at 71–102.

In the same way, these 'tutelary' guarantees lead to a broadening of the material and coercive powers of states acting 'collectively,' in cases where the territorial state, which has primary responsibility, is unwilling or unable to protect fundamental interests. The force exerted is therefore to be considered as 'internal force' and not as 'international force.' As a result, this type of humanitarian intervention is not subject to the prior authorization of the Security Council. In specific cases such an action is to be considered legitimate provided that the appropriate UN bodies – the General Assembly and the Security Council – have not censured the intervention.[126]

Enforcement Mechanisms to Safeguard the Peace Process

Another enforcement mechanism put into effect by states and the UN for the implementation of objective international law is derived from the international practice. It is directed at bringing an end to serious breaches of basic international norms that have led to an international conflict (as in the case of the multinational force operating against Iraq bringing hostilities to an end in 1992) and is used chiefly to safeguard the peace process and democracy in countries torn by civil war.[127] Joint administration by states and the UN is put into effect by the incorporation of the Accord reached by the parties to the conflict (usually with the mediation of third-party states) in a Security Council resolution. In incorporating the Accord, which provides a plan for implementing the peace process, the Security Council, agreeing to implement it under the aegis of the UN, exercises the functions of supervision and control over action by states and non-UN organizations. Acting on behalf of the international community, it controls the legality of the Accord (compliance of the objectives and conditions for implementing the peace plan with the fundamental principles

---

126 On this point, see *infra* chapter 6, under the heading 'A General Framework for Addressing Problems Related to the 'Tutelary' Protection of Global Values'.

127 See, e.g., the following resolutions: SC Res. 783 (Oct. 13, 1992) and SC Res. 792 (Nov. 30, 1992), on the implementation of the Paris Accords (UN Doc. A/46/608–S/23177 (Oct. 30, 1991)) for the election of a constitutive assembly, the adoption of a constitution, and the formation of a new government in Cambodia; SC Res. 788 (*supra* note 114, para. 2), passed to ensure respect and implementation of the Yamoussoukro IV Accord of 30 October 1991 (UN Doc. S/24815), considered 'the best possible framework for a peaceful resolution of the Liberian conflict' in that it created 'the necessary conditions for free and fair elections in Liberia'. See also SC Res. 782 (Oct. 13, 1992) and SC Res. 797 (Dec. 16, 1992), in which the Council expresses pleasure at the signature of a General Peace Agreement for Mozambique on 4 October 1992 (S/24635), takes note of the parties' joint declaration that they 'accept the role of the United Nations in monitoring and guaranteeing the implementation of the General Peace Agreement' (S/24406), and determines to establish a UN Operation in Mozambique; and SC Res. 1236 (May 7, 1999), with which the Council at once incorporates the General Agreement between Indonesia and Portugal on 5 May 1999, on the transfer of authority in East Timor to the UN (Art. 6) and provides for its implementation with two supplementary accords stipulated between the UN and the two governments concerned, regarding the modalities for the popular consultation (S/1999/513, Annexes I to III) and deciding on the deployment of the United Nations Mission in East Timor (UNAMET) with a view to assisting in the implementation of the Arrangements in order to supervise the peaceful implementation of the consultation process.

of democracy, human rights, and so on); it acts as guardian for implementation, entrusting states with the application of measures deemed necessary for that purpose. It places restrictions on the sovereignty of the state concerned in the peace process, taking away some of that state's policing, administrative, and judicial functions, which it entrusts either to non-UN international organizations or to international agencies set up by the Council, which operate under Council direction. The dual capacity in which the UN acts is often evident in this procedure: hence, the Security Council sometimes addresses 'all' states in the resolutions themselves; at other times, it addresses only member states, specifying that it is acting under the terms of the Charter.[128] This occurs especially when it is setting up peace-keeping forces and/or specific organisms operating on behalf of the UN to provide enforcement of its own decisions.[129]

The Osmotic Relationship Between the Inter-State Community and the United Nations

The enforcement procedures we have just examined support the perspective we have proposed (and examined in depth) in earlier studies of the current 'vertical' trends in international society; they also confirm the integrated approach to the organization of the decision-making functions of the international legal order (creation and implementation of law) that we put forward in those studies.[130]

In our view, although we judge the current international community to be still largely unorganized, we believe that by conferring ever wider general functions on international institutions for the shared governance of public interests together with states, the international order is evolving towards forms of institutionalization of power. This new trend has already set in motion the building of a constitutional system establishing legal procedures for performance of the social functions of the international legal order, carried out jointly by states, international organizations, and the UN bodies acting as co-agents of the global community. The integrated collective enforcement system we have outlined above has developed outside the legal framework of the Charter and the enforcement system provided thereunder (Chapter VII); in order to function, it uses the UN bodies, which have been assigned general functions with *erga omnes* validity by virtue of general norms, both substantive and procedural. These rules envisage modalities of implementation and mechanisms for integrating state action with the action of UN bodies. Accordingly, the UN bodies now appear to be vested by the international legal order with functions

128 See *supra* notes 59, 82, where it is noted that when coercive action is carried out by UN peace-keeping or peace-enforcement forces, UN member states have a responsibility to support the institutions previously created by the Security Council to achieve its objectives. See Chinkin, *supra* note 118, at 846.

129 As regards the modalities of use of unilateral force by one or a group of states, emphasis has been placed on the need for the Security Council to indicate the objectives for which the force may be used and the duration of the authorization in clear language and unambiguous terms. See Lobel & Ratner, *supra* note 107, at 138, 141, 143.

130 See *supra* notes 2, 3, 44, 48, 103.

other than the institutional functions conferred on them by the Charter; by virtue of this empowerment, UN bodies not only act on behalf of the Organization on the basis of powers conferred by the Charter, but also on behalf of the international community as its 'agents' and on the basis of rules of general international law. The mechanisms for joint governance, and the integrated procedures consolidated by the trend outlined above, are accepted by states and can now be considered established as constitutional norms of the international legal order. These procedures and mechanisms are acquiring ever greater weight, and show a tendency to expand further.

As a result, we do not subscribe to the theory that the UN Charter is the constitution of the international community in its entirety.[131]

There can be no doubt about the contribution of international organizations towards the verticalization of the world community, and this is especially true of organizations with a universal calling that are either political or economic in character. We believe, however, that from the above examination of the practice, it has become clearer and more explicit that the contribution of these organizations towards 'verticalization' cannot be interpreted as meaning that their structure has substituted or been superimposed onto the structure of the international community; what is meant is that in a world community that is still prevalently unorganized, such organizations have promoted the development of mechanisms of control over state action and processes of joint governance by states and international institutions.

The fact is that although the UN has played a dominant role in establishing international norms protecting collective values of the world community, it is restricted by a pact that has now fallen behind the times, endowed as it is with an inadequate collective enforcement system with regard to the progress international law has made. Hence, even the great achievement of the Charter in 1945, with its imposition on states of the absolute prohibition of the use of international force, is revealing its limits today in relation to emerging new actors and principles protecting public interests of international law and the need to ensure their effective implementation; such a need is not guaranteed by Chapter VII, which focuses on the maintenance of peace and whose precepts are addressed only to states. A significant factor limiting the effective implementation of the system is that the Charter voting procedures can paralyse the Security Council, the body empowered to enforce observance of the non-use of force. International law has underlined the importance of 'human security' over the past few years, thanks also to the activity of the UN bodies. International law today not only seeks to protect individuals from the horrors of wars of aggression, but also has other aims: it seeks to protect individuals and peoples from any inhuman and cruel forms of generalized violence (genocide, slavery, ethnic cleansing, trafficking in human beings, terrorism, etc.), demanding from both state bodies and individuals or groups the implementation of humanitarian law and human rights; it seeks to protect the common heritage of humanity (the environmental and artistic heritage, resources, and so on) and looks to the achievement of social justice and fair economic relations between the rich and the poor countries of the world. The emergence of non-state actors has reduced

131 See *supra* notes 14, 78 and corresponding text.

the scope of UN action. The unilateral action of states to protect such collective values has posed the problem of its lawfulness, both from the angle of whether it is compatible with the obligations undertaken by states under the Charter and from the viewpoint of its 'objectivity' – an indispensable factor for public activity, which is clearly absent from the action of a state or group of states that claims to be acting in the common interest. The UN has responded to these two charges in the following terms: without claiming to hold the exclusive right to protect world values, it has put its institutional structure at the service of the community of states, so as to ensure the 'objectivity' of state action carried out in a collective capacity, reducing the risk of abuse. The integrated collective enforcement system that has developed, outlined above, restricts state sovereignty, placing the authority of UN bodies above states and fulfilling the conditions for the objective protection of the fundamental interests and values of global law.

Thus, a realistic analysis of modern society and the phenomenon of international organization that characterizes it can hardly fail to take account of the osmotic relation and deep interpenetration now established and operating between the international substantial community (inter-state community) and the UN, and, as a result, the growing institutionalization of the international legal order. The UN has made a significant contribution to the integrated system of the protection of global values, a flexible system of collective guarantees that, due to its particular characteristics, changes over time, reflecting the need for change.

1. Based as it is on a 'multipolar' system, it makes provision for participation in enforcement, monitoring, and coercive functions not only on the part of states and bodies set up by state representatives (as is the case with the system of the Charter), but also by non-governmental actors representing civil society in a global perspective.
2. It moderates the unilateralism of state sanctions imposed 'in the common interest', by placing them under institutional control.
3. It extends the powers of the UN bodies (above all of the General Assembly) in relation to those laid down by the Charter, conferring on them powers of verification and sanction *erga omnes*; it introduces procedural rules and mechanisms to overcome the veto (Article 27 (2), UN Charter) and therefore moves beyond the blockage of the UN system of collective security, in cases in which it is used; at the same time, it contains means for 'getting round' the veto in an institutional context.[132]
4. It sets up integrated structures and mechanisms jointly managed by the international institutions and state organisms in order to implement global values and principles (e.g., in promoting the principle of individual responsibility and the trial and sentencing of those responsible for international crimes, it has made provision for the setting up by the Security Council of *ad hoc* international and mixed criminal tribunals, and procedures that require state bodies to collaborate).

132 See Franck, *supra* note 103. On the humanitarian interventions see also *supra* notes 118–119 and corresponding text.

5. It makes provision for the setting up of integrated structures and regimes for the protection and management of heritage sites for the entire world in order to ensure that they can be saved for future generations.

The challenge that has to be faced by international law and the UN is: firstly, to continue with the integration between states, institutions, and the forces of globalization (multinational economic networks, the media, NGOs) in order to channel these forces into existing institutional mechanisms, both regional and global; secondly, to develop forms of participation in decision-making processes, in order to prevent them from developing out of control; and thirdly to promote increasingly representative processes for the forces that operate in the global community (also for 'citizens' of the global community and of world public opinion), enabling them to become more democratic and transparent.

Concluding Remarks: Moving Towards Shared International Governance

In concluding our study, we express a degree of cautious optimism over the increased level of 'legality' in the international order[133] and the way it is attempting to collectively protect public interests not guaranteed by the UN Charter.

Nonetheless, we need to underline the fact that the integrated collective enforcement system in its present form is not entirely satisfactory. This is due both to the fact that provisions regulating mechanisms and modalities of integration between the community of states and international organizations have crystallized insufficiently, and chiefly to the margin of abuse inherent in action performed in the common interest by states, even where one holds the view (as we ourselves do) that such action requires UN endorsement. The participation of states (especially hegemonic ones) as co-agents in the decision-making process in implementing public international law nourishes the misgivings of those who emphasize the weakness of the current integrated system of collective guarantee and the weakness of the UN itself – a participant in the system. These scholars judge the Security Council authorization method to be a sign of UN weakness, as compared with the centralized system of collective security envisaged by the Charter.[134]

Undoubtedly there is a risk that world crises are controlled predominantly by the permanent members of the Security Council, or by certain of these members; an attempt is made to ward off this very real risk by the effective participation of the General Assembly in different decision-making functions of the integrated enforcement system, aiming in this way to affirm a role for the Assembly in the

133 See Thomas Franck, *Fairness in the International Legal and Institutional System*, 240 Recueil des Cours 9 (1993–III). See also our work, *supra* note 2, inquiring into the content of 'constitutional principles of legality' in the international legal system emerging since 1945.

134 See, e.g., William Michael Reisman, *The Constitutional Crisis in the United Nations*, *in* Dupuy, Le Développement, *supra* note 74, at 400; Giovanni Battaglini, Il Diritto Internazionale come Sistema di Diritto Comune 221 (1999).

current constitutive process.[135] In the silence of the Charter, also the International Court of Justice is attempting to strike a balance between the powers of the UN bodies that ensures international legality.[136] To this end the Court is acquiring a role with supervisory powers, in order to guarantee international legality, with regard to the two main political bodies. In this way it contributes to the development of the legality of the international juridical system.[137]

The fact is that 'co-management' mechanisms and 'integrated' procedures are acquiring greater importance, with a tendency towards further expansion; they require regulation, giving rise to specific obligations for all the actors in the system. The aim for the new world system of developing an effective and legitimate constitutional order will therefore be achieved only if the international community manages to carry out the following actions.

Firstly, it must consolidate the 'central role' and position of superiority of the UN in relation to states and the other actors in the process of globalization; this position is assured by the control or supervisory function assigned to the UN bodies as part of an 'integrated' system, a function that is still not fully defined in terms of implementation. The Secretary-General of the UN in the Report presented to the

---

135 In some cases the General Assembly has performed functions of determination of grave violations of human rights and the principle of democracy, requesting economic sanctions and allowing states to adopt them (see *supra* notes 43–44, 79 and corresponding text); in other cases it has performed functions of control over economic sanctions adopted by states in a collective capacity (see *supra* notes 84–85, 88–89 and corresponding text).

136 See Thomas M. Franck, *The 'Powers of Appreciation': Who Is the Ultimate Guardian of UN Legality?*, 82 Am. J. Int'l. L. 519 (1992); *Id.*, *UN Checks and Balances: The Role of the ICJ and the Security Council*, *in* American Society of International Law/ Nederlandse Vereniging Voor Internationaal Recht, Contemporary International Law Issues: Opportunities at a Time of Momentous Change 280 (René Lefeber ed., 1994); Geoffrey R. Watson, *Constitutionalism, Judicial Review, and the World Court*, 34 Harv. Int'l L.J. 1 (1993), at 14 *et seq.*; Mohammed Bedjaoui, Nouvel Ordre Mondial et Contrôle de la Légalité des Actes du Conseil de Sécurité 46 (1994); Lucius Caflisch, *Is the International Court Entitled to Review Security Council Resolutions Adopted under Chapter VII of the United Nations Charter?*, *in* International Legal Issues Arising Under the United Nations Decade of International Law 633 (Najeeb Al-Nauimi ed., 1995). Some authors have argued in favour of a widening of the powers of the Court and have proposed solutions in this regard. See the authoritative opinions of Louis B. Sohn, *How New Is the New International Legal Order?*, 20 Denver J. Int'l L & Pol'y 205 (1992), at 209; Stephen M. Schwebel, *Authorizing the Secretary-General of the United Nations to Request Advisory Opinions of the International Court of Justice*, *in* Essays in International Law in Honour of Judge Manfred Lachs 519 (Jerzy Makarczyk ed., 1984); George Abi-Saab, *De l'Evolution de la Cour Internationale. Réflexions sur Quelques Tendances Récentes*, 96 Rev. Gen. D.I.P. 273 (1992–II), at 293; *An Agenda for Peace*, *supra* note 101, Parts III and IV. See also *supra* note 83. See also *infra* chapter 3 of this book.

137 Giuliana Ziccardi Capaldo, *Tendenze Evolutive della Politica Giudiziaria della Corte internazionale di Giustizia*, *in* Il Ruolo del Giudice Internazionale nell'Evoluzione del Diritto Internazionale e Comunitario, Atti del Convegno di Studi in Memoria di Gaetano Morelli 257 (Francesco Salerno ed., 1995).

General Assembly on 21 March 2005[138] outlined certain guidelines or criteria for the Security Council to adopt in the exercise of the supervisory function over the use of force on the part of states: 'When considering whether to authorize or endorse the use of military force, the Council should come to a common view on how to weigh the seriousness of the threat, the proper purpose of the proposed military action; whether means short of the use of force might plausibly succeed in stopping the threat; whether the military option is proportional to the threat at hand; and whether there is a reasonable chance of success'. He then recommended adopting a resolution setting out the principles and criteria, and complying with them: 'I therefore recommend that the Security Council adopt a resolution setting out these principles and expressing its intention to be guided by them'.[139]

What is needed is a more adequate regulation of the mechanisms and means of integration between the international community and organized communities, and, above all, a structuring of international power in which a supervisory role for the General Assembly is laid down, with regard to the proper application of unilateral economic measures in order to prevent a violation of human rights. Finally, there is a need for the judicial control function of the International Court of Justice to be consolidated and to eliminate the confusion between those exercising and those subject to control. At present, there is an element of confusion between the hegemonous states who are the guiding force in the international community and the Security Council, the body currently entrusted with the supervisory function, which is dominated by the states over which it is intended to exert control. On this point the Report cited above is silent.

The second action of the international community must be to improve the institutions, restructuring the main governing bodies of the UN and developing international institutions with effective power to promote, create, and apply legal norms. Changes to the Charter are now urgently needed, extending the decision-making powers of the General Assembly, allowing for the veto to be set aside in cases in which the system of collective security is blocked. There is a need to provide mechanisms, and where appropriate, institutionalise those that are present so far only in embryonic form; one possibility is provided by the procedure indicated by the General Assembly Resolution *Uniting for Peace*,[140] that which has now emerged from the 'limbo' to which it was confined after the ruling by the International Court of Justice.[141]

Thirdly, the international community must widen participation in decision-making processes to include new forces of globalization. There is a risk that the

---

138 *In Larger Freedom: Towards Development, Human Rights for All*, Report of the Secretary-General, UN Doc A/59/2005 (March 21, 2005) [hereinafter *In Larger Freedom*, Report of the Secretary-General].

139 *Id.*, at para. 126.

140 *Uniting for Peace*, GA Res. 377 (V) (Nov. 3, 1950).

141 See *infra* chapter 3, under the heading 'Judicial Protection of Human Rights Beyond the ICJ Statute', chapter 4, under the heading 'Concluding Remarks: Effectiveness is Not Supplanting Legality, *Evolution of Integrated Processes to Implement International Legality*, and chapter 8, under the heading 'An Integrated Monitoring System and Action Programme'.

governance of world interests will be monopolized by a select group consisting of hegemonic states with permanent seats on the Security Council or by a certain number of them, and that certain components of the international community will be excluded or kept on the margins of the decision-making process.[142] So far the mechanisms of joint government have not managed to prevent this risk in specific situations, in spite of attempts to achieve wider participation in the decision-making process in the General Assembly and the regional organizations, especially those in crisis areas on various occasions.[143] The Secretary-General in the Report cited above argued that among its priorities the UN 'must be open not only to states but also to civil society, which at both the national and international levels plays an increasingly important role in the world affairs';[144] he then expressly renewed his request to the General Assembly (made on a number of occasions)[145] 'to establish mechanisms enabling it to engage fully and systematically with civil society'.[146]

In conclusion, the new international order that is currently being shaped requires improved mechanisms of integration between states of various cultures and geographical regions, international organizations, and other forces of globalization (with attention to world public opinion) to strengthen the central role of the UN and to improve public institutions, in order to give rise to multilateral decision-making processes that are more democratic and transparent and therefore better able to protect fundamental 'global' interests. There is also a need to strike a balance between the powers of the governing bodies of the UN and to achieve tangible results in the institutionalisation of the control of legitimacy of the International Court of Justice over the decisions of the Security Council,[147] which is fundamental for achieving more legitimate governance for a global community.

---

142 In general, see M. Cherif Bassiouni, Crimes against Humanity in International Criminal Law 499–527 (1992).

143 The authority of regional decisions (in the crisis area concerned) increasingly represents a valid basis for collective enforcement actions. See the recognition given by the UN to the activity carried out by the OSCE in the case of the Italian intervention in Albania (SC Res. 1101 (March 28, 1997)), which obtained the prior authorization of the OSCE (27 March) and the European Union (24 March); the activity carried out in Kosovo by the OSCE, the European Union, and the Contact Goup (SC Res. 1160, *supra* note 59), by the Contact Group and the Monitoring Mission of the European Community (SC Res. 1199, *supra* note 71), and by NATO (SC Res. 1203, *supra* note 121); the activity carried out by ECOWAS, supported by the OAU, in the cases of Liberia and Sierra Leone (*supra* note 114) by the OAU to obtain the extradition from Ethiopia of the three individuals suspected of the assassination attempt on President Mubarak of Sudan (SC Res. 1054, *supra* note 59, preamble); and the OAU, the League of Arab States, the Non-Aligned Movement, and the Islamic Conference over the question of the extradition of Libyan terrorists (SC Res. 1192, *supra* note 69).

144 *In Larger Freedom*, Report of the Secretary-General, *supra* note 138, para. 153.

145 See *Report of the Secretary-General in Response to the Report of the Panel of Eminent Persons on United Nations–Civil Society Relations*, UN Doc. A/59/354 (Sept. 13, 2004).

146 *In Larger Freedom*, Report of the Secretary-General, *supra* note 138, para. 162.

147 See David D. Caron, *The Legitimacy of Collective Authority of the Security Council*, 87 Am. J. Int'l. L. 552 (1993). See generally Daniel Bodansky, *The Legitimacy of International Governance: A Coming Challenge for International Environmental Law?*, 93 Am. J. Int'l. L. 596 (1999).

SECTION III
Global Justice

Chapter 3

The International Court of Justice – From Judicial Organ to Global Court*

Introduction

In recent years, the attention paid by scholars and states to the activity of the International Court of Justice (hereinafter ICJ or 'the Court') has notably increased.[1] The background is the inter-state community's move towards a global human society and the search for a new political-institutional order that can legitimize international decision-making authority.

---

* This chapter is based on the paper by Giuliana Ziccardi Capaldo, *Global Trends and Global Court: The Legitimacy of World Governance*, 4 The Global Community. Yearbook of International Law and jurisprudence [hereinafter GCYILJ] 127 (2004–I). That early text has been updated and modified. The changes to international law I detail therein have been summarized in Table 6.

1 Amongst the most significant studies on the ICJ during this period, see Hersch Lauterpacht, The Development of International Law by the International Court (1958); Gerald Fitzmaurice, The Law and Procedure of the International Court of Justice (1986); The International Court of Justice at the Crossroads (Lori Fisler Damrosch ed., 1987); Hugh Thirlway, *The Law and Procedure of the International Court of Justice 1960–1989, Part Two*, 61 British Yearbook of International Law [hereinafter BYIL] 1 (1990); *Id., The Law and Procedure of the International Court of Justice 1960–1989, Part Ten*, 70 BYIL 1 (1999); Elihu Lauterpacht, Aspects of the Administration of International Justice (1991); Shigeru Oda, *The International Court of Justice Viewed from the Bench (1976–1993)*, 244 Recueil des Cours 9 (1993–VII); Fifty Years of the International Court of Justice. Essays in Honour of Sir Robert Jennings (Vaughan Lowe & Malgosia A. Fitzmaurice eds, 1996); The International Court of Justice, Process, Practice and Procedure (Derek W. Bowett, James Crawford & Arthur Watts eds, 1997); Robert Y. Jennings, *The Role of the International Court of Justice*, 68 BYIL 1 (1997); Shabtai Rosenne, The Law and Practice of the International Court, 1920–1996 (3rd ed., 1997); The International Court of Justice: Its Future Role After Fifty Years (Alexander S. Muller, David Raic & J.M. Thuranzsky eds, 1997); International Law and The Hague's 75th Anniversary (Wybo P. Heere ed., 1999); John G. Merrills, *New Horizons for International Adjudication*, 6 GCYILJ 47 (2006–I). See the systematic cataloguing of the Court's jurisprudence, *World Court Digest*, prepared by Rainer Hofmann, Juliane Kokott, Karin Oellers-Frahm, Stefan Oeter & Andreas Zimmermann, (Vol. I, 1992), (Vol. II, 1997); Giuliana Ziccardi Capaldo, Repertory of Decisions of the International Court of Justice/Répertoire de la Jurisprudence de la Cour Internationale de Justice (1947–1992), 2 vols., (1995) [hereinafter Ziccardi Capaldo, Repertory]. See further the literature cited below.

Towards the end of the twentieth century, the international legal order faced a double challenge: the ineffectiveness of existing institutions in the management of fundamental global interests and goods (e.g., the fight against terrorism, human rights safeguards, expansion of democracy to all peoples, ensuring a clean and safe environment, enjoyment of cultural heritage, and, generally, a better quality of life), and growing doubts, also amongst scholars, about the legitimacy of such institutions.[2]

The international legal order has experienced growing pains to adjust to the changed circumstances, to resolve the intrinsic contradictions in the international legal system and to address the ineffectiveness of existing procedures and institutions. The classic 'horizontal' and anarchic international legal order is clearly not able to handle these new challenges. Evidence of this is the UN's tendency, increasing since the 1980s, to overcome structural deficiencies of the international legal system and manage global functions through its organs, widening the powers of the Security Council beyond the Charter system.[3] Be that as it may, nowadays we are witnessing the deterioration of the UN system under the increasing weight of old and new world problems[4] (e.g., gross violations of human rights, the world's hunger, the rise of international organized crime, etc.), the return of American unilateralism, the disruptive power of global terrorism, and the reduced UN role due to the rise of non-state forces (Islamic and other religious groups, large multinational companies, mass media, etc.) that act on a global level and affect the world's decision-making processes. All these phenomena heighten and reveal the problems the UN has in assuming a general role. This incapacity is structural, worsened by the present concentration of power within the Security Council, the veto which can incapacitate the Council; the large discretionary powers of the Security Council;[5] the absence in the Charter of mechanisms of control of its activity; and a system of checks and balances.[6] In fact, the field of the maintenance of peace and security, which, under the Charter, is to be carried out by a collective security system, and mainly under the guidance of the Council (Chapter VII of the Charter), has been expanded so much that the protection of any other general interest has been subsumed under this general heading.

---

2 Thomas M. Franck, The Power of Legitimacy Among Nations (1990); David D. Caron, *The Legitimacy of the Collective Authority of the Security Council*, 87 American Journal of International Law [hereinafter Am. J. Int'l. L.] 552 (1993); Daniel M. Bodansky, *The Legitimacy of International Governance: A Coming Challenge for International Environmental Law?*, 93 Am. J. Int'l. L. 596 (1999).

3 See *supra* chapter 2 of this book and the studies cited *infra* notes 38–39.

4 For a first critical analysis, see Piero Ziccardi, *Caratteri Istituzionali delle Nazioni Unite. Considerazioni Preliminari*, 25 La Comunità Internazionale 468 (1970); *Id.*, *Règles d'Organisation et Règles de Conduite en Droit International. Le Droit Commun et les Ordres Juridiques*, 152 Recueil des Cours 119 (1976–IV).

5 See Le Développement du Rôle du Conseil de Sécurité/The Development of the Role of the Security Council, Peace-Keeping and Peace-Building, Colloque, La Haye, 21–23 Juillet 1992, (René-Jean Dupuy ed., 1993) [hereinafter Dupuy, Le Développement].

6 William Michael Reisman, *The Constitutional Crisis in the United Nations*, *in* Dupuy, Le Développement, *supra* note 5, at 400 *et seq*.

The Court, which has always understood and adapted to the evolutionary trends of the international system,[7] is central in this context. During almost eighty years of activity, it has interpreted its role *vis-à-vis* the most pressing needs of change in the international community in a progressive, developmental manner. One can identify two major phases in this evolutionary process: in a first phase the Court acted mostly as a judicial organ of the inter-state society. In a second phase, which is currently ongoing, it overcame the limits of the Statute and the Charter. In this phase, the Court is acting as builder of the vertical system of the global community and supreme guardian of constitutional values, thus legitimizing global governance.

The First Phase

In the first phase – from its establishment to the early 1980s – the judicial politics of the Court have been dominated by the need to entrench its judicial functions. In an unstructured society, characterized by the decentralization of the general organizational functions, the establishment of the Permanent International Court of Justice (PCIJ) by the Covenant of the League of Nations was a first attempt to institutionalize those functions. The PCIJ, the predecessor of the ICJ, was a response to the new need to resolve disputes between states with means other than the use of force and the principle of effectivity, which had hitherto been the standard. Although it is defined by the Charter as a mere 'organ' of the UN, and despite the fact that its roots are traceable to the institute of arbitration, the ICJ has aptly interpreted the assigned role, as specified in Article 35 of the Charter, and the universalistic inspirations of the World's Organization.

Since the outset, the Court has strongly affirmed its judicial-organ character, which requires it to be independent from the parties to the dispute, both in regard to the procedure and substantive law. The Court considers central attributes of its judicial function: the interpretation of the parties' conclusions;[8] the examination of all the elements of the dispute, not only those formally raised by the parties;[9] the

---

7 Giuliana Ziccardi Capaldo, *Tendenze Evolutive della Politica Giudiziaria della Corte internazionale di Giustizia, in* Il Ruolo del Giudice Internazionale nell'Evoluzione del Diritto Internazionale e Comunitario, Atti del Convegno di Studi in Memoria di Gaetano Morelli 257 (Francesco Salerno ed., 1995).

8 Certain German Interests in Polish Upper Silesia, Merits, Judgment No. 7, (May 25, 1926), 1926, PCIJ, Series A, No. 7, at 34–35; Reservations to the Convention on Genocide, Advisory Opinion, 1971 ICJ Reports 15 (May 28, 1951), at 26; Minquiers and Ecrehos (France/United Kingdom), Merits, Judgment, 1953 ICJ Reports 47 (Nov. 17, 1953), at 52; Nottebohm (Liechtenstein v. Guatemala), Second Phase, Judgment, 1955 ICJ Reports 4 (April 6, 1955), at 16; Nuclear Tests (Australia v. France), Judgment, 1974 ICJ Reports 253 (Dec. 20, 1974), paras 29–30, at 262–263; Nuclear Tests (New Zealand v. France), Judgment, 1974 ICJ Reports 457 (Dec. 20, 1974), paras 30–31, at 466–467.

9 Emprunts Brésiliens, Judgment No. 15, (July 12, 1929), 1929, PCIJ, Series A, No. 21, at 124; Fisheries Jurisdiction (United Kingdom v. Iceland), Merits, Judgment, 1974 ICJ Reports 3 (July 25, 1974), para. 48, at 21–22; Fisheries Jurisdiction (Federal Republic of Germany v. Iceland), Merits, Judgment, 1974 ICJ Reports 175 (July 25, 1974), para. 40, at 190; Nuclear Tests (Australia v. France), *supra* note 8, paras 30–31, at 263–264; Nuclear Tests (New Zealand

reaching of decisions that transcend the arguments and the solutions proposed by the parties;[10] and the free examination of evidence, while within the limits imposed by the Court's Statute and the Rules.[11] The Court has declared that the validity of its judgments cannot depend upon the acceptance of the judgment by the parties.[12] Further, it has construed Article 62 of the Statute as giving it power to permit an intervention even though it be opposed by one or both parties to the case,[13] and, in the *Lotus* case,[14] has affirmed that it has power to determine the applicable law, on the basis of the *jura novit curia* principle,[15] to consider on its own initiative all rules of international law that may be relevant to the settlement of the dispute.

The ICJ has striven to strengthen its judicial functions by pushing the limits of compulsory jurisdiction. It has done so both by interpreting extensively Articles 36 (3) and 37 of the Statute, concerning the transfer of the acceptance of mandatory jurisdiction of the PCIJ to the ICJ,[16] and by identifying the deposit of the declaration of acceptance with the Secretary-General as the only formal requirement for the

---

v. France), *supra* note 8, paras 31–32, at 467–468; Military and Paramilitary Activities in and against Nicaragua (Nicaragua v. United States of America), Merits, Judgment, 1986 ICJ Reports 14 (June 27, 1986), para. 30, at 25.

10 Free Zones of Upper Savoy and the District of Gex, Judgment No. 17, (June 7, 1932), 1932, PCIJ, Series A/B, No. 46, at 138; Case concerning the Application of the Convention of 1902 Governing the Guardianship of Infants (Netherlands v. Sweden), 1958 ICJ Reports 55 (Oct. 28, 1958), at 62; Temple of Preah Vihear (Cambodia v. Thailand), Merits, Judgment, 1962 ICJ Reports 6 (June 15, 1962), at 36; Delimitation of the Maritime Boundary in the Gulf of Maine Area (Canada v. United States of America), Judgment, 1984 ICJ Reports 246 (Oct. 12, 1984), para. 190, at 325.

11 Military and Paramilitary Activities, *supra* note 9, para. 60, at 40; Frontier Dispute (Burkina Faso/Republic of Mali), Judgment, 1986 ICJ Reports 554 (Dec. 22, 1986), para. 42, at 575.

12 Free Zones, *supra* note 10, at 161; Military and Paramilitary Activities, *supra* note 9, para. 27, at 23–24.

13 Continental Shelf (Libyan Arab Jamahiriya/Malta), Application to Intervene, Judgment, 1984 ICJ Reports 3 (March 21, 1984), para. 46, at 28; Land, Island and Maritime Frontier Dispute (El Salvador/Honduras), Application to Intervene, Judgment, 1990 ICJ Reports 92 (Sept. 13, 1990), para. 96, at 133.

14 Lotus, Judgment No. 9, (Sept. 7, 1927), 1927, Judgment PCIJ, Series A, No. 10, at 31.

15 Fisheries Jurisdiction (United Kingdom v. Iceland), *supra* note 9, para. 17, at 9; Fisheries Jurisdiction (Federal Republic of Germany v. Iceland), *supra* note 9, para. 18, at 181; Military and Paramilitary Activities, *supra* note 9, para. 29, at 24–25.

16 Aerial Incident of 27 July 1955 (Israel v. Bulgaria), Preliminary Objections, Judgment, 1959 ICJ Reports 127 (May 26, 1959), at 136–145; Temple of Preah Vihear (Cambodia v. Thailand), Preliminary Objection, Judgment, 1961 ICJ Reports 17 (May 26, 1961), at 25–26; Barcelona Traction, Light and Power Company, Limited (Belgium v. Spain), Preliminary Objections, Judgment, 1964 ICJ Reports 6 (July 24, 1964), at 29, 31–39; Aegean Sea Continental Shelf (Greece v. Turkey), Judgment, 1978 ICJ Reports 3 (Dec. 19, 1978), para. 34, at 14; Military and Paramilitary Activities in and Against Nicaragua (Nicaragua v. United States of America), Jurisdiction and Admissibility, Judgment, 1984 ICJ Reports 392 (Nov. 26, 1984), paras 28–30, at 405–406.

validity of the acceptance and, thus, the existence of the jurisdiction.[17] It has argued that even the deposit of a notice terminating the declaration under the optional clause does not affect the jurisdiction of the Court.[18]

While, on the one hand, the Court has repeatedly reaffirmed that the basis of its jurisdiction is ultimately the consent of the parties,[19] on the other hand, it has proceeded to undermine the principle of consent by way of the *forum prorogatum* doctrine[20] and the general principle contained in the Statute (Article 36 (6)) according to which, in any given dispute, the Court judges of its own competence.[21] Furthermore, as it emerges from a consistent jurisprudence, the principle of consensual jurisdiction

---

17 Right of Passage over Indian Territory (Portugal v. India), Preliminary Objections, Judgment, 1957 ICJ Reports 125 (Nov. 26, 1957), at 146–147; Temple of Preah Vihear, *supra* note 16, at 31; Military and Paramilitary Activities, *supra* note 16, para. 45, at 412.

18 Right of Passage over Indian Territory (Portugal v. India), Preliminary Objections, Judgment, 1957 ICJ Reports 125 (Nov. 26, 1957), at 146–147; Temple of Preah Vihear, *supra* note 16, at 31; Military and Paramilitary Activities, *supra* note 16, para. 45, at 412.

19 Mavrommatis Palestine Concessions, Judgment No. 2, (Aug. 30, 1924), 1924, PCIJ, Series A, No. 2, at 16; Corfu Channel (United Kingdom v. Albania), Preliminary Objections, Judgment, 1947–48 ICJ Reports 15 (March 25, 1948), at 27; Reparation for Injuries Suffered in the Service of the United Nations, Advisory Opinion, 1949 ICJ Reports 174 (April 11, 1949), at 177–178; Interpretation of Peace Treaties with Bulgaria, Hungary and Romania, 1st Phase, Advisory Opinion, 1950 ICJ Reports 65 (March 30, 1950), at 71; Anglo-Iranian Oil Co. (United Kingdom v. Iran), Jurisdiction, Judgment, 1952 ICJ Reports 20 (July 22, 1952), at 114; Ambatielos (Greece v. United Kingdom), Merits, Judgment, 1953 ICJ Reports 10 (May 19, 1953), at 19; Monetary Gold Removed from Rome in 1943 (Italy v. France, United Kingdom and United States of America), Judgment, 1954 ICJ Reports 19 (June 15, 1954), at 32; Temple of Preah Vihear, *supra* note 10, at 31; Appeal Relating to the Jurisdiction of the ICAO Council, Judgment, 1972 ICJ Reports 46 (Aug. 18, 1972), para. 13, at 52; Western Sahara, Advisory Opinion, 1975 ICJ Reports 12 (Oct. 16, 1975), paras 32–33, at 25; Continental Shelf (Libyan Arab Jamahiriya/Malta), *supra* note 13, paras 14, 34, at 10, 22; Military and Paramilitary Activities, *supra* note 16, para. 45, at 412; Application for Revision and Interpretation of the Judgment of 24 February 1982 in the Case concerning the Continental Shelf (Tunisia/Libyan Arab Jamahiriya) (Tunisia v. Libyan Arab Jamahiriya), Judgment, 1985 ICJ Reports 192 (Dec. 10, 1985), para. 43, at 216; Military and Paramilitary Activities, *supra* note 9, para. 44, at 32; Applicability of Article VI, Section 22, of the Convention on the Privileges and Immunities of the United Nations, Advisory Opinion, 1989 ICJ Reports 177 (Dec. 15, 1989) para. 31, at 188–189; Land, Island and Maritime Frontier Dispute, *supra* note 13, para. 51, at 113–114, para. 95, at 133; Certain Phosphate Lands in Nauru (Nauru v. Australia), Preliminary Objections, Judgment, 1992 ICJ Reports 240 (June 26, 1992), para. 53, at 260; Land, Island and Maritime Frontier Dispute (El Salvador/Honduras; Nicaragua intervening), Judgment, 1992 ICJ Reports 351 (Sept. 11, 1992), para. 378, at 585.

20 Haya de la Torre case (Colombia v. Peru), Judgment, 1951 ICJ Reports 71 (June 13, 1951), at 78; Anglo-Iranian Oil Co. case, *supra* note 19, at 114.

21 Nottebohm case, *supra* note 8, at 119–120; Fisheries Jurisdiction (United Kingdom v. Iceland), Jurisdiction of the Court, Judgment, 1973 ICJ Reports 3 (Feb. 2, 1973), para. 45, at 21; Fisheries Jurisdiction (Federal Republic of Germany v. Iceland), Jurisdiction of the Court, Judgment, 1973 ICJ Reports 49 (Feb. 2, 1973), para. 45, at 66; Military and Paramilitary Activities, *supra* note 9, para. 27, at 23–24; Arbitral Award of 31 July 1989 (Guinea-Bissau v. Senegal), Judgment, 1991 ICJ Reports 53 (Nov. 12, 1991), para. 46, at 68–69.

is applicable only to contentious, and not advisory, procedures,[22] whose judicial character has been reaffirmed by the Court itself.[23]

By developing the notion of *intrinsic limits* to jurisdiction, the Court both increased its independence from the parties and, at the same time, emphasized its nature of judicial organ in charge of settling disputes. The notion of intrinsic limits gave the Court a power/duty to renounce to exercise its functions, both contentious and advisory, even when it has jurisdiction.[24] Among other things, these intrinsic limits, outlined by the Permanent Court in the renowned judgment about the *Free Zones* case,[25] mandate the Court to ascertain whether a dispute exists in the first place. In the merits phase the Court checked whether, after the submission of the case, circumstances developed to make the case moot.[26] In other words, the Court held that it could dismiss the case as moot, thus renouncing to exercise its functions, even when the applicant does not want to withdraw the case in compliance with the rules of procedure.[27]

The theme of this first phase of the Court's judicial politics is basically the one outlined by the Permanent Court in the *Free Zones* case: the Court is not to take a stand in questions that do not pertain to a judicial body, whose role is applying the law to settle actual disputes.[28] While in theory the Court claimed the power to render a declaratory judgment that defines a norm of international customary law or interprets a treaty, thus influencing the relationships between states that are not party

---

22 Interpretation of Peace Treaties, *supra* note 19, at 71; Western Sahara, *id.*, para. 21, at 20; Applicability of Article VI, Section 22, *id.*, para. 31, at 188–189; Legal Consequences of the Construction of a Wall in the Occupied Palestinian Territory, Advisory Opinion, (July 9, 2004) [hereinafter Construction of a Wall], paras 47–48.

23 Status of Eastern Carelia, Advisory Opinion, (July 23, 1923), 1923, PCIJ, Series B, No. 5, at 29; Judgment of the Administrative Tribunal of the ILO upon Complaints Made Against the UNESCO, Advisory Opinion, 1956 ICJ Reports 77 (Oct. 23, 1956), at 84–85; Constitution of the Maritime Safety Committee of the Inter-Governmental Maritime Consultative Organization, Advisory Opinion, 1960 ICJ Reports 150 (June 8, 1960), at 153; Case Concerning the Northern Cameroons (Cameroon v. United Kingdom), Preliminary Objections, Judgment, 1963 ICJ Reports 15 (Dec. 2, 1963), at 30.

24 Haya de la Torre case, *supra* note 20, at 79; Certain Expenses of the United Nations (Article 17, paragraph 2, of the Charter), Advisory Opinion, 1962 ICJ Reports 151 (July 20, 1962), at 155; Northern Cameroons, *supra* note 23, at 29–30; Nuclear Tests (New Zealand v. France) *supra* note 8, para. 23, at 463; Western Sahara, *supra* note 19, para. 23, at 21; Frontier Dispute (Burkina Faso/Republic of Mali), *supra* note 11, para. 45, at 577.

25 Free Zones of Upper Savoy and the District of Gex, Order, (Aug. 19, 1929), PCIJ, Series A, No. 22, at 15; Free Zones, *supra* note 10, at 161–162.

26 Northern Cameroons, *supra* note 23, at 38; Nuclear Tests (Australia v. France), *supra* note 8, paras 55–59, at 270–272; Nuclear Tests (New Zealand v. France), *supra* note 8, paras 58–62, at 477.

27 Nuclear Tests (Australia v. France), *supra* note 8, paras 52, 54, at 270; Nuclear Tests (New Zealand v. France), *supra* note 8, paras 55, 57, at 475.

28 Free Zones, *supra* note 10, at 162; Northern Cameroons, *supra* note 23, at 33–34.

to the dispute, now and in the future,[29] in concrete cases, when requested to do so, the Court declined to render such a judgment.[30]

During this first phase, the Court interpreted narrowly its judicial role by adhering to a literal and strict reading of the existent international law, and by drawing only from classic sources (i.e., those listed in Article 38 of the Statute). For what concerns the substantive aspects of the case, it applied norms of international law relevant for the actual situation, including those specified in the *compromis* if applicable, for they are the expression of the parties' will sanctioned by an international act.[31] For what concerns the procedural aspects, it interpreted and applied the rules of the Charter and its Statute.

The Second Phase

The second phase of the Court's judicial politics, which will be covered shortly,[32] is conversely characterized by the evolving interpretation and the application of general judicial principles – both substantive and procedural. MacWhinney has very well described this change in the Court's judicial policy. He identified in President Lachs the 'intellectual bridge'[33] between the old and the Court's new interpretative approach, allowing it to move 'from the earlier, positivistic, strict-and-literal approach' to a new 'policy oriented approach'.[34] This makes it possible for the Court to tackle the challenges of the global international community's socio-political transformations.

Although hampered by states' diffidence, in general, and in particular that of Socialist countries, during the first phase the Court addressed some important issues and needs of the international community by: (1) declaring unlawful the use of force and imposing on the parties to the dispute a settlement in conformity with international law;[35] (2) fostering respect for international law in the states' conscience; and (3) institutionalizing the international judicial function and strengthening compulsory jurisdiction, while, at the same time, reaffirming its character as an UN organ.

---

29 Interpretation of Judgments Nos 7 and 8 (Factory at Chorzów), Judgment No. 11, (Dec. 16, 1927), 1927, PCIJ, Series A, No. 11, at 20; Aegean Sea Continental Shelf, *supra* note 16, paras 39, at 16–17.

30 Northern Cameroons, *supra* note 23, at 37; Nuclear Tests (Australia v. France), *supra* note 8, para. 30, at 263; Nuclear Tests (New Zealand v. France), *supra* note 8, para. 31, at 467.

31 Continental Shelf (Tunisia/Libyan Arab Jamahiriya), Tunisia v. Libyan Arab Jamahiriya, Judgment, 1982 ICJ REPORTS 18 (Feb 24, 1982), para. 23, at 37; Frontier Dispute (Burkina Faso/Republic of Mali), *supra* note 11, para. 42, at 575; Land, Island and Maritime Frontier Dispute, *supra* note 19, para. 27, at 380; para. 40, at 386.

32 See *infra* next section of this chapter.

33 Edward MacWhinney, *The Role and Mission of the International Court in an Era of Historical Transition*, *in* PERSPECTIVES ON INTERNATIONAL LAW 217 (Nandasiri Jasentuliyana ed., 1995).

34 *Id.*, at 217–218.

35 Corfu Channel case (United Kingdom v. Albania), Judgment, 1949 ICJ REPORTS 4 (April 9, 1949), at 32, 33; Military and Paramilitary Activities, *supra* note 9, paras 188–192, at 99–102.

In the second phase, which began in the mid-1970s, and which is still in progress, the Court is paying great attention to the transition of the community of states towards an organized world system based on global constitutional principles. During the last three decades, the Court consolidated its role at the service of world's society[36] by claiming independence from the West.[37] During this phase, its judicial politics are aimed at strengthening the process of regulatory and structural 'verticalization' of the international community.

We use the term 'verticalization'[38] to refer to the ongoing process of reorganization of international power in a centralized fashion, by gradually subtracting it from states and the classical egalitarian, horizontal, management. This process was started by the need to manage the emerging global values and to compensate the shortcomings of both the classical international system and the UN itself. Verticalization is epitomized by the growing tendency of the UN and its organs to carry out general social functions, along with or in lieu of states, and with other international organizations, both on a global and regional level, as well as non-governmental organizations, for the management, or co-management, of goods and interest of the whole of human kind. This is done by overcoming the Charter system, as well as the sovereignty of the states, and by gradually integrating the substantive community with the organized community. We called such system of shared governance 'integrated system'.[39]

We already examined the general activities performed by the Security Council and General Assembly to safeguard fundamental global interests (peace and international security, human rights, self-determination, democracy, health, etc.), bypassing the Charter to operate on behalf of the growing global community.[40] We now want to illustrate the parallel, simultaneous activity performed by the Court to achieve the same goals, as an interpreter of the pressing needs created by globalization. By sidestepping the Charter and the Statute, widening its competence and powers, the ICJ acts as 'global supreme court'.[41] The Court strengthens its provisional and advisory powers and uses them to safeguard peace and human rights. It consolidates

---

36 Georges Abi-Saab, *The International Court as a World Court*, *in* FIFTY YEARS OF THE INTERNATIONAL COURT OF JUSTICE, *supra* note 1, at 3 *et seq.*; Gilbert Guillaume, *La Mondialisation et la Cour Internationale de Justice*, 2 INTERNATIONAL LAW FORUM DU DROIT INTERNATIONAL 242 (2000).

37 Georges Abi-Saab, *De l'Evolution de la Cour Internationale. Reflèxions sur Quelques Tendances Récentes*, 96 REVUE GÉNÉRALE DE DROIT INTERNATIONAL PUBLIC [hereinafter REV. GEN. D.I.P.] 273 (1992–II).

38 See Giuliana Ziccardi Capaldo, *Verticalità della Comunità Internazionale e Nazioni Unite. Un Riesame del Caso Lockerbie*, *in* INTERVENTI DELLE NAZIONI UNITE E DIRITTO INTERNAZIONALE 61 (1995) [hereinafter Ziccardi Capaldo, *Verticalità*]; *Id.*, *Da Yalta ad un Nuovo Ordine Politico Internazionale*, 45 LA COMUNITÀ INTERNAZIONALE 210 (1990); *Id.*, *Democratizzazione all'Est e Diritto Internazionale Generale*, *in* DEMOCRATIZZAZIONE ALL'EST E DIRITTO INTERNAZIONALE 27 (Giuliana Ziccardi Capaldo ed., 1998).

39 Giuliana Ziccardi Capaldo, *The Law of the Global Community: An Integrated System to Enforce 'Public' International Law*, 1 GCYILJ 71 (2001).

40 See *supra* notes 38–39.

41 The quote is from Philip Allott, *The International Court and the Voice of Justice*, *in* FIFTY YEARS OF THE INTERNATIONAL COURT OF JUSTICE, *supra* note 1, at 39.

its authority over the organs of states and international institutions, and judicial and political organs (that is to say, the Court's 'vertical trends'). It claims the power to control the acts of the organs of the UN and the Security Council in order to safeguard the values shared by the world community. During this second phase the Court is acting to safeguard universal constitutional values/principles, and the legitimacy of global governance has became the central focus of its judicial politics. The Court's global reach beyond the confines of the Charter is becoming the rule of the new global constitutional system.

The ICJ as the Builder of the Vertical Global System

In the past few decades, the Court has increased its authority and gained states' trust: nowadays not only European and American, but also African,[42] Asian, and Caribbean States are increasingly relying on it to settle significant disputes about land and sea boundaries.[43]

---

42 Bola A. Ajibola, *Africa and the International Court of Justice*, *in* LIBER AMICORUM 'IN MEMORIAM' OF JUDGE JOSÉ MARÌA RUDA 253 (Calixto A. Armas Barea ed., 2000).

43 Minquiers and Ecrehos, *supra* note 8; Sovereignty over certain Frontier Land (Belgium/Netherlands), Judgment, 1959 ICJ REPORTS 209 (June 20, 1959); Arbitral Award Made by the King of Spain on 23 December 1906 (Honduras v. Nicaragua), 1960 ICJ REPORTS 192 (Nov. 18, 1960); Temple of Preah Vihear, *supra* note 10; Continental Shelf (Tunisia/Libyan Arab Jamahiriya), Tunisia v. Libyan Arab Jamahiriya, *supra* note 31; Continental Shelf (Libyan Arab Jamahiriya/Malta), Judgment, 1985 ICJ REPORTS 13 (June 3, 1985); Frontier Dispute (Burkina Faso/Republic of Mali), *supra* note 11; Land, Island and Maritime Frontier Dispute (El Salvador/Honduras; Nicaragua intervening) *supra* note 19; Maritime Delimitation and Territorial Questions between Qatar and Bahrain (Qatar v. Bahrain), Jurisdiction and Admissibility, 1994 ICJ REPORTS 112 (July 1, 1994); Land and Maritime Boundary between Cameroon and Nigeria (Cameroon v. Nigeria), Provisional Measures, Order, 1996 ICJ REPORTS 13 (March 15, 1996); Kasikili Sedudu Island (Botswana/Namibia), 1999 ICJ REPORTS 1045 (Dec. 13. 1999), Maritime Delimitation and Territorial Questions between Qatar and Bahrain (Qatar v. Bahrain), Merits, Judgment, 2001 ICJ REPORTS 40 (March 16, 2001) (on the literature concerning this last case, see John R. Crook, *The 2001 Judicial Activity of the International Court of Justice*, 96 AM. J. INT'L. L. 397 (2002)); Shabtai Rosenne, *Introductory Note, The International Court of Justice. 1 July 1999–31 December 2001*, 2 GCYILJ 207, 221 (2002–I); John G. Merrills, *Introductory Note, The International Court of Justice in 2002*, 3 GCYILJ 277 (2003–I) [hereinafter Merrills, *Introductory Note*]; Barbara Kwiatkowska, *The Law of the Sea Related Cases in the International Court of Justice During the Presidency of Judge Stephen M. Schwebel (1997–2000) and Beyond*, 2 GCYILJ 27 (2002–I); Case Concerning the Land and Maritime Boundary between Cameroon and Nigeria (Cameroon v. Nigeria: Equatorial Guinea intervening), Judgment, (Oct. 10, 2002); Case Concerning Sovereignty over Pulau Ligitan and Pulau Sipadan (Indonesia/Malaysia), (Dec. 17, 2002); Case Concerning the Frontier Dispute (Benin/Niger), Order, (Nov. 27, 2002); Application for Revision of the Judgment of 11 September 1992 in the Case Concerning the Land, Island and Maritime Frontier Dispute (El Salvador/Honduras: Nicaragua intervening) (El Salvador v. Honduras), Judgment, (Dec. 18, 2003); Territorial and Maritime Dispute (Nicaragua v. Colombia), Order, 2002 ICJ REPORTS (Feb. 26, 2002); Maritime Delimitation between Nicaragua and Honduras in the Caribbean Sea (Nicaragua v. Honduras), Order, (March 21, 2000); Sovereignty over

Recently, the Court has heard cases dealing with violations of human rights and fundamental social values.[44]

The Court in Charge of the World's Territorial Order

The Court is increasingly in charge of the peaceful maintenance of the world's territorial order.[45] Its increasing use to settle boundary delimitation disputes is accompanied by an increased power of its decisions, as the parties to the dispute generally comply with them, with the help of the Court itself or of international organizations. These are processes of 'functional integration' – as Rosenne calls them[46] – where the parties cooperate with international organs[47] and the Court. The demarcation of the Eritrea/Ethiopia boundary fixed by the 2002 UN Commission[48] was facilitated by the extension of the UN Mission in Ethiopia and Eritrea until 15 September 2004, by the unanimous UN Security Council Resolution of 12 March 2004.[49] Also, in the *Cameroon v. Nigeria* case, 'a major African boundary dispute',[50]

Pedra Branca/Pulau Batu Puteh, Middle Rocks and South Ledge (Malaysia/Singapore), Order, (Sept. 1, 2003); Proceedings Instituted by Romania against Ukraine (Romania v. Ukraine), Order, (Nov. 19, 2004). The ongoing Belize/Guatemala territorial and maritime settlement and the Joint Legal Opinion (available at <http://www.belize-guatemala.gov.bz/library/legal_opinion/welcome.html>) are ably appraised in the pioneering analysis of John G. Merrills, *The Belize–Guatemala Territorial Dispute and the Legal Opinion of January 2002*, 2 GCYILJ 77 (2002–I).

44 See *infra* third section of this chapter.

45 On the meaningful contribution of the Court to the development of international law in this field and to the solution of complex territorial controversies with multiple political implications, see especially Robert Y. Jennings, *Contributions of the Court to the Resolution of International Tensions*, *in* Increasing the Effectiveness of the International Court of Justice 78 (Connie Peck & Roy S. Lee eds, 1997); John G. Merrills, *The International Court of Justice and the Adjudication of Territorial and Boundary Disputes*, 13 Leiden Journal of International Law [hereinafter LJIL] 873 (2000); Barbara Kwiatkowska, *Equitable Maritime Boundary Delimitation, as Exemplified in the Work of the International Court of Justice During the Presidency of Judge Gilbert Guillaume (2000–2003) and Beyond*, 5 GCYILJ 51 (2005–I)

46 Rosenne, *supra* note 1, Vol. I, at 265.

47 See the Anglo-Iranian Oil Co. case, the Arbitral Award of the King of Spain case, the Military and Paramilitary Activities in and against Nicaragua case, and the Territorial Dispute (Chad/Libya) case.

48 UN Eritrea/Ethiopia Boundary Commission, Decision, 41 International Legal Materials [hereinafter Int'l Legal Mat.] 1057 (2002); 42 Int'l Legal Mat. 1010 (2003).

49 SC Res. 1531 (March 12, 2004), available at <http://www.un.org/News/Press/docs/2004/sc8023.doc.htm>, <http://www.un.org/apps/news/story.asp?NewsID=10055&Cr=ethiopia&Cr1=eritrea> and Progress Report S/2004/180, including the 12th EEBC President's Report, available at <http://www.eritreadaily.net/documents/thedailynews04/U30804.pdf> and <http://www.un.org/Docs/sc/>.

50 John G. Merrills, *The Land and Maritime Boundary Case – Judgment on the Merits*, 52 International & Comparative Law Journal [hereinafter Int'l & Comp. L.Q.] 788 (2003); Peter H. Bekker, *Land and Maritime Boundary Between Cameroon and Nigeria*, 97 Am. J. Int'l. L. 387 (2003).

after the Court's decision about the administration of Lake Chad,[51] the relentless Nigerian opposition to the Court's ruling is waning thanks to the creation of an *ad hoc* commission to demarcate the boundary, as requested by the parties to the UN Secretary-General.[52]

The Court simplifies its procedures and facilitates access. The last innovation includes changes to its Statute and its Practice Directions enacted in 2001[53] and 2002.[54] The Court reminds the states of the possibilities offered by Articles 29 and 26 of the Statute: the first dealing with Chambers of summary procedure and the second dealing with Chambers for specific kinds of disputes (Article 26 (1) and (2)).[55] In the past, *ad hoc* Chambers have been created to settle important territorial disputes,[56] and in more recent times they have been used for two boundary disputes: *Benin v. Niger* and *Salvador v. Honduras*.[57]

The Court's 'Authority' Over State Organs

The ICJ increasingly consolidates its authority over states. It demands fairness and shows determination against opportunistic states clearly abusing the process.[58] Its

---

51 Land and Maritime Boundary between Cameroon and Nigeria, Judgment, *supra* note 43, para. 325.

52 The Communiques of all – so far nine (9th was held on 7–8 April 2004 in Yaounde) – meetings of the UN Cameroon/Nigeria Mixed Commission charged with delicate task of demarcating the land and maritime boundaries delimited by the 2002 ICJ Judgment (available at <http://www.icj–cij.org) are at <http://www.un.org/Depts/dpa/prev_dip/africa/office_for_srsg/cnmc/preleas/comlist.htm>. See also in parallel Two UN Mediations between Guyana/Venezuela, available at <http://www.scoop.co.nz/mason/stories/WO0309/S00353.htm> and Gabon/Equatorial Guinea, available at <http://www.irinnews.org/report.asp?ReportID=39104&SelectRegion=West_Africa&SelectCountry=EQUATORIAL_GUINEA–GABON>.

53 Rosenne, *supra* note 43, at 209–214.

54 Merrills, *Introductory Note*, *supra* note 43, at 277.

55 In July 1993 the Court established an environmental chamber.

56 Delimitation of the Maritime Boundary in the Gulf of Maine Area (Canada v. United States of America), Constitution of Chamber, Order, 1982 ICJ Reports 3 (Oct. 8, 1982); Frontier Dispute (Burkina Faso/Republic of Mali), Constitution of Chamber, Order, 1985 ICJ Reports 6 (April 3, 1985); Land, Island and Maritime Frontier Dispute (El Salvador/Honduras), Constitution of Chamber, Order, 1987 ICJ Reports 10 (May, 8, 1987).

57 Frontier Dispute (Benin/Niger), *supra* note 43; Application for Revision of the Judgment of 11 September 1992 in the Case Concerning the Land, Island and Maritime Frontier Dispute (El Salvador/Honduras: Nicaragua intervening) (El Salvador v. Honduras), Order, (Nov. 27, 2002). The latter case was submitted to the Court in September 2002 by El Salvador, which asked, according to Art. 60 of the Court's Statute, the revision of the ruling in the *Land, Island and Maritime Frontier Dispute* case, *supra* note 19, for the sixth sector relative to the river Goascoràn.

58 Fisheries Jurisdiction (Spain v. Canada), Jurisdiction of the Court, Judgment, 1998 ICJ Reports 432 (Dec. 4, 1998), para. 49, at 454; Cases Concerning Legality of Use of Force (Serbia and Montenegro v. Belgium), Request for the Indication of Provisional Measures, Order, 1999 ICJ Reports 124 (June 2, 1999), para. 30, at 135; Case Concerning the Aerial

authority over states' organs becomes more direct,[59] as it specifically demands them to perform certain tasks. By invoking the principle stating that the conduct of a state's organ, 'even an organ independent from the executive',[60] must be considered as an act of the state itself, therefore implying its responsibility, the Court declares violations of international law committed by executive and judicial national organs alike, and dictates the behaviour they are to adhere to.

In the advisory opinion *Immunity from Legal Process*, the ICJ applied for the first time Article VIII, Section 30, of the 1946 General Convention on the United Nations' Privileges and Immunities, which provides that whenever a dispute arises between the UN and one of its members as to the interpretation or application of the Convention, the Court can exercise its advisory functions 'with binding effects' on the parties.[61] In the specific case, a disagreement arose between the UN and the Malaysian Government with respect to the immunity from legal process of Datò Param Cumaraswamy, a UN agent and Special Rapporteur of the UN Commission on Human Rights. The Court scrutinized the actions of Malaysian organs, and pointed out the violation of the Convention both by the Malaysian Government and Courts: the former for not having conveyed to the competent courts the Secretary-General's notice to the UN on the immunities guaranteed by the Convention; the latter for having disregarded the generally recognized procedural principle according to which '[q]uestions of immunity are [...] preliminary issues which must be expeditiously decided *in limine litis*'.[62] Eventually it ordered the Malaysian Government to communicate to the national courts the advisory opinion so that Malaysia's international obligations would be given effect.[63]

The Court returned to the rule of immunity from criminal jurisdiction in the *Arrest Warrant* case,[64] where it was urged to examine it in the light of the present context shaped by international responsibility of individuals and the principle of universality of criminal jurisdiction.[65] Referring to practice,[66] the Court stated that

---

Incident of 10 August 1999 (Pakistan v. India), Jurisdiction of the Court, Judgment, 2000 ICJ REPORTS 12 (June 21, 2000), para. 40, at 30.

59 John R. Crook, *The 2000 Judicial Activity of the International Court of Justice*, 95 AM. J. INT'L. L. 685 (2001), at 687; *Id.*, *supra* note 43; *Id.*, *The 2002 Judicial Activity of the International Court of Justice*, 97 AM. J. INT'L. L. 352 (2003), at 353; Ian Brownlie, *Remedies in the International Court of Justice*, *in* FIFTY YEARS OF THE INTERNATIONAL COURT OF JUSTICE, *supra* note 1, at 557.

60 Difference Relating to Immunity from Legal Process of a Special Rapporteur of the Commission on Human Rights, Advisory Opinion, 1999 ICJ REPORTS 62 (April 29, 1999), para. 62, at 87–88.

61 *Id.*, para. 10, at 66–69.

62 *Id.*, para. 63, at 88.

63 *Id*,. para. 65, at 88.

64 Case Concerning the Arrest Warrant of 11 April 2000 (Democratic Republic of the Congo v. Belgium), Judgment, 2002 ICJ REPORTS 3 (Feb. 14, 2002).

65 M. Cherif Bassiouni, *Universal Jurisdiction for International Crimes*, 42 VIRGINIA JOURNAL OF INTERNATIONAL LAW 81 (2001); Georges Abi-Saab, *The Proper Role of Universal Jurisdiction*, 1 JOURNAL OF INTERNATIONAL CRIMINAL JUSTICE 596 (2003).

66 This reveals the superficiality of the analysis of the practice performed by the Court.

under the customary rule on immunity, incumbent Foreign Ministers/state officials enjoy immunity from criminal jurisdiction of other states/foreign states, even when accused of serious violations of human rights. By pointing out that immunity does not mean impunity, the Court declared that state officials can be subject to criminal proceedings before domestic courts, when out of office. In any event, even when still in office, they can be tried by international courts. In the specific case, the Court decided that the arrest warrant issued by a Belgian investigating judge against the incumbent Congolese Foreign Minister constituted a violation of international customary law.[67] Accordingly, the Court ordered Belgium to cancel the warrant and to forward the judgment to the authorities of those states to whom the warrant was circulated so that *restitutio in integrum* could be effectuated.

This latter aspect of the decision, which profoundly divided the Court,[68] has also been extensively discussed in literature.[69] Judgments of the Court affecting decisions of domestic organs, like the ones just mentioned, threaten the independence and authority of national courts.[70] The ruling in the *Arrest Warrant* case had an immediate impact on the domestic level as the 1999 Belgian law was amended in 2003.[71] However, before the law was amended, the ICJ's ruling profoundly changed the interpretation of the international rule of immunity by Belgian courts, which, obvious difficulties notwithstanding, implemented the ICJ's ruling by interpreting the 1999 law accordingly.[72]

Also, in the *LaGrand* case,[73] the Court found a breach of international law committed by domestic executive and judicial organs. First, German citizens had

---

67 Law Concerning the Punishment of Grave Breaches of International Humanitarian Law of 16 June 1993, as amended by Law of 10 February 1999, Belgian Official Gazette, 5 August 1993 and 23 March 1999.

68 It was adopted with six judges opposed. Arrest Warrant, *supra* note 64, Dissenting Opinions of Judge Al-Khasewneh, at paras 1–2, 4, and Judge *ad hoc* Van den Wyngaert, at paras 20–21; Joint Opinion of Judges Higgins, Kooijmans, and Buergenthal, at paras 81–83.

69 See Steffen Wirth, *Immunity for Core Crimes?*, *id.*, at 877; Marc Herzelin, *La Compétence Pénale Universelle, Une Question non Résolue par l'Arrêt Yerodia*, 106 Revue Générale de Droit International Public 819 (2002).

70 Chanaka Wickremasinghe & Malcolm D. Evans, *Difference Relating to Immunity from Legal Process of a Special Rapporteur of the Commission on Human Rights*, 49 Int'l & Comp. L.Q. 724 (2000), at 729–730.

71 Belgian Official Gazette, 7 May 2003.

72 See Belgian Court of Cassation, Judgment of 12 February 2003, available at <http://www.indictsharon.net/12feb2003dectrans.pdf>; Cour d'appel de Bruxelles, Chambre des Mises en Accusation, Judgment of 10 June 2003, available at <http://www.ulb.ac.be/droit/cdi/fichiers/arret–CMA–Yaron.pdf> and the considerations on the case by Jan Wouters, *The Judgement of the International Court of Justice in the Arrest Warrant Case: Some Critical Remarks*, 16 LJIL 253 (2003), at 266.

73 LaGrand (Germany v. United States of America), Provisional Measures, Order, 1999 ICJ Reports 9 (March 3, 1999). Together with Germany, other States (Paraguay and Mexico) asked the Court for temporary measures to delay the execution of some of their citizens, to whom the protection described in Art. 36 of the Vienna Convention had been denied (Vienna Convention on Consular Relations (Paraguay v. United States of America), Provisional Measures, Order, 1998 ICJ Reports 248 (April 9, 1998); Avena and Other Mexican Nationals

been sentenced to death in the US, in violation of the rules set by Article 36 (1)(b) of the 1963 Vienna Convention on Consular Relations.[74] Second, US organs had not complied with the provisional measures the Court indicated on 3 March 1999.[75] These violations ascertained, the Court ordered the US to provide, by means of its own choice, for the 'review and reconsideration of the conviction and sentence' of any cases implicating the death penalty towards German and foreign citizens where violations due to omission of consular assistance has been committed.[76]

In the same *LaGrand* case, the ICJ also affirmed its authority over national legislative organs and claimed it could assess the compatibility of a domestic law – both substantively and procedurally – with the state's international obligations.[77] In this case it concluded that American laws do conform to the 1963 Vienna Convention.[78] This general statement made by the Court on its competence to examine the conformity of domestic laws to international law opens the way to international control on the procedures national systems follow to conform to international law.[79]

In the perspective of the evolution of the international community and a firmer control over domestic organs, the Court demands from states increasingly specific behaviours, going as far as contemplating the obligation of responsible states to repair material damages caused to individuals. In the advisory opinion on the *Construction of a Wall in the Occupied Palestinian Territory*,[80] after having ascertained the Israeli responsibility for having illegally built the wall on occupied Palestinian land, the Court specifies the legal consequences of that act. Reinterpreting the obligation to repair affirmed by the PCIJ,[81] the ICJ, in accordance with the applicable rules of international law, included in the obligation to compensate 'all natural or legal persons having suffered any form of material damage as a result of the wall's construction'[82] and demanded 'appropriate compensation for individuals whose homes or agricultural holdings have been destroyed'.[83] The Court also considered

---

(Mexico *v*. United States of America), Provisional Measures, Order, (Feb. 5, 2003)). Amongst the scholars, see Keith Highet, *The Emperor's New Clothes. Death Row Appeals to the World Court?*, *in* Liber Amicorum 'in Memoriam' of Judge José Marìa Ruda, *supra* note 42, at 435. On the issue see also *infra* notes 138–143 and corresponding text.

74 21 UST 77, TIAS No. 6820, 596 UNTS 261. Done at Vienna on April 24, 1963 and entered into force on March 19, 1967.

75 See LaGrand, *supra* note 73, para. 29, at 16.

76 LaGrand (Germany v. United States of America), Judgment, (June 27, 2001), para. 128; see also *infra* notes 149–150 and corresponding text.

77 *Id*., at para. 125, as summarized by Giuliana Ziccardi Capaldo *in* 2 GCYILJ 310 (2002–I).

78 The Court concluded: 'The Court … can determine the existence of a violation of an international obligation. If necessary, it can also hold that a domestic law has been the cause of this violation.' *Id*., at para. 125.

79 See *infra* chapter 5 of this book, under the heading 'International Minimum Standards for Internal Applicability of Treaty Law'.

80 Construction of a Wall, *supra* note 22.

81 Factory at Chorzów, Merits, Judgment No. 13, (Sept. 13, 1928), 1928, PCIJ, Series A, No. 17, at 47.

82 Construction of a Wall, *supra* note 22, para. 153.

83 *Id*., at para. 145.

the possibility of demanding from the responsible state 'guarantees and assurances of non-repetition'.[84] Such a measure opens the way to a further control by the Court over domestic organs' conduct and creates a deterrent for the state in question, which could be held responsible for successive violations of the Court's ruling.[85] This tool, together with the competence claimed by the Court over issues like the use of force and the violation of human rights, could provide a useful means to foster respect of international legality and fundamental rights.[86]

States respond to the heightened prestige of the Court by increasingly trusting it and submitting to its authority. An example of this is the resort to procedure under Article 38 (5) of the Court's Rules. In 2002, the Democratic Republic of Congo filed a case against France[87] on the alleged violation of the Congolese President's immunity, demanding 'to declare that the French Republic shall cause to be annulled the measures of investigation and prosecution taken by several French courts and the investigating judges of those courts'. As a basis for the Court's jurisdiction, Congo cited the aforementioned Article,[88] which provides that when the applicant state proposes to found the jurisdiction of the Court upon a consent thereto yet to be given or manifested by the state against which such application is made, the application shall be transmitted to that state. By a letter dated 8 April 2003, France consented explicitly to the jurisdiction of the Court to entertain the application on the basis of that Article, even if the precedent set by the *Arrest Warrant* case was in favour of immunity of state's high officials.[89] This is the first occasion in which Article 38 (5) has been actually applied, since its inclusion in the Court's Rules in 1978. This is a clear signal of great trust in the Court. It increases chances of actual compliance with its judgments. It creates hope even for the institution of compulsory jurisdiction, whose effectiveness is doubtful in the case of reluctant states.[90]

The Court as the Director of the Development of International Law

The Court leads the institutionalization of the international normative functions. This is necessarily so, as the international legal system lacks an organ formally charged with *law-making* functions. Nowadays the Court, by ascertaining principles and customary norms, carries out functions that go well beyond those of a typical

84 LaGrand, *supra* note 76, paras 121–124; Construction of a Wall, *supra* note 22, para. 145.

85 Martin Mennecke, *Towards the Humanization of the Vienna Convention of Consular Rights*, 44 German Yearbook of International Law 430 (2001), at 455.

86 See *infra* later in this chapter under the headings 'Judicial Protection of Human Rights …' and 'Judicial Protection of Peace …'.

87 Certain Criminal Proceedings in France (Republic of the Congo v. France), Application and Request for the Indication of Provisional Measures (available at <http://www.icj–cij.org/icjwww/idocket/icof/icoforder/icof_iapplication_20020209.pdf>).

88 *Id.*, at para. 10.

89 Arrest Warrant, *supra* note 64.

90 Shigeru Oda, *The Compulsory Jurisdiction of the International Court of Justice: A Myth?*, 49 Int'l & Comp. L.Q. 251 (2000), at 264; Dire Thadi, *Reviving the Debate on the Efficacy of the ICJ*, 25 South African Yearbook of International Law 232 (2000), at 236.

judicial body. Before applying the appropriate rule to a specific question, it ascertains the existence and the applicability of norms in an 'innovative, developmental way';[91] sometimes it treats norms while they are in the making, thus directing and contributing to the development of international law. This is the case, in particular, in the field of the law of the sea, where the Court's contribution has been substantial, in the opinion of the Court itself.[92] Further, in exercising advisory jurisdiction – which is a function that transcends the protection of the rights and interests of specific parties and instead serves the need of the larger community – the Court ascertains and proclaims norms and general principles, performing a 'quasi-legislative' function.[93]

The case law of the Court has clarified and brought about developments on questions like the way international law is created (mostly custom and its codification[94] and treaties[95]), as well as the content of customs and principles concerning: non-intervention; non-use of force; aggression; self-defence;[96] countermeasures;[97] genocide;[98] diplomatic and consular law;[99] immunity of state officials[100] and UN

---

91 In general, on the Court's contribution to the development of international law, see LAUTERPACHT, *supra* note 1; Stephen M. Schwebel, *The Contribution of the International Court of Justice to the Development of International Law*, *in* INTERNATIONAL LAW AND THE HAGUE'S 75TH ANNIVERSARY, *supra* note 1, at 405; Elihu Lauterpacht, *The Development of the Law of International Organization by the Decisions of International Tribunals*, 152 RECUEIL DES COURS 377 (1976–IV).

92 Delimitation of the Maritime Boundary in the Gulf of Maine Area, *supra* note 10, para. 83, at 290–291.

93 See Giuliana Ziccardi Capaldo, *Il Parere Consultivo della Corte Internazionale di Giustizia sul Sahara Occidentale: Un'Occasione per un Riesame della Natura e degli Effetti della Funzione Consultiva*, 15 COMUNICAZIONI E STUDI 532 (1978), at 556 [hereinafter Ziccardi Capaldo, *Il Parere Consultivo*]; *Id.*, *Foreword*, ZICCARDI CAPALDO, REPERTORY, *supra* note 1, at lix. See generally Edward MacWhinney, *The International Court and Judicial Law-making. Nuclear Tests Re-visited*, *in* THEORY OF INTERNATIONAL LAW AT THE THRESHOLD OF THE 21ST CENTURY. ESSAYS IN HONOUR OF KRZYSZTOF SKUBISZEWSKI 509 (Jerzy Makarczyk ed., 1996).

94 North Sea Continental Shelf (Denmark/Federal Republic of Germany), Judgment, 1969 ICJ REPORTS 3 (Feb. 20, 1969), para. 88, at 48–49; Military and Paramilitary Activities, *supra* note 9, para. 177, at 94–95; paras 184, 186, at 97–98; para. 188, at 100; para. 207, at 108–109. See also ZICCARDI CAPALDO, REPERTORY, *supra* note 1, vol. I, Nos 1000–1025, at 5–25.

95 *Id.*, Nos 1082–1149, at 85–155.

96 *Id.*, Nos 1044–1052, at 41–51.

97 Military and Paramilitary Activities, *supra* note 9, paras 188–211, at 99–111.

98 Application of the Convention on the Prevention and Punishment of the Crime of Genocide (Bosnia and Herzegovina v. Yugoslavia), Provisional Measures, Order, 1993 ICJ REPORTS 325, (Sept. 13, 1993), para. 42, at 345; Legality of Use of Force, *supra* note 58, para. 40, at 273. See also ZICCARDI CAPALDO, REPERTORY, *supra* note 1, vol. I, Nos 1066, at 67. See in general WILLIAM A. SCHABAS, *GENOCIDE IN INTERNATIONAL LAW* (2000).

99 United States Diplomatic and Consular Staff in Tehran (United States of America v. Iran), Merits, Judgment, 1980 ICJ REPORTS 3 (May 24, 1980), para. 86, at 40; para.92, at 42–43. See also ZICCARDI CAPALDO, REPERTORY, *supra* note 1, vol. I, Nos 1059–1061, at 59–61.

100 Arrest Warrant, *supra* note 64.

agents;[101] the principle of *uti possidetis juris*;[102] self-determination;[103] and humanitarian law.[104] It articulated the notion of *erga omnes* obligations in international law,[105] and it determined the consequences deriving from their violations for the responsible state,[106] and for all other states.[107] It developed the notion of equity,[108] and developed

---

101 Applicability of Article VI, Section 22, *supra* note 19; Immunity from Legal Process, *supra* note 60.

102 Frontier Dispute (Burkina Faso/Republic of Mali), *supra* note 11, paras 23–26, at 566–567; Land, Island and Maritime Frontier Dispute (El Salvador/Honduras; Nicaragua intervening), *supra* note 19, paras 41–42, at 386–387. See also Ziccardi Capaldo, Repertory, *supra* note 1, vol. I, Nos 1055–1058, at 55–59.

103 Legal Consequences for States of the Continued Presence of South Africa in Namibia (South West Africa) notwithstanding Security Council Resolution 276 (1970), Advisory Opinion, 1971 ICJ Reports 16 (June 21, 1971), para. 52, at 31; Western Sahara, *supra* note 19, paras 54–55, at 31–32; East Timor (Portugal v. Australia), Judgment, 1995 ICJ Reports 90 (June 30, 1995), para. 29, at 102; Construction of a Wall, *supra* note 22, paras 88, 115–122, 155–156. See also Ziccardi Capaldo, Repertory, *supra* note 1, vol. I, Nos 1053–1054, at 53–55.

104 Military and Paramilitary Activities, *supra* note 9, paras 216–220, at 112–115; Legality of the Threat or Use of Nuclear Weapons, Advisory Opinion, 1996–I ICJ Reports 226 (July 8, 1996), para. 26, at 240, mainly paras 78–79, 87, 90–92, 105, at 257, 260–262, 265–267; Construction of a Wall, *supra* note 22, para. 157. See also Ziccardi Capaldo, Repertory, *supra* note 1, vol. I, Nos 1062–1065, at 63–67. Amongst the scholars, see Theodor Meron, *The Humanization of Humanitarian Law*, 94 Am. J. Int'l. L. 239 (2000); Rosalyn Higgins, *The International Court of Justice and Human Rights*, *in* International Law: Theory and Practice. Essays in Honour of Eric Suy, 691, 702 (Karel Wellens ed., 1998); Judith Gardam, *The Contribution of the International Court of Justice to International Humanitarian Law*, 14 LJIL 349 (2001). Particularly important is the advisory opinion, *Construction of a Wall*, *supra* note 22, paras 104–113; on this opinion see our remarks *infra*, under the heading 'Judicial Protection of Human Rights …'.

105 Barcelona Traction, Light and Power Company, (Belgium v. Spain), Limited, Judgment, 1970 ICJ Reports 3 (Feb. 5, 1970), paras 33–34, at 32; Legality of the Threat or Use of Nuclear Weapons, *supra* note 104, para. 79, at 257; Construction of a Wall, *supra* note 22, paras 89–101, 155–157. See also Ziccardi Capaldo, Repertory, *supra* note 1, vol. I, Nos 1070–1071, at 69–71. See Robert Y. Jennings, *The Judicial Function and the Rule of Law in International Relations*, International Law at the Time of its Codification. Essays in Honour of Roberto Ago 139, 142 (1987–III); Vera Gowlland-Debbas, *Judicial Insights into Fundamental Values and Interests of the International Community*, *in* The International Court of Justice: Its Future Role After Fifty Years, *supra* note 1, at 327, 335.

106 Haya de la Torre case, *supra* note 20, at 82; United States Diplomatic and Consular Staff, *supra* note 99, para. 95, at 44; Military and Paramilitary Activities, *supra* note 9, para. 292.13, at 149; Construction of a Wall, *supra* note 22, paras 150–153.

107 South West Africa, *supra* note 103, para. 44, at 32–33; Construction of a Wall, *supra* note 22, para. 159–160. See also Ziccardi Capaldo, Repertory, *supra* note 1, vol. I, Nos 1585–1586, at 615–619.

108 North Sea Continental Shelf, *supra* note 94, para. 88, at 48–49; Continental Shelf (Tunisia/Libyan Arab Jamahiriya), *supra* note 31, para. 71, at 60; Frontier Dispute (Burkina Faso/Republic of Mali), *supra* note 11, para. 28, at 567–569. See also Ziccardi Capaldo, Repertory, *supra* note 1, vol. I, Nos 1072–1078, at 73–79.

some of the principles and norms of the law of the sea, eventually incorporated in the 1982 United Nations Convention on the Law of the Sea (UNCLOS). In 1984, the Court noted that the principle whereby maritime delimitation 'must be based on the application of equitable criteria' is a fundamental norm of customary international law governing maritime delimitation.[109] It also noted that this principle, which had been invoked by the Court repeatedly in its previous jurisprudence,[110] had been officially sanctioned by the proceedings and conclusions of the Third Conference on the Law of the Sea. The Court also built in the international system the general principles of a judicial procedure of competence and evidence, and, most of all, the principles *audi alteram partem*, *jura novit curia*, and that of the equality of the parties.[111] The Court applied this latter principle in the case of the opinions on the judgments of the administrative tribunals (UN Administrative Tribunal and ILO Administrative Tribunal), where it held that there must be equality between the employee and the organization, despite the 'seeming or nominal' inequality deriving from Article 66 of the Statute.[112]

The Court has systematically referred to conventions codifying international law, to ascertain the principles and the general norms dealing with the various different subject areas of international law. It did so when it stated the general character of many dispositions of the 1969 Vienna Convention on the Law of the Treaties[113] or when it declared that the Vienna Conventions of 1961 and 1963 on diplomatic and consular relations largely codify customary international law.[114] Although denying that these conventions have general character, it stated in a sentence dealing with the

109 Delimitation of the Maritime Boundary in the Gulf of Maine Area, *supra* note 10, para. 113, at 300.

110 In the case concerning the North Sea Continental Shelf, *supra* note 94, para. 92, at 50, and then in its judgment of 24 February 1982, in the case concerning Continental Shelf (Tunisia/Libyan Arab Jamahiriya), *supra* note 31, para. 44, at 47.

111 On the subject of competence, see, for instance: Nottebohm case, *supra* note 8, at 119–120; Land, Island and Maritime Frontier Dispute (El Salvador/Honduras; Nicaragua intervening), *supra* note 19, para. 402, at 600; on the subject of proof, see Military and Paramilitary Activities, *supra* note 9, paras 58, 60, at 39–40; on the subject of equality of the parties, *id.*, para. 31, at 26; on the principle *audi alteram partem*: Nuclear Tests (Australia v. France), *supra* note 8, para. 33, at 265; Nuclear Tests (New Zealand v. France), *supra* note 8, para. 34, at 469; Application for Review of Judgement No. 273 of the United Nations Administrative Tribunal, Advisory Opinion, 1982 ICJ Reports 325 (July 20, 1982), para. 59, at 356. On the *jura novit curia* principle, see also *supra* note 15. Amongst the scholars, see Gaetano Morelli, Nuovi Studi sul Processo Internazionale (1972); Rosenne, *supra* note 1; Hugh Thirlway, *Procedural Law and the International Court of Justice*, *in* Fifty Years of the International Court of Justice, *supra* note 1, at 389; Ziccardi Capaldo, Repertory, *supra* note 1, vol. II: Procedural Law; Stefania Negri, I Principi Generali del Processo Internazionale nella Giurisprudenza della Corte Internazionale di Giustizia (2002).

112 Application for Review of Judgement No. 158 of the United Nations Administrative Tribunal, Advisory Opinion, 1973 ICJ Reports 166 (July 12, 1973), para. 35, at 180; Application for Review of Judgement No. 273, *supra* note 111, para. 29, at 338–339.

113 Arbitral Award of 31 July 1989, *supra* note 21, para. 48, at 69–70.

114 United States Diplomatic and Consular Staff in Tehran, *supra* note 99, para. 45, at 24.

law of the sea that 'it is in codifying conventions that principles and rules of general application can be identified'.[115] Finally, the Court, fulfilling its role of ultimate interpreter and innovator of substantive and procedural principles of international law, often made reference to the law-making activities of the General Assembly, which takes the form of non-binding declarations of principles (e.g., those referring to the notions of aggression or legitimate defence or the self-determination principle[116]). By doing so, the Court seems to have meant to confer upon those acts a general binding character,[117] which, *per se*, they lack.[118]

The 'Intrinsic Authority' of the Court's Decisions

By operating as the organ of the whole global community, the ICJ has placed itself at the apex of the international judicial system.[119] The 'authority' of the judgments of the world's Court warrants this pre-eminent position. The Court is the main interpreter of international law, whose members represent 'the main forms of civilization and the principal legal systems of the world' (Article 9 of the Statute). The concept of 'intrinsic authority' of the Court's decisions,[120] authoritatively expressed by the former President, Stephen Schwebel, and supported along similar lines by Sir Hersch

115 Delimitation of the Maritime Boundary in the Gulf of Maine Area, *supra* note 10, para. 83, at 291. Concerning the 1982 Convention on the Law of the Sea, the Court held that 'although the Convention had not yet come into force … some of its provisions constitute the expression of customary international law in the matter' (Continental Shelf (Libyan Arab Jamahiriya/Malta), *supra* note 13, paras 26–27, at 29–30; Delimitation of the Maritime Boundary in the Gulf of Maine Area, *supra* note 10, paras 94–95, at 294). Similarly, in the case *Maritime Delimitation between Qatar and Bahrain*, given the need to ground findings on customary international law, the Court applied the provisions of the Law of the Sea Convention that it considered to be customary international law, for the purposes of drawing the boundary in the southern sector of the territorial sea. In particular, it relied on Art. 15 (Delimitation of the territorial sea between States with opposite or adjacent coasts) and Art. 121 (Regime of islands) of that Convention. See Maritime Delimitation and Territorial Questions between Qatar and Bahrain (Qatar v. Bahrain), Merits, *supra* note 43, para. 169, at 55, and paras 185, 195, at 97 and 99, respectively.

116 South West Africa, *supra* note 103, para. 52, at 31; Western Sahara, *supra* note 19, paras 55, 57–58, at 31–33; Military and Paramilitary Activities, *supra* note 9, para. 177, at 94–95; paras 193, 195, at 102–104; East Timor, *supra* note 103, para. 29, at 102; Construction of a Wall, *supra* note 22, paras 88, 156.

117 The 'jural significance' acquired by the General Assembly Declaration of Principle on the Friendly Relation between the States from 1970 by way of ICJ's jurisprudence is analysed by V.S. Mani, *The Friendly Relations Declaration and the International Court of Justice, in* Legal Visions of the 21st Century. Essays in Honour of Judge Christopher Weeramantry 527, 533, 540 (Antony Anghie & Garry Sturgess eds, 1998).

118 On the non-binding character of Declarations of Principles, see Gaetano Arangio Ruiz, *The Normative Role of the General Assembly of the United Nations and the Declaration of Principles of Friendly Relations*, 137 Recueil des Cours 431 (1972–III).

119 Ziccardi Capaldo, *supra* note 7, at 259.

120 Schwebel, *supra* note 91.

Lauterpacht,[121] is also cited in literature as the tool of choice to preserve and enhance the Court's authority.[122]

The Court construed the concept of 'authority' of its decisions throughout the years, by referring to its own past case law, as well as decisions of arbitral tribunals, which it sometimes regarded to be on a par with its own decisions. Citing a wide spectrum of jurisprudence, including, besides its own decisions, those of arbitral tribunals, other third-party fora, and national courts, and by interpreting and scrutinizing those judgments, the Court reinforced its role as the supreme judicial organ, in harmony with the other courts. This concept has acquired a new dimension in the present era of proliferation of specialized international courts and tribunals.[123] We are entering a sensitive phase of coordination and harmonization of the judgments of various international courts and tribunals, which suggests a pyramid-like structure for the international judicial system.[124] In particular, the *ad hoc* international criminal tribunals are active in determining general principles and customary norms of both substantive and procedural law.[125] The fact that the International Criminal Tribunal for the Former Yugoslavia held as customary law Article 7 (2) of its Statute (i.e., the non-applicability of immunity towards high officers guilty of international crimes), thus partially (dis)agreeing with the interpretation of the same customary norm made by the Court in the famous *Arrest Warrant* case,[126] is a clear example of the issues faced by the international judicial system.[127]

---

121 Lauterpacht, *supra* note 1.

122 See Barbara Kwiatkowska, Decisions of the World Court Relevant to the UN Convention on the Law of the Sea. A Reference Guide (2002), who emphasizes this concept and our considerations on the matter in *Book Review*, 50 Netherlands International Law Review [hereinafter Neth. Int'l L. Rev.] 88 (2003), at 89.

123 Alan E. Boyle, *The Proliferation of International Jurisdictions and Its Implications for the Court*, *in* The International Court of Justice, Process, Practice and Procedure 124 (Derek W. Bowett, James Crawford & Arthur Watts eds, 1997); Jonathan I. Charney, *The Impact on the International Legal System of the Growth of International Courts and Tribunals*, 31 New York University Journal of International Law & Politics 697 (1999); Hugh Thirlway, *The Proliferation of International Judicial Organs and the Formation of International Law*, *in* International Law and the Hague's 75th Anniversary, *supra* note 1, at 433.

124 See generally Jonathan I. Charney, *Is International Law Threatened by Multiple International Tribunals?*, 271 Recueil des Cours 101 (1998–I); Henry G. Schermers, *The International Court of Justice in Relation to Other Courts*, *in* The International Court of Justice: Its Future Role After Fifty Years, *supra* note 1, at 261.

125 For the corresponding jurisprudence see GCYILJ 491–655 (2001); *Id.*, 661–1080 (2002–II); *Id.*, 591–730 (2003–I); *Id.*, 621–1063 (2004–I–II); *Id.*, 621–1013 (2005–II).

126 *Infra* note 155. See also: The Prosecutor v. Anto Furundzjia, Case No. IT–95–17/1, Trial Chamber II, Judgment, (Dec. 10 1998), para. 140, Prosecutor v. Charles Ghankay Taylor, Case No. SCSL-2003-01-I, (May 31 2004), at <http://www.sc-sl.org/SCSL-03-01-I-059.pdf>.

127 See *supra* notes 64-66; *infra* notes 153-156 and corresponding text.

The Court's Authority on International Institutions

The ICJ takes great care in establishing a cooperative relationship with the UN and other international institutions. In the most recent judgments and opinions the Court quite clearly equated the UN with the international community[128] and explored ways to integrate the international community with the organized community.[129] The Court promotes a concentration of the global functions in a public international organization, such as the UN, and fosters the creation of a balance of powers between the organizations' organs to ensure international legality. By doing so, it goes beyond the limits of the Charter, acting as an organ of the whole international community, and it affirms its role as the ultimate interpreter of international law and guardian of international legality, even in competition with the two major political organs (i.e., the General Assembly and the Security Council).

The ICJ as Guardian of Global Constitutional Values

Given the absence of a clear separation of the powers of the Security Council and the ICJ in the Charter, and the inadequacy of the distinction between judicial and political disputes, as in Chapter VI of the UN Charter (Article 26 (3)), the relationship the Court is building with the Security Council will largely determine the face of the emerging global legal system.

Recently, the Court has ruled in several cases dealing with human rights and maintenance of international peace and security issues.[130] In so doing, it has been inspired by the constitutional principle of cooperation with the Security Council, while stressing the separation of the two different international powers. Whenever asked not to meddle in questions regarding the use of force under consideration by the Security Council, the Court has stressed the political nature of the Council's functions, as opposed to the judicial nature of its own functions, concluding that they can be exercised in parallel. Both organs can carry out their respective functions, 'distinct but complementary', regarding the same events.[131] Once competence has

128 In the 8 April 1993 ruling, Application of the Convention on the Prevention and Punishment of the Crime of Genocide, Provisional Measures, Order, 1993 ICJ Reports 11 (April 8, 1993), in particular at 12–13, about the request to indicate provisional measures in the *Bosnia and Herzegovina v. Yugoslavia* case, the Court overcame the Yugoslav Republic's objection to allow Mr Alija Izetbegovic to represent Bosnia before the Court by stating that he was considered by the UN as the Head of State of the Republic of Bosnia and Herzegovina and that the power of the head of state to act on behalf of his/her own state in international relations is universally recognized and affirmed in Art. 7 (2)(a) of the Vienna Convention on the Law of Treaties.

129 See *infra* notes 270–275 and corresponding text.

130 See Giuliana Ziccardi Capaldo (ed.), *International Court of Justice, Legal Maxims: Summaries and Extracts from Selected Case Law*, GCYILJ 155–266 (2001); *Id.*, 205–339 (2002–I); *Id.*, 295–383 (2003–I); *Id.*, 321–412 (2004–I); *Id.*, 351–395 (2005–I); *Id.*, 235–272 (2006–I)..

131 United States Diplomatic and Consular Staff, *supra* note 99, paras 39–40, at 21–22; Military and Paramilitary Activities, *supra* note 9, paras 93–96, at 433–435; para. 98, at 436;

been established, the Court considers itself entitled to control the legitimacy of the Council's decisions, because of its role as the UN's 'principal judicial organ'.[132] Thus, the Court uses its advisory function and provisional measures to safeguard common interests when peace and security (matters over which the Security Council has principal but not exclusive competence), human rights, etc. are violated. In sum, because of the expansion of the two organs' competence,[133] conflicts between them are not only possible but also concrete.

Judicial Protection of Human Rights Beyond the ICJ Statute

The expansion of the Court's advisory and provisional functions. In provisional measures involving cases dealing with human rights issues, the Court has assumed a bold position. It did so because it is acutely aware of its indispensability to a community that is evolving towards a universal human society but which is also still missing an adequate system of safeguards due to the UN General Assembly's lack of binding powers and the ineffectiveness of specific human rights institutions, both global (Human Rights Council) and regional (European and Inter-American Courts for human rights), *vis-à-vis* some powerful states.[134] The Court follows the lead of the Universal Declaration of Human Rights[135] when it intervenes with provisional measures to ensure the judicial protection of human rights for peoples, groups, and also individuals.[136] As stated by Judge Higgins, it does not fail to recognize 'the humanitarian realities behind disputes' between states.[137]

---

see also the submissions of Libya in the Orders of 14 April 1992, Questions of Interpretation and Application of the 1971 Montreal Convention arising from the Aerial Incident at Lockerbie (Libyan Arab Jamahiriya v. United Kingdom), Provisional Measures, Order, 1992 ICJ Reports 3 (April 14, 1992), para. 36, at 14; Questions of Interpretation and Application of the 1971 Montreal Convention arising from the Aerial Incident at Lockerbie (Libyan Arab Jamahiriya v. United States of America), Provisional Measures, Order, 1992 ICJ Reports 114 (April 14, 1992), para. 39, at 126.

132 On this subject see *infra*, section headed 'Judicial Control Over the Acts of UN Political Organs' later in this chapter.

133 See *supra* notes 3–5 and corresponding text.

134 See Alison Duxbury, *Saving Lives in the International Court of Justice: The Use of Provisional Measures to Protect Human Life*, 31 California Western International Law Journal 141 (2000), at 175.

135 Universal Declaration of Human Rights, GA Res. 217 A (III), (Dec. 10, 1948).

136 United States Diplomatic and Consular Staff in Tehran (United States of America v. Iran), Provisional Measures, Order, 1979 ICJ Reports 7 (Dec. 15, 1979), at 19; Frontier Dispute (Burkina Faso/Mali), *supra* note 11, at 10; Application of the Convention on the Prevention and Punishment of the Crime of Genocide, *supra* note 128, at 24; Land and Maritime Boundary between Cameroon and Nigeria, Order, *supra* note 43, at 22–23. See also Legality of the Threat or Use of Nuclear Weapons, *supra* note 104, para. 26, at 240; para. 36, at 244.

137 See Rosalyn Higgins, *Interim Measures for the Protection of Human Rights*, *in* Politics, Values and Functions. International Law in the 21st Century. Essays in Honour of Professor Louis Henkin 101, 103 (Jonathan I. Charney, Donald K. Anton & Mary Ellen O'Connell eds, 1997). See also *Id.*, *The International Court of Justice and Human Rights*, *in*

The Court was asked to indicate provisional measures meant to safeguard the life of certain individuals in three distinct cases filed against the US for the infringement of the 1963 Vienna Convention on Consular Relations (i.e., *Paraguay v. United States of America*;[138] *Germany v. United States of America*;[139] and *Mexico v. United States of America*[140]). The provisional measure adopted in this circumstance, justified by the 'extreme urgency' of the matter (Article 41 of the Statute) and pending the decision on the merits, was the suspension of the application for the execution of death sentences against nationals of the applicants.[141] Consistently with the rise on the international scene of individuals as 'new actors', the Court has interpreted Article 36 of the Vienna Convention on Consular Relations as conferring on individuals the right to receive consular assistance. Hence, it construed non-compliance with this provision as a violation of an individual's right rather than states' rights, thus departing from the traditional approach that granted diplomatic protection and entrusted the state the right to protect its citizens abroad. Despite the ICJ's stated refusal to act as an 'ultimate court of appeal in national criminal proceedings',[142] in practice the Court has become a virtual 'universal supreme court'[143] in respect to US courts in these particular cases.

The request for suspension of executions in those three cases[144] is evidence of the Court's determination to safeguard the public interest of the global community, even when it means limiting states' sovereignty (in this case the sovereignty of the world's most powerful state). This resolve is particularly evident when the general interests at stake are respect for fundamental human rights. This attitude acquires a tangible effect when it is coupled with the fact that in the *LaGrand* case the Court stated that its provisional measures are, indeed, binding.[145] This was the first time the Court felt compelled to pronounce itself on the binding/non-binding nature of provisional measures under Article 41 of the Statute since, for too long, as the Court said, the issue 'has been the subject of extensive controversy in the literature'.[146] The Court did not consider the power and clout of the US or the fact that executions had ultimately been carried out as an obstacle. Nor was there an obstacle over the disagreement

International Law: Theory and Practice. Essays in Honour of Eric Suy, 691, 703 (Karel Wellens ed., 1998).

138 Vienna Convention on Consular Relations, *supra* note 73.

139 LaGrand, *supra* note 73.

140 Avena and Other Mexican Nationals, *supra* note 73.

141 Vienna Convention on Consular Relations, *supra* note 73, para. 41, at 258; LaGrand, *id.*, para. 29, at 16; Avena and Other Mexican Nationals, *id.*, at para. 59.

142 LaGrand, *supra* note 73, para. 52, at 485–486.

143 *Id.*

144 See *supra* note 141.

145 LaGrand, *supra* note 76, paras 109–110. The Court has reaffirmed that its 'orders on provisional measures under Article 41 have binding effect' (see Case Concerning Armed Activities on the Territory of the Congo (Democratic Republic of the Congo v. Uganda), Judgment, 19 December, 2005, para. 263). See, amongst scholars, John G. Merrills, *The International Court of Justice, Introductory Note*, 6 GCYILJ 211 (2006–I).

146 *Id.*, at para. 99.

– not smoothed, bur rather highlighted[147] – with the US Solicitor General, whose 'categorical statement' about the measures' force was harshly criticized.[148] In the merits phase, stating the binding character of provisional measures, the Court found that the US had committed a breach of international law for having disregarded the provisional measures order that demanded the US adopt 'all measures at its disposal to ensure that Walter LaGrand is not executed pending the final decision in these proceedings'.[149] Subsequently, the Court demanded that the US reconsider any other similar rulings against German/foreign citizens carried out in violation of Article 31 (1)(b) of the Vienna Convention on Consular Relations.[150]

The ICJ between over-reaching and over-caution. The Court has decided to step boldly into the field of human rights, despite statutory limitations and the opinion of several scholars who consider it an 'inappropriate forum' to discuss human rights, due to both the incompatibilities between its primary judicial function – to settle disputes between states[151] – and the judicial safeguard of individual rights, and the Court's limited power to enforce its own decisions.[152]

Scholars have also accused the Court of not doing enough to safeguard human rights and have criticized it for having put limits (i.e., immunities attached to official capacities) to the principle of universal jurisdiction and for having deemed international prosecution 'a viable substitute' for national extraterritorial prosecution of incumbent state officials who are accused of having committed core crimes (*Arrest Warrant* case).[153]

We rather think that the Court's approach to the universality of jurisdiction in this case signals a global vision of the international order.[154] The ruling in the *Arrest Warrant* case focused on balancing two interests equally safeguarded by the new international criminal law of the global community: on the one hand, the necessity of a fair process guaranteed by the internationalization of the judicial means of human rights safeguards, and, on the other hand, the need to punish and deter the most serious international crimes. The Court has been careful in ensuring the ultimate fairness of

147 See Avena and Other Mexican Nationals, *supra* note 73, para. 14.

148 LaGrand, *supra* note 76, para. 115.

149 LaGrand, *supra* note 73, para. 29, at 16.

150 LaGrand, *supra* note 76, para. 128.7. See also Avena and Other Mexican Nationals (Mexico *v*. United States of America), Judgment, (March 31, 2004), para. 153.11.

151 Yoshiyuki Iwamoto, *The Protection of Human Life Through Provisional Measures Indicated by the International Court of Justice*, 15 LJIL 345 (2002), at 346.

152 Duxbury, *supra* note 134, at 171.

153 Steffen Wirth, *Immunity for Core Crimes?*, 13 European Journal of International Law [hereinafter Eur. J. Int'l L.] 877 (2002), at 893.

154 The Court eschews the question of procedural limitations to universal jurisdiction, that is to say, whether its exercise *in absentia* for the most heinous international crimes is allowed under international law. It sets substantial limits to the principle of universality by relying on a rather superficial analysis of states' practice. Some judges wrote in favour of universal jurisdiction *in absentia*, while others favoured conditional universal jurisdiction. See Jan Wouters, *The Judgment of International Court of Justice in the Arrest Warrant Case*, 16 LJIL 253 (2003), at 264.

the prosecution of perpetrators of international crimes and, at the same time, has shown concern for the possible instrumental use of extraterritorial jurisdiction, especially when applied to incumbent state officials. Because of this, it has come to the conclusion that, in the case of incumbent high state officials, prosecution by unbiased international courts is a better option. Again, the Court has striven to strike a compromise between two principles: the judge's impartiality and the fairness of the process protecting human rights. It has done so on the one hand by advocating the prosecution of incumbent state officials by unbiased international organs, like an *ad hoc* criminal court or the International Criminal Court,[155] and on the other hand by stating that immunity does not mean impunity, thus reaffirming the principle of universality and prompting national courts to carry it out, both in cases other than those involving incumbent high state officials and when the mandate of these officials has been terminated. The Court's approach is probably too advanced. In the present state of still uncertain functioning of international criminal institutions, this could thwart the activity of international courts[156] and, ultimately, the achievement of the objective of the international system: punishment of serious violations of human rights.

Another contribution to the protection of human rights, both from a regulatory/ substantive and a procedural standpoint, is the advisory opinion on the *Construction of a Wall*.[157] By using the 'quasi-legislative' powers implicit in the advisory function,[158] the Court has reinterpreted certain principles of humanitarian law and norms of the Geneva Conventions, stating the cogent nature of many of them and the *erga omnes* character of those obligations.[159] Further, by strengthening its advisory functions, it created a mechanism that can be used to safeguard human rights even when the Security Council is blocked. This process can be activated by the General Assembly, acting on the basis of the *Uniting for Peace* precedent (Resolution 377/V). With this opinion, the Court has reactivated the UN. It has asked the political organs of the Organization – the Security Council and the General Assembly – to address the situation of illegality created by Israel in the occupied territories and to 'consider what further action is required to bring to an end the illegal situation'.[160]

This is an historical and innovative opinion. However, it is also true that the Court could have done more for the protection of human rights in times of armed conflicts.[161]

---

155 Arrest Warrant, *supra* note 64, para. 61, at 22. See also ICC Article 27(2); ICTY Article 7(2), ICTR Article 6(2); and SCSL Article 6(2).

156 Antonio Cassese, *When May Senior State Officials Be Tried for International Crimes?*, 13 Eur. J. Int'l L. 853 (2002).

157 Construction of a Wall, *supra* note 22.

158 See *supra* note 93 and corresponding text.

159 Construction of a Wall, *supra* note 22, paras 104–113, 155–156. See in general M. Cherif Bassiouni, *Accountability for Violations of International Humanitarian Law and Other Serious Violations of Human Right*, 1 GCYILJ 3 (2001).

160 Construction of a Wall, *supra* note 22, paras 160, 163.E.

161 GA Res. 377 A (V) (Nov. 3, 1950). See *infra* chapter 8 of this book, under the heading 'Terrorist Acts Committed on behalf of "Peoples" '.

Judicial Protection of Peace Beyond the UN Charter

Functional parallelism: Court-Council. The Court's advisory function and provisional powers play an equally important role in the field of the maintenance of peace. Traditionally, the Court has been respectful of the constitutional principle enunciated in the *Nicaragua* case, whereby the Court and the Council have complementary but distinct functions in the field of maintenance of peace.[162] For example, in the *Hostages* case,[163] when indicating provisional measures, the Court embraced Resolution 457 (1979) with which the Council had demanded the immediate liberation of the hostages. The same happened in the *Bosnia-Herzegovina v. Yugoslavia* case, where the Court's incidental ruling strengthened the Council's actions.[164] In the first series of the 1999 *Armed Activities* cases, filed by the Republic of Congo against its neighbours,[165] the Court relied on the Council's Resolution 1034 of 16 June 2000, stating that the situation in Congo 'continues to constitute a threat to international peace and the security in the region',[166] to ascertain the 'urgency' of the situation (which is the requisite for the Court to be able to indicate provisional measures, under Article 41 of the Statute[167]). Further, the provisional measures eventually ordered both parties (Congo and Uganda) to refrain from armed actions, to conform to international obligations, and to comply with the Council's Resolution.[168] Finally, in the cases, *Use of Force*[169] and *Armed Activities (New*

---

162 United States Diplomatic and Consular Staff, *supra* note 99, para. 40, at 21–22; Military and Paramilitary Activities, *supra* note 16, para. 95, at 434–435; Application of the Convention on the Prevention and Punishment of the Crime of Genocide, *supra* note 128, para. 33, at 19; Armed Activities on the Territory of the Congo (Democratic Republic of the Congo v. Uganda), Provisional Measures, Order, 2000 ICJ Reports 111 (July 1, 2000), para. 36, at 126–127.

163 United States Diplomatic and Consular Staff in Tehran, *supra* note 136, para. 23, at 15.

164 See Resolution 819 (April 16, 1993), with which the Council acknowledges the provisional measures adopted by the Court in the 8 April 1993 decision, which the government of the Yugoslavian Republic 'should immediately take', and decides to dispatch a mission of its members to assess and report on the situation (32 Int'l Legal Mat. 931 (1993)).

165 Congo initially filed cases against Burundi, Rwanda, and Uganda in June 1999. The Court indicated provisional measures in the Uganda case on 1 July 2000 (Armed Activities (Congo v. Uganda), *supra* note 162); Congo discontinued proceedings against Burundi and Rwanda in January 2001 (Armed Activities on the Territory of the Congo (Democratic Republic of the Congo v. Burundi), Order, 2001 ICJ Reports 3 (Jan. 30, 2001); Armed Activities on the Territory of the Congo (Democratic Republic of the Congo v. Rwanda), Order, 2001 ICJ Reports 6 (Jan. 30, 2001)). See Shabtai Rosenne, *Introductory Note to the Activity of the ICJ in 1999–2001*, 2 GCYILJ 207 (2002–I).

166 Armed Activities (Congo v. Uganda), *supra* note 162, paras 44–45.

167 *Id.*, at para. 39; see also La Grand, *supra* note 73, paras 22–23.

168 *Id.*, at para. 47.

169 Cases Concerning Legality of Use of Force (Yugoslavia v. Spain), Request for the Indication of Provisional Measures, Order, 1999 ICJ Reports 761 (June 2, 1999); Cases Concerning Legality of Use of Force (Yugoslavia v. United States of America), Request for the Indication of Provisional Measures, Order, 1999 ICJ Reports 916 (June 2, 1999).

Application),[170] although the Court rejected the request for provisional measures due to 'a lack of jurisdiction' *prima facie*,[171] it reaffirmed its competence in the field of the maintenance of peace, by acknowledging the Council's main responsibility in the field[172] and by warning the parties against violating their obligations under international law, the UN Charter, and, above all, humanitarian law.[173] The most alert scholars have noticed the issuing of this warning.[174]

This practice suggests that there is an actual ongoing collaboration between the Court and the Council. However, there is always the concrete possibility of conflict between the decisions of the two organs whenever the Court is involved in situations under the scrutiny of the Council. For instance, the Court could be requested to indicate provisional measures that contradict the actions of the Council.[175] Thus, considering the binding nature of provisional measures of the Court, states violating resolutions to comply with provisional measures would not be in breach of international law.

In the *Lockerbie* case the two organs almost conflicted.[176] In fact, Libya's request for provisional measures to safeguard its rights under the Montreal Convention (that is to say, to not extradite Libyan citizens suspected of international terrorism to the authorities in the US and the UK) contrasted with the measures adopted by the Council with Resolution 731 (1992), which had 'recommended' the surrender of the alleged terrorists.[177] Had the Court exercised its provisional powers, it would

---

170 Case Concerning Armed Activities on the Territory of the Congo (New Application: 2002) (Democratic Republic of the Congo v. Rwanda), Request for the Indication of Provisional Measures, Order, (July 10, 2002).

171 Legality of Use of Force (Yugoslavia v. Spain), *supra* note 169, paras 33, 40; Legality of Use of Force (Yugoslavia v. United States of America), *supra* note 169, paras 25, 34; Armed Activities (New Application: 2002), *supra* note 170, paras 89, 94; in the former case the Court, concluding that it 'manifestly lacked jurisdiction', removed the case from the list. However, it did not do so in the latter case when it denied Rwanda's request.

172 Legality of Use of Force (Yugoslavia v. Spain), *supra* note 169, paras 17, 39; Legality of Use of Force (Yugoslavia v. United States of America), *supra* note 169, paras 17, 33; Armed Activities (New Application: 2002), *supra* note 170, para. 55.

173 Legality of Use of Force, *supra* note 169, para. 19; Armed Activities (New Application: 2002), *supra* note 170, paras 56, 93.

174 John R. Crook, *The 2002 Judicial Activity of the International Court of Justice*, 97 AM. J. INT'L. L. 352 (2003), at 357.

175 On several occasions the Court has been requested to indicate provisional measures in cases involving UN political organs. See, for instance, Anglo-Iranian Oil Co. case, Interim Protection, Order, 1951 ICJ REPORTS 89 (July 5, 1951); Aegean Sea Continental Shelf (Greece v. Turkey), Interim Protection, Order, 1976 ICJ REPORTS 3 (Sept. 11, 1976); United States Diplomatic and Consular Staff, *supra* note 136; Military and Paramilitary Activities in and Against Nicaragua (Nicaragua v. United States of America), Provisional Measures, Order, 1984 ICJ REPORTS 169 (May 10, 1984).

176 In the 14 April 1992 ruling relative to the *Lockerbie* case, the Court rejected the Libyan request to indicate provisional measures because such measures would have prejudiced the rights that Resolution 748 (March 31, 1992) seemed to have *prima facie* given to the US (Lockerbie (Libyan Arab Jamahiriya v. United States of America), *supra* note 131, paras 42, 44, at 126–127).

177 On this point see the individual opinion of Judge LACHS, 1992 ICJ REPORTS, at 138.

have interfered with the Council's powers in the field of peace and security. By the same token, the adoption of Resolution 748 (1992), which imposed the surrender of the alleged terrorists and was adopted by the Council while the Court was about to pronounce on the provisional measures, trampled the Court's powers by interfering with the exercise of its judicial functions.[178] Evidence of this is the fact that the Court justified the refusal to indicate provisional measures by stressing both the binding nature and primacy over the Montreal Convention of Resolution 748.[179] According to the Court, the Resolution had modified the legal situation. Once adopted, under Articles 25 and 103 of the Charter, the rights claimed by Libya under the Convention could not be regarded any longer 'as appropriate for protection'[180] because provisional measures would interfere with superior rights that Resolution 748 (1992) seemed, *prima facie*, to have granted to the US. This Resolution, which, in the interim phase was to be presupposed valid, would have nullified the rights claimed by Libya under the Convention.[181] The Court rejected the Libyan request by interpreting literally Article 41 of the Statute and by relying on its case law according to which the goal of provisional measures is to safeguard 'the respective rights of *each* party'.[182] By focusing on the conflict between norms, the Court eschewed the crucial question: '*si un organe peut agir de telle manière à rendre impossible la mission de l'autre*'.[183] Once again, the Court evaded the problem of the difficult issue of its relationship with the Council.

In domestic legal systems, the problems of concurrent jurisdiction are avoided by the application of several principles and norms. In the judicial context, the principle of litispendence carries out this function. Litispendence is the principle whereby simultaneous proceedings pertaining to the same matter are prevented by establishing that a question pending before one tribunal may not be brought before or decided by another tribunal. On the international level, this principle is also, in a way, applicable.[184] For instance, some sort of litispendence principle is incorporated in the Charter. Article 12 regulates the intersection of the competence of the principal

---

178 SC Res. 748, *supra* note 176. Resolution 748 is believed to be *ultra vires* because it conflicts with Art. 92 of the Charter. On this point, see the dissenting opinion of Judge El-Kosheri, *id.*, at 210. Judge Bedjaoui wrote about 'chevauchement d'attributions' because the Council addressed the question of extradition, an issue which was under consideration by the Court, *id.*, at 144 *et seq.*, 150 *et seq.*

179 *Lockerbie* (Libyan Arab Jamahiriya v. United Kingdom), *supra* note 131, paras 37, 39, at 14.

180 *Id.*, at para. 40, at 15.

181 See the dissenting opinion of Judge Bedjaoui, *id.*, at 156. On this point see also *supra* note 178.

182 See the individual opinion of Judge Shahabuddeen, *id.*, at 148.

183 See Bedjaoui, *supra* note 178, para. 25.

184 Dan Ciobanu, *Litispendence Between the International Court of Justice and the Political Organs of the United Nations*, *in* The Future of the International Court of Justice 209, 214 *et seq.*, 220 *et seq.* (Leo Gross ed., 1976); Karin Oellers–Frahm, *Multiplication of International Courts and Tribunals and Conflicting Jurisdiction,* 5 Max Planck Yearbook of United Nations Law 67 (2001); Yuval Shany, The Competing Jurisdictions of International Courts and Tribunals (2003).

political organs of the UN: General Assembly and Security Council. Yet, the Charter lacks a similar article on the relationship between the Council and the Court. Scholars talk about 'functional parallelism', meaning that both organs have the competence to deal with the same issues.[185] On the other hand, as we already pointed out,[186] the Court deems perfectly appropriate the simultaneous exercise of each organ's respective functions regarding the same issue. In the well-known *Certain Expenses* opinion,[187] the Court clarified that the expression 'principal responsibility' in Article 24 of the Charter does not mean the Council's exclusive responsibility. Moreover, it highlighted that there is no hierarchy between Court and Council. While Article 12 clearly forbids the General Assembly to make recommendations on disputes or situations under the scrutiny of the Security Council, similar restrictions do not apply to the Court.[188] In sum, according to the Court, '[t]he Council has functions of a political nature assigned to it, whereas the Court exercises purely judicial functions. Both organs can therefore perform their separate but complementary functions with respect to the same events'.[189]

Complementarity: Court-Council. Once it embraced the Council/Court functional parallelism, the Court enunciated the concept of complementarity. In the Court's view this is a relationship based on coordination and cooperation aimed at achieving the Organization's goals rather than competition and mutual exclusion.[190] Scholars point out that the Court/Council model creates a new complementarity notion, unlike domestic constitutional models, which are inspired by competition between institutions.[191] In an essay on the *Lockerbie* case, we touched upon several of the aspects of this complex issue. We expressed the hope that the Court could address the issue of possible conflicts between its own decisions and those of the Council and other constitutional organs from an institutional standpoint (i.e., considering the relationship between institutions) rather than use of a literal approach, as it did in that case.[192] The Court needs to clarify the concept of complementarity. It needs to make it clear whether the concept implies a full separation of the two organs' powers. If so, the activity of each would be 'separated',[193] albeit both would remain structurally

---

185 Rosenne, *supra* note 1, at 87.

186 See *supra* note 131.

187 Certain Expenses of the United Nations, *supra* note 24, at 163.

188 United States Diplomatic and Consular Staff, *supra* note 99, para. 40, at 21–22; Military and Paramilitary Activities, *supra* note 9, para. 93, at 433–434.

189 Military and Paramilitary Activities, *supra* note 9, para. 95, at 434–435.

190 In this sense, Judge Ni, 1992 ICJ Reports, at 134. Judge Lachs outlined that the Charter's drafters, when creating the main organs, 'did not effect a complete separation of powers, nor indeed is one to suppose that such was their aim'. He asserts that the system implies that the two organs (Court and Council) act in a 'fruitful interaction', so that neither of them impinges on the exercise of powers by the other organ (*id.*, at 139 *et seq.*).

191 See Edward MacWhinney, Judicial Settlement of International Disputes. Jurisdiction, Justiciability and Judicial Law-Making on the Contemporary International Court 142 *et seq.* (1991).

192 Ziccardi Capaldo, *Verticalità*, *supra* note 38, at 88–89.

193 Judge Ni, *supra* note 190.

necessary to the functioning of the organization and the achievement of its goals. Or, rather, whether it means that their respective activities overlap each other and that there is a duty to cooperate. It needs to specify the terms of such a duty obligation for the constitutional organs and to decree the limits on their discretion, keeping in mind they are applicable both in the case of the Council and the Court.

In the case of the Court, one needs to consider the impact of such an obligation on the question of the evaluation of the circumstances that must exist for provisional measures to be granted. If an obligation of cooperation with the Council exists, this could restrict the discretionary powers in this field that Article 41 of the Statute gives the Court. The Court could be obliged to refuse to 'indicate' requested measures or could be obliged to 'indicate' measures (even when not requested or different from the requested ones) to honour the duty to cooperate with other constitutional organs. In the Court's jurisprudence, the key to avoiding conflicts between the two organs during the provisional measures phase is the correct use of the discretionary powers granted by Article 41 of the Statute, which gives the Court competence to examine in the merits phase the validity of the Council's resolutions.[194] *Mutatis mutandis*, this approach recalls a distinction made by the Court on other occasions between competence and opportunity to exercise its functions.[195]

Overcoming veto rule of Art. 27 of the UN Charter. The issues raised by the Court/Council relationship are crucial. As far as the maintenance of peace is concerned, the widening of provisional powers is the harbinger of great developments, provided the Court consolidates them and uses them to overcome the Charter's deficiencies and supersede the veto of the permanent members. Since the Court, consistently with its case law, has reiterated its competence to adjudicate on matters of which the Council is seized,[196] nothing bars it from ascertaining violations of peace and acts of

194 See Lockerbie case (Libyan Arab Jamahiriya v. United Kingdom), *supra* note 131, para. 40, at 22–23. In the dispute between Greece and Turkey on the *Aegean Sea*, Greece requested the Court to indicate provisional measures to prevent the deterioration or the widening of the dispute. Yet, the Security Council, with Resolution 395 (Aug. 25, 1976), had already adopted these kinds of measures. Although the Court did not address the question of whether Art. 41 of the Statute confers on it the power to indicate such measures, it rejected the request because it held that the 'circumstances' in the specific case made it clear that the Security Council had already taken concrete steps (albeit mere recommendations, lacking binding power) to maintain peace and security and because the parties are bound to respect the Charter.

195 Both in the contentious and advisory proceedings the Court has ruled that, even when its competence is established, it might need to decline to exercise jurisdiction, from time to time, to remain true to its judicial functions. See, for instance, Certain Expenses of the United Nations, *supra* note 24, at 155; Northern Cameroons, *supra* note 23, at 29–30; Nuclear Tests (Australia v. France), *supra* note 8, paras 57–58, at 271; Nuclear Tests (New Zealand v. France), *supra* note 8, paras 60–61, at 477; Western Sahara, *supra* note 19, para. 23, at 21; Frontier Dispute (Burkina Faso/Republic of Mali), *supra* note 11, para. 45, at 577; Legality of the Threat or Use of Nuclear Weapons, *supra* note 104, para. 14, at 235; Immunity from Legal Process, *supra* note 60, para. 29, at 78–79.

196 Application of the Genocide Convention, *supra* note 128, para. 33, at 19; Armed Activities (New Application: 2002), *supra* note 170, para. 36.

aggression, and adopting provisional measures even when permanent UN members are threatening or violating the world's peace themselves. In fact, resolutions adopted under Chapter VII of the Charter fly in the face of the *nemo judex in re sua* principle which, according to Article 27 (3), applies only to issues under Chapter VI.[197] Only in the case of decisions taken under Chapter VI must members party to the controversy abstain from voting.[198]

In the *Use of Force* cases,[199] the Court rejected Yugoslavia's request for provisional measures to impose upon NATO members (US and Spain) the suspension of bombing and other military activities, because it deemed its own jurisdiction manifestly absent.[200] Be that as it may, it restated its responsibility in the maintenance of peace[201] and its competence to adjudicate on states' compliance with international law, thus sowing the seeds of future provisional pronunciations about activities violating fundamental international norms, even when committed by the Security Council's permanent members. This especially applies to violations of peace, in which permanent members are *de facto legibus soluti*, for the Council cannot condemn and sanction their unlawful behaviours because of their veto power.

To safeguard global fundamental values and peace, the Court strengthens its advisory functions: it has resorted to advisory opinions to ascertain violations of *erga omnes* obligations and to define their judicial consequences not only for the responsible state but also for all other states and UN organs. In the important opinion *Construction of a Wall*, once the illegality of the wall and the legal consequences deriving from it were assessed, the Court stressed the 'definitive' character of the ascertainment of Israel's responsibility[202] and demanded the UN organs to adopt all necessary measures to bring violations of international law to an end, 'taking due account' of its own conclusions.[203] In this specific case, the use of the advisory function to further fundamental values of the global community is evident, bypassing the veto of the permanent members. The request for an advisory opinion on the construction of the wall in the occupied Palestinian territory[204] had a double effect: it gave the Court the chance to ascertain Israel's international legal responsibility with effects *erga omnes*, and it made it possible for the General Assembly to adopt the coercive measures outlined in the opinion,[205] thus bypassing vetoes blocking the Security Council. This way, the Court's opinion strengthened the power of the Assembly.

The Court's ascertainment of violations of fundamental obligations by way of advisory opinions and its provisional activities to safeguard peace do not contradict one another but are rather complementary to the Council's activity pursuing

---

197 Charter of the United Nations, signed at San Francisco on 26 June 1945, entered into force on 24 October 1945.

198 Benedetto Conforti, Le Nazioni Unite 77 (2000).

199 See *supra* note 169.

200 See *supra* note 171.

201 See *supra* note 172.

202 Construction of a Wall, *supra* note 22, para. 147.

203 *Id.*, at paras 160, 163.E.

204 GA Res. ES–10/14 (Dec. 8, 2003).

205 See GA Res. A/ES–10/L.18/Rev.1 (July 20, 2004).

the Charter's objectives. They integrate the Charter and transcend it, filling the institutional loophole created by the voting system under Article 27 (3) on Chapter VII decisions.[206]

Weakness of Enforcement Remedies

The Court's forays into human rights and maintenance of peace fields create anticipation about new directions in which the Court might move. States increasingly turn to the Court for advice. The Court strengthens and widens its advisory and provisional functions[207] to address serious violations of humanitarian law and peace. The innovative position assumed by the Court in the *Construction of a Wall* opinion is part of this trend.[208] Consistent with the idea, repeatedly affirmed in principle, of the 'judicial character' of the advisory function,[209] the Court gave impetus to greater cooperation with UN political organs. It strongly urged them to give effect to its findings.[210] Heeding the call of international legal scholars, including our own,[211] the Court has finally acted on the idea that when exercising advisory functions it does not act as a mere expert body but rather as a judicial organ. As the Permanent Court did at the times of the Society of Nations, the Court has denied the downgrading of advisory functions to mere cooperation of the Court with the other organs of the Organization.[212]

As already mentioned,[213] the Court interpreted at length Article 41 of the Statute. It stated the binding nature of provisional measures[214] and expanded the ambit of procedural norms regulating the exercise of provisional powers under Article 41 of the Statute and Article 75 (1) of the Rules of Procedure, making their exercise independent from the will of the parties. For instance, the Court can indicate

---

206 On the creation of procedures to overcome the veto problem, see *infra* chapter 4, under the heading 'Overcoming the Ineffectiveness of Decision-Making Institutions; also chapter 8, under the heading 'Introduction'.

207 See *supra* the sections headed 'Judicial Protection of Human Rights ...' and 'Judicial Protection of Peace ...' earlier in this chapter.

208 See *supra* note 22.

209 Interpretation of Peace Treaties, *supra* note 19, at 71; Judgments of the Administrative Tribunal of the ILO upon Complaints Made against UNESCO, *supra* note 23, at 84; Constitution of the Maritime Safety Committee, *supra* note 23, at 153; Application for Review of Judgement No. 158, *supra* note 112, para. 24, at 175; Western Sahara, *supra* note 19, para. 23, at 21; paras 32–33, at 24 *et seq.*; paras 46–47, at 28 *et seq.*

210 Construction of a Wall, *supra* note 22, paras 160–161.

211 See Georges Scelle, *Règles Générales du Droit de la Paix*, 46 Recueil des Cours 331, 581 *et seq.* (1933–IV); Dharma Pratap, The Advisory Jurisdiction of the International Court 230–231 (1972); Michla Pomerance, The Advisory Function of the International Court in the League and UN Eras 379–380 (1973); Ziccardi Capaldo, *Il Parere Consultivo*, *supra* note 93, at 539 *et seq.*, 543 *et seq.*

212 See Judges Loder, Moore, and Anzilotti, in PCIJ, Series E, No. 4, at 72 *et seq.*, 75 *et seq.*

213 See *supra* note 145 and corresponding text.

214 LaGrand, *supra* note 76.

measures partly or totally different from those requested.[215] It can examine *motu proprio* whether the circumstances warrant provisional measures.[216] According to the interpretation of the Statute and the Rules given, in case of extreme urgency, it can also indicate provisional measures without holding oral hearings.[217]

The Court's provisional activity might seem to be lacking effectiveness, for effective remedies in case of non-compliance do not support it. In the *LaGrand* case, the Court stated that the part of the Charter's Article 94 (1), where it is said that the decisions of the Court are binding, applies to any decision it takes, thus also orders indicating provisional measures; on the other hand, by way of what looks like *obiter dicta*, it established that the Charter's Article 94 (2), refers 'only to judgments'.[218] It can therefore be gathered that the provision whereby '[i]f any party to a case fails to perform the obligations incumbent upon it under a judgment rendered by the Court, the other party may have recourse to the Security Council, which may, if it deems necessary, make recommendations or decide upon measures to be taken to give effect to the judgment'[219] applies only to judgments and not to provisional measures. Nowadays the Court participates more actively in the implementation of its own decisions, which can be held to be its prerogative,[220] and recently it demanded that the states, according to Article 78 of the Rules, keep it informed of the measures adopted to implement its rulings.[221] The Court can and must strengthen its powers of implementation and enforcement of its own decisions, and scholars have repeatedly called attention to the problem (i.e., silence of the Statute on the matter and lack of advanced procedures for judicial enforcement)[222] and have suggested possible solutions.[223]

---

215 Land and Maritime Boundary between Cameroon and Nigeria, Order, *supra* note 43, para. 41; Armed Activities (Congo v. Uganda), *supra* note 162, paras 44–45. The Court has claimed the power to indicate provisional measures to prevent the worsening or spreading of a dispute independently from any such request by the parties 'whenever it considers that circumstances so require' (Frontier Dispute (Burkina Faso/Republic of Mali), *supra* note 11, para. 18, at 9; Certain Criminal Proceedings in France (Republic of the Congo v. France), Request for the Indication of Provisional Measures, Order (June 17, 2003), para. 39).

216 LaGrand, *supra* note 73, para. 21, at 14; Armed Activities (Congo v. Uganda), *supra* note 162, para. 38.

217 LaGrand, *supra* note 73, para. 21, at 14.

218 LaGrand, *supra* note 76, para. 108.

219 United Nations Charter, *supra* note 197, Art. 94 (2).

220 Mutlaq Al-Qahtani, *The Role of the International Court of Justice in the Enforcement of Its Judicial Decisions*, 15 LJIL 781 (2002).

221 LaGrand, *supra* note 73, para. 29.

222 Robert Y. Jennings, *The Judicial Enforcement of International Obligations*, 47 Zeitschrift für Ausländisches Öffentliches Recht und Völkerrecht 3 (1987), at 15; Rosenne, *supra* note 1, at 219, 258.

223 William Michael Reisman, *Enforcement of International Judgments*, 63 Am. J. Int'l. L. 1 (1969) at 3–4; Jonathan I. Charney, *Disputes Implicating the International Credibility of the Court: Problems of Non-Appearance, Non-Participation, and Non-Performance*, *in* The International Court of Justice at the Crossroads, *supra* note 1, at 288, 305.

The ICJ as a Supreme Constitutional Court

Judicial Control Over the Acts of UN Political Organs

The Court exercises control over the legality of the UN organs' acts.[224] This seems to be a general trend of the Court's jurisprudence, but one that is neither supported by the Charter nor the Statute. In the advisory opinion on *South-West Africa*, despite recognizing that the Charter does not give it powers of judicial control or of appeal over the UN organs' decisions,[225] the Court examined nonetheless the validity of the relevant resolutions adopted by the General Assembly and the Security Council and pronounced on their legal consequences.[226] Consistently with its previous pronouncement in the advisory opinion on *Certain Expenses*,[227] the Court reaffirmed the presumption of validity of those resolutions.[228] On another occasion, the Court examined its own relationship with the General Assembly, stressing the difference between its role and that of the Assembly, and outlined the consequences arising from its possible pronunciation on the alleged illegality of the Assembly's resolutions in the specific case.[229]

Be that as it may, these are episodes. The trend is still unclear. The Court has generally eluded making its own pronouncements on the issue of the control over the legality of the Security Council's acts.[230] The question is still debated amongst

---

224 See mainly Thomas M. Franck, *The Powers of Appreciation: Who Is the Ultimate Guardian of UN Legality?*, 86 Am. J. Int'l. L. 519 (1992); Elihu Lauterpacht, *Judicial Review of the Acts of International Organisations*, *in* International Law, the International Court of Justice and Nuclear Weapons (Laurence Boisson de Chazournes ed., Cambridge University Press, Cambridge, 1999).

225 South West Africa, *supra* note 103, para. 89, at 45.

226 Judges Ammoun, Onyeama, Fitzmaurice, and Gros (*id.*, respectively at 72, 143, 226, 331) supported judicial review of the Council's decisions under Chapter VII. Also, the International Criminal Tribunal for the former Yugoslavia (ICTY) asserted competence to scrutinize the legality of the act by which the Security Council created the ICTY itself (*Prosecutor v. Duzko Tadic*, Case No. IT–94–1, Decision on the Defence Motion on Jurisdiction, Trial Chamber (Aug. 10, 1995), paras. 3–9, 12; *Prosecutor v. Duzko Tadic*, Case No. IT–94–1, Decision on the Defence Motion for Interlocutory Appeal on Jurisdiction, Appeals Chamber (Oct. 2, 1995), paras. 20–22).

227 Certain Expenses of the United Nations, *supra* note 24, at 168.

228 South West Africa, *supra* note 103, para. 20, at 22.

229 Northern Cameroons, *supra* note 23, at 33.

230 In the *Lockerbie* case (*supra* note 131, at 25 and 155) examination of this matter was deferred to the merits phase. On this point, see specifically Judges Bedjaoui and Ajibola (*id.*, at 156, 196, respectively). On this question, see, amongst scholars, Bernhard Graefrath, *Leave to the Court What Belongs to the Court. The Libyan Case*, 4 Eur. J. Int'l L. 184 (1993); Vera Gowlland-Debbas, *The Relationship Between the International Court of Justice and the Security Council in the Light of the* Lockerbie *Case*, 88 Am. J. Int'l. L. 643 (1994), at 667. Likewise, Bosnia-Herzegovina raised before the Court the question of the legality of SC Resolution 713 (Sept. 25, 1991), imposing an arms-trade embargo on and with the whole of Yugoslavia, thus violating Bosnia-Herzegovina's right of self-defence under Art. 51 of the Charter (Application of the Convention on the Prevention and Punishment of the

scholars.[231] We dwelt on the issue of the powers the Court attributed to itself and the powers it claims over UN organs because the consolidation of this trend has great impact on the safeguard of the global values. In previous writings on this point, we expressed the opinion, increasingly popular,[232] that both the Charter and general international law limit the Council's exercise of Chapter VII sanctionary powers. Specifically, these limits are: proportionality, necessity, and respect of *jus cogens*.[233]

The question of the power of the Court to review Chapter VII Council decisions, which contain not only a finding of a threat or violation of peace or an act of aggression, but also the finding of a specific violation by a specific state or non-state entity of a fundamental international legal obligation (i.e., violation of the principles of self-determination, non-use of force, democracy, human rights, humanitarian law) is still undetermined. The question was raised in the *Lockerbie* case,[234] where Council's Resolution 748, whose legality was disputed by Libya, determined the responsibility of that state by indicating it was the one responsible for the bombing of flights Pan Am 103 and UTA 772, thus in violation of Article 2 (4) of the Charter, and the general international law against terrorist acts.[235]

In this case, the crucial question is: can the Court scrutinize the legality of determinations of responsibility undertaken by the Council when acting under the Charter's Article 39? This Article does indeed give the Council full discretion in evaluating threats to peace. It is a political evaluation, and it can be subject to the scrutiny of the Court only when abused (i.e., excess of competence). But when the Council determines a state's legal responsibility, verifying that state's behaviour against fundamental norms of international law, it carries out a legal determination,

---

Crime of Genocide (Bosnia and Herzegovina v. Yugoslavia), Provisional Measures, Order, 1993 ICJ Reports 325 (Sept. 13, 1993), para. 2, and, in favour of a judicial review, see the individual opinion of Judge *ad hoc* Lauterpacht, in the Court's order of 13 September 1993, paras 99–104, at 439–441). Finally, the Court eschewed the question in the advisory opinion on the legality of the use of nuclear weapons (see *supra* note 104). See Marcelo G. Kohen, *L'Avis Consultatif de la CIJ sur la Liceité de la Menace ou de l'Emploi d'Armes Nucléaires et la Fonction Judiciaire*, 8 Eur. J. Int'l L. 337 (1997), at 357. In general, on this subject see Shabtai Rosenne, The World Court 37 (5th ed., 1995).

231 See, mainly, Franck, *supra* note 224; Edward MacWhinney, *The International Court as Constitutional Court and the Blurring of the Arbitral/Judicial Processes*, 6 LJIL 279 (1993); Geoffrey R. Watson, *Constitutionalism, Judicial Review, and the World Court*, 34 Harvard International Law Journal 1 (1993); Mohammed Bedjaoui, The New World Order and the Security Council (1994); Terry D. Gill, *Legal and Some Political Limitations on the Power of the UN Security Council To Exercise Its Enforcement Powers Under Chapter VII of the Charter*, 26 Netherlands Yearbook of International Law 33 (1995); Judith C. Gardam, *Legal Restraints on Security Council Military Enforcement Action*, 17 Michigan Journal of International Law 285 (1996); Josè E. Alvarez, *Judging the Security Council*, 90 Am. J. Int'l. L. 1 (1996).

232 Peter Malanczuk, *Reconsidering the Relationship Between the ICJ and the Security Council*, *in* International Law and The Hague's 75th Anniversary, *supra* note 1, at 87.

233 Ziccardi Capaldo, *Verticalità*, *supra* note 38, at 94.

234 *Id.* at 94–95.

235 SC Res. 748, *supra* note 176. See also *supra* under the heading 'Judicial Protection of Peace' earlier in this chapter.

not a political one. Such a determination, even when carried out by a political organ with different methods from those applied by the Court, is subject to control by the Court, the guardian of the system's legality. In these cases, the Court cannot resort to the concept of 'inherent limitations',[236] which it has used before to avoid stepping into political issues, even when its jurisdiction is established, to avoid compromising its judicial functions. The Court could agree with the Council on the question of the state's responsibility, which would reinforce the determination made by the political organ. However, should there be disagreement the Court/Council cooperation cannot be invoked, for they would both be acting beyond the ambit of their discretionary power. The powers of the Security Council are constrained by international law and the UN Charter, as mandated by the Charter's Articles 1 (1), and 24 (2). These limits to the Council's activity, and, at the same time, the Court's role as supreme judicial organ, are to be kept in mind while thinking about the Court's obligation to cooperate and give maximum effect to the UN political organs' decisions. In the exercise of its functions, the Court is independent from the other UN organs but, in any event, subject to the application of international law.[237]

Decisions Regarding Ultra Vires *Acts*

Scholars have paid insufficient attention to the question of the value of the Court's finding of illegality of UN organs' *ultra vires* acts. Although this is not the place to debate this issue, let us just outline some concerns that have been expressed in literature. First, the Court's control functions are limited by its incidental nature. Second, advisory opinions are not binding. Third, the Court's rulings are, in principle, binding only for the disputing parties and the particular case.[238] We dealt

236 See Northern Cameroons, *supra* note 23, at 29–31; South West Africa, Second Phase (Ethiopia v. South Africa; Liberia v. South Africa), Judgment, 1966 ICJ Reports 6 (July 18, 1966), para. 57, at 36; Nuclear Tests, *supra* note 8, para. 23, at 463; para. 23, at 259–260; Construction of a Wall, *supra* note 22, para. 41.

237 Judge Weeremantry has particularly stressed the need for the Court to preserve its independence. Citing the separate opinion of Judge Tarazi (1976 ICJ Reports, at 33) and the principles that he believes should inform the role of the Court, including the principle whereby '[t]he Court, if the circumstances so require, ought to collaborate in the accomplishment of this fundamental mission' (*that is*, maintenance of peace and security), he argued that '[t]he judge of the question whether the circumstances so require is surely the Court in the exercise of its independent judgment' (1992 ICJ Reports, at 168, 176).

238 On the legal effect of international organizations' *ultra vires* acts, see, in particular, Hersh Lauterpacht, *The Legal Effect of Illegal Acts of International Organizations*, *in* Cambridge Essays in International Law, Essays in Honour of Lord Mcnair 88 (Arnold Duncan McNair ed., 1965); Leo Gross, *The International Court of Justice and the United Nations*, 120 Recueil des Cours 313, 327 (1967–I); Ebere Osieke, *The Legal Validity of Ultra Vires Decisions of International Organizations*, 77 Am. J. Int'l. L. 239 (1983); Hubert Thierry, *Les Résolutions des Organes Internationaux dans la Jurisprudence de la Cour Internationale de Justice*, 167 Recueil des Cours 385, 414 *et seq.* (1980–II); Geoffrey R. Watson, *Constitutionalism, Judicial Review, and the World Court*, 34 Harvard International Law Journal 1 (1993) at 14 *et seq.*; Rudolf A. Bernhardt, *Ultra Vires Activities of International Organizations*, *in* Theory of International Law at the Threshold of the 21st Century. Essays in Honour of

with these issues in a previous study, where we argued that advisory opinions, which are judicial acts that authoritatively declare the law, while not binding *per se*, could have a 'definitive' character with *erga omnes* effects.[239] This means that the illegality (or legality) of actions or behaviours determined by the opinions is binding in any other judgment where it might arise, even incidentally.[240] The opinion, *Construction of a Wall*,[241] confirmed the definitive, general *erga omnes* value of the determination of responsibility contained in advisory opinions. The Court held that, because the construction of the wall violated Israel's international obligations, 'it follows that the responsibility of that state is engaged under international law'.[242] The definitive character of the opinion can be inferred by analogy from Article 60 of the Court's Statute and by the fact that advisory opinions are decisions made by a judicial organ in the exercise of a judicial function. Advisory opinions state the law and are neither binding for states nor are actionable.[243] However, the Court maintains that the lack of binding force does not transform its judicial activity into a merely consultative one. Being judicial acts, advisory opinions have a legitimizing effect: given that findings by the Court are supported by a presumption of correctness, we believe that states' behaviour violating political organs' resolutions regarded as unlawful by the Court in advisory proceedings ought to be considered lawful. This applies both to the recommendations and to the binding decisions of the Security Council.

As for the use of contentious proceedings to ascertain lawfulness of UN organs' actions, Article 59 of the Statute limits the binding effect of the Court's decision to the disputing parties. Nevertheless, the Court has claimed that, Article 59 of the Statute notwithstanding, its own pronouncements on the validity of a legal act 'may have implications in the relations between states other than [the Parties]'.[244] Referring to the Permanent Court's jurisprudence, it deemed 'indisputable' the right to pass 'in an appropriate case' a judgment holding 'a continuing applicability'.[245]

Krzysztof Skubiszewski 599 (Jerzy Makarczyk ed., 1996); Mary Ellen O'Connell, *Debating the Law of Sanctions*, 13 Eur. J. Int'l L. 63 (2002) at 64.

239 See Ziccardi Capaldo, *Il Parere Consultivo*, *supra* note 93, at 557.

240 *Id.*, at 562.

241 Construction of a Wall, *supra* note 22.

242 *Id.*, at para. 147. In the words of the Court: 'Since the Court has concluded that the construction of the wall ... and its associate régime are contrary to various of Israel's international obligations it follows that the responsibility of that state is engaged under international law'.

243 When rendering advisory opinions, the Court does not demand states to carry out specific acts. It simply states the law and the norms applicable in a determinate situation, and the rights and duties arising therefrom.

244 Aegean Sea Continental Shelf, *supra* note 16, para. 39, at 16–17. In that case, the Court had to determine whether the 1928 General Act for the Peaceful Settlement of Disputes was still in force and what its legal status was.

245 Northern Cameroons, *supra* note 23, at 37. The declaratory character of judgments of the Court about the legality or illegality of acts is also evidenced by the advisory opinion on *Reservations to the Genocide Convention.* In that opinion the Court declared that its eventual finding of incompatibility of a given reservation with the object and aim of a treaty would imply the exclusion of the state making the given reservation from the Convention. This means that the Court's findings in advisory proceedings do transcend the mere relationship

Such a judgment is 'to ensure recognition of a situation at law, once and for all ... so that the legal position thus established cannot again be called in question in so far as the legal effects ensuing therefrom are concerned'.[246] It thus seems that the Court's pronouncement on the legal validity of the UN organs' resolutions has the character of a declaratory judgment[247] and *mutatis mutandis*, in the Court's words, 'that the Court make a declaration ... which would clarify the legal situation for the entire international community'.[248] Therefore it must be accorded an effect going beyond that of the disputing parties. Of course, a judgment declaring 'illegal' a Security Council's decision does not nullify the decision;[249] nonetheless, the declaration of illegality is opposable to all states. Besides, consistently with the duty of cooperation between UN organs, the Court's decision should induce the political organ to re-evaluate the unlawful act.

Concluding Remarks: The Road Ahead for the ICJ Towards the Legitimacy of Global Governance

During the past thirty years, the judicial policy of the Court has significantly evolved. Currently, the Court is fully aware of its new role in the global community. It addresses the urgent needs of verticalization of the international system[250] and contributes to the building of a coherent legal system for a universal human society.

As the foregoing evidenced, the ICJ's global trends stem from the need to compensate for the structural deficiencies of the international system and the UN Charter, which are incapable of satisfactorily answering the challenges arising

---

between the state making the reservation and the states objecting to it in the specific case (Reservations to the Convention on Genocide, *supra* note 8, at 26–27).

246 Interpretation of Judgments Nos 7 and 8 (Factory at Chorzów), *supra* note 29, at 20; Northern Cameroons, *supra* note 23, at 37.

247 Bosnia-Herzegovina tried to obtain a similar ruling in the case against the Republic of Yugoslavia (Serbia and Montenegro) about the Genocide Convention. Bosnia argued that the arms-trade embargo decided by the Security Council with Resolution 713 (*supra* note 230), by including Bosnia, was denying it the possibility to exercise its 'natural law' right of self-defence, guaranteed by Art. 51 of the Charter. The Court denied the request, remarking that the applicant's aim was not so much to safeguard its own rights but rather to obtain a declaratory judgment. The Court believed that such a request transcended the limits set by Art. 41 of the Statute. However, it did not rule out the possibility that the request by Bosnia could be satisfied in the merits phase. See Application of the Genocide Convention, *supra* note 128, para. 41, at 345.

248 *Id.*, para. 40, at 345.

249 Constitution of the Maritime Safety Committee, *supra* note 23, at 171. See Lauterpacht, *supra* note 238, at 104 *et seq.*; Osieke, *supra* note 238, at 244. On the voidness *ab initio* caused by the violation of a norm of *jus cogens*, see the individual opinion of Judge Lauterpacht, *in* 1993 ICJ Reports 441. On the voidness of acts in international law, see, in general, Paul Guggenheim, Traité de Droit International Public 181, 184 (2nd ed., 1967); Jean Paul Jacqué, *Acte et Norme en Droit International Public*, 227 Recueil des Cours 357 (1991–II).

250 See *supra* the second section of this chapter.

from and the needs of globalization. These trends are an answer to the need to centralize the management of fundamental global values, subtracting it from states and the UN collective security system based on veto-power: the aim is to ensure international legality by creating a supreme judicial forum that can interpret and guide the development of international law and that can monitor the respect of global constitutional principles both by domestic and international organs. By going beyond the Charter and the Statute, the Court is becoming a global Court, widening its functions and powers. It is involved in the protection of human rights and the maintenance of peace. It asserts its power of judicial control over the UN political organs, standing as the 'ultimate guardian'[251] of the constitutive principles of the emerging international global community.[252] The task of the Court to the evolving needs of the global community is, thus, twofold: it increases the verticalization of both the regulatory/normative and the operative functions of the international system.

The Court leads the development of international law and contributes to the protection of the fundamental principles of the emerging global community and strengthens their judicial functions/powers. It expands the scope of its advisory function and powers on provisional measures under Article 41 of the Statute. By decoupling powers on provisional measures from the will of the parties,[253] and by stating the binding force of such measures,[254] the Court has given itself an extraordinary tool to safeguard human rights and international peace.

The Court strives to protect human life by using provisional measures. It completes the institutional international system for safeguarding human rights and tries attempts to address two fundamental weaknesses: the facultative and non-binding nature of interim measures under the Optional Protocol to the International Covenant on Civil and Political Rights, and the regional nature of the European and Inter-American human rights systems.[255]

The Court affirms its 'responsibility' in the field of the maintenance of international peace and security, as well. The establishment of the binding character of interim measures and the strengthening of advisory powers open new ways to the future exercise of interim and advisory powers for the protection of human rights and the maintenance of peace, even when the collective security system under Chapter VII of the Charter is paralysed by veto and the Security Council is unable to determine the existence of a threat or violation of international peace and security and to take measures against the responsible state.[256]

The rocky journey of the Court towards the protection of the principles of the universal legal order has started. It is clear that Article 41 of the Statute has limits.

---

251 The quote is from Franck, *supra* note 224; see also the authors cited *supra* notes 230–233.

252 See *supra* the third section of this chapter.

253 See *supra* notes 214–215 and corresponding text.

254 See *supra* note 145.

255 See *supra* note 134 and corresponding text.

256 See *supra* in this chapter under the heading 'Overcoming Veto Rule of Art. 27 of the UN Charter'.

Provisional measures are often disregarded and their implementation is difficult to monitor. Besides, individuals cannot request them, only states can do so, and this is a large limitation when it comes to human rights. A possible improvement could be the strengthening of remedies against violations of decisions in contentious proceedings. 'Guarantees of non-repetition' are to be welcomed. The Court should also heed, in the merits phase, requests to recover damages caused by the use of force.[257]

The Court leads the reorganization of international power. It consolidates its authority over the state's organs and international institutions.

It affirms its competence to review acts of domestic organs, not only executive, but also legislative and judicial organs, and their consistency with international law, and issues specific orders directly to them.[258] In the dispositive part of certain judgments, it included generic provisional measures ordering the parties to 'refrain from [...] any armed action',[259] to respect international law and the obligations arising under the Charter, and to ensure respect of human rights and humanitarian law. Even outside the strict framework of the measures, the Court makes a separate general statement appealing to states party to the dispute[260] that violations of international law carried out by their organs entails international responsibility of the states themselves.

At the global level, by strengthening its institutional role and armed with its 'intrinsic authority', the Court has placed itself at the apex of the international judicial system, as supreme interpreter of international law.

It cooperates with the political organs of the UN to the building of the universal constitutional system. It declares its responsibility in areas such as peace and security and human rights, over which the Charter gives competence to the General Assembly and the Security Council. It is inspired by the principle of cooperation and, despite the silence of the Charter, it claims a power of control on the acts of these organs. After all, the power of judicial control on the legality of decisions of political organs is typical of domestic constitutions and is on the rise.[261]

The needs of certainty and rule of law,[262] and of the emerging organized structure of the global society, demand that the judicial supremacy claimed by the Court over the political organs is formally defined. Procedures for states and organs to raise issues of international constitutionality need to be fixed, as well as time limits for

---

257 The Court did not follow up on Cameroon's request to award on damages caused by the occupation by Bakassi on behalf of Nigeria. It held the evacuation order imparted to Nigeria a sufficient remedy for the 'injury suffered by Cameroon by reason of the occupation of its territory' (Land and Maritime Boundary between Cameroon and Nigeria, Judgment, *supra* note 43, para. 319).

258 See *supra* notes 77–78 and corresponding text.

259 Armed Activities (Congo v. Uganda), *supra* note 162, para. 47.

260 See *supra* notes 173–174 and corresponding text.

261 Erika De Wet, *Judicial Review as an Emerging General Principle of Law and Its Implications for the International Court of Justice*, 47 Neth. Int'l L. Rev. 181 (2000).

262 See Graefrath, *supra* note 230, especially at 199 *et seq.*; Louis B. Sohn, *How New Is the New International Legal Order*, 21 Denver Journal of International Law & Policy 205 (1992).

judicial review.[263] Finally, the Court needs to be conferred powers *erga omnes*. Until the day these reforms are enacted, the 'final' character of advisory opinions,[264] and the legitimacy effect arising therefrom,[265] are definitively assets; so is the power of the Court to adjudicate on the legality of acts of political organs, with declaratory effects that can go beyond the parties to the dispute.[266]

The formalization of the Court's power to review the acts of the Security Council, invoked by many scholars,[267] is the keystone of the new system of organization of world power. The ongoing integration between the community of states and the UN hinges on the balancing of powers between UN organs, and of UN organs *vis-à-vis* the Security Council. If an organized global society is to be built, checks and balances need to be applied to the Security Council, which is tantamount to subjecting the power of superpowers to controls and restrictions. Their powers need to be limited if such an organized universal society is ever to be built.[268]

This is what the ICJ did in the above-mentioned opinion, *Construction of a Wall*.[269] The Court was seized of the matter by the General Assembly[270] while the Security Council was 'unable to make a decision',[271] and it used the landmark and unorthodox procedure created by the *Uniting for Peace* resolution.[272] In the opinion, the Court restated its power of control over the legality of acts of UN organs by examining the powers of the General Assembly in the field of the maintenance of peace and security. It extended the powers of the General Assembly by resorting to

---

263 Christopher Greenwood, *The Impact of Decisions and Resolutions of the Security Council on the International Court of Justice*, *in* International Law and The Hague's 75th Anniversary, *supra* note 1, at 81, 86.

264 See *supra* the subsection earlier in this chapter headed 'Decisions Regarding *Ultra Vires* Acts', in particular, note 239 and corresponding text.

265 See *supra* the introduction to this chapter.

266 See *supra* notes 247–249 and corresponding text.

267 See, amongst others, the solution proposed by Sohn, *supra* note 262.

268 This explains why whenever attempts are made to constrain great powers by introducing controls of legitimacy of Security Council decisions, great powers answer by turning down proposals to enlarge powers of the Court. Had the proposal of the Secretary-General to enlarge access to the Court been adopted, this would have probably resulted in a reduction of the powers of the permanent members (see *An Agenda For Peace: Preventive Diplomacy, Peacemaking and Peace-Keeping. Report of the Secretary-General*, UN SCOR, 47th Sess., UN Doc. S/24111 (June 17, 1992) [hereinafter *An Agenda For Peace*], chap. III and IV). On this proposal, see Stephen M. Schwebel, *Authorizing the Secretary-General of the United Nations to Request Advisory Opinions of the International Court of Justice*, *in* Essays in International Law in Honour of Judge Manfred Lachs 519 (Jerzy Makarczyk ed., 1984); Francisco Orrego Viçuna, *The Settlement of Disputes and Conflict Resolution in the Context of a Revitalized Role for the United Nations Security Council*, *in* Dupuy, Le Développement, *supra* note 5, at 41, in particular, at 44–45.

269 See *supra* note 22.

270 See *supra* note 204.

271 Construction of a Wall, *supra* note 22, para. 31. See *supra* the subsection headed 'Overcoming Veto Rule of Art. 27 of the UN Charter' in this chapter and note 256 with corresponding text.

272 See *supra* note 161.

an evolutionary interpretation, in the light of the Assembly's practice, of the relevant Articles of the Charter (i.e., Articles 12 and 14).[273] It endorses judicially the practice of the General Assembly of taking over functions in the field of the maintenance of peace and security when the Security Council is unable to decide because of the veto of one of its permanent members. By so doing, it strikes a balance between the powers of the two organs. By determining the admissibility of the request for the advisory opinion and the regularity of the meeting of the General Assembly where the request was adopted, the Court did not fail to specify the conditions under which the *Uniting for Peace* procedure can be resorted to.[274]

The increasing scrutiny by the Court of the acts of the General Assembly and the Security Council provide a solid basis for the legitimacy of global governance; it is particularly momentous in the current transitional phase from a system where international power is parcelled out between states to a system where decision-making power is being concentrated in international organs. It takes place at a time when the General Assembly is widening its normative powers in several fields touching upon fundamental interests of the global community, and when the Security Council is increasingly acting as the decision-making authority of those interests.[275] In both organs, states' influence is still overwhelming (quantitatively in the former and, because of the weight of some states, in the case of the latter).[276] *Mutatis mutandis*, this change for legitimacy of global governance is as weighty as the one that, according to Hans Kelsen, took place in constitutional monarchies when courts asserted a power of judicial control over legislation and administration, the two powers of government over which the monarch still had influence.[277]

---

273 See *supra* note 161.

274 *Id.*, at para. 30.

275 See recently, Cora True-Fros, *The UN Security Council Marks Seventh Anniversary of Resolution 1325 on Women, Peace and Security with Open Debate*, ASIL Insight (Dec. 17, 2007), Volume 11, Issue 29.

276 Certain ideas contained in the famous report of the UN Secretary-General of 17 June 1992 point in this direction. This is the case of both actions to restore international peace and the creation of a permanent army of the UN, to whom such actions should be entrusted to lessen the determinant role played by superpowers in this field. It is also the case of the proposal to allow the Secretary-General to request from the Court advisory opinions under Art. 96 (2) of the Charter (see *An Agenda for Peace*, *supra* note 268).

277 Hans Kelsen, General Theory of Law and State (1999).

PART II
Legality Principles and Common Global Values

Chapter 4

Legality Versus Effectivity in the Global Legal System*

Introduction

During the intervention in Iraq of 2003, the US and UK invoked two legal bases for their action: Article 51 of the UN Charter and the illegitimacy of Saddam Hussein's government due to gross violations of human rights, support of terrorism, and alleged possession of weapons of mass destruction, which had been used against the Kurds in the 1980s. In fact, these violations of international law had already been ascertained and reaffirmed by the UN Security Council with Resolution 1441.[1] Ultimately, the US and the coalition that offered direct and indirect support intervened in Iraq on the platform of safeguarding the values of democracy in the world and allowing the Iraqi people to establish democracy in their own country.

The military intervention has been harshly criticized by many governments, by most of the world's public opinion, and by scholars,[2] not only because it lacks authorization by the UN, but also because it violated the sovereignty of Iraq and the effectivity of its government. Does international law allow one state, or a coalition of states, to intervene in defence of a people victimized by a murderous government which is disrespectful of human rights and democracy? Is this unlawful meddling with the internal affairs of such a country? Is the removal of a dictator a legitimate measure to sanction the violation of the principle of democracy? Can this be done unilaterally and with the use of force? To answer these questions one must first analyse the scope of the classical principle of effectivity. This also implies determining to what degree this principle has been eroded by the onset of another principle, that of legality. Indeed, the dawning of the principle of legality is the hallmark of the transition from a community of states to a global community, where the sovereignty of a state is limited in favour of the safeguard of fundamental human rights. Answering those questions also requires verifying to what extent the principle of democracy has taken roots in contemporary international law, what its actual

---

* This chapter is based on the paper by Giuliana Ziccardi Capaldo, *Legality vs. Effectivity in the Global Community: The Overthrowing of Saddam Hussein,* 3 The Global Community. Yearbook of International Law and Jurisprudence [hereinafter GCYILJ] 107 (2003–I). That early text has been updated and modified. The changes to international law I detail therein have been summarized in Tables 1 and 2.

1 SC Res. 1441 (Nov. 8, 2002), preamble, para. 1.

2 See generally *Agora: Future Implications of the Iraq Conflict*, 97 American Journal of International Law 553 (2003) [hereinafter *Agora*].

scope is, and whether, by bestowing the right of self-determination in an 'internal' sense, it has ultimately overtaken the effectivity of sovereignty.

These questions concern the very structure of contemporary international law and its evolution towards becoming the law of a universal community. The creation of a global community posits both the gradual erosion of the principle of effectivity and increasing limitations to sovereignty of individual states. We are currently facing a transition from the classical inter-state community, egalitarian and unorganized, to a global community, which is concerned with the protection of the individual and mankind, and which focuses on human rights. This particular juncture makes it necessary to question the relationship between the principles of effectivity and legality. How can these two principles coexist? What protection can the emerging principle of legality provide to the subjects of sovereign states as opposed to the effectivity of their governments? Which measures can be internationally taken to shield defenceless people (and all the people in the world, for that matter) from the barbarity of some governments? Which decision processes are to be followed internationally in the implementation of the principle of democracy? This chapter will address these questions. It is organized in five paragraphs which will examine, respectively:

1. The justifications for the intervention in Iraq and whether they fit the framework of Article 51 of the Charter. Either the intervention is construed as an act of self-defence by the US or as an Anglo-American intervention to safeguard international legality and democracy;
2. The notion of democracy in the global community's legal system and its impact on the principle of sovereignty:
    - the relationship between legality and effectivity in contemporary international law;
    - the sanctions that can be lawfully imposed on a murderous dictatorship; in particular, whether international law allows the overthrowing of a government in the name of international legality;
3. The coercive implementation of the principle of international legality: the present multilateral decision processes co-managed by states and UN organs and international organizations to safeguard democracy;
4. The peculiar role played by the UN in the Iraqi situation, that is to say the question of whether Security Council Resolution 1472 (2003) modified the role of the UN by shifting the participation in the integrated decision-making process attributed respectively to intervening states and institutions;
5. The recognition by the UN of the temporary government of the 'occupying power': does the principle of effectivity make a resurgence on the principle of legality?

The Question of International Legality in the Overthrow of Saddam Hussein: The Legal Basis for Allied Intervention in Iraq

The Iraqi conflict raises thorny issues, such as how the Anglo-American intervention should be qualified. Besides Article 51 of the Charter, the US invoked the need to safeguard democracy and the necessity to oust a dictator, responsible for major violations of human rights, allegedly possessing weapons of mass destruction, and supporting international terrorism. Can the intervention be justified under Article 51 and be qualified as the exercise of the right to self-defence by the US and its allies in response to the September 11 attacks and/or feared future attacks or is it rather a social action pursued by states to protect common interests and values in response to the violation of international law?

Self-Defence

In order to consider the intervention as a legitimate implementation of the right of self-defence, sanctioned by Article 51 of the UN Charter, it is necessary to ask whether being targeted by a terrorist attack is enough to trigger the exercise of that right. The issue was already raised in the 1980s, when the US and Israel invoked the right to self-defence to justify military responses to certain terrorist attacks. In 1986, the US attacked Libya (bombing of Tripoli and Benghazi). Israel invaded Lebanon in 1978 and bombed Palestine Liberation Organization (PLO) offices in Tunisia in 1985 and 1988. These attacks were all condemned by the UN, and by most countries. In those instances, the international community denied that Article 51 could justify the use of force against those countries that had offered logistical and financial aids to the terrorists who carried out the attacks.[3]

In 1986, the International Court of Justice corroborated this view in its judgment on *Military and Paramilitary Activities in and against Nicaragua*. In an *obiter dictum*, the Court clarified the concept of 'armed attack' according to customary international law: by quoting the General Assembly's Declaration of Principles on Aggression,[4] it stated that 'in customary law, the prohibition of armed attacks may apply to the sending by a state of armed bands to the territory of another state …'.[5] Moreover, the Court declared inconsistent with international law the idea 'that the concept of "armed attack" includes not only acts by armed bands where such acts

3 See, in particular, the following resolutions: SC Res. 425 (March 19, 1978); SC Res. 573 (Oct. 4, 1985); SC Res. 611 (April 25, 1988); GA Res. 41/38 (Nov. 20, 1986). For further discussion of the issue, see, Giuliana Ziccardi Capaldo, Terrorismo Internazionale e Garanzie Collettive/International Terrorism and Collective Guarantees 40–45, 55–56, 111–113 (1990).

4 GA Res. 3314 (XXIX) (Dec. 14, 1974), Art. 3 (g).

5 Military and Paramilitary Activities in and Against Nicaragua (Nicaragua v. United States of America), Merits, Judgment, 1986 ICJ Reports 14 (June 27, 1986), para. 195, at 103–104. See also Giuliana Ziccardi Capaldo, Repertory of Decisions of the International Court of Justice/Répertoire de la Jurisprudence de la Cour internationale de Justice (1947–1992), 2 vols, (1995) [hereinafter Repertory], vol. I, Nos 1048, 1589, at 47, 621, respectively.

occur on a significant scale but also assistance to rebels in the form of the provision of weapons or logistical or other support'.[6] The Court pointed out 'gravity' (i.e., its significant scale) as the determining factor in qualifying the acts as an 'armed attack'.

Resolution 1368, which was adopted in the wake of the September 11 attacks, upheld this view by recognizing the right sanctioned by the UN Charter to individual and collective self-defence.[7] Evidently, the Security Council recognized that the attacks carried out against the US that day were profoundly different in nature from those that occurred hitherto and, because of this and their scale and effects, they could be qualified as 'armed attack'. Clearly, the gravity of that terrorist attack led the Security Council to hold legitimate the exercise of the inherent right of the US to self-defence.

In the *Nicaragua* case, while ascertaining customary international law, the ICJ held also that for an act to be qualified as 'armed attack', and thus to justify the exercise of the right of self-defence, hostile forces must be sent by a state, or be susceptible of being qualified as agents of the sending state. Moreover, the attack must be such as to require an 'immediate, irresistible'[8] response, which leaves no choice of means and no time for a decision. This particular requisite reveals that there must be a temporal causality link between offence and reaction for response to be lawful.

The question of whether the American intervention in Afghanistan, launched on 7 October 2001, was a lawful implementation of the principle of self-defence has been raised in an ample doctrinal dispute.[9] To summarize, it has been objected that self-defence implies an immediate reaction, that Al Qaeda is not a state, that the

---

6 *Id.*

7 SC Res. 1368 (Sept. 12, 2001); SC Res. 1373 (Sept. 28, 2001), the latter was reaffirmed in SC Res. 1440 (Oct. 24, 2002); SC Res. 1450 (Dec. 13, 2002); SC Res. 1452 (Dec. 20, 2002); and SC Res. 1465 (Feb. 13, 2003). On the question of a terrorist attack as an 'armed attack', see *supra* chapter 2 of this book, under the heading 'States Acting in the Common Interest and Institutional Control', also chapter 7 under the heading 'The Requirement that an "Armed Attack" be Attributable to a State'; Sean D. Murphy, *Terrorism and the Concept of 'Armed Attack' in Article 51 of the U.N. Charter*, 43 HARVARD INTERNATIONAL LAW JOURNAL 41 (2002); Carsten Stahn, *Terrorist Acts as 'Armed Attack'*, 27 THE FLETCHER FORUM OF WORLD AFFAIRS 35 (2003); Karl Matthias Meessen, *Unilateral Recourse to Military Force against Terrorist Attacks*, 28 THE YALE JOURNAL OF INTERNATIONAL LAW 341 (2003).

8 American Secretary of State Daniel Webster in the dispute between US and UK on the *S.S. Caroline* case. On this: Fausto Pocar, *Uso della Forza in Risposta agli Eventi dell'11 Settembre e Legittima Difesa*, DIRITTI DELL'UOMO. CRONACHE E BATTAGLIE 55 (2001). See also the authors quoted *infra* note 9.

9 See especially William Michael Reisman, *In Defense of World Public Order*, 95 AMERICAN JOURNAL OF INTERNATIONAL LAW [hereinafter AM. J. INT'L L.] 833 (2001); Jonathan Charney, *The Use of Force Against Terrorism and International Law*, *id.*, at 835; Thomas M. Franck, *Terrorism and the Right of Self-Defence*, *id.*, at 839. See also Karl Zemanek, *Self-Defence against Terrorism, Reflexions on An Unprecedented Situation*, *in* EL DERECHO INTERNACIONAL EN LOS ALBORES DEL SIGLO XXI: HOMENAJE AL PROFESSOR JUAN MANUEL CASTRO–RIAL CANOSA 695 (Fernando M. Mariño Menendez ed., 2002); John C. Yoo, *International Law and the War in Iraq*, 97 AM. J. INT'L L. 563 (2003); Jordan J. Paust, *Use of Armed Force*

Taliban had not carried out the September 11 attacks themselves, and that no sure proof of the link between them and the terrorists was ever provided. It will be only noted that, on the occasion of the intervention in Afghanistan, NATO thoroughly assessed the intelligence collected by the US about the involvement of Osama Bin Laden's terrorist organization, Al Qaeda, in the attacks and the link between this latter organization and the Taliban. The links between Bin Laden and the Taliban were well known within the UN. In previous resolutions, the Security Council had taken note of them and repeatedly condemned 'the Afghan faction known as the Taliban, which also calls itself the Islamic Emirate of Afghanistan', for the support given to Al Qaeda terrorists, for the protection granted to their leader, Osama Bin Laden, and for the use of the Afghani territory 'for the sheltering and training of terrorists and planning of terrorist acts'.[10] The Taliban controlled most of the Afghani territory, and thus was the effective government of the country. Al Qaeda operated in Afghanistan with the blessing and support of the Taliban, and thus the Taliban and the Islamic Emirate of Afghanistan could be considered as the instigators of the September 11 attacks. After the Security Council reiterated economic and diplomatic sanctions, an immediate armed response was the only possible action to thwart the terrorist threat.[11]

By and large, the intervention in Afghanistan has been considered by states and international organizations as self-defence. Such was the opinion of NATO, which considered the events of September 11 'an armed attack', invoked the application of Article 5 of the Washington Treaty and gave support to the US military operations against Al Qaeda and the supporting Taliban regime.[12] Most UN member states have supported the American intervention in Afghanistan. Lack of explicit authorization by the Security Council is not really at issue, since the intervention is clearly an enforcement of Article 51 of the Charter. Indeed, to exercise the right of self-defence there is no need for an authorization by the Security Council, which only needs to

---

Against Terrorists in Afghanistan, Iraq, and Beyond, 35 Cornell International Law Journal 533 (2002).

10 SC Res. 1267 (Oct. 15, 1999), preamble. After determining the Taliban's responsibility, the Council imposed sanctions to halt the repeated violations of consolidated rules of international law, according to Chapt. VII (*id.*; see also SC Res. 1333 (Dec. 19, 2000); SC Res. 1363 (July 30, 2001); SC Res. 1367 (Sept. 10, 2001)).

11 Bin Laden was in the US crosshairs well before September 11. Already in 1999, the UN had asked the Taliban to surrender Bin Laden, against whom an arrest warrant had already been issued by the US as the person responsible for the attacks against the US embassies in Kenya and Tanzania (SC Res. 1267, *supra* note 10, para. 2).

12 NATO, North Atlantic Council, Invocation of Article 5 confirmed (Oct. 2, 2001) (available at <http://www.nato.int/docu/update/2001/1001/e1002a.htm>); Statement to the Press by NATO Secretary General Lord Robertson on the North Atlantic Council Decision on Implementation of Article 5 of the Washington Treaty following the 11 September Attacks against the United States (Oct. 4, 2001) (available at <http://www.nato.int/docu/speech/2001/s011004b.htm>); NATO's Response to Terrorism, Statement issued at the Ministerial Meeting of the North Atlantic Council (Dec. 6, 2001), para. 3 (available at <http://www.nato.int/docu/pr/2001/p01–158e.htm>).

be informed immediately of the actions undertaken.[13] Only in the case the Council should decide to take measures to protect peace and security, then the actions taken in self-defence should be suspended.

This point should be stressed because some have claimed that the right to self-defence of the US was superseded by the measures adopted by the Security Council, under Chapter VII, by Resolution 1373, of 28 September 2001.[14] Professor Michael Reisman is right in qualifying the September 11 attack as an aggression against the US and, at the same time, against the 'values of a system of world public order'.[15] Indeed, in Resolution 1373, the individual and the social action coexist. That Resolution, as the one adopted on September 12,[16] while reinforcing the inherent right of the US to self-defence, at the same time established the existence of a major threat to the world's peace, which was tackled by way of sanctions. When, after the adoption of Resolution 1373, the US and the UK informed the Council of the military action carried out in Afghanistan, performed according to Article 51, no objection was raised.[17]

Conversely, the intervention in Iraq was condemned by many states, which considered it unlawful, because it lacked the authorization of the Security Council. The fact that such authorization was considered necessary by many states, international organizations, and the world's public opinion, makes it apparent that the Anglo-American intervention was not considered to be an expression of the inherent right to self-defence according to Article 51 of the UN Charter. Its legal basis must be sought somewhere else.

The Safeguard of Democracy

Although US officials invoked Article 51 as a justification for the intervention in Iraq, they actually fell short of using the September 11 events as a justification. While presenting evidence of the alleged liaison between Saddam Hussein and Al Qaeda, US representatives illustrated how his regime constituted a *present* and *future* threat to democracy, both for the Iraqi people and all mankind,[18] rather than actually proving its involvement in the September 11 plot. At the eve of the intervention in Iraq, when addressing the Security Council about why the ousting of Saddam Hussein by military force was needed, the US Secretary of State, Colin Powell, did not characterize the threatened intervention as a reprisal against the September 11 attacks but rather as an action needed to ward off a present and future menace.

---

13 Franck is substantially in agreement with this point. See Franck, *supra* note 9.

14 SC Res. 1373, *supra* note 7, paras 1–2.

15 Reisman, *supra* note 9.

16 SC Res. 1368, *supra* note 7.

17 See Letters of the Permanent representatives of the US and the UK to the President of the Security Council dated 7 October 2001 (UN Docs. S/2001/946 and S/2001/947).

18 Once the intervention has been qualified as self-defence, the allegedly limited role played by international organizations should be an issue. On this, see Eric P.J. Myjer & Nigel D. White, *The Twin Towers Attack: An Unlimited Right to Self-Defence*, 7 Journal of Conflict and Security Law 5 (2002). For what concerns NATO's role, see also NATO Statement, *supra* note 12.

Its objective was to overthrow a dictatorship that had committed gross violations of human rights against its people, had hidden weapons of mass destruction, had actively supported terrorist organizations (in fact, Secretary Powell illustrated in detail the liaisons between Baghdad, Al Qaeda, and other terrorist organizations), and had seriously infringed well-established principles of international law, the Council's requirements, and the values of democracy both *vis-à-vis* the Iraqi people and the whole world, thus constituting – at that time and in the future – a serious threat to the world's population.[19]

US officials have justified the intervention by pointing to the illegitimacy, under international law, of Saddam Hussein's government: illegitimacy that arises from the blatant disregard of democratic principles of rightful authority. Moreover, other justifications have also been brought forward, such as a customary international law right of pre-emptive self-defence, and Article 51 of the Charter, interpreted in such a way as to include the use of force in anticipatory self-defence.[20] However, this is much shakier ground and the international scholars have time and again rejected these further legal bases.[21]

A New Concept of Worldwide Democracy

Once determined that Article 51 of the Charter provides no legal basis for the intervention in Iraq, one of the possible arguable bases is construing the American intervention as a social action to safeguard democracy. The objective pursued and its implementation are consistent with a long tradition of American foreign policy, ever struggling to affirm the values of democracy in every place and by every means.

Yet, what is the notion of democracy outlined by American representatives? Does it correspond to the accepted notion in contemporary international law? What are legitimate means to safeguard it? What sanctions can be taken against dictatorships that infringe such values?

---

19 Secretary of State Colin L. Powell, *Remarks to the United Nations Security Council* (Feb. 5, 2003), available at <http://www.state.gov/secretary/former/powell/remarks/2003/17300.htm>.

20 See Yoo, *supra* note 9; William H. Taft IV & Tood F. Buchwald, *Preemption, Iraq, and International Law*, 97 Am. J. Int'l L. 557 (2003); Ruth Wedgwood, *The Fall of Saddam Hussein: Security Council Mandates and Preemptive Self-Defence*, *id.*, at 576; Christopher Greenwood, *International Law And The Pre-Emptive Use of Force. Afghanistan, Al-Qaida, and Iraq*, 4 San Diego International Law Journal 7 (2003); Abraham D. Sofaer, *On the Necessity of Pre-emption*, 14 European Journal of International Law [hereinafter Eur. J. Int'l L.] 209 (2003); Surya S. Prakash, *The American Doctrine of 'Pre-emptive Self-defence'*, 43 Indian Journal of International Law 215 (2003); Robert M. Lawrence, *The Preventive/Preemptive War Doctrine Cannot Justify the Iraq War*, 33 Denver Journal of International Law & Policy 16 (2004); Robert Kolb, *Self-defence and Preventive War at the Beginning of the Millenium*, 59 Zeitschrift für Offentliches Recht 111 (2004); Joseph J. Darby, *Self Defense in Public International Law. The Doctrine of Pre-emption and Its Discontents*, Internationale Gemeinschaft und Menschenrechte 29 (2005).

21 Richard A. Falk, *What Future for the UN Charter System of War Prevention*, 97 Am. J. Int'l L. 590 (2003).

The international safeguard of the values of democracy has long been a constant and firm foreign policy objective of the US and its Western allies. In fact, the long and difficult ideological conflict between the two superpowers, known as the Cold War, originated from the infringement of civil and political rights carried out by the authoritarian regimes under the USSR influence. The strenuous opposition of the US against dictatorships was articulated in the doctrines first of Woodrow Wilson and later of Ronald Reagan.[22] Traditionally, the violation of fundamental freedoms has caused firm reactions on the part of the US, which intervened both militarily and with economic sanctions against right- and left-wing dictatorships. To name a few: the refusal to accept Bulgaria, Rumania, and Hungary as part of the UN because of their violation of basic human rights;[23] the suspension, in 1981, of the Most Favoured Nation Clause for the GATT area countries considered illiberal and dictatorial, like Poland; the adoption of major economic sanctions against Panama, Chile, Nicaragua, and Cuba in the 1970s and 1980s;[24] and the military interventions against Central and South American dictatorships in the 1980s (Grenada in 1983, Haiti in 1986, Puerto Rico, Nicaragua and Panama in 1989, the air strike in Manila in support of the newborn democracy of the government of Corazón Aquino).[25]

On the international level, the principle of democracy started prevailing towards the middle of the twentieth century.[26] From the 1950s on, the activity of the UN and other regional organizations led to the conclusion of several treaties aimed to safeguard several rights and freedoms that were already constitutionally granted by most developed countries. However, for a long time the international protection of human rights remained confined to treaty law and could not be elevated to customary international law because the Socialist countries (a considerable part of the international community) claimed that civil and political rights were matters for

---

22 Charles Rousseau, *Élaboration d'une Nouvelle Doctrine sur les Rapports des Etats-Unis avec les Régimes Dictatoriaux (Message du Président Reagan au Congrès, 14 mars 1986), Chronique des Faits Internationaux,* 90 Revue Générale de Droit International Public [hereinafter Rev. Gen. D.I.P.] 646 (1986).

23 UN SCOR, 2nd year, 203rd–206th meetings.

24 See United States Economic Measures against Cuba. Proceedings in the United Nations and International Law Issues (Michael Krinsky & David Golove eds, 1993).

25 See *infra* note 107 and corresponding text.

26 See, in general, The International Dimensions of Human Rights (Karel Vasak & Philip Alston eds, 1982); Philip Alston, *A Third Generation of Solidarity Rights: Progressive Development or Obfuscation of International Human Rights Law?*, 29 Netherlands International Law Review 307 (1982); Christian Tomuschat, *Human Rights in a World-Wide Framework – Some Current Issues*, 45 Zeischrift für ausländisches Offentliches Recht und Völkerrecht 547 (1985); Jack Donnelly, Universal Human Rights in Theory and Practice (1989); Bruno Simma & Philip Alston, *The Sources of Human Rights Law: Custom, Ius Cogens, and General Principles*, 12 Australian Yearbook of International Law 241 (1992); Thomas M. Franck, *Fairness in the International Legal and Institutional System. General Course on Public International Law*, 240 Recueil des Cours 9 (1993–III); Bruno Simma, *International Human Rights and General International Law: A Comparative Analysis*, 4 Collected Courses of the Academy of European Law 153 (1995). See Giuliana Ziccardi Capaldo, *Democratizzazione all'Est e Diritto Internazionale Generale*, *in* Democratizzazione all'Est e Diritto Internazionale 27 (Giuliana Ziccardi Capaldo ed., 1998), at 30.

domestic jurisdiction, thus removing their protection from the reach of international law. For this reason, despite Western pressure within the UN, the safeguard of civil and political freedoms became a value shared by the international community only after the revolutions in the Eastern bloc that culminated with the acceptance of democratic rules and the safeguard of the civil and political rights of the individual in those countries.[27] After these events, in the 1990s the debate within the UN and other international organizations intensified and a general consensus was eventually reached about the principle of democratic legitimacy, humanitarian intervention, international criminal responsibility, and the punishment of perpetrators of *crimina juris gentium*.

The UN activated the safeguard of human rights and implemented sanctions against gross violations in this field. The General Assembly insisted on the necessity of holding periodic and free elections. Respect of the principle of democratic legitimacy has been granted by directly controlling the regular occurrence of free elections,[28] by pressuring authoritarian regimes, by firmly requesting free expression of popular will, and also by the use of force, as in the case of Haiti.[29]

The safeguard of civil freedoms, which is a fundamental characteristic of contemporary democratic states, is guaranteed under international law, mostly by treaty law. On a customary level, a list of fundamental freedoms is emerging; yet, despite the fact that most modern constitutions enumerate fundamental civil freedoms, there are significant variations, and they do not always follow the template of the 1948 Universal Declaration of Human Rights or the 1966 Covenant on Civil and Political Rights and the Covenant on Economic and Social Rights.[30] The Human Rights Committee (now Council), which monitored compliance with the 1966 Covenant on Civil and Political Rights, time and again has stressed the shortcomings of many states in adapting national laws to the Pact's provisions and making the rights outlined therein justiciable. Starting from the 1980s, the Committee intensified its activity by examining the actual democracy of various regimes and

---

27 In the second half of the 1980s, the Soviet Union formally accepted the principle of democratic legality. In this regard see the Geneva summit of November 1985 between Reagan and Gorbachev, and the following meetings between the two leaders (the summits in Washington (Nov. 7, 1987); Moscow (May 29, 1988); Malta (Dec. 2, 1989)). The new Soviet Union's approach brought about the immediate broadening of the international safeguard of human rights.

28 See, e.g., GA Res. 51/31 (Dec. 6, 1996). See also GA Res. 52/18 (Nov. 21, 1997); GA Res. 53/31 (Nov. 23, 1998); GA Res. 54/36 (Nov. 29, 1999); GA Res. 55/43 (Nov. 27, 2000); GA Res. 56/96 (Dec. 14, 2001); GA Res. 58/180 (Dec. 22, 2003); GA Res. 59/193 (March 18, 2005), preamble; GA Res. 60/162 (Feb. 28, 2006), para. 2; GA Res. 60/164 (March 2, 2006), paras 2, 6; see also <http://www.unhchr.ch/democracy/resolutions.htm>.

29 On the topics, see *supra* chapter 1 of this book, at notes 18–22 and corresponding text.

30 On the International Covenant on Civil and Political Rights ((Dec. 16, 1966), 999 UNTS 171) as customary international law, see especially Theodor Meron, Human Rights and Humanitarian Norms as Customary Law 80–81 (1989); Louis B. Sohn, *Generally Accepted International Rules*, 61 Washington Law Review 1073 (1986), at 1077–1078.

the respect of their people's will.[31] Reservations to the Covenant, particularly those worded loosely, clearly illustrate states' hesitance to give full implementation to the Covenant. Moreover, it should be considered that the safeguard of fundamental freedoms does not depend only on the adaptation of domestic laws to international standards, but also on less tangible cultural and legislative traditions and religious beliefs. The definition of a consolidated list of inalienable fundamental freedoms is something that could be fully accomplished only in some regions, like the European Union.[32] On a global level, the emergence of the global community is bringing about a minimum standard of fundamental freedoms, which includes freedom of association and peaceful assembly and of expression and opinion, the freedom of religion, the freedom to leave one's country, and respect for cultural diversity.[33]

Let us not dwell for too long on the essential elements of democracy in contemporary international law and the definition of a normative legal standard of governmental legitimacy. Important studies of what Thomas Franck dubs 'democratic entitlement'[34] have traced the development in international law of the concept of democracy, of its substantial and procedural aspects, and the legal innovations relative to democratic governance.[35] It is rather necessary to point out the new dimension of the notion of democracy in international law, embodied in the concept of 'democracy worldwide', as invoked by the US during the current Iraqi

---

31 *Viz.*, Spain (UN Doc. A/34/40 (1979), para. 208; UN Doc. A/40/40 (1985), paras 478–479); Soviet Union (UN Doc. A/40/40 (1985), para. 260); Korea (UN Doc. A/43/40 (1988), para. 428); Panama (UN Doc. A/46/40 (1991), paras 422–423); Madagascar (*id.*, at paras 531–533); Colombia (UN Doc. A/47/40 (1992), paras 352, 377, 391); Nepal (UN Doc. A/50/40 (1995), para. 64); Morocco (*id.*, at para. 104); Argentina (*id.*, at para. 147); Paraguay (*id.*, at para. 196); Haiti (*id.*, at para. 226 *et seq.*); Ukraine (*id.*, at para. 310); Russian Federation (*id.*, at para. 379). See generally Egon Schwelb, *Entry into Force of the International Covenants on Human Rights and the Optional Protocol to the International Covenant on Civil and Political Rights*, 70 Am. J. Int'l L. 511 (1976); Dana D. Fisher, *Reporting under the Covenant on Civil and Political Rights: The First Five Years of the Human Rights Committee*, 76 Am. J. Int'l L. 142 (1982); Dominic McGoldrick, The Human rights Committee. Its Role in the Development of the International Covenant on Civil and Political Rights (1991). See also *supra* chapter 1 of this book, under the heading 'The Principle of Democratic Legitimacy …'.

32 See Charter of Fundamental Rights of the European Union, *reprinted* in Official Journal No. C–364/1 (Dec. 18, 2000) (also available at <http://ue.eu.int/df/docs/en/CharteEN.pdf>); Treaty establishing a Constitution for Europe (July 18, 2003) (available at <http://europa.eu.int/constitution/index_en.htm>); Lisbon Treaty <http://europa.eu/lisbon_treaty/full_text/index_en.htm>.

33 See, e.g., GA Res. 56/151 (Dec. 19, 2001), paras 3 (j), 5; GA Res. 59/201 (March 23, 2005), para. 1; CHR Res. 2003/63 (April 24, 2003), para. 4 (k) ; CHR Res. 2005/32 (April 19, 2005).

34 Thomas M. Franck, *The Emerging Right to Democratic Governance*, 86 Am. J. Int'l L. 46 (1992), at 61–77.

35 See, e.g., Gregory H. Fox & Brad R. Roth, *Democracy and International Law*, 27 Review of International Studies 327 (2001), at 331, 338.

crisis. Numerous acts of the UN and other international organizations,[36] as well as various declarations of state representatives,[37] portray a notion of democracy that has a broader range than in the past and that is suitable to build an international community on the basis of common humanity. In these documents, human rights and fundamental freedoms are described as universal and everyone is entitled to enjoy them to a full extent. The international community must treat human rights globally and promote a 'democratic international order'.[38] The global dimension of human rights and democracy necessitates a widening of the obligation of states 'to promote universal respect for, and observance and protection of, all human rights and fundamental freedoms for all', beyond their own territory.[39] This obligation is 'regardless of [states'] political, economic and cultural systems'.[40] The necessity of multilateral decision processes to manage global values, and the need of global policies and measures,[41] stress the global dimension of the concept of safeguard and the move away from unilateralism.

On the occasion of the Iraqi crisis, the US and the UK pointed out this 'extra-territorial' widening of the obligations to safeguard the values of democracy – introduced by the concept of 'democracy worldwide'. States must protect democracy not only in their own territory and for the sake of their own citizens, but also for every individual and people in the world. This argumentation was used not only to point out gross violations of human rights and fundamental freedoms by Saddam Hussein, but also to affirm the obligation and the right of all states to guarantee their implementation anywhere. Several international organizations, including the EU Council, have stated that terrorism constitutes one of the most serious violations of the universal values of human dignity, freedom, equality, and the principles of democracy and the rule of law.[42] Based on this concept, the US and the UK asserted that Saddam Hussein's regime breached the principle of democracy by its systematic violations of human rights and the freedom of the Iraqi and Kurdish people, by sponsoring international terrorism, and by the manufacturing of weapons of mass

36 See generally GA Res. 55/107 (Dec. 4, 2000); GA Res. 56/151, *supra* note 33. See also CHR Res. 2001/65 (April 25, 2001); CHR Res. 2002/72 (April 25, 2002); CHR Res. 2003/36 (April 23, 2003); CHR Res. 2003/63, *supra* note 33; CHR Res. 2004/30 (April 19, 2004).

37 See Warsaw Declaration adopted by the First Ministerial Conference of the Community of Democracies; and Seoul Plan of Action, Second Ministerial Conference of the Community of Democracies (Seoul 10–12 November 2002).

38 GA Res. 56/151, *supra* note 33, preamble, para. 5; GA Res. 57/213 (Dec. 18, 2002); GA Res. 59/193, *supra* note 28, para. 4; CHR Res. 2003/63, *supra* note 33, para. 6; CHR Res. 2004/64 (April 21, 2004).

39 A/60/L.1 (20 Sept. 2005), paras. 138–139. See also CHR Res. 2003/63, *supra* note 33, preamble.

40 *Id.*, at para. 6.

41 *Id.*, at paras 3 (n), 8.

42 EU Council Framework Decision of 13 June 2002 on Combating Terrorism 2002/475/JHA, paras 1–2. See also, in the same sense, Council of Europe, Parliamentary Assembly, Recommendations: 982 (May 9, 1984), paras 3–4; 1426 (Sept. 23, 1999), para. 3, and 1534 (Sept. 26, 2001), para. 2; Resolution 1258 (Sept. 26, 2001), para. 3; see also the Council of Europe Convention on the Prevention of Terrorism (May 16, 2005), preamble.

destruction. By doing so, it endangered human rights and freedoms of any individual or people.[43] Further, the US and the UK asserted a close link between the safeguard of democracy and the fight against terrorism, by widening the scope of the obligation and right to safeguard the values of democracy across national frontiers and states' sovereignties.

Is There a Right to Overthrow an Illegitimate Regime?

The allied intervention in Iraq has been considered illegitimate under international law and has stirred reactions from different countries, international organizations, and the world's public opinion. It is held that this intervention was a major violation of the principle of sovereignty and the principle of effectivity, which is its corollary, and a major infringement of the ban of the use of force in international relations sanctioned by Article 2 (4) in the UN Charter. The question is whether international law permits sanctions against murderous dictatorial governments that violate fundamental universal values, and whether these sanctions can take the form of actions that eventually lead to the overthrowing of governments. If so, with what modality should this be accomplished?

The issue is not new to scholars.[44] In the late 1980s, a well-known article by Oscar Schachter questioned: 'Is there a right to overthrow an illegitimate regime?'.[45] In examining the modalities of armed interventions against regimes considered illegitimate, he wondered what are the internationally accepted instruments that can be used to safeguard the values of democracy and to sanction the violations committed by governments. Professor Schachter considered the conflict between effectivity and legality, and recognized effectivity as an 'objective standard' to ensure the respect of states' sovereignty;[46] he excluded that a regime's illegality could justify an armed intervention and its unilateral overthrow. He invoked Article 2 (4) of the Charter, aimed at 'protecting all states, irrespective of politics or "legitimacy" of its ruling authority'[47] and concluded his study by considering it 'not unrealistic to anticipate more effective collective measures in the future…'.[48]

Starting from Schachter's conclusions on the future of 'collective measures', we will examine whether the international legal system has actually evolved towards the direction he was hoping for; how much the development of human rights in the global system has eroded the principle of sovereignty; and how, and to what extent,

43 Powell, *supra* note 19.

44 See generally William Michael Reisman, *Sovereignty and Human Rights in Contemporary International Law*, 84 Am. J. Int'l L. 866 (1990), at 871; Thomas M. Franck, The Empowered Self: Law and Society in the Age of Individualism (2001).

45 Oscar Schachter, *Is There a Right to Overthrow an Illegitimate Regime?*, Le Droit Interne au Service de la Paix, de la Justice et du Développement. Mélanges Michel Virally 423 (1991).

46 *Id.*, at 424.

47 *Id.*, at 425. For a different view, see William Michael Reisman, *Coercion and Self-Determination: Construing Charter Article 2(4)*, 78 Am. J. Int'l L. 642 (1984).

48 Schachter, *supra* note 45, at 430.

the principles of effectivity and legality coexist in the current international legal system.

The Difficult Coexistence Between the Principles of Legality and Effectivity

Effectiveness in Classical International Law

Historically, effectivity has overridden legality. The principle of effectivity, one of the tenets of classical international law, required one to carefully consider the actual territorial situation,[49] disregarding the legality of the title of acquisition, and the way it was governed. The *ex factis oritur jus* principle legitimized any effective situation. Important twentieth-century studies found the basis of sovereignty in effectivity alone.[50] Hans Kelsen efficiently claimed that the only test of legitimacy of territorial acquisitions is the effectivity of control of that territory; effectivity rectifies the illegality of the title of acquisition.[51] At the end of the 1970s, Rolando Quadri observed that the international community had not yet developed democratic-legitimist notions according to which the only effective power was that which had been established peacefully and in respect to so-called human rights. According to him, oppressive regimes have the same right to claim respect for territorial sovereignty.[52]

In classical international law, the problem of the legal consequences arising out of the 'illegitimate' practice of governments was not an issue; attempts to subordinate the birth of a new state to criteria of legality never reached legal articulation.[53] Towards the end of the eighteenth century, the international community ceased to consist of European Christian states only, and its membership started being questioned. In this period, the practice of states' recognition developed. Certain politics of that period and legal scholars of the 1800s used this practice to ascertain the legitimacy of newly created states and, at the same time, welcome them as part of the international community. Certain new states, in particular those led by revolutionary governments, were denied recognition because of the illegitimacy of

49 During the twentieth century, the effectivity principle found full affirmation in jurisprudence and application of arbitral common practice. See Tinoco case (Great Britain v. Costa Rica), 1 Review of International Arbitral Awards 369 (1923); Albert de La Pradelle & Nicolas Politis, II Recueil des Arbitrages Internationaux (1856–72) (1932), at 404; Claude H. M. Waldock, *Disputed Sovereignty in the Falkland Islands Dependencies*, 25 British Yearbook of International Law [hereinafter BYILL] 311 (1948).

50 See James Crawford, The Creation of States in International Law (1979).

51 Hans Kelsen, *Théorie Générale du Droit International Public*, 4 Recueil des Cours 121, 261, 323–324 (1932–IV).

52 Rolando Quadri, Diritto Internazionale Pubblico (5th ed., 1968).

53 On this and the relevance of democracy to ensure recognition, see Thomas M. Franck, The Power of Legitimacy Among Nations (1990); Sean D. Murphy, *Democratic Legitimacy and the Recognition of States and Governments*, 48 International and Comparative Law Quarterly 545 (1999), at 546, 566; Brad Roth, Governmental Illegitimacy in International Law (1999).

their origins.[54] Legitimacy remained essentially a political issue, without becoming a real legal principle;[55] although the so-called 'legitimist doctrines' tried to spell out precise criteria for recognition. This process is illustrated by the 'principle of monarchic legitimacy' sanctioned by the Troppau Protocol on 19 November 1820, and invoked by the powers of the Holy Alliance to justify the refusal to recognize the rebellious Spanish provinces in Latin America, as well as the Austrian intervention in the Kingdom of Two Sicilies of 2 July 1820. However, this principle did not outlive the Holy Alliance. The doctrine of democratic legitimacy outlined by Julio Tobar, Ecuador's Minister of Foreign Affairs, was more successful. This doctrine was formulated in the Washington Treaty of 20 December 1907, and affirmed the duty of the contracting parties (Costa Rica, Guatemala, Honduras, Nicaragua, and El Salvador) to deny the recognition of any revolutionary government that could arise in those troubled countries, unless and until the people had a chance to elect their representatives and the new power structure had been sanctioned by the amended constitution.[56] The principle of democratic legitimacy inspired the British practice until the first World War, and it was also followed by the US, under President Wilson, who made 'constitutionalism' the inspiring principle of his political agenda in Latin America.[57]

This practice – and other efforts directed towards setting limits to territorial sovereignty and granting the safeguard of the individual from the national state – did not become general international law until at least the first half of the

54 See generally M. Philip Marshall Brown, La Reconnaissance des Nouveaux Etats et des Nouveaux Gouvernements (1933); John F. Williams, *La Doctrine de la Reconnaissance en Droit International et Ses Développements Récents*, 44 Recueil des Cours 203 (1933–II); Roland Hall Sharp, Non-Recognition as a Legal Obligation 1775–1934 (1934); Arnhold Raestad, *La Reconnaissance Internationale des Nouveaux Etats et des Nouveaux Gouvernements*, 27 Revue de Droit International et de Legislation Comparée 257 (1936); Georges Scelle, *Quelques Réflexions sur une Institution Juridique Primitive: la Reconnaissance Internationale*, Introduction à l'Etude du Droit Comparé, Recueil d'Etudes en l'Honneur d'Edouard Lambert 123 (1938–III); Hans Kelsen, *Recognition in International Law. Theorical Observations*, 35 Am. J. Int'l L. 606 (1941); Charles G. Fenwick, *The Recognition*, 38 Am. J. Int'l L. 448 (1944); Herbert W. Brigg, *Recognition of States: Some Reflections on Doctrine and Practice*, 43 Am. J. Int'l L. 113 (1949); Jean Charpentier, La Reconnaissance Internationale et l'Evolution du Droit des Gens 123 *et seq.*, 174 *et seq.* (1956). For developments, see Joe Verhoeven, La Reconnaissance Internationale dans la Pratique Contemporaine (1975); P.K. Menon, The Law of Recognition in International Law (1994); Mildred J. Peterson, Recognition of Governments. Legal Doctrine and State Practice 1815–1995 (1997).

55 On the question that '*aucun principe légitimiste n'est obligatoire pour dévenir membre de la communauté internationale*' see Jean J.A. Salmon, La Reconnaissance d'Etat 36 (1971). International jurisprudence widely concords that recognition of new states does not establish international personality. In this sense, see Hans Blix, *Contemporary Aspects of Recognition*, 130 Recueil des Cours 587 (1970–II).

56 Salmon, *supra* note 55, at 31.

57 See, e.g., Hersch Lauterpacht, Recognition in International Law 116 *et seq.*, 124 *et seq.* (1948); Ti-Chiang Chen, The International Law of Recognition, with Special Reference to Practice in Great Britain and the United States (1951).

twentieth century. The principle of effectivity was predominant in the Westphalian international community,[58] as clearly stated by James Monroe, President of the US, who had announced in his famous Message of 1823 that *de facto* governments were to be considered legitimate.[59] The thesis of President Monroe was further developed by George Canning, the British Minister of Foreign Affairs, in a note of 1825 addressed to the Spanish Government.[60] The principle of effectivity, as enunciated by these two statesmen, inspired the international praxis of the nineteenth century, as reflected by numerous cases of recognition of new revolutionary governments, such as those of Bulgaria, Belgium, Romania, Germany, and Italy. The recognition of *de facto* situations continued in the period immediately following the First World War. The so-called 'Estrada doctrine', named after the Mexican Foreign Affairs Minister, criticized the practice of recognition based on democratic legitimacy; it outlined its shortcomings, namely, the fact that it let the legitimacy of a government depend on the whim of foreign governments. '*Cette pratique, en effet, met ces pays dans une situation où leurs affaires domestiques pourront étre jugées ... par d'autres gouvernements qui, en fait, prennent une attitude de censure en décidant favorablement ou défavorablement sur la légalité d'un régime étranger*'.[61]

The weakness of legitimistic theories has been pointed out by Schachter: the unilateral and unorganized system of compliance-control typical of international law cannot be objective enough to support social actions that safeguard the international legality. Only the objective determination of a regime's illegitimacy and concerted multilateral UN sanctions could set free 'human rights, self-rule and justice' from the dictates of effectiveness.[62]

Yet, what makes Schachter's idea difficult to apply is the fact that the UN Charter is the ultimate guarantor of sovereignty and guardian of domestic jurisdiction (Article 2 (7)), and it is not easy to find in its words an authorization to remove illegitimate governments to sanction the violation of the values of democracy. Article 1 (3) enunciates the duty to safeguard human rights and fundamental freedoms, but it does not provide a system of sanctions. The collective security system, provided for in Chapter VII, focuses on maintaining peace and lists a series of measures that can be taken to sanction threats or violations of international peace and security (Article 41). Article 42 gives the Security Council the power to allow the use of force to restore peace and security. On the one hand, the aim of the Charter is to safeguard the sovereignty of states and defend their domestic sphere, which includes democracy and good governance. On the other hand, Article 1 of the Charter has eventually breached the limits of domestic jurisdiction and, starting from mere programmatic formulations, given birth to new principles, which have eroded the traditional

58 See, in particular, LAUTERPACHT, *supra* note 57, at 98, 141 *et seq.*, and 331 *et seq.*; HANS KELSEN, GENERAL THEORY OF LAW AND STATE 228–229 (1949); JEAN TOUSCOZ, LE PRINCIPE D'EFFECTIVITÉ DANS L'ORDRE INTERNATIONAL 122 (1964); CRAWFORD, *supra* note 50, at 44–45.

59 CHARLES DE MARTENS, NOUVELLES CAUSES CÉLÈBRES DU DROIT DES GENS 236 *et seq.* (1843).

60 *British and Foreign State Papers*, XII, at 909 *et seq.* See also HAROLD TEMPERLEY, HAROLD TEMPERLEY, THE FOREIGN POLICY OF CANNING, 1822-1827 (1925).

61 Foreign Policy Association Reports (U.S.A.), VII, I, at 203.

62 Schachter, *supra* note 45, at 430.

freedom of the states. By relying on Article 1, UN organs have questioned some of the classical modes of territorial acquisition – like occupation – have negated the legitimacy of colonies, and condemned gross violations of human rights. In sum, because of the pointed and constant UN action – both in terms of treaty-making and practice – in the second half of the twentieth century, certain state behaviour that hitherto was legitimate because of effectivity was outlawed. Imperative general principles that limited the traditional rights inherent in states' sovereignty were developed. These led to the practice of collective coercive measures that sometimes might go beyond the limits set by the UN Charter.

The UN Practice of Non-Recognition of Unlawful Territorial Situations

The principle of effectivity was gradually eroded by UN practice. Starting from the 1960s, on the basis of the principle of international legality, the organization declared some territorial situations illegitimate. The General Assembly and the Security Council repeatedly sanctioned actions harming populations subject to the authority of states. The determination of the illegality of territorial situations resulting from violations of obligations *erga omnes* (e.g., occupation, colonialism, apartheid, and other major human rights violations), was usually accompanied by a request to member states to withhold recognition of the effects of such unlawful situations, both on the domestic and international level.

This Copernican revolution shifted the centre of gravity of international law from states to individuals. Principles of international legality were stated, and these became criteria according to which the legitimacy of power, which was hitherto founded on effectivity, could be monitored.[63]

By asking states to withhold recognition of 'unlawful' territorial situations, the UN has followed the practice of the League of Nations, which, following the 1932 Stimson Declaration, maintained that territorial acquisitions obtained with the use of force are unlawful.[64] In reality, the UN went further. It expanded the practice of withholding recognition to illegitimate governments. Examples of this are the declaration of illegality and the refusal to recognize the possession of the Arab territories occupied by Israel after 1967;[65] the South African presence in Namibia;[66]

---

63 For broader reflections on the principle of legality, and the relationship between legality and effectivity in the international system, see Giuliana Ziccardi Capaldo, Le Situazioni Territoriali Illegittime nel Diritto Internazionale/Unlawful Territorial Situations in International Law 14–18, 122–128, and *Summary* in English, at 129–135 (1977).

64 Available at <http://courses.knox.edu/hist285schneid/stimsondoctrine.html>. See Robert Langer, Seizure of Territory. The Stimson Doctrine and Related Principles in Legal Theory and Diplomatic Practice (1947); David Turns, *The Stimson Doctrine of Non-Recognition, Its Historical Genesis and Influence on Contemporary International Law*, 2 Chinese Journal of International Law 105 (2003); Stefan Talmon, *The Constitutive Versus the Declaratory Theory of Recognition: Tertium Non Datur?*, 75 BYILL 101 (2004).

65 SC Res. 252 (May 21, 1968); SC Res. 478 (Aug. 20, 1980).

66 GA Res. 2145 (XXI) (Oct. 27, 1966); SC Res. 276 (Jan. 30, 1970).

the racist minority regime in South Rhodesia between 1965 and 1979;[67] the apartheid in South Africa between 1948 and 1994;[68] the independence of the *Bantustans*;[69] the Iraqi aggression on Kuwait in 1990; and the construction of the wall being built by Israel in the Occupied Palestinian Territory.[70] These resolutions reinforced the trend in international law towards greater enforcement of human rights norms, which were migrating from the private to the public sphere (i.e., from being confined to the internal affairs of a state to matters of concern to the international community at large). This practice made it possible to ascertain and sanction major violations of human rights, including not only the apartheid practised by Ian Smith's government in Southern Rhodesia and the government of South Africa, but also the crimes perpetrated by Pol Pot's government against the Cambodians; those of Saddam Hussein against the Kurds; the ethnic cleansing pursued by Milosevic in Bosnia; and the gross violations to human rights in Rwanda, Sierra Leone, and Liberia, just to mention some of the most significant cases.

This practice cleared the path for the protection of the individual from his/her own state, bypassing the roadblock of the effectivity principle and the classical notion of 'domestic jurisdiction'. It started a constituent process aimed at making tangible the great intellectual movement in defence of the human being. The novelty of this practice lies in the fact that the UN not only started promoting the development and codification of human rights instruments, but also took concrete steps to ascertain their violations and enforce them and, by doing this, effectively expressed *erga omnes* the judgment of the whole international community. The International Law Commission (ILC) Articles on State Responsibility for Internationally Wrongful Acts provide in Article 41(2) that 'no state shall recognize as lawful a situation created by a serious breach' of an obligation arising under a peremptory norm of general international law.[71]

The objective ascertainment of illegality has provided the basis for the development of international multilateral processes, in addition to those provided for by the Charter, that actually have made it possible to sanction violations of human rights. The international order was thus profoundly changed:

---

67 Myres S. McDougal & William Michael Reisman, *Rhodesia and the United Nations: The Lawfulness of International Concern*, 62 AM. J. INT'L L. 1 (1968).

68 GA Res. 3151 (XXVIII) (Dec. 14, 1973); GA Res. 39/72 (Dec. 13, 1984); SC Res. 554 (Aug. 17, 1984).

69 GA Res. 31/6 (Oct. 26, 1976). On the UN practice of non-recognition, see ZICCARDI CAPALDO, *supra* note 63, at 41 *et seq.*

70 The obligation of non-recognition was reiterated by the International Court of Justice (ICJ) in the advisory opinion on Legal Consequences of the Construction of a Wall in the Occupied Palestinian Territory, (July 9, 2004), para. 159. See *supra* chapter 3 under the heading 'The ICJ between over-reaching and over-caution' and *infra* chapter 8 under the heading 'Terrorist Acts Committed on Behalf of "Peoples" '.

71 GA Res. 56/83 (Dec 12, 2001), Annex, Art. 41 (2), at 9. General Assembly Resolution took note of the articles and 'commend[ed] them to the attention of Governments without prejudice to the question of their future adoption or other appropriate action' (*id.*, at para. 3).

1. the *ex injuria jus non oritur* principle was counterposed to the *ex factis oritur jus* principle;
2. the individual became central in the changing international structure, thus eroding state sovereignty; and
3. a system of collective safeguards to sanction the illegality of governments, based on the UN task to objectively ascertain violations of human rights, was created. In these matters, the authority of the UN was held greater than that of the states themselves, thus denting the *superiorem non recognoscentes* principle. The UN was empowered to act as agent of the international community, and this was above and beyond what the Charter provides, as it does not gives the organization the power to determine international legal responsibility in the human rights field (Article 39 of the Charter notoriously deals only with the violations and threats to peace and security).

Co-Managing Action Against Illegitimate Regimes

At the beginning of the second half of the twentieth century international standards for the safeguard of human rights grew in importance. This raised the issue of their objective implementation, for that could not be left to states without risking abuse. To this end, the international legal system was 'only partially effective'. Of the four configurations described by Michael Reisman, it fell under the heading 'effective but limited',[72] because it lacked the power to effectively enforce the principles created. Neither states nor the UN had the power to implement them by themselves. In classical international law, due to its unorganized nature and decentralized system, a state was entitled to self-defence if one of its rights had been infringed and the safeguarding of its own material interests affected; so it was evident that, until *Barcelona Traction*, there was no legal interest in the observance of a general principle and protection of common interests and social values. Not even the UN had sufficient power to implement human rights principles that are not enforceable in the Charter (Chapter VII collective security system, guaranteeing only the maintenance of peace).

The international enforcement system of the 1950s had not yet developed rules and procedures to coordinate the actions of states and international institutions that could further safeguard the collective interests of the global community. In the 1960s, the UN gave way to the call of the international community for the actual safeguard of those interests and started the aforementioned practice of non-recognition. Going beyond the limits of the Charter and the respect of domestic jurisdiction, the UN organs created a collective system that distributed the responsibility for managing social values between states and international institutions. The dynamics of shared governance (states/UN) that arose made the international legal order capable of enforcing human rights standards. The consensus amongst most states on some of the standards of objective legality stated by the UN, together with the introduction of an external scrutiny of territorial issues and the exercise of power by governments,

72 William Michael Reisman, *Unilateral Action and the Transformations of the World Constitutive Process*, 11 Eur. J. Int'l L. (2000).

reduced the leeway of states. This also settled the ground for the development of a public-law function, wielded multilaterally, to safeguard human and social values. Nowadays, the international legal system for the protection of human rights and the public-law interests of the global community is characterized by the fact that states, the UN, and other international institutions partaking the decision-making functions and cooperate in the activities aimed at safeguarding the common interests. We have called this decision process the 'integrated system'.[73] It encompasses various functions, including:

1. UN ascertainment that a behaviour constitutes a serious violation of human rights and/or other *erga omnes* obligations;
2. decision and application of the sanction (i.e., activities by third/agent states) – the coercive function – to the actual case (i.e., peaceful enforcment measures and authorized uses of force); and
3. institutional control over states' coercive action to sanction the objectively established illegality and the execution of agreed program for restoration of the illegal situation and national institutions.

During the past fifty years, the classical international system of enforcement – moulded on states and the safeguard of their own 'private' interests – evolved into a system capable of safeguarding 'public' interests of the international community. The distribution of participation in various decision-making functions is the crucible of the integrated system; a system that is still lacking an equilibrium between those states that want to confer on the UN the monopoly of decision-making power on the use of force against illegitimate governments (i.e., those governments responsible for gross violations of human rights and international law) and those dominant states that want to keep this power for themselves and for the regional organizations of which they are members. Although this is, by far, the most pressing problem, it is certainly not the only one. Another issue is the demand of Western states to enhance the safeguard of human rights and sanction illegitimate governments with measures increasingly encroaching on sovereignty. Gradually, the UN decision-making power (where gross violations of human rights were concerned) dwindled and states began participating. The expansion of the safeguard of human rights demanded by Western states has led to drastic coercive measures against illegitimate governments; this has resulted in a gradual erosion of state sovereignty.

Overcoming the Ineffectiveness of Decision-Making Institutions

The creation of the 'integrated system' has been a three-stage dynamic process leading to the definition of some norms, both substantive and procedural. During this process, the variables at stake have been: (1) the distribution of participation (among its components); (2) the breadth of the safeguarded human rights; and (3)

---

73 See *supra* 'Introduction' to chapter 2 of this book. See Giuliana Ziccardi Capaldo, *The Law of the Global Community: An Integrated System to Enforce 'Public' International Law*, 1 GCYILJ 71 (2001), at 73.

the effectiveness of the permitted coercive measures, their capacity to reduce the freedom of 'illegitimate' governments, and their effectivity. These three phases of the constitutive process will be examined below.

The Concentration of Decision-Making Power Within the UN

The first phase began in the 1960s and was characterized by the concentration within the UN of the competence to implement international law. The UN specified the principles safeguarding human rights that were stated in the Charter only in a programmatic fashion; it ascertained whether a given territorial situation conformed to international law and, if this was not the case, declared the situation 'illegal' and decided the measures to be taken by member states. The UN acted as the agent of the whole international community: it put at everyone's disposal its structure and aided the international system, which still lacked institutions and procedures to implement 'public' international law principles.[74] In sum, during this phase it acted as the organ implementing international law on behalf of the whole community, rather than within the narrower limits of the Charter. Its organs – Security Council and General Assembly – took on powers of ascertainment and sanctioning not contemplated in the Charter, and new forms of action (such as the non-recognition of the acts of illegitimate governments[75]). The notion of threat to peace and security, which authorizes the Council to determine responsibility (Article 39) and sanction violations (Articles 41 and 42), was extended to encompass the protection of human rights and peoples' right to self-determination (and subsequently, any situation of non-compliance with international law).

During this first phase, individuals were protected from the horrors of opprobrious government practices (e.g., occupation, colonialism, and other generalized serious violations to human rights) by the emerging practice of non-recognition of illegitimate governments. It is in this period that the UN started to scrutinize the legality of certain territorial situations (modes of acquisition of territory and rightful exercise of government authority);[76] the determination of a situation as illegal made by a competent organ of the UN is an authoritative international act, which could lead to an unquestionable declaration of illegitimacy. Effectivity could not legalize illegitimacy, and situations declared 'illegal' were stigmatized until legality was restored. This UN determination represents the verdict of the international community and has *erga omnes* effects, according to the judgment of the International Court of Justice on Namibia.[77] In this case, the International Court of Justice drew both

74 This term is here used differently from what it is commonly meant in international law. That is to say, it is used to indicate the set of norms regarding the safeguard of fundamental social values.

75 See *supra* under the heading of 'The UN Practice of Non-Recognition …' earlier in this chapter.

76 See Ziccardi Capaldo, *supra* note 63, at 34 *et seq.*

77 See Legal Consequences for the States of the Continued Presence of South Africa in Namibia (South-West Africa) notwithstanding Security Council Resolution, Advisory Opinion, 1971 ICJ Reports 16 (June 21, 1971), para. 126, at 56; Repertory, *supra* note 5, vol. I, No. 1600, at 632–633.

from international law and the Charter the obligation for all states to implement sanctions – both economic and of other kinds – against governments not recognized by the UN.[78] The objective determination of illegality made by an international institution was the tenet of the new integrated system, and it was never questioned in its successive refinements. By non-recognizing, the UN was actually isolating the illegitimate government with economic and diplomatic measures; it was up to the member states to carry out the sanctions imposed by the Security Council and to take the necessary steps to prevent the illegitimate situation from producing legal effects. The Security Council did not always take similar steps. Resolution 569 started the practice of 'authorized procedures', by transferring decision-making powers to states. In that resolution, the Council did not decide on sanctions itself, but it rather merely authorized states to undertake 'voluntary' economic sanctions against South Africa, thus leaving them free to decide whether to do so and what measures to adopt. Although the Charter gives the Council the power to take binding measures (i.e., 'what measures ... are to be employed to give effect to its decisions') (Article 41), this resolution started a new practice, which we have dubbed 'integrated decision-making process', where the Council and states share international law-enforcement powers and, in particular, the exercise of coercive measures.[79]

States Claim a Role in the Decision-Making Process

In the 1980s, following the progressive democratization of the Eastern bloc, states joined the UN in the task of guaranteeing internationally the rights protection of individuals rights. States were bound to respect democracy, civil and political rights, and fundamental freedoms. The war against terrorism, construed as a violation of peace and fundamental human rights, was endorsed by different governments. States demanded independence in their decisions and sanctions against governments which, in the opinion of the UN, had committed violations of human rights. In this period, Western states started applying economic and diplomatic sanctions against violations of human rights and other fundamental values of the international community, even without a specific authorization of the Security Council. This practice marked a turning point in the redistribution of decision-making power in the integrated process between states and international institutions. Because these steps were taken to safeguard common values, they were lawful. The result of the debate between UN member states on the role of the organization – especially in relation to the state's power to unilaterally apply sanctions to countries sponsoring terrorism – was the acceptance of only unilateral measures that did not imply the use of force, provided that illegitimacy had been objectively ascertained by the UN and/or other international organizations. Thus, in this phase, the Security Council and the General Assembly carried out an *ex post* control of peaceful countermeasures in

78 *South-West Africa* case, *supra* note 77, paras 121–124, at 55–56.

79 SC Res. 569 (July 26, 1985). See also *supra*, note 73, and chapter 2.

order to evaluate their legitimacy and their conformity to the criteria of necessity and proportionality. Sometimes they urged states to discontinue them.[80]

It is in this period that force started being used against illegitimate governments responsible of gross violations of human rights and democracy. The decision power remained mostly in the hands of the Security Council. However, new forms of participation of states in the maintenance of international peace and security were developed, including the use of force to end gross violations of human rights, once these had been ascertained by the Security Council. The UN practice of 'authorizations' to use force, albeit outside the strict framework of Article 42 of the Charter, has evolved into a customary legal obligation.

Processes of Multilateral Authoritative Decision-Making

Towards the end of the twentieth century, whenever institutions proved to be ineffective or incapable of acting, the non-institutional components of the global community (i.e., states) reclaimed the decision-making powers. During this third phase, states claim that they are able to use force without the authorization of the Security Council against governments whose responsibility for serious violations to human rights has been ascertained by the Council. They claim they have the right to use force in cases when the Council already determined the illegality of the situation but cannot take the necessary steps to restore legality. The apex of this sensitive phase was the Kosovo crisis, during which NATO countries, with the approval of other states, used force against the Yugoslav government to halt serious and flagrant violations of human rights that had been ascertained by the Security Council.[81] The Kosovo intervention, not authorized because of Russia's and China's veto, was largely approved by states and international organizations. A vast majority of states, public opinion, and eventually the UN, endorsed NATO actions. Upon completion of military operations, the Security Council took back its leading role by legalizing the intervention *ex post*.[82]

The Kosovo crisis was yet another turning point in the process of redistribution of the decision-making powers on the use of force in the integrated process between states and multilateral institutions. The non-institutional component claimed the power to override ineffective institutions; this will, although subject to certain conditions, promptly developed into a legal international rule. Therefore, to be legitimate, unilateral actions taken in lieu of ineffective institutions need the backing of a large number of states, international regional organizations, and the world's public opinion; the following conditions must be met:

---

80 See *supra* chapter 2 under the heading 'Mechanisms to Co-Manage Peaceful Enforcement Measures'.

81 SC Res. 1160 (March 31, 1998); SC Res. 1199 (Sept. 23, 1998); SC Res. 1203 (Oct. 24, 1998).

82 See *supra* chapter 2 under the heading 'Unauthorized Humanitarian Interventions', and the authors quoted above.

1. the Security Council must have determined the existence of serious violations of human rights and other *erga omnes* obligations;[83]
2. the armed intervention to halt the violation must be necessary and urgent;
3. the Security Council must be incapable of acting, because blocked by veto;
4. unilateral action must receive the support of a large majority of states, regional organizations and the world's public opinion; and
5. upon the end of the crisis, control of the situation must be given back to competent international institutions, and representative governments must be restored.

The integrated system allows for unauthorized use of force against illegitimate governments, provided that the aforementioned procedures are met. Whenever the Council reckons that the procedural and substantive requirements (i.e., that force was used in compliance with the international law criteria of necessity, proportionality, and respect of *jus cogens*) were met, it regains control of the situation and takes over the final phase of the integrated process (administration of the territory and restoration of national institutions).

The Unlawfulness of the Unilateral Intervention in Iraq

To determine whether the allied intervention in Iraq is lawful it is necessary to examine whether it was carried out in compliance with the relevant rules of the integrated system of international law described above, which require that decisions be taken multilaterally. It is argued here that it did not.[84] Let us briefly review the facts.

From the outset, the American proposal to use force against Saddam Hussein's regime to stop reiterated and serious violations of international law committed in Iraq was backed by the UK, but was opposed by France, Russia, Germany, and other states and international organizations, including the Arab League. An agreement on the allied plan could not be reached within the regional organizations (NATO and EU) to which the two allied countries belong (the US to NATO only, and the UK to both). No resolution authorizing the use of force was submitted to the Security Council, because both Russia and France had threatened to use their veto power. In the wake of the intervention, the number of states disapproving the unauthorized use of force swelled. Those states were first concerned about the safeguard of national economic interests in Iraq and the region but were also genuinely concerned with US unilateralism. They feared the monopolization of the power to decide the use of force and the ensuing loss of objectivity and potential abuse. On top of this, France and Germany would have liked to see the European Union play a greater role, more independent and of higher profile, in the decisions regarding the maintenance of world peace and security. Last, but not least, Third World and Islamic countries were concerned with the imposition of an American *Pax*, the presence of American troops

---

83 *Id.* See also chapter 2 under the heading 'Some Mechanisms of Joint Governance'.

84 See *supra*, the third phase of the integrated constituent process, as discussed under the heading 'Processes of Multilateral Authoritative Decision-Making'.

in the region, and the dominance of Western culture to the detriment of their economy as well as their political, cultural and religious identity. The military intervention was not considered to be the last resort. Some states, led by France, believed that inspections carried out by the UN and collaboration with the Iraqi government, albeit difficult and unreliable, were still possible. Other states, like Russia and other Arab countries, wanted to give diplomacy another chance and started various initiatives aimed at Saddam Hussein's exile,[85] thus implicitly recognizing that effectivity was to yield to legality.

International organizations did not endorse the intervention. During the military operations, Arab countries, gathered in international regional organizations, unanimously declared the intervention illegal.[86] Although not explicitly declaring the intervention unlawful, other regional organizations like NATO and the EU claimed for the UN a central role in Iraq's reorganization and administration.[87] Ever since the first resolution adopted after the intervention, while military operations were still under way, the Security Council has defined the Iraqi territory as 'occupied', qualified the US and the UK in Iraq as 'occupying powers', and reminded them of their obligations towards the Iraqi people under Article 55 of the Fourth Geneva Convention.[88] Once the operations were concluded, the Security Council intervened with Resolution 1483:[89] it reaffirmed the unlawfulness of the unilateral intervention; it did not mend the breach to integrated legal procedures.

The Effectiveness of the 'Occupying Powers'

With Resolution 1483, the Council accomplished three goals:

(1) It established that US and UK are 'occupying powers'; thus, they have obligations and responsibilities under international law

The determination by the Council that the US and UK are in Iraq as 'occupying powers'[90] contains two elements: the ascertainment of the effectivity of power; and the illegality of the title to administer the territory. In international law, effective control gives rise to obligations and responsibilities, whether the title is legal or not. Occupation does not give legal title to administer a territory. Be that as it may, the occupying powers are not freed from the obligations towards other states and from

85 See *infra* note 110 and corresponding text.

86 Arab League Ministerial Council Resolution (March 24, 2003). This Resolution refers to 'the position opposing war of the African Union, the Organization of Islamic Conference, the Non-aligned Movement'. See also Arab League Council, Res. 227 (March 28, 2002); Res. 243 (March 1, 2003).

87 See the Conclusions of the Extraordinary European Council on Iraq (Feb. 17, 2003) and the European Council's Statement on Iraq (March 20, 2003), both available at <http://europa.eu.int/comm/external_relations/iraq/news/>.

88 SC Res. 1472 (March 28, 2003), preamble.

89 SC Res. 1483 (May 22, 2003).

90 *Id.*, at preamble.

the responsibilities that derive from controlling the territory. The fact that the US and UK do not have a valid legal title to administer Iraq does not release them from their obligations and responsibilities under international law.[91] In the Advisory Opinion on South-West Africa, the International Court of Justice confirmed that '[p]hysical control of territory, and not sovereignty or legitimacy, is the basis of state liability for actions affecting other states'.[92]

(2) It recognized the effectivity of the occupying powers

International law deems the occupation as unlawful and sanctionable by non-recognition. It does not recognize *de facto* situations created with the use of force and denies them extraterritorial legal effects. The legal tenet of the doctrine of non-recognition, formulated in 1932 by the late American Secretary of State Henry Stimson, is that violations of international law can not produce a territorial situation affecting third states. Theoretically, the practice of not recognizing the legal effects of acts arising from an illegal situation, as occupation is, can be traced back to the principle *ex iniuria jus non oritur*, which can be found in domestic legal systems, as well as in the international legal system. It is usual UN and states' practice of non-recognition to deny the legality of occupation and the legal effects of the acts performed by the occupier for the occupied territory. This can be found in the Declarations of Principles of the General Assembly, as a corollary of the outlawing of the use of force. Paragraph 10 of the Declaration of Principles of 18 November 1987, dictates that 'neither acquisition … nor any occupation of territory resulting from the threat or use of force in contravention of international law will be recognized as legal …'.[93]

According to the jurisprudence of the International Court of Justice, the Security Council's determination that a state is an occupying power brings certain consequences. In the case of South-West Africa, the Court stated that both under general international law and the Charter, states must refrain from entering into relationships of economic or other nature 'which may imply a recognition that the authority of that state [responsible] on the territory unlawfully detained is legal'.[94] They are under the obligation to not recognize the validity and the effects of domestic or international acts performed for the territory occupied by the government responsible for the illegal situation. The occupying state must withdraw from the occupied territory.

The holding of the ICJ in the South-West Africa case can help in understanding the legal implications of the recognition of the US/UK 'Authority' in Resolution 1483: '… recognizing the specific authorities, responsibilities, and obligations under applicable

91 *Id.*, at paras 4–5.

92 *South-West Africa* case, *supra* note 77, para. 118, at 54; Repertory, *supra* note 5, vol. I, No. 1601, at 633.

93 Declaration on the Enhancement of the Effectiveness of the Principle of Refraining from the Threat or Use of Force in International Relations, GA Res. 42/22 (Nov. 18, 1987), para. 10.

94 *South-West Africa* case, *supra* note 77, paras 121–124, 126, at 55–56.

international law of these states as occupying powers under unified command …'.[95] The recognition is an authoritative act of the Council and it carries out a specific legal effect: it implies the renunciation to sanction the situation's illegitimacy created by the Authority. That is to say, it suspends *erga omnes* the legal consequences arising out of the illegal presence in Iraq of the US and UK, classified by the Council as an 'occupation'. This suspension is subordinate to the conditions set by the Authority in the Resolution; the Council 'decides' to control its implementation.[96] The UN recognition precludes the sanctioning of the Anglo-American occupation by denying legal effect to the official acts performed by the occupying power on behalf of Iraq; it also precludes the adoption of economic sanctions.

(3) It defined the role of the UN as 'vital'

Resolution 1483 indicated in the Authority the only institution that has effective governing power, albeit temporarily, that is to say, until an 'internationally recognized, representative [Iraqi] government' is built.[97] Non-occupying states and international organizations can operate 'under the Authority'[98] to contribute to the stability and safety of Iraq, and to assist the Iraqi people in reforming their institutions and rebuilding the country. The UN has 'a vital role in humanitarian relief, the reconstruction of Iraq, and the restoration and establishment of national and local institutions for representative governance'.[99] Clearly, this is not comparable to the central role performed by the UN in similar situations, when it takes over the administration of certain territories waiting to rebuild a representative national government[100] (especially in Kosovo and East Timor).[101] In this case, the UN control function has been emptied of its actual contents and has been downgraded to mere supervision of the implementation of the conditions contained in the Resolution.

The question is whether Resolution 1483 actually mended the breach of integrated legal procedures that took place during the crisis and re-established a link between intervening states and competent international institutions; in other words, whether it restored the short-circuited decision process by modifying the distribution of power in the decision-making process between the participants

---

95 SC Res. 1483, *supra* note 89, preamble. See Sean D. Murphy, *Contemporary Practice of the United States Relating to International Law*, 97 Am. J. Int'l L. 681 (2003).

96 SC Res. 1483, *supra* note 89, at paras 16, 25.

97 *Id.*, at para. 9.

98 *Id.*, at preamble; see also *id.*, at para. 13.

99 *Id.*, at preamble.

100 The UN Special Representative has 'independent responsibilities' of coordination of humanitarian assistance and reconstruction and the task to 'restore and establish national and local institution' that accomplish 'working intensively with the Authority' (see SC Res. 1483, *supra* note 89, para. 8). The Development Fund for Iraq also features a representative of the General Secretary, although the funds 'shall be disbursed at the direction of the Authority'.

101 Ruth Wedgwood & Harold K. Jacobson, *Symposium: State Reconstruction after Civil Conflict, Foreword*, 95 Am. J. Int'l L. 1 (2001); Michael J. Matheson, *United Nations Governance of Postconflict Societies*, *id.*, at 76; Samuel H. Barnes, *The Contribution of Democracy to Rebuilding Postconflict Societies*, *id.*, at 86.

(i.e., between the Council and those states which have the capacity and the will to enforce international law). In previous instances of interruption of the 'integrated process', as happened in the case of Kosovo, the UN restored the decision process by endorsing states' actions *ex post*, and terminated – with states' collaboration – the final phase of the integrated decision process by regaining control over the social action. Resolution 1483 is not an attempt by the Security Council to resume the procedural process that had begun with the determination of serious violations of human rights in Iraq and was later interrupted by the Anglo-American intervention. In fact, the Council has qualified the US and UK as occupying powers, and therefore the intervention remains illegal. By recognizing the Authority's government powers, the UN did not render the intervention lawful. It did not take over the administration of the country. It did not cooperate with those states in the administration of Iraq, nor complemented their actions with its own impartial actions. It merely agreed to the temporary control of Iraq by the US and UK, which is an activity imputable only to the occupying states. The check performed by the Council of the Authority's administration, as contemplated in the Resolution, is only subsidiary to the main activity performed by the occupying states, and its aim is to verify adherence to the resolution's requirements. It does not purport *to integrate* the occupying Authority's administration. In conclusion, the Resolution does not give the UN a new role in the integrated decision process. It does not modify the customary procedures and the linchpin role of the UN in the use of force and the administration and reconstruction in post-conflict peace-building. After all, this 'incident' is the result of US pressures. Washington strove to obtain an endorsement of some sort, after it had been severely chastised both by the majority of the international community and international organizations, which did not stop claiming multilateral decisions and a central role for the UN.[102]

Concluding Remarks: Effectiveness Is Not Supplanting Legality

Since the UN Declaration on Human Rights, sixty years ago, the safeguard of human rights and fundamental freedoms has gone a long way both in a legal sense and in the practice of states and international organizations. Eventually, legality has prevailed over effectivity. Three pieces of evidence, which can be found in the current Iraqi crisis, illustrate the legal notion of legality and its endurance against effectivity.

---

102 On the necessity of multilateralism in the management of social values and on the central role assigned to the UN in these processes, see also resolutions of international organizations, like CHR Res. 2003/63, *supra* note 33: the UN Commission on Human Rights reinforced the 'integrated' nature of the enforcement system by 'stressing that the responsibility for managing ... threats to international peace and security, must be shared among the nations of the world and should be exercised multilaterally that in this regard the central role must be played by the United Nations …' (preamble), and also 'express[ing] its rejection of unilateralism and stress[ing] its commitment to multilateralism and multilaterally agreed solutions, in accordance with the Charter of the United Nations and international law, as the only reasonable method of addressing international problems' (para. 8); see also NATO Statement, *supra* note 12, para. 9.

Promotion of a Democratic International Order

A new legal notion of democracy has emerged in legal texts and common practice of international organizations, which aims at providing democracy as a system of governance for both civil societies and the global society. This notion of democracy encompasses procedure and substance, laws and their enforcement; the full realization of 'all human rights for all' and democratic institutions, both domestic and international. The aim of the democratic process is to build a 'democratic international order'.[103] Once the concept of international community based on the idea of common humanity is adopted, the international legal obligations of states – such as those assigning states the duty to safeguard human rights and fundamental freedoms, not only of their own citizens, but of all individuals – are bound to expand. As a result, the notion of gross violations is expanded to include the sponsoring of terrorism and the illicit production of weapons of mass destruction, two activities that could infringe the fundamental rights and freedoms and thwart the economic and social development of all individuals and peoples.

Gradual Tightening of Sanctions Against 'Illegitimate' Governments

Measures taken to sanction illegitimate governments are beginning to be increasingly invasive of sovereignty. They are no more solely economic sanctions, but measures, as in the case of Iraq, include actions taken to implement an international weapons-monitoring system,[104] including the duty to allow inspectors to enter the country and examine its arsenals.[105] It is to be noted that there has never been substantial disagreement amongst states on the fact that Saddam Hussein needed to be removed from power. The point of contention was whether this was to be done unilaterally or multilaterally.

In the past, governments that have seriously violated human rights and the principle of democracy have rarely been overthrown either by way of multilateral actions under the aegis of the UN or regional organizations. It did not happen in the case of Kosovo in 1998 nor in that of Iraq in 1990, when the Security Council authorized operations to free Kuwait but refrained from mandating the removal of Saddam Hussein's regime. The case of Haiti in 1994, when the Security Council authorized the US to use force to prevent the interruption of the democratization process and to restore the lawfully elected government of Aristide, is an exception.[106] All other cases of government-ousting due to violation of the principle of democracy and other fundamental norms of international law have been unilateral. Many of them are the result of the American policy to export democracy everywhere and

103 See GA Res. 56/151, *supra* note 33 and pronouncements of the UN Commission on Human Rights.

104 See the system introduced under SC Res. 687 (April 3, 1991); SC Res. 1284 (Dec. 17, 1999). Lori Fisler Damrosch, *The Permanent Five as Enforcers of Controls on Weapons of Mass Destruction*, 13 Eur. J. Int'l L. 305 (2002).

105 SC Res. 1441, *supra* note 1, para. 5.

106 SC Res. 940 (July 31, 1994).

with every means. This is the case of the ousting of Marcos in the Philippines and Duvalier in Haiti, the military intervention in Grenada, and the imprisonment of Noriega in Panama,[107] just to mention the most recent.

In the case of the current Iraqi situation, the toppling had already been foreshadowed by Resolution 1441, in which the Security Council decided to give the Iraqi regime ‘a final opportunity’,[108] and warned Saddam Hussein of the ‘serious consequences’ that he would face if he did not comply with the Resolution. Resolution 1441 did not contain an ‘automatic’ authorization of the use of force, as promptly pointed out by the Arab countries.[109] After this, the fact that Saddam Hussein’s regime had to step down from power was accepted also by the Arab countries and Russia, which actually floated diplomatic plans and offered to negotiate the exile of the dictator and his top officials.[110] The decision of the Economic Community of Western African States (ECOWAS) to dispatch a peace contingent in Liberia to deal with civil war and the serious violations of human rights[111] is the validation of the fact that contemporary international law allows the overthrow of murderous dictators by way of multilateral action, even in the form of unauthorized armed intervention carried out by regional organizations. The Liberian President, Charles Taylor, was ‘invited’ to leave the country. The UN endorsed the decision of the region’s states and regained control of the situation in Liberia.[112]

Evolution of Integrated Processes to Implement International Legality

The development of international law in the human rights field has been characterized by the continuous erosion of sovereignty and the birth of a multilateral system of

107 The opinions of authors on the unilateral use of force differ. See, e.g., Anthony D’Amato, *The Invasion of Panama Was a Lawful Response to Tyranny*, 84 Am. J. Int’l L. 516 (1990); Malvina Halbestram, *The Copenhagen Document: Intervention in Support of Democracy*, 34 Harvard International Law Journal 163 (1993); Richard A. Falk, *The Haiti Intervention: A Dangerous World Order Precedent for the United Nations*, 36 Harvard International Law Journal 341 (1995); Vera Gowlland-Debbas, *The Limits of Unilateral Enforcement of Community Objectives in the Framework of UN Peace Maintenance*, 11 Eur. J. Int’l L. 361 (2000). See also the authors quoted *supra* notes 7, 9, and 72.

108 SC Res. 1441, *supra* note 1, para. 2.

109 Arab League Council, Res. 227, Res. 243, *supra* note 86. See Franck, *What Happens Now? The United Nations After Iraq, Agora, supra* note 2, at 610.

110 The United Arab Emirates’ plan to exile Saddam Hussein was discussed within the international organizations of the Arab world: Arab League Summit in Sharm El Sheik (March 1, 2003) (available at <http://news.bbc.co.uk/2/low/middle_east/2808729.stm>); Gulf Cooperation Council in Qatar (March 3, 2003) (available at <http://www.islamonline.net/english/News/2003–03/03/article15.shtml>); Islamic Conference (March 5, 2003) (available at <http://www.oic–un.org/home/Exsum.html>. The proposal had the consensus mostly within the Gulf Cooperation Council. Yet it was not formally approved; Saddam Hussein’s firm refusal to leave the country was followed by a growing concern amongst Arab leaders about ‘attempts to impose changes in the region’ (see Arab League Council, Res. 243, *supra* note 86, para. 8 and Point 6 of the Statement of the Islamic Conference).

111 ECOWAS Decision of 17 May 2002.

112 SC Res. 1497 (Aug. 1, 2003).

intervention against dictatorial and immoral regimes. The advent of this system deeply modified the traditional balance between effectivity and legality. In the face of the UN Charter's inadequacy to safeguard human rights, the international structure has developed a multilateral system of safeguarding international legality, co-managed by states and international institutions. In the integrated decision process, the UN holds the central role, and its responsibilities include: (1) objective determination of illegality; (2) management of operations to restore legality; and (3) control of the activity of the states and the regional organizations working to this end. The integrated system for the safeguard of human rights, albeit recent, holds a high degree of legitimacy, since it is founded on the extended practice of the UN and regional organizations. The dynamics and procedures of 'shared governance', applied in practice, are gradually becoming general international norms.[113]

The integrated system is evolving. At the present time, in order to overcome the limit imposed by veto powers, force can be used without UN authorization, provided that the action is endorsed by the majority of states and regional organizations and supported by public opinion. The UN controls *ex post* whether the actions taken are genuinely multilateral and whether military operations conform to the parameters of legality. If these tests are met, the link between states and the UN is restored. The latter resumes the direction of operations and brings to its conclusion the process of restoration of legality by taking care of the administration and the reconstruction of democratic institutions in the concerned country. This is what happened in Kosovo and what legitimized that situation. The integrated system evolves towards overcoming the veto, and safeguards and strengthens the multilateral nature of the decisions deemed indispensable in the processes of safeguarding international legality.[114] Whenever the Security Council is blocked by a veto, or a threat of veto, unilateralism trumps the collective character of the decision-making process. This is all the more disturbing when the veto-wielding state is opposed by a large number of states and regional international organizations. Thus, the dynamics of co-managing the integrated system must be developed and institutionalized. Changes of such importance are aimed at replacing the imperialistic role of the dominant states with the 'public' action and imply and demand an institutional restructuring of the international community, or at least its sufficient integration with the UN and other organizations to prevent abuses committed in the name of fundamental values. Clearly, once it is perfected institutionally, the undergoing process of shared governance, inspired by the safeguard of legality rather than considerations of brute force, can be a major addition to the international structure.

---

113 See *supra* Introduction to this book, under the headings 'Verticality' and 'Collective Guarantees'; see chapter 2 under the heading 'The Osmotic Relationship Between the Inter-State Community and the United Nations'.

114 See the debates on Security Council reform at the General Assembly and the recommendations to refrain from the use of the veto in the event of genocide, crimes against humanity and serious violations of international humanitarian law (A/60/L.49, 17 March 2006, Annex; GA/10484 , 20 July 2006). For the activity performed by the International Court of Justice in this field, see *supra* chapter 3 of this book, under the heading 'Overcoming veto rule of Art. 27 of the UN Charter'; also see *infra* chapter 8, 'Introduction'.

This chapter aimed to demonstrate that the concept of 'legitimacy' has become a norm of modern international law: the legitimacy of governments is monitored by international institutions on the basis of well-defined parameters. Illegality can be sanctioned by overthrowing illegitimate governments, provided that the action is accomplished multilaterally. In our time, legality has won supremacy over effectivity. This triumph is partially overshadowed by the 'recognition' of the Authority's effectivity to temporarily govern Iraq. However, there is the risk that some states might monopolize the functions of common guarantee by claiming to act on behalf of all and thus depriving the action from the necessary objectivity. Recognition of effectivity might sideline the UN and reduce its centrality. Those states might alter the equilibrium among the participants in the integrated system. Even though the Security Council has qualified the US and the UK in Iraq as 'occupying powers' – thus reaffirming the widespread accusations of unilateralism. This raises the question of whether effectivity is about to make a comeback on legality.

This worry was not lessened by Resolution 1551.[115] Indeed, it is a hybrid. On the one hand, it reaffirms the need for multilateral action to safeguard democracy under the UN aegis (the Security Council '*authorizes* a multinational force under unified command to take all necessary measures to contribute to the maintenance of security and stability in Iraq'[116]). On the other hand, the UN does not take on the administration of the territory, and its role is not 'central' anymore, although it remains 'vital'.[117] Again, on the one hand, Resolution 1551 does not confer on the Governing Council effective power to administer the territory, but, on the other hand, it affirms that the Governing Council 'embodies the sovereignty of the state of Iraq during the transitional period';[118] sovereignty has been emptied of the content that is normally attributed to it by international law. In reality, Resolution 1551 restored to the Authority 'the specific responsibilities, authorities, and obligations under applicable international law recognized and set forth in Resolution 1483' by virtue of its effectivity in the territory, while, at the same time, it explicitly reaffirms its temporary nature.[119] Finally, the Resolution does not contain any mention of the states of the coalition as 'occupying powers'. In sum, it is a surrender to effectivity. Yet, this incident is not sufficient to conclude that Resolution 1483 has created a new practice. Because of this, its reach does not extend beyond this specific case and therefore does not modify the future of the integrated decision method.

To conclude, nowadays integrated decision-making processes play a paramount role. They are increasingly relied upon in international practice to implement the legality and morality in the new world order. At this critical juncture, and until the day the Charter is radically overhauled, the future of the UN Charter system and the equilibrium between law and force ultimately depend on the capacity of the UN to rein in these processes.

---

115 SC Res. 1511 (Oct. 16, 2003).

116 *Id.*, at para. 13.

117 *Id.*, at para. 8.

118 *Id.*, at para. 4.

119 *Id.* at para. 1.

PART III
Integration of Legal Systems in the Direction of Global Law

Chapter 5

State Law and International Law in a Globalizing Legal System*

Introduction

In recent years, due to the profound transformations taking place in international society and its legal order, the issue of the relationship between internal law and international law has forcefully come to the forefront of states' attention. Forty years after Friedmann's seminal study on the changing structure of international law, with its notorious distinction between the law of 'coexistence' and the law of 'cooperation',[1] there seems to be little doubt that international law of the beginning of the third millennium is increasingly a law of 'integration'.

Undoubtedly, one of the consequences of globalization is the acceleration of emphasis on the osmosis between internal law and international law, and the blurring of boundaries between the two legal orders. Globalization processes currently under way have focused the international community's attention on national political systems. International human rights treaties, which confer fundamental rights and freedoms to individuals, often including procedural guarantees for the protection of such rights, necessitate the adaptation of national legal systems. Important regulatory functions have been taken away from states both by supranational organizations, which strive to achieve uniform standards in economic matters, and by universal organizations, which create and oversee compliance with minimum social standards. Moreover, international criminal judicial bodies' statutes provide for cooperation in criminal matters and set limits on the judicial activity of states.[2]

In other words, increasingly, rules of general international law and treaty law govern issues that were formerly left to the states' exclusive competence, thus reducing states' freedom and multiplying grounds of conflict between two categories

---

* This chapter is based on the paper by Giuliana Ziccardi Capaldo, *Treaty Law and National Law in a Globalizing System*, 2 The Global Community. Yearbook of International Law and Jurisprudence [hereinafter GCYILJ] 143 (2002–I). That early text has been updated and modified.

1 Wolfgang Friedmann, The Changing Structure of International Law 60–67 (1964). See generally Piero Ziccardi, *Règles d'Organisation et Règles de Conduite en Droit International. Le Droit Commun et les Ordres Juridiques*, 152 Recueil des Cours 119, 123 (1976–IV).

2 Brian F. Havel, *The Constitution in an Era of Supranational Adjudication*, 78 North Carolina Law Review 257 (2000).

of norms: domestic and international.[3] States that have not equipped their legal systems with institutions and procedures to cope with rapid changes in international law face a double risk. On the one hand, they might breach international obligations and thus undermine their international reputation. On the other hand, the domestic balance of powers might come under severe strain. This is true especially in the case of those states that have regulated treaty-making powers inadequately; that is to say, those states where the executive, on the basis of the residual power doctrine,[4] has the ultimate power to undertake international obligations. Thus, the sheer mass of international norms, and their rapid expansion created chiefly by executives, raises a serious of sensitive issues about law-making functions in democratic societies.

The danger has not gone unnoticed. A remarkable process of constitutional regulation of the internal effect of international law, which has also affected considerably the countries of Eastern Europe,[5] is currently taking place. Since the middle of the twentieth century, scholars and decision-makers have increased their attention towards the *lacunae* of a great number of municipal legal systems and have begun an earnest search for criteria and mechanisms to facilitate the internal application of international law. Likewise, constitutional organs of both established and newer democracies have increased efforts towards endowing national legal systems with rules and instruments to bring the internal legal system in line with the international legal order.[6]

As mentioned earlier, states do pay great attention to the effects of international treaties on the domestic legal order. The need to coordinate treaties with possibly conflicting internal norms has become urgent as a result of the enormous expansion (not only quantitative) of treaties, by their tendency to govern relations between

3 Giuseppe Sperduti, *Le Principe de Souveraineté et le Problème des Rapports entre le Droit International et le Droit Interne*, 153 RECUEIL DES COURS 319 (1976–V); CONSTANTIN P. ÉCONOMIDÈS, THE RELATIONSHIP BETWEEN INTERNATIONAL AND DOMESTIC LAW (1994); Dermott J. Devine, *Relationship Between International Law and Domestic Law in Domestic Courts*, 24 SOUTH AFRICAN YEARBOOK OF INTERNATIONAL LAW 317 (1999); Benedetto Conforti, *Notes on the Relationship Between International and National Law*, 3 INTERNATIONAL LAW FORUM DU DROIT INTERNATIONAL 18 (2001); CONTEMPORARY ISSUES IN THE LAW OF TREATIES (Malgosia A. Fitzmaurice ed., 2005).

4 According to the residual power doctrine, the executive possesses all powers inherent to the conduct of foreign affairs, unless they have been expressly taken from it.

5 Eric Stein, *International Law in Internal Law: Toward Internationalization of Central–Eastern European Constitutions?*, 88 AMERICAN JOURNAL OF INTERNATIONAL LAW [hereinafter AM. J. INT'L L.] 427 (1994); *Id.*, *International Law and Internal Law in the New Constitutions of Central-Eastern Europe*, *in* RECHT ZWISCHEN UMBRUCH UND BEWAHRUNG 865 (Ulrich Beyerlin ed., 1995); Gennady M. Danilenko, *The New Russian Constitution and International Law*, 88 AM. J. INT'L L. 451 (1994); Vladlen S. Vereshchetin, *New Constitutions and the Old Problem of the Relationship Between International Law and National Law*, 7 EUROPEAN JOURNAL OF INTERNATIONAL LAW [hereinafter EUR. J. INT'L LAW] 29 (1996).

6 Paul de Visscher, *Les Tendences Internationales des Constitutions Modernes*, 80 RECUEIL DES COURS 511, 560 (1952–I); Nicolas Maziau, *Le Costituzioni Internazionalizzate*, 4 DIRITTO PUBBLICO COMPARATO ED EUROPEO 1397 (2002). For more details, as well as bibliographical references, see *infra*, under the heading 'Recent Trends …' later in this chapter, especially note 52.

individuals of various nature (e.g., commercial, social, or economic) and by the need to protect the rights of private persons. States' attention is all the more necessary as increasingly binding and effective compliance-control and enforcement mechanisms are created at the international level. This is particularly true of supranational organizations of a regional character, such as the European Community, but also applies to international organizations of a universal character operating in the economic, social, financial, and defence sectors. Over the years, several treaty-based bodies have been equipped with specific organs entrusted with the task of ascertaining and sanctioning breaches of treaty rules, and of instituting binding enforcement measures. Contracting states might wish to avoid the consequences of any breach and to protect their reputation as trustworthy members of the international community.

It is for these reasons that most states have amended or supplemented their constitutions to implement international treaty obligations, and they have done so by adhering to international principles, such as the rule *pacta sunt servanda* and its corollaries, such as good faith, primacy, and direct and immediate applicability of treaties. These principles have been repeatedly upheld by international judicial bodies. They regulate the way states implement agreed treaty obligations in the internal legal system. They give concrete meaning to the rule *pacta sunt servanda*, and, therefore, their non-observance is a breach of the cardinal rule of the international legal system.

The growing concern about the internal effect of international obligations in domestic legal systems is confirmed by the stance taken by the International Court of Justice in the *LaGrand* case, where the Court declared that it has the power to 'hold that domestic law has been the cause of [a] violation of [an international treaty obligation]'.[7]

Italy, too, has taken steps to regulate the internal applicability of treaty law/ European Community law by amending its Constitution. Such regulation was hitherto lacking in the Italian legal order. The Italian Constitution of 1948 was silent on the effect of treaties in internal law. For a long time, and unlike its European partners,[8] Italy left several constitutional issues arising out its membership to the European Union unaddressed (e.g., allocation of powers between Parliament and the Government and procedures for the national instruction of EU matters). Article 11 of the Italian Constitution was left to bear the brunt of it. The *Corte Costituzionale* (the Italian Constitutional Court) and scholars relied on Article 11 of the Constitution to determine the effects and status of Community law (both the founding treaties and Community legislation, known as 'secondary law') in the Italian legal system.[9] Yet, Article 11 surely had not been drafted to cope with the process of European

7 *LaGrand* Case (Germany v. United States of America), Judgment, (June 27, 2001), para. 125.

8 Joël Rideau, *Constitution et Droit International dans les Etats Membres des Communautées Européennes*, 3 Revue Française de Droit Constitutionnel 425 (1990).

9 See Art. 11 of the Italian Constitution [hereinafter Ital. Const.], translated in Constitutions of the Countries of the World (Albert P. Blaustein & Gisbert H. Flanz eds, 1987) [hereinafter Constitutions].

integration but rather with the substantially different goal of the eventual accession to the UN.

It is only towards the end of the 1990s that steps were undertaken to address this issue. Despite the failure of the Parliamentary Commission for Constitutional Reforms (i.e., the *Bicamerale* Commission),[10] changes were introduced by the law 'Amendments to Title V Part Two of the Constitution of Italy' (hereinafter 'Amendments'),[11] approved by referendum on 18 October 2001. The Amendments rearranged the relations between the central state and the regions, as well as the system of legal sources, defining the relationship between internal law and treaty law/EC law but falling short of what was needed. Ideally, a more comprehensive approach would have been preferable, covering both treaty power and the relationship between treaties and domestic law, and paying specific attention to the process of European integration.[12] This would have avoided the many interpretative doubts that did not fail to emerge soon after the approval of the Amendments.[13]

With the Amendments, Italy has conformed to the recent state habit of regulating at the constitutional level the internal effect of treaty obligations. By doing so, Italy has significantly moved towards compliance with established and widely respected international standards that will be examined in the paragraph below.

As we will discuss, this trend has been reinforced by transformations that the international community is undergoing, moving away from a community of self-reliant states towards a tightly knitted 'world community'. The remarkable scope of these changes question the traditional view of a large part of the doctrine which holds that states have the unfettered freedom to choose how to implement a treaty. They conversely suggest that, under international law, the state might be subject to certain international minimum standards when implementing its international treaty obligations.

---

10 Established by Legge Costituzionale No. 1, of 24 January 1997, GAZZETTA UFFICIALE No. 22 (Jan. 28 1997); the Commission's Project was transmitted to the Chambers of Parliament on 4 November 1997.

11 Legge Costituzionale No. 3, of 18 October 2001, GAZZETTA UFFICIALE No. 248 (Oct. 24, 2001). English text of Constitution, as modified by Law No. 3, available at <http://english.camera.it>. For a critical survey see *infra* later in this chapter under the heading 'Reducing State Freedom …'.

12 In this sense, see our proposals for possible reform that were drawn up while the *Bicamerale* Commission was working (see Giuliana Ziccardi Capaldo, *Riforme Istituzionali e Trattati Internazionali: Contributo alla Commissione Bicamerale*, XLIV NORD E SUD 89 (1997) [hereinafter Ziccardi Capaldo, *Riforme Istituzionali*]) and were later re-elaborated and reproposed in the ensuing critical evaluation of the Project (*Id.*, *I Rapporti tra Diritto Interno e Diritto Internazionale. I Cocci della Commissione Bicamerale e le Prospettive di Riforma*, RIFORME COSTITUZIONALI. PROSPETTIVA EUROPEA E PROSPETTIVA INTERNAZIONALE 159 (2000) [hereinafter Ziccardi Capaldo, *I Rapporti*]). There has been considerable debate about this subject, for a detailed examination and doctrinal references see *id.*, *passim*.

13 See the debate at the *Symposium* ATTUAZIONE DEI TRATTATI INTERNAZIONALI E COSTITUZIONE ITALIANA. UNA RIFORMA PRIORITARIA NELL'ERA DELLA COMUNITÀ GLOBALE (Giuliana Ziccardi Capaldo ed., 2003) [hereinafter ATTUAZIONE DEI TRATTATI]. For some remarks and suggestions for possible reform, see *infra* text under the heading 'Reducing State Freedom …' later in this chapter.

In sum, this chapter will discuss:

1. the international minimum standards for the domestic implementation of treaty obligations dictated by general principles of international law, as interpreted and applied by international courts (under the heading 'International Minimum Standards ...');
2. the *de facto* application of such international standards by domestic courts, and the growing practice of incorporating *de jure* those standards in constitutions (the two following sections);
3. the Italian practice on implementing international obligations in the domestic legal system. While the 1948 Constitution was silent on the matter, Italian practice in the second half of the twentieth century was evolved by way of rulings of the *Corte Costituzionale*. The 2001 constitutional Amendments followed along the path traced by the *Corte Costituzionale* and incorporated the court's ruling in the letter of the Constitution (under the heading 'The Italian Solution ...'); and
4. the upheaval the internal balance of powers might experience when state constitutions implement international standards; also the repercussions on the democratic nature of internal and international law that may ensue from failure to grant parliaments an adequate role in the various phases of the treaty-making process (the last two sections).

International Minimum Standard for Internal Applicability of Treaty Law

The considerations just outlined define the heart of the current debate about whether states must follow international minimum standards – besides the generic good faith requirement – in implementing international treaty obligations in their internal legal order. The question is intensely debated among international legal scholars. Eric Stein cast doubt on 'the continued functionality of the rule that a state is free, subject only to the broad international "good faith" standard to choose the ways and means of implementing a treaty to which it is a party'.[14]

The well-known doctrinal dispute of the last century between 'dualism' and 'monism' is no more relevant to this issue, as many commentators agree.[15] Others maintain that, considering the absence of criteria for uniform implementation, it should be left to any given treaty to indicate the way in which it should be implemented in domestic law. This would serve two purposes: fostering uniformity of application and facilitating the selection of the implementing procedure most consonant with the contents and scope of the given treaty. In practice, however, rarely do treaties

---

14 Stein, *supra* note 5, at 450. See also Stefan Kadelbach, *International Law and the Incorporation of Treaties into Domestic Law*, 42 German Yearbook of International Law 66 (1999).

15 Patrick Daillier, *Monisme et Dualisme: Un Débat Depassé?*, *in* Droit International et Droits Internes, Dévéloppements Récentes 9 (Rafaâ Ben-Achour & Sadok Belaïd eds, 1999). See also Giuseppe Sperduti, *Dualism and Monism. A Confrontation to Overcome*, 3 Israel Yearbook of International Law 31 (1977); David Feldman, *Monism, Dualism and Constitutional Legitimacy*, 20 The Australian Yearbook of International Law 10 (1999);

indicate the way in which they should be implemented in the domestic legal systems of the contracting states, leaving it to states to decide.

Admittedly, it cannot be denied that well-established general rules and principles, some of which have also been codified in the Vienna Convention on the Law of Treaties (the Vienna Convention),[16] require states to observe certain modalities in the implementation of treaties. Responsibility for breach will ensue from states' failure to observe such requirements. In codifying the principle *pacta sunt servanda*, Article 26, Section I of Part III, entitled 'Observance, application and interpretation of treaties' of the Vienna Convention provides that 'Every treaty *in force* is binding upon the parties to it and *must be performed* by them in good faith'. Article 27, entitled 'Internal law and observance of treaties', clearly states the primacy and the immediate applicability of treaties, by providing that 'A party may not invoke the provisions of its internal law as justification for its failure to perform a treaty…'.

These provisions of the Vienna Convention are customary international law, as the International Court of Justice and other international courts time and again have confirmed, identifying the principles of good faith, primacy and direct applicability of treaties as the minimum standards for internal implementation of treaty obligations. This is confirmed also by consistent and widespread international practice, to which we will return later (see under the next three subheadings in this chapter).

Because of this, states' unfettered freedom in implementing treaties in their internal legal system cannot be claimed anymore. It is rather a question of freedom of choice of forms and means that a state considers it suitable to ensure its observance of the standards prescribed by those principles.[17]

States may comply with these minimum standards *de jure* (i.e., by way of constitutional and/or legislative provisions) or *de facto* (i.e., by practice of state organs). The former option provides greater guarantee that the obligations undertaken will be performed, thus reinforcing the state's trustworthiness at the international level. Because of this consideration, it is the practice of choice by states today. The latter, however, gives more flexibility. Moreover, domestic courts often implement those international standards even in the absence of internal rules, to protect the state from incurring sanctions for breach of international obligations.

Yet, the question is what the international minimum standards of internal implementation of treaties are which, at the present time, exist in international law. Three can be identified: direct applicability, good faith, and primacy of treaties.

Direct Applicability

The principle *pacta sunt servanda* requires the simultaneous and uniform binding effect of the contractual relationship entered into. It may be inferred from Articles

---

16 Vienna Convention on the Law of Treaties, 23 May 1969, 1155 UNTS 331 [hereinafter VIENNA CONVENTION].

17 See the ECJ on the principle of good faith in Portuguese Republic v. Council of the European Union, Case C–149/96, Judgment of 23 November 1999, 1999 ECR I–8395, para. 35 (as summarized in 1 GCYILJ 1127 (2001)).

26 and 27 of the Vienna Convention[18] that compliance with the standard of the direct and immediate applicability allows the states to realize the simultaneousness and uniformity required by the principle *pacta sunt servanda*.

Under Article 26, treaties must be performed from the date of their entry into force, and without altering their content in any way. Any national procedures of implementation, be they laws or otherwise (e.g., executive orders, decisions by local competent authorities, rulings by national courts, etc.), that delay the implementation of treaties within a state's legal system or modify its contents breach the rule *pacta sunt servanda*. This may occur, for instance, when the implementation of self-executing agreements is made dependent upon the adoption of *ad hoc* legislation. This is an issue in so-called dualist countries, such as Italy and Germany, which embrace the theory of the 'transformation' of international law into domestic law.[19]

Under Article 27 of the Vienna Convention, provisions of internal law cannot be invoked to justify failure to perform obligations undertaken.

The International Court of Justice (ICJ) confirms that

> '… there is a duty of a state not to impede the due implementation of a treaty to which it is a party, that is not a duty imposed by the treaty itself … it is a duty arising under customary international law independently of the treaty, … it is implicit in the rule *pacta sunt servanda*'.[20]

To avoid hindering the due implementation of a treaty, states should equip themselves with the appropriate legal procedures in advance. This would ensure the integrity of treaty provisions domestically and their implementation from the very moment the

---

18 VIENNA CONVENTION, *supra* note 16.

19 Italian practice opts to paraphrase the language of binding decisions of the Security Council. On the detrimental effects of the theory of 'transformation' on the implementation of treaties in the Italian legal system, see notes 78–89 and corresponding text. See also note 144. The French constitutional system of 1958 has distanced itself from the theory of transformation of international law into domestic law. See Louis Dubouis, *Le Juge Administratif Français et les Règles du Droit International*, 17 ANNUAIRE FRANÇAIS DE DROIT INTERNATIONAL [hereinafter ANN. FR. D.I.]15 (1971).

20 Military and Paramilitary Activities in and Against Nicaragua (Nicaragua v. United States of America), Merits, Judgment, 1986 ICJ REPORTS 14 (June 27, 1986), para. 270, at 135. See GIULIANA ZICCARDI CAPALDO, REPERTORY OF DECISIONS OF THE INTERNATIONAL COURT OF JUSTICE/RÉPERTOIRE DE LA JURISPRUDENCE DE LA COUR INTERNATIONALE DE JUSTICE (1947–1992), 2 vols (1995) [hereinafter REPERTORY], vol. I, No. 1030, at 29. The following declaration of principle by the PCIJ has remained isolated: 'an international agreement cannot, as such, create direct rights and obligations for private individuals' (Jurisdiction of the Courts of Danzig, Advisory Opinion No. 15 (March 3, 1928), 1928, PCIJ, Series B, No. 15, at 3). In the case it was called on to decide (i.e., whether the Beamtenabkommen, an agreement between Poland and Danzig, was directly applicable in the Danzig courts) the Court itself decided in favour of direct applicability (*id.*, at 18). See Thomas Buergenthal, *Self-Executing and Non-Self-Executing Treaties in National and International Law*, 235 RECUEIL DES COURS 303, 322 (1992–IV); Zhaojie Li, *Effects of Treaties in Domestic Law*, 16 DALHOUSIE LAW JOURNAL 62 (1993); Carlos Manuel Vázquez, *The Four Doctrines of Self–executing Treaties*, 89 AM. J. INT'L L. 695 (1995).

treaty comes into force internationally. State must be equipped with a system capable of ensuring that self-executing treaties, and acts based on treaty law (i.e., 'complete' treaty provisions that do not require internal implementing acts to integrate their content), can be directly invoked by individuals before domestic courts without the need of further measures.[21] States must also ensure that the entry into force of implementing measures (whenever they are necessary) in the domestic legal system is contemporaneous with the entry into force of the treaty internationally.

The Court of Justice of the European Communities (ECJ) has contributed extensively to precisely define the concept of direct applicability of agreements, both with regard to the Community law capacity to produce direct effects within the legal order of member states[22] and with regard to agreements entered into by the European Community and third countries. According to the well-established jurisprudence of the ECJ,

> 'A provision of an agreement entered into by the Community with non-member countries must be regarded as being directly applicable when, regard being given to the wording, purpose, and nature of the agreement, it may be concluded that the provision contains a clear, precise, and unconditional obligation that is not subject, in its implementation or effects, to the adoption of any subsequent measure.'[23]

21 Joe Verhoeven, *La Notion d''Applicabilite Directe' du Droit International*, 15 Revue Belge de Droit International [hereinafter Rev. Belge D.I.] 243 (1980); Buergenthal, *supra* note 20, at 317; Denis Alland, *L'Applicabilité Directe du Droit International Considerée du Point de Vue de l'Office du Juge: Des Habits Neufs pour une Vielle Dame?*, 102 Revue Générale de Droit International Public [hereinafter Rev. Gen. D.I.P.] 203 (1998); Thomas Cottier, *A Theory of Direct Effect in Global Law*, European Integration and International Co-Ordination. Studies in Transnational Economic Law in Honour of Claus-Dieter Ehlermann 99 (Armin von Bogdandy, Petros C. Mavroidis & Yves Mény eds, 2002).

22 See, e.g., Costa v. ENEL, Case 6/64, Judgment of 15 July 1964, 1964 ECR 585, 596. See also Baumbast, R and Secretary of State for the Home Department, Case C–413/99, Judgments of 17 September 2002, 2002 ECR I–7091, para. 80; Manufacture Française des Pneumatiques Michelin v. Commission of the European Communities, Case T–203/01, Judgment of 30 September 2003, 2003 ECR II–4071, para. 112; Kunqian Catherine Zhu, Man Lavette Chen v. Secretary of State for the Home Department, Case C–200/02, Judgment of 19 October 2004, 2004 ECR I–9925, para. 26. More broadly on this point, see Buergenthal, *supra* note 20, at 325. For the direct applicability of Community acts in Italy, see *infra* note 91. On primacy and direct effects of Community law, see also the recent judgment of the European Court of Human Rights in the Case of Bosphorus Hava Yollari Turizm Ve Ticaret Anonim Şirketi v. Ireland, Application No. 45036/98, Judgment of 30 June 2005, paras 92–93, 145 (available at <http://www.echr.coe.int>).

23 See Parfums Christian Dior SA and Others, Joined Cases C–300/98 and C–392/98, Judgment of 14 December 2000, 2000 ECR I–1307, para. 42; The Queen v. Secretary of State for the Home Department, Cases C–63/99, C–235/99, C–257/99, Judgment of 27 September 2001, 2001 ECR I–6359, 6427, 6557, paras 30, 31, 31, respectively (as summarized by Bernardo Cortese in 2 GCYILJ 2002, 1188 (2003–II)). See also Demirel, Case 12/86, Judgment of 30 September 1987, 1987 ECR 3719, para. 14; Sevince, Case C–192/89, Judgment of 20 September 1990, 1990 ECR I–3461, para. 15; The Queen v. Minister of Agriculture, Fisheries and Food, *ex parte* Anastasiou and Others, Case C–432/92, Judgment of 5 July 1994, 1994 ECR I–3087, para. 23; A. Racke GmbH & Co. v. Hauptzollamt Mainz, Case C–162/96,

The direct effect that must be accorded to such a provision 'implies that the individuals to which it applies have the right to rely on it before the courts of Member States'.[24] The ECJ affirmed the direct effect of provisions while deciding disputes involving association agreements. It specified that the fact that the association agreement aims essentially to favour the economic development of the third country, involving therefore an imbalance in the obligations assumed by the Community towards the non-member country concerned, 'is not such as to prevent recognition by the Community of the direct effect of certain of its provisions'.[25] It is true that the case law of the ECJ constantly denies direct effect to the rules of the GATT and the WTO Agreement and annexes thereto.[26] But it is also true that the ECJ has not been completely consistent on this issue,[27] as highlighted by ECJ judgments on the

---

Judgment of 16 June 1998, 1998 ECR I–3655, para. 31 (as summarized by Giuliana Ziccardi Capaldo *in* 1 GCYILJ 722 (2001)); Sürül, Case C–262/96, Judgment of 4 May 1999, 1999 ECR I–2685, para. 60; Omer Nazli, Caglar Nazli, Melike Nazli and Stadt Nürnberg, Case C–340/97, Judgment of 10 February 2000, 2000 ECR I–957, paras 26–28 (as summarized by Bernardo Cortese in 2 GCYILJ 1133 (2002–II)); The Queen v. Secretary of State for the Home Department, *ex parte* Abdulnasir Savas, Case C–37/98, Judgment of 11 May 2000, 2000 ECR I–2927, para. 39, *in* 2 GCYILJ 1146 (2002–II)).

24 *Ex parte* Savas, *supra* note 23, para. 54.

25 Sürül, *supra* note 23, para. 72 and The Queen, *id.*, at paras 36, 37, 37, respectively. See also Bresciani, Case 87/75, Judgment of 5 February 1976, 1976 ECR I–199, para. 21; 12 December 1995, Case C–469/93, Chiquita Italia, ECR I–4533, para. 34; Land Nordrhein-Westfalen and Beata Pokrzeptowicz-Meyer, Case C–162/00, Judgment of 29 January 2002, 2002 ECR I–1049, para. 27; Wählergruppe Gemeinsam Zajedno/Birlikte Alternative und Grüne GewerkschafterInnen/UG, Case C–171/01, Judgment of 8 May 2003, 2003 ECR I–4301 para. 65.

26 Portuguese Republic, *supra* note 17, paras 47–48; see also The Queen and Secretary of State for the Environment, Transport and the Regions, *ex parte* Omega Air Ltd and Others, Joined Cases C–27/00 and C–122/00, Judgment of 12 March 2002, 2002 ECR I–2569, para. 93; Petrotub SA and Republica SA v. Council of the European Union, Case C–76/00 P, Judgment of 9 January 2003, 2003 ECR I–79, para. 53; Biret International v. Council of the European Union, Case C–93/02 P, Judgment of 30 September 2003, 2003 ECR I–10497, para. 52; Léon Van Parys NV v. Belgisch Interventie – en Restitutiebureau (BIRB), Case C–377/02, Judgment of 1 March 2005, 2005 ECR I–1465, para. 39.

27 In Portuguese Republic, *supra* note 17, recalling its previous case law (see Fediol v. Commission, Case 70/87, Judgment of 22 June 1989, 1989 ECR 1781, paras 19–22 and Nakajima All Precision Co. Ltd. v. Council, Case C–69/89, Judgment of 7 May 1991, 1991 ECR I–2069, para. 31), the Court confirmed that 'where the Community intended to implement a particular obligation assumed in the context of WTO, or where the Community measure refers expressly to precise provisions of the WTO agreements, it is for the Court to review the legality of the Community measure in question in the light of the WTO rules' (para. 49). In the same direction, see also OGT Fruchthandelsgesellschaft mbH and Hauptzollamt Hamburg-St. Annen, Case C–307/99, Order of 2 May 2001, 2001 ECR I–3159, para. 27 (as summarised by Enrica Adobati, in 2 GCYILJ 1175 (2002–II)); Biret International, *supra* note 26, para. 53; Léon Van Parys, *id.*, at para. 40. For extensive discussion on the interpretation and application of the *Nakajima* case law, see Chiquita Brands International, Inc., Chiquita Banana Co. BV, and Chiquita Italia, SpA v. Commission of the European Communities, Case T–19/01, Judgment of 3 February 2005, para. 114 *et seq.* (available at <http://www.curia.eu.int>). In

application of the TRIPs Agreement.[28]

It follows that national implementing procedures should be limited only to instances of non-self-executing treaties and to cases where the adoption of internal measures is *effectively* necessary to integrate the content of the treaty or its rules, which would otherwise be inapplicable. In these instances, domestic measures ought to be adopted – or at least declared applicable – as of the date of entry into force of the international act or the date set for its implementation.[29] Otherwise, responsibility for breach would ensue, provided that, of course, that delay, or failure to adopt the necessary domestic measures, concerns rules imposing obligations on the parties and not simply rules granting them powers.[30]

Many national systems tend to favour direct applicability.[31] Still, there is a troubling tendency to claim the non-self-executing nature of a politically problematic treaty to prevent its immediate application.[32] Although this behaviour seems to be tolerated on the international plane, it is at variance with the principle of good faith.

---

general, see Judson Osterhoudt Berkey, *The European Court of Justice and Direct Effect for the GATT: A Question Worth Revisiting*, 9 Eur. J. Int'l L. 626 (1998); Paolo Mengozzi, *La Cour de Justice et l'Applicabilité des Règles de l'OMC en Droit Communautaire à la Lumière de l'Affaire Portugal c. Conseil*, Revue du Droit de l'Union Européenne 509 (2000).

28 Annex 1C to the WTO Agreement. While reasserting its constant jurisprudence, the Court affirmed that with reference to sectors in which the TRIPs Agreement applies and in which the Community has not legislated – and which do not, therefore, fall under Community law – member states have competence to recognize the right of individuals to invoke the rules of the TRIPs Agreement directly. See Parfums Christian Dior, *supra* note 23, paras 46–49. See also Schieving-Nijstad vof and Others, Case C–89/99, Judgment of 13 September 2001, 2001 ECR I–5851, para. 55; Anheuser-Busch Inc. v. Budějovický Budvar, Národní Podnik, Case C–245/02, Judgment of 16 November 2004, 2004 ECR I–10989, paras 54–57.

29 The *Corte Costituzionale* dealt with this issue in connection with the question of the application of EU law. Consistently with ECJ case law (Inter-Environnement Wallonie ASBL, C–129/96, Judgment of 18 December 1997, 1997 ECR I–7411), the Italian Court held that in the period between the entry into force of a directive and the date set for its implementation, 'a situation of pre-conformation to the obligation to conform is created which precludes the adoption of acts conflicting with the Directive' (Capezzone e altri, 7 February 2000, Sentenza No. 45, para. 3, Vincenzo Starace & Andrea Cannone, La Giurisprudenza Costituzionale in Materia Internazionale e Comunitaria 2661 (2001) [hereinafter La Giurisprudenza].

30 The *Corte Costituzionale* has excluded direct applicability for treaty norms that confer powers, not obligations, see Di Lazzaro, 16 May 1994, Sentenza No. 183, para. 4, *in* La Giurisprudenza, *supra* note 29, at 1852, and Priebke, 3 March 1997, Sentenza No. 58, paras 4–5, *id.*, at 2241. It has denied the direct applicability to the European Social Charter, Ordinanza of 2 December 2005, No. 435.

31 See *infra* notes 53, 55, 65 and corresponding text.

32 See, in general, Implementing The Tokyo Round: National Constitutions and International Economic Rules (John Jackson, Jean-Victor Louis & Mitsuo Matsushita eds, 1984) [hereinafter Implementing the Tokyo Round]; Ronald A. Brand, *Direct Effect of International Economic Law in the United States and the European Union*, 17 Northwestern Journal of International Law & Business 556 (1996/97). On the debate in the US and the tendency of Congress to consider treaties such as the one establishing the WTO and the Covenant on Civil and Political Rights non-self-executing (138 cong. rec. S8068–72, April 2, 1992), see Yuji Iwasawa, *The Doctrine of Self-Executing Treaties in the United States: A*

Be that as it may, several states have moved away from previous ambiguous stances.[33] This shift has been strongly influenced by globalization and the need for a higher degree of trust in international relations.

Likewise, the Italian Court of Cassation (*Corte di Cassazione*) changed its previous orientation by holding that Article 5 (1)(f) and Article 5 (4) of the European Convention on Human Rights are directly applicable.[34] The *Corte di Cassazione* headed the call of the European Court of Human Rights (ECHR) to contracting parties to ensure the direct applicability and primacy of the provisions of the Convention. The Court has recently held that 'the Convention, which lives through the Court's case law, is now directly applicable in practically all the States Parties'.[35]

Critical Analysis, 26 VANDERBILT JOURNAL OF INTERNATIONAL LAW 627 (1986); Havel, *supra* note 2; on German case-law concerning GATT, see Jochen Frowein, *The Federal Republic of Germany*, *in* UNITED KINGDOM NATIONAL COMMITTEE OF COMPARATIVE LAW, THE EFFECT OF TREATIES IN DOMESTIC LAW 96 (Francis G. Jacobs & Shelly Roberts eds, 1987) [hereinafter THE EFFECT OF TREATIES]. For Japanese practice, see Mitsuo Matsushita, *Japan and the Implementation of the Tokyo Round Results*, *in* IMPLEMENTING THE TOKYO ROUND, *supra*; Kenneth L. Port, *The Japanese International Law 'Revolution': International Human Rights Law and Its Impact in Japan*, 28 STANFORD JOURNAL OF INTERNATIONAL LAW 139 (1991), at 154; Tokyo District Court and Others v. State of Japan, 30 November 1998, para. 2. For Dutch Law, see Henry G. Schermers, *Some Recent Cases Delaying the Direct Effect of International Treaties in Dutch Law*, 10 MICHIGAN JOURNAL OF INTERNATIONAL LAW 266 (1989).

33 On this point and for the relative practice, see Joe Verhoeven & Olivier Lhoest, *Jurisprudence Belge Relative au Droit International Public*, 27 REV. BELGE D.I. 691 (1994); Denis Alland, *Jurisprudence Française de Droit International Public*, 99 REV. GEN. D.I.P. 1013 (1995); see also *supra* text at notes 27–28.

34 Corte di Cassazione, 8 May 1989, Sentenza No. 15. In two cases brought by the Commission before the ECHR, the Italian Government based its objection on failure to exhaust national remedies, arguing 'that the applicants had omitted to rely on Art. 6 (1) before the national authorities, notwithstanding the direct applicability of that provision in Italian law'. See Foti and Others v. Italy, Applications Nos 7604/76; 7719/76; 7781/77; 7913/77, Merits (Dec. 10, 1982), 56 Eur. Ct. H. R. (ser. A), para. 45 Corigliano v. Italy, Application No. 8304/78, Merits and Just Satisfaction (Dec. 10, 1982), 57 Eur. Ct. H. R. (ser. A), para. 28.

35 Scordino and Others (No. 1) v. Italy, Application No. 36813/97, Decision on Admissibility (March 27, 2003), Eur. Ct. H. R. Reports of Judgments and Decisions 2003–IV. Among legal scholars, see Vincenzo Starace, *European Court of Human Rights, Introductory Note*, 1 GCYILJ 659 (2001); *Id.*, 989 (2003–II); *Id.*, 1285 (2005–II).

In general, see, e.g., De Wilde, Ooms and Versyp, Applications Nos 2832/66; 2835/66; 2899/66, Merits (June 18, 1971), 12 Eur. Ct. H. R. (ser. A), para. 95; Van Oosterwijck, Application No. 7654/76, Preliminary Objections (Nov. 6, 1980), 40 Eur. Ct. H. R. (ser. A), para. 33; Van Droogenbroeck v. Belgium, Application No. 7906/77, Merits (June 24, 1982), 50 Eur. Ct. H. R. (ser. A), para. 55; Ahmet Sadik v. Greece, Application No. 18877/91, Preliminary objections (Nov. 15, 1996), Eur. Ct. H. R. Reports of Judgments and Decisions 1996–V, para. 31. Domestic courts of the states parties have also pronounced on the primacy and direct applicability of the European Convention on Human Rights. See especially: for Belgium, Cour de Cassation, Case of Fromagerie Franco-Suisse 'Le Ski', Pasicrisie belge, Judgment of 27 May 1971, 1971, I, at 886–920; Cour de Cassation, Pasicrisie belge, Judgment of 21 September 1959 and 26 September 1978, 1979, I, at 126–128; for the Netherlands, Hoge Raad, Judgment of 18 January 1980, Nederlands Jurisprudentie 1980, No. 462; and for the

The Strasbourg Court has long insisted on the subsidiary character of the machinery established by the Convention and on the national courts' obligation to apply the Convention *ex officio*. To ensure the effectiveness of the system for the protection of fundamental human rights, in states where the above conditions are fulfilled, the subsidiary character of the conventional machinery of protection is 'all the more pronounced'.[36]

Good Faith

On various occasions, the ICJ has declared '[t]rust and confidence ... inherent in international co-operation', along with the principle of good faith, to be 'one of the basic principles' that govern the formation and implementation of conventional obligations, and also their interpretation.[37]

Scholars and international courts constantly point to good faith as the key standard to which a state is subject in implementing treaties. But the uncertain contours of the 'good faith' concept make it hard to define precisely its content.

The ECJ reaffirmed the general applicability of the principle of good faith in the fulfilment of 'every agreement'. In specifying its content, the Court maintained that 'each contracting party is responsible for executing fully the commitments which it has undertaken'; nevertheless, it is 'free to determine the legal means appropriate for attaining that end in its legal system, unless the agreement interpreted in the light of its subject-matter and purpose, itself specifies those means'.[38]

Articles 26 and 31 of the Vienna Convention, which require states, respectively, to perform and interpret treaties in good faith,[39] lead to the conclusion that states have a duty to trust and have confidence in other contracting parties' implementation in due consideration in order that treaty rules should be applied by the internal organs

---

Grand-Duchy of Luxembourg, Supreme Court of Justice, Journal des Tribunaux, Judgment of 2 April 1980, 1980, at 491.

36 Klass and Others v. Germany, Application No. 5029/71, Merits (Sept. 6, 1978), 28 Eur. Ct. H. R. (ser. A), para. 55; Eckle v. Germany, Application No. 8130/78, Merits (July 15, 1982), 51 Eur. Ct. H. R. (ser. A), para. 66; see the Dissenting Opinion in the *Ahmet Sadik* case of Judge Martens, joined by Judge Foighel, note 12 and the relative part of the text.

37 Nuclear Tests (Australia v. France), Judgment, 1974 ICJ Reports 253 (Dec. 20, 1974), para. 46, at 268; Nuclear Tests (New Zealand v. France), Judgment, 1974 ICJ Reports 457 (Dec. 20, 1974), para. 49, at 473; Border and Transborder Armed Actions (Nicaragua v. Honduras), Jurisdiction and Admissibility, Judgment, 1988 ICJ Reports 69 (Dec. 20, 1988), para. 94, at 106; Military and Paramilitary Activities in and Against Nicaragua (Nicaragua v. United States of America), Jurisdiction and Admissibility, Judgment, 1984 ICJ Reports 392 (Nov. 26, 1984), para. 63, at 419; see also Repertory, *supra* note 20, vol. I, Nos 1079–1080, at 81; *id*., vol. II, Nos 2096–2097, at 723. See Robert Kolb, *Aperçus sur la Bonne Foi en Droit International Public*, 54 Revue Hellénique de Droit International [hereinafter Rev. Hell. D.I.] 1 (2001).

38 Portuguese Republic, *supra* note 17, para. 35. The Court drew its argument from the Statement cited above to declare that 'the WTO agreements, interpreted in the light of its subject-matter and purpose, do not determine the appropriate legal means of ensuring that they are applied in good faith in the legal order of the contracting parties' (para. 41).

39 Vienna Convention, *supra* note 16.

of each state in full respect of the fact that such rules belong to the international legal order from which they originated and are therefore applicable on the domestic plane 'as such', just as they are effective and applied in the international legal order. Still, the view that treaties must be interpreted in conformity with international law is also shared by those authors and national courts, that maintain that treaties must be 'transformed' into internal law and, so to speak, 'nationalized', in order to confer rights and impose duties on individuals.[40]

Primacy

The principle that international law prevails over municipal law has been widely upheld by international courts and tribunals. It was originally endorsed in the *Alabama Arbitration* of 14 September 1872 in the dispute between the US and Great Britain,[41] and was later reaffirmed by the Permanent Court of International Justice (PCIJ). In the case of the *Greco-Bulgarian Communities*, the PCIJ held that 'it is *a generally accepted principle of international law* that in the relations between Powers who are contracting parties to a treaty, *the provisions of municipal law cannot prevail over those of the treaty*'.[42] The ICJ reaffirmed the status of the principle of primacy of treaties by stating that it is a 'fundamental principle of international law'.[43] Evoking its predecessor's jurisprudence,[44] the Court went as far as declaring the existence of a well-established rule of international law, according to which both general and conventional international law prevail not only over municipal laws but also over constitutional norms, by stating that 'a State cannot adduce as against another State its own Constitution with a view to evading obligations incumbent upon it under

40 See, e.g., Corte Costituzionale, Ruggerini, 30 July 1997, Sentenza No. 288, *in* La Giurisprudenza, *supra* note 29, at 2311; see also *infra* text under the heading 'Reducing State Freedom …' later in this chapter.

41 Text in Alexander M. Stuyt, Survey of International Arbitrations 1794–1989, 96 (1990).

42 The Greco-Bulgarian 'Communities', Advisory Opinion No. 17, 1930, (July 31, 1930), 1930, PCIJ, Series B, No. 17, at 32 (emphasis added).

43 Applicability of the Obligation to Arbitrate under Section 21 of the United Nations Headquarters Agreement of 26 June 1947, Advisory Opinion, 1988 ICJ Reports 12 (April 26, 1988), para. 57, at 34–35; see Repertory, *supra* note 20, vol. I, No. 1147, at 151. See also on this point Case Concerning the Arrest Warrant of 11 April 2000 (Democratic Republic of the Congo v. Belgium), hearings of 22 November 2000 (CR 2000/34) and 15 October 2001 (CR 2001/5) oral arguments of the representatives of the Democratic Republic of the Congo. On 14 February 2002, the Court affirmed the primacy of customary international rule relating to immunities accorded to Ministers of Foreign Affairs over Art. 5 (3) of the Belgian Law of 19 February 1999 'concerning the Punishment of Serious Violations of International Humanitarian Law' (Arrest Warrant of 11 April 2000 (Democratic Republic of the Congo v. Belgium), Judgment, 2002 ICJ Reports 3 (Feb. 14, 2002), para. 70).

44 Treatment of Polish Nationals in Danzig, Advisory Opinion No 23, (Feb. 4, 1932), 1933, PCIJ, Series A/B, No. 44, at 24.

international law or treaties in force'.[45] The primacy of international law over internal norms, even of constitutional status, has similarly been upheld by the ECJ.[46]

As it was described, Article 27 of the Vienna Convention codifies the principle of the primacy of treaty law by prohibiting states from invoking provisions of internal law to justify failure to perform a treaty. In other words, the Convention states that, in order to avoid responsibility for breach, each state party must implement the treaty giving it priority over prior and subsequent conflicting domestic laws.

However, the majority of states, and, above all, domestic supreme courts, seems to be inclined to defend the primacy of constitutional principles[47] by removing such core constitutional norms from the reach of the rule of absolute primacy of international law over municipal law, upheld by international courts and tribunals.[48]

---

45 Case Concerning the Land Island and Maritime Frontier Dispute (El Salvador v. Honduras; Nicaragua intervening), Judgment, 1992 ICJ Reports 351 (Sept. 11, 1992), para. 377, at 584–585; see also Repertory, *supra* note 20, vol. I, No. 1149, at 152.

46 Handelsgellschaft v. Einfuhr-und Vorratsstelle fur Getreide-und Futtermittel, Case 11/70, Judgment of 17 December 1970, Internationale, 1970 ECR 1125, para. 3; Staatliche Finanzverwaltung v. Spa Simmenthal (Simmenthal II), Case 106/77, Judgment of 9 March 1978, 1978 ECR 629, paras 14–23. See also Consorzio Industrie Fiammiferi (CIF) and Autorità Garante della Concorrenza e del Mercato, Case C–198/01, Judgment of 9 September 2003, 2003 ECR I–8055, para. 48; Debra Allonby, and Accrington & Rossendale College, Education Lecturing Services, trading as Protocol Professional, Secretary of State for Education and Employment, Case C–256/01, Judgment of 13 January 2004, para. 77; Kühne & Heitz NV and Productschap voor Pluimvee en Eieren, Case C–453/00, Judgment of 13 January 2004, 2004 ECR I–873, paras 27–28; Werner Mangold v. Rudiger Helm, Case C–144/04, Judgment of 22 November 2005, para. 78 (<available at http://www.curia.eu.int>). On the application of the principle of primacy by the ECJ, also with reference to treaties concluded by the Community with Third States, see Eric Stein, *External Relations of the European Community: Structure and Process*, 1 Collected Courses of the Academy of European Law 115 (1990), at 168–177.

47 Such a safeguard is ensured by states both by means of provisions protecting basic principles (e.g., Art. 28 (3), Greek Constitution) and by those that expressly declare the absolute primacy of the Constitution (Art. 3, Constitution of Kenya; Art. 15, Constitution of Uzbekistan), even over treaties (e.g., Art. 182, Constitution of Nicaragua) (for the English texts, see Constitutions, *supra* note 9), and in the practice of their courts. Besides the well-known judgment of the US Supreme Court (Reid v. Covert, 354 U.S. 1 (1957)), see, e.g.: Supreme Court of Nigeria, General Sani Abacha & Others v. Chief Gani Fawehinmi, 28 April 2000, No. SC 45/1997 (Why African Charter Cannot Be Superior to the Constitution); Kenya, Ogunda v. AG, E A 19 (1970); Conseil d' État, Ass. 3 July 1996, 101 Rev. Gen. D.I.P. 237 (1997); Conseil Constitutionnel, Decision 93–325 DC of 13 August 1993, Loi relative à la maîtrise de l'immigration et aux conditions d'entrée et séjour des étrangers en France, RJC I–539, published in OJFR (Aug. 18, 1993), at 11722. On the point under examination, see, e.g., Frowein, *supra* note 32; Michel Sastre, *La Conception Américaine de la Garantie Judiciaire de la Supériorité des Traités sur les Lois*, 103 Rev. Gen. D.I.P. 149 (1999), at 155; Vincent Kronenberger, *A New Approach to the Interpretation of the French Constitution in Respect to International Conventions: From Hierarchy of Norms to Conflict of Competence*, 47 Netherlands International Law Review 323 (2000), at 339 and 346 (note 65). For the judicial practice of the Italian *Corte Costituzionale*, see *infra* note 130.

48 *Supra* notes 42–46.

Although this might be the general trend, in the human rights field states seem to be inclined otherwise, indicating the prevailing uncertainty on this matter. By having recourse to criteria such as that of conformity, combined with that of the greater degree of protection, national courts give priority to the international rule whenever it ensures fuller rights than those guaranteed constitutionally,[49] or interpret constitutional rules broadly.[50]

Recent Trends in Domestic Implementation of Treaty Obligations

To summarize, currently international law mandates that states implement international obligations in good faith, give international rules direct applicability, and accord them primacy over domestic law. These three standards apply both to obligations deriving from treaty law (the specific subject of this chapter) and to obligations deriving from general rules of international law. These minimum international standards are widely followed in state practice. Whenever domestic courts happen to divert from them, they always go at great length in justifying their reason for not doing so, even though the reasons given might not always be completely sound and logical.[51]

---

49 See, e.g., Art. 23 of the Venezuelan Constitution of 1999: 'treaties, covenants and conventions relative to human rights signed and ratified by Venezuela, have constitutional status and prevail in the internal order as far as the norms they contain are more favourable than the norms established by the Constitution and the laws of the Republic, and they are of immediate and direct application before the tribunals and other organs of public power' (available at <http://www.georgetown.edu/pdba/Constitutions/Venezuela/venezuela.html>); however, the Venezuelan Supreme Court, in giving constitutional rank to international human rights conventions, did not consider such treaties as having primacy over the Constitution (Decision of 21 November 2000, Supreme Court of Justice (Cas. Pen.), Exp. No. 00–00743). See also the new Constitutions of Eastern European countries (e.g., Art. 10, Czech Constitution of 1993; Art. 11, Slovak Constitution of 1992) and reflections on this point by: Danilenko, *supra* note 5, at 461; Vereshchetin, *supra* note 5, at 32–33. On this point see also *infra* text at note 75.

50 See, e.g., Potenziani, 28 April 1994, Sentenza No. 168, para. 3, *in* La Giurisprudenza, *supra* note 29, at 1841. See also *infra*, note 150.

51 Among the judgments excluding the application of primacy to international law that have received most criticism for the ambiguity of the grounds given for the decisions, see especially District Tribunal of New York, United States of America v. O.L.P., 29 June 1988, with critical comment by Brigitte Stern, *L'Affaire du Bureau de l'O.L.P. Devant les Juridictions Internes et Internationales*, 34 Ann. Fr. D.I. 165 (1988); U.S. Supreme Court, Breard v. Greene, 523 U.S. 371 (1998), 14 April 1998, 37 International Legal Material [hereinafter Int'l Legal Mat.] 824 (1998), and relative comment by Sastre, *supra* note 47. See Conseil d'État, Ass. 30 October 1998, Sarran; Cour de Cassation, Ass. 2 June 2000, Fraisse), and considerations by Kronenberger, *supra* note 47, at 344. See also Michel Cosnard, *Quelques Observations sur les Décisions de la Chambre des Lords du 25 Novembre 1998 et du 24 Mars 1999 dans l'Affaire Pinochet*, 103 Rev. Gen. D.I.P. 309 (1999), at 325–328. Moreover, domestic courts have also unjustifiably excluded direct applicability by pointing to the existence of implementation clauses in the treaty or the 'indeterminateness' or 'flexibility' of the treaty provisions, which could be inferred from the presence of clauses that provide for conciliation procedures, or

Several states have also taken care to give these standards constitutional dignity.[52] In certain cases, this has been done by declaring the direct applicability of treaties in the state's legal system[53] – although sometimes restricting direct applicability only to human rights treaties. In other instances, it has been done by providing expressly for the supremacy of treaties over domestic legislation.[54] However, in this case, too,

---

make application of the treaty dependent on reciprocity. On the point, see generally, Frowein, *supra* note 32, at 69; Benedetto Conforti, *Cours Général de Droit International Public*, 212 Recueil des Cours 9, 45 (1988–V); George Slyz, *International Law in National Courts*, 28 New York University Journal of International Law & Policy 65 (1996).

52 Many important works deal with the various national systems of treaty application and contain extensive bibliographies, see, e.g., de Visscher, *supra* note 6; *Id.*, *La Constitution Belge et le Droit International*, 19 Rev. Belge D.I. 5 (1986); Antonio Cassese, *Modern Constitutions and International Law*, 192 Recueil des Cours 331 (1985–III); The Effect of Treaties, *supra* note 32; Constitutional Adjudication in European Community and National Law. Essays for the Hon. Mr. Justice T. F. O'Higgins (Deirdre Curtin & David O'Keeffe eds, 1992); Constantin P. Économidès, *La Position du Droit International dans l'Ordre Juridique Interne et l'Application des Règles du Droit International par le Juge National*, 49 Rev. Hell. D.I. 207 (1996); L'Integration du Droit International et Communautaire dans l'Ordre Juridique National. Etude de la Pratique en Europe/The Integration of International and European Community Law into the National Legal Order 11 (Pierre M. Eisemann ed., 1996) [hereinafter The Integration]; see also the literature quoted *supra* note 5.

53 See, e.g., the following constitutions actually in force: Art. 5, Albanian Constitution; Art. 8; Art. 7 (1), Constitution of Costa Rica; Art. 52, Constitution of the Czech Republic; Art. 18, Ecuadorian Constitution; Art. 53, French Constitution; Art. 28 (1), Greek Constitution; Art. 7, Hungarian Constitution; Art. 12 (3), Constitution of Kyrgyzstan; Art. 115, Constitution of Mali; Art. 93, Constitution of the Netherlands; Art. 76, Omani Constitution; Art. 55, Peruvian Constitution; Art. 91 (1), Polish Constitution; Art. 11 (2) Romanian Constitution; Art. 15 (4), Russian Constitution Art. 5, Russian Law of 15 July 1995 on international treaties; Art. 231 (3) (4), South African Constitution; Art. 191, Swiss Constitution; Art. 32, Tunisian Constitution; Art. 9 (1), Ukrainian Constitution; Art. VI, United States Constitution; Arts. 23, 153, Venezuelan Constitution. For the English texts, see Constitutions, *supra* note 9. In particular, on Art. VI, US Constitution, see Carlos Manuel Vázquez, *Treaty-Based Rights and Remedies of Individuals*, 92 Columbia Law Review 1082 (1992); Martin S. Flaherty, *History Right?: Historical Scholarship, Original Understanding, and Treaties as 'Supreme Law of the Land'*, 99 Columbia Law Review 2095 (1999). *Contra*, see John C. Yoo, *Treaties and Public Lawmaking: A Textual and Structural Defense of Non-Self-Execution*, *id.*, at 2218; *Id.*, *Globalism and the Constitution: Treaties, Non-Self-Execution, and the Original Understanding*, *id.*, at 1955. See also the response of Carlos Manuel Vázquez, *Laughing at Treaties*, *id.*, at 2154.

54 See, e.g., the following constitutions actually in force: Art. 31, Argentinian Constitution; Art. 6 (4), Armenian Constitution; Art. 151, Azerbaijani Constitution; Art. 5 (4), Bulgarian Constitution; Art. 45, Constitution of Cameroon; Art. 7 (1), Constitution of Costa Rica; Art. 123 (2), Estonian Constitution; Art. 55, French Constitution; Art. 6 (2), Constitution of Georgia; Art. 28 (1), Greek Constitution; Art. 7, Hungarian Constitution; Art. 4 (3), Constitution of Kazakhstan; Art. 87, Ivory Coast Constitution; Art. 116, Constitution of Mali; Art. 4 (2), Moldovan Constitution; Art. 94, Constitution of the Netherlands; Art. 72, Omani Constitution; Arts. 137 and 141, Constitution of Paraguay; Art. 91 (2), Polish Constitution; Art. 20 (2), Romanian Constitution; Art. 15 (4), Russian Constitution; Art. 96

restrictions apply. For instance, sometimes supremacy is granted only on condition of reciprocity, while in other cases it is limited only to cases where treaties have been approved by the legislature. Of course, constitutions may also provide that treaties shall be observed in good faith, as in the case of Japan (Article 98 of the Japanese Constitution).

This trend is particularly conspicuous in the most recent constitutions. Most of the former Socialist countries have expressly regulated treaty power in a more or less organic way and declared the primacy of treaties and/or their direct applicability in the domestic legal system.[55] Many other countries have moved in the same direction, including not only recent but also established democracies.[56] International scholars highlight the growing presence of 'primacy clauses' in new constitutions. These clauses give *de jure* recognition to a widespread practice.[57]

In general, however, states show great caution when defining the relationship between treaties and constitutional norms.[58] Cases like that of the Constitution of the Oman (Article 72), which clearly provide for the supremacy of treaties over the Constitution are rare.

Even in the absence of express provisions, domestic courts seem to be willing to uphold not only the direct applicability of treaties, but also their primacy over statutory law.[59] Typically, national judges achieve this by interpreting laws in such a way as to ensure the supremacy of treaty provisions over subsequent domestic laws. In fact, it is emerging judicial practice to abandon the *lex posterior derogat anterior* rule, which allows prior treaty norms to be superseded by subsequent contrasting national legislation, in favour of criteria that guarantees the primacy of the international norm. This may be achieved by considering treaties *lex specialis* (as the Italian courts do)[60] or by relying on the assumption that domestic norms conform to treaty law,[61] combined with the doctrine that the later national rule prevails only if

---

(1), Spanish Constitution; Art. 98, Constitution of Senegal; Art. 10, Constitution of Tajikistan; Art. 32, Tunisian Constitution; Arts. 23; 153, Venezuelan Constitution. For the English texts, see CONSTITUTIONS, *supra* note 9. See Hervé Bribosia, *Applicabilité Directe et Primauté des Traités Internationaux et du Droit Communautaire*, 29 REV. BELGE D.I. 33 (1996).

55 On the trend followed by the new Constitutions of Eastern European countries and judicial practice in favour of the direct applicability and primacy of treaties, see Wladiyslaw Czaplinsky, *Relationship Between International Law and Polish Municipal Law in the Light of the 1997 Constitution and of the Jurisprudence*, 31 REV. BELGE D.I. 259 (1998); Stein, *supra* note 5, at 444–446; Vereshchetin, *id.*, at 36. See also *infra* note 75.

56 For Italy, see *infra* under the heading 'Reducing State Freedom …' later in this chapter.

57 Vereshchetin, *supra* note 5, at 41. See also *supra* note 54.

58 See text and note 47 *supra*.

59 See generally the practice and literature quoted *supra*, see under the headings 'Direct Applicability' and 'Good Faith' earlier in this chapter and note 53. See also note 65.

60 See *infra* note 88.

61 See end of the section headed 'Primacy' earlier in this chapter, and text at notes 88–89 *infra*.

it is clear that it is intended to prevail, or if it expressly provides that it has priority over the earlier international norm.[62]

Treaty Obligations Embodying Jus Cogens

The foregoing considerations are particularly meaningful in the context of the issue of the domestic applicability of treaties incorporating fundamental principles of the international legal order; that is to say, those treaties containing peremptory rules of the international legal order (*jus cogens*), and treaties establishing international organizations.

In this context, one of the crucial questions is whether such treaties require specific procedures of incorporation. In particular, the issue is whether international law requires states incorporating such treaties in the domestic legal order to attribute to them a rank higher than ordinary treaties and laws.[63]

Clearly, this particular approach to the issue is an upshot of the dualist theory, whereby treaties need to be transformed into domestic law to become part of the national legal system. Although the dualist theory was generally relied on in Europe in the twentieth century, it has been gradually foresworn, both by national legislatures and in Europe, where it has been challenged by the Court of Justice of the European Communities.[64]

These days, the prevailing idea is that states are supposed to apply international law as such (that is to say, as formally belonging to the legal order of their origin, without the need to restate them as national laws); therefore, international law is to be applied and interpreted according to the rules of the international legal order and not the domestic one. As the foregoing review of the constitutions of several countries illustrated, there is a clear trend towards direct applicability.[65] This trend can also be found in several decisions of domestic courts, which, while holding to the theory of 'transformation', assert that international law cannot be interpreted in

62 RESTATEMENT (III) OF THE FOREIGN RELATIONS LAW OF THE UNITED STATES, § 115 (1)(a); US Supreme Court, Chae Ping v. United States, 103 U.S. 581 (1889); Supreme Court of Nigeria, 28 April 2000 (*supra* note 47). Similarly, the *Corte Costituzionale* has found the will of the Italian legislature to modify certain clauses of Art. 22 of the Warsaw Convention of 12 October 1929, in Law No. 84 of 26 March 1983, executed in Italy by Law No. 841 of 19 May 1932, and thus its will to 'suspend the execution of the treaty in those parts' (Società Sibram di Canestri e C. c. Alitalia S.p.a., 6 June 1989, Sentenza No. 323, para. 4, *in* LA GIURISPRUDENZA, *supra* note 29, at 1252). In later judgments the Court has ruled out the possibility for the legislator to abrogate treaty provisions by law. See *infra* text and note 95.

63 See Kadelbach, *supra* note 14, at 68.

64 See paragraphs under the heading 'Reducing State Freedom …' in this chapter, especially text at notes 87–94. See also note 144.

65 See *supra* notes 53, 55. For the direct applicability of human rights treaties, see Marc Bossuyt, *The Direct Applicability of International Instruments on Human Rights*, 15 REV. BELGE D.I. 317 (1980); Jacques Velu, *Les Effets Directs des Instruments Internationaux en Matière de Droits de l'Homme*, *id.*, at 293.

the light of municipal law.[66] This approach requires national judges to resort directly to international law whenever an international norm is to be applied or interpreted.

These observations raise the question of the internal applicability of treaties embodying international norms of a fundamental character. This is best left to the international judge, who will take into account the criteria governing the application of this category of treaty at the international level.

On various occasions the ICJ has considered the question of the application of treaties embodying norms of *jus cogens*. According to the Court, '[t]he fact that [the principles of general and customary international law], recognized as such, have been codified or embodied in multilateral conventions does not mean that they cease to exist and to apply as principles of customary law, even as regards countries that are parties to such conventions'.[67] Therefore, in the ICJ's view, treaties containing *jus cogens* norms maintain in any case their peremptory norm status, prevailing over all other norms of both general international law and treaty law.

This means that, when applying international treaties, national courts must take into consideration which kind of treaty is at issue and the nature of the provisions in question, so as to give priority to treaties containing rules of *jus cogens* over other 'ordinary' treaties. As a matter of fact, *jus cogens* norms enjoy a rank higher than any other in the hierarchy of international norms.[68]

Hence, as underlined by the ICJ, whenever applying treaties, judges in national courts must take into account the fact that, even if peremptory norms of international law are embodied in international conventions, such norms 'continue to exist and to apply separately from international treaty law',[69] and they must therefore receive a treatment different from that given to conventional norms of identical content, 'by reference to the methods of interpretation and application'.[70] The ICJ has insisted

66 The *Corte Costituzionale* rules out the possibility of interpreting such international norms in the light of domestic law, even though it maintains that treaty norms are transformed into domestic law through the order of execution (see, e.g., Ruggerini, *supra* note 40, at para. 7).

67 Military and Paramilitary Activities, *supra* note 37, at 424, para. 73; see also Repertory, *supra* note 20, vol. I, No. 1024, at 23.

68 It should be added that, when applying international treaties, the national judge must also take into account the presence in the text of the treaty of so-called 'compatibility' clauses, that is to say, provisions that define the relation between the treaty and other pre-existing and/or later accords (see, above all, Art. 103 of the UN Charter providing that Charter obligations prevail over obligations assumed by Member States under any other international agreement, whether earlier or later; Art. 307 of the EC Treaty (*Official Journal No. C 325 (Dec. 24, 2002)*); Art. 82 of the 1944 Chicago Convention on Civil Aviation (15 UNTS 289); Art. 311 of the Montego Bay Convention of 1982 (21 Int'l Legal Mat. 1261). Art. 30 (2) of the Vienna Convention (*supra* note 16) lays down that 'When a treaty specifies that it is subject to, or that it is not to be considered as incompatible with, an earlier or later treaty, the provisions of that other treaty prevail'. Further, the rules contained in Arts. 30 (3) and 30 (5) of the Vienna Convention (*supra* note 16) will be applied, governing the relationship between incompatible treaty provisions (i.e., between provisions of an earlier and later treaty relating to the same subject matter, where it is not possible to apply them both).

69 *Military and Paramilitary Activities*, *supra* note 20, paras 179, 190, at 96, 100.

70 *Id*., paras 178–179, at 96.

that 'there are no grounds for holding that when customary international law is comprised of rules identical to those of treaty law, the latter "supervenes" the former, so that the customary international law has no further existence of its own'.[71]

Evidently, this necessitates the duty for national law-makers to grant treaty provisions of a general character the treatment reserved in the domestic legal system to principles and norms of customary international law. Some legal systems give to such norms constitutional rank,[72] ensuring their supremacy over domestic norms.

National courts normally grant treaty rules of the type under consideration priority over domestic norms, even over conflicting constitutional law, except fundamental constitutional principles. But even this last exception should be overruled in the case of peremptory norms of international law. State practice and the case law of some domestic courts point in this direction. This orientation is supported greatly by a recent judgment of the EC Court of First Instance that has considered '*jus cogens* as a body of higher rules of public international law binding on all subjects of international law [...] from which no derogation is possible'.[73]

However, certain domestic courts have taken the opposite stance, denying the 'general rule' character of treaty provisions embodying peremptory norms.[74] Language in the constitution, *expressis verbis*, that treaties of the type being considered here enjoy a rank higher than any other laws ensures legal certainty and safeguards the state from the risk of inadvertent breach for failure to apply peremptory rules of international law. Some new constitutions have done so by expressly attributing constitutional status to international treaties protecting human rights and/or international acts embodying universal principles, such as the UN Charter and the Universal Declaration of Human Rights. National courts are bound to interpret constitutional norms in conformity with such pacts.[75]

---

71 *Id.*, para. 177, at 95; see also Repertory, *supra* note 20, vol. I, No. 1025, at 25.

72 See, for instance, Art. 10 of the Italian Constitution and references *infra* notes 79, 116. See also the new Constitutions, such as Art. 8, Constitution of Belarus; Art. 6 (2), Constitution of Georgia; Art. 6, Constitution of Turkmenistan.

73 Yusuf and Al Barakaat International Foundation v. Council of the European Union and Commission of the European Communities, Case T–306/01, Judgment of 21 September 2005, para. 277. See the Swiss Supreme Court and references in Kadelbach, *supra* note 14, at 71, notes 22–24.

74 See Corte Costituzionale, Sentenza 8 June 2005, No. 224, para. 2.3.

75 See, above all: Art. 31, Cambodian Constitution; Art. 5, Chilean Constitution; Arts. 10 and 87, Czech Constitution; Art. 4 (1), Moldovan Constitution; Art. 4 (Final and Transitory Provisions), Peruvian Constitution; Art. 20 (1), Romanian Constitution; Art. 11, Slovak Constitution; Art. 10 (2), Spanish Constitution; Art. 23, Venezuelan Constitution. For the English texts, see Constitutions, *supra* note 9.

The Italian Solution Regarding the *Status* of Treaties

Italian Norms and Practice Before the Amendments to the Constitution

The Amendments to the Italian Constitution, approved on 18 October 2001, follow the trend of giving pre-eminent place to international law in the domestic legal order. The Amendments fill a gap in the Constitution of 1948, which did not regulate the effect of treaties in internal law, and aim at putting an end to the uncertainty of the practice. In fact, the previous constitutional *lacuna* left the solution to the numerous problems relating to the effect of treaties and of European Community law in the national order (such as modalities of implementation, resolution of conflicts with domestic norms, and interpretation) to the practice of state organs and the legal doctrine. This case-by-case approach was, of course, uncertain and contradictory, relying on axioms inspired by, as Stein writes, 'the strictest form of dualism'.[76]

According to the theory of the 'transformation' of international norms, which is held by most Italian legal scholars,[77] the transposition of international law into the domestic sphere not only incorporates it in the internal legal order, but also transforms it in domestic law. In other words, international law becomes, so to speak, nationalized. In previous writings we have underlined how that theory has made it more difficult for Italy to solve the already complex problems pertaining to relationships between internal and international law.[78]

Despite the general monist slant of the Italian Constitution, as evidenced by Article 10,[79] which provides that general international law has direct effect and is superior to internal law, the practice in Italy has been to give internal force to international treaties by way of an 'act of incorporation', the so-called *ordine di esecuzione* (i.e., order of execution or implementation). An *ordine di esecuzione* is either a law passed by the competent law-making organ or a mere administrative act. The domestic applicability of the treaty is subordinate to it.[80]

This practice is supported by the extensive case law of the *Corte Costituzionale*, which excludes international treaties from the reach of Article 10, even when they are of a general character (such as treaties embodying peremptory norms of customary law), on the grounds that 'the principle of automatic incorporation into Italy's legal system of the generally recognized principles of international law must be deemed to refer exclusively to rules of customary law'.[81] In fact, it has been affirmed that

76 See Stein *supra* note 5, at 428.

77 See, e.g., Giorgio Gaja, *Italy*, *in* The Effect of Treaties, *supra* note 32, at 87; Conforti, *supra* note 51.

78 Ziccardi Capaldo, *Riforme Istituzionali*, *supra* note 12, at 94–97; *Id.*, *I Rapporti*, *supra* note 12, at 190–194.

79 Ital. Const., Art. 10, translated in Constitutions, *supra* note 9.

80 The *Corte Costituzionale* has confirmed that by virtue of the order of execution, the treaty acquires the force of 'self-application', or rather, it is directly applicable in private relations between individuals (Di Lazzaro, *supra* note 30, at para. 4).

81 Corte Costituzionale, S.r.l. Tubettificio Robbiese c. S.n.c. Edilsistem, 26 February 1993, Ordinanza No. 75 (La Giurisprudenza, *supra* note 29, at 1649); Lintrami e altri, 22 December 1980, Sentenza No. 188, para. 5, *id.*, at 1359. See also Servizio riscossione

without an order of execution, 'the treaty has no value for the Italian legal order',[82] even if it has been duly ratified.

To some extent, Italian parliamentary practice has overcome the problem, since, in the case of self-executing treaties, the Parliament orders its 'execution' with the very same law authorizing its ratification, thus permitting its immediate internal applicability. This is a twisted artifice, since execution is ordered *before* the treaty comes into force, not *after* as it should logically be.[83]

This ruse does not address, however, treaties stipulated in simplified form by the executive, which do not require a law authorizing their ratification, as well as binding acts of international organizations. These are usually implemented by way of *ad hoc* legislation, which sometimes alters their content, and, in any event, their entry into force is dependent on such implementing measures. Of course, the sole exception is Community law, which is granted immediate and direct applicability by virtue of Article 11 of the Constitution.[84]

The 'nationalization' of international norms, making them homologous with domestic norms, creates two problems: (1) that of the proper rank of international norms in the domestic legal hierarchy; and (2) that of their survival. It is generally maintained, in fact, that international norms incorporated in the domestic legal order have the same rank as the domestic norm incorporating them. Yet, placing treaties within the national legal hierarchy with the rank of ordinary law (or administrative act)[85] exposes them to a twofold risk. First, they might be overridden by later domestic norms by virtue of the *lex posterior* rule. Second, they might be disregarded by virtue of the procedure envisaged by Article 134 (1) of the Constitution on the control of constitutional legitimacy.[86] Both cases would eventually entail Italy's responsibility for breach. The negative impact that the transformation theory has had on the application of Community law in Italy (specifically, regarding the effect

---

tributi, 29 January 1996, Sentenza No. 15, para. 2, *id.*, at 2062 and Pandolfi e altro, 7 May 1996, Sentenza No. 146, para. 2, *id.*, at 2109; Ruggerini, *supra* note 40, para. 7; Groppi, 18 December 1997, Ordinanza No. 421, *id.*, at 2346. In addition, Belton S.r.l. c. Ministero delle poste e delle telecomunicazioni, 13 May 1987, Sentenza No. 153, para. 14, *id.*, at 777; Legler Industria tessile S.p.a. c. Amministrazione delle finanze, 20 May 1982, Sentenza No. 96, para. 5, *id.*, at 286; Soc. Immobiliare Sobrim c. Russel, 18 June 1979, Sentenza No. 48, para. 3, *id.*, at 68; Leoni *et al.*, 8 July 1969, Sentenza No. 104, para. 5 *in* Vincenzo Starace & Carmela Decaro, La Giurisprudenza Costituzionale in Materia Internazionale 225 (1977), [hereinafter La Giurisprudenza]; Regione Trentino-Alto Adige c. Presidente dei Ministri, 18 May 1960, Sentenza No. 32, para. 3, *id.*, at 68. *Contra*, Rolando Quadri, Diritto Internazionale Pubblico 64–65 (5th ed., 1968).

82 Corte di Cassazione, 23 March 1972, Sentenza No. 867; 17 April 1972, Sentenza No. 1196; 8 June 1972, Sentenza No. 1773.

83 On the relationship between the order of execution and ratification, see Franco Mosconi, *Ordine di Esecuzione e Mancata Ratifica*, 19 Rivista di Diritto Internazionale Privato e Processuale 580 (1983).

84 See text at note 9 *supra* and note 91 *infra*.

85 Concerning the theory of the 'transformation' of international norms, see *supra* text at notes 77–82 and *infra* text at note 121.

86 Ital. Const., Art. 134, translated in Constitutions, *supra* note 9. See *infra* text at notes 119–121.

and hierarchic status of acts of European Community bodies in Italian law) triggered reactions by the European Court of Justice and engendered considerable confusion within the *Corte Costituzionale*.[87]

In practice, both ordinary courts and the Constitutional Court have tried to avoid the negative consequences of the theory of 'nationalization'. To save Italy from international responsibility for breach of international treaty-based obligations, Italian courts, following the opinion of Italian and foreign scholars, have given international treaties primacy over ordinary laws. To achieve this, Italian courts have resorted to several criteria, including that of the speciality of treaties (a multiple-edged criterion)[88] or the presumption of conformity of domestic laws to international obligations. These interpretative stratagems notwithstanding, the *Corte Costituzionale* has considered treaties, or, to be precise, the executing law, to be subject in any event to the control of constitutional legitimacy and potential annulment provided for by Article 136 of the Constitution.[89]

Still, it was the Italian Constitutional Court itself that dismantled the thesis of 'nationalization' of international norms. In the mid-1970s, as Community law gained clout, and following pressure from the ECJ, the *Corte Costituzionale* recognized the direct effect of Community law and its supremacy over inconsistent domestic law, even over conflicting constitutional law.[90] This position, however, was to change time and again.[91]

---

87 See *infra* notes 90–91 and corresponding text.

88 Società Sibram, *supra* note 62, the *Corte Costituzionale* declared that it is the task of ordinary courts to give treaties priority over laws: any conflict between the two categories of norms, and the eventual application of the principle of 'special status of treaties' does not raise the issue of constitutional legitimacy. It is the Court's firm practice to exclude international conventional norms from the scope of Art. 10 of the Constitution (see text at note 81 *supra*).

89 See *infra* notes 124–127. Ital. Const., Art. 136, translated in Constitutions, *supra* note 9.

90 See particularly Corte Costituzionale, Società Industrie chimiche dell'Italia centrale c. Ministero del commercio con l'estero, 30 October 1975, Sentenza No. 232, para. 8, *in* La Giurisprudenza, *supra* note 81, at 414.

91 In 1984 (Società Granital c. Amministrazione delle Finanze, 8 June 1984, Sentenza No. 170, paras 4–5, *in* La Giurisprudenza, *supra* note 29, at 438), the *Corte Costituzionale* abandoned the thesis it had upheld in 1975, according to which breach of Community law through later legislation entailed a violation of Art. 11 of the Constitution, since the priority of Community law should itself be ensured by the same Court with the procedure for control of constitutional legitimacy provided by Art. 134 of the Constitution (Società Industrie chimiche, *supra* note 90). In the *Simmenthal* case (*supra* note 46), the ECJ held that the transformation procedure could not ensure the proper application (i.e., the direct applicability) of Community law because, whenever EC law is inconsistent with domestic norms, it could be applied by domestic courts only if, and after, the *Corte Costituzionale* declared the inconsistent domestic law constitutionally illegitimate. Thus, once abolished, the conflicting domestic law 'ceases to have effect *ex nunc* from the day following the publication of the decision' (Ital. Const., Art. 136, *supra* note 89). In keeping with the case-law of the ECJ (see Costa v. Enel, *supra* note 22) and stressing one of its own earlier pronunciations (Frontini e S.r.l. Commercio Prodotti Alimentari c. Amministrazione delle Finanze *et al.*, 27 December 1973, Sentenza No. 183, *in* La Giurisprudenza, *supra* note 81, at 364), the *Corte Costituzionale* specified

It is only in 1984 that the Constitutional Court, referring to a previous judgment made in 1973,[92] described the relationship between Community law and domestic laws as relations between 'autonomous and independent legal systems', not comparable to the ordinary relationships between norms belonging to the same legal order. In the Court's words, Community legislation 'does not become a part of domestic law, neither is it in any way subjected to the regime existing for laws (and acts having the force of law) of the State'.[93] Accordingly, the Court declared that it did not have jurisdiction to control the constitutional legitimacy of Community norms, since such control is limited by Article 134 (1) of the Constitution to 'laws and enactments having the force of law issued by the State and the regions'.[94]

The Court has been more cautious in applying the same reasoning also to treaties. A 1993 ruling, which justifies the priority of treaties over ordinary laws for reasons different from those used in previous decisions, seems to point in this direction. In this decision, the Court construed international treaty-based norms as 'norms deriving from a source traceable back to an *extraordinary competence* and, as such, not amenable to abrogation or modification by provisions of ordinary law'.[95]

The Amended Italian Constitution

The Amendments to Title V of the Constitution are clear evidence of the will of Italian authorities to respect Italy's international treaty-based obligations. This may be inferred both from Article 120, granting the Government power to act in

---

that 'Community norms … must have … direct application in all Member States, without the need for laws of reception and adjustment … so that they enter into force contemporaneously everywhere, attaining equal and uniform application in relation to all subjects to whom they are addressed' (Società Granital, *id.*, at para. 4). See also *infra* note 98.

92 Frontini, *supra* note 91, para. 7.

93 Società Granital, *supra* note 91, para. 4; see also Judgments: S.p.a. BECA c. Amministrazione delle Finanze, 23 April 1985, Sentenza No. 113, paras 3.1, 5, *in* LA GIURISPRUDENZA, *supra* note 29, at 554; Provincia autonoma di Bolzano c. Presidente del Consiglio dei Ministri, 11 July 1989, Sentenza No. 389, para. 3, *id.*, at 1275; Russo, Galletti e Ottaviano, 2 February 1990, Sentenza No. 64, para. 2.2, *id.*, at 1325; Regione Emilia Romagna c. Presidente del Consiglio dei Ministri, 14 June 1990, Sentenza No. 285, para. 4.2, *id.*, at 1362; S.p.a. Industria Dolciaria Giampaoli, 18 April 1991, Sentenza No. 168, paras 4, 5, *id.*, at 1440; Capezzone e altri, 7 February 2000, Sentenza No. 41, para. 3, *id.*, at 2654.

94 Frontini, *supra* note 91, para. 9; Società Industrie chimiche, *supra* note 90, paras 9–10; Zandonà c. I.N.P.S., 18 December 1995, Sentenza No. 509, para. 2, *in* LA GIURISPRUDENZA, *supra* note 29, at 2037. The Court reserved the right to review the constitutionality of Community acts only where they conflict with the supreme principles of the Italian legal order. See ITAL. CONST., Art. 134, *supra* note 86.

95 See Corte Costituzionale, Mujanovic – Hakimi, 19 January 1993, Sentenza No. 10, para. 2, *in* LA GIURISPRUDENZA, *supra* note 29, at 1621 (confirmed by the Corte di Cassazione, Judgment No. 6672 of 8 July 1998). See also Di Lazzaro, *supra* note 30, para. 3, where the Court affirmed that Art. 6 (1) of the Strasbourg Convention of 24 April 1967, ratified by Italy by Law No. 357 of 22 May 1974, cannot be deemed to be abrograted 'either wholly or in part' by Law No. 184 of 1983; in an earlier judgment, the Court had stated that the legislature may abrogate treaty norms by law. See *supra* note 62.

lieu of bodies of the regions, metropolitan cities, provinces, and municipalities, if the latter fail to comply with international rules and treaties or EU legislation. It is also evidenced by Article 117, which rearranges the system of sources of law and regulates the relationship between internal law and international treaty-based obligations. The new hierarchy of sources reflects a multiplicity of decision-making centres. In the new system, the domestic and international norms are now sources belonging to distinct legal systems.

Under the first paragraph of Article 117, the legislative powers of the state and the regions must comply not only with the Constitution, but also 'with the constraints deriving from EU legislation and international obligations'.[96] The loose wording of Article 117 (1) suggests that the legislator is required to comply with *all* treaty obligations, be they international treaties, Community law, or binding secondary law of international organizations (hereinafter, collectively called 'treaty law'), that is to say, with all those international rules that are not part of international customary law and so are normally excluded from the provision of Article 10 of the Constitution.

In sum, the new Article 117 (1) governs the internal effect of treaty law, achieving conformity with international minimum standards. The supremacy of treaty law is established, for Article 117 (1) requires state and regional legislatures to act in compliance with treaty-based obligations. This entails that precedence shall be accorded to treaty law over conflicting domestic law, even over domestic later-in-time rules.

The legislator's obligation to comply with treaty law (as well as the Constitution) automatically conforms the Italian legal order to treaties. Legislative acts of transformation are no longer required. In adopting this principle, the Italian legal system has done nothing but restate what is already written in Article 10 of the Constitution, whereby Italy accepts to 'conform' the legal system to the generally recognized principles of international law. Supremacy is conferred on treaty norms over laws to the extent they are international norms, and not because they are norms of a higher rank in the hierarchy of domestic norms.[97] They are to be complied with by the legislative power on a par with constitutional norms, to which they are not, however, assimilated. In fact, the two sources (i.e., the Constitution and international treaty law) are indicated separately.

The law-makers have rejected the theory of the transformation of international law into domestic law with regard to Community law, just as the *Corte Costituzionale*

96 Ital. Const., Art. 117, provides: 'Legislative power shall be vested in the State and the Regions in compliance with the Constitution and with the constraints deriving from EU legislation and international obligations. (...) In the areas falling within their responsibilities, Regions may enter into agreements with foreign States and with local authorities of other States in the cases and according to the forms laid down by State legislation. (…)' (available at web site, *supra* note 11).

97 The adoption by the Italian Constitution of international standards for treaty implementation is a welcome development. On several occasions, we pleaded to this effect (*supra* note 12). However, the unclear formulation of the new constitutional provision has raised interpretative doubts and risks perpetuating the old uncertainties about the applicability of treaties. For our approach, see Ziccardi Capaldo, *Riforme istituzionali*, *supra* note 12, at 101–108; *Id.*, *I Rapporti*, *id.*, at 194–199.

had done before. When drafting Article 117 it was deliberately decided to ensure singleness of application to all international treaty law, recognizing its priority over domestic laws and respecting the fact that international law belongs to a legal order different from the domestic system. International norms are to be applied as formally belonging to the legal order of their origin. This is confirmed by the references made in Article 117 to compliance with constraints deriving from the Community legal order and international obligations. By doing so, the law-makers heeded the call of the *Corte Costituzionale,* which, for some time, upheld the supremacy and effect *proprio vigore* of Community law on the grounds that it belongs to an 'independent and autonomous' legal order.[98]

The conformity of legislation with all international treaty law, required by Article 117, also aims to achieve a gradual integration, in the long run, between the internal and the international legal orders.

Despite the limits of the new provision, which will be treated in the next part, it does have unquestionable merits. First, the long-standing practice of the Italian courts is given constitutional blessing. It makes it harder for the legislator to abrogate treaties,[99] bringing about greater certainty of the law. Second, creating a single legal status for all international treaty law eliminates the double standard between Community law and international treaties. This allows important conclusions to be drawn, both as regards the control of constitutional legitimacy of treaties[100] and their interpretation by the domestic courts. The contradiction inherent in the thesis of the 'nationalization' of treaties, where international criteria of interpretation are applied to norms that have become national, is also eliminated.[101]

The new Article 117 (1) effectuates the coordination between domestic law and international law consistently with the national constitutional system (i.e., Article 10). Moreover, it conforms to general international law by ensuring the primacy of international treaty law over national laws.

---

98 See note 93 and text at notes 90–94 *supra*. Art. 117 confirms and extends to treaties and other acts of conventional origin the most recent orientation of the *Corte Costituzionale*, which gives Community law priority over domestic norms. In the Court's view, mere adjustments to the Constitution, such as Art. 11, do not nationalize Community norms but rather coordinate domestic law and international law. Community norms are applied inasmuch as they belong to the legal order of origin. The ordinary judge (i.e., non-constitutional judge) is bound to apply Community law and to disregard domestic norms that conflict with it. Conflicting domestic norms are not repealed but merely set aside (Società Granital, *supra* note 91, para. 5; *S.p.a. BECA*, *supra* note 93, para. 3.1; *Provincia autonoma di Bolzano*, *id.*, at para. 3). It is worth recalling that this thesis reversed an earlier orientation of the Court that held that laws contrary to Community norms were constitutionally illegitimate as being in breach of Art. 11 of the Constitution (see *supra* note 91).

99 Even before the amendment to Art. 117 of the Constitution, the supremacy of treaty law over conflicting ordinary law was asserted and given effect in the practice of the Italian Courts (see text at notes 88 and 95 *supra*, and lastly, Corte Costituzionale, Priebke, *supra* note 30, para. 3). The primacy of treaties is also endorsed in some Italian laws, e.g., Arts. 696 and 705, Code of Criminal Procedure, concerning extradition.

100 See *infra* section headed 'Reducing State Freedom …' later in this chapter.

101 See *supra* note 98.

Unlike some commentators did immediately after the referendum approving the Amendments, it is not possible to claim that Article 117 (1) 'constitutionalized' treaties. Those arguing this did so by relying on the fact that the incorporation of treaties is regulated in the Constitution. But the same claim is not made in numerous other countries that, like Italy, regulate the relationship between treaties and laws in their constitutions, and that attribute supremacy to the former over the latter.

To say that treaties have constitutional status because the incorporation of treaties is regulated in the Constitution means clinging to the dualist concept of 'nationalization' of international law, which, we have seen, was rejected in the constitutional amendments. Above all, it would mean reading more into Article 117 (1) than it actually says.

In reality, while Article 10 of the Constitution, requiring the conformity of 'the Italian legal system'[102] (and thus, also the Constitution) with the generally recognized principles of international law, endorses the priority of the latter even over conflicting constitutional norms, the new Article 117 (1) does not have such a wide reach. It does not cover the relationship between international treaty norms and constitutional norms. The fact that in the revised Article 117 legislative power is subordinated to both the Constitution *and* international treaty obligations corroborates the interpretation given above, since only ordinary law is thus subordinated to international treaty norms. It follows that Article 117 (1) establishes the primacy of international treaty law 'only' over ordinary laws.

Shortcomings of the Amended Italian Constitution

Although the changes introduced by the Amendments are significant and a step in the right direction, they still fall short of what was hoped for. Partly because of its position in the Constitution, Article 117 leaves several issues unsettled: we now examine these.

The supremacy of treaty law. Under Article 117 (1), legislative powers must be exercised in compliance with international obligations, but the provision does not indicate which organ is entrusted with exercising control over the conformity of laws to treaties. Consistently with the most recent judgments of the *Corte Costituzionale*, it may be argued that treaties are not to be given priority by ordinary (i.e., non-constitutional) judges.[103] However, this should have been stated explicitly by the drafters of the Amendments, so as to avoid uncertainty. The same kind of problem is posed by Article 55 of the French Constitution, which is equally ambiguous

---

102 We obviously also rule out the so-called 'constitutionalization' of general international law, allegedly effectuated by Art. 10 of the Constitution. By providing for the conformity of Italy's legal system with general norms of 'international law', Art. 10, too, recognizes the fact that such norms belong to a different legal order. It grants them direct effect and priority over domestic norms by virtue of their international nature and in application of international standards. ITAL. CONST., Art. 10, *supra* note 79.

103 See judgments n. 348/2007 and n. 349/2007.

about which state organ has the power to determine the compatibility of laws with treaties.[104]

In case of conflicts between domestic laws and treaty provisions, domestic law will just be disregarded, but not repealed, because the abrogation of laws remains a privilege of the law-making organs endowed, be they at state or regional level. Indeed, as the *Corte Costituzionale* declared about domestic laws conflicting with Community law, the supremacy of international norms does not entail abrogation nor have the effect of extinguishing or derogating from domestic norms. It will be necessary for the legislative organs to make the required changes to domestic law to eliminate any contradictions with the international norms. Doing so would fulfil the need for legal certainty domestically, while internationally it is the 'specific obligation for states' to do so.[105] In this regard, the PCIJ declared the existence of a 'principle which is self-evident, according to which a State which has contracted valid international obligations is bound to make in its legislation such modifications as may be necessary to ensure the fulfilment of the obligations undertaken'.[106]

Obviously, mechanisms for ensuring that this obligation is fulfilled remains to be found. Some scholars, writing on the subject of conflicts between domestic laws and Community law, have proposed the introduction of an 'implied abrogation clause'. Such a clause could be appended to and modelled on Article 15 of the General Provisions of the Italian Civil Code, which treats the issue of incompatibility between prior and later legislation. Obviously, a similar device would not involve reciprocity because it is impossible for national laws to abrogate international law.[107]

The direct applicability of treaty law. Article 117 leaves undetermined the question of the direct applicability of treaty law. In particular, it could be queried whether it dictates the direct applicability of treaties and binding acts of international organizations (e.g., UN Security Council measures under Article 41 of the Charter) on a par with the treatment already given to Community law in accordance with the decisions of the *Corte Costituzionale*.[108]

---

104 Conseil Constitutionnel, Decision 74–54 of 15 January 1975, Loi relative à l'avortement; Cour de Cassation, Société des Café Jacques Vabres, Ch. Mixte 24 May 1975; Conseil d'État, Nicolo, Ass. 20 October 1989 and Meyet, Sect. 2 June 1999. On this point see especially, Kronenberger, *supra* note 47, at 331–333.

105 Corte Costituzionale, *S.p.a. BECA*, *supra* note 93, para. 3.1; Provincia autonoma di Bolzano, *id.*, at para. 4.

106 *Exchange of Greek and Turkish Populations*, Advisory Opinion No. 10 (Feb. 21, 1925), 1925, PCIJ, Series B, No. 10, at 20.

107 In this sense, see Alessandro Pizzorusso, *Percorsi, Contenuti e Aspetti Problematici di una Riforma del Quadro Normativo Relativo all'Attuazione degli Obblighi Comunitari*, L'Europa in Italia. Verso Nuovi Strumenti di Attuazione delle Normative Comunitarie, Quaderni Internazionali di Vita Italiana, Presidenza del Consiglio dei Ministri, Dipartimento per l'informazione e l'Editoria, Istituto Poligrafico e Zecca dello Stato 61 (1999).

108 *Supra* notes 90–91. In Italy, Law No. 86 of 9 March 1989 (Gazzetta Ufficiale No. 58 (March 10, 1989)) governs the implementation of Community obligations. See Antonio La Pergola, *Il Recepimento del Diritto Comunitario. Nuove Prospettive del Rapporto tra*

Article 117 (1) requires legislative powers to be exercised in compliance with 'constraints deriving from EU legislation and international obligations'. The reasoning of the drafters in coordinating state and regional laws with treaty law is therefore the same followed by Article 10 of the Constitution. In the words of the *Corte Costituzionale,* the formula used by Article 10, by which 'Italy's legal system conforms with the generally recognized principles of international law', entails 'the automatic coordination (i.e., direct applicability)' of the Italian legal system to general international law.[109]

This solution guarantees the effective implementation of treaties and binding acts of international organizations. Yet, it contrasts with the stance of Italian legislative and administrative organs, which gives treaties different status from Community law, making applicability subject to *ad hoc* implementing measures. In absence of *ad hoc* implementing measures, even self-executing treaty-based norms are not enforceable in the Italian legal system.[110] However, because the Amendments have given identical status to both treaty law and Community law, this practice must cease.

Once the automatic applicability of treaty norms has been recognized, the use of *ad hoc* acts of execution is to be restricted to integrating non-self-executing treaty norms, and for the sole purpose of ensuring greater certainty of the law, but without affecting their internal applicability.

Such an interpretation of Article 117 (1) is consistent with the idea underlying it, that is to say, to ensure compliance by legislative powers with all treaty-based obligations. It remains to be seen what line will be followed in practice.

No evolution is to be seen in the recent case law in which the *Corte Costituzionale* for the first time has interpreted that provision of the Constitution. The Court remains anchored to the theory of nationalization of international law; it confirms the non-direct applicability of European Convention on Human Rights (ECHR), while attributing to it a sub-constitutional level (judgments n. 348/2007 and n. 349/2007 paras. 4.7 and 6.1.2 respectively). Also the Italian *Corte di Cassazione* backs down, rejecting the direct applicability of that Convention already asserted in some previous case law (Cass. Civ. Sez. I, no. 28507/05 (Dec. 15, 2005); Cass. Pen. Sez. I, no. 2800 (Dec. 1, 2006)). The Italian Courts have failed to grasp the opportunity to leave behind the political-legal culture of the past century and to enable the Italian legal system to meet the needs of the global community of the twenty-first century.

Of course, for the sake of certainty, it would have been advisable to state clearly that all international self-executing treaty-based measures are directly applicable, without need for an order of execution.[111] The Italian legal requirement of publicity, of which the practice of issuing orders of execution is an embodiment, could be

---

Norme Interne e Norme Comunitarie alla Luce della Legge 9 Marzo 1989, n. 86, La Corte Costituzionale fra Diritto Interno e Diritto Comunitario 18 (1991).

109 See *supra* note 79 and text at note 81.

110 See text at notes 80–82 *supra.*

111 In Italy, steps in this direction have been taken by Law No. 839 of 11 December 1984, Gazzetta Ufficiale No. 345, (Dec. 17, 1984).

equally satisfied by mere publication, as it already happens in other countries.[112] Still, publication should not be made an indispensable precondition for treaties to have internal legal force[113] since, if delayed, it would hinder their implementation.

The conflict between treaties and the Constitution. Another limit of the Amendments concerns the relationship between treaty law and constitutional norms.[114] Article 117 (1) leaves unsettled the question of the admissibility of controlling the constitutional legitimacy of treaties under Article 134 of the Constitution.[115] Two types of control should be examined separately: (1) the control of *substantive* constitutional legitimacy; and (2) the control of *formal* constitutional legitimacy.

Let us first consider *control of substantive constitutional legitimacy*. The *Corte Costituzionale* lacks a coherent approach to the control of constitutional legitimacy of international norms and, in the past, wove between contradictory solutions. First, it removed norms of general international law from the purview of control of substantive constitutional legitimacy provided by Article 134 (1), granting them constitutional rank in the hierarchy[116] and thus subscribing to the view of prominent scholars. Then, after various hesitations,[117] it also excluded Community norms from such control, though on a different premise. Since Community norms belong to a legal order independent from the domestic one, they escape the review of constitutional legitimacy reserved by Article 134 (1) to legislative acts.[118]

By contrast, the Italian Constitutional Court has always stated (and reaffirmed in the well-known *Baraldini* case)[119] that it does have power to review the constitutional legitimacy of treaties[120] and, where necessary, declare them unconstitutional. This

---

112 Jochen A. Frowein & Karin Oellers-Frahm, *L'Application des Traités dans l'Ordre Juridique Interne*, *in* THE INTEGRATION, *supra* note 52, at 15.

113 It does not, for example, in the new Russian Constitution, see Danilenko, *supra* note 5, at 456; it is required, for instance, in the Constitutions of: Mali (Art. 116); Senegal (Art. 98); Spain (Art. 96 (1)). For the English texts see CONSTITUTIONS, *supra* note 9.

114 See text at note 102 *supra*.

115 ITAL. CONST., Art. 134, *supra* note 86.

116 On various occasions the Court has declared that a law contrary to customary international law would be in violation of the Constitution, see Judgments: Penso e Baracchini, 22 December 1961, Sentenza No. 67, *in* LA GIURISPRUDENZA, *supra* note 81, at 108; Governo della Gran Bretagna c. Guerrato, 13 July 1963, Sentenza No. 135, *id.*, at 126; Hartmann e Pude, 18 May 1967, Sentenza No. 48, *id.*, at 183; Zennaro, 8 April 1976, Sentenza No. 69, *id.*, at 427; Legler Industria Tessile S.p.a. c. Amministrazione delle Finanze, 20 May 1982, Sentenza No. 96, para. 6, *in* LA GIURISPRUDENZA, *supra* note 29, at 286; Klieber, 17 June 1992, Sentenza No. 278, *id.*, para. 2, at 1557.

117 See text at and notes 91–94 *supra*.

118 The Court never entirely abandoned the theory of transformation, and its orientation has often been ambiguous (see text at note 130 *infra*). In general, see Antonio La Pergola & Patrick Del Duca, *Community Law and the Italian Constitution*, 79 AM. J. INT'L L. 598 (1985). See also *supra* note 87.

119 Baraldini, 22 March 2001, Sentenza No. 73, para. 3.1, 3 GIURISPRUDENZA COSTITUZIONALE 428 (2001).

120 Di Lazzaro, *supra* note 30; Lee, 12 October 1990, Sentenza No. 446, *in* LA GIURISPRUDENZA, *supra* note 29, at 1380; Coccia e altra c. Soc. Turkish Airlines, 6 May 1985,

is because, according to the Court, by virtue of incorporation into the domestic legal system, by way of the order of execution, treaties have acquired the status of ordinary law.[121] The Court pushed the theory of nationalization to the extreme, arriving at the absurd pronouncement that even norms of general international law should receive the same treatment as ordinary laws, whenever such norms are incorporated in international treaties.[122] The Court held so, despite the fact that in practice it consistently excluded rules of general international law from review, and despite the International Court of Justice's pronouncement, on several occasions, that general norms do not lose their status as such even when they are embodied in international treaties.[123]

Admittedly, notwithstanding statements of principle, in practice the *Corte Costituzionale* has been cautious in declaring the constitutional illegitimacy of legislation implementing international treaties, doing so only in case of conflict with

---

Sentenza No. 132, *id.*, at 566; De Bettin e Manzan c. Ministero della difesa, 10 March 1966, Sentenza No. 20, *in* La Giurisprudenza, *supra* note 81, at 171. In addition, see the references contained in notes 125–128.

121 Fasoli *et al.*, 17 February 1999, Sentenza No. 32, *in* La Giurisprudenza, *supra* note 29, at 2520; Ruggerini, *supra* note 40; Società Sibram, *supra* note 62.

122 The Court stated that because Italy's accession to the International Covenant on Civil and Political Rights of 16 December 1966, ratified by Italy by ordinary Law No. 881 of 25 October 1977, ensued from an ordinary law, this prevented principles contained in the Covenant from being used as parameters in the judgment of constitutionality of laws and from constitutional value being attributed to such principles (Servizio riscossione tributi, *supra* note 81, at para. 2). In the same direction, see Lintrami e altri, *supra* note 81, at para. 5, Belton S.r.l., *id.*, at para. 14, Società Sibram, *supra* note 62, at para. 4.; Fasoli et al., *supra* note 121, followed by Ordinanza of 23 December 2005, No. 464; Sentenza No. 224, *supra* note 74.

123 See *Military and Paramilitary Activities*, *supra* note 20, para. 179, at 96; Delimitation of the Maritime Boundary in the Gulf of Maine Area, Judgment, 1984 ICJ Reports 246 (Oct. 12, 1984), para. 94, at 294; Continental Shelf (Tunisia v. Libyan Arab Jamahiriya), Judgment, 1982 ICJ Reports 18 (Feb. 24, 1982), para. 24, at 38; North Sea Continental Shelf, Judgment, 1969 ICJ Reports 3 (Feb. 20, 1969), para. 63, at 39; Repertory, *supra* note 20, vol. I, Nos 1015, 1017–1018, at 17, 19. See also text at notes 67–71 *supra*.

basic constitutional principles,[124] such as the prohibition of the death penalty[125] or principles in matters of labour law[126] and extradition of minors.[127]

After the adoption of the Amendments, it is all the more difficult to defend the different treatment given by the *Corte Costituzionale* to treaties and to Community law. Article 117 (1) grants treaties, like Community acts, supremacy over laws and distinguishes them from laws by virtue of the fact that treaties belong to the international legal order. This excludes the applicability of Article 134 (1) of the Constitution to treaties, since that provision expressly provides for control only of 'laws and acts having the force of law emanating from central and regional governments'.[128]

This is true notwithstanding the reasoning of the *Corte Costituzionale* in the *Baraldini* case. On that occasion, and recalling its own previous case law, the Court resorted to the 'transformation' of international acts approach, removing from review of constitutional legitimacy international norms possessing a 'particular constitutional foundation'. These are: general norms, supported by Article 10 of the Constitution; norms contained in treaties establishing international organizations having in view the objectives set out in Article 11 of the Constitution or secondary legislation of such organizations; and bilateral norms with which the state and the Catholic Church regulate their reciprocal relations under Article 7 (2) of the Constitution. If the Court's reasoning is followed, even treaties should now be excluded from review under Article 134 (1), by virtue of Article 117, which mandates compliance with treaties. International treaties can no longer be held to be lacking any 'particular constitutional foundation'.[129]

---

124 See, in this direction, the case law quoted *infra* at notes 125–127, with the exception of Coccia e altra, *supra* note 120, declaring the constitutional illegitimacy of Art. 1 of Law No. 841 of 19 May 1932 and of Art. 2 of Law No. 1832 of 3 December 1962 in the parts where they execute Art. 22 (1) of the Warsaw Convention of 12 October 1929 on international air transport, as modified by Art. IX of the Hague Protocol of 28 September 1955.

125 See Cuillier *et al.*, 21 June 1979, Sentenza No. 54, *in* La Giurisprudenza, *supra* note 29, at 74, and Venezia c. Ministero di grazia e giustizia, 27 June 1996, Sentenza No. 223, *id.*, at 2133, declaring the constitutional illegitimacy, respectively, of the laws executing the Treaty of 1870 between Italy and France and the extradition treaty between Italy and the US of 13 October 1983, in the parts permitting extradition for crimes punishable by the death penalty.

126 Nitti e altri c. S.p.A. Vetrerie meridionali, 24 July 1986, Sentenza No. 210, *in* La Giurisprudenza, *supra* note 29, at 719, declaring the constitutional illegitimacy of Law No. 1305 of 2 August 1952, in the part executing Art. 3 of the International Labour Organization (ILO) Convention of 9 July 1948 concerning evening work for women in industrial employment.

127 Sciacca, 15 April 1987, Sentenza No. 128, *in* La Giurisprudenza, *supra* note 29, at 769, declaring the constitutional illegitimacy of part of Law No. 632 of 9 October 1974 (giving execution to the Treaty between Italy and the US of 18 January 1973). The unconstitutional part was the one providing for the extradition of accused persons of more than 14 but less than 18 years of age, when they are not considered minors by US laws.

128 Ital. Const., Art. 134, *supra* note 86.

129 See *Baraldini* case, *supra* note 119.

The Court's case law, including the *Baraldini* judgment, consistently indicates that there can be no derogation from the fundamental principles of the constitutional order. These constitute 'obstacles to the entry into the Italian legal system' for all international norms (both general and conventional).[130] Actually, most states set such a limit to the supremacy of international norms over national norms. The *Corte Costituzionale* has arrogated the jurisdiction to assess the non-conformity of international norms to basic constitutional principles, even if Article 134 of the Constitution does not expressly grant it this power.

The Constitutional Court's practice regarding the control of constitutionality of treaties *ex post* exposes Italy to the risk of incurring responsibility for breach of its treaty obligations. Some countries have been induced to anticipate the control of constitutionality of international law to actual ratification, thus reducing the risks of conflicts between treaties and the national Constitution.[131]

Italy could provide for preventive control of constitutionality by amending Article 134 (1) of the Constitution. The request for prior review should be addressed to the *Corte Costituzionale* by the President of the Republic, the Prime Minister, and the Presidents of the two Chambers of Parliament.[132] The exclusion of judicial organs is dictated by logic. Despite the fact that the judiciary has general recourse to the control of constitutionality of laws, it always acts *ex post*, while the control at issue is *ex ante*. Preventive control of constitutionality would not only be consistent with the principle of supremacy of international law, but also contribute to reconcile the constitutional system with the spirit of Article 80 of the Constitution, according

---

130 *Id.* The Court had repeatedly stressed that basic constitutional principles are a limit to the 'admission'/incorporation of general international norms (Soc. Immobiliare Sobrim, *supra* note 81, para. 3) and of Community law (Judgments: Frontini, *supra* note 81, para. 9; Regione Emilia Romagna c. Presidente del Consiglio dei Ministri, 19 November 1987, Sentenza No. 399, *in* La Giurisprudenza, *supra* note 29, para. 2, at 915; S.p.a FRAGD c. Amministrazione delle Finanze, 21 April 1989, Sentenza No. 232, para. 3, *id.*, at 1211; Zerini, 31 March 1994, Sentenza No. 117, para. 2, *id.*, at 1821; Provincia Autonoma di Trento c. Presidente del Consiglio dei Ministri, 24 April 1996, Sentenza No. 126, para. 5 (c), *id.*, at 2093; Regione Umbria c. Presidente del Consiglio dei Ministri, 11 April 1997, Sentenza No. 93, para. 3, *id.*, at 2265; Zandonà, *supra* note 94, para. 2, and of bilateral norms with which the state and the Church regulate their relations (in re Otto richieste di referendum abrogativo, 7 February 1978, Sentenza No. 16, para. 4, *id.*, at 45; in re Marella *et al.*, 2 February 1982, Sentenza No. 16, para. 7, *id.*, at 222; Di Filippo c. Gospodinoff *et al.*, 2 February 1982, Sentenza No. 18, para. 4, *id.*, at 235).

131 The control of constitutionality *ex ante* is provided for in the constitution of various countries: France (Art. 54); Netherlands (Art. 73); Portugal (Art. 278 (1)); Romania (Art. 91); Spain (Art. 95 (1) and (2)); and in some recent Constitutions: the Ivory Coast (Art. 86); Russia (Art. 125 (2)(d)); Senegal (Art. 97); Ukraine (Art. 9 (2)); Venezuela (Art. 336 (5)); also by German practice of the *Bundesverfassungsgericht* and by practice of Costa Rica (Advisory Opinion on the constitutionality of the draft law of approbation of the Rome Statute on the International Criminal Court, Supreme Court of Justice (Constitutional Chamber) Costa Rica, 1 November 2000).

132 In this field, and within their responsibilities, the regions may play a role. During the works of the *Bicamerale* Commission, the preventive control of the *Corte Costituzionale* came under attack. See *supra* note 10.

to which Parliament and the Government share the treaty-making power. It is their prerogative to denounce treaties, and judicial organs cannot do so by their own act.[133]

Let us now move to the second type of control, that of *formal constitutional legitimacy*. Control of formal constitutionality means controlling whether state organs (i.e., the legislator at state and regional level and the executive) have observed the norms of the Italian Constitution that regulate treaty-making powers, namely, Articles 80 and 87 and the new Article 117, last paragraph, conferring competence on the regions to conclude treaties.[134] French courts have addressed the question in a case where private citizens challenged the validity of a treaty that had been stipulated without due regard for domestic norms on competence to ratify.[135]

In the Italian legal system, by virtue of paragraph 2 of Article 134 of the Constitution, it is the task of the *Corte Costituzionale* to verify the formal constitutionality of treaties.[136] In fact, issues about the conformity of treaties to constitutional norms that regulate their conclusion (i.e., norms on treaty-making powers) relate to 'controversies arising over constitutional assignment of powers within the state', and Article 134 (2)[137] grants the *Corte Costituzionale* jurisdiction exactly over such issues.

It is certainly expedient that the task to decide on formal constitutionality is entrusted to a supreme court (as in Germany, under Article 93 (1)) rather than the ordinary courts. This ensures greater uniformity of application of treaties.[138]

This type of control, and the potential declaration of unconstitutionality of the treaty, does not contrast with the principle of primacy of treaty norms over domestic

---

133 In this sense, see GIULIANA ZICCARDI CAPALDO, LA COMPETENZA A DENUNCIARE I TRATTATI INTERNAZIONALI. CONTRIBUTO ALLO STUDIO DEL TREATY POWER 108 (1983).

134 ITAL. CONST., Art. 117 (9) provides: 'In the areas falling within their responsibilities, Regions may enter into agreements with foreign states and with local authorities of other states in the cases and according to the forms laid down by state legislation.' (available at web site, *supra* note 11).

135 Conseil d'État, SARL du Parc d'activités de Blotzheim, 18 December 1998; Kronenberger, *supra* note 47, at 335–339.

136 S.r.l. Medusa Distribuzione e altre c. Ministero del Turismo e dello spettacolo e altra, 19 December 1984, Sentenza No. 295, *in* LA GIURISPRUDENZA, *supra* note 29, at 491. Giovanni Battaglini, *Riflessione Breve su di un Tema della Sentenza n. 295, con Variazioni*, 2 GIURISPRUDENZA COSTITUZIONALE 1334 (1985).

137 For the text of this Article see *supra* note 86. The Court holds that it can hear cases about division of competences under the Constitution, not only in case of encroachment of constitutionally guaranteed power, but also when such a distribution is accomplished by Community acts. Indeed, Art. 11 of the Constitution equates Community norms with constitutional norms. Community law may therefore distribute competences differently from provisions of the Constitution, provided this is done in specific instances under Community provisions and consistently with basic constitutional principles. See Regione Emilia Romagna, *supra* note 130, para. 2; Provincia Autonoma di Trento, *id.*, at para. 5 (c); Regione Umbria, *id.*, at para. 3.

138 Frowein & Oellers-Frahm, *supra* note 112, at 22. Besides, by prohibiting the Court from carrying out such a supervision, political organs would be granted the power to decide whether or not to observe norms on treaty power, and even to derogate from them.

laws. In fact, Article 27 of the Vienna Convention permits states party to treaties to invoke as justification for failure to perform a treaty the violation of a rule of fundamental importance of its internal law on competence to conclude treaties.[139] Thus, any judgment by the *Corte Costituzionale* annulling *a posteriori* treaty norms, on the ground of violation of fundamental internal rules on treaty-making powers, is consistent with international law.

An Important Step but Only the First

The new Article 117 of the Italian Constitution provides sound constitutional basis for the regulation of the relationship between internal law and international treaty law. It resonates with the same spirit underlying Articles 10 and 11 of the Italian Constitution and is consistent with the decisions of the *Corte Costituzionale* giving effect to Community law.

Still, because of the position it occupies in the constitutional framework (i.e., Title V Regions-Provinces-Municipalities), Article 117 falls short of what is needed. The Amendments neither ensure full observance of treaty and Community obligations, nor do they address the issue of the internal balance of powers.

Although the Amendments fill a gap in the Constitution, regulate the relationship between internal norms and international treaty norms in conformity with international standards, and are consistent with the Italian constitutional system, they still have some important shortcomings.[140] They fail to regulate the treaty – and Community acts – formation phase.

Italy has not yet taken measures to regulate the participation of the Parliament in the national preparation of acts, agreements, and other measures to be decided in the ambit of the European Union. Although Article 80 of the Constitution provides for parliamentary participation in the stipulation of international treaties, this provision is not adequate to ensure the effective participation of Parliament in the whole decision-making process, including the negotiating phase. Practice shows that the Parliament is usually involved only at a later stage, when a text, negotiated by the Government, has already been agreed upon, and concerning which the chambers are called upon to accept or reject *in toto*. Besides, in the Italian legal system, the power to amend and to denounce treaties is not regulated, and there are no norms on reservations to treaties, nor on treaties in simplified form and treaties' provisional implementation.

These flaws are so significant that the creation of treaty norms and Community norms in Italy is mainly entrusted to the executive, on the basis of the residual power theory.[141] The Amendments bring a large number of treaty-based norms into the Italian legal system that prevail over statutory law and escape the control of the legislature. The democratic character of the law-making function is endangered

139 Vienna Convention, *supra* note 16.

140 *Supra* under the heading 'Recent Trends…' of this chapter.

141 In this sense, see particularly Antonio La Pergola, Costituzione e Adattamento dell'Ordinamento Interno al Diritto Internazionale 162 (1961); Costantino Mortati, Istituzioni di Diritto Pubblico 669 (9th ed., 1976).

by the lack of a definition of the Parliament's role in the decision-making process relating to the formation and life of treaties and Community law.

The process of European unification and the proliferation of treaty obligations suggest the need to seek a better balance between Parliament and Government through co-participation in decision-making and specific institutional safeguards in those sectors, which pertain to interests and values of general significance that simply cannot be entrusted to the readiness of the Government. In seeking to strike an admittedly delicate balance between a nimble foreign policy decision-making process and the democratic principle of participation by the elected organ (i.e., Parliament), it must be decided which foreign policy decisions must be shared by the Government and the Parliament.

These procedures should permit Parliament to take decisions in a reasonable length of time to satisfy the rapidity that is demanded from decision-making processes in the contemporary world.

This reform has long been called for and needs to be carried out according to the 'constitutional principle of the co-participation of Parliament and the Government in treaty power', enshrined in Article 80 of the Constitution.[142] All that remains to be done is to put into practice the principles already inscribed in the Constitution with an organic revision enhancing the role of Parliament in international policy-making processes and involving in the decision-making procedures all constitutional bodies with a stake in the creation of international treaty law and Community law (the Government, Parliament, and the regions). In this sense, one of the merits of the Amendments is the role given to the regions in the stipulation of treaties, under the new Article 117, last paragraph,[143] although this is subject to implementing norms.

The Amendments to Article 117 of the Italian Constitution dealt with the issue of internal effects of treaty law and Community law. They did so consistently with the principles of direct applicability and primacy of international law. Admittedly, these principles were already enshrined in Article 10 of the Italian Constitution. However, the Amendments, while filling a significant *lacuna* in the Constitution, fall short of providing an overall organic revision of treaty-making powers (including the power to negotiate, administer, amend, and terminate the treaty), which could ensure the effective participation of the Parliament. In spite of a recent reform,[144] the Italian legal system has not adopted procedures sufficient to prepare for the internal law-making and implementation of European Union treaties.

It is necessary to create appropriate treaty-making procedures that ensure the effective participation of the domestic legal institutions that the Constitution recognizes as having an interest in the creation of international treaty law and Community law (i.e., the Government, Parliament, and the regions). Provision should also be made for the preventive judicial review of the constitutional legitimacy of treaties.

While applauding the constitutionalization of the primacy of treaties and Community law over statutory law, a step which fosters their effective observance,

142 See Ziccardi Capaldo, *Riforme istituzionali*, *supra* note 12, at 97–108.

143 See *supra* note 134.

144 Legge No. 11, of 4 February 2005, Gazzetta Ufficiale No.37 (Feb. 15, 2005).

we cannot fail to stress that the Amendments cannot be considered a point of arrival but are merely an important step towards an organic reform to be achieved by means of constitutional and/or legislative provisions. Such a reform, building upon the international principles of direct applicability, primacy, and good faith, and the principle of democratic law-making functions, will eventually keep Italy apace with the progressive integration of the European Union and of the world community at large.

Reducing State Freedom in the Internal Applicability of Treaties

States look with increasing concern to the issue of implementation of international law in their own legal system. In the keynote address to the 2003 annual meeting of the American Society of International Law, Justice Stephen Breyer declared that nothing could be 'more exciting for an academic, practitioner, or judge than the global legal enterprise that is now upon us'.[145] The approach taken by law-makers towards international law is changing: barriers are coming down, and the wall of diffidence epitomized by dualism is crumbling.[146] Internal and international law share fundamental aims and values, placing the individual at the centre of common interests.

Internal law is opening up to international law and integrating with it.[147] Starting from the middle of the twentieth century, gradually and increasingly both constitutional norms and ordinary statutory law of many countries have given direct application to treaties, affecting individuals directly. Such enactments have compelled legislators to eliminate contradictions of domestic law with international law, to guarantee the latter's long-term integration. Likewise, they pressured judicial organs to grant treaties supremacy over domestic legislation, including priority over subsequent legislation. Integration is also favoured by the bearing of international

---

145 Stephen Breyer, *Keynote Address*, 97 AMERICAN SOCIETY OF INTERNATIONAL LAW: PROCEEDINGS OF THE ANNUAL MEETING 268 (2003).

146 Gaetano Arangio-Ruiz, *Dualism Revisited. International Law and Interindividual Law*, 86 RIVISTA DI DIRITTO INTERNAZIONALE 909 (2003); Jean d'Aspremont Lynden, *Du Dualisme au Monisme*, 4 REVUE BELGE DE DROIT CONSTITUTIONNEL 397 (2003); Pierre Pescatore, *Monisme, Dualisme et 'Effet Utile' dans la Jurisprudence de la Cour de Justice de la Communauté Européenne*, in UNE COMMUNAUTÉ DE DROIT. FESTSCHRIFT FÜR GIL CARLOS RODRÍGUEZ IGLESIAS 329 (Ninon Colneric, David Edward, Jean-Pierre Puissochet & Dámaso Ruiz-Jarabo Colomer eds, 2003). The UK system is considered the forerunner of dualism. See the decision of the Privy Council in Higgs & Aron v. Minister of National Security & Others, 23 December 1999. Other countries have legal systems based on the English system, such as: Australia (see the High Court of Australia in the cases of Simsek v. McPhee (1980), Koowarta v. Bjelke Petersen (1981), Tasmania v. Commonwealth (1982), Minister for Immigration v. Teoh (1995), 128 AUSTRALIAN LAW REPORTS 353); Finland (Constitution, Section 94); Malaysia (Constitution, Art. 76 (1)(a)); Nigeria (*General Sani, supra* note 47); Norway (Constitution, Art. 26); Zimbabwe (Constitution, Section 111 (B)). For the English texts see CONSTITUTIONS, *supra* note 9.

147 Leonard F.M. Besselink, *The Constitutional Duty to Promote the Development of the International Legal Order*, 34 NETHERLANDS YEARBOOK OF INTERNATIONAL LAW 89 (2003).

law on the interpretation of municipal statutes and laws: national courts interpret domestic law as closely as possible to international law. Supreme courts in various countries give international norms constitutional status, making it impossible for laws to derogate from them. Further, they look to international law as an instrument to interpret basic constitutional law which, whenever international law is more favourable, ensures fuller protection of human rights.[148] The US Supreme Court has accorded a broad role to international law in some of its adjudications, giving weight to decisions reached by international tribunals.[149] Similarly, the Italian *Corte Costituzionale* has used international conventions on human rights and the protection of minors to which Italy is a party, as well as decisions of the EC Court, to interpret the Italian Constitution along evolutionary lines.[150]

Some constitutions expressly mandate observance of principles laid down in international acts of a universal character (the UN Charter, the Universal Declaration of Human Rights of 1948, and other human rights Conventions) and give them constitutional status and pre-eminence over internal norms. Similar universal acts sometimes contain references to other multilateral treaties of a general character, and this means that an increasing number of international norms are brought within the framework of national constitutions.

The case-by-case approach to the implementation of treaty law in the national sphere is gradually relinquished by states, in favour of express regulations on the internal effect of international law in the state system. This has become a compelling priority for both stable democracies and newly democratic countries. Equally, there is a widespread recognition of the idea that international law imposes an obligation on states to provide for observance of common international standards concerning the internal effect of treaties. To avoid states' international responsibility, domestic courts have generally ensured the observance of such standards spontaneously, even in the absence of specific domestic rules. With increasing frequency, various countries

148 See *supra*, note 49.

149 See Atkins v. Virginia, 536 U.S. 304 (2002); Lawrence v. Texas, 123 S. Ct. 2472 (2003). For a discussion on this topic see generally Harold Hongju Koh, *International Law as Part of Our Law*, 98 Am. J. Int'l L. 43 (2004); Roger P. Alford, *Misusing International Sources to Interpret the Constitution, id.*, at 57; Gerald L. Neuman, *The Uses of International Law in Constitutional Interpretation, id.*, at 82, 84; Michael D. Ramsey, *International Materials and Domestic Rights, id.*, at 69; Thomas A. Aleinikoff, *International Law, Sovereignty, And American Constitutionalism. Reflections on the Customary International Law Debate, id.*, at 91; Paul B. Stephan, *Us Constitutionalism and International Law, What the Multilateralist Move Leaves Out*, 2 Journal of International Criminal Justice 11 (2004). See also Daniel Bodansky, *The Use of International Sources in Constitutional Opinion*, 32 Georgia Journal of International & Comparative Law 421 (2004); Michael Wells, *International Norms in Constitutional Law, id.*, at 429.

150 See Corte costituzionale, 24 May 2002, Sentenza No. 135; 12 November 2002, Sentenza No. 445; 28 November 2002, Sentenza No. 494; 9 May 2003, Sentenza No. 149; 13 January 2004, Sentenza No. 7; 24 June 2004, Sentenza No. 185; 23 December 2004, Sentenza No. 413.

have constitutionalized certain key international standards, such as implementation of treaties in good faith, direct applicability, and primacy over domestic norms.[151]

This increasing regulation at the constitutional level brings about closer coordination between the two legal orders and reinforces certainty of the law in the internal and international legal orders.

The growing process of transformation occurring within international society and its legal order has led to the gradual merging of the two orders. Numerous factors have contributed to the trend, including the democratization process of authoritarian regimes.[152]

The international legal order is progressively developing into a legal system based on common values shared by states; a system that is mindful of individuals and of future generations. The globalization of values and decision-making processes has brought about the acceptance by states of international standards in the fields of human rights, democracy, punishment for international crimes, and the economy.

The international community wishes to see fundamental common values safeguarded and its own norms applied by states.[153] These norms are increasingly addressed directly to individuals and cover areas previously reserved for exclusive domestic regulation.[154] This has strengthened the convergence of interests between internal law and international law but also has heightened any conflicts which might arise between the two, thus making the need for coordination imperative.[155]

The international legal order now shows greater determination than it once did in regulating economic processes and significant sectors of social life, with the creation of organs and organized structures capable of expressing general principles and treaty norms. It is also more determined to assert due and uniform application of such norms by compelling states both to observe international common minimum standards for due implementation of obligations and to adopt appropriate mechanisms to ensure international supervision over observance of international commitments.

---

151 See *supra* under the heading 'Recent Trends …' earlier in this chapter.

152 As Stein pointed out in his analysis of the new Constitutions of the countries of Eastern Europe after the dissolution of the Soviet bloc (*supra* note 5).

153 On the use of 'global opinions of humankind' to interpret constitutional provisions, see Harold Hongju Koh, *Paying Decent Respect to International Tribunal Rulings*, 96 American Society of International Law: Proceedings of the Annual Meeting 45 (2002); *Id., Paying 'Decent Respect' to World Opinion on the Death Penalty*, 35 University of California Davis Law Review 1085 (2002), at 1129; Anne Marie Slaughter, *A Global Community of Courts*, 44 Harvard International Law Journal 191 (2003), at 203.

154 Gaetano Arangio-Ruiz, Dualism Revisited. *International law and Interindividual Law*, 86 Rivista di Diritto Internazionale 909 (2003).

155 Paul Schiff Berman, *Judges as Cosmopolitan Transnational Actors,* 12 Tulsa Journal of Comparative & International Law 109 (2004); Bruce Carolan, *The Search for Coherence in the Use of Foreign Court Judgments by the Supreme Court of Ireland, id.*, at 123.

Concluding Remarks: Towards an Integrated Global Legal System Arranged in Concentric Circles

The first conclusion is that the international legal order is moving towards the development of an integrated world system, arranged in concentric circles, with the aim of governing key issues, such as economy, environment, cultural heritage, health, and work, by means of integrated enforcement mechanisms and decision-making processes. General policy approaches agreed upon by the international society are transposed into legislation of supranational organizations and/or into treaties, obliging states to make them directly enforceable in their national legal systems.

The area in which this phenomenon of integration is most evident is that of human rights protection, where initiatives of international organizations have grown exponentially, generating interlinked norms of both a universal and regional character. To illustrate, regional human rights treaties expressly refer to the norms of treaties of a general character (e.g., UN Charter; Universal Declaration of Human Rights; UN Covenants on Human Rights) and thus make them directly enforceable domestically by way of their own incorporation in the legal order of states.[156] It is in the human rights field that states have taken the boldest steps in domestic implementation, by way of constitutional provisions or through the interpretative practices of their constitutional courts.[157]

Another field where close collaboration between inter-state and domestic legal institutions and structures is fundamental is that of the punishment of international crimes committed by individuals. The developments of integrated systems of co-management of judicial initiatives, such as the creation of international criminal courts and mixed courts, is mandated by international statutes (statutes of *ad hoc* tribunals and the Statute of the International Criminal Court), which sometimes also require constitutional amendments to be enforced within national legal systems.[158]

Peremptory common values have emerged in the international community, and it is from states' acceptance of these values that full integration in the world community arises. At the same time, states benefit from cooperation and take part in the international decision-making processes. These transformations have made evident how prospects for economic and social development and the development of national security are linked to the sharing and observance of those values, and to a higher degree of trust in implementing treaty commitments undertaken at the international level.

---

156 See, e.g., the Maastricht Treaty (Official Journal No. C 325 (Dec. 24, 2002)), Art. 6 (2).

157 See e.g., Gerald L. Neuman, *Human Rights and Constitutional Rights, Harmony and Dissonance*, 55 Stanford Law Review 1863 (2003); Daphne Barak-Erez, *The International Law of Human Rights and Constitutional Law. A Case Study of an Expanding Dialogue*, 2 International Journal of Constitutional Law 611 (2004). See also *supra* notes 49, 50, 75.

158 For a comparative analysis, see Anna Oriolo, *Ratifica e Attuazione in Italia dello Statuto di Roma: Questioni di Compatibilità Costituzionale e Opportunità di un'Armonizzazione Legislativa*, *in* Attuazione dei Trattati, *supra* note 13 at 265. In general, on the development of integrated systems of safeguards, see *supra* Introduction of this book.

The second conclusion is that, by permitting the expansion of the prerogatives of supranational institutions and constitutionalizing international standards for the domestic implementation of international law, states conform their own domestic system to international common values, limiting their own sovereignty.

In the face of state constitutions' increasing observance of international minimum standards, the classical notion that states have freedom to choose the ways and means by which they implement international law in the domestic legal system becomes increasingly questionable.[159]

The concept of sovereignty is changing. The traditional state attitude towards the exclusive protection of national interests is shifting.[160] The modern sovereign state cannot protect its own interests and safeguard its economy but by participating in the international decision-making process. This awareness has substantially transformed the classical concept of sovereignty. The term sovereignty can no longer be translated as *jus escludendi alios* but must be interpreted as the state's power to contribute with other states and subjects to building the new world order and to its management.

The third conclusion is that the trend towards integration between internal law and international law, and the progressive inclusion within constitutions of international standards for domestic implementation of international law, creates two fundamental problems for states: safeguarding basic constitutional principles; and preserving the balance of internal powers.

On the one hand, these problems require states to take greater care in eliminating contradictions between domestic law and international law before they turn into overt conflict, for instance, during the treaty-making process. On the other hand, they solicit states' action to ensure participation of parliaments in the treaty-making process. Leaving treaty-making powers completely in the hands of the executive, to the exclusion of elected bodies, such as the Parliament, encroaches on the principle of the separation of powers, especially when international treaties become directly applicable and prevail over domestic norms.[161] If treaty-making procedures do not provide for effective democratic participation there is a risk of severe institutional imbalances within state systems, subverting the very principle of democracy in law-making processes both at the national and international levels.[162]

While giving constitutional status to the principles of primacy and direct applicability, states must also endow their domestic legal systems with adequate legislative and judicial checks and balances over the creation and administration of international treaty norms.

159 See *supra* under the heading 'International Minimum Standards …' earlier in this chapter.

160 See recently, Thomas A. Aleinikoff, *Thinking Outside the Sovereign Box, Transnational Law and the U.S. Constitution*, 82 Texas Law Review 1989 (2004).

161 See the further concerns expressed by Jackson regarding policies that favour the higher status of directly applied norms/DAHS system, *supra* note 32, at 330.

162 Eric Stein has approached the nexus between integration and democracy from a different perspective. See Eric Stein, *International Integration and Democracy: No Love at First Sight*, 95 Am. J. Int'l L. 488 (2001).

PART IV
Collective Guarantees: An Embryonic New System

SECTION I
Actions to Combat Global Terrorism

Chapter 6

Heteronomous Actions Against Terror: The Military Interventions

Introduction

Collective guarantees have emerged at an international level based on norms safeguarding universal values and the interests of the global community. These norms impose obligations on states, individuals, and groups with an *erga omnes* effect. The UN Charter established, in principle, the formal opposition of the international community to the unilateral use of force (Article 2 (4)). The Charter also provides a system of collective security, centred in the Security Council, for the maintenance of peace and the adoption of sanctions against offending parties, all with a view to preventing unilateral law enforcement measures by individual states (Chapter VII).

In the second half of the twentieth century, the practice of states and UN bodies promoted the development of other norms protecting global interests and values, as well as peace and international security. These norms were of a 'public' nature, with the result that other legal principles were established along the lines of constitutional principles of global law.[1] These principles in turn gave rise to other obligations under peremptory norms of general international law (*jus cogens* norms). *Jus cogens* norms imposed such principles on sovereign states, individuals, and groups as the prohibitions on colonialism, genocide, apartheid, inhumane treatment, and dictatorial regimes, as well as on international terrorism, organized crime, the narcotics trade, and large-scale pollution, among others. Due to the inadequacy of UN security procedures, which are applicable only to states and are implemented only to protect peace and security, states have occasionally taken unilateral action for safeguarding global interests, even when the interests of those states have not been directly violated. Such states act on a 'collective' basis, on behalf of the global community, under the supervision of UN bodies, but going beyond the UN Charter system. The development of this practice has resulted in a system of international collective guarantees and integrated mechanisms that have been put in place for the implementation of provisions that are 'public' in character – i.e., those concerning obligations under peremptory norms of general international law. In order to protect global interests, a principle has been established that states may be entitled to uphold the rule of law even though they have suffered no material prejudice themselves (states acting 'in the common interest', or *uti universi*). States may do so, however, only with the participation of UN bodies, to which the international order has granted general supervisory powers. This supervision by international institutions

1 See *supra*, Introduction to this book.

provides actions carried out 'unilaterally' with the objectivity necessary for them to be recognised as carrying out a public function.[2]

Mechanisms to collectively protect fundamental global values have been established, giving rise to integrated decision-making systems as states and international institutions jointly uphold the law. These integrated mechanisms for the implementation of international constitutional principles, though making use of the institutional structure of the UN, are not carried out within the normative limits of the Charter and therefore fall outside the system of collective security laid down by Chapter VII. The Charter system in fact established a set of sanctions to be taken only against states, and only with a 'punitive' function.

These mechanisms for co-managing the protection of collective interests, which grew from state practice and gave rise to customary norms, have led to the 'public' management of the fundamental values of the global order and to a system of guarantees intended to function in the universal community in relation not only to states, but also individuals, movements, and groups, and having not only a 'punitive', but also a 'tutelary,' character. This is the evolutionary process we are calling the 'verticalization' of the international community and its legal order, from which 'the integrated system of collective guarantees' derives.

The Dual Functions of Collective Guarantees – Punitive and Tutelary

One aim of this book is to elaborate a theoretical construction of the integrated system of collective guarantees through empirical research. The focus will be on the mechanisms of co-management of the integrated system of collective guarantees; we argue that this system performs a dual function: the punitive function – i.e., guaranteeing global interests by means of sanctions against those responsible for internationally wrongful acts infringing public interests (Chapters 2, 8); and the tutelary function – i.e., policing actions aimed at protecting these interests in themselves (Chapter 6).

In Chapter 2, we identify the processes and mechanisms of the integrated system of law-enforcement – including measures involving and those not involving the use of force – aimed at moving forward from the system of collective security provided by the UN Charter. The attention is, therefore, on unilateral state action to apply sanctions on behalf of the collectivity and in order to protect the general interest, as well as the parallel activity of UN bodies outside the institutional framework to integrate and to legitimate the range of sanctions adopted by states acting in the common interest, *uti universi*.[3]

The mechanisms under discussion must be seen as constituting collective guarantees of a 'punitive' nature. The mechanisms for 'institutional' sanctions provided in Chapter VII of the UN Charter, Articles 41 and 42, may be said to have an analogous character. Such mechanisms may be regarded as a response to states

2 Chapter 2 of this book, under the heading 'States Acting in the Common Interest and Institutional Control'.

3 *Supra*, chapter 2 under the headings 'Mechanisms to Co-Manage Peaceful Enforcement Measures' and 'Mechanisms to Co-Manage Involving the Use of Force'.

responsible for grave violations of *jus cogens* norms. These new mechanisms entail an expansion of the law enforcement capacity of states.

The 'punitive' measures within the integrated system of collective security also consist of economic sanctions that require the cooperation of states, the UN, and other international organizations that are imposed against individuals, groups, and movements responsible for serious breaches of obligations under peremptory norms of general international law (i.e., smart sanctions and other measures, examined in Chapters 8 and 9).[4]

In this chapter we highlight the fact that at the international level another category of collective guarantees belonging to the integrated system is emerging. In previous studies we have called such collective guarantees 'tutelary',[5] since they provide protection for fundamental collective interests and values, regardless of punitive measures taken against those responsible for violating international norms. This tutelary protection of global interests is achieved by widening the authority or jurisdiction of states operating in the common interest (as 'agents' of the international community, or 'agent states'). Agent states can exercise jurisdictional, material, coercive, and regulatory powers that are more extensive than those normally conferred by customary law on sovereign states within their own territory (i.e., territorial sovereignty) and over their citizens abroad (i.e., personal sovereignty). The exercise of these powers on behalf of the international community, however, is subject to institutional control.

With regard to jurisdictional powers, the principle of 'universal' jurisdiction allows states to exercise powers over individuals who have committed crimes against humanity (*crimina juris gentium*), even when the territorial or personal link normally required between the crime and the state community (i.e., the social attachment) is lacking. Legal scholars argue that the principle of the universality of the criminal jurisdiction allows that crimes against humanity may be linked to any legal system, wherever and by whomever they have been committed.

As an example of material and coercive governmental powers, the fight against international terrorism includes cases of states exercising such powers – over and above the limits laid down by international law – on ships or planes flying the flag of another state, or even within the territory of another state, in order to put an end to a terrorist act and to bring those responsible to justice. This practice has not provoked significant reactions on the part of the international community or the UN. Another example of this trend can be seen in international practice relating to the prevention and abatement of large-scale pollution of the sea and air, which has entailed the expansion of the powers of neighbouring states.

The following discussion will focus on international practice relating to the repression of international terrorism, underlining how certain cases reflect the dual approach to collective guarantees with regard to the 'general powers' exercised by

---

4 *Infra*, chapter 8 under the heading 'The Concept of "Smart Sanctions" ' and chapter 9, 'Introduction'.

5 See Giuliana Ziccardi Capaldo, Terrorismo Internazionale e Garanzie Collettive/International Terrorism and Collective Guarantees (1990) [hereinafter Ziccardi Capaldo, Terrorismo Internazionale], at 75–102. See also *supra* chapter 2 of this book.

states in combating terrorism in the common interest. The term 'general powers' will be used to cover all the limitations that the international order places on the sovereign rights of individual states and of individuals, as justified by the higher purposes of the global community. As a result, this term must be understood as including not only punitive actions by states acting *uti universi* against states, individuals, and groups responsible for supporting or funding acts of terrorism, but also the exceptional expansion of governmental powers of a jurisdictional, material, and coercive nature exercised over individual terrorists on an extraterritorial basis. Such powers arise beyond the normal limits for the exercise of state power, restricting the sovereign rights of other states for the benefit of the collectivity. Clearly, these are two instances of a 'public' guarantee function, albeit of an embryonic kind, which in the first case takes the form of sanctions or punitive actions to repress grave violations of international law, and in the second case takes the form of security measures affording protection for society and the maintenance of public order.

From our point of view, in any investigation of the fight against terrorism, particular attention should be paid to the fact that terrorism carried out by individuals or organized groups in order to achieve certain objectives, with or without the support of states, is an attack on the values and interests of the international community as a whole, even though attacks on these interests entail a breach of the rights of one or more individual states. As a result, the interest of the community in repressing the phenomenon can, in our view, be seen as a corollary of the more general maintenance of peace and international security that terrorist actions seriously threaten due to their frequency and intensity. Particular attention should also be paid to grave violations of humanitarian law and human rights in the fight against terrorism.

At this point in our enquiry it is important to underline that this perspective brings together both the actions of states taken on behalf of the collectivity against other states, movements, and groups sponsoring terrorism, as well as the exercise of extraterritorial state powers in relation to individual terrorists, all with significant implications for the definition of the integrated system of collective guarantees. Starting from support for fundamental interests, which *all* states, not just the injured party,[6] are potentially permitted to protect, our position is that those extraterritorial forms of protection that include special powers of a material, coercive, and jurisdictional kind in relation to individual terrorists are legitimate in certain circumstances. It is thus our intention to make a case for the concept of 'tutelary protection' of the values of the international community.

The State Practice of Military Incursions in the Fight Against Terrorism

Actions of states combating terrorism reflect significant support for the position that underlines the 'public' role of international law in the repression of terrorism and the broadening of the concept of collective guarantees: we recall in particular certain responses to Middle Eastern terrorism, and certain episodes that are particularly significant in terms of the expansion of state powers of a material, coercive, and

6 See *supra* chapter 2, under the heading 'Introduction'; see also *infra* note 44.

jurisdictional kind carried out to rescue hostages, to capture terrorists, and to put them on trial.

Since the 1980s, international news reports have increasingly focused on the exercise of governmental authority by certain states in the territory of other states in order to secure the liberation of their citizens or other individuals taken hostage by terrorists, and to bring those responsible to justice. In many cases the government of the country concerned gave its consent prior to the operation, as in the case of the incursion by German forces at the airport of Mogadishu in October 1977,[7] and the Egyptian raid on the airport of La Valletta in November 1985.[8] But the most challenging cases, which have attracted the greatest interest among international scholars, are those cases in which consent has not been given and where, in spite of the manifest infringement of customary international law, the community of states and the UN have not expressed a firm and unanimous condemnation of the 'violation' of the sovereignty of the affected state. In many cases, these operations have elicited a positive response from third-party states, underlining the legitimacy of operations aimed at combating international terrorism, as well as the right and duty of states to protect their citizens even when they are abroad and the right to legitimate self-defence laid down by Article 51 of the UN Charter. Examples include the following: the Israeli incursion at Entebbe in Uganda in June 1976;[9] the Egyptian incursion in

---

7 The German incursion in Somalia at the Mogadishu airport, where the hijacking of a Lufthansa airliner by Arab terrorists ended on the night of 17 October 1977 with the liberation of all the hostages (Charles Rousseau, *Chronique des Faits Internationaux* [hereinafter Rousseau, Chronique], 82 Revue Générale de Droit International Public 627 (1978); New York Times, 18 October 1977), was successful due to the intervention of a West German special police corps that had been set up in 1972 to combat terrorism after the dramatic Palestinian attack on the Olympic games in Munich. The intervention of the German special forces was carried out with the consent of the Somali government and with the unanimous support of Western countries. In the debate on air piracy at the UN that immediately followed, Arab States expressed concern that their sovereignty had been violated, but Germany was not censured. The Arab States managed to add to the text of the resolution, which was unanimously approved by the General Assembly with the abstention of Cuba, an amendment prohibiting States from responding to hijacking in a way that would infringe on the sovereignty or territorial integrity of other States (GA Res. 32/8 (Nov. 3, 1977)).

8 On 23 November 1985, a terrorist group hijacked an Egyptian airliner and diverted it to Malta. The hijacking was brought to an end with a massacre resulting from an armed engagement between the hijackers and Egyptian special forces, intervening with the consent of the Maltese government. The States concerned rejected the offer of intervention on the part of American special forces. In this case, similar to the *Achille Lauro* incident, there was an attempt by the US to promote the idea that the Sixth Fleet, and in particular the Delta force, could police the Mediterranean, as an anti-terrorist force. The classic concept of territorial sovereignty here began to show signs of weakness.

9 The Israeli operation met with a positive response in almost all Western countries. However, the summit of the Organization of African States issued a unanimous declaration condemning the Israeli incursion. The African members of the UN Security Council drafted a resolution drawing attention to the 'violation of sovereignty' resulting from the Israeli action (and this draft resolution was widely supported by the Communist countries: see UN Doc. S/12139 (1976)). The Security Council did not manage to adopt a resolution on this matter.

Cyprus in February 1978;[10] the crisis between Iran and the US that was sparked by the occupation of the US Embassy in Teheran, with diplomatic staff taken hostage and held from November 1979 to January 1981, which resulted in an incursion by American special forces in Tabas in April 1980;[11] and the hijacking of the *Achille Lauro*, leading to the interception and forced landing at Sigonella of the Egyptian plane that was transporting the terrorists in October 1985.[12] It is also the case that some armed incursions into the territory of other states resulting in the death of terrorists – and at times civilians – have provoked a significant reaction neither from the affected state, nor from the international community. One such example was the US airstrike on the village of Damadola, Pakistan, on 15 January 2006, in which a number of Al Qaeda terrorists were killed.[13]

There is a need to make a distinction here between military incursions involving the extraterritorial exercise of *jurisdiction*, which are not intended as punitive actions or sanctions, and armed operations involving the use of force 'against' a state in order to impose sanctions by means of force. As underlined in the following analysis, the different juridical connotations of these two types of operations require a different frame of reference in addressing each one.[14]

The divergent views of the states in the UN and the emergence of a degree of tolerance for the interventions of the first type – i.e., those interventions that are

---

The draft resolution proposed by the US and the UK (UN Doc. S/12138 (1976), put to a vote, was rejected (31 UN SCOR, 1943rd mtg, UN Doc. S/PV.1943 (1976), at 81).

10 On 18 February 1978, two Palestinian terrorists made their way into the Hilton Hotel in Nicosia, where a meeting was being held of the Organization for Solidarity with Afro-Asian Peoples, and assassinated the Egyptian minister Youssef Al Sebai, who was closely connected to then-President Sadat. Many aspects of this incident remain unclear. Above all, it has never been clarified whether the Egyptian intervention was sanctioned by the Cypriot authorities. It is significant, however, that Egypt invoked the right to combat international terrorism.

11 It is also the case that in April 1980, US military forces in Iranian territory attempted to rescue the US diplomatic personnel taken hostage in Teheran. The US defended the action by invoking Art. 51 of the UN Charter on the right to self-defence. There were no significant reactions on the part of other States or even on the part of the Iranian government. The Security Council, which had unanimously requested the release of the hostages (SC Res. 457 (Dec. 4, 1979), para. 1), did not adopt any resolutions condemning the US intervention. The International Court of Justice, to which the US referred the case on 29 November 1980, expressed its concern but did not formally condemn the US operation, which was considered, in the circumstances, '*de nature à nuire au respect du règlement judiciaire*' (United States Diplomatic and Consular Staff in Tehran), Merits, Judgment, 1980 ICJ Reports 3 (May 24, 1980), para. 93, at 43.

12 The American interception and forced landing of the Egyptian plane (with the terrorists on board) did not give rise to a consistent reaction on the part of the international community or protests about the infringement of Egyptian and Italian sovereignty. See *infra* this chapter under the heading 'Interventions on the High Seas or in Free Spaces'.

13 The international community condemned the killing in Tunisian territory of the deputy leader of the PLO, Abu Jihad, on 16 April 1988. A UN Security Council resolution, which the US did not veto, refuted the Israeli claim that the State of Israel was entitled to strike down terrorist leaders anywhere and at any time (SC Res. 611 (April 25, 1988)).

14 See this and the preceding sections of this chapter.

not intended as punitive actions – in spite of the range of different justifications put forward, undermines the traditional interpretation of the principle of sovereignty. This growing tolerance also opens up the possibility of considering as lawful the extra-territorial exercise of state powers of a material and coercive kind in areas normally reserved for the jurisdiction of other states, while posing questions about the circumstances that render such interventions lawful and, above all, about their classification in the system of international law.

Under What Authority Can a State Exercise Its Sovereign Powers Beyond Its Borders?

It is not the purpose of this section, which is aimed at investigating the structure of the international order and the nature of collective guarantees, to define the limits of state power in the capture or detention of terrorists.[15] It suffices for the moment to note that in connection with the practice outlined above, legal scholars recognise the rights of a state to exercise its sovereign powers over terrorists beyond its borders. In fact, this practice and these opinions are not incompatible with the main features of the international order and do not have such a significant impact on the system as it may at first appear. There is a need to underline the fact that the history of international relations, even in earlier periods, includes cases of the 'exceptional' exercise of governmental powers by states in relation to certain violations of international law. The classic example is that of piracy, which allows any state to capture pirates on the high seas and to punish them.[16] However, on the basis of an older opinion that is attracting renewed interest, we argue that similar powers should also be recognised for states in the case of other serious crimes – in particular *crimina juris gentium*, or crimes against humanity.[17] The range of such 'exceptional' cases has tended to increase over the years, with legal scholars particularly focused

---

15 This is covered later in this chapter under the heading 'Conditions Legitimizing the Exercise…'.

16 See Arts 14–21 of the 1958 Geneva Convention on the High Seas (April 29, 1958, 450 UNTS 11) and Arts 100–107 of the United Nations Convention on the Law of the Sea (UNCLOS) (Dec.10, 1982, Doc. A/CONF.62/122 and Corr.1 to 11) [hereinafter Montego Bay Convention], 21 International Legal Materials [hereinafter Int'l Legal Mat.] 1261; the Convention for the Suppression of Unlawful Acts Against the Safety of Maritime Navigation and its related Protocol (1988), amended by the Diplomatic Conference on the Revision of the SUA Treaties held in 2005. For a doctrinal analysis of the jurisdictional aspects of piracy and for bibliographical references, see Alfred P. Rubin, *The Law of Piracy*, 15 Denver Journal of International Law & Policy 173 (1987); Joseph G. Starke, An Introduction to International Law (7th ed., 1972), at 284–288; George R. Constantinople, *Towards a New Definition of Piracy: The Achille Lauro Incident*, 26 Virginia Journal of International Law 723 (1986); Hugh W. Stephens, *Not Merely the* Achille Lauro: *The Threat of Maritime Terrorism and Piracy*, 9 Terrorism 285 (1987); Eric F. Ellen, Piracy at Sea (1989); Ethan C. Stiles, *Reforming Current International Law to Combat Modern Sea Piracy*, 27 Suffolk Transnational Law Review 299 (2004).

17 Interest in this concept dates back to the American proposal of 15 November 1946 (UN Doc. A/CN.4/25, Yearbook of International Law Commission [hereinafter Y. Int'l L.

on individual responsibility under international law for grave violations of human rights law.[18]

However, despite the interest in the international nature of such crimes, and the widely debated status under international law of those indicted, there is a lack of theoretical work concerning the legal basis of the wide-ranging powers conferred on states.[19]

In our opinion, the legal basis for this expansion of state authority is related to the existence of the essential values and interests of the global community, which go beyond the particular interests of individual states.[20]

Moreover, legal scholars are calling for the international protection of these values, and this is cited as a legal basis for the international prosecution of individual criminals for actions violating international norms. However, we would argue that the need for international protection of these interests should also be seen as providing the legal basis for the 'exceptional' widening of state powers in relation to criminal activity. This would give rise to *erga omnes* powers, strengthening state authority to protect the fundamental values of the international system.

In our view, the 'exceptional' powers conferred upon states and exercised in the common interest, *uti universi*, should not be limited to an extension of the internal criminal jurisdiction over foreign nationals, but should also, in certain cases and under certain conditions to be specified below,[21] give rise to derogations from the rights of individual criminals as well as of the state in whose jurisdiction the

---

COMM.] (1950), Vol. II, (Part One), paras 11–13, at 256) to the UN General Assembly to adopt a general codification of the principles drawn up and applied by the Nuremberg Tribunal.

18 For the activities of the two Tribunals in the years 1999–2006, see *supra*, Introduction to this book, note 68.

19 In the past, legal scholars debated the nature of the power exercised by the State in relation to piracy, in particular as to whether a State capturing pirates acted on behalf of the collective will of all States (see JOHN WESTLAKE, ETUDES SUR LES PRINCIPES DU DROIT INTERNATIONAL (1895), at 1–2; HANS KELSEN, DAS PROBLEM DER SOUVERÄNITÄT UND DIE THEORIE DES VÖLKERRECHTS (1960), at 165, or whether it acted as a subject in the 'exercise of freedom' (see ROLANDO QUADRI, LA SUDDITANZA NEL DIRITTO INTERNAZIONALE (1936), at 79 *et seq.*; ALFRED VERDROSS, DIE VERFASSUNG DER VÖLKERRECHTSGEMEINSCHAFT (1926), at 158), and therefore whether the State exercises power on behalf of the international community or on behalf of the State itself. Recently, see Leticia Diaz & Barry Hart Dubner, *On the Problem of Utilizing Unilateral Action to Prevent Acts of Sea Piracy and Terrorism*, 32 SYRACUSE JOURNAL OF INTERNATIONAL LAW AND COMMERCE 1 (2004).

20 In the US, the *Achille Lauro* case gave rise to a debate about the international legitimacy of the territorial extension of American jurisdiction in relation to terrorist acts committed outside US territory by foreign nationals (US House, Committee on the Judiciary, 4 March 1986, 99th Cong. 2nd sess.), especially after the adoption by the Senate of the Antiterrorism Act of 1986. See on this point, Catherine Collier Fisher, *US Legislation to Prosecute Terrorists: Antiterrorism or Legalized Kidnapping?*, 18 VANDERBILT JOURNAL OF TRANSNATIONAL LAW [hereinafter VAND. J. TRANSNAT'L L.] 915 (1985); Patrick L. Donnelly, *Extraterritorial Jurisdiction over Acts of Terrorism Committed Abroad: Omnibus Diplomatic Security and Antiterrorism Act of 1986*, 72 CORNELL LAW REVIEW 599 (1987). See also *infra* under the heading 'Under What Authority …?' earlier in this chapter.

21 See later this chapter under the heading 'Conditions Legitimizing the Exercise…'.

crimes are taking place or the criminals are situated (hereinafter, the 'territorial state'). This extends the material and coercive powers of the agent state beyond its jurisdiction, and subordinates the territorial state, which is obliged to tolerate (*pati*) the infringement of its sovereignty (hereinafter, the 'affected state'), although claims for damages may be made. This principle should apply to all cases of the lawful extra-territorial exercise of governmental authority (police, internal public order and regulatory powers), and therefore in all cases in which the international order entrusts states with the protection of fundamental interests for the global community, thus granting 'exceptional' powers.

If we bear these considerations in mind, it becomes clear that the exceptional widening of the powers granted to the agent state is closely connected to the interests they are intended to defend and the values they are intended to uphold. They are therefore functional powers, in the sense that they can be exercised only to the extent that they are 'necessary' to satisfy the specific interests that are being protected (i.e., human rights, environmental protection, cultural resources, health, energy, nuclear power, among others) and within the limits laid down by the detailed norms dealing with particular cases in each specific sector of the law. Since these powers – linked as they are to the protection of collective interests – go beyond the normal authority of the sovereign state over its territory and citizens, they are generally suitable for extending the powers of the state acting on behalf of the entire international community beyond the limits normally laid down by international law, even to the extent of infringing the rights of an individual or an individual state. As a result, the expansion of the powers of the agent state, and the corresponding restriction of the powers of the territorial state or of individuals gives rise to improved conditions for the protection of the collective interest, resulting in a form of guarantee of the international legal order that may be defined as 'heteronomous' and 'tutelary'.

The Scholars' Approach to the Problem

We argue that the protection of global interests and rights offers a legal basis for extra-territorial coercion and jurisdictional powers that can be exercised by states on an exceptional basis, beyond the typical limits of their jurisdiction. The solutions proposed here for problems connected to the fight against terrorism thus diverge from those applied in legal doctrine and international diplomacy. In those arenas, these problems have been discussed in an unsatisfactory manner, due to the tendency not to consider the issues as connected to the objective implementation of the international order.

We must first address situations in which states allegedly violate the sovereignty of another state in an effort to rescue individual victims of terrorism or to arrest those responsible for terrorist acts.[22] The most common approach among politicians, diplomats, and legal scholars is to view such allegations in light of the general prohibition of armed force found in the UN Charter and in customary international law. This, however, is not the appropriate starting point.

---

22 See *supra* notes 7–13, *infra* note 51 and corresponding text.

Following the usual approach, a number of authors have deemed this type of intervention to be unlawful, as it is a violation of the principle of the non-use of force. On the other hand, other authors have attempted to show that it is not a violation of this principle. Such arguments focus on the right to intervene found in Article 51 of the UN Charter relating to legitimate self-defence, or on the humanitarian aspects of the intervention, linking it to the right of states to protect their own citizens with the use of force, a right and practice that is upheld in derogation of Article 2 (4). Scholars also find a justification in the fact that the prohibition on force is diminished in cases in which, at a practical level, the system of collective security laid down by the UN Charter in Chapter VII is not capable of functioning.[23]

The question arising from these operations and incursions – classified before as 'interventions' of a non-punitive character[24] – does not relate to the legitimate use of force in international relations. As a result, the question is not whether such operations violate the principle in Article 2 (4) prohibiting the use of 'international' force. Rather, it is entirely a matter of the international regulation of the *jurisdiction* of states – i.e., the 'internal' use of force – raising the question of the lawfulness

---

23 With regard to the incursions occurred since the 1970s, see H.H. Anthony Cooper, *Hostage Rescue Operations: Dénouement at Algeria and Mogadishu Compared*, 26 Chitty's Law Journal 91 (1978); Jeffrey A. Sheehan, *The Entebbe Raid: The Principle of Self-Help in International Law as Justification for State Use of Armed Force*, 1 The Fletcher Forum of World Affairs 135 (1977); Jordan J. Paust, *Entebbe and Self-Help: The Israeli Response to Terrorism*, 2 The Fletcher Forum of World Affairs 86 (1978); Robert A. Friedlander, *Retaliation as an Anti-Terrorist Weapon: The Israeli Lebanon Incursion and International Law*, 8 Israel Yearbook on Human Rights 63 (1978), at 68; M. McDougal & William Michael Reisman, New York Times (July 16, 1976); Mark D. Larsen, *The Achille Lauro Incident and the Permissible Use of Force*, 9 Loyola of Los Angeles International and Comparative Law Journal 481 (1987). On humanitarian intervention and in general support of a State's right to intervene, see Richard B. Lillich, *Forcible Self-Help by States to Protect Human Rights*, 53 Iowa Law Review 325 (1967); *Id.*, *Humanitarian Intervention: A Reply to Ian Brownlie and a Plea for Constructive Alternatives*, *in* Law and Civil War in the Modern World 229 (John N. Moore ed., 1974) [hereinafter Law and Civil War]; Donald W. Greig, International Law (2nd ed., 1976) at 879–880; Jean-Pierre L. Fonteyne, *Forcible Self-Help by States to Protect Human Rights: Recent Views from the United Nations*, *in* Humanitarian Intervention and the United Nations 197 (Richard B. Lillich ed., 1973). For an opposing view, see Haro F. Van Panhuys, The Role of Nationality in International Law (1959), at 113 *et seq.*; Ian Brownlie, International Law and the Use of Force by States 255–256 (1963); *Id.*, *Humanitarian Intervention*, *in* Law and Civil War, *supra*, at 217–228; James L. Brierly, The Law of Nations 413–421 (6th ed., 1963); Tom J. Farer, *The Regulation of Foreign Intervention in Civil Armed Conflict,* 142 Recueil des Cours 291 (1974–II), especially at 387–393; Grigorij I. Tunkin, Theory of International Law 385–395 (1974); Natalino Ronzitti, Rescuing Nationals Abroad Through Military Coercion and Intervention on Grounds of Humanity (1985) (and references therein). For recent views on the theory of humanitarian intervention, see *supra* chapter 2 of this book, under the heading 'Unauthorized Humanitarian Interventions'.

24 See earlier this chapter under the heading 'The Dual Functions of Collective Guarantees…'.

of the extra-territorial exercise of governmental powers over citizens and foreign nationals in free spaces or in spaces under the jurisdiction of other states.[25]

Those military operations we classify as interventions in the internal or external affairs of another state do not in themselves constitute the 'use of force' prohibited by Article 2 (4) of the UN Charter. [26] They should be distinguished (with admitted difficulty) from 'armed interventions' of a 'punitive' nature in the form of military strikes against states deemed to be sponsoring terrorist groups and organizations. Only in such cases does it make sense to speak of the lawfulness of the use of force at an international level.

Support for this distinction between military incursions involving the extraterritorial exercise of governmental power, or 'internal' force, and military incursions of a punitive character, or 'international' force, prohibited under Article 2 (4) of the UN Charter, can be found in the workings of UN bodies and the opinions expressed by state representatives during official debates on the fight against international terrorism[27] and in the reactions of the affected states. We are reminded again that on various occasions in relation to operations classified as the first type

---

25 With regard to the incursion at Entebbe, the French representative on the Security Council, Jacques Lecompt, considered the Israeli intervention '*une violation de la souveraineté*' of Uganda, though it was not intended to undermine the '*intégrité territoriale ni à l'indépendence*' of that country (UN Doc. S/PV.1943, *supra* note 9, at 31). Also, in the case of the incursion in Iran, the US underlined the 'humanitarian' aspect of the mission, defined as a 'rescue operation' (TV and radio broadcast by President Carter on 25 April 1980 and a White House official communiqué issued on the same day). Finally, the interception of the Egyptian plane in the *Achille Lauro* case was considered to be a matter relating to the extraterritorial exercise of US jurisdiction, rather than as a matter of the use of 'international' force. See Jeffrey A. McCredie, *Contemporary Uses of Force Against Terrorism: The United States Response to Achille Lauro; Questions of Jurisdiction and Its Exercise*, 16 Georgia Journal of International and Comparative Law 435 (1986).

26 With reference to the cases under discussion, diplomatic sources, especially American ones, and legal scholars refer to a use of force other than that prohibited by Art. 2 (4) as 'limited force in intention and effect' and as permitted, on an exceptional basis, in certain well-defined circumstances. See in general Daniel P. O'Connell, International Law 303 (2nd ed., 1970).

27 See the opinions expressed by certain Western representatives, and above all those of the US, on the UN Security Council in relation to the Entebbe intervention (UN Doc. S/PV. 1939 (1976)). See also *supra* note 9. For a more extensive legal analysis of the applicable juridical principles, and for bibliographical references, see M. Knishbacher, *The Entebbe Operation: A Legal Analysis of Israel's Rescue Action*, 12 Journal of Internal Law & Economics 57 (1977); Helmut Strebel, *Nochmals zur Geiselbefreiung in Entebbe*, 37 Zeitschrift für Ausländisches Offentliches Recht und Völkerrecht 691 (1977); Atimomo A. Emiko, *The Impact of International Terrorism and Hijacking of Aircraft on State Sovereignty: The Israeli Raid on Entebbe Airport Re-visited*, 23 Journal of the Indian Law Institute 90 (1981), at 100 *et seq.*; Francis A. Boyle, *The Entebbe Hostages Crisis*, 29 Netherlands International Law Review 32–71 (1982), especially at 34–38; Leslie C. Green, *Humanitarian Intervention: 1976 Version*, 24 Chitty's Law Journal 217 (1976); *Id.*, *Rescue at Entebbe. Legal Aspects*, *in* 6 Israel Yearbook on Human Rights 312 (1976). Cf. also *supra*, note 25 and *infra*, notes 36, 38, 58.

(e.g. the incursions at Entebbe, Mogadishu, Larnaca, and the American incursion in Iran), the UN Security Council did not pass a resolution condemning the state's action as a use of force. However, the Security Council managed to condemn as unlawful uses of force, in no uncertain terms, operations that were clearly aggressive, such as the Israeli invasion of Lebanon in 1978,[28] or the two Israeli incursions into Tunisia in 1985 and 1988, and the US/UK military intervention in Iraq,[29] with a clear reference to a breach of the peace and to Article 2 (4) of the UN Charter.[30] In addition, the injured parties threatened military retaliation only in cases in which they were victims of armed intervention.[31] The ICJ, moreover, in the case of *Military and Paramilitary Activities in and against Nicaragua*, in 1986, determined that 'what is unlawful, in accordance with [the principle of the non-use of force], is recourse to either the threat or the use of force against the territorial integrity or political independence of any State'.[32]

Accordingly, we consider that in relation to operations in the first category, a military response should not be allowed (pursuant to Article 51 of the Charter). As the *ultra vires* exercise of jurisdictional powers, these operations would constitute the violation of a norm other than the Article 2 (4) prohibition of the use of force – namely, the principle of non-intervention in the internal affairs of another state.

The distinction proposed between the use of internal and international force in armed interventions against terrorism could usefully contribute to the definition of the principle of non-intervention in the internal affairs of other states, and to the identification of a particular application of this principle distinct from the prohibition of the threat or the use of force. This would overcome the theoretical and interpretive difficulties found in the case law[33] and in acts of the UN, such as General Assembly Resolution 36/103,[34] which have been highlighted by scholars.

Nor, in our view, can 'interventions' involving the extra-territorial exercise of governmental powers be deemed to be forms of justifiable self-defence. Moreover, in many instances the state in which the incursion took place, and which lodged a protest about an infringement of its sovereignty, had not breached any international obligation. In any event, even in cases in which an internationally wrongful act had

---

28 SC Res. 425 (March 19, 1978).

29 Chapter 4 of this book, under the heading 'The Unlawfulness of the Unilateral Intervention in Iraq'.

30 SC Res. 573 (Oct. 4, 1985); SC Res. 611 (April 25, 1988). On the general implications of this point, see Derek Bowett, *Reprisals Involving Recourse to Armed Force*, 66 American Journal of International Law 1 (1972), at 10 *et seq.*; Serge Regoud, *Raids 'Antiterroristes' et Developments Récents des Atteintes Illecites au Principe de Non-Intervention*, 32 Annuaire Francais de Droit International [hereinafter Ann. Fr. D.I.] 79 (1986).

31 For a more extensive analysis and general references on the topic, see also *supra* chapter 4 of this book, under the heading 'The Question of International Legality…', subheading 'Self-Defence'.

32 Military and Paramilitary Activities in and Against Nicaragua (Nicaragua v. United States of America), Merits, Judgment, 1986 ICJ Reports 14 (June 27, 1986), para. 227, at 118.

33 *Id.*, at paras 195, 205 at 103, 197 respectively.

34 GA Res. 36/103 (Dec. 9, 1981).

been committed by the 'affected' state, normally the intervention was not deemed by the agent state as a response to an injury to its own interests. Here we should mention the American intervention in Iran after the kidnapping of the American diplomats in 1979, which was said to be aimed *solely* at rescuing the hostages. In this case the US imposed economic sanctions against Iran for injury to its interests in relation to the kidnapping.[35] At the same time, the US also intercepted an Egyptian airliner that was forced to land at Sigonella. This action was only indirectly linked by the US to the failure of the Egyptian government to comply with the Convention of 1979 on the taking of hostages.[36]

A Theory Arguing for the 'Tutelary' Intervention of the 'Agent' State

We now come to another, closely related consideration. In the traditional approach, which is still prevalent, the problems posed by interventions involving 'internal force' have been addressed by taking as a starting point the principle of the non-use of force and/or the classical principle of sovereignty (understood as the right of a state to exercise sovereign powers without external interference in the spaces under its jurisdiction: its territory, coastal waters, air space, and on vessels or aircraft flying its flag in free spaces). Under this approach, the norm discussed above would render unlawful the exercise of extra-territorial powers over individuals in spaces covered by the jurisdiction of other states, unless the state whose sovereignty was infringed had given its consent.

While this conclusion is generally considered to be correct, the underlying principles are not fully respected in practice, considering that in recent years interventions by states in what may be termed 'reserved' spaces (territory, vessels, and aircraft), in order to safeguard their own citizens or foreign nationals who are subjected to terrorist violence, have not elicited strong reactions on the part of the international community or the UN, even in the case of interventions taking place without the consent of the territorial state or the flag state. On the basis of this practice, some legal scholars, while considering such interventions to be unlawful, have argued that they are 'tolerated' by the international community.[37] At the same

35 See *supra* chapter 2 under the heading 'States Acting in the Common Interest and Institutional Control'.

36 The peculiarity of these incursions, which were not exactly of a warlike character, was underlined by the States who pointed out the limited size of the military force deployed and the 'limited' objective to be achieved. See e.g., the American authorities on the incursion into Iran (*supra*, notes 11, 25). See also the speech of the Israeli ambassador Herzog at the UN in the debate on Entebbe, who underlined that 'Israel's rescue was not directed against Uganda' (UN Doc. S/PV.1939, *supra* note 27, at 51–59).

37 See Luigi Migliorino, *International Terrorism in the United Nations Debates*, 2 Italian Yearbook of International Law 102 (1976), at 120; Ulrich Beyerlin, *Die Israelische Befreiungsaktion von Entebbe in Völkerrechtlicher Sicht*, 37 Zeitschrift für Ausländisches Offentliches Recht und Völkerrecht 213 (1977); Henri Labayle, *Droit International et Lutte contre le Terrorisme*, 32 Ann. Fr. D.I. 105 (1986), at 134 *et seq.*

time, other scholars have argued that such interventions are lawful under a theory of necessity of self-defence.[38]

Here we should underline the general reservations in the international order to recognizing such a state of necessity. Although the International Court of Justice, citing the Draft Articles on Responsibility of States (Article 25),[39] has recently asserted that 'the state of necessity is a ground recognized by customary international law',[40] this rule is difficult to apply due to the indeterminate nature of the conditions that legitimise its application. Thus, as the Court has asserted, the state that relies on it 'is not the sole judge of whether those conditions have been meet'.[41]

Above all, this approach starts from a classical perspective that considers the international order as a set of norms intended to regulate relations between states on a reciprocal basis.

If we consider these phenomena in a concrete manner, in light of changes in international law, there is a need to widen the traditional perspective. Thus we argue that the classical principle of sovereignty is not able to provide a legal basis for exclusive governmental powers in relation to situations and events that, though taking place in 'reserved' areas (territory, vessels, and aircraft subject to a state sovereignty), affect interests that by their nature go beyond the powers of the sovereign state considered *uti singulus*. Such interests are 'public' in character, and are therefore not subject to exclusive sovereignty. In these cases, the 'individual' right of the sovereign state to exercise powers of government without external interference is subject to limitations.

This point becomes clear if we consider that the new offensive strategies of international terrorism and major technological changes are undermining the international community and its fundamental rules. This is true both in terms of parity – meaning that a plurality of sovereign bodies operate in the community – and

---

38 See, e.g., in the Entebbe case the interventions at the Security Council by the British delegate in the meeting of 12 July 1976 (UN Doc. S/PV.1940 (1976), at 46) and of the Israeli delegate on 9 July 1976. The Israeli delegate, in line with the classical formulation of the 'Caroline' case, invoked 'a necessity of self-defense, instant, overwhelming, leaving no choice of means and no moment for deliberation' (UN Doc. S/PV.1939, *supra* note 27, at 58 *et seq.*). In general, references to the state of necessity may be found also in legal doctrine that considers humanitarian interventions to be legitimate. See e.g. Claude H.M. Waldock, *The Regulation of the Use of Force by Individual State in International Law*, 81 Recueil des Cours 455 (1952–II), at 466, 503; Gerald Fitzmaurice, *The General Principles of International Law Considered from Standpoint of the Rule of Law*, 92 Recueil des Cours 5–67 (1957–II); Derek W. Bowett, Self-Defense in International Law (1958), at 89, 105, and *supra*, note 23.

39 *Draft Articles on Responsibility of States for Internationally Wrongful Acts, Report of the International Law Commission on the work of its 53rd Session* (23 April–1 June and 2 July–10 August 2001), Art. 25, UN Doc. A/56/10, chp.IV.E.1, at 56 *et seq.*, available at <http://untreaty.un.org/ilc/reports/2001/english/content.pdf>.

40 Legal Consequences of the Construction of a Wall in the Occupied Palestinian Territory, Advisory Opinion, 2004 ICJ Reports 136 (July 9, 2004), para. 140, at 194.

41 Case Concerning the Gabcíkovo-Nagymaros Project (Hungary/Slovakia), Judgment, 1997 ICJ Reports 7 (Sept. 25, 1997), para. 51, at 40.

in terms of the exclusivity and effectiveness of each sovereign body in exercising authority over its own spaces of reserved jurisdiction.

The recent strategy of global terrorism, aimed above all at harming the interests of communities and states in the West, which have become the target of systematic and publicly announced attacks *wherever* they are to be found, has made it extremely difficult for states to effectively ensure stable government of their societies. The interest of states in protecting their citizens and national interests abroad under the threat of terrorist action cannot be achieved in a satisfactory manner by means of the classical rule of diplomatic protection, given the characteristics of global terrorism, which is not aimed at individuals or specific groups, but against the community as a whole at a global level.

Phenomena of this kind, which give rise to difficulties for states in governing their communities, have occurred with an increasing intensity in the international arena since the 1980s and are linked to profound changes arising from technological progress. A case in point is the use of nuclear energy for peaceful purposes, which is potentially liable to nullify the anti-nuclear policies of governments in neighbouring states. Some international bodies see the need for new measures in international law providing for forms of cooperation and co-management between states, and certain areas have been identified that could be internationalized or managed on a collective basis.

As a result, on the assumption that the problems arising from international terrorism necessarily concern the entire international community, a solution to these problems cannot be found without taking into account the harmonization of the interests involved. Therefore, the starting point for an approach to these problems is an in-depth analysis of the relationship between the liberty of each sovereign state to regulate activities carried out within its jurisdiction and the necessity of the international order to defend universal values, including taking over powers from states acting *uti singuli* where necessary.

Therefore, with reference only to 'legitimate' interventions involving the extraterritorial exercise of governmental powers, it is our view that they constitute a form of collective guarantee, when carried out under certain conditions.[42] In such cases, it is not 'intervention' itself that is the guarantee of the international order. Rather, the international guarantee derives from the extension of the juridical sphere of the agent state, operating on behalf of the international community, *uti universi*. In this light, it becomes possible for a state to exercise coercive and jurisdictional powers on an exceptional basis within the sphere of rights assigned to another sovereign state – including state power over its own territory, and also over communities, vessels, and aircraft in free spaces under the jurisdiction of the state. This reflects the resolve of the global legal system to safeguard its fundamental interests by means of actions that are 'public' in character – i.e., taken by states in the common interest. Such actions need to take place under the supervision of international bodies.[43]

Restrictions on the jurisdiction of an individual state resulting from an action taken in protection of the collective interest are not in themselves specifically

---

42 See later in this chapter under the heading 'Conditions Legitimizing the Exercise…'.

43 *Id.*

'punitive' in character. Rather, the result is a derogation of the sovereign rights of individual states, who are required to tolerate (*pati*) the authoritative interference of states acting in the common interest, by virtue of the higher value of the common good as against the particular interests of individual states. It may also be argued that the force which accompanies the intervention in question takes the form of policing operations, as it is exercised on an exceptional basis in order to safeguard supreme global interests. This type of guarantee has become part of the body of international law, and as a result it should be implemented in strict compliance with the criteria of necessity and proportionality in relation to the task to be performed, in order that any infringement of the sovereignty of the affected state is reduced to a minimum.

Insufficient Regulation of Extraterritorial Powers to Safeguard Global Interests

The conclusion reached in favour of recognizing in general international law the existence of norms granting exceptional coercive and jurisdictional powers to states – that is to say, powers granted in relation to the particularly collective nature of values to be safeguarded – does not conflict with the fact that the response to terrorist attacks normally comes from states that are the direct target of such attacks.

This matter has been the subject of extensive debate on the part of legal scholars in connection with issues arising from the identification of the states who are entitled to react in order to safeguard collective rights.

In a general statement the International Court of Justice has asserted that 'all States can be held to have a legal interest in (the) protection … of obligations towards the international community as a whole' (i.e., obligations *erga omnes*).[44] This means that states whose rights are infringed may react on their own behalf to protect their own interests *and* on behalf of the collectivity to protect the public interest against breaches of *erga omnes* obligations. They have a right to act to safeguard the public interest, but only in the context of separate actions that comply with relevant principles and legal rules.

Support for this conclusion is to be found in the official declarations of states whose private rights are breached, yet who justify their intervention in the internal affairs of another state by citing their 'tutelary' right to combat terrorism and to safeguard common interests. Normally, an agent state does not portray an intervention of this kind as a response to material prejudice suffered.[45] Separate actions of a 'punitive' nature, however, deriving from the right to self-protection or self-help, may be taken by an agent state in response to breaches of its own material interests[46] as well as for the breaches of *erga omnes* obligations (e.g., economic sanctions against

44 Barcelona Traction, Light and Power Company (Belgium v. Spain), Limited, Judgment, 1970 ICJ Reports 3 (Feb. 5, 1970), paras 33–34, at 32.

45 See *supra* notes 24–27.

46 Reference is also made to the right to self-defence laid down by Art. 51 of the Charter, but UN bodies have objected to the legitimacy of this provision. On this topic see *supra* chapter 4 ,under the heading 'The Question of International Legality …', subheading 'Self-Defence'.

territorial state for possible support to terrorists) in accordance of the relevant rules of international law. The territorial state, of course, is entitled to claim damages resulting from a 'tutelary' action for the protection of collective guarantees (e.g., damages to airport structures).

Concerns may be raised about this conclusion, especially because of the indeterminate character of the norms that confer on states the exceptional 'power' to act outside their own jurisdiction, and the wide margin of discretion associated with non-institutional heteronomous action. The contrasting positions taken in diplomatic practice and the lack of legal studies in this area, together with the lack of international instruments or treaty rules, make it particularly difficult to provide a general framework in which to find solutions on a case-by-case basis. Official government positions on the extraterritorial exercise of governmental powers that go beyond 'normal' international limits are well known. At times governments react favourably, and at other times they are more cautious, or even openly critical.

In the following discussion we outline certain general principles that can be derived from international practice in these matters, with particular reference to the exceptional powers conferred on states in the fight against terrorism. But we would like to point out in advance the need for further legal studies, and above all the need for specific legal provisions, by means of international conventions, specifying the spatial limits within which agent states may act for the common good, or *uti universi* (in the fight against terrorism, but also, *inter alia*, against organised crime, the narcotics trade, and large-scale pollution). Specific provisions are also needed to identify, in each specific case, the states that have a legal right to act in the common interest and to regulate potentially competing claims.[47]

An attempt to codify this general trend by means of international agreement is to be found above all in Articles 100–111 of the UN Convention on the Law of the Sea.[48] The Convention specifies the cases in which there is a right to coercion and to jurisdiction on the high seas over persons or ships not subject to the sovereignty of the intervening state – i.e., rights belonging to states other than those 'normally' entitled to intervene. In addition to the classic cases of piracy on the high seas and the transportation of slaves, already subject to the principle of universal jurisdiction under the Geneva Convention on the High Seas (Articles 14–22), the third Convention lays down in other cases (such as the illegal trade in narcotic drugs and unauthorized dumping at sea) the *erga omnes* right of cooperation between member states and specifies those states authorized to intervene alongside, or in place of, the flag state (Articles 108 and 109).

---

47 The need for a preventive agreement among the members of the Western European Union (WEU), aimed at dealing with the problems arising from decision-making powers and the use of force in 'active defence' operations against terrorism (special units from State police forces, where necessary to be deployed by members also outside their own territorial jurisdiction), was raised in 1978 at the Assembly of the Union by the Rapporteur M. Muller on behalf of the General Affairs Commission. *Rapport de la Commission des Affaires Générales, Le terrorisme international*, Assemblée de l'Ueo, XXIV Sess. ord., première partie, Doc. 771, Part III, Arts. 33 *et seq.*, 39–40.

48 Arts 100–111 of the Montego Bay Convention, *supra* note 16.

A connection may be made between the current uncertainty and the troubling tendency of certain states to react to the escalation of terrorist violence either by monopolizing the function of safeguarding collective interests or by moving in the direction of a widening of the coercive powers to be exercised *uti universi* against terrorists (objectives pursued, e.g., by the US and Israel). There has been an attempt to invoke an *erga omnes* right to combat terrorism *wherever it may be* (also in recent political attitudes of the Russian Government)[49] and as a result it is assumed that *all* states may employ coercive and/or jurisdictional powers outside their own jurisdiction, in cases and under conditions that are not clearly defined. This assertion of authority applies not only in free spaces, such as vessels and aircraft of other states, but also in the very territory of other states. It remains to be seen, however, whether these trends will be consolidated in practice.

Principles and Criteria Based on International Practice: The Subsidiarity Principle

With all of the flux and uncertainty in this area of the law, it is no simple matter to provide an assessment, on the basis of contemporary general international law, of the powers that may be exercised by states over terrorist suspects on behalf of the collectivity. In making this attempt, there is a need, above all, to underline the general trend of international law towards extending the normal criminal jurisdiction that may be exercised by a state in its own sphere of sovereignty. Indeed it is now widely recognized that states are entitled to take action against terrorists within their own territory, even in the absence of a link between the suspects and the territorial community.

A number of scholars argue that on the basis of general international norms, there is an obligation on the part of the territorial state to bring to justice or to extradite terrorist suspects to a requesting state (the rule known as *aut dedere aut judicare*). This principle has been upheld, above all in the West, in a number of declarations of intent – starting with the Bonn Declaration in 1978[50] – that aim to overcome the jurisdictional limits of the participating countries and to lay down general principles. This approach is evident in the policies of the participating countries. There are a number of cases in which these states clearly intend to bring the terrorist suspects to justice and to put them on trial, in contrast with a more permissive approach taken by other states.[51] States that fail to comply with their obligations do not usually contest those obligations, but often hasten to find justifications for their failure to comply.

---

49 See also chapter 8 of this book.

50 See 14 U.S. Weekly Compilation of Presidential Documents 1038 (July 24, 1978), 17 Int'l Legal Mat. 1285 (1978).

51 For example, in the well-known *Achille Lauro* case, Italy and Egypt attempted to justify their failure to arrest the terrorists by trading accusations with each other (see documentary evidence cited by Antonio Cassese, Terrorism, Politics And Law. The Achille Lauro Affair (1989) (transl. by S.J.K. Greenleaves of: Antonio Cassese, Il Caso 'Achille Lauro'. Terrorismo, Politica e Diritto nella Comunità Internazionale (1987)).

Although these trends are particularly significant, and despite the orientation of certain international conventions and the attempts at codification by the International Law Commission,[52] the customary application of the obligations at issue still appears to be uncertain.

It is now necessary to consider in greater depth the key issue under consideration, which is how to determine in practice the content of 'general' material and coercive powers that may be exercised in an extra-territorial dimension over terrorist suspects in accordance with general international law. We need to make a distinction here on the basis of the spaces and the situations in which these powers are to be exercised. An adequate definition of these general powers cannot be established without taking account not only of the customary rights that the state exercises over its territory and other spaces on the basis of the fundamental principle of sovereignty, but also the general powers to be exercised on behalf of the international community. In principle, the latter powers belong first to the territorial state itself, in that it safeguards an 'autonomous' public interest on behalf of the community as a whole (e.g., in the fight against international terrorism) distinct from private legal interests deriving from the right to sovereignty.

Sovereign rights and legal rights to general powers of the territorial state are closely related and affect the specific rights of protection exercised on an exceptional basis by other states who may operate on behalf of the international community, also known as 'agent states'. That is to say they can be said to defend a public interest that has been breached, and thus they may intervene alongside, or as a substitute for, the territorial state.

At this point, there is a need to distinguish between the coercive powers that agent states are entitled to exercise over terrorists on the high seas or on vessels or aircraft flying the flag of another state (the 'flag state'), and the powers that such states are entitled to exercise on an exceptional basis in the territory of other states, including cases in which the terrorist action takes place on vessels and aircraft in the ports and airports of another state (the 'territorial state').

Interventions on the High Seas or in Free Spaces

With regard to free spaces, we should underline the fact that the principle of exclusive jurisdiction of the flag state (or 'registration state') has been subject to limitations in recent practice in connection with the repression of terrorism. This is the case, as underlined by legal scholars and diplomatic sources, when the flag state is 'unable or unwilling'– i.e., the flag state does not possess sufficient means or is not inclined to intervene in an effective manner to bring an end to a terrorist action on a ship or aircraft flying the flag of that state. In such cases, from our perspective, other states

52 Art. 4 of the proposed articles on the draft Code on Offences against the Peace and Security of Mankind, UN Doc. A/CN.4/404, Y. Int'l L. Comm. (1950), Vol. II, (Part One), at 3–4. *Report of the International Law Commission on the Work of its 48th Session* (6 May – 26 July 1996), Art. 9, UN Doc. A/51/10, Y. Int'l L. Comm. (1996), Vol. II, (Part Two), available at <http://untreaty.un.org/ilc/texts/instruments/english/draft%20articles/7_4_1996.pdf>.

may engage in coercive action *uti universi* in place of the sovereign state in order to put a stop to terrorist action, save the hostages, and bring the suspects to justice.[53]

A similar intervention by a agent state, acting as an agent of the international community, should be allowed on the high seas or in free spaces in relation to the ships or aircraft of states that fail or refuse to arrest and bring to justice those responsible for the terrorist action immediately after the conclusion of the act, wherever it may have been committed, but rather allow them to escape. An intervention of this kind, the purpose of which is to bring the suspects to justice, may be regarded as an act of international policing, substituting for the flag state that fails to intervene or acts as an accomplice to the terrorist group. However, there is a need for 'continuity' between the act of terrorism and the material and coercive action of the agent state – reflecting an *animus comprehendi* on the part of this state – so that the actions take place in a logical and temporal sequence, and the various phases of the process constitute a coherent whole.

Under such circumstances, the limits on the jurisdiction of the flag state are also significant with respect to ships in foreign ports or in the territorial waters of other states. In these cases there is an evident need to take into account the customary sovereign powers of the coastal state – either exclusive of or concurrent with those of the flag state – and, at the same time, the entitlement of the coastal state to general powers that may be exercised on behalf of the entire international community.

The identification of the states with the authority to act in a collective capacity, in place of a flag state that is either unable or unwilling to intervene, is a matter for careful consideration. In practice there have been few operations of this kind, and they have generally aimed to comply with the customary principles of criminal jurisdiction – i.e., the principles of territoriality, active personality, and passive personality (defence). The trend has been to seek legitimation not only from the state in whose sphere of reserved jurisdiction the act of terrorism takes place, and the suspects' state of citizenship, but also from any state whose national interests have been violated and the victims' state(s) of citizenship.

It has been argued that terrorism, like piracy, should be treated as a universal crime, therefore granting *all* states authority to capture terrorists in free spaces, regardless of the nationality of the ship or aircraft involved.[54] This broad interpretation of the

53 The relevance of circumstances of this kind is today accepted by legal scholars. For past issues, see especially American diplomatic sources which, in order to justify interventions of this type, have made reference to the presence of 'an imminent threat of injury or death,' together with the claim that the territorial state was 'unwilling or unable' to protect the hostages. See, e.g., the opinion expressed at the UN Security Council by the US representative, Ambassador W. Scranto, in the debate on the Entebbe case (UN Doc. S/PV.1941 (1976), at 31). See also, from the same point of view, Brierly, *supra* note 23, at 627. A further significant factor is the reference to the arbitration ruling in the dispute between the UK and Spain in 1925, reported in Bowett, *supra* note 38, at 87.

54 The *Achille Lauro* case and successive events led to the passing by the US Senate on 19 February 1986 of the Terrorist Prosecution Act (S 1429, 99th Cong., 2nd sess., 132 Cong. Rec. S 1382–1388 (1986)). This Act extended the criminal jurisdiction of the US on an extraterritorial basis in relation to individuals responsible for terrorist actions committed

principle of universality[55] is not at present supported by international practice, which would appear to grant authority to a third-part state to act only under certain accepted circumstances – i.e., a failure or refusal to intervene by the flag state, and continuity between the terrorist action and the policing action.[56]

In this light, the interception by the US of the Egyptian aircraft that was intended to take the *Achille Lauro* terrorists into hiding, and the capture of the terrorists by Italian authorities belonging to the territorial state after the forced landing at Sigonella, should be seen as a policing operation by the US acting in place of the Egyptian government, to whom the terrorists had handed themselves over.

In this particular case, the request by US authorities to the Egyptian government for custody of the terrorists responsible for the death of an American citizen, so that they may be brought to justice or extradited, brings together both the terrorist act and the third-party act of coercion. This is because it reflects an *animus comprehendi* of the agent state, which is entitled, like all other states, to engage in *erga omnes* operations in the repression of terrorism. In this particular case, the coercive act of interception was legitimated under the principle of subsidiarity, since the agent state (the US) – faced with the inertia of the flag state (Egypt) – was the state of a hostage who had been killed. Also, the subsequent policing action by the US against Abu Abbas was intended to substitute for action by the territorial state after the Italian

---

abroad to the detriment of US citizens. It also allowed for the use of material coercion, if necessary, to capture the terrorists and to bring them to justice in the US.

55 On this principle and in general on the five traditional principles of jurisdiction (those of territoriality, nationality, protection, passive personality, and universality), see *Harvard Research in International Law, Draft Convention on Jurisdiction with Respect to Crime*, 29 AM. J. INT'L L. SUPPLEMENT 435 (1935), at 445, 563 *et seq*., 569; Christopher L. Blakesley, *United States Jurisdiction over Extraterritorial Crime,* 73 JOURNAL OF CRIMINAL LAW AND CRIMINOLOGY 1109 (1982), at 1139; Ernst M. H. Hirsch Ballin, *Beyond the Limits of the Territoriality Principle*, *in* REFLECTIONS ON INTERNATIONAL LAW FROM THE LOW COUNTRIES IN HONOUR OF PAUL DE WAART 278 (Erik Denters ed., 1998); Yoram Dinstein, *The Universality Principle and War Crimes*, *in* THE LAW OF ARMED CONFLICT: INTO THE NEXT MILLENNIUM 17 (Michael N. Schmitt ed., 1998); Albin Eser, *National Jurisdiction Over Extraterritorial Crimes Within the Framework of International Complementary: A Comparative Survey on Transnational Prosecution of Genocide According to the Principle of Universality*, *in* MAN'S INHUMANITY TO MAN. ESSAYS ON INTERNATIONAL LAW IN HONOUR OF ANTONIO CASSESE 279 (Lal Chand Vohrah ed., 2003).

In favour of the application of the principle of universality on the basis of international law grounded in current practice, also with references to international terrorism, see Jordan J. Paust, *Extradition and United States. Prosecution of the Achille Lauro Hostage-Takers: Navigating the Hazards*, 20 VAND. J. TRANSNAT'L L. 235 (1985), at 235–237, 250–254; Malvina Halberstam, *Terrorism on the High Seas: The Achille Lauro, Piracy and the IMO Convention on Maritime Safety*, 82 AM. J. INT'L L. 269 (1988), at 272 *et seq.*, 299; Robert Kolb, *Universal Criminal Jurisdiction in Matters of International Terrorism: Some Reflections on Status and Trends in Contemporary International Law*, 50 REVUE HELLENIQUE DE DROIT INTERNATIONAL 43 (1997); James D. Fry, *Terrorism as a Crime Against Humanity and Genocide: The Backdoor to Universal Jurisdiction,* 7 UCLA JOURNAL OF INTERNATIONAL LAW AND FOREIGN AFFAIRS 169 (2002).

56 See later in this chapter under the heading 'Conditions Legitimizing the Exercise…'.

authorities, who were primarily responsible for taking action against the terrorist suspects, allowed them to escape. Before Abu Abbas was allowed to escape, the US Department of Justice had charged him with hijacking the ship, and issued a warrant for his arrest that was transmitted to the Italian authorities.[57]

On the other hand, one example of state action that may be regarded as unlawful is that of the Israeli authorities when they intercept vessels or civilian aircraft of other states in free spaces when the Israelis suspect them of carrying wanted terrorists. The Israeli government, engaged above all in coercive action against individuals and groups, has repeatedly and publicly defended the right of Israel to strike at terrorist targets *wherever* they may be.[58] It is therefore the case that, in addition to repeated incursions into Lebanese territory to strike at Palestinian terrorist bases, Israel has implemented a practice of inspecting civilian vessels and aircraft of other states operating in free spaces when they are suspected of carrying terrorists. These inspections are considered by the Israeli authorities to be routine operations against Palestinian terrorism. Reference may be made here to the Israeli interception and inspection of an Iraqi aircraft in 1973. The UN Security Council passed a resolution condemning the Israeli action,[59] and a similar response came from the Council of the Extraordinary Assembly of the OACI.[60] Other examples of Israeli action include the interception on the high seas of the Panamanian vessel *Blanco* on 29 June 1984, the inspection on 18 July 1984 of another merchant ship, the *Ulah*, chartered by the PLO, and the interception and inspection of a Libyan civilian aircraft bound for Damascus on 4 February 1986. Israel sought to justify the action against the Libyan plane with a generic reference to striking terrorist targets wherever they are to be found and specifically to the amendment of the Convention on International Civil Aviation (the Chicago Convention), according to which any state-party has the right to intercept civil aircraft if it has reason to believe that they are being used for purposes contrary to the spirit of the convention (Article 3 *bis* (b)).[61]

The UN Security Council promptly convened regarding the issue of the Libyan plane, but failed to agree on a draft resolution presented by a number of African states to condemn this intervention, since the US, though 'deploring' the Israeli action, vetoed the resolution. The US ambassador underlined the fact that his government rejected the draft resolution because it did not take account of the fact that 'in some

---

57 District of Columbia (Oct 10, 1985), 24 Int'l Legal Mat. 1553 *et seq.* (1985). After these events, the White House spokesperson, Dill Protrosky, stated that it was the intention of the US authorities to trace Abbas wherever he might be hiding. Later, an Italian court tried Abbas in absentia and sentenced him to life in prison. On 16 April 2003, US forces captured terrorist Abu Abbas in Baghdad.

58 For the Israelis the fight against terrorism takes place on three levels. The first consists of action taken against States that actively support terrorism, to be achieved by means of international isolation and military operations. The second involves the use of coercion against leaders of terrorist organizations, also in areas under the jurisdiction of other States. The third consists of armed incursions against terrorist bases located in the territory of other States.

59 SC Res. 337 (Aug. 15, 1973).

60 The text of the resolution adopted by the Assembly is to be found in 36 Revue Générale de l'Air et de l'Espace 265 (1973).

61 UN Doc. S/PV.2651 (1986), at 112–113.

cases' the interception of an aircraft may be justified (he was evidently referring to the interception in the Sigonella incident).[62] These Israeli operations did not take place on a continuous basis with acts of terrorism. The resulting lack of support for these practices in the international community, which was practically unanimous, was recorded in the international bodies that condemned the practice.

Interventions in the Territory of Other States

At this stage, we should turn to the second type of intervention – action taken on the territory of another state – and the definition of the governmental powers to be exercised on behalf of the collectivity in such interventions.

In the territory of other states, the exercise of governmental powers against terrorists by agent states is extremely limited, and therefore there is a need to apply more restrictive and rigid rules than those relating to interventions on vessels and aircraft of other states in free spaces.

This is entirely in line with the importance that is given in the international system to the fundamental principle of territorial sovereignty, and the greater sovereign power exercised by a state over its territory than over its vessels and aircraft.

That being said, the international practice of consent reflects an approach giving wider scope to the collective interest, as compared to 'normal' exclusivity. Authorization is often granted by a state in whose territory a hijacked aircraft has landed to allow the state with which the aircraft is registered, or even agent states, to carry out a military intervention in order to bring the hijacking to an end and to free the hostages. This extension of powers is also to be found in cases, albeit of an exceptional nature, in which governments make their own airports available to the military forces of another country. The most prominent example of this was the request of the West German government after the dramatic Palestinian attack on the Munich Olympics in 1972 to use the airports of other countries. This met a favourable response from the airports of Algiers, Barcelona, Mumbai (at that time, Bombay), Istanbul, and Tripoli.[63] This practice is undoubtedly indicative of a will to cooperate and to jointly manage certain events considered to go beyond the 'individual' interests of states, and to overcome the 'domestic' connotation of events taking place within a national territory, which is implicit in the classical principle of sovereignty, that grants the territorial state exclusive power to carry out acts of internal force within its own territory.

Even in the absence of consent on the part of the territorial state, current trends in international practice indicate that it is legitimate to carry out interventions in the territory of other states solely to liberate hostages – i.e., victims of a terrorist action that is taking place. This is true as long as attempts to reach a negotiated solution have been made with the territorial state, and that state is unwilling or unable to intervene to restore order, to put an end to the terrorist action, and to arrest the terrorists and to bring them to justice.

---

62 *Id.*

63 Rousseau, Chronique, *supra* note 7, at 630.

However, it would appear to be unlawful to arrest terrorists in the territory of another state when that state has expressed the intention to institute law-enforcement proceedings against those suspects. The strong reaction by states to the capture of terror suspects in their territory by other states lends support to this view.[64]

In concluding this analysis, it may be said that at present, in areas of reserved jurisdiction, the balancing of the particular interests of sovereign states and the general interest in the fight against terrorism and the protection of global values is being achieved by means of the progressive evolution of a practice. In this balance, a sovereign state has a legal right to protect the public interest in spaces reserved to its authority, taking priority over other states, while other states are entitled to act in these same spaces only in special circumstances, such as when the territorial state is unwilling or unable to safeguard the collective interest. In the case of competing claims between third-party states, and in the absence of international instruments, conventions, and norms, international practice tends to give priority to states that have a right based on the general criteria of criminal jurisdiction. Under current international law, there does not appear to be any way to identify the states that have a legal right to act to defend the public interest other than on a case-by-case basis.

In conclusion, it may be useful to make one further point at this stage, which is linked to the argument that the 'tutelary' intervention of a third-party state in the sphere of authority of another state should be considered, not as a sanction, but as a policing operation carried out in place of action by a sovereign state that is unwilling or unable to act. It is important to underline the right of the agent state, as with all other states, to impose sanctions and other 'punitive' measures on a territorial state for possible breaches of *erga omnes* obligations in the fight against terrorism (as well as in response to breaches of its own private interests).

States are under no international obligation to repress terrorist actions taking place in their sovereign territories or to arrest those responsible and bring them to justice. However, it is evident that other states, without affecting the customary right to act of those directly affected, may be entitled to act as the guarantor of the general interest in response to acts of a territorial state in support of terrorist groups. Such agent states may take punitive collective measures in response to a breach of the *erga omnes* obligation to refrain from carrying out terrorist actions or collaborating with those responsible for them.[65] But in this case the international responsibility of states sponsoring terrorism, as well as the responsibility of individuals, groups, and organizations committing terrorist and other criminal actions (*crimina juris gentium*), is to be determined by international organs. The consequent implementation of punitive measures permitted on a collective basis by the international order, such as smart sanctions, will be discussed below.[66]

---

64 The most prominent example of such a reaction can be seen in the determination of the Italian police force in the face of the attempt by US military personnel to arrest the *Achille Lauro* hijackers after the interception by the American military of the Egyptian aircraft that was forced to land at the American air base of Sigonella.

65 See *supra* chapters 2 and 4 of this book.

66 The Taliban/Al Qaeda sanctions regime and the related resolutions of the Security Council are examined in chapter 8 of this book, under the sub-heading 'The Concept of

Concept and Structure of the Embryonic System of Collective Guarantees

This analysis requires that the international norms on heteronomous safeguards to which collective guarantees belong be classified into two categories. The first category comprises international norms that impose on states obligations towards the international community as a whole to safeguard fundamental global interests (*erga omnes* obligations). In view of the importance of the rights involved, these obligations are generally guaranteed by a special safeguard: under current international law all states have a legal interest in vindicating the infringement of these rights even if they have suffered no material prejudice themselves.[67] All states may be deemed to have a right to impose sanctions against those responsible, be they states, individuals, or groups.

The second category comprises international norms that grant all states legal rights and 'exceptional' powers in order to safeguard global values. These exceptional powers, which are governmental in nature (jurisdictional, material, coercive, etc.), may be exercised by all states, acting *uti universi*, to safeguard the public interest 'in itself'. The exclusive aim of such powers is to put an end to the threat to the public interest. Therefore, all states may be regarded in principle as having a right to take such protective action. Since the agent state is granted 'exceptional' powers, these powers must be limited to safeguarding the specific interest for which they were granted. Moreover, the exceptional powers exercised by agent states must be consistent with commitments arising from relevant instruments or rules of law.

It is important to underline the fact that the concept of collective guarantees must be understood as including not only law enforcement actions in the common interest of a 'punitive' kind, but also the exercise by the agent state of extraterritorial policing powers of a 'tutelary' character. In both cases, as members of the international community, states share the *erga omnes* right to safeguard collective interests, in the sense that each of them has rights in relation to all the others and therefore, in principle, all of them may be subject to the power of the agent state acting in vindication of a public interest. In both cases, the heteronomous action is subject to institutional control.

From a theoretical point of view, any concerns about the wider scope of the concept of collective guarantees should be set aside, given that in the two categories of norms outlined above, the nature of the interests protected by law and the content of the juridical positions of the states regarding their rights to protect the public interest are comparable. The characteristic feature of the normative regime in each case consists of the fact that, alongside the *erga omnes* right to protect the fundamental values of the international legal order, these norms potentially allow all states to act on behalf of the international community for their own protection, either implementing sanctions to repress an internationally wrongful act or exercising extraterritorial powers.

"Smart Sanctions"'.

67 South West Africa, Second Phase (Ethiopia v. South Africa; Liberia v. South Africa), Judgment, 1966 ICJ Reports 6 (July 18, 1966), para. 44, at 32; *Barcelona Traction* case, *supra* note 44.

In this context, the concept of collective guarantees appears to be broader than mere sanctions, and must be understood as including operations classified as 'tutelary,' because such actions are undertaken in the name of the global community, and are aimed exclusively at protecting fundamental social interests 'in itself'.

A General Framework for Addressing Problems Related to the 'Tutelary' Protection of Global Values

Harmonizing Liberty with Necessity

In an attempt to define the conditions in the presence of which states may legitimately exercise extraterritorial powers in the common interest, we should first point to some of the distinctive features of tutelary collective guarantees in current practice.

The first consideration is that, with the rise of norms protecting the fundamental interests and the values of the global community, the sphere of governmental authority of individual states has been significantly eroded. As a result of these norms, the means of guaranteeing global interests have also evolved beyond classical legal provisions and have profoundly changed and limited the principle of sovereignty, as well as the principle of exclusivity of territorial state authority.

At present, the balancing of the 'particular' interest of the sovereign state in defending its prerogatives and the 'general' interest of the international order in protecting global values and interests, when under threat, may be found in an increasingly accepted rule. According to this rule, the exclusivity of the jurisdiction of the sovereign state – in whose territory, vessels, or aircraft those responsible for criminal activity are located – is subject to limitations in cases in which that state is 'unable or unwilling' to act to protect the common good. In such cases, other states may undertake coercive and jurisdictional measures.

The exercise of extraterritorial powers 'in the common interest' is therefore exceptional and subsidiary, and is closely linked to the balancing of the interests at stake that are internationally protected. These interests include the public interest in upholding peremptory international principles – i.e., putting an end to breaches of these rules and bringing the suspects to justice in order to prevent future violations, the 'private' interest of the territorial state in guaranteeing its own sovereign rights – i.e., the exclusive exercise of the powers of government in the areas and over the individuals normally subject to such governmental powers, and the interest of responsible individuals and groups aimed at the respect of personal rights and procedural guarantees to which they are entitled on the basis of internal and international norms.

Derogations from the classical principle of sovereignty and the exclusivity of state jurisdiction must be founded on the priority assigned to the protection of collective values, as compared to the 'individual' interests of states and private individuals.

The second consideration derives from the fact that all states are potentially entitled to the exercise of extra-territorial governmental powers for protecting public and global interests; it raises the question of how to deal in specific cases with competing claims to the exercise of powers for the common good. A further problem is how to identify in each specific sector (human rights and environmental protection, among others) any deviations or derogations from the norms laid down by the international order that may be allowed in the interests of protecting universal values and interests. The essential requirement is to identify the states entitled to act on behalf of 'all' on a case-by-case basis, in strict compliance with the principle of subsidiarity as well as general criteria and relevant instruments or norms.

As to the third point, we should also be concerned about arrangements that conflict with the traditional norm of sovereignty in the practice of states. These arrangements have not been sufficiently formalized in agreements or other international instruments, and as a result heteronomous actions are characterized by a margin of discretion of the agent state. On this subject we would consider that the extra-territorial exercise of sovereign powers has been classified as a guarantee of the international order. Taking it to be a 'collective' guarantee belonging to the integrated system, the exercise of these powers is subject not only to the general criteria of lawfulness (necessity, proportionality, and respect for peremptory norms, or *jus cogens*), but also to an objective 'control of legitimacy'[68] on the part of international institutions. However, it may be argued that actions in the common interest cannot be achieved without institutional support, or at least the assurance, in each case, that such operations will not be condemned as unlawful by UN bodies. In our view, the limitations on the authority of states and the rights of individuals necessitated by the protection of global interests, together with institutional participation, may be seen as a consequence of the trend in the international order towards greater verticalization of international power. This tendency is characterized by the increasing weight of the UN and other international institutions in the management of the general functions of the international legal order.

The development of collective guarantee mechanisms is the result of a progressive integration of the organized community, with the community of states taking action both by enforcing general guarantees through international organizations, and by measures in which individual states take action *uti universi* with institutional authorization or consent (or at least take action that has not been censured *ex post facto* by the UN).

This analysis is also supported by recent domestic and international jurisprudence and by the practice of the UN political bodies. It is well known that domestic courts have asserted their jurisdiction over individuals accused of international terrorism or other *crimina juris gentium*, even in cases in which the legitimacy of the arrest was contested due to cross-border abduction or a failure to comply with the terms of extradition treaties. These courts have often invoked the principle of *male captus, bene detentus*, according to which a tribunal can exercise its jurisdiction over an individual accused of international crimes, regardless of the lawfulness of the arrest.[69] While

68 See *supra* chapter 2 under the heading 'States Acting in the Common Interest and Institutional Control'.

69 For a discussion of this principle and the cases in which this rule has been applied, see Fritz A. Mann, *Reflections on the Prosecution of Persons Abducted in Breach of International Law*, *in* International Law at a Time of Perplexity. Essays in Honour of Shabtai Rosenne 407 (Yoram Dinstein ed., 1989); Alonso Gómez-Robledo Verduzco, United States vs Alvarez Machain (1993); Carlos Darío Espósito, *Male Captus, Bene Detentus: A Propósito*

avoiding any statement about the question of the compatibility of the mode of capture with general international norms (i.e., the principle of sovereignty) or international conventions (i.e., respect for procedures laid down in extradition treaties[70]), domestic tribunals have based their jurisdiction on the principle of passive personality, or defence.[71] The International Criminal Tribunal for the Former Yugoslavia (ICTY), in *Prosecutor v. Dragan Nikolic*,[72] examined internal jurisprudential practice in an attempt to identify its basic elements.[73] The court pointed out that, while respecting the variety of domestic jurisprudence in national systems, there is a need to take into account the 'gravity' of the wrongful act as well as the attitude of the affected state. This argument led domestic courts to defend their right to try defendants under their own jurisdiction,[74] in spite of the derogation from the formal rules for capture or arrest and from extradition procedures. Moreover, these domestic tribunals did not take into account the question of compliance with international treaties, since it was argued, among other things, that the defendants could not invoke international extradition treaties, as they were not directly applicable and could not serve as the basis for a claim.[75] The domestic tribunals also pointed to the need for 'a weightier nexus' between the capture and the alleged acts of terrorism, requiring a logical and temporal continuity, and for evidence of an *animus comprehendi* to be identified from conclusive evidence.

---

de la Sentencia del Tribunal Supremo de Estados Unidos en el Caso Alvarez-Machain, 62 Lecciones y Ensayos 17 (1995).

70 See US Supreme Court, United States v. Alvarez-Machain, 504 U.S. 655 (1992). Among legal scholars, see Michael J. Glennon, *State-Sponsored Abduction: A Comment on United States v. Alvarez Machain*, 86 Am. J. Int'l L. 746 (1992); Derek C. Smith, *Beyond Indeterminacy and Self-Contradiction in Law: Transnational Abductions and Treaty Interpretation in U.S. v. Alvarez-Machain*, 6 European Journal of International Law 1 (1995); William J. Aceves, *The Legality of Transborder Abductions: A Study of United States v. Alvarez-Machain*, 3 Southwestern University Journal of Law and Trade in the Americas 101 (1996); Paul Mitchell, *English-Speaking Justice: Evolving Responses to Transnational Forcible Abduction After Alvarez-Machain*, 29 Cornell International Law Journal 383 (1996); Myint Zan, *US v Alvarez-Machain 'Kidnap' Case Revisited*, 70 The Australian Law Journal 239 (1996); Mark S. Zaid, *Military Might Versus Sovereign Right: The Kidnapping of Dr. Humberto Alvarez-Machain and the Resulting Fallout*, 19 Houston Journal of International Law 829 (1997); Jennifer J. Veloz, *In the Clinton Era, Overturning Alvarez-Machain and Extraterritorial Abduction: How a Unified Western Hemisphere, Through the OAS, Can Win the War on Drugs and Do It Legally*, 12 Temple International and Comparative Law Journal 241 (1998).

71 See *supra* note 55.

72 Prosecutor v. Dragan Nikolic, Case No. IT–94–2–PT, Decision on Defense Motion Challenging the Exercise of Jurisdiction by the Tribunal, Trial Chamber II (Oct. 9, 2002).

73 *Id.*, at paras 79–93.

74 Malvina Halberstam, *In Defense of the Supreme Court Decision in Alvarez-Machain*, 86 Am. J. Int'l L. 736 (1992), at 744–745; Rosalyn Higgins, Problems and Process: International Law and How We Use It 69 (1994).

75 Rodrigo Labardini, La Magia del Intérprete: Extradición en la Suprema Corte de Justicia de Estados Unidos: El Caso Álvarez Macháin (2000).

At the request of defendants accused of *crimina juris gentium* and international terrorism, international tribunals have also handed down rulings on the legitimacy of states exercising extra-territorial powers. Such defendants generally contest the legitimacy of the arrest, arguing that it breached extradition treaties and individual rights, and have refused to recognize the jurisdiction of such tribunals. We have just cited *Prosecutor v. Dragan Nikolic*: another was the *Ocalan* case[76] in the European Court for Human Rights (ECHR).

Both the ICTY and the ECHR upheld their own rights of jurisdiction in these cases. They also accepted the idea of limits on sovereign territorial powers in the capture of an accused on foreign soil by means of forcible cross-border abduction,[77] in spite of the alleged violation of international norms safeguarding the rights of the individual, as well as the derogations from extradition treaty procedures and the due process of law.

In not directly addressing the question of the violation of the principle of sovereignty, and in upholding the legitimacy of the arrests, these courts expounded the idea that in the case of an extraterritorial arrest, in the words of the ICTY, 'much ... depends on the reaction of the injured state itself'.[78] Similarly, in the *Ocalan* case, the ECHR defended its right to hear the case and underlined the fact that the capture of the defendant by the Turkish government had not given rise to protests at an international level by the Kenyan authorities.[79] At the same time they expounded the idea that 'informal extradition' and 'extradition in disguise' (i.e., extradition arising from cooperation between states) are not in themselves illegal,[80] and ruled that they could constitute 'a legal impediment to the exercise of jurisdiction' only in cases where the accused 'is very seriously mistreated, maybe even subjected to inhumane, cruel or degrading treatment, or torture'. This concept, first proposed by the ICTY,[81] was upheld by the ECHR in the *Ocalan* case.[82]

---

76 Ocalan v. Turkey, Application No. 46221/99, Merits and Just Satisfaction, Judgment (March 12, 2003). See, with reference to this case, Juan-Antonio Carrillo Salcedo, *La Peine de Mort, Peut-Elle Etre Considérée en Soi, en l'Absence d'Autres Eléments, Comme un Peine Inhumaine Et Dégradante? Quelques Réflexions sur la Pratique Subséquente des Etats Parties dans l'Arrêt de la Cour Européenne des Droits de l'Homme du 12 Mars 2003 (Affaire Ocalan c. Turquie)*, 1 Libertés, Justice, Tolérance 385 (2004); Annemarieke Künzli, *Ocalan v. Turkey: Some Comments*, 17 Leiden Journal of International Law 141 (2004); Stefania Negri, *Interpreting the European Convention on Human Rights in Harmony with International Law and Jurisprudence: What Lessons from* Ocalan v. Turkey*?*, 4 GCYILJ 243 (2004–I).

77 Douglas Kash, *Abducting Terrorists Under PDD–39: Much Ado About Nothing New*, 13 American University International Law Review 139 (1997).

78 Prosecutor v. Dragan Nikolic, *supra* note 72, para. 97.

79 The ECHR deemed the arrest of Ocalan on the part of Turkish agents to be legitimate on the basis of the court's findings of fact, with the agreement of the Kenyan authorities. In actuality, the circumstances of the arrest remain obscure, though it should be noted that Kenya did not lodge any complaint in relation to the arrest.

80 Ocalan v. Turkey, *supra* note 76, paras 90–91.

81 Prosecutor v. Dragan Nikolic, *supra* note 72, para 114.

82 Ocalan v. Turkey, *supra* note 76, para. 228. Negri, *supra* note 76.

This orientation of the courts corresponds to the notion, reiterated by the ECHR, that 'inherent in the whole of the [the European Convention on Human Rights] is a search for a fair balance between the demands of the general interest of the community and the requirements of the protection of the individual's fundamental rights'.[83]

The derogations from the procedural rights of particular individuals and from the sovereign powers of individual states upheld by these tribunals are justified since they fulfil a public safety function, reflecting the gravity of the crimes and responding to the need to bring those responsible to justice. At the same time, there is a need to ensure that the capture, detention, and trial of the defendants are not carried out in such a way as to constitute a grave breach of human rights and the right to a fair trial. Derogations from international norms found in the sovereignty principle and in extradition treaties are allowed in the presence of grave violations of fundamental values – classified as crimes against the international order – provided that the action to safeguard the public interest does not represent a violation of the basic rights of the individual.

UN bodies have also accepted the idea of a limitation on the authority of states for the purposes of safeguarding fundamental global values. In certain specific cases they have failed to censure the exercise of extraterritorial powers intended to safeguard the general interest, to put an end to terrorist actions, and to bring those responsible to justice. The UN Security Council placed explicit limits on Libyan sovereignty in the *Lockerbie* affair and approved the claims of some states to perform activities as a substitute for action by the Libyan authorities, who were unable or unwilling to hold a fair trial for the terrorist suspects (some of whom were found to be Libyan agents). In this way, the Security Council enabled the collective guarantee to be fulfilled.

In the presence of the grave violation of human rights perpetrated by Libyan terrorists in the Lockerbie attack, and in response to requests from the US and the UK, the Security Council approved resolutions 731 (1992), para. 3 e) and 748 (1992), para. 1, requiring Libya to extradite the alleged terrorists to the requesting states in order to ascertain their involvement in the attacks and to enable a fair trial to take place. The request was approved by the Council in spite of Libyan claims that its sovereignty would be violated and Libyan demands for the application of the extradition treaty between Libya and the UK.[84] This treaty did not place Libya under an obligation to extradite the alleged terrorists, but rather to implement the principle of *aut dedere aut judicare* – i.e., that Libya would state its willingness to hold a fair trial. The cited resolutions adopted by the Security Council gave rise to deeply debates among state's delegations to the Security Council, ICJ's judges and

83 Soering v. The United Kingdom, Application No. 14038/88, Merits and Just Satisfaction, Judgment (July 7, 1989), 161 Eur. Ct. H. R. (ser. A), para. 89; Ocalan, *supra* note 76, para. 90.

84 It should be noted that the obligation on the part of Egypt to arrest the terrorist 'assassins' was also based on the Convention of 1979 on hostage-taking (Dec. 18, 1979), to which the US, together with Egypt, was a State-Party. However, the US made scant references to this instrument.

legal scholars, pointing out the risk that damage precedent be established.[85] It is our opinion that the request made by the Security Council to Libya may be placed in the framework of collective guarantees and may be seen as a 'tutelary' measure (to ensure a fair trial and the punishment of those responsible for crimes) taken by the Council at the initiative of states acting *uti universi*. Para. 3 e) of Resolution 731 (1992) and para. 1 of Resolution 748 (1992) are in line with the current trends to seek to reconcile the 'particular' interests of the sovereign state and the 'general' interest of the fight against terrorism, in compliance with the rule that the principle of the exclusivity of territorial state authority (on whose territory the individuals suspected are to be found) is subject to limitations when the state in question is unable or unwilling to exercise its jurisdiction; in such cases, other states can exercise the related jurisdictional powers. The decision of the Security Council to require Libya to hand over the alleged suspects for a fair trial in either the UK or the US is not a 'punitive' sanction: rather, as noted above, it may be seen as a true tutelary guarantee, aimed at limiting the rights of an individual state for the purpose of protecting collective interests, and at identifying the states with a legitimate right to exercise jurisdiction on a subsidiary basis, in place of the state with primary jurisdiction (Libya), who is unable to do so. Accordingly, the preamble to Resolution 731 makes explicit reference to the fact that the suspected terrorists were 'agents of the Libyan Government'. This meant that Libya was unable to prosecute them, on the basis of the general principle '*nemo judex in re sua*': Libya would be both 'judge' and 'defendant' at the same time.[86] The development in the Security Council of a legal basis for the exercise of extraterritorial criminal jurisdiction over alleged terrorists by the requesting countries conferred the legal character of a 'public action' on this non-institutional collective action by individual states acting in the common interest. In an earlier study we made a case for the legitimacy of Paragraph 3 of Resolution 731 (1992) and Paragraph 1 of Resolution 748 (1992). By adopting these resolutions, the Security Council did not violate general international law – i.e., the principle of sovereignty. The limitation on Libyan sovereignty resulting from the authorization of the US and the UK to exercise jurisdiction over the alleged terrorists (lacking an international criminal court) was justified on the basis of a collective guarantee that was 'tutelary' in character. This category of guarantees can be deemed to have become part of the body of global law.[87] Subsequent developments in the Libya case highlighted difficulties relating to the identification of states authorized to perform

85 On this question, see, UN Doc. S/PV. 3033 (Jan. 21, 1992), at. 73, 77, 78 *et seq*., 82, 96. See judge *ad hoc* El-Kosheri, in 1992 ICJ Reports at 202 *et seq*. and judge Ajibola, *ibidem*, at 193. Amongst scholars, see Bernhard Graefrath, *Leave to the Court What Belongs to the Court. The Libyan Case*, 4 European Journal of International Law 184 (1993); Christian Tomuschat, *The Lockerbie Case Before the International Court of Justice*, 48 International Commission of Jurists. The Review 38 (1992); Vera Gowlland-Debbas, *The Relationship Between the International Court of Justice and the Security Council in the Light of the* Lockerbie *Case*, 88 American Journal of International Law 643 (1994), at 667.

86 This concern was clearly expressed by Judge Bedjaoui, in 1992 ICJ Reports, at 147.

87 Giuliana Ziccardi Capaldo, *Verticalità della Comunità Internazionale e Nazioni Unite. Un Riesame del Caso Lockerbie*, in Interventi delle Nazioni Unite e Diritto Internazionale 61 (1995), and the references therein, at 77.

the general safeguarding function and to ensure the 'objectivity' of collective action.[88] The Security Council's decision about the states entitled to exercise criminal jurisdiction over terrorists was based on the classic principles of territoriality and the passive personality, since the UK was the State where the disaster occurred, and the US was the country where the aircraft was registered and the country of nationality of most of the victims (those principles have been included in Montreal Convention, Articles 5, paras 2 and 3). The jurisdictional function of the two designated states was to be carried out on an exceptional basis, as underlined in the interventions of the states' representatives in the Council, preceding the vote on the resolution, and in substitution for the State on whose territory the alleged suspected terrorists were to be found. It also highlighted the urgent need for impartial international judicial bodies to try terrorist suspects for the protection of global values and interests.

Conditions Legitimizing the Exercise of Extraterritorial Powers in the Common Interest

On the basis of the discussion so far, it is possible to outline certain conditions in the presence of which the extraterritorial exercise of state powers 'in the common interest' is currently permitted by international law (leaving out of consideration the consent or acquiescence on the part of the territorial state that suffers the consequences of the heteronomous action):

1. a grave threat of injury or of a serious breach, in terms of scale and effect, of a fundamental global interest safeguarded by an obligation arising under a peremptory norm of general international law;
2. a failure or refusal to act on the part of the territorial state, which must normally be deemed to have priority in safeguarding the common good, but is unwilling or unable to do so in a given case;
3. an entitlement of the state acting in place of the territorial state and in the common interest on the basis of relevant international instruments, the rule of law, or other legal criteria;
4. an exclusively 'tutelary' aim of safeguarding the interests of the collectivity (and not of imposing sanctions against the territorial state or individuals responsible);

88 See the conclusion of the *Lockerbie* case (Questions of Interpretation and Application of the 1971 Montreal Convention arising from the Aerial Incident at Lockerbie (Libyan Arab Jamahiriya v. United Kingdom), Provisional Measures, Order, 1992 ICJ Reports 3 (April 14, 1992); Questions of Interpretation and Application of the 1971 Montreal Convention arising from the Aerial Incident at Lockerbie (Libyan Arab Jamahiriya v. United States of America), Provisional Measures, Order, 1992 ICJ Reports 114 (April 14, 1992); Questions of Interpretation and Application of the 1971 Montreal Convention arising from the Aerial Incident at Lockerbie (Libyan Arab Jamahiriya v. United Kingdom), Preliminary Objections, Judgment, 1998 ICJ Reports 9 (Feb. 27, 1998); Questions of Interpretation and Application of the 1971 Montreal Convention arising from the Aerial Incident at Lockerbie (Libyan Arab Jamahiriya v. United States of America), Preliminary Objections, Judgment, 1998 ICJ Reports 115 (Feb. 27, 1998)).

5. a minimal intrusion on the sovereignty of the territorial state that stays within the boundaries that are strictly necessary for achieving the established aim of international guarantees – i.e., to put the injury to an end and to provide for the preservation of global interests;
6. respect for fundamental individual rights and the right to due process for the defendants at the arrest, detention, and trial stages, which is guaranteed by internal and international norms against, among other things, inhumane, cruel, or degrading treatment and torture;
7. an *animus comprehendi* and a logical-temporal connection between the capture of the defendants and the specific offence with which they are charged; and,
8. control by international institutions over compliance with these conditions.

The exercise of extraterritorial powers in the common interest is subject to institutional control of an objective kind. Based on current practice, actions performed as safeguards are to be regarded as unlawful if they are not approved by the majority of states in the international community and in UN bodies. Thus, the legality of a given action is to be determined on a case-by-case basis.

Concluding Remarks: A Working System of Collective Guarantees Limiting Private Rights for the Collective Good

The collective guarantees classified here as 'tutelary' protect the primary values of the global community by expanding the authority of the agent state acting on behalf of the collectivity, while limiting the private rights and powers of the territorial state, of other states, and of individuals. The exercise of these exceptional powers is subject to the control of institutional bodies integrating the 'public' activity of the agent state.

The construction of an integrated system of tutelary collective guarantees is still at an embryonic stage. In domestic law the power to limit individual rights for the collective good, or to deprive an individual of them entirely, is one of the fundamental powers of public administration and serves to guarantee higher social interests. The difficulties in identifying the states that in a given case are entitled to act in the common interest, and the slow progress made in defining in each specific sector (e.g., human rights, environmental protection, organized crime, the narcotics trade, nuclear power, and the production of weapons of mass destruction) the limitations, in the name of universal interests, on the 'normal' powers granted to states and individuals by the international order, indicate the need for further study in this area. Above all, these difficulties highlight the need for international conventions regulating these actions, and the urgent need to institutionalize the integrated processes for defining and strengthening institutional control over the legitimacy of such operations. This is necessary to secure the strict compliance of the exercise of exceptional governmental powers with relevant instruments and the rule of law, thus reducing the arbitrary use of extra-territorial state actions for heteronomous purposes and ensuring the 'public' character of such operations.

Chapter 7

An Integrated Self-Defence System Against Large-Scale Attacks by Irregular Forces: The Israeli-Hezbollah Conflict*

Introduction

During the escalation of the conflict between Israel and Hezbollah, the UN Security Council ('SC') intervened with Resolution 1701 on 11 August 2006.[1] The ambiguity of this resolution does not appear to provide any help in the debate among political scientists and legal scholars on the highly complex Israeli-Lebanese crisis in understanding the positions of the two parties to the dispute on the basis of norms of international law.

One particularly controversial matter is the legality of Israel's use of armed force in Lebanon. In this regard, Resolution 1701 expresses generic 'concern at the continuing escalation of hostilities in Lebanon and in Israel since Hizbollah's attack on Israel on 12 July 2006';[2] '[*c*]*alls for* a full cessation of hostilities based upon, in particular, the immediate cessation by Hizbollah of all attacks and the immediate cessation by Israel of all offensive military operations';[3] '[*c*]*alls for* Israel and Lebanon to support a permanent ceasefire and a long-term solution'[4] based, in part, on 'the disarmament of all armed groups in Lebanon'[5] so that, pursuant to the Lebanese cabinet decision of 27 July 2006, 'there will be no weapons or authority in Lebanon other than that of the Lebanese State';[6] and decides 'to authorize an increase in the force strength of UNIFIL [the United Nations Interim Force in Lebanon],' which shall assist the government of Lebanon.[7]

This resolution gives rise to certain questions, such as how to define 'Hizbollah's attack' of 12 July. It is not clear if it is considered a terrorist attack or whether it is attributable to the Lebanese government, or to Syria or Iran. Also, the force exercised

* This chapter is based on the article by Giuliana Ziccardi Capaldo, *Providing a Right of Self-Defense Against Large-Scale Attacks by Irregular Forces: The Israeli-Hizbollah Conflict*, 48 HARV. INT'L L.J. ONLINE 101 (2007), available at <http://www.harvardilj.org/online/115>.

1 SC Res. 1701, (Aug. 11, 2006).

2 *Id.*, preamble.

3 *Id.*, para. 1.

4 *Id.*, para. 8.

5 *Id.*

6 *Id.*

7 *Id.*, para. 11(f).

by Israel is generically referred to in terms of 'offensive military operations',[8] but there is no reference to 'aggression' or 'occupation'. It appears to the writer obvious from the entire tenor of Resolution 1701 and the reference to 'Hizbollah's attack on Israel' that this resolution is intended to exclude the hypothesis of a preventive Israeli self-defence against terrorists in Lebanon. The resolution seems to consider the Israeli military action as a response to Hezbollah's 'attack'. However, it cannot be qualified as an 'armed attack', according to Article 51 of the UN Charter; therefore, the Israeli 'military operations' are qualified as 'offensive' since they cannot be regarded as an implementation of the right to self-defence, lacking the necessary requirement of the armed attack.

In addition, the resolution makes no reference to any chapter of the UN Charter, giving rise to debate among legal scholars about where it should be placed in the UN framework.[9]

The present study is directed at addressing an important issue – the right of self-defence in the case of armed attack by a non-state armed group.[10] The analysis provides a conceptual framework for describing and critically assessing the contribution of Resolution 1701 to this crucial issue in normative and practical terms. It concludes that Resolution 1701 has actually made a step in the direction of allowing states attacked by non-state actors to retaliate. Some reflections on the position of the resolution in the Charter system are also contained below.

But, first of all, mention should be made of an issue in the analysis of the legality of Israel's use of armed force in Lebanon. This obviously includes the concept of proportionality in the context of legitimate self-defence, which raises questions of methodology as well as others of interpretation and thus requires priority.

The Proportionality of Self-Defence

Scholars, diplomats, and political leaders have concentrated their attention on the 'proportionality' of the Israeli intervention in Lebanon: they have put forward arguments both for and against, with some commentators considering the Israeli reaction to be disproportionate and therefore illegitimate. The discussion about whether or not Israel's actions are proportionate to the actions of Hezbollah has been based on the traditional view, recently expressed by Professor Frederic Kirgis, according to which 'the intensity of force used in self-defence must be about the same as the intensity defended against'.[11]

---

8 *Id.*, para. 1.

9 *See* Anthony D'Amato, *The UN Mideast Ceasefire Resolution Paragraph-by-Paragraph*, Jurist's Forum (Aug. 13, 2006), available at <http://jurist.law.pitt.edu/forumy/2006/08/un-mideast-ceasefire-resolution.php>.

10 William V. O'Brien, *Reprisals, Deterrence, and Self-Defense in Counterterror Operations*, 30 Virginia Journal of International Law 421 (1990); Yoram Dinstein, War, Aggression and Self-Defence (4th ed., 2005).

11 *See* Frederic Kirgis, *Some Proportionality Issues Raised by Israel's Use of Armed Force in Lebanon*, ASIL Insight (Aug. 17, 2006), available at <http://www.asil.org/insights/2006/08/insights060817.html>.

In connection with this doctrinal opinion, we would like to propose an alternative reading of the relevant pronouncements of the International Court of Justice ('ICJ'). We submit that the principle of the proportionality of legitimate defence could be taken to mean that the degree of force used in self-defence must be commensurate with the end to be achieved – the restoration of the rights violated as the result of an armed attack. This means that force must be 'strictly necessary' in any situation and 'directed' at the removal of the violation and the restoration of the violated rights.

For example, in the case of *Congo v. Uganda*, the ICJ considered that 'the taking of airports and towns many hundred kilometres from Uganda's border would not seem proportionate to the series of transborder attacks it [Uganda] claimed had given rise to the right of self-defence, nor to be necessary to that end'.[12] According to the Court, that the armed intervention of Uganda took place a great distance from where the violation occurred meant that the use of force for legitimate defence was not proportionate, since it was not suited to stopping the attacks along the border and therefore to achieving the object of restoring the rights of the state asserting a violation of its borders. The same reasoning underlies the advisory opinion on the *Threat of Use of Nuclear Weapons*, in which the Court even contemplated the use of nuclear armaments 'in an extreme circumstance of self-defence, in which the very survival of a state would be at stake'.[13]

The proportionality principle also requires the action taken in self-defence to be halted when the 'end' has been achieved. In *Military and Paramilitary Activities in and Against Nicaragua* ('*Nicaragua v. United States*'), the ICJ considered 'not to have been proportionate' the US's activities relating to the mining of Nicaraguan ports and attacks on ports and installations,[14] noting that 'the reaction of United States in the context of what it regarded as self-defence (against Nicaraguan-supported rebels in El Salvador) was continued long after the period in which any presumed armed conflict by Nicaragua could reasonably be contemplated'.[15]

An analysis of the proportionality of the Israeli military action raises a methodological issue. Clearly, implicit in any discussion of proportionality is compliance with Article 51 of the UN Charter since, if it were to be found that the preconditions for the exercise of the right to self-defence were lacking, it would make no sense to discuss whether Israel's military operations were proportionate. This was the pronouncement of the ICJ in the *Congo v. Uganda* case.[16] From a methodological point of view therefore, there is a need to establish as a matter of priority whether Israel made proper use of force in self-defence (since it is not obvious!), and, in the case of an affirmative response, to establish whether the Israeli military action was necessary and proportionate under international law.

---

12 Armed Activities on the Territory of the Congo (Democratic Republic of Congo v. Uganda), Judgment, 2005 ICJ Reports116, para. 147 (Dec. 19, 2005).

13 Legality of the Threat or Use of Nuclear Weapons, Advisory Opinion, 1995 ICJ Reports 226, at 263, para. 97 (July 8, 1996).

14 Military and Paramilitary Activities in and Against Nicaragua (Nicaragua v. United States), 1986 ICJ Reports 14, at 122, para. 237 (June 27, 1986).

15 *Id.*

16 *See supra* note 12, para. 147.

Legal Basis for Israel's Right to Resort to Self-Defence

The Requirement that an 'Armed Attack' Be Attributable to a State

The UN Charter and general international law provide for an absolute prohibition on the use of force by states, except in the case of legitimate self-defence laid down by Article 51 of the Charter (a norm of general international law, according to the ICJ).[17] Self-defence is 'legitimate' according to Article 51 when a state is subject to an 'armed attack' or act of aggression. One particularly complex point is whether the 'attack' by Hezbollah may be characterized as an 'armed attack' pursuant to Article 51.[18]

In general, the Security Council and the international community have discussed whether attacks by terrorist organizations and groups or irregular forces can be considered 'armed attacks' or acts of aggression, which would allow for the exercise of the right to resort to armed force pursuant to Article 51. In connection with international terrorism, an affirmative interpretation, supported above all by Israel and the US (and recently also by Uganda and Congo[19]) has generally been rejected in the past. In the late 1980s, the UN denied that Article 51 could justify the use of force or the right of self-defence as a response to terrorist attacks such as the bombing of Tripoli and Bengasi by the US (1986) and the bombing of the Palestine Liberation Organization offices in Tunisia by Israel (1985 and 1988).[20]

In contrast, after the attack on the US by Al Qaeda on 11 September 2001, the Security Council, which was immediately convened, recognized the US's right of legitimate self-defence and, as a result, deemed legitimate the armed intervention by the US against Afghanistan.[21] Still, in the advisory opinion *Construction of a Wall*,[22] the ICJ rejected Israeli claims that the construction of a wall in Palestinian territory was legitimate. Israel, referencing the US's armed intervention in Afghanistan, had claimed that the legitimacy for constructing the wall was founded on its right to self-defence.[23] The Court underlined the difference between the two situations and stated that 'Article 51 of the Charter … recognizes the existence of an inherent right of self-defence in the case of armed attack by one State against another State. However, Israel does not claim that the attacks against it are imputable to a foreign State'.[24]

---

17 See Nicaragua v. United States, *supra* note 14, at 102–103, para. 193.

18 See, e.g., Sean D. Murphy, *Terrorism and the Concept of 'Armed Attack' in Article 51 of the U.N. Charter*, 43 Harvard International Law Journal [hereinafter Harv. Int'l L.J.] 41 (2002).

19 See Dem. Rep. Congo v. Uganda, *supra* note 12, paras 147, 253, 254, 278, 286.

20 See, e.g., SC Res. 425 (Mar. 19, 1978); SC Res. 573 (Oct. 4, 1985); SC Res. 611 (Apr. 25, 1988); GA Res. 41/38 (Nov. 20, 1986).

21 See, e.g., Steven R. Ratner, Jus ad Bellum *and* Jus in Bello *After September 11*, 96 American Journal of International Law [hereinafter Am. J. Int'l L.] 905 (2002).

22 Legal Consequences of the Construction of a Wall in the Occupied Palestinian Territory, Advisory Opinion, 2004 ICJ Reports 136 (July 9, 2004).

23 *Id.*, at 194, paras 138–139.

24 *Id.*, at 194, para. 139.

Standards for Attribution to a State of Non-State Acts

In connection with the ICJ's interpretation, the right of self-defence has long required the 'armed attack' to be imputable to a state. As a result, in cases in which an attack comes from a non-state armed group, there is a need to demonstrate that it can be attributable to a state. In *Nicaragua v. United States*, decided in 1986, the Court recognized 'effective control' as the standard for the attribution to a state of the act of a non-state armed group.[25]

This line of reasoning was once again adopted in *Congo v. Uganda* (and, recently, in *Bosnia and Herzegovina v. Serbia and Montenegro*),[26] in which the Court found 'that the legal and factual circumstances for the exercise of a right of self-defence by Uganda against the Democratic Republic of the Congo (DRC) were not present.' Despite arguments by Uganda to the contrary, the Court found that 'there is no satisfactory proof of the involvement in these attacks, direct or indirect, of the Government of the DRC. The attacks did not emanate from armed bands or irregulars sent by the DRC or on behalf of the DRC …'.[27]

On the basis of these considerations, what might be the legal basis for Israel's right to resort to armed force in the recent conflict in Lebanon and northern Israel? It only remains to ascertain whether Hezbollah's 'armed attacks' can be attributed to a state, be it Lebanon, Syria, or Iran, and whether these acts are of 'such gravity' as to amount to large-scale armed attacks.

It appears to be difficult to claim, on the basis of the normative acts available, that the Hezbollah attacks on Israel can be imputed to a state. The acts of the UN organs (Security Council Resolution 1701 and the Secretary-General's Report on its implementation[28]) do not deal specifically with this point – neither the overall tone nor the language enables us to ascertain this element with a degree of certainty. Resolution 1701 does not provide an assessment of responsibility on the basis of the existence of 'effective control' over the Hezbollah attacks by a state (under Article 39 of the Charter), nor does it make reference to support for Hezbollah by third-party states such as Syria and Iran. With regard to Lebanon, the context of the resolution leads us to rule out any involvement, either direct or indirect, on the part of the Lebanese government. Certain paragraphs memorialize the intention of the Lebanese government to disarm and render inoperative the Hezbollah fighters.[29] This leads us to rule out the possibility that the Israeli military operations can be founded on Article 51 of the Charter, even if the long list of deplorable actions on the part of the Hezbollah – such as launching missiles against Haifa – could be regarded

25 Nicaragua v. United States., *supra* note 14, at 65, para. 115.

26 Dem. Rep. Congo v. Uganda, *supra* note 12. *See also* Application of the Convention on the Prevention and Punishment of the Crime of Genocide (Bosnia and Herzegovina v. Serbia and Montenegro), 2007 ICJ Reports 91, paras 377–415 (Feb. 26, 2007).

27 Dem. Rep. Congo v. Uganda, *supra* note 12, para. 146.

28 The Secretary-General, *Report of the Secretary-General on the Implementation of Security Council Resolution 1701*, UN Doc. S/2006/730 (Sept. 12, 2006).

29 SC Res. 1701, *supra* note 1, paras 3, 12.

as 'cumulative in character'[30] and as having the characteristics of gravity pertaining to acts of war.

This is the case because, even if responsibility is assigned to the Lebanese government for having failed to take measures to prevent the action or to bring to justice those behind the terrorist actions, this would not grant Israel the right to resort to armed force (but rather to use other forms of international sanctions); such actions still remain non-attributable to Lebanon. In this case, the armed non-state activities cannot be attributed to a state according to current doctrinal opinion and case law rulings.[31]

If one reaches the conclusion that Hezbollah's 'attack' is not imputable to a state, then the Israeli reaction cannot be founded on Article 51 of the Charter in conformity with contemporary international law. This seems to be confirmed also by the Security Council, which determined Israel's military operations to be 'offensive,' thus stating that they cannot be founded on the right of legitimate self-defence.

The Need for New Standards Less Rigid in Their Application

The lack of a right of self-defence against armed attacks from irregular forces and/or terrorist groups not attributable to a state, even in the case of large-scale armed attack, is a grave *lacuna* in international law. This *lacuna* is all the more serious if we consider the widespread (but difficult to prove) connivances between states and terrorist organizations and their autonomy in terms of resources and action even in respect of states sponsoring.

'Effective control' as the basis for attribution to a state of non-state armed acts is too rigid a criterion. For a state to 'effectively control' a non-state actor, *Nicaragua v. United States* requires 'financing, organizing, supplying and equipping … the selection of its military or paramilitary targets and the planning of the whole of its operation'.[32] A more recent decision requires 'overall control', involving also participation in the planning and supervision of military operations.[33] These high standards stand in contrast to the 1974 Resolution of the General Assembly, which required merely 'substantial involvement'.[34] Moreover, 'effective control' is not easy to ascertain in concrete cases, as there is a need for 'clear evidence' of a State having exercised such a degree of control 'in all fields' so as to justify treating a non-state actor as acting on its behalf.[35]

This point is by no means easy to resolve because it is risky to argue for equating non-state actors to states, thereby providing an automatic extension of the right to legitimate defence under Article 51 of the Charter to armed attacks from non-state

30 See Dem. Rep. Congo v. Uganda, *supra* note 12, para. 146.

31 See, e.g., Jonathan Somer, *Acts of Non-State Armed Groups and the Law Governing Armed Conflict*, ASIL Insight (Aug. 24, 2006), available at <http://www.asil.org/insights/2006/08/insights060824.html>; United States Diplomatic and Consular Staff in Tehran (United States v. Iran), 1980 ICJ Reports 3, at 16–34, paras 27–68 (May 24).

32 *Supra* note 14, at 64, para. 115.

33 Prosecutor v. Tadic, Case No. IT–94–1-A, paras 120, 122, 123, 131 (July 15, 1999).

34 GA Res. 3314 (XXIX), Art. 3(g), UN Doc. A/RES/3314.

35 Nicaragua v. United States, *supra* note 14, at 62, para. 109.

organizations. However, the emergency remains, and international law must find a way to deal with the fact that international society has grown to include new actors who possess and deploy military equipment comparable to that of sovereign states. Because of this danger, there is a need for new rules of attribution and standards less rigid in their application, together with objective institutional mechanisms, to allow for self-defence in the face of a non-state armed attack. This should act as a deterrent for terrorist groups and the states sponsoring them. It is for this reason that certain legal scholars have proposed adopting, in addition to 'effective control,' the standard of 'due diligence' as a basis for attribution.[36]

Who should step in at an international level to fill this normative void? Certainly the UN bodies that, within the changing institutional framework of the international community that has evolved to deal with new international issues, have set in motion procedures to provide international norms that go beyond the classical procedures of customary law.[37] That the UN bodies should fill this gap aligns with Thomas Franck's forceful argument for 'the capacity of law to adapt to new circumstances'.[38]

In the 1970s, the UN General Assembly made an important contribution to the definition of aggression; it did so at a time when international terrorism had not taken on the global character that it has today. The General Assembly does not have binding normative powers, but, by means of its Declarations of Principle, it carries out the function of encouraging 'the progressive development of international law' (Article 13 (1) (a) of the UN Charter), and it is the primary forum for the adoption of principles of international law of an instantaneous character.[39] However, a significant limit on the effective ability of the General Assembly to provide for a right of self-defence against non-state actors arose from a disagreement within the UN on the definition of 'terrorism'[40] and how to distinguish between terrorism, which it condemned, and violence on the part of national liberation movements, which it considered possibly legitimate.[41]

Even the ICJ has not specifically dealt with this matter. In the above-mentioned case of *Congo v. Uganda*, the Court did not consider it appropriate 'to respond to the contentions of the Parties as to whether and under what conditions contemporary international law provides for a right of self-defence against large-scale attacks by irregular forces'.[42] Even in the Advisory Opinion *Construction of a Wall*, the Court failed to take advantage of the opportunity given to it by Israel's claim that the

---

36 Robert P. Barnidge Jr., *States' Due Diligence Obligations with Regard to International Non-State Terrorist Organisations Post-11 September 2001: The Heavy Burden that States Must Bear*, 16 Irish Stud. Int'l Aff. 103 (2005).

37 See, e.g., José E. Alvarez, International Organizations as Law-Makers (2005).

38 Thomas M. Franck, *The Power of Legitimacy and the Legitimacy of Power: International Law in an Age of Power Disequilibrium*, 100 Am. J. Int'l L. 88, (2006), at 104–105.

39 See, e.g., Bin Cheng, *UN Resolutions on Outer Space: 'Instant' International Customary Law?*, 5 Indian Journal of International Law 23 (1965).

40 See generally M. Cherif Bassiouni, *Legal Control of International Terrorism*, 43 Harv. Int'l L. J. 83 (2002), at 101.

41 See, e.g., GA Res. 3314 (XXIX), *supra* note 34, at Art. 7.

42 Congo v. Uganda, *supra* note 12, para. 147.

construction of a wall constituted an exercise of the right of self-defence in the face of terrorist attacks.[43]

One of the functions of the Court is to interpret the norms of international law and, therefore, Article 51 of the Charter. But the Court takes a cautious approach toward intervening in a matter entrusted primarily to the Security Council by Article 24 of the Charter. Thus, it hesitates to extend the application of Article 51 to non-state actors, which would be possible according to the language of Article 51. Commentators have underlined that the letter of this Article does not expressly require that an armed attack triggering the right to self-defence must come to be attributable to a state.[44] In the words of Article 51 of the UN Charter, '[n]othing in the present Charter shall impair the inherent right of individual or collective self-defence if an armed attack occurs against a Member of the United Nations'.[45]

So, the body that has really dealt with this, easing the way for future advances of the other two bodies – the ICJ and the General Assembly – is the Security Council.

A Mechanism for Attribution Established by Security Council Resolution 1701

Although the Security Council has not made an explicit effort to change the standard for a right to self-defence from 'effective control', it has made a step in the right direction by making it easier to attribute terrorist attacks to states.

The Security Council made provision for a more extensive application of Article 51 after the terrorist attacks of 11 September 2001 in the US, considering as legitimate the exercise of the right of self-defence in response to an armed attack by a non-state group involved in terrorist activities.[46] In that case, the Security Council did so by attributing the actions of the Taliban to Afghanistan. Following from this proposition, Resolution 1701 introduces what may be considered to be a 'rule-based model of attribution' that aims to overcome the legal obstacle of 'effective control.' This is especially appropriate in the unclear Lebanese situation in which Hezbollah appears to have close links with the Lebanese government. Although it has not yet been proven, there is a strong suspicion that there were links and a secret agreement with the government of Lebanon that Hezbollah's members would not be disarmed and would be allowed to continue to import arms.[47]

The Security Council approaches the question of attribution only indirectly and at a practical level. The resolution aims to re-establish effective control by the Lebanese government over its territory, to enable it to be free and, at the same time,

---

43 Construction of a Wall, *supra* note 22, at 194, para. 139.

44 See, e.g., Karl Zemanek, *Self-Defence Against Terrorism, Reflexions on an Unprecedented Situation*, *in* El Derecho Internacional en Los Albores del Siglo XXI: Homenaje al Professor Juan Manuel Castro-Rial Canosa 695, 702 (Fernando M. Mariño Menendez, ed. 2002).

45 UN Charter.

46 SC Res. 1368 (Sept. 12, 2001); SC Res. 1373 (Sept. 28, 2001) (reaffirmed in SC Res. 1440 (Oct. 24, 2002)); SC Res. 1450 (Dec. 13, 2002); SC Res. 1452 (Dec. 20, 2002); and SC Res. 1465 (Feb. 13, 2003).

47 *See* D'Amato, *supra* note 9.

to make it responsible for its political actions. To this effect, it '[c]*alls upon* the Government of Lebanon to secure its borders and other entry points … and *requests* UNIFIL … to assist the Government of Lebanon'[48] to prevent the entry into Lebanon of arms or related material 'without its consent'.[49] The resolution clearly states that 'no foreign forces [may be] in Lebanon without the consent of its government [and that] no sales or supply of arms and related material [should go] to Lebanon except as authorized by its government'.[50] The resolution's aims can be identified through the wording chosen: that of 'assist' and 'consent'. On the basis of these provisions, the Lebanese government is permitted to make the voluntary choice as to whether to support the terrorist actions of Hezbollah or to oppose them. It alone has the power to decide whether to disarm the Hezbollah fighters or to allow weapons in to equip them – it all depends on the political will of the government, and UNIFIL cannot interfere with it.

In this way, the entire scenario can be seen as providing a sort of mechanism for attribution, a context within which any further armed activity on the part of terrorist groups based in Lebanon would be deemed the 'deliberate official policy'[51] of the government of Lebanon. If the Lebanese government was forced to take responsibility for large-scale attacks, it would leave open the way for legitimate self-defence on the part of Israel under the terms of Article 51. These attacks will be imputable to the authorities of Lebanon, since the 'consent' provides a clear and unequivocal act of 'acknowledgment and adoption' of the conduct in question.

The 'acknowledgement and adoption' standard of attribution, already adopted by the Security Council in Resolution 138 in the case of Eichmann's capture[52] and formalized by the International Law Commission (ILC) in Article 11 of the Report on State Responsibility of 2001,[53] originated in the *Diplomatic and Consular Staff* case, in which the ICJ ruled that 'the Iranian State … itself was internationally responsible'[54] for attacks by Iranian militants on the US embassy in Teheran. These attacks were the outcome of a change in policy adopted by the Iranian authorities and of 'the approval' given to the conduct of the militias that transformed the initial legal situation. The Court found that there was a substantive difference in terms of the legal consequences between the initial negligence of the Iranian State for having failed 'to take appropriate steps' in order to prevent the attacks on the embassy, and the subsequent behaviour, during which the Iranian authorities were 'aware of their obligation', and, 'due to more than mere negligence or lack of appropriate means', 'failed to use the means which were at their disposal to comply with their obligations'.[55] In essence, the Court made a distinction between 'mere negligence'

48 SC Res. 1701, *supra* note 1, para. 14. See also paras 6, 11(d), (e), (f), 12.

49 *Id.*, at para. 14.

50 *Id.*, at para. 8.

51 Nicaragua v. United States, *supra* note 14, para. 155.

52 SC Res. 138 (June 23, 1960).

53 Draft Articles on Responsibility of States for Internationally Wrongful Acts with Commentaries, Art. 11, *in International Law Commission, Report of the International Law Commission on the Work of Its 53rd Session*, UN Doc. A/56/10 (2001).

54 Diplomatic and Consular Staff, *supra* note 31, para. 74.

55 *Id.*, at paras 63, 68.

and what may be called 'awareness/conscious negligence' – only in the latter case is the conduct in question to be attributed to the state.

The *Diplomatic and Consular Staff* standard of attribution has a far wider significance in connection with the standard laid down in Article 11 of the ILC Report, which 'provides for attribution to a State of conduct that was not or may not have been attributable to it at the time of commission, but which is subsequently acknowledged and adopted by the State as its own',[56] i.e., 'retroactive' attribution.

The resolution seems to lay the legal basis for Lebanon's responsibility for possible armed attacks on Israel by Hezbollah on the 'conscious negligence' (i.e., awareness and failure on the part of a state to use the means that were at its disposal to prevent terrorist activities) of the Lebanese government.

The Security Council consolidates a rule of attribution, around which there is much uncertainty, expressing a preference for the ICJ's interpretation. Moreover the Security Council has applied such a norm in an original manner, as a law-maker, setting it as the basis for a mechanism of shared governance and contributing to the gradual establishment of an integrated enforcement system, on which we have largely focused (and have systematically reconstructed) in previous writings.[57] Already, the substantial international community (i.e., the inter-state community) has developed mechanisms of integration with the organized international community (i.e., the international organizations and the global NGO community) and, above all, the UN.[58]

Concluding Remarks: A Courageous Reorganization of International Law-Enforcement Through the Institutionalization of Integrated Mechanisms

Security Council Resolution 1701, although characterized by ambiguity, makes an operative and normative contribution to creating an effective tool for providing the right of self-defence in response to an armed attack by a non-state armed group.

From an operational point of view, the resolution aims to provide a response to the problems posed by weak and/or acquiescent governments that offer sanctuary to terrorist networks preparing attacks on other states. It puts in place a mechanism to dissuade the government of Lebanon from supporting Hezbollah fighters by setting up a UN support force to restore territorial control and to assist the Lebanese army while allowing the Lebanese government to decide whether to ensure respect for the arms embargo and disarm the terrorist groups or to allow weapons to enter and permit terrorist groups to equip themselves.

In normative terms, what I am arguing for is also a sort of mechanism for the attribution of the acts of armed groups operating on its territory to the Lebanese

---

56 Draft Articles on Responsibility of States, *supra* note 53, commentary to Art. 11, at 119.

57 Giuliana Ziccardi Capaldo, *The Law of the Global Community: An Integrated System to Enforce 'Public' International Law*, 1 The Global Community. Yearbook of International Law and Jurisprudence 71 (2001), at 97.

58 I first used this difference in Giuliana Ziccardi Capaldo, Terrorismo Internazionale e Garanzie Collettive (1990), at 127–130.

government. This attribution is based upon 'acknowledgement and adoption' (with the meaning of 'awareness/conscious negligence') – a less rigid standard than the criterion of 'effective control', which itself was a more cautious approach than the earlier-espoused standard of 'due diligence/mere negligence'.

The resolution institutes a mechanism of law-enforcement that follows in the wake of the ongoing process of change in the system of international guarantee toward new forms. This is a change determined by the need to make up for the inability of classical forms of guarantee and the UN system itself to protect collectively new fundamental values of the global community (such as peace, human rights, self-determination, sustainable development, the environment, international commons, etc.). The shortcomings of the Charter are well known. It is not only those that are procedural (blocking of the system due to vetoes, the lack of decision-making power of the General Assembly, etc.); but also that the UN system of collective security foreseen by Chapter VII is solely focused on safeguarding the peace in the event of 'threats to peace, violation of the peace and acts of aggression'. In any case, even for maintaining the peace, the UN does not possess the necessary tools, since the 'special agreements' foreseen by the Charter (for instance, in Articles 43–47) for the creation of a permanent standing UN army have never been stipulated.

It is therefore particularly important to focus attention on mechanisms of joint governance and processes of multilateral authoritative decision-making between states and international organizations acting jointly. The UN participates in a position of superiority, carrying out the function of control and legitimization of multilateral activity, which is a new role for it compared to its strictly institutional one.

We believe the mechanism put in place by Resolution 1701 should be placed outside the normative system of the UN Charter, with regard to both Chapters VI and VII, as well as Articles 42 and 51. It serves as the model for a more effective, integrated system for a new era in the enforcement of international law under the authority of the UN. It is a response to the problems arising from the conflict in Lebanon, which could also be effective in analogous unlawful territorial situations if the mechanism, currently in its embryonic form, is perfected and formalized.

This is only an initial step, and there remains a need for normative and operational interventions with a courageous reorganization of international law enforcement, through the formalization and institutionalization of integrated mechanisms.

SECTION II
Global Enforcement Mechanisms Against Terrorism

Chapter 8

Joint Mechanisms Against Terrorists, Insurgents and Other Non-State Actors*

Introduction

In the wake of the tragedy in Beslan, in the Russian Republic of North Ossetia, and the downing of two jets claimed by the so-called 'black widows' (female Chechen terrorists), the Russian President, Vladimir Putin, talked about 'the direct intervention of international terror',[1] and General Yuri Baluevsky, chief of Russia's general staff, declared his commitment to fight terrorism like the US[2] 'in any region of the world' and even talked of launching 'preventive strikes'.[3] This is another clear and disturbing signal of a unilateral drift menacing the world's legal system. The prompt and straightforward warning of the UN Secretary-General to Russia[4] testifies to the seriousness of the situation.

Global terrorism holds the world in its deadly grip, causing destruction, destabilizing national democracies and the rules *in fieri* of the international democratic system.[5] It hit democratic states (the US and Spain respectively, with the 11 September 2001, and 11 March 2004 attacks) and forced them to stiffen their institutions, to curtail democratic achievements, and to renounce civil liberties.[6] It shattered 'human

---

* This chapter is based on the paper by Giuliana Ziccardi Capaldo, *Editorial: Fighting Global Terrorism: Through Global Enforcement Mechanisms*, 4 The Global Community. Yearbook of International Law and Jurisprudence [hereinafter GCYILJ] xv (2004–I). That early text has been updated and modified

1 Putin's Speech of 4 September 2003, available at <http://president.kremlin.ru/eng/text/speeches/2004/09/04/1958_76332.shtml>.

2 The National Security Strategy of the United States of America, 17 September 2002, chapt. V (Prevent our Enemies from Threatening Us, Our Allies, and Our Friends with Weapons of Mass Destruction), at 13, available at <http://www.usembassy.it/pdf/other/nss0902.pdf>.

3 <Http://www.civil.ge/eng/article.php?id=7773>.

4 Press encounter with the Secretary-General at the Mexican Foreign Ministry (Sept. 8, 2004), available at <http://www.un.org/apps/sg/offthecuff.asp?nid=628>.

5 See William Michael Reisman, *In Defense of World Public Order*, 95 American Journal of International Law [hereinafter Am. J. Int'l L.] 833 (2001).

6 Uniting and Strengthening America by Providing Appropriate Tools Required to Intercept and Obstruct Terrorism Act of 2001 (USA Patriot Act), Pub. L. No. 107–56, 115 Stat. 272 (2001); Ley 12/2003 de 21 de mayo 2003, de prevencion y bloqueo de la financiaciòn del terrorismo, Boletín Oficial del Estado (May 22, 2003), at 19490–19494. See also the decree of President Vladimir Putin introducing urgent measures to increase the effectiveness of the war on terrorism, adopted on 13 September 2004 (available at <http://www.mosnews.

rights and freedoms of any individual or people'.[7] It crept into both historical and more recent conflicts (Palestine, Iraq, Chechnya, and Pakistan), exploiting legitimate expectations of peoples, fuelled by sponsoring states and terror networks inspired by ideological and religious extremism. By infiltrating armed conflicts, no matter what the causes and their qualifications (i.e., their national or international nature), it becomes endemic and therefore even more dangerous. Terrorism camouflages itself, blending into the struggle for self-determination of peoples, operating in their name, eluding observation and the rules of international law. Once wormed in, terrorism fuels conflicts and paralyses structures and democratic decisional processes of the global community. The international community is paralysed by terror, and its institutions and structures are incapacitated. In the Iraqi crisis, the incapacity of the Security Council to find an agreement between its permanent members to terminate Saddam Hussein's regime led to the unilateral intervention of the US and the UK, and a fracture in the world's government that is yet to be mended.[8]

The Palestinian crisis is in an age-old deadlock, too. Not only are all negotiations at a standstill, but so is the Road Map:[9] the most relevant effort towards a solution based on negotiations, and the most modern and articulate platform born out of an 'integrated' decisional process, engaging states and international organizations under UN supervision.[10] The Security Council, frozen by the veto, was not able to decide on the construction of the wall in Palestine. The veto of a permanent member on draft resolutions on 'Israeli actions in the Occupied Palestinian Territory',[11] coupled

---

com/news/2004/09/14/ukaz.shtml> and <http://www.washingtonpost.com/wp–dyn/articles/A17838–2004Sep13.html>).

7 Secretary of State Colin L. Powell, *Remarks to the United Nations Security Council* (Feb. 5, 2003), available at <http://www.state.gov/secretary/former/powell/remarks/2003/17300.htm>. See, in general, Anthony McGrew, *Cosmopolitanism and the War on Terror*, 6 GCYILJ 35 (2006–I).

8 See Lori Fisler Damrosch & Bernard H. Oxman, *Editors' Introduction, Agora: Future Implications of the Iraq Conflict*, 97 Am. J. Int'l L. 553 (2003); William H. Taft IV & Todd F. Buchwald, *Preemption, Iraq, and International Law, id.*, at 557; John C. Yoo *International Law and the War in Iraq, id.*, at 563; Ruth Wedgwood, *The Fall of Saddam Hussein: Security Council Mandates and Preemptive Self-Defense, id.*, at 576; Richard N. Gardner, *Neither Bush nor the 'Jurisprudes', id.*, at 585; Richard A. Falk, *What Future for the UN Charter System of War Prevention?, id.*, at 590; Miriam Sapiro, *Iraq: The Shifting Sands of Preemptive Self-Defense, id.*, at 599; Thomas M. Franck, *What Happens Now? The United Nations After Iraq, id.*, at 607; Tom J. Farer, *The Prospect for International Law and Order in the Wake of Iraq, id.*, at 621; Jane E. Stromseth, *Law and Force After Iraq: A Transitional Moment, id.*, at 628; see also *supra* chapter 4 of this book.

9 The text has been prepared by the Quartet (consisting of representatives of the US, the European Union, the Russian Federation, and the UN) and was transmitted by the UN Secretary-General to the Security Council (Letter dated 7 May 2003 (UN Doc. S/2003/529)), which approved it on 19 November (SC Res. 1515 (Nov. 19, 2003)).

10 See *supra* Introduction to this book, under the heading 'Collective Guarantees' and *supra* chapter 2.

11 See the rejection by Security Council, on 7 March and 21 March 1997, as a result of negative votes by a permanent member, of two draft resolutions concerning certain Israeli settlements in the Occupied Palestinian Territory (see, respectively, UN Docs. S/1997/199,

with the acknowledgment that there existed a threat to international peace,[12] created the conditions for an extraordinary convocation of the General Assembly[13] based on the historical, but dubious, procedure set by Resolution 377/V, which had been adopted in 1950, in the depth of the Cold War, in the equally dramatic circumstances of the Korean crisis. The *Uniting for Peace* Resolution established that, when the Security Council, facing a threat or breach to peace or aggression, is unable to act, the General Assembly can adopt the necessary measures, including the use of armed force.[14] In the case of the Occupied Palestinian Territory, both the validity of the procedure followed by the Tenth Emergency Special Session and the action of the General Assembly in lieu of the Council, were objected to.[15]

In such a dangerous situation of paralysis of international politics, the International Court of Justice stepped up to the plate. It intervened on the Palestinian question, at the request of the General Assembly,[16] as ultimate guardian of international legality, to provide an advisory opinion on the legal consequences of the construction of a wall by Israel in the occupied Palestinian Territory. The intervention of the principal judicial organ of the organization was necessary to overcome the impasse of the veto because the Court, by validating the procedure set by the *Uniting for Peace* Resolution, dispelled doubts as to the regularity of the procedure that the General Assembly followed to request the opinion.[17]

Terrorist Acts Committed on Behalf of 'Peoples'

In the Advisory Opinion *Construction of a Wall*, the Court attempted to fill the legal void and the institutional impasse arising from the increasing incapacity of the Charter to answer the needs of the global community. The Court should be praised for having risen, consistently with its advisory practice, to be the world's legislator, the ultimate guardian of the global legal system. In the opinion on the construction of the Palestinian wall, the Court fittingly analyses international human rights and humanitarian law, both customary and treaty-based, 'as it evolved from the Charter

S/PV.3747, S/1997/241 and S/PV.3756) and again the rejection, on 14 October 2003, of a draft resolution concerning the construction by Israel of the wall in the same Territory (UN Docs. S/2003/980, S/PV.4841 and S/PV.4842).

12 GA Res. ES–10/2 (April 25, 1997), preamble.

13 Tenth Emergency Special Session on 'Illegal Israeli Actions in Occupied East Jerusalem and the Rest of the Occupied Palestinian Territory', convened on 24 and 25 April 1997, subsequently reconvened 11 times.

14 GA Res. 377 A (V) (Nov. 3, 1950), Section A, para. 1. *See* Piero Ziccardi, *L'Intervento Collettivo delle Nazioni Unite e i Nuovi Poteri dell'Assemblea Generale*, 12 La Comunità Internazionale 221–236, 415–447 (1957).

15 See *infra* note 17.

16 GA Res. A/ES–10/14 (Dec. 8, 2003).

17 See Written Statement of the Government of Israel on Jurisdiction and Propriety (Jan. 30, 2004), Part Two, chapt. IV, at 57–81, available at <http://www.icj–cij.org/icjwww/idocket/imwp/imwpframe.htm> and the Court's remarks, Legal Consequences of the Construction of a Wall in the Occupied Palestinian Territory, Advisory Opinion, 2004 ICJ Reports 136 (July 9, 2004) [hereinafter Construction of a Wall], paras 29–34, at 150–152.

and from UN practice'.[18] It asserts its applicability in the occupied territories.[19] It spells out the obligations deriving from it for the occupying state and the *erga omnes* nature of some of them.[20] It concludes that the obligations *erga omnes* violated by Israel are the obligation to respect the right of the Palestinian people to self-determination and certain of its obligations under international humanitarian law.[21] Following a consistent practice that begun with the *Barcelona Traction*[22] and *Namibia*[23] cases, the Court defines the legal regime for the violations of *erga omnes* obligations, filling the gap left behind by the International Law Commission.[24] In the opinion in question, it details the legal consequences of the violation of such obligations not only for the occupying state (in other words, Israel's obligation towards the Palestinian people, the international community, and damaged individuals and institutions),[25] but also for third-party states[26] and the UN.[27] It demands that UN organs – especially the Security Council and the General Assembly – consider 'what further action is required to bring to an end the illegal situation resulting from the construction of the wall and the associated regime, taking due account of the (...) Advisory Opinion'.[28] By doing so, it strengthens its advisory functions and implicitly reasserts its judicial power of control on the political organs for the safeguard of the constitutional values of peace and human rights.

The 'human rights' approach of the Court to self-determination issues,[29] raised in the specific case, is consistent with its jurisprudence. The Court strives to safeguard individuals' fundamental rights, and, in doing so, it is attuned to the priorities of the contemporary global community. Although with this opinion the Court greatly contributed to the clarification of *erga omnes* principles and structural rules for the new global community, it lost the opportunity to build upon the new 'global trends'[30] emerging from its most recent judicial pronouncements. When it defines the consequences of the violation of *erga omnes* obligations in international

---

18 Construction of a Wall, *supra* note 17, para. 156, at 199.

19 *Id.*, at paras 89–101 and 105–113, at 172–177 and 177–181.

20 *Id.*, at paras 155–157.

21 *Id.*, at para. 155.

22 Barcelona Traction, Light and Power Company (Belgium v. Spain) Limited, Judgment, 1970 ICJ Reports 3 (Feb. 5, 1970), paras 33–35, at 33–34.

23 Legal Consequences for States of the Continued Presence of South Africa in Namibia (South West Africa) notwithstanding Security Council Resolution 276 (1970), Advisory Opinion, 1971 ICJ Reports 16 (June 21, 1971), paras 111, 117, 122–126, at 40, 42, 43–44, respectively.

24 Pierre-Marie Dupuy, *A General Stocktaking of the Connections Between the Multilateral Dimension of Obligations and Codification of the Law of Responsibility*, 13 European Journal of International Law 1053 (2002).

25 Construction of a Wall, *supra* note 17, paras 149–153.

26 *Id.*, at paras 154–159.

27 *Id.*, at para. 160.

28 *Id.*, at paras 160, 163 E.

29 See generally Robert McCorquodale, *Self-Determination: A Human Rights Approach*, 43 International and Comparative Law Quarterly 857 (1994).

30 See *supra* chapter 3 of this book, under the heading 'The ICJ between over-reaching and over-caution'.

humanitarian law, it analyses states' responsibilities and duties within the traditional international law framework, made of states interacting in an inter-state society, but it fails to do the same for non-state actors, thus overlooking the new structure of the international community, which nowadays clearly includes them. The Court does not define the Palestinian people's obligations, and, more generally, the obligations of groups/movements struggling against foreign occupation, arising from *erga omnes* norms, although it does refer to its jurisprudence and states that 'a great many rules of humanitarian law applicable in armed conflict '... are to be observed ... because they constitute intransgressible principles of international customary law'. These rules include obligations 'which are essentially *erga omnes*'.[31] At the end of the Opinion, the Court limits itself to a generic warning for Israel and Palestine to respect 'scrupulously' the norms of humanitarian law, 'one of the paramount purposes of which is to protect civilian life'.[32]

The Court lost the chance to address doubts about the application of humanitarian law to armed conflicts.[33] It did not touch upon the need to distinguish between terrorism and struggle for national liberation, and the need to punish terrorist acts, committed on behalf of 'peoples' fighting for their rights to self-determination consistently with humanitarian law, as 'grave breaches'.[34] It lost the occasion to give effect to the spirit of the Fourth Geneva Convention,[35] which the Court itself deems to 'guarantee the protection of civilians in time of war, regardless of the status of the occupied territories'.[36]

The Court did not dwell on the link between terrorism and legitimate resistance against occupation but to exclude that Israel can invoke the resolutions adopted by the Security Council after 11 September 2001,[37] to support its claim to be exercising the right of self-defence in the face of terrorist attacks.[38] In its reasoning, the Court greatly contributed to the political and scholarly debate on the applicability of the Charter's Article 51 to terrorist attacks,[39] by deeming it applicable 'in the case of

31 See Construction of a Wall, *supra* note 17, para. 157; see also Legality of the Threat or Use of Nuclear Weapons, Advisory Opinion, 1996–I ICJ REPORTS 226 (July 8, 1996), para. 79, at 257.

32 Construction of a Wall, *supra* note 17, para. 162.

33 In general, see George H. Aldrich, *The Taliban, Al Qaeda, and the Determination of Illegal Combatants*, 96 AM. J. INT'L L. 891 (2002).

34 ELIZABETH CHADWICK, SELF–DETERMINATION, TERRORISM AND THE INTERNATIONAL HUMANITARIAN LAW OF ARMED CONFLICT (1996); Fausto Pocar, *Human Rights Under the International Covenant on Civil and Political Rights and Armed Conflicts*, MAN'S INHUMANITY TO MAN. ESSAYS ON INTERNATIONAL LAW IN HONOUR OF ANTONIO CASSESE 729 (Lal Chand Vohrah ed., 2003).

35 Geneva Convention Relative to the Protection of Civilian Persons in Time of War (Aug. 12, 1949), 75 UNTS 287, No. 973.

36 Construction of a Wall, *supra* note 17, para. 95.

37 SC Res. 1368 (Sept. 12, 2001); and SC Res. 1373 (Sept. 12, 2001).

38 Construction of a Wall, *supra* note 17, para. 139, at 194.

39 See Jonathan I. Charney, *The Use of Force Against Terrorism and International Law*, 95 AM. J. INT'L L. 835 (2001); Thomas M. Franck, *Terrorism and the Right of Self-Defense*, *id.*,

armed attack by one state against another state'.[40] It stresses that Israel 'exercises control in the Occupied Palestinian Territories', and, thus, the situation in question 'is ... different from that contemplated by Security Council Resolutions' invoked by Israel.[41]

The Court had a chance to explore the issue of the 'morality' of the use of force by state and non-state actors, the connivance with terrorism, and the use of terrorist tactics by national liberation movements. It could have distinguished between terrorism and the fight for self-determination, both internal and external, and claim international control over the use of terrorist tactics in armed conflicts. The Court needed to set the premises for the collective action against acts of terrorism by liberation forces and domestic belligerents in armed conflicts, by restoring control in the hands of the UN and taking it away from states' unilateralism. By declaring the obligation of the Palestinian Authority to stay clear of terrorist groups and methods that cause 'grave injury to human beings' (i.e., suicide attacks by Hamas and the Jihad), the Court would have created the basis for a subsequent UN action in this regard. By doing so, the Court would have acted according to the priorities outlined by the Security Council in its resolutions on the protection of civilians in armed conflicts: the areas set out in the Secretary-General's ten-point platform include '(i) developing further measures to promote the responsibility of armed groups and non-state actors'.[42] Had the Court taken this occasion, it would have acted consistently with the multi-institutional cooperative approach implicit in the Opinion's analysis of states' *erga omnes* obligations and the processes granting their implementation (i.e., the obligations of the UN and its organs in the restoration of legality 'taking due account' of the Opinion).

A New Global Approach to Terrorist Activities in Armed Conflicts: Principles and Mechanisms

The global community is no more a community made of states only. To protect its principles, and particularly human rights, which are at its basis, obligations of non-state actors, as well as legal consequences in case of their violations, need to be defined. Armed conflicts need to be 'humanized' by severing any link between terrorism and the self-determination struggle, whether internal or external. We need to give concrete content to the UN mantra whereby all forms of terrorism ought to be fought multilaterally,[43] and to question the ambiguous formula that legitimizes

---

at 839; see also *supra* chapter 4, under the heading 'The Question of International Legality…', subheading 'Self-Defence'.

40 Construction of a Wall, *supra* note 17, para. 139.

41 *Id.*

42 Report of the Secretary-General to the Security Council on the Protection of Civilians in Armed Conflict, UN Doc. S/2004/431 (May 28, 2004), para. 16. The Report examines areas already identified by the Security Council as priorities (see SC Res. 1265 (Sept. 17, 1999) and SC Res. 1296 (April 19, 2000)), which form the basis of the ten-point platform.

43 In its resolutions, the Security Council, acting under Chapter VII of the UN Charter, 'condemns in the strongest terms all acts of terrorism irrespective of their motivation, whenever

national liberation struggle carried out 'by all available means'.[44] We need to find an answer to terrorism that is consistent with the protection of human rights and international humanitarian law,[45] which encompasses everyone and is devoid of lacunae and ambiguities.[46]

The struggle for self-determination needs to be placed in an appropriate legal framework; i.e., the human rights law. The paramount interest of the international community to safeguard human rights and to fight terrorism 'in all its forms'[47] posits a new global approach to the problems created by the use of terrorism in the fight for national liberation and armed conflicts in general. We now examine what it necessitates.

A Coherent Legal Framework Applicable to Non-State Actors

An effective legal framework should be created, based on respect for international humanitarian law/human rights law, applicable to all armed conflicts and providing for international responsibility of all parties (States, liberation movements, resistance groups, leaders) and prosecution of terrorist activities as 'grave breaches' of essential humanitarian principles. As well, protection of human rights must be central to an effective strategy to counter terrorism. It is from the principles, embodied in the Fourth 1949 Geneva Convention, and from agreed minimum standards of treatment to which people are entitled as human beings, that the UN framework for the protection of civilians in armed conflict has arisen and evolved.[48] In the

---

and by whomsoever committed, as one of the most serious threats to peace and security' (SC Res. 1566 (Oct. 8, 2004), para. 1); see also SC Res. 1530 (March 11, 2004), para. 1; SC Res. 1516 (Nov. 20, 2003), para. 1.

44 GA Res. 36/9 (Oct. 28, 1981), para. 2; GA Res. 37/43 (Dec. 3, 1982), para. 2; GA Res. 38/17 (Nov. 22, 1983), para. 2; GA Res. 39/17 (Nov. 23, 1984), para. 2; GA Res. 40/25 (Nov. 29, 1985), para. 2; GA Res. 41/101 (Dec. 4, 1986), para. 2; GA Res. 42/95 (Dec. 7, 1987), para. 2; GA Res. 46/106 (Dec. 8, 1988), para. 2; GA Res. 44/79 (Dec. 8, 1989), para. 2; GA Res. 45/130 (Dec. 14, 1990), para. 2; GA Res. 46/87 (Dec. 16, 1991), para. 2; GA Res. 47/82 (Dec. 16, 1992), para. 2; GA Res. 48/94 (Dec. 20, 1993), para. 2; see also GA Res. 26/49 (Nov. 30, 1970), para. 1.

45 M. Cherif Bassiouni, *Legal Control of International Terrorism*, 43 Harvard International Law Journal 83 (2002). See also *infra* note 62.

46 See, for its ambiguity, the Declaration of Arab League (<http://www.corriere.it/Primo_Piano/Esteri/2005/01_Gennaio/18/diario_iraq.shtml>).

47 See SC Res. 1566, *supra* note 43, preamble; see also Commission on Human Rights Resolutions on Human Rights and Terrorism (UN Docs. E/CN.4/RES/1997/42 (April 11, 1997), preamble, paras 4, 5; E/CN.4/RES/1998/47 (April 17, 1998), preamble, paras 5, 6; E/CN.4/RES/1999/27 (April 26, 1999), preamble, paras 5, 6; E/CN.4/RES/2000/30 (April 20, 2000), preamble, paras 5, 6; E/CN.4/RES/2001/37 (April 23, 2001), preamble, paras 5, 6; E/CN.4/RES/2002/35 (April 22, 2002), preamble, paras 5, 7; E/CN.4/RES/2003/37 (April 23, 2003), preamble, paras 5, 7; E/CN.4/RES/2004/44 (April 19, 2004) preamble, paras 7, 9).

48 Report of the Secretary-General to the Security Council on the Protection of Civilians in Armed Conflict, *supra* note 42. This is the fourth Report; three other Reports on the subject were presented under request of the Council (see UN Docs. S/1999/957 (Sept. 8, 1999); S/2001/331 (March 30, 2001); S/2002/1300 (Nov. 26, 2002)). See also SCR Publications,

context of the fight against terrorism, a legal basis for a proper coordinated action of the international community against those responsible for terrorist activities in armed conflicts and their sponsors (states, organizations, movements, groups, and leaders) has to be developed. In particular, rules, standard operational procedures, and sanctions regimes to fight terrorism have to be established and implemented. Such a system of international norms and collective mechanisms designed to prevent and sanction the use of terrorist methods during civil wars would sever the link between: (1) terrorism and legitimate resistance against foreign occupation; (2) terrorism and weak democracies and countries in transition; and (3) terrorism and resistance against non-democratic governments. The human rights approach to the fight against terrorism in armed conflicts makes possible international control over terrorist acts committed by groups and movements allegedly in the name of peoples. At the same time, it forestalls states' unilateral fight against terrorism in 'domestic' armed conflicts.

An Integrated Monitoring System and Action Programme

Fighting global terrorism in armed conflicts (even those qualified as 'domestic' conflicts) consistent with human rights law necessitates international monitoring not only of the force used by states, but also of the legitimacy of the means used by resistance movements. It requires a coordinated multilateral action to ensure effective implementation of measures against violations.[49] This would forestall states' unilateral actions. When fighting Chechen terrorism, Vladimir Putin's Russia cannot resort to means typical of international conflicts and invoke the concept of domestic jurisdiction. At the same time, the massacres committed by Chechens in Russia, by way of international terrorism and terrorist strategies, are large-scale human rights violations. They must be subject to the UN collective security system and international mechanisms established by 'integrated systems' safeguarding global values.[50]

Within the UN system, the Security Council should consider establishing a monitoring framework to review the conduct of parties to conflicts. This would enable it to call upon the parties to refrain from using terrorist tactics, to condemn violations, and to apply targeted measures. Consistent with the Security Council's commitment to the protection of civilians in armed conflicts, terrorism in armed conflicts could be formally placed on the Security Council's agenda and be the object of specific action. This is the case, for instance, of the issue of war-affected

---

Update Report No. 4, Protection of Civilians in Armed Conflict 16 November 2007, available at <http://www.securitycouncilreport.org/site/c.glKWLeMTIsG/b.3588183/k.1B40/Update_Report_No_4brProtection_of_Civilians_in_Armed_Conflictbr16_November_2007.htm>. On this topic see Theodor Meron, *The Humanization of Humanitarian Law*, 94 AM. J. INT'L L. 239 (2000).

49 See *Uniting Against Terrorism: Recommendations for a Global Counter-Terrorism Strategy*, Report of the Secretary-General, UN Doc. A/60/825 (April 27, 2006).

50 See *supra* note 10.

children, on which the Secretary-General has reported yearly since 1998.[51] The goal would be the establishment of an integrated system providing monitoring and accountability by way of blacklisting the parties to the conflict employing terrorist strategies and their sponsors. Such a monitoring system would involve both UN bodies and participants outside the UN system, in particular, national governments, regional organizations, and non-governmental organizations.

Appropriate integrated sanction-enforcement procedures are to be developed, as well.[52] The interaction between the UN, regional organizations, and individual states in applying sanctions against terrorists and their sponsors is to be reconsidered, especially in the light of the new prerogatives of the Security Council and the General Assembly in the fields of human rights and peace, and in consideration of the cooperation between these organs and the Court.[53]

There is also the need to improve the emerging procedures of functional integration to safeguard collective values created by new forms of institutional cooperation between UN organs, like the recent one between the Court and the Assembly, which makes it possible to bypass the impasse of Security Council caused by the permanent members. A significant precedent in this regard is the cooperation between the Court and the Assembly in the above-mentioned Israeli-Palestinian dispute. The advisory opinion, requested on the basis of the *Uniting for Peace* procedure, gave the Court the chance to carry out an 'objective determination' of violations of obligations *erga omnes* and the consequences deriving therefrom, and the Assembly the capacity to acknowledge the measures determined by the Court. The combination of ascertainment of violations of *erga omnes* obligations by way of advisory opinions, and the adoption by UN organs of coercive measures, is practice in the human rights field,[54] but it can function against terrorism in armed conflicts, as well. The prerequisites are the willingness of states, within UN organs, to distinguish between terrorism and legitimate armed resistance, and the inclusion in the Court's probing of gross violations of *erga omnes* obligations by all components of the global community, including non-state armed groups.

---

51 The third Report of the Secretary-General on the protection of civilians in armed conflict, highlighted the changing environment for the protection of civilians and, in particular, the rise of terrorism in armed conflicts (S/2002/1300 (Nov. 26, 2002)). See also the steps undertaken by the General Assembly for the effective follow-up of 'The United Nations Global Counter-Terrorism Strategy' (A/RES/60/288 (Sept. 20, 2006)). It 'decides' to invite the Secretary-General to contribute to the future deliberations of the GA on the review of the implementation and updating of the Strategy (para. 3 lett. (c)). In the Annex Plan of Action, the Members of the United Nations encourage the Secretary-General to institutionalize the Counter-Terrorism Implementation Task Force within the Secretariat (Annex III, para. 5); and invite the GA and the SC to develop guidelines for the necessary cooperation and assistance in the event of a terrorist attack using weapons of mass destruction (Annex II, para 17).

52 See *infra* note 56 and corresponding text.

53 See *supra* note 51; and chapter 3, under the headings 'Judicial Protection of Human Rights Beyond the ICJ Statute' and 'Judicial Protection of Peace Beyond the UN Charter'.

54 This happened with the construction of the wall in occupied Palestinian territories. See UN General Assembly Resolution 'acknowledging' the Advisory Opinion of the ICJ on Israel's Wall on 9 July 2004 (*supra* note 17), GA Res. A/ES–10/L.18/Rev.1 (July 20, 2004).

A System of Properly Targeted Collective Measures

Measures capable of striking organizations/groups/leaders that use terrorist tactics in armed conflicts or support terrorist activities should be wide-ranging; that is to say, linked to other sanctions against illegal activities supporting and financing terrorism. Until new forms of sanctions are introduced, effective means to undermine perpetrators of terrorist activities (movements, leaders, and non-governmental parties) could be one or more of the following measures.

The concept of 'smart sanctions'. These are constraining selective measures (such as financial sanctions, travel bans, and embargoes on weapons or specific products) pressuring particular individuals and entities, which, at the same time, minimize the negative humanitarian impact on the civilian population. The 'smart sanction' concept is central to a current scholarly debate;[55] it inspired the Security Council's sanctions programmes aimed at the prevention and repression of financing, planning, or supporting terrorist acts. Individuals and entities belonging or related to the Taliban, Osama Bin Laden, and the Al Qaeda organization are among the targets of a UN sanctions programme aimed at blocking funds or 'freezing' assets supporting global terrorism.[56] The Security Council maintained a list of individuals/entities for this purpose and established a Committee charged to oversee the implementation by states of the sanctions imposed.[57] The Taliban/Al Qaeda sanctions regime is a key instrument in the fight against terrorism. This Security Council action is particularly significant in the context of the organization of the global community. By adopting measures against non-state actors, the Security Council went beyond the UN enforcement system, for the Charter confers upon the Council only the power to take measures against states. The Security Council acted as an organ of the global human society. In the light of this experience, these kinds of measures are to be developed,[58] and the various problems created to all involved in their implementation need to be resolved. For instance, within the European Union, the implementation of these sanctions has created problems.[59] Targeted economic sanctions and embargoes

55 Peter Fitzgerald, *Managing 'Smart Sanctions' Against Terrorism Wisely*, 36 New England Law Review 957 (2002).

56 Under SC sanctions regime, all states are obliged to freeze the assets, prevent the entry into or the transit through their territories, and prevent the direct or indirect supply, sale, and transfer of arms and military equipment with regard to the individuals, entities, or groups involved in or associated with terrorist activities. See SC Res. 1267 (Oct. 15, 1999), para. 4(b); SC Res. 1333 (Dec. 19, 2000), para. 8 (c); SC Res. 1373, *supra* note 37, para. 1; SC Res. 1390 (Jan. 16, 2002), paras 1, 2; SC Res. 1455 (Jan. 17, 2003), preamble, para. 1; SC Res. 1526 (Jan. 30, 2004), para. 1. The Security Council has established Committees to monitor the implementation of these resolutions (SC Res. 1267, *supra*, para. 6; SC Res. 1373, *supra* note 37, para. 6; SC Res. 1540 (April 28, 2004), para. 4.

57 SC Res. 1267, *supra* note 56, para. 6.

58 See, in this direction, SC Res. 1566, *supra* note 43, para. 9.

59 See the objections raised within the EU on the application of measures against terrorism adopted by the Security Council in the Case T–306/01 (Abdirisak Aden, Abdulaziz Ali, Ahmed Yusuf, and Al Barakaat International Foundation v. Council of the European

have also been used by the Security Council and regional organizations[60] against liberation movements (e.g., against UNITA, to compel it to cooperate with the peace process[61]). Any counter-terrorism measures must be in accordance with international human rights law and recognized international standards,[62] as well as fundamental principles of necessity and proportionality.[63] Some UN Human Rights bodies have expressed concern that counter-terrorism measures (i.e., the multiplication of policies, legislation, and practices increasingly being adopted by many countries in the name of the fight against terrorism) may affect the enjoyment of non-derogable human rights – civil, cultural, economic, political, and social.[64]

Political-diplomatic measures. The denial of recognition of national liberation movements is a sanction that ought to be explored and developed. In international practice, organized groups fighting against foreign occupation, colonial and racist regimes, are recognized, *de jure* or *de facto*, by the UN, by regional international organizations, and/or states as 'legitimate representatives' of peoples entitled to self-determination. Consequently, they have *locus standi* in the international community as beneficiaries of the norms ensuring self-determination. These norms make legal otherwise illegal states' actions (for instance states' granting economic and military assistance and/or logistical or military bases). Further, these movements often establish political/diplomatic relations with states and international organizations.

Union and Commission of the European Communities), Order (May 7, 2002), 2002 ECR II–2387.

60 See, e.g., SC Res. 917 (May 6, 1994) on the situation in Haiti; SC Res. 1054 (April 24, 1996) on the situation in Sudan; SC Res. 1132 (Oct. 8, 1997) and SC Res. 1171 (June 5, 1998) on the situation in Sierra Leone; SC Res. 1483 (May 22, 2003) and SC Res. 1518 (Nov. 24, 2003) on the situation in Iraq; and recently, SC Res. 1803 (March 3, 2008) concerning individuals engaged in Iran's proliferation sensitive nuclear activities. For the EU, see: Regulation (EC) No. 1705 (July 28, 1998) and Council Regulation (EC) No. 146/2003 (Jan. 27, 2003) against UNITA and Regulation (EC) No. 1294 (June 15, 1999), Council Regulation (EC) No. 2488 (Nov. 10, 2000) against individuals/entities related to Milosevic.

61 SC Res. 864 (Sept. 15 1993); SC Res. 1127 (Aug. 28, 1997); SC Res. 1130 (Sept. 29, 1997); SC Res. 1173 (June 12, 1998); SC Res. 1176 (June 24, 1998).

62 See generally SC Res. 1373, *supra* note 37, para. 3(f); SC Res. 1456 (Jan. 20, 2003), para. 6; SC Res. 1566, *supra* note 43, preamble; GA Res. 48/122 (Feb. 14, 1994), preamble, para. 2; GA Res. 49/183 (Oct. 26, 1995), preamble, para. 3; GA Res. 50/186 (March 6, 1996), preamble, paras 3, 4; GA Res. 52/133 (Feb. 28, 1998), preamble, paras 4, 5; GA Res. 54/164 (Feb. 24, 2000), preamble, paras 4, 5; GA Res. 56/180 (Feb. 13, 2002), para. 1; GA Res. 57/219 (Feb. 27, 2003), preamble, para. 2; GA Res. 58/187 (Dec. 22, 2003), preamble, paras 1, 4, 7; GA Res. 58/174 (March 10, 2004), preamble, paras 6, 7, 9; see also the Reports of the Secretary-General to the General Assembly, UN Docs. A/50/685 (Oct. 26, 1995); A/54/439 (Oct. 6, 1999); A/56/190 (July 17, 2001), A/58/533 (Oct. 24, 2003); *Digest of Jurisprudence of the UN and Regional Organizations on the Protection of Human Rights While Countering Terrorism*, available at <http://www.unhchr.ch/html/menu6/2/digest.doc>.

63 UN Docs. A/58/266 (Aug. 8, 2003), para. 31; A/59/404 (Oct. 1, 2004), paras 11, 20.

64 UN Doc. E/CN.4/2004/4 (Aug. 5, 2003), Annex 1; see also UN Docs. E/CN.4/RES/2003/37, *supra* note 47, and E/CN.4/RES/2003/68 (April 25, 2003)). See Report of Secretary-General, *supra* note 49, Section VI, para. 112.

The denial of recognition would deprive national liberation movements responsible for terrorist acts of the benefits of international cooperation.[65]

Amongst political measures, greater consideration should be given to the possibility of holding armed groups, which aspire to be incorporated in the new state's structures, accountable for past behaviour against civilians and violations of humanitarian law. Groups that have been involved in gross human rights violations should be excluded from new governmental structures. For instance, in Resolution 1648 (2003) on the Democratic Republic of Congo, the Security Council asked the parties involved in the conflict to take into account respect for human rights in selecting individuals to be placed in the key positions of the transitional government.[66]

An International Judicial System for the Prosecution and Punishment of Terrorists

This objective has not yet been completely achieved. The Statute of the International Criminal Tribunal for Rwanda includes terrorist acts amongst the 'serious violations of Article 3 common to the Geneva Convention of 12 August 1949 for the Protection of War Victims, and of Additional Protocol II thereto of 8 June 1977'.[67] Yet, the omission of international terrorism *per se* from the list of crimes under the International Criminal Courts' jurisdiction might have serious consequences. It makes it difficult for the Security Council to refer situations to the Prosecutor for investigation under Article 13 (b) of the Rome Statute,[68] where national jurisdictions are unwilling or unable to act. Besides, as the International Court of Justice held in the *Arrest Warrant* case, while immunity of jurisdiction for incumbent state officials who have committed core crimes can be invoked in cases of foreign national prosecution,[69] it cannot be invoked in cases of international prosecution.[70] Hopefully, the 2009 Rome Statute Review Conference, provided for by Article 23 of the Court's Statute, will fill this gap, as recommended in the final resolutions of the 1998 Rome

65 Giuliana Ziccardi Capaldo, Terrorismo Internazionale e Garanzie Collettive/International Terrorism and Collective Guarantees 136 (1990). The Palestine Liberation Organization (PLO) enjoys the status of special observer in the work of the General Assembly (UN Doc. A/INF/59/4/Add.1 (Dec. 14, 2004)), together with other advantages, after the proclamation of the State of Palestine in 1988, and participates in Security Council sessions according to Art. 31 of the Charter.

66 SC Res. 1468 (March 20, 2003), para. 4.

67 ICTR Statute, Art. 4 (d) (SC Res. 955 (Nov. 8, 1994)).

68 Rome Statute of the International Criminal Court, UN Doc. A/CONF.183/9 (July 17, 1998) Art. 13 (b) (available at <http://untreaty.un.org/cod/icc/statute/romefra.htm>).

69 In a recent Declaration on the issue of combating terrorism, the Security Council decided that 'States must bring to justice those who finance, plan, support or commit terrorist acts or provide safe havens, in accordance with international law, in particular on the basis of the principle to extradite or prosecute' (SC Res. 1456, *supra* note 62, para. 3).

70 Case Concerning the Arrest Warrant of 11 April 2000 (Democratic Republic of the Congo v. Belgium), Judgment, 2002 ICJ Reports 3 (Feb. 14, 2002), para. 61; see also *supra* chapter 3, under the heading 'The Court's "Authority" Over State Organs'.

Conference.[71] The possibility of establishing an international fund to compensate victims of terrorist acts and their families is a concern of the Security Council.[72]

Concluding Remarks: A Comprehensive and Integrated Approach to the Fight Against Terrorism

In conclusion, terrorism must be attacked at its roots, by addressing the causes. Sanctions alone are not sufficient to eliminate terrorism. Integrated processes of negotiated solution of armed conflicts should be planned and set up. The International Court of Justice called the attention of UN organs to foster efforts to resolve the Israeli–Palestinian crisis on the basis of the Road Map.[73] By doing this, the Court underlined the need for a renewed spirit of cooperation between UN organs and states, and the need of integrated processes, under UN aegis, to resolve international crises.

This comprehensive and integrated approach to the problem of effective eradication of terrorism in armed conflicts is innovative and may yield results in the fight against global terrorism.

---

71 UN Doc. A/CONF. 183/10 (July 17, 1998).

72 SC Res. 1566, *supra* note 43, para. 10. *See* M. Cherif Bassiouni, *The Right to Restitution, Compensation, and Rehabilitation for Victims of Gross Violations of Human Rights and Fundamental Freedoms*, UN Doc. E/CN.4/2000/62 (Jan. 16, 2000). *See also Guidelines on Reparations for Victims of Human Rights Violations, Prohibiting Torture, Combating Defamation of Religions among Other Issues*, GA/10437 (Dec. 16, 2005).

73 Construction of a Wall, *supra* note 17, para. 139, at 200.

Chapter 9

The UN Counter-Terrorism System

Introduction

The central position that the individual has come to assume in the current global legal order has led to an expansion of the international systems safeguarding human rights, with a consequent evolution in enforcement mechanisms. The responsibility for violations of human rights and humanitarian law is charged not only to countries themselves but also to new actors. The individual perpetrators of *crimina juris gentium* are considered responsible at an international level.[1] International criminal courts have been set up to pass judgment on and to sentence criminals, and forms of targeted sanctions, of an economic-administrative nature, aimed at depriving or reducing the benefits an individual may enjoy from personal liberties (freedom of movement, patrimony, etc.) have been established by the UN and by states themselves against single individuals, entities, and groups (i.e., smart sanctions).[2]

We are coming from a traditional inter-state, inorganic-egalitarian perspective – which, emphasizing the sovereignty of states and their legal equality, configured the system of implementation of international law-enforcement as a system capable of functioning between the offended state and the offending state, exclusively on the basis of 'equality' – to an organic and vertical global law-enforcement system.[3] Current sanctions systems subject individuals 'directly' to international law and make them answerable to international bodies. They also see individuals making direct use of means of safeguarding their rights before judicial or quasi-judicial bodies; that is to say, having the right to be awarded damages though an evaluation of the damage suffered at an international level.

---

1 *See* M. Cherif Bassiouni, *Accountability for Violations of International Humanitarian Law and Other Serious Violations of Human Rights*, 1 The Global Community. Yearbook of International Law and Jurisprudence 3 (Giuliana Ziccardi Capaldo ed., 2001) [hereinafter GCYILJ].

2 As to the UN, see SC Res. 864 (Sept. 15, 1993); SC Res. 917 (May 6, 1994); SC Res. 1132 (Oct. 8, 1997); SC Res. 1267 (Oct. 15, 1999); SC Res. 1333 (Dec. 19, 2000); SC Res. 1390 (Jan. 16, 2002); SC Res. 1483 (May 22, 2003); SC Res. 1803 (March 3, 2008). As to the EU, see Council Regulation (EC) No. 1081/2000 of 22 May 2000, *Official Journal L 122, 24.5.2000, at 29–38;* Council Regulation (EC) No. 2488/2000 of 10 November 2000, *Official Journal L 287, 14.11.2000, at 19–37;* Council Regulation (EC) No. 2580/2001 of 27 December 2001, *Official Journal L 344, 28.12.2001, at 70–75;* Council Regulation (EC) No. 310/2002 of 18 February 2002, *Official Journal L 50, 21.2.2002, at 4–12;* Council Regulation (EC) No. 881/2002 of 27 May 2002, *Official Journal L 139, 29.5.2002, at 9–22.*

3 Giuliana Ziccardi Capaldo, *The Law of the Global Community: An Integrated System to Enforce 'Public' International Law*, 1 GCYILJ 71 (2001).

The safeguarding of human rights involves individuals more and more as injured parties and actors on an international stage. This trend, which is also becoming consolidated at a regional level, does not always prove to be coherent in practice and within global sanctions systems. We refer to those regimes established by international bodies that exercise public and coercive power directly on individuals, operating as imposers of sanctions of an administrative nature.[4]

The most advanced sanctions system of this type, both because of its noted institutionalization and by its worldwide coercion, is that instituted by the Security Council (SC), with resolutions adopted under Chapter VII of the UN Charter, which is intended to prevent and suppress all acts of terrorism wherever and by whomever committed and which obliges 'all' countries (therefore, not only those that are members of the UN) to cooperate against terrorism and to adopt measures denying terrorists and related entities financial support (freezing funds and other financial assets or economic resources) and denying terrorists access to travel, including flight restrictions and others. The basic Resolution 1267 (1999)[5] and subsequent resolutions 1333[6] and 1390[7] created a complex structure, through the institution of subsidiary bodies of the Security Council –i.e., the Sanctions Committee Concerning Al-Qaeda and the Taliban and Associated Individuals and Entities ('Sanctions Committee')[8] and the Monitoring Group[9] – which were charged with: preparing and updating periodically, with the help of international organizations (regional and sub-regional) and countries themselves, the 'UN List' of suspected individuals and entities belonging to or associated with the Taliban and Al-Qaeda Organization;[10] receiving the reports presented by individual states on the enactment of sanctions and examining petitions for exemption on humanitarian grounds, drafting periodic reports to send to the Security Council,[11] assisting national states in applying these self-same sanctions, as well as supporting the SC in exercising functions of control over the relevant activities of each state.

Subsequent and reiterated SC resolutions gradually extended the initial personal and spatial limits (Afghan territory controlled by the Taliban) established by Resolution 1267/99, as the terrorist acts committed by the Al Qaeda group operating in Afghanistan extended its deadly actions to the whole world. After the bloody

4 *See supra* note 2.

5 SC Res. 1267, *supra* note 2.

6 SC Res. 1333, *supra* note 2.

7 SC Res. 1390, *supra* note 2.

8 See SC Res. 1267, *supra* note 2, para. 4; SC Res. 1333, *supra* note 2, paras 5 (a), 8 (c); SC Res. 1390, *supra* note, para. 2.

9 See SC Res. 1363 (July 30, 2001), paras 3, 4; SC Res. 1390, *supra* note 2, para. 9; SC Res. 1455 (Jan. 17, 2003), para. 8.

10 UN List of Individuals and Entities Belonging to or Associated with the Taliban and Al-Qaeda Organization, available at <http://www.un.org/Docs/sc/committees/1267/1267ListEng.htm>.

11 See Guidelines of the Security Council Committee established pursuant to Resolution 1267 (1999) concerning Al-Qaeda and the Taliban and associated individuals and entities for the conduct of its work (adopted on 7 November 2002, as amended on 10 April 2003 and revised on 21 December 2005) [hereinafter Guidelines], section 5.

events of 11 September 2001, Resolution 1373 represents an important turn in the broadening of the SC's strategy against terrorism: the SC, obliging states to adopt further counter-terrorism measures, recommended respect for 'international standards of human rights',[12] emphasizing the need to coordinate forces at national, sub-regional, regional, and international levels 'in order to strengthen a global response' to the threat of terrorism.[13]

The sphere of spatial and personal activity relating to initial counter-terrorism measures has gradually evolved and has been perfected into the system that exists today. It affects 'all' states and subjects all persons 'who commit or attempt to commit'[14] acts of terrorism and the entities that control them, wherever they may operate, to the sanctions regime. As far as the structure is concerned, it has been imbued with the characteristics of a world-integrated system in which the participants are the UN, states themselves, and international governmental and non-governmental organizations, etc. The current system is centred on the SC, which is the flywheel of the system, with coordinating and controlling functions, supported in these roles by *ad hoc*-created bodies with binding resolutions (the Sanctions Committee,[15] the Counter-Terrorism Committee (CTC),[16] the Counter-Terrorism Committee Executive Directorate (CTED)[17], and Monitoring Team[18] which replaced the Monitoring Group for the application of Sanctions.

This enforcement system, not only from an institutional point of view but also for its sphere of application, was conceived of to harmonize an integrated cosmopolitan vision of the global legal order and to modernize the development of the safeguarding of human rights.

Nevertheless, the UN counter-terrorism system lacks an independent, international body whose task it is to decide, in law and in fact, on petitions brought by individuals against decisions pertaining to them adopted by the SC and the Sanctions Committee. The Sanctions Committee is in fact responsible for the regular updating of the list of persons and entities whose funds must be frozen pursuant to SC decisions. SC resolutions foresee a periodic re-examination of the general sanctions regime[19] and have set up a procedure for re-examining individual cases by the Sanctions Committee (for the purpose of having the person concerned removed from the list of persons affected by the sanctions, in other words a de-listing procedure), basing itself on the institution of diplomatic protection and enabled through the mediation of the Member

12 SC Res. 1373 (Sept. 28, 2001), para. 3 (f).

13 *Id.*, at para. 4.

14 SC Res. 1373, *supra* note 12, para. 1 (c), (d).

15 See *supra* note 8 and corresponding text.

16 The CTC was instituted with Resolution 1373 (SC Res. 1373, *supra* note 12, para. 6) and is supported by the Counter-Terrorism Committee Executive Directorate (SC Res. 1535 (March 26, 2004), para. 2).

17 *Id.*

18 See SC Res. 1526 (Jan. 30, 2004), para. 6; SC Res. 1617 (July 29, 2005), para. 19, Annex I.

19 See SC Res. 1333, *supra* note 2, para. 23; SC Res. 1526, *supra* note 18, para. 3; SC Res. 1617, *supra* note 18, para. 21.

State of the individual's nationality or country of residence.[20] The *Guidelines of the Sanctions Committee* ('the Guidelines') provides that a petitioner (individual(s), groups, enterprises, and/or entities on the 1267 Committee's consolidated list) may petition the government of residence and/or citizenship to request review of the case. In this circumstance, the petitioner should provide justification for the de-listing request, offer relevant information and request support for de-listing. If, after reviewing any additional information, the petitioned government wishes to pursue a de-listing request, it should submit jointly or separately a request for de-listing to the Sanctions Committee. The Committee will reach decisions by consensus of its members. If consensus cannot be reached even after further consultations, the matter may be submitted to the SC.[21]

Even recent actions taken which were supposed to improve this mechanism have been shown to be inadequate. On 29 November 2006, the Sanctions Committee amended the Guidelines regarding inclusion in these lists and asked individual states for more detailed information on the listing of individuals and entities.[22] Furthermore, the Security Council, with its resolution of 19 December 2006 has created a mechanism whereby those persons wishing to present de-listing petitions directly may do so to a 'focal point' of the UN Secretariat.[23] In any case, removal from the list requires the consensus of all the governments present in the Committee.[24] Petitioners seeking to submit a request for de-listing can do so either through the focal point process outlined below or through their state of residence or citizenship.[25]

Obviously, this is a procedure that is still anchored to the traditional, inter-state vision of international law and one that excludes the subjectivity of individuals and their capacity to act on an international level and make use of legal means of recourse directly. The mechanism is badly suited to achieving effective safeguards over an individual's basic human rights, both in substance and procedural terms – something which the new approach to international human rights safeguards wishes to ensure.

This UN sanctions system, which is being perfected, poses obvious problems of legitimacy. Some objections regarding the legitimacy of the system, as well as the lawfulness of the measures meted out against them have already been raised by certain affected individuals who have raised challenges; in other words, alleging infringement of the right to a defence, the right to effective judicial protection, the right of access to documents, and the right of property before the Court of First Instance of the European Communities (CFIEC).

---

20 See Guidelines, *supra* note 11, section 8, entitled 'De-listing'.

21 *Id.*, at section 8 (e).

22 See Report of the Security Council Committee established pursuant to resolution 1267 (1999) concerning Al-Qaida and the Taliban and associated individuals and entities, UN Doc. S/2007/59 (Feb. 7, 2007), para. 9.

23 SC Res. 1730 (Dec. 19, 2006), para. 1, Annex. The Security Council requested the Secretary-General to establish, within the Secretariat (Security Council Subsidiary Organs Branch), a focal point to receive de-listing requests.

24 See Chia Lehnardt, *European Court Rules on UN and EU Terrorist Suspect Blacklists*, ASIL Insight (Jan. 31, 2007), Vol. 11, Issue 1, available at <http://www.asil.org/insights/2007/01/insights070131.html>, Paragraph III.

25 SC Res. 1730 *supra* note 23, Annex.

The European Union has given effect to the UN sanctions regime through certain acts: the European Community institutions, among them the CFIEC, have had great difficulty in applying Security Council counter-terrorism measures and reconciling such SC decisions with mechanisms of guarantee to which they are accustomed.[26] The CFIEC, which was asked to grant relief in the form of annulment of the restrictive measures imposed upon certain individuals by Community Regulations enacted to accomplish SC resolutions in the struggle against terrorism,[27] issued important statements on this issue.[28] Such sentences were the subject of doctrinal works and comments of legal scholars.[29]

The following pages will discuss the legitimacy of the counter-terrorism system set up by the SC and to shed some light on it, taking into account the issue of the conditions under which a *lex specialis* rule may derogate from a universal one (see next section). The world community has great expectations for the future of a global legal order providing for security, stability, economic well-being, justice, and the protection of fundamental human rights. These rights need to be safeguarded, even in

---

26 Paolo Mengozzi, *Court of First Instance and Court of Justice of the European Communities Introductory Note, The European Union Balance of Powers and the Case Law Related to EC External Relations*, 6 GCYILJ 817 (2006–II), at 827–830.

27 The SC's resolutions directed against the Islamic terrorist network of Al Qaeda (SC Res. 1267, *supra* note 2; SC Res. 1333, *supra* note 2; SC Res. 1390, *supra* note 2) have been implemented with the Council of the European Union's Regulation No. 881 of 2002, *supra* note 2; Resolution 1373 was adopted with Council Common Position 2001/931/PESC (Council Common Position 931/2001 of 27 December 2001 on the application of specific measures to combat terrorism, *Official Journal L 344, 28.12.2001, at 93–96)* and with Regulation No. 2580/2001, *supra* note 2. See also Regulations No. 1081, No. 2488, and No. 310, *supra* note 2. As for the EU, Cfr. Mengozzi, *supra* note 26, at 828.

28 Segi, Araitz Zubimendi Izaga, Aritza Galarraga v. Council of the European Union, Case T–338/02, Order, 7 June 2004, 2004 ECR II-1647; Case C-355/04 P, Judgment, 27 February 2007, 2007 ECR I-1657; Jose Maria Sison v. Council of the European Union, Joined Cases T-110/03, T-150/03 and T-405/03, Judgment, 26 April 2005, 2005 ECR II-1429; Ahmed Ali Yusuf and Al Barakaat International Foundation v. Council of the European Union and Commission of the European Communities, Case T–306/01, Judgment of 21 September 2005, 2005 ECR II–3533; Yassin Abdullah Kadi v. Council of the European Union and Commission of the European Communities, Case T–315/01, Judgment of 21 September 2005, 2005 ECR II–3649; Chafiq Ayadi v. Council of the European Union, Case T–253/02, Judgment of 12 July 2006, 2006 ECR II–2139; Faraj Hassan v. Council of the European Union, Case T–49/04, Judgment of 12 July 2006, 2006 ECR II–52*; Organisation des Modjahedines du Peuple d'Iran, v. Council of the European Union, Case T–228/02, Judgment of 12 December 2006, 2006 ECR II–4665.

29 See August Reinisch, *Introductory Note to Court of First Instance of the European Communities: Yassin Abdullah Kadi v. Council of the European Union and Commission of the European Communities*, 45 International Legal Materials 77 (2006); Christian Tomuschat, *Case T–306/01, Ahmed Ali Yusuf and Al Barakaat International Foundation v. Council and Commission, Judgment of the Court of First Instance of 21 September 2005; Case T–315/01, Yassin Abdullah Kadi v. Council and Commission, Judgment of the Court of First Instance of 21 September 2005*, 43 Common Market Law Review 537 (2006); Giuliana Ziccardi Capaldo & Michele Nino, *Globalization of Law Enforcement Mechanisms: Issues of Legality and Legitimacy*, in International Criminal Law (3rd ed., M. Cherif Bassiouni ed., forthcoming).

the struggle against terrorism. This is, after all, the aim of the strong statements made in support of safeguarding human rights standards in combating terrorism contained in many acts of UN organs (General Assembly,[30] the Commission and Committee for Human Rights, and also the SC) (see under the heading 'Non-Derogable Human Rights Norms …'). What is needed is an optimization of the current system in terms of the balance between the counter-terrorism measures and human rights safeguards (see under the heading 'The Lack of Respect …'). The global vision of the UN sanctions regime needs global review mechanisms. It is necessary to build and implement a broad strategic plan based on the rule of law, justice, and human rights, combining mechanisms and regulations to combat terrorism together with a system of judicial safeguards at various levels (national, sub-regional, regional, and universal) to develop and implement this process (see the two sections thereafter).

Special Treaty-Regimes *vis-à-vis* General International Law: Is the Security Council Permitted to Derogate to Key Human Rights?

The UN counter-terrorism system poses questions about both its value with respect to general international law and its compatibility with other legal systems (mainly EC systems).

This chapter does not deal with the relationship between the UN system and the EC order. The question now under discussion of the legitimacy of the UN system against terrorism falls under the more general question of the relationship between general and special law, namely, the conditions under which a *lex specialis* rule may derogate from a universal one. The term *lex specialis* rule is here understood as a rule belonging to special treaty regimes – a special set of secondary rules, or a special branch of international law with its own principles, institutions, and system for dispute settlement, as well as an enforcement system to sanction violations – called 'self-contained regimes'[31] or 'sub-systems'.[32] Our attention is drawn to the question of the relationship between general international law and the special counter-terrorism regime created by the SC under Chapter VII of the UN Charter,[33] as a question of the ability of this regime to derogate from general international law.

30 GA Res. 57/219 (Dec. 18, 2002); GA Res. 58/187 (Dec. 22, 2003); GA Res. 59/191 (Dec. 20, 2004); GA Res. 60/1 (Sept. 16, 2005); GA Res. 60/158 (Dec. 16, 2005).

31 United States Diplomatic and Consular Staff in Tehran (United States of America v. Iran), Merits, Judgment, 1980 ICJ Reports 3 (May 24, 1980), para. 86, at 41. See also Giuliana Ziccardi Capaldo, Repertory of Decisions of the International Court of Justice/ Répertoire de la Jurisprudence de la Cour internationale de Justice (1947–1992), 2 vols, (1995) [hereinafter Repertory], vol. I, No. 1061, at 61.

32 See Third Report on the content, forms and degrees of international responsibility (Part Two of the draft articles on State Responsibility), by Mr Willem Riphagen, Special Rapporteur of the International Law Commission, A/CN.4/354 and Corr.1 and Add.1 & 2 (12 and 30 March and 5 May 1982), para. 54; see also Third Report on State responsibility, by Mr Gaetano Arangio-Ruiz, Special Rapporteur of the International Law Commission, A/ CN.4/440 and Add.1 (19 July 1991), para. 84, note 167.

33 Report of the International Law Commission, 57th Session (2 May–3 June and 11 July–5 August 2005), A/60/10, para. 459.

The discussion concerning the universality or fragmentation of international law is at the centre of a doctrinal debate[34] and holds the attention of the International Law Commission (ILC).[35]

In the *Yusuf* and *Kady* cases,[36] the CFIEC adopted a stance on the question of the universality of international law. The Court has considered *jus cogens* 'as a body of higher rules of public international law binding on all subjects of international law, including the bodies of the UN, and from which no derogation is possible'.[37] In the Court's opinion, there cannot be self-contained regimes; nor sub-systems exempting from mandatory *jus cogens* principles, so that even the SC's powers of sanction in the exercise of responsibility under UN Chapter VII 'must therefore be wielded in compliance with international law'.[38]

These conclusions reinforce our vision of an integrated and vertically structured global legal system.[39] The Court's opinion about the hierarchical superiority of *jus cogens* norms, to which all legal systems at various levels, national, regional, and universal (including the UN system) must submit, comfortably supports the widespread opinion, even among international lawyers, of the universality and unity of general international law,[40] through the empire of its universal principles of *jus cogens*. Structurally, the verticality of the global system is ensured by the central position of the UN with regard to other international organizations (under Chapter VIII, UN Charter) and by the primacy of the obligations assumed on the basis of the Charter (pursuant to Article 103). This brings about both the supremacy of SC decisions over obligations set by other treaty-regimes or sub-systems, in the event of conflict,[41] and the fact that not only do the Member States' organs themselves have to

---

34 Martti Koskenniemi & Päivi Leino, *Fragmentation of International Law? Postmodern Anxieties*, 15 Leiden Journal of International Law 553 (2002); Matthew Craven, *Unity, Diversity and the Fragmentation of International Law*, 14 The Finnish Yearbook of International Law 3 (2003); Gerhard Hafner, *Pros and Cons Ensuing from Fragmentation of International Law*, 25 Michigan Journal of International Law 849 (2004); Karel Wellens, *Fragmentation of International Law and Establishing an Accountability Regime for International Organizations. The Role of the Judiciary in Closing the Gap*, *id.*, at 1159.

35 See Report of the International Law Commission, 55th session (5 May–6 June and 7 July–8 August 2003), A/58/10, para. 429; Report of the International Law Commission, 56th session (3 May–4 June and 5 July–6 August 2004), A/59/10, para. 303; Report of the International Law Commission, 57th Session, *supra* note 33, paras 462, 466.

36 See *supra* note 28.

37 Case T–306/01, *supra* note 28, para. 277; Case T–315/01, *supra* note 28, para. 226.

38 Case T–306/01, *supra* note 28, para. 280; Case T–315/01, *supra* note 28, para. 229.

39 Giuliana Ziccardi Capaldo, *Editorial. A New Dimension of International Law: The Global Law*, 5 GCYILJ xvi (2005–I).

40 See Robert Y. Jennings, *Universal International Law in a Multicultural World*, *in* International Law and The Grotian Heritage: A Commemorative Colloquium on the occasion of the fourth centenary of the birth of Hugo Grotius 187 (1985).

41 See Arts 53, 64, Vienna Convention on the Law of Treaties (May 23, 1969); Questions of Interpretation and Application of the 1971 Montreal Convention arising from the Aerial Incident at Lockerbie (Libyan Arab Jamahiriya v. United Kingdom), Provisional Measures, Order, 1992 ICJ Reports 3 (April 14, 1992), para. 37, at 14–15; Questions of Interpretation and Application of the 1971 Montreal Convention arising from the Aerial Incident at Lockerbie

give effect to these decisions but so do international organizations and their bodies. The result is an integrated structure of global legal order and its organization into concentric circles, described in previous writings,[42] within which the various legal systems (national, sub-regional, regional, international/global), ordered hierarchically and subordinated between themselves, are dominated by the system of the Charter from a legal and structural point of view, all of which (including the UN system and its bodies), in turn, is subject to the supreme principles of global law (*jus cogens*). The CFIEC itself has affirmed that we must reject the view that the Community legal order 'is a legal order independent of the United Nations, governed by its own rules of law'.[43] According to the Court, 'the Community may not infringe the obligations imposed on its Member States by the Charter of the United Nations;'[44] even though such an obligation derives from the same EC Treaty rather than directly from general international law.[45] Undoubtedly, community law and bodies (as well as the UN system and the SC) are subject to *jus cogens*.

The verticality of the global system poses problems of coordination between various different legal systems, and many of these emerged during the enactment of SC resolutions through Community acts.[46] The CFIEC has pointed out, amongst other things, the inability of jurisdictional bodies belonging to treaty-regimes (and its own inability) to verify the legitimacy of SC decisions and reached the conclusion that it is empowered to check, 'indirectly,' the legitimacy of the resolutions of the SC with 'exclusive' regard to *jus cogens*.[47] This conclusion is accentuated by the statement that the UN Charter lacks an organ that is expressly entitled to verify the lawfulness of binding acts of the SC with regard to the Charter itself and to general international law.[48]

This favourable opinion of admitting the application of *jus cogens* to self-contained regimes represents a highly evolved trend of the judicial international bodies entitled to solve these controversies in such treaties. The European Court of Human Rights (ECHR), in a general statement of principle, declared that the European Convention on Human Rights 'should be interpreted as far as possible in harmony with other principles of international law of which it forms part'.[49] Likewise,

---

(Libyan Arab Jamahiriya v. United States of America), Provisional Measures, Order, 1992 ICJ Reports 114 (April 14, 1992), para. 42, at 126. *See also* Repertory, *supra* note 31, vol. I, No. 1496, at 521.

42 See Giuliana Ziccardi Capaldo, *Treaty Law and National Law in a Globalizing System*, 2 GCYILJ 139 (2002–I).

43 Case T–315/01, *supra* note 28, para. 208.

44 Case T–306/01, *supra* note 28, para. 254; Case T–315/01, *supra* note 28, para. 204.

45 '[I]t is not under general international law [...] but by virtue of the EC Treaty itself, that the Community was required to give effect to the Security Council resolutions [...].' See Case T–306/01, *supra* note 28, para. 257; Case T–315/01, *supra* note 28, para. 207.

46 See *supra* 'Introduction' in this chapter, notes 26–29 and corresponding text.

47 Case T–306/01, *supra* note 28, paras 272, 276; Case T–315/01, *supra* note 28, paras 221, 225.

48 Case T–306/01, *supra* note 28, para. 345; Case T–315/01, *supra* note 28, para. 290.

49 Vlastimir and Borka Bankovic, Zivana Stojanovic, Mirjana Stoimenovski, Dragana Joksimovic and Dragan Sukovic v. Belgium, The Czech Republic, Denmark, France, Germany,

and before the ECHR, the European Court of Justice (ECJ) stated that '... the rules of customary international law ... are binding upon the Community institutions and form part of the Community legal order'.[50] In the same way, the judicial bodies of the WTO questioned the legitimacy of behaviour by Member States, justified by safeguarding intransgressible global values and interests, even in cases where this brought about a limitation of the objectives of the Treaty and the use of measures that were incompatible with WTO rulings.[51] This trend is highlighted by that famous and fundamental statement emanating from the WTO's appellate body, according to which Treaty regulations 'should not be read in clinical isolation from public international law'.[52]

In conclusion, treaty-regimes are abandoning the idea of self-sufficient systems, based on 'internal' rules and guarantee mechanisms, with the exclusion of 'external' rules of general international law. The construction of a global community guaranteed by a minimum of absolutely non-derogable norms, which are binding on all, is now a constant of the international jurisprudence; today, 'systemic integration' is an increasingly accepted principle of international jurisprudence and legal interpretation.[53] With reference to human rights, the International Court of Justice (ICJ) stated that:

> 'The superior rules of international law falling within the ambit of *jus cogens* have been observed, in particular, the mandatory provisions concerning the universal protection of human rights, from which neither the Member States nor the bodies of the UN may derogate because they constitute 'intransgressible principles of international customary law'.[54]

These conclusions are also echoed by the President of the ILC, according to whom these regimes do not constitute 'closed legal circuits;'[55] he observed that 'the term

---

Greece, Hungary, Iceland, Italy, Luxembourg, the Netherlands, Norway, Poland, Portugal, Spain, Turkey and the United Kingdom, Application No. 52207/99, Decision on Admissibility (Dec. 12, 2001), Eur. Ct. H. R. Reports of Judgments and Decisions 2001–XII, para. 57.

50 A. Racke GmbH & Co. v. Hauptzollamt Mainz, Case C–162/96, Judgment of 16 June 1998, 1998 ECR I–3655, para. 46.

51 Appellate Body Report, United States Import Prohibition of Certain Shrimps and Shrimp Products, 12 October 1998, WT/DS58/AB/R, paras 152–153.

52 Appellate Body Report, United States Standards for Reformulated and Conventional Gasoline, 29 April 1996, WT/DS2/AB/R, para. 182. See Gabrielle Marceau, *A Call for Coherence in International Law, Praises for the Prohibition Against 'Clinical Isolation' in WTO Dispute Settlement*, 33 Journal of World Trade 87 (1999).

53 Report of the International Law Commission, 56th session, *supra* note 35, para. 321.

54 Legality of the Threat or Use of Nuclear Weapons, Advisory Opinion, 1996–I ICJ Reports 226 (July 8, 1996), para. 79, at 226. See also, to that effect, Advocate General Jacobs's Opinion in Case C–84/95, Bosphorus Hava Yollari Turizm ve Ticaret AS v. Minister for Transport, Energy and Communications and Others, para. 65.

55 Report of the International Law Commission, 56th session, *supra* note 35, para. 317; see also the Report of the Study Group Chairman, Mr. Martti Koskenniemi, on 'Study on the Function and Scope of the *lex specialis* rule and the question of "self-contained regimes"' (ILC(LVI)/SG/FIL/CRD.1 (7 May 2004) and Add.1 (4 May 2004)).

"self-contained" was a misnomer in the sense that no set of rules … was isolated from general law,'[56] and that this has been affirmed especially as regarding human rights regimes[57] and WTO law.[58]

Non-Derogable Human Rights Norms While Countering Terrorism

There is some criticism of the doctrinal and jurisprudential treatment of the question of the ability of self-contained regimes to derogate from general international law. Apart from the formal issue of the non-derogability of *jus cogens*, the problem of the permissibility to derogate from norms of general law in concrete situations has remained a subject that has not been sufficiently clarified.

Obviously, the issue under discussion of the legitimacy of the SC counter-terrorism sanctions regime is not only a formal question of hierarchy between sources (i.e., referred to non-derogation in situations where the general law was of a *jus cogens* nature); the question of the ability of the SC and its subsidiary bodies to derogate from general law in the field of human rights depends upon the content of the rights alleged to have been violated and their evaluation in the specific context of the fight against terrorism and the safeguard of public interests. This is a question of a context-dependent nature. The concept involved in this scenario is: if an element is mandatory at the abstract level, must it be included at the concrete level?

It follows that it is necessary to examine which human rights should be considered 'non-derogable', even within the sphere of the fight against terrorism. In this regard, it is appropriate to stress the importance of what is defined as a 'pragmatic hierarchy' between international norms. It is important to note that 'there was a kind of informal hierarchy which emerged pragmatically 'as a "forensic" or "natural" aspect of legal reasoning'.[59]

Our analysis therefore shifts from the abstract level of priority between legal sources (i.e., the ability of special SC measures to derogate from general international law) to a concrete one, that of the priority of legal interests, which focuses on the relationship between human rights protection and counter-terrorism measures.

---

56 Report of the International Law Commission, 56th session, *supra* note 35, para. 318.

57 See IACHR, Velásquez-Rodríguez Case, Judgment of 29 July 1988, Series C No. 4, para. 184; Loizidou v. Turkey, Application No. 15318/89, Merits and Just Satisfaction, Judgment (Dec. 18, 1996), Eur. Ct. H. R. Reports of Judgments and Decisions 1996–VI, para. 43; Al-Adsani v. The United Kingdom, Application No. 35763/97, Merits, Judgment (Nov. 21, 2001), Eur. Ct. H. R. Reports of Judgments and Decisions 2001–XI, para. 55; McElhinney v. Ireland, Application No. 31253/96, Merits, Judgment (Nov. 21, 2001), Eur. Ct. H. R. Reports of Judgments and Decisions 2001–XI, para. 36; Fogarty v. The United Kingdom, Application No. 37112/97, Merits, Judgment (Nov. 21, 2001), Eur. Ct. H. R. Reports of Judgments and Decisions 2001–XI, para. 35; Bankovic, Application No. 52207/99, *supra* note 49, para. 57.

58 Report of the International Law Commission, 56th session, *supra* note 35, para. 321. See also United States Standards for Reformulated and Conventional Gasoline, *supra* note 52, para. 182; United States Import Prohibition of Certain Shrimps and Shrimp Products, *supra* note 51, paras 127–131; Panel Report, Korea – Measures Affecting Government Procurement, 1 May 2000, WT/DS163/R, para. 7.96.

59 Report of the International Law Commission, 56th session, *supra* note 35, para. 307.

On the one hand, safeguarding basic human rights and protecting the 'individual' rights of alleged terrorists and, on the other hand, safeguarding 'general' interests as reflected in asset-freezing and in the SC sanctions regime.

Attention is to be drawn to two specific issues in this context, namely: (1) the balance set up under by general acts of the UN and judicial practice between counter-terrorism measures and human rights obligations; that is to say, identifying those non-derogable human rights under 'states of emergency'[60]; and (2) the point at which the SC counter-terrorism measures, which are claimed to derogate from fundamental human rights, disrupt the pragmatically reached balance (between private and public interests) by international bodies.

In international judicial practice, in specific cases in which the problem has arisen, the trend has been inspired by the concept reiterated by the ECHR, that 'inherent in the whole of [the European Convention on Human Rights] is a search for a fair balance between the demands of the general interest of the community and the requirements of the protection of the individual's fundamental rights'.[61]

One prominent example was the case of *Prosecutor v. Dragan Nikolic*[62] in the International Criminal Tribunal for the Former Yugoslavia (ICTY); another was the *Ocalan* case[63] in the European Court for Human Rights (ECHR). Both the ICTY and the ECHR debated on possible derogations from extradition procedures and the due process of law for those accused of international terrorism and other *crimina juris gentium*.[64] Both the ECJ and the ECHR in the *Bosphorus* case were not adverse, under community law and the European Convention on Human Rights, respectively, to the confiscation of an aircraft owned by a resident of the Federal Republic of Yugoslavia, which had been hired to an 'innocent' operator in good faith, bearing in mind, of course, the general interest in the confiscation (that is to say, the state of war in that region and the massive violations of human rights).[65]

At the same time, the international judicial bodies themselves and the UN, expressing concern about the deprivation of human rights deriving from counter-

---

60 See M. Cherif Bassiouni, *International Crimes: Jus Cogens and Obligatio Erga Omnes*, 59 Law and Contemporary Problems 63 (1996).

61 Soering v. The United Kingdom, Application No. 14038/88, Merits and Just Satisfaction, Judgment (July 7, 1989), 161 Eur. Ct. H. R. (ser. A), para. 89.

62 Prosecutor v. Dragan Nikolic, Case No. IT–94–2–PT, Decision on Defense Motion Challenging the Exercise of Jurisdiction by the Tribunal, Trial Chamber II (Oct. 9, 2002), para. 114.

63 Ocalan v. Turkey, Application No. 46221/99, Merits and Just Satisfaction, Judgment (March 12, 2003).

64 They expounded the idea that 'informal extradition' and 'extradition in disguise' (i.e., extradition arising from cooperation between states) are not in themselves illegal, and ruled that they could constitute 'a legal impediment to the exercise of jurisdiction' in cases where the accused 'is very seriously mistreated, maybe even subjected to inhumane, cruel or degrading treatment, or torture.'

65 Bosphorus Hava Yollari Turizm ve Ticaret AS v. Minister for Transport, Energy and Communications and Others, Case C–84/95, Judgment of 30 July 1996, 1996 ECR I–3953; Bosphorus Hava Yollari Turizm Ve Ticaret Anonim Sirketi v. Ireland, Application No. 45036/98, Merits, Judgments (June 30, 2005), 2005 VI Reports of Judgments and Decisions.

terrorism measures, were faced with providing details as to the extent of admissibility of derogations and listing those individual rights that were non-derogable, even at a time of national and international public emergency.

The Lack of Respect for Non-Derogable Human Rights in the UN Counter-Terrorism Regime

We now turn our attention to the assessment of the legitimacy of the SC counter-terrorism system in the light of the minimum standards required for the protection of human rights and, specifically, the right to due process of law that general acts of the UN and judicial practice have stated as being non-derogable, even during a state of emergency. These have been aptly described in the Report of the Policy Working Group on the UN and Terrorism, established in October 2001 by the UN Secretary-General, and in the following human rights-related recommendation:

> 'All relevant parts of the UN system should emphasize that key human rights must always be protected and may never be derogated from. The independence of the judiciary and the existence of legal remedies are essential elements for the protection of fundamental human rights in all situations involving counter-terrorism measures.'[66]

The aim of the Working Group was to identify the long-term implications and broad policy dimensions of terrorism for the UN and to formulate recommendations on steps that the UN system might take to address the issue.

Despite this recommendation, the sanctions system instituted by the SC and its Sanctions Committee does not contain 'essential' legal remedies for the protection of individuals against arbitrary public power. First of all, there is no hearing in connection with the inclusion on the list of persons whose funds are to be frozen, and the relevant SC resolutions do not provide individuals affected by the sanctions with the right to be heard on the subject of their inclusion on the list, nor to express their own point of view on the facts communicated to the Sanctions Committee by states and regional organizations, as well as on the evidence adduced against them; facts and evidence are not communicated to them. Under paragraph 18 of its Resolution 1526 (2004), the SC only '… encourages all States to inform, to the extent possible, individuals and entities included in the Committee's list of the measures imposed on them.'[67]

The adoption of the contested sanctions and the re-examination of individual situations fall within the complete competence of the SC and its Sanctions Committee, the only authority competent to issue a decision on a petition for re-examination. There is no judicial remedy available to the individuals affected to be heard in person regarding the correctness and relevance of the facts and evidence relied on by the SC in support of the measures it has taken and/or the legality of these measures.

---

66 Report of the Policy Working Group on the United Nations and Terrorism, para. 52, Recommendation 4, available at <http://www.globalsecurity.org/security/library/report/2002/un-wrkng-grp-terrorism-recommendations.htm>.

67 SC Res. 1526, *supra* note 18, para. 18.

The mechanism for the re-examination of individual cases, formalized by the 'Guidelines',[68] empowers the government of residence and/or citizenship (i.e., the petitioned government) with deciding 'whether' and 'when' to forward to the Sanctions Committee the request of the petitioner either to be removed from the list or to obtain exemption from the freezing of funds. However even the Security Council's recently adopted resolution 1730, which allows individuals to petition directly for de-listing, does not constitute an effective revision procedure that the interested party might participate in.[69]

Mandatory prescriptions of the public international order require that SC decisions and sanctions respect the criteria of proportionality, necessity, non-discrimination, and legal parameters for substantive and procedural correctness. The principle of legality and the rule of law require that fundamental requirements of a fair trial be respected during a state of emergency (namely, the right to be informed promptly; the right to a hearing by an independent and impartial body), including the presumption of innocence (inclusion in the lists is based on a presumption of guilt on the basis of a summary assessment – *fumus boni juris* – typical of the precautionary safeguards of civil procedures).

From the viewpoint of substantive rights, the right to compensation for damages suffered as a result of the unfair inclusion on the lists should, even in emergency situations, be considered non-derogable for persons affected by the sanctions (such as when a petition for de-listing has been approved by the Committee). Asset-freezing measures significantly affect the right of property, which is barely safeguarded on account of the fact that the SC provides a mechanism for the review of their applicability after a period of 12[70] to 18 months.[71] The right of property is recognized as fundamental by the ICJ, which, in its well-known Advisory Opinion, *Construction of a Wall in the Occupied Palestinian Territory*, stated the obligation *erga omnes* of Israel to award compensation for damages to property belonging to individuals and entities incurred from the construction of the wall.[72]

In addition to the lack of respect for non-derogable human rights, problems of the legitimacy of the SC counter-terrorism regime arise from its questionable conformity with the overall system of the Charter (e.g., problems of constitutional legitimacy). Doubts can be aired especially regarding the competence of the SC to exercise, over individuals, those same powers of sanction conferred by Chapter VII, which were hitherto exercised over states that threatened peace, violated peace, or acted as aggressors. Furthermore, the precautionary measures adopted by the Council are difficult to be seen as stemming from Article 40 of the Charter (provisional measures). They should rather be included amongst those listed in Article 41 as measures which,

---

68 See *supra* under the heading 'Introduction' earlier in this chapter, notes 20–21 and corresponding text.

69 See *supra* under the heading 'Introduction' earlier in this chapter, notes 23–25 and corresponding text.

70 See SC Res. 1333, *supra* note 2, para. 23.

71 See SC Res. 1526, *supra* note 18, para. 3.

72 Legal Consequences of the Construction of a Wall in the Occupied Palestinian Territory, Advisory Opinion, (July 9, 2004), para. 153.

by their nature, require a prior ascertainment of responsibility by the SC pursuant to Article 39 of the Charter. The sanctions adopted by the SC against individuals and entities suspected of terrorism can be assimilated into what is termed, in legal parlance, as 'accessory punishments,' that is to say, those further punishments that can be an adjunct to the principal sanction but which cannot be imposed independently, subject to the faculty reserved to the judge for their provisional application before sentencing (Article 140, Italian Penal Code). Such a faculty has been exercised by the SC without ensuring the legal guarantees of a criminal trial.

It certainly refers to authoritative prerogatives of the SC to determine whether there exists a threat to international peace and security and to adopt those measures it considers appropriate. These are discretionary political assessments that judicial bodies belonging to national and regional systems cannot control; they have not been entitled to do so under SC resolutions. It is noticeable too that the Charter does not designate a body to exercise powers of control over the legitimacy of SC decisions – over their compliance with international law or the Charter. UN bodies may ask the ICJ for an advisory opinion on any judicial question (Article 96, UN Charter; Article 65, ICJ Statute), which, however, is not compulsory. Furthermore, the contentious jurisdiction of the Court is limited by Article 34 of its Statute to disputes between states.

In addition, the ineffectiveness of the delisting procedure provided for in section 8 of the 'Guidelines'[73] is also complained about because of the discretionary power attributed to states to which the petition is submitted, the various formal consultation mechanisms between the countries involved in the procedure, provided for in section 8(b) to (e) of 'Guidelines,' and the difficulty encountered by the Sanctions Committee in reaching the required consensus of its members for decisions.

Proposals for Eliminating Deficiencies

The deficiencies identified above have prompted national and international courts and legal scholars to suggest solutions to bring the UN counter-terrorism system into conformity with standards of international effectiveness and legality.[74] We now examine some of the common characteristics amongst proposed solutions.

1. That the SC resolutions should oblige states to grant individuals a minimum standard of processual guarantees in the acquisition of the facts and evidence for listing and de-listing procedures.[75] It is in this direction that the CFIEC has

73 Guidelines, *supra* note 11, section 8.

74 *See* The Watson Institute for International Studies, 'Strengthening Targeted Sanctions Through Fair and Clear Procedures' (30 March 2006), available at <http://www.watsoninstitute.org/pub/Strengthening_Targeted_Sanctions.pdf>, at 4, 43, 58 [hereinafter Watson Project].

75 See Case T–253/02, *supra* note 28, para. 149; Case T–49/04, *supra* note 28, para. 119.

been heading recently, departing from previous jurisprudence.[76] The Court has interpreted section 8 of the 'Guidelines'[77] and Article 6 of the Treaty on European Union (EU Treaty) as imposing an obligation on Member States 'to respect the fundamental rights of the persons involved',[78] and therefore: to inform individuals and entities included in the Committee's List of the measures imposed on them; to act promptly to ensure that such persons' cases are presented without delay and fairly and impartially to the Committee;[79] to ensure, so far as is possible, that interested persons are placed in a position to present 'their point of view before the competent national authorities when they present a request for their case to be reviewed';[80] to bring an action for judicial review based on the domestic law of the state of the petitioned government against any wrongful refusal by the competent national authority to submit their cases to the Sanctions Committee for re-examination and, more generally, against any infringement by that national authority of the right of the persons involved to request the review of their case.[81]

2. That the SC resolutions should authorize regional organizations (and therefore the European Community) to provide for mechanisms for the examination or re-examination of individual situations.[82] In the case of *Organisation des Modjahedines du Peuple d'Iran (OMPI) v. Council of the European Union* [83] the CFIEC annulled, in so far as it concerns the applicant,[84] Council decision to freeze funds,[85] implementing SC resolution 1373 (2001).[86] According to the Court, such a resolution (unlike the preceding Resolution 1267 (1999) of

76 See *a contrario* Case T–306/01, *supra* note 28, para. 240; Case T–315/01, *supra* note 28, para. 190.

77 See Case T–253/02, *supra* note 28, para. 145; Case T–49/04, *supra* note 28, para. 115.

78 Case T–253/02, *supra* note 28, para. 146; Case T–49/04, *supra* note 28, para. 116.

79 Case T–253/02, *supra* note 28, para. 149; Case T–49/04, *supra* note 28, para. 119.

80 Case T–253/02, *supra* note 28, para. 147; see also Case T–49/04, *supra* note 28, para. 117.

81 For example, see a decision given by a court of a Member State ordering that State to request, as a matter of urgency, the Sanctions Committee to remove the names of two persons from the list in question, on pain of paying a daily penalty (Tribunal de première instance de Bruxelles (Court of First Instance, Brussels), Fourth Chamber, Judgment of 11 February 2005 in the case of Nabil Sayadi and Patricia Vinck v. Belgian State).

82 See Case T–306/01, *supra* note 28, para. 328; Case T–315/01, *supra* note 28, para. 258.

83 See Case T–228/02, *supra* note 28.

84 By order of 28 March 2001of the United Kingdom Secretary of State for the Home Department the OMPI was included in the list of unlawful organizations under the *Terrorism Act* 2000.

85 Council Decision No. 930 of 21 December 2005 (*Official Journal L 340, 23.11.2005*, at 64–66) which enacts Art. 2 (3) of EC Regulation No. 2580 (*supra* note 2), abrogating Council Decision No. 848 of 19 November 2005 (*Official Journal L* 314, 30.11.2005, at 46–47). See Case T–228/02, *supra* note 28, para. 17.

86 SC Res. 1373, *supra* note 12.

the Security Council,[87] examined in previous cases brought before it[88]) does not specify individually the persons, groups and entities who are to be the subjects of those measures and therefore involves discretionary assessment by Member States and the Community. Therefore, respect for the rights of defence and the right to effective judicial protection of the parties involved is imposed as a line of principle on community institutions;[89] this is effectively ensured by the right the parties concerned have to bring an action before the Court against a decision to freeze their funds. The Court affirmed its competence 'to review the lawfulness and merits of the measures to freeze funds without it being possible to raise objections that the evidence and information used by the Council is secret or confidential'.[90]

3. That the SC resolutions should confer 'directly' upon the persons affected the right to be heard by the Sanctions Committee with regard to the challenge to the validity of its decisions (as well as the SC decisions).
4. That the effectiveness of the re-examination procedures should be ensured by an interpretation of UN acts further safeguarding the individuals affected, on the one hand, drawing from general principles of international law to oblige UN Member States to act in good faith,[91] thereby ensuring speed in the de-listing procedure and obtaining consensus from the body of the Sanctions Committee for its own decisions (the Sanctions Committee takes its decisions by consensus) and, on the other hand, drawing from the SC resolutions (i.e., from paragraph 9 of Resolution 1267 (1999), paragraph 19 of Resolution 1333 (2000), and paragraph 7 of Resolution 1390 (2002))[92] an obligation from

87 For the cited resolution see *supra* note 2.

88 In the *Yusuf* and *Kadi* cases which we mentioned previously (see *supra* note 28) the Court rejected the request for annulment of the contested EC Council Regulation ('the contested regulation, adopted in the light of Common Position 2002/402'), which constituted the implementation at Community level of the obligation placed on the Member States of the Community, of Resolutions 1267 (1999), 1333 (2000) and 1390 (2002), which imposed the freezing of funds of the parties concerned. The Court sustained that: 'In that situation, … [the institutions] had no autonomous discretion. … Any review of the internal lawfulness of the contested regulation, especially having regard to the provisions or general principles of Community law relating to the protection of fundamental rights, would therefore imply that the Court is to consider, indirectly, the lawfulness of those resolutions.' (See Case T–306/01, *supra* note 28, paras 265–266; Case T–315/01, *supra* note 28, paras 214–215).

89 In the Court's reasoning: 'Since the identification of the persons, groups and entities contemplated in Security Council Resolution 1373 (2001), and the adoption of the ensuing measure of freezing funds, involve the exercise of the Community's own powers, entailing a discretionary appreciation by the Community, the Community institutions concerned, in this case the Council, are in principle bound to observe the right to a fair hearing of the parties concerned when they act with a view to giving effect to that resolution. … [W]ith respect to the safeguard relating to the right to effective judicial protection, this is effectively ensured by the right the parties concerned have to bring an action before the Court against a decisi*on to freeze their funds* …' (See Case T–228/02, *supra* note 28, paras 107, 152).

90 *See* Case T–228/02, *supra* note 28, para. 155.

91 See Art. 26, Vienna Convention on the Law of Treaties, *supra* note 41.

92 Case T–253/02, *supra* note 28, para. 142; Case T–49/04, *supra* note 28, para. 112.

all states to cooperate fully with the Sanctions Committee in the fulfilment of its tasks.

Providing the UN Counter-Terrorism Regime with a System of Judicial Remedies Based on the UNAT-ICJ Model

The compliance of the UN counter-terrorism regime with human rights obligations cannot be entirely ensured by the aforementioned interpretative and administrative proposed solutions as they do not provide the 'essential elements' for the protection of human rights (such as impartiality and independence of the review mechanism and direct access to it) that must be respected even during a state of emergency.[93] The Sanctions Committee, formed by members of the SC, which decides on the petitions for de-listing, is the self-same body that provides inclusion on the list itself.

It is in light of this need that some form of review mechanisms has been proposed. In this regard, our approach to the problems enumerated above is based on the need that the SC, through its own resolutions, should establish proceedings before a judicial or quasi-judicial body to whom the interested parties should have direct access. This body should be empowered to rule, in law and in fact, on actions involving individual decisions taken by the Sanctions Committee and to check the legality of the measures established and their appropriateness, proportionality, and compliance with general international law and with the UN Charter. Besides, the SC – *mutatis mutandis* – has already extensively interpreted its own powers in this direction when it instituted *ad hoc* international criminal tribunals, which are entitled to judge individuals accused of *crimina juris gentium*.[94]

The institution of an independent international body is even more necessary due to the fact that the individuals affected cannot even petition internal courts with respect to the sanctions adopted against them, given the rule of immunity that exempts the UN from judicial action from internal courts of Member States. The CFIEC considers such a limitation (established by the rule of immunity) on the right of access to the courts 'inherent in that right as it is guaranteed by *jus cogens*',[95] by which argument it affirms that the re-examination mechanism as set in place by the SC system is adequate for ensuring the protection of fundamental human rights.[96]

We would remind ourselves that, quite to the contrary, the same circumstance (the restriction on the right of access to the courts as a result of the aforementioned

---

93 See *supra* under the heading 'The Lack of Respect...' earlier in this chapter..

94 SC Res. 827 (May 25, 1993); SC Res. 955 (Nov. 8, 1994).

95 Case T–306/01, *supra* note 28, para. 343; Case T–315/01, *supra* note 28, para. 288.

96 Case T–306/01, *supra* note 28, para. 345; Case T–315/01, *supra* note 28, para. 290. The Court stated that 'the right of access to the courts, a principle recognised by both Article 8 of the Universal Declaration of Human Rights and Article 14 of the International Covenant on Civil and Political Rights, adopted by the United Nations General Assembly on 16 December 1966, is not absolute. On the one hand, at a time of public emergency which threatens the life of the nation, measures may be taken derogating from that right, as provided for on certain conditions by Article 4 (1) of that Covenant.' See Case T–306/01, *supra* note 28, para. 342; Case T–315/01, *supra* note 28, para. 287.

immunity from jurisdiction rule) has been considered quite differently at the UN by the General Assembly, extensively interpreting the Charter.[97] In explaining the power of the Assembly, in its given advisory opinion, the ICJ not only supported the competence of the General Assembly to create the Court but actually urged it to do so in the name of 'justice' as inspired by the Charter and, therefore, towards 'the expressed aim of the Charter to promote freedom and justice for individuals and with constant preoccupation of the UN Organization to promote this aim …'.[98] These same reasons (the right to be heard and the right of access to the courts) also convinced some specialized agencies of the UN to set up administrative tribunals entitled to decide disputes between those international organizations and members of their staff.[99]

In international law, though very limited and incomplete, there exist judicial or quasi-judicial procedures to which individuals and entities may appeal decisions regarding their interests. One example of which is the system foreseen by Article 230 of the EC Treaty, with its double system of justice involving the CFIEC and the ECJ, a kind of administrative jurisdiction governing the legitimacy of Community acts; they also, however, include the experience of judicial and quasi-judicial control systems concerning the respect for human rights in special treaty-regimes.[100]

The UN system is not very amenable to the direct safeguarding of individuals' own rights. The controlling mechanism of the Human Rights Council allows for an examination of petitions presented by individuals against a contracting state, but only under certain pre-set conditions. In any case, the Council's acts are not binding. There exist, however, in the UN system, administrative and jurisdictional instances that are available to individuals for solving questions of an administrative nature, as has already been mentioned.

As stated at the beginning of this Part, placing counter-terrorism within a rule-of-law framework is consistent with international law and with the UN system. It is our opinion, which therefore differs from those that are based on a judicial form of review mechanism of de-listing decisions, that a solid base in this direction and in defence of human rights could be ensured by a system of judicial safeguards based upon the UN Administrative Tribunal (UNAT)-ICJ model, according to the procedure foreseen by Article 11 of the UNAT Statute. In the same way, recourse to a judicial body (or a quasi-judicial body), which we shall term the 'Administrative Tribunal for Sanctions,' could be coupled with a mechanism of review for challenging judgments of such a tribunal before the ICJ through the machinery of a request, which emanates from a body duly authorized,[101] of an advisory opinion having a conclusive effect. Such a system might protect individuals against wrongful SC action in imposing

97 GA Res. 351 (IV) (Nov. 24, 1949).

98 Effect of Awards of Compensation Made by the UN Administrative Tribunal, Advisory Opinion, 1954 ICJ Reports 47 (July 13, 1954), para. 57, at 57–58. See also Repertory, *supra* note 31, vol. I, No. 1519, at 545.

99 Art. I, Statute of the Administrative Tribunal of the International Labour Organization, adopted by the International Labour Conference on 9 October 1946.

100 European Court of Human Rights and Inter-American Court of Human Rights.

101 A body similar to the Committee on Applications for Review of Administrative Tribunal (UNAT) Judgments, composed of Member States, with the task to decide whether

targeted sanctions; including such exercise of discretionary powers as may have been determined to be in violation of fundamental procedural and substantive norms of the UN Charter.

Within its overall review of the internal legal system of the UN, the General Assembly decided, by a resolution adopted on 11 December 1995, to delete Article 11 from the Statute of the UNAT, which established the review procedure.[102]

It may also be observed that the ICJ, interpreting the powers of UNAT, has stated that the Tribunal does not possess any powers of judicial review or appeal in respect of the decisions taken by the General Assembly, powers which the Court itself does not possess.[103] This might lead us to cast doubt on the possibility of judicial control over the SC's discretionary powers. It should be added however, that when taking into account the powers of the UNAT with respect to the Secretary-General (where the Secretary-General has been invested with discretionary powers), the Court itself stated that 'such discretionary powers must be exercised without improper motive so that there shall be no misuse of power, since any such misuse of power would call for the rescinding of the decision';[104] therefore, the Court has emphasized as being the 'essential point' that the Tribunal 'does not abandon all claim to test such exercise against the requirements of the Charter'.[105] This statement on the powers of the UNAT *vis-à-vis* the discretionary powers of the Secretary-General might point towards limits to the SC's discretionary powers in imposing targeted sanctions and create an opening to the possibility of the ICJ's judicial control over such power on the grounds that it is contrary to the requirements of the Charter and to the standard of protection of fundamental rights as recognized by the international legal order.

Certainly the question of judicial review of the legality of SC decisions is a much debated topic in legal doctrine[106] and one that we will refer back to our previous writings.[107] For the present, we wish to emphasize only that, apart from certain

---

there is a substantial basis for the application to have the matter reviewed. This function could be entrusted by the Sanctions Committee.

102 This procedure is thus no longer applicable for judgments of the Tribunal delivered as of 1 January 1996.

103 Legal Consequences for States of the Continued Presence of South Africa in Namibia (South West Africa) notwithstanding Security Council Resolution 276 (1970), Advisory Opinion, 1971 ICJ Reports 16 (June 21, 1971), para. 89, at 45. *See also* Repertory, *supra* note 31, vol. II, No. 2404, at 1011.

104 Application for Review of Judgement No. 333 of the United Nations Administrative Tribunal, Advisory Opinion, 1987 ICJ Reports 18 (May 27, 1987), para. 65, at 53. *See also* Repertory, *supra* note 31, vol. II, No. 2473, at 1081.

105 Application for Review of Judgement No. 333 of the United Nations Administrative Tribunal, *supra* note 104, para. 75, at 57. *See also* Repertory, *supra* note 31, vol. II, No. 2473, at 1082.

106 See, e.g., Elihu Lauterpacht, *Judicial Review of the Acts of International Organisations*, in International Law, The International Court of Justice and Nuclear Weapons (Laurence Boisson de Chazournes ed., 1999). *See also supra*, chapter 3, notes 230–233 and the literature quoted therein.

107 Giuliana Ziccardi Capaldo, *Global Trends and Global Court: The Legitimacy of World Governance*, 4 GCYILJ 127 (2004–I), at 161, notes 230–233 and the literature quoted therein.

statements of principle, in concrete cases in which the question has emerged, the ICJ has extensively interpreted its powers in not hesitating to exercise power of control on Council decisions, acting as a 'global Court'.[108] Certainly, the proposed UNAT-ICJ model for a double system of jurisdiction in the counter-terrorism regime needs adjustments; the requirements of the judicial process depend on the circumstances and conditions of each particular system. Nevertheless, certain requisites of advisory jurisdiction being used for judicial review of contentious proceedings to which individuals were parties have already been expressed by the Court in its sentences and those of greatest importance can be synthesized as follows:

1. The procedure before the ICJ is not intended to be part of a procedure of appeal on the merits of the case, the Court acting as the supreme judge of legitimacy. In fact, under Article 65 of the Court's Statute, the Court is authorized to give an advisory opinion only on a legal question.[109]
2. An application for petition to the ICJ could be filed not only by the persons in respect to whom the judgment has been rendered by the tribunal, but also by UN Member States and other institutions in order to allow for decisions pronounced by the Court 'in the interest of law' and to guarantee an interpretation of law by the Court that may be used as a precedent in future sentences.
3. The request for an advisory opinion must be submitted to the Court by a duly authorized body. The Court has underlined that 'if that were not so, as neither a member state, nor the Secretary-General, nor individuals is authorized by the Charter to request an advisory opinion of the Court, their request would not be admissible'.[110]

The system of judicial safeguards that have been outlined above is in accordance with the general principles governing the judicial process and is consistent with the UN system both from a structural standpoint and a substantive due process perspective. Establishing the rule of a law-based UN counter-terrorism system (i.e., transparency in Sanctions Committee procedures and access to effective and independent judicial review mechanisms) has a vital role in promoting adherence to international human rights law, and it is equally crucial to reinforce the verticality and legitimacy of the world order, the integration between UN sanctions programmes and measures of implementation adopted by various institutions (national, regional, and international) that operate for the efficacy of the counter-terrorism regime. These aims constitute future challenges, and their achievement is a coherent duty of the SC with the principles of law that have already been enacted by UN bodies to help guide states

108 *Id.*, at 152 *et seq.*

109 Application for Review of Judgement No. 158 of the United Nations Administrative Tribunal, Advisory Opinion, 1973 ICJ Reports 166 (July 12, 1973), para 41, at 183–185. *See also* Repertory, *supra* note 31, vol. II, No. 2457, at 1065.

110 Application for Review of Judgement No. 273 of the United Nations Administrative Tribunal, Advisory Opinion, 1982 ICJ Reports 325 (July 20, 1982), para. 24, at 335. See also Repertory, *supra* note 31, vol. II, No. 2442, at 1049.

in protecting human rights in the context of their efforts to eradicate terrorism.[111] The General Assembly in the 2005 World Summit Outcome urged the SC to ensure, with the support of the Secretary-General, 'due process and fair and clear procedures of listing and de-listing'.[112] It has a long way to go before building and implementing a broad strategic plan, coherent with the need of legitimacy of global governance, based on cooperation between the various institutions of the system and the states engaged in developing a vision of counter-terrorism strategies that are fully respectful of human rights.[113]

Concluding Remarks: A Fair Balance Between Public Safety and the Safeguarding of Individual Human Rights

In establishing, with Resolution 1267 (1999) and subsequent measures, a sanctions regime against terrorism placed under its immediate responsibility, the SC has interpreted the trend in the international community to shift from an inter-state community to a universal human community.[114] It has faced the evil of global terrorism by creating and imposing a targeted sanctions regime against individuals and entities. Through binding resolutions, adopted in accordance with Chapter VII of the Charter, the SC has placed itself as the 'world public authority' over individuals and entities suspected of involvement in acts of terrorism and/or belonging to terrorist networks by deciding upon and setting up procedures for imposing targeted sanctions. It has targeted suspects' goods and interests by ordering states and international institutions to freeze funds belonging to suspected individuals and entities and preventing the movement of terrorists. SC public authority has become more and more prominent, spreading all over various legal systems, in such a way as to be exercised through interaction between national, regional, and global institutions.

The sanctions system which is centred on the SC and the Sanctions Committee, its subsidiary body, is the expression of the highest exercise of public power which, however, is not provided with minimum due process guarantees. Although giving effect to UN Sanctions Committee decisions, various states and international

---

111 The same SC subsidiary bodies created to control states implementation of Resolutions 1267 and 1373 (especially the Committee, CTC, CTED, Monitoring Team, and UNODC) are preparing general principles of law.

112 GA Res. 60/1, *supra* note 30, para. 109.

113 Cooperation between the SC and its bodies with the Secretary-General, the OHCHR, the new Human Rights Council, has begun. See Report of the UN Secretary-General 'Uniting Against Terrorism: Recommendations for a Global Counter-terrorism Strategy', A/60/825, (April 27, 2006), para. 117. On 6 August 2002, the Secretary-General submitted the Report of the Policy Working Group to the General Assembly and the Security Council (A/57/273 – S/2002/875). See *supra* note 66. See also the 'Digest of Jurisprudence of the UN and Regional Organizations on the Protection of Human Rights while Countering Terrorism' (July 2003), which has been prepared by the United Nations Office of the High Commissioner for Human Rights (OHCHR).

114 Giuliana Ziccardi Capaldo, *Editorial*, 1 GCYILJ xix (2001).

institutions and bodies have expressed concerns about the lack of fairness of listing and de-listing procedures.

The choice of the institution of diplomatic protection as a review mechanism against the arbitrariness of public power,[115] whilst demonstrating the ineffectiveness of the chosen mechanism of safeguarding the basic rights of the individuals, betrays the inconsistency of the tools used in relation to the objective of creating a sanctions system against global terrorism designed to guarantee protection for public values (such as security, welfare, and human rights), which is integrated into an organized global legal framework acting as a flywheel for the government of a global human society, respectful of international law.

Such a broadly based sanctions system must be provided with coherent guarantee mechanisms for its global nature and must not become defiled or polluted by rumblings of sovereignty which remain present even in the amendment provided by the Security Council to the procedure for the re-examination of individual situations.[116] It must be perfected and moulded to ensure reasonable standards of legality by following the guidelines that the UN bodies themselves are processing so as to grant respect for basic human rights, even in the fight against terrorism.[117]

Even the CFIEC has strongly affirmed, in the above-mentioned case *Organisation des Modjahedines du Peuple d'Iran (OMPI) v. Council of the European Union*,[118] individuals must be able to avail themselves of effective judicial protection of the rights they have under the Community legal order, as the right to such protection is part of the general legal principles deriving from the constitutional traditions common to the Member States and has been enshrined in Articles 6 and 13 of the ECHR.[119] This also particularly applies to measures to freeze the funds of persons or organizations suspected of terrorist activities.[120] In the Court's opinion rights of defence may necessitate, in cases concerning national security and, more specifically, terrorism, certain restrictions on the right to a fair hearing;[121] it is necessary to ensure that a fair balance is struck between the need to combat international terrorism and the protection of fundamental rights.[122] Therefore, the restrictions on the rights of the

---

115 See *supra* Introduction to this chapter.

116 See SC Res. 1730, *supra* note 23.

117 Reports of the Special Rapporteur M. Cherif Bassiouni on the situation of human rights in Afghanistan (A/59/370, 21 September 2004 and E/CN.4/2005/122, 11 March 2005). See *supra* notes 111–112. In general, see Theodor Meron, The Humanization of International Law (2006).

118 See Case T–228/02, *supra* note 28.

119 *Id.*, para. 110; Degussa AG v. Commission of the European Communities, Case T–279/02, Judgment of 5 April 2006, 2006 ECR II–897, para. 421, and case law cited therein.

120 See Case T–228/02, *supra* note 28, para. 111; see also, to that effect, Article XIV of the 'Guidelines on Human Rights and the Fight Against Terrorism', adopted by the Committee of Ministers at the 804th meeting of the Ministers' Deputies (July 11, 2002).

121 See Case T–228/02, *supra* note 28, paras 133–135.

122 *Id.*, at para. 155.

defence of the parties must be offset by 'a strict judicial review which is independent and impartial'.[123]

Making provision for the needs of legality and harmonization of the sanctions system under discussion with new claims of legitimacy of public authority within the global community and respect for fundamental human rights requires:

1. procedural fairness in listing, exemptions, and de-listing procedures;[124]
2. a system of review with the requirements of judicial process, providing for an independent and truly judicial or quasi-judicial body, before which individuals and entities affected may exercise the right to be heard and to issue challenges relating to the decisions of international organs;
3. the possibility of petitioning the ICJ, using the advisory jurisdiction of the Court, for judicial review of legitimacy over the SC's exercise of discretionary power to test any 'misuse' of such power against the requirements of the Charter and mandatory provisions of general international law; and
4. granting, apart from the parties involved, states and regional organizations and other international institutions the power to request from the ICJ an advisory opinion 'in the interests of law'.

The adoption by the UN of a system of judicial safeguards, based on the proposed comprehensive system of review (double system of review taken from the UNAT-ICJ model), answers the problems that are being faced by the targeted sanctions regime instituted by the SC – problems of legality and legitimacy. Addressing the issue of placing counter-terrorism within a rule-of-law framework is vital in a system of multi-level governance in order to secure both the procedural fairness of decisions affecting individuals and entities, and their compliance with due process of law and the legitimacy of world governance carried out in the global order, through the control of the World Court. A judicial review which is independent and impartial would appear to be the only procedural protection ensuring a fair balance between public safety and the safeguarding of an individual's human rights.

---

123 *Id.*; see also, to that effect Eurofood IFSC Ltd, Case C–341/04, Judgment of 2 May 2006, 2006 ECR I–3813, para. 66.

124 Watson project, supra note 74, at 3, 6, 7, 24, 39, 49.

Conclusions

Global law is in an embryonic phase. That is the way legal scholars, who are used to more articulated systems, view it. It is growing as the law of a common humanity brings with it the emergence of an organizational model of the world's society based on the gradual integration of various systems of organization (legal, social, economic, mediatic, etc.) at different aggregation levels, local to worldwide (that is, national states, regional and universal organizations, multinational corporations, NGOs, media networks, etc.). Framed this way, global law is the third stage of development of international law,[1] the preceding two phases being those described by Wolfgang Friedmann[2] (i.e., the international law of coexistence and the international law of cooperation).

This book describes the main changes to rules and structure of the international legal system caused by the process of globalization. This is only the beginning of a complex process and still far away from the achievement of a harmonic legal system for a universal society, capable of safeguarding humanity and each and every human being.

Encouraging this process, the UN General Assembly has underlined the fact that 'it is imperative for the international community to ensure that globalization becomes a positive force for all the world's people…';[3] it has asserted that 'the international community should strive to respond to the challenges and opportunities posed by globalization for the full enjoyment of all human rights',[4] reaffirming that 'the United Nations has a central role in promoting international cooperation for development and in promoting policy coherence on global development issues, including in the context of globalization and interdependence'.[5]

Currently, the world is a large laboratory where, by means of diplomatic conferences and through various institutions, norms and procedures to achieve a global legal system are researched. Globalization is a reality. To dispel fears, it needs

---

1 See Giuliana Ziccardi Capaldo, *Verso una Regolamentazione del Rapporto tra Ordinamento Italiano e Trattati Internazionali. Contenuti di una Riforma Possibile dopo le Modifiche al Titolo V della Parte Seconda della Costituzione*, in ATTUAZIONE DEI TRATTATI INTERNAZIONALI E COSTITUZIONE ITALIANA. UNA RIFORMA PRIORITARIA NELL'ERA DELLA COMUNITÀ GLOBALE (Giuliana Ziccardi Capaldo ed., 2003); see also chapter 5 of this book, under the heading 'Introduction'.

2 WOLFGANG FRIEDMANN, THE CHANGING STRUCTURE OF INTERNATIONAL LAW 60–67 (1964).

3 Promotion of a Democratic and Equitable International Order, GA Res. 59/193, (March 18, 2005), preamble.

4 Globalization and Its Impact on the full Enjoyment of All Human Rights, GA Res. 59/184 (March 8, 2005), para. 10.

5 GA Res. 62/199 (Feb. 29, 2008), preamble

to be reined in by rules[6]; integrated processes and the central role of the UN need to be consolidated. The powers of international institutions need to be calibrated and balanced; there must be a judicial control of the legitimacy of world governance. Finally, participation in decision-making processes of the forces driving globalization and of the 'new powers' must be enlarged to ensure that neither develops nor acts outside of institutional supervision in formulating global policies (policies which address the needs and protect the rights of human beings) and in taking global action.

The road ahead for the ICJ towards the legitimacy of global governance has begun.[7] As well as efforts to increase the involvement of all States and participation by and interaction with NGOs and other non-state actors, other avenues are being pursued, both within and outside institutional procedures, in the practices of international bodies and in the UN's work towards increasing the number of interactive meetings, such as the open debates in the UNGA and UNSC on thematic issues of current global relevance.[8] This also takes place through substantive and interactive debates in the UN General Assembly, of consideration of special subject-oriented reports submitted by the SC to the GA,[9] and several other types of interface with civilian society, such as informal meetings — bilateral meetings, briefings, and occasional invitations, known as the 'Arria Formula', initiated in 1992.[10]

Mechanisms are being set up to enhance the active engagement of non-governmental actors to participate directly in decision-making and to have access to justice, and to develop and implement uniform standards in the areas of human rights, international criminal law, international environmental law, and trade law, as important elements for globalization. There is also wide support for a strengthened role for non-governmental actors/NGOs in international courts and tribunals and UN bodies as well as in compliance mechanisms set up through international conventions, especially in environmental matters.[11]

Although there are still major gaps and challenges to be overcome between the various actors, this practice of increased interaction between all global players bypasses the inter-governmental character of the UN and other international institutions; it overlooks the drawbacks of the classic international order under which decision-making is necessarily an inter-governmental process; and it

6 Philip Allott, Towards the International Rule of Law: Essays in Integrated Constitutional Theory (2005).

7 See *supra* chapter 3 under the heading 'Concluding Remarks'.

8 SC Report Publications on Thematic and General Issues, available at <www.securitycouncilreport.org>.

9 GA Res. 59/313 (Sept. 12, 2005), paras 2(b) to 2(f).

10 For more information, see Global Policy Forum, at <http://www.globalpolicy.org/security/mtgsetc/brieindx.htm>.

11 See the adoption of the UN/ECE Convention on Access to Information, Public Participation in Decision-making and Access to Justice in Environmental Matters – the Aarhus Convention. The Convention was adopted on 25 June 1998; it entered into force on 30 October 2001. The third meeting of the Parties will be held in Riga, Latvia, on 11–13 June 2008. See also Responsibility to Protect-Engaging Civil Society (R2PCS) at <http://www.responsibilitytoprotect.org/index.php>.

increasingly realizes the implementation of formalized processes for the integrated management of global social issues, both in the formulation of policies and in their implementation.[12] This is a prerequisite for meaningful progress towards a global community and the legitimacy of global law.

12 See *supra* chapters 1 and 2 of this book.

Tables

WESTPHALIAN SYSTEM (1648)

PRINCIPLES/CONCEPTS	**PLAYERS**	**FUNCTIONS**	**PROCESSES**	**POWER**
• **Sovereignty principle** - independence and supreme authority possessed by states within their territory (*superiorem non recognoscentes, jus excludendi alios*) • **Effectivity principle/criterion (*ex factis oritus jus*)** - force not prohibited; - occupation, legitimate means of acquiring title to territory • **Coexistence concept** - International law as a law of coexistence between states	**States the only international actors**	**Performed by the players themselves (i.e., states)**	• **Rule-formation processes** - Based on custom, treaties (states as law-makers) • **Rule-enforcement processes** - Based on self-defense (states acting by themselves) • **Arbitration** -Based on special agreement (compromis) between the states parties to the dispute	**Decentralized, not organized, absence of superior power**

Table 1 The Westphalian System

UN CHARTER SYSTEM (San Francisco 1945)

PRINCIPLES/ CONCEPTS*	PLAYERS	FUNCTIONS/ PROCESSES	POWERS*	UN SUPREMACY
• **Principle of sovereign equality (Art. 2 (1))** • **Fundamental values and legality principles (Art. 1 (1) (2) (3))** - peace and security; - self-determination; - human rights • **Force, occupation prohibited (Art. 2 (4))** • **Legality vs. effectivity (*ex iniuria jus non oritur*)** • **Authority** - prescriptive/ binding powers (Arts. 17 (2), 25); - majority principle (Arts. 18 (2), 27 (2), 67 (2), 89 (2), Charter and Art. 55, ICJ Statute) veto rule (Art. 27 (3)) • **Cooperation concept (Art. 1 (3))** ***States' sovereignty limited by legality principles and Authority***	• **States** - system limited to inter-state relationships; - exclusion of new powers/actors	• **Rule-making** - codification (Art. 13 (1)(a)); - GA Declarations of Principles (not binding); - ICJ quasi-legislative function: advisory opinions (Art. 96); - SC binding decisions (Art. 25) • **Enforcement System** - suspension, expulsion (Arts. 5, 6); - Collective Security System (Chap. VII) • **Ascertainment and Judicial functions** - SC Political ascertainment (Art. 39); - ICJ judicial functions (Arts. 92, 94) • **Administrative lawgivers:** - Secretariat (Chapter XV); - ECOSOC (Chapter X); - Trusteeship Council (Chapter XIII); - UNAT	• **Characters and limits:** - organized decision-making power; - legislative weakness; - preeminence of executive; - imbalance of powers; - veto power (Art. 27 (3)) blocking SC decisions Chapter VII; - weakness of judicial control ***Collective Security System not able to guarantee respect for global values***	• **Preeminence of the Charter's obligations (Art. 103)** • **Regional arrangements or agencies (Chap. VIII)** - activities consistent with the purposes and Principles of the UN (Art. 52 (1)); - no enforcement action shall be taken without the authorization of the SC (Art. 53 (1)) • **Specialized Agencies** - agreements to co-ordinate the activities with the UN (Arts. 57, 63); - the GA approves financial and budgetary arrangements and examines the administrative budgets (Art. 17 (3))

Table 2 The UN Charter System

GLOBAL LEGAL SYSTEM
LEGAL SYSTEM FOR A UNIVERSAL HUMAN SOCIETY

THE PILLARS	PRINCIPLES/ CONCEPTS*	PLAYERS	GLOBAL FUNCTIONS/ PROCESSES*	GLOBAL GOVERNANCE*
• **Verticality** - regulatory: universally defined principles; - functional: integrated decisional processes with institutions' participation • **Legality** - legality principle (*ex iniuria jus non oritur*); - control of legality over global governance • **Integration** - organizational model of the world's society based on the gradual integration between various systems of organization (legal, social, economic, religious, and mediatic) at different aggregation levels (local to worldwide) • **Collective guarantees** - integrated mechanisms of monitoring, ascertainment, and coercive implementation measures	• **Global constitutional principles/values** - prohibition on the use of force; safeguarding self-determination, human rights; common heritage concept; sustainable development • **Multilateral Regimes** - to formulate regulations, to manage, protect, and conserve environment, global commons, natural resources, cultural goods • **Global Economy** - WTO/GATT rules, world financial regulations • **Integration concept** - harmonization/ integration of legal systems in the direction of global law - global law is the third stage of development of international law, the preceding two phases being the international law of coexistence and the international law of cooperation **The emergence of rules oriented towards individuals, ethnic groups, humankind, marks the transition from inter–state society to global community*	• **States** • **Non-state actors/global forces** (IGOs, NGOs and different forms of power i.e., new powers)	• **Rule-formation** - quasi–organic processes; - public and private participation, together with transparency • **Regime of compliance and enforcement** - integrated systems for monitoring and action • **Global judicial function** - global courts and tribunals to protect global values and commons - participation of civil society in international courts and tribunals (e.g., Human Rights Courts, International Criminal Court) **Multilateral normative processes and actions for managing worldwide economic and social development as well as threats to international peace and security*	• **Co-management of global values and commons** • **Integrated decision-making processes (institutional participation and control)** • **Multilateral actions and shared responsibility** • **Central role of UN** • **Judicial control over the executive** **Shared governance under UN control involving the forces of the global community (UN organs, states, non-state actors, IGO, NGOs, civil society, and the private sector)*

Table 3 The Global Legal System

RULE-FORMATION PROCESSES IN GLOBAL LAW

SYSTEMS AND TREATY REGIMES

- **NORMATIVE REGIMES FOUNDED IN INTERNATIONAL INSTITUTIONS**
  - **UN Charter System**
  - **The Bretton Woods System/WTO**
  - **Regional treaty regimes**
- **LEGAL REGIMES** for co-management of the environment, cultural goods, natural resources, and global commons (the Oceans; Antarctica; Outer Space; the Atmosphere)
- **INFORMAL LAW-MAKING** promulgated by international arbitral panels, networks of regulatory entities, or non-state accreditation and standard-setting bodies

GENERAL RULES AND PROCESSES

PROCESSES

A) CUSTOM

- **Notion**
  - general practice accepted as law (Art. 38 (1)(b), ICJ Statute)
- **Characters**
  - general international rules, substantive and procedural (e.g., *pacta sunt servanda* and customary treaty law)
- **Requirements**
  - *diuturnitas, opinio juris sive necessitatis*
- **Formation Process**
  - uniform and constant behavior of "each" individual member of the international community;
  - accompanied by acceptance. The will of "each" member remains distinct
- **Decline of Custom**

B) GENERAL PRINCIPLES OF LAW

- **Notion**
  - general principles of law recognized by civilized nations (Art. 38 (1)(c), ICJ Statute)
- **Characters**
  - principles of legal logic (*ne bis in idem, nemo judex in re sua, etc.*) and principles of natural law (prohibition of genocide, slavery, other gross violations of human rights)
- **Formation Process**
  - universal principles of law posed at the level of national legal orders;
  - accepted internationally/applied by international tribunals

C) INTEGRATED PRINCIPLES OF LAW

- **Notion/Characters**
  - principles of the shared management of global interests/values
  - immediate and direct expression of the will of the global community;
  - without the need for custom/each state's acceptance (i.e., *omisso medio*)
- **Formation Process***
  - intersection of prevailing forces and the public interest:
  - "proposal" of dominant powers/global forces;
  - accepted as law in institutional *fora* (quasi-organic process).

  Proposal and consent represent the basic elements of a dynamic, democratic process for the adoption of general international norms

Security Council's Open Debates;
G8 as a forum for proposals, vested with power to initiate

BASIC RULES/JUS COGENS

- **Notion and Characters**
  - global constitutional principles, peremptory norms of general international law (*jus cogens*);
  - binding on all actors of the global community;
  - no derogation is permitted (Arts. 53, 64, Vienna Convention);
  - can be modified only by a subsequent norm of general international law having the same character (Art. 53, Vienna Convention)
- **Formation Processes**
  - processes indexed in A), B), C), before. Not all general rules produced by these processes (customary norms, general principles of law; integrated principles of law) are peremptory norms

  These processes do not include soft law (i.e. the General Assembly's declarations of principles;the ICJ's advisory opinions) that is not binding but can only produce another legal effect: the "effect of lawfulness"

Table 4 Rule-Formation Processes in Global Law

GLOBAL LAW-ENFORCEMENT SYSTEM

UN COLLECTIVE SECURITY SYSTEM (Chap. VII, Charter)

CONCEPTS

- **Managed by Security Council**
- **Centralized (Arts. 11 (2); 24-25; 39-50)**
- **Veto rule (Art. 27 (3))**

REQUIREMENTS

- **Threats to the peace, breaches of the peace, and acts of aggression**
- **Ascertainment by Security Council (Art. 39)**

MECHANISM AND MEASURES

- **Provisional measures (Art. 40)**
- **Measures not involving the use of armed force**: these may include complete or partial interruption of economic relations and of rail, sea, air, postal, telegraphic, radio, and other means of communication, and the severance of diplomatic relations (Art. 41)
- **Measures involving the use of force:** peace operations (Art. 42)

COLLECTIVE GUARANTEES/ INTEGRATED SYSTEMS

CONCEPTS

- **Enforcement measures co-managed**: responsibility shared between states, UN, global/regional IOs; NGOs
- **Cooperative approach**
- **States acting in the common interest (*uti universi*)**
- **Central role of the UN/organs acting as community agents**
- **Overcoming the veto rule**

REQUIREMENTS

- **Serious violations of peace, human rights, democracy, and other *erga omnes* obligations**
- **Objective ascertainment of violations by UN organs**
- **Institutional control over states acting in the common interest**

SYSTEMS AND MEASURES

- **Unilateral/multilateral military actions**

A) Authorized by the Security Council

B) Non-authorized

- Requirements
  - taken in lieu of ineffectiveness of institutions/SC blocked by veto;
  - necessity and urgency;
  - support of a large majority of states, regional IO, NGOs, and world's public opinion;
  - UN legitimation: control of necessity, proportionality, respect of *jus cogens*

- **Economic coercion/peaceful measures**
  - Unilateral/multilateral economic, diplomatic, and others peaceful measures against responsible state;
  - Targeted sanctions pressuring individuals and entities (*i.e.*, smart sanctions);
  - UN ascertainment of violations and control

- **Co-managed regimes/systems**
  - Human rights implementation systems;
  - Integrated monitoring systems;
  - Integrated diplomatic systems to settle conflicts (e.g., the Road Map);
  - Mixed systems to enforce peace process in countries ravaged by civil war;
  - Integrated judicial systems to enforce crimes committed by individuals and to provide redress to victims: cooperation between state organs and international bodies (*ad hoc*, mixed criminal tribunals, ICC) according to the Statutes;
  - Integrated UN counter-terrorism system
  - Regime compliance and enforcement in the global Commons;
  - Pollution control regimes

Table 5 The Global Law-Enforcement System

GLOBAL JUDICIAL SYSTEM

WORLD'S JUDICIAL BODIES AND TRIBUNALS

- **International Tribunal of the Law of the Sea (ITLOS)**
- **WTO Dispute Settlement Body (WTODSB)**
- **International Criminal Bodies**
  - International Criminal Court (ICC)
  - International Criminal Tribunal for the Former Yugoslavia (ICTY)
  - International Criminal Tribunal for Rwanda (ICTR)
  - Mixed/internationalized criminal jurisdictions (in Sierra Leone, Cambodia, East Timor, Lebanon)
- **Arbitration**
  - Permanent Court of Arbitration (PCA)
  - International Centre for Settlement of Investment Disputes (ICSID)
- **international compliance bodies** based on multilateral conventions (especially in the environmental field).

INTERNATIONAL COURT OF JUSTICE (ICJ)

ICJ PRINCIPAL JUDICIAL ORGAN OF THE UN (ART. 92, CHARTER and ART. 1, STATUTE)

- **Contentious Jurisdiction**
  - Competence:

    -only states may be parties (Art. 34 (1), Statute)
  - Jurisdiction:

    - all legal disputes (Art. 36 (1), Statute);
    - acceptance of the compulsory jurisdiction through declaration made under Article 36 (2), Statute
  - Applicable law:

    - the Court decides in accordance with international law (Art. 38 (1) Statute);
    - power to decide *ex aequo et bono* (Art. 38 (2), Statute)
  - Decision/judgment:

    - binding character, between the parties only (Art. 94 (1), Charter; Art. 59, Statute);
    - final and without appeal (Art. 60, Statute);
    - remedies of enforcement (Art. 94 (2), Charter)
- **Advisory Function**

  (Art. 96, Charter; Chapter IV, Statute)

ICJ GLOBAL TRENDS*

- **The Court as the Guide directing the development of human rights law, humanitarian law, self-determination**
  - The Advisory function as quasi–legislative function
- **Court protection of human rights, peace, and other global values beyond the Charter veto and Statute:**
  - The expansion of the power to indicate (Art. 41, Statute): the binding nature of provisional measures (*LaGrand case*);
  - The expansion of advisory function and the "definitive" ascertainment of violations of *erga omnes* obligations;
  - The validation of the procedure "Uniting for Peace" (GA Res. 377 (V) A)
- **Court's Authority**
  - authority over states' organs;
  - judicial supremacy: the "intrinsic authority" of the Court's decisions;
  - authority in law-making processes
- **Court's control over the UN organs**
  - Relationship Court/ Security Council
    - functional parallelism;
    - complementarity Court/Council;
    - judicial control over the SC decisions;
    - overcoming of the veto rule

The Court as a Supreme Constitutional Court, guardian of global constitutional values – providing legitimacy to world governance

Table 6 The Global Judicial System

Bibliography

Randall S. Abate, *Dawn of a New Era in the Extraterritorial Application of U.S. Environmental Statutes: A Proposal for an Integrated Judicial Standard Based on the Continuum of Context*, 31 Columbia Journal of Environmental Law 87 (2006)

George Abi-Saab, *La Coutume dans Tous Ses Etats ou le Dilemme du Developpement du Droit International General dans un Monde Eclaté*, Il Diritto Internazionale al Tempo della sua Codificazione. Studi in Onore di Roberto Ago 53 (Giuffré, Milano, 1987–I)

George Abi-Saab, *De l'Évolution de la Cour Internationale. Réflexions sur Quelques Tendances Récentes*, 96 Revue Générale de Droit International Public 273 (1992–II)

Georges Abi-Saab, *The International Court as a World Court*, *in* Fifty Years of the International Court of Justice. Essays in Honour of Sir Robert Jennings 3 (Vaughan Lowe & Malgosia A. Fitzmaurice eds., Cambridge University Press, Cambridge, 1996)

Georges Abi-Saab, *The Proper Role of Universal Jurisdiction*, 1 Journal of International Criminal Justice 596 (2003)

Domingo E. Acevedo, *The U.S. Measures Against Argentina Resulting from the Malvinas Conflict*, 78 American Journal of International Law 323 (1984)

William J. Aceves, *The Legality of Transborder Abductions: A Study of United States v. Alvarez-Machain*, 3 Southwestern University Journal of Law and Trade in the Americas 101 (1996)

Mohsen Aghahosseini & Hossein Piran, *Iran-U.S. Claims Tribunal, Introductory Note*, The Global Community. Yearbook of International Law and Jurisprudence 1597 (2005–II); *id.* 1435 (2006–II); *id.* 1787 (2007–II).

Roberto Ago, *Obligations* Erga Omnes *and the International Community*, *in* International Crimes of States: A Critical Analysis of the ICL's Draft Article 19 on State Responsibility 237 (Joseph H. H. Weiler ed., de Gruyter, Berlin, 1989)

Agora: Future Implications of the Iraq Conflict, 97 American Journal of International Law 553 (2003)

Bola A. Ajibola, *Africa and the International Court of Justice*, *in* LIBER AMICORUM "IN MEMORIAM" OF JUDGE JOSÉ MARÌA RUDA 353 (Calixto A. Armas Barea ed., Kluwer Law International, The Hague, 2000)

George H. Aldrich, *The Taliban, Al Qaeda, and the Determination of Illegal Combatants*, 96 AMERICAN JOURNAL OF INTERNATIONAL LAW 891 (2002)

Thomas A. Aleinikoff, *International Law, Sovereignty, And American Constitutionalism. Reflections on the Customary International Law Debate*, 98 AMERICAN JOURNAL OF INTERNATIONAL LAW 91 (2004)

Thomas A. Aleinikoff, *Thinking Outside the Sovereign Box, Transnational Law and the U.S. Constitution*, 82 TEXAS LAW REVIEW 1989 (2004)

Roger P. Alford, *Misusing International Sources to Interpret the Constitution*, 98 AMERICAN JOURNAL OF INTERNATIONAL LAW 57 (2004)

Gudmundur Alfredsson, Jonas Grimheden, Bertram G. Ramcharan & Alfred de Zayas eds., INTERNATIONAL HUMAN RIGHTS MONITORING MECHANISMS: ESSAYS IN HONOUR OF JAKOB TH. MÖLLER (Nijhoff, The Hague, 2001)

Jean Allain, *The True Challenge to the United Nations System of the Use of Force. The Failures of Kosovo and Iraq and the Emergence of the African Union*, 8 MAX PLANCK YEARBOOK OF UNITED NATIONS LAW 237 (2004) and DENIS ALLAND, JUSTICE PRIVÉE ET ORDRE JURIDIQUE INTERNATIONAL. ÉTUDE THÉORIQUE DES CONTRE-MEASURES EN DROIT INTERNATIONAL PUBLIC (Pedone, Paris, 1994)

Denis Alland, *Jurisprudence Française de Droit International Public*, 99 REVUE GÉNÉRALE DE DROIT INTERNATIONAL PUBLIC 1013 (1995)

Denis Alland, *L'Applicabilité Directe du Droit International Considerée du Point de Vue de l'Office du Juge: Des Habits Neufs pour une Vielle Dame?*, 102 REVUE GÉNÉRALE DE DROIT INTERNATIONAL PUBLIC 203 (1998)

Sara E. Allgood, *United Nations Human Rights "Entitlements". The Right to Development Analyzed Within the Application of the Right of Self-determination*, 31 GEORGIA JOURNAL OF INTERNATIONAL & COMPARATIVE LAW 321 (2003)

Philip Allott, EUNOMIA. NEW ORDER FOR A NEW WORLD (Oxford University Press, Oxford, 1990)

Philip Allott, *The International Court and the Voice of Justice*, *in* FIFTY YEARS OF THE INTERNATIONAL COURT OF JUSTICE. ESSAYS IN HONOUR OF SIR ROBERT JENNINGS 389 (Vaughan Lowe & Malgosia A. Fitzmaurice eds., Cambridge University Press, Cambridge, 1996)

Philip Allott, TOWARDS THE INTERNATIONAL RULE OF LAW: ESSAYS IN INTEGRATED CONSTITUTIONAL THEORY (Cameron May, London, 2005)

Najeeb Al-Nauimi ed., INTERNATIONAL LEGAL ISSUES ARISING UNDER THE UNITED NATIONS DECADE OF INTERNATIONAL LAW (Martinus Nijhoff Publishers, The Hague/ London, 1995)

Mutlaq Al-Qahtani, *The Role of the International Court of Justice in the Enforcement of Its Judicial Decisions*, 15 LEIDEN JOURNAL OF INTERNATIONAL LAW 781 (2002)

Philip Alston, *A Third Generation of Solidarity Rights: Progressive Development or Obfuscation of International Human Rights Law?*, 29 NETHERLANDS INTERNATIONAL LAW REVIEW 307 (1982)

Philip Alston, THE UNITED NATIONS AND HUMAN RIGHTS: A CRITICAL APPRAISAL (Clarendon Press, Oxford, 1992)

Philip Alston, *The Myopia of the Handmaidens: International Lawyers and Globalization*, 8 EUROPEAN JOURNAL OF INTERNATIONAL LAW 435 (1997)

Josè E. Alvarez, *Judging the Security Council*, 90 AMERICAN JOURNAL OF INTERNATIONAL LAW 1 (1996)

José Alvarez, *Editorial Comment: Hegemonic International Law Revisited*, 97 AMERICAN JOURNAL OF INTERNATIONAL LAW 873 (2003)

Josè E. Alvarez, INTERNATIONAL ORGANIZATIONS AS LAW-MAKERS (Oxford University Press, Oxford, 2005)

Kim Anderson & Richard Blackhurst eds., REGIONAL INTEGRATION AND THE GLOBAL TRADING SYSTEM (Harvester Wheatsheaf, New York, 1993)

Antony Anghie & Garry Sturgess eds., LEGAL VISIONS OF THE 21ST CENTURY. ESSAYS IN HONOUR OF JUDGE CHRISTOPHER WEERAMANTRY (Kluwer Law International, The Hague, 1998)

Gaetano Arangio Ruiz, *The Normative Role of the General Assembly of the United Nations and the Declaration of Principles of Friendly Relations*, 137 RECUEIL DES COURS 419 (1972–III)

Gaetano Arangio Ruiz, *The Establishment of the International Criminal Tribunal for the Former Yugoslavia and the Doctrine of Implied Powers of the United Nations*, *in* DAI TRIBUNALI PENALI INTERNAZIONALI *AD HOC* A UNA CORTE PERMANENTE, ATTI DEL CONVEGNO, ROMA 15–16 DICEMBRE 1995, 36 (Flavia Lattanzi & Elena Sciso eds., Editoriale Scientifica, Napoli, 1996)

Gaetano Arangio-Ruiz, *Dualism Revisited. International Law and Interindividual Law*, 86 RIVISTA DI DIRITTO INTERNAZIONALE 909 (2003)

Daniele Archibugi, David Held & Martin Köhler eds., RE-IMAGINING POLITICAL COMMUNITY: STUDIES IN COSMOPOLITAN DEMOCRACY (Polity Press, Cambridge, 1998)

Calixto A. Armas Barea ed., LIBER AMICORUM "IN MEMORIAM" OF JUDGE JOSÉ MARÌA RUDA 253 (Kluwer Law International, The Hague, 2000)

Harry W. Arthurs, *The Collective Labour Law of a Global Economy*, *in* LABOUR LAW AND INDUSTRIAL RELATIONS AT THE TURN OF THE CENTURY. LIBER AMICORUM IN HONOUR OF ROGER BLANPAIN 143 (Chris Engels ed., Kluwer Law International, The Hague, 1998)

John. B. Attanasio ed., MULTILATERALISM V. UNILATERALISM, POLICY CHOICES IN A GLOBAL SOCIETY (British Institute of International and Comparative Law, London, 2004)

Daphne Barak-Erez, *The International Law of Human Rights and Constitutional Law. A Case Study of an Expanding Dialogue*, 2 INTERNATIONAL JOURNAL OF CONSTITUTIONAL LAW 611 (2004)

Samuel H. Barnes, *The Contribution of Democracy to Rebuilding Postconflict Societies*, 95 AMERICAN JOURNAL OF INTERNATIONAL LAW 86 (2001)

Robert P. Barnidge Jr., *States' Due Diligence Obligations with Regard to International Non-State Terrorist Organisations Post-11 September 2001: The Heavy Burden that States Must Bear*, 16 IRISH STUDIES IN INTERNATIONAL AFFAIRS 103 (2005)

M. Cherif Bassiouni, CRIMES AGAINST HUMANITY IN INTERNATIONAL CRIMINAL LAW (Nijhoff, Dordrecht, 1992)

M. Cherif Bassiouni, *International Crimes:* "Jus Cogens" *and* "Obligatio Erga Omnes", 59 LAW & CONTEMPORARY PROBLEMS 63 (1996)

M. Cherif Bassiouni, *The Right to Restitution, Compensation, and Rehabilitation for Victims of Gross Violations of Human Rights and Fundamental Freedoms*, UN Doc. E/CN.4/2000/62 (Jan. 16, 2000)

M. Cherif Bassiouni, *Universal Jurisdiction for International Crimes: Historical Perspectives and Contemporary Practice*, *in* POST-CONFLICT JUSTICE (M. Cherif Bassiouni ed., Transnational Publishers, Ardsley, New York, 2002)

M. Cherif Bassiouni, *Legal Control of International Terrorism*, 43 HARVARD INTERNATIONAL LAW JOURNAL 83 (2002)

M. Cherif Bassiouni, *International Criminal Justice in the Era of Globalization: Rising Expectations*, 6 THE GLOBAL COMMUNITY. YEARBOOK OF INTERNATIONAL LAW AND JURISPRUDENCE 3 (2006–I)

M. Cherif Bassiouni ed., INTERNATIONAL CRIMINAL LAW (3rd ed., *in print*)

Giovanni Battaglini, *Riflessione Breve su di un Tema della Sentenza n. 295, con Variazioni*, 2 GIURISPRUDENZA COSTITUZIONALE 1334 (1985)

Giovanni Battaglini, IL DIRITTO INTERNAZIONALE COME SISTEMA DI DIRITTO COMUNE (Cedam, Padova, 1999)

Richard R. Baxter, *Treaties and Custom*, 129 RECUEIL DES COURS 25 (1970–I)

Mohammed Bedjaoui ed., INTERNATIONAL LAW: ACHIEVEMENTS AND PROSPECTS (Unesco, Martinus Nijhoff Publishers, Paris, 1991)

Mohammed Bedjaoui, *Les Organizations Internationales Devant la Cour Internationale de Justice: Bilan et Perspectives*, GAOR 49th sess. (Oct. 24, 1994)

Mohammed Bedjaoui, NOUVEL ORDRE MONDIAL ET CONTRÔLE DE LA LÉGALITÉ DES ACTES DU CONSEIL DE SÉCURITÉ (Bruylant, Bruxelles, 1994)

Mohammed Bedjaoui, THE NEW WORLD ORDER AND THE SECURITY COUNCIL. TESTING THE LEGALITY OF ITS ACTS (Nijhoff, Dordrecht, 1994)

David Beetham, *Human Rights as a Model for Cosmopolitan Democracy*, *in* RE-IMAGINING POLITICAL COMMUNITY: STUDIES IN COSMOPOLITAN DEMOCRACY 58 (Daniele Archibugi, David Held & Martin Köhler eds., Polity Press, Cambridge, 1998)

Peter H. Bekker, *Land and Maritime Boundary Between Cameroon and Nigeria*, 97 AMERICAN JOURNAL OF INTERNATIONAL LAW 387 (2003)

Rafaâ Ben-Achour & Sadok Belaïd eds., DROIT INTERNATIONAL ET DROITS INTERNES, DÉVÉLOPPEMENTS RÉCENTES. COLLOQUE DES 16–17–18 AVRIL 1998 (Pedone, Paris, 1999)

Mohammed Bennouna, *L'Obligation Juridique dans le Monde de l'Après-Guerre Froide*, 39 ANNUAIRE FRANÇAIS DE DROIT INTERNATIONAL 41 (1993)

Mohamed Bennouna, *Les Sanctions Economiques des Nations Unies*, 300 RECUEIL DES COURS 9 (2002)

Judson Osterhoudt Berkey, *The European Court of Justice and Direct Effect for the GATT: A Question Worth Revisiting*, 9 EUROPEAN JOURNAL OF INTERNATIONAL LAW 626 (1998)

Paul Schiff Berman, *Judges as Cosmopolitan Transnational Actors,* 12 TULSA JOURNAL OF COMPARATIVE & INTERNATIONAL LAW 109 (2004)

Rudolf A. Bernhardt, *Ultra Vires Activities of International Organizations*, *in* THEORY OF INTERNATIONAL LAW AT THE THRESHOLD OF THE 21ST CENTURY. ESSAYS IN HONOUR OF KRZYSZTOF SKUBISZEWSKI 599 (Jerzy Makarczyk ed., Kluwer International Law, The Hague, 1996)

Rudolf A. Bernhardt ed., ENCYCLOPEDIA OF PUBLIC INTERNATIONAL LAW, Max-Planck-Institut für Ausländisches Öffentliches Recht und Völkerrecht, Heidelberg North-Holland Amsterdam, 1992-2003)

Leonard F.M. Besselink, *The Constitutional Duty to Promote the Development of the International Legal Order*, 34 NETHERLANDS YEARBOOK OF INTERNATIONAL LAW 89 (2003)

Daniel L. Bethlehem, THE KUWAIT CRISIS: SANCTIONS AND THEIR ECONOMIC CONSEQUENCES (Grotius Publisher, Cambridge, 1991)

Mario Bettati, LE DROIT D'INGERENCE, MUTATION DE L'ORDRE INTERNATIONAL (Jacob, Paris, 1996)

Ulrich Beyerlin, *Die Israelische Befreiungsaktion von Entebbe in Völkerrechtlicher Sicht*, 37 ZEITSCHRIFT FÜR AUSLÄNDISCHES ÖFFENTLICHES RECHT UND VÖLKERRECHT 213 (1977)

Ulrich Beyerlin ed., RECHT ZWISCHEN UMBRUCH UND BEWAHRUNG (Springer, Berlin/Heidelberg, 1995)

Henry Bienen & Robert Gilpin, *Economic Sanctions as a Response to Terrorism*, 3 JOURNAL OF STRATEGIC STUDIES 89 (1980)

Paolo Biscaretti Di Ruffia, COSTITUZIONI STRANIERE CONTEMPORANEE. TESTI SCELTI E COMMENTATI A CURA DI PAOLO BISCARETTI DI RUFFIA (Giuffrè, Milano, 1996–I)

Adelle Blackett, *Global Governance, Legal Pluralism and the Decentered State: A Labor Law Critique of Codes of Corporate Conduct*, 8 INDIANA JOURNAL OF GLOBAL LEGAL STUDIES 401 (2001)

Christopher L. Blakesley, *United States Jurisdiction over Extraterritorial Crime*, 73 JOURNAL OF CRIMINAL LAW AND CRIMINOLOGY 1109 (1982)

Albert P. Blaustein & Gisbert H. Flanz eds., CONSTITUTIONS OF THE COUNTRIES OF THE WORLD. A SERIES OF UPDATED TEXTS, CONSTITUTIONAL CHRONOLOGIES AND ANNOTATED BIBLIOGRAPHIES (Oceana Publications, Dobbs Ferry, New York, 1987)

Hans Blix, *Contemporary Aspects of Recognition*, 130 RECUEIL DES COURS 587 (1970–II)

Niels M. Blokker & Henry G. Schermers eds., PROLIFERATION OF INTERNATIONAL ORGANIZATIONS: LEGAL ISSUES (Kluwer Law International, The Hague, 2001)

John D. Blum, *The Role of Law in Global E-Health, a Tool for Development and Equity in a Digitally Divided World*, 46 SAINT LOUIS UNIVERSITY LAW JOURNAL 85 (2002)

Armin von Bogdandy, Petros C. Mavroidis & Yves Meny eds., EUROPEAN INTEGRATION AND INTERNATIONAL CO-ORDINATION. STUDIES IN TRANSNATIONAL ECONOMIC LAW IN HONOUR OF CLAUS-DIETER EHLERMANN (Kluwer Law International, The Hague, 2002)

Daniel Bodansky, *The Legitimacy of International Governance: A Coming Challenge for International Environmental Law?*, 93 AMERICAN JOURNAL OF INTERNATIONAL 596 (1999)

Daniel Bodansky, *The Use of International Sources in Constitutional Opinion*, 32 GEORGIA JOURNAL OF INTERNATIONAL & COMPARATIVE LAW 421 (2004)

Laurence Boisson de Charzournes ed., IMPLICATIONS OF THE PROLIFERATION OF INTERNATIONAL ADJUDICATORY BODIES FOR DISPUTE RESOLUTION. PROCEEDINGS OF A FORUM CO-SPONSORED BY THE AMERICAN SOCIETY OF INTERNATIONAL LAW AND THE GRADUATE INSTITUTE OF INTERNATIONAL STUDIES; GENEVA, SWITZERLAND, MAY 13, 1995 AMERICAN SOCIETY OF INTERNATIONAL LAW BULLETIN NO. 9, 2 (American Society of International Law Publ., Washington, D.C., 1995)

Laurence Boisson de Chazournes, Cesare Romano & Ruth Mackenzie eds., INTERNATIONAL ORGANIZATIONS AND INTERNATIONAL DISPUTE SETTLEMENT. TRENDS AND PROSPECTS (Transnational Publisher, Ardsley, New York, 2002)

Marc Bossuyt, *The Direct Applicability of International Instruments on Human Rights*, 15 REVUE BELGE DE DROIT INTERNATIONAL 317 (1980)

Derek W. Bowett, SELF-DEFENSE IN INTERNATIONAL LAW (University Press, Manchester, 1958)

Derek W. Bowett, *Reprisals Involving Recourse to Armed Force*, 66 AMERICAN JOURNAL OF INTERNATIONAL LAW 1 (1972)

Derek W. Bowett, *Economic Coercion and Reprisals by States*, 13 VIRGINIA JOURNAL OF INTERNATIONAL LAW 1 (1972)

Derek W. Bowett, James Crawford & Arthur Watts eds., THE INTERNATIONAL COURT OF JUSTICE, PROCESS, PRACTICE AND PROCEDURE (British Institute of International and Comparative Law, London, 1997)

Francis A. Boyle, *The Entebbe Hostages Crisis*, 29 NETHERLANDS INTERNATIONAL LAW REVIEW 32 (1982)

Alan E. Boyle, *The Proliferation of International Jurisdictions and Its Implications for the Court*, *in* THE INTERNATIONAL COURT OF JUSTICE, PROCESS, PRACTICE AND PROCEDURE 124 (Derek W. Bowett, James Crawford & Arthur Watts eds., British Institute of International and Comparative Law, London, 1997)

Ronald A. Brand, *Direct Effect of International Economic Law in the United States and the European Union*, 17 NORTHWESTERN JOURNAL OF INTERNATIONAL LAW & BUSINESS 556 (1996/97)

Stephen Breyer, *Keynote Address*, 97 AMERICAN SOCIETY OF INTERNATIONAL LAW: PROCEEDINGS OF THE ANNUAL MEETING 268 (2003)

Hervé Bribosia, Applicabilité Directe et Primauté des Traités Internationaux et du Droit Communautaire, 29 REVUE BELGE DE DROIT INERNATIONAL 33 (1996)

James L. Brierly, THE LAW OF NATIONS. AN INTRODUCTION TO THE INTERNATIONAL LAW OF PEACE (6th ed., Clarendon Press, Oxford, 1963)

Herbert W. Brigg, *Recognition of States: Some Reflections on Doctrine and Practice*, 43 AMERICAN JOURNAL OF INTERNATIONAL LAW 113 (1949)

Aron Broches, *The Convention on the Settlement of Investment Disputes between States and Nationals of Other States*, 136 RECUEIL DES COURS 331 (1972–II)

Hartmut Brosche, *The Arab Oil Embargo and the United States Pressure Against Chile*, 7 CASE WESTERN RESERVE JOURNAL OF INTERNATIONAL LAW 30 (1974)

N. Brower, *The Iran-United States Claims Tribunal*, 224 RECUEIL DES COURS 123 (1990–V)

Edith Brown Weiss, *The New International Legal System*, *in* PERSPECTIVES ON INTERNATIONAL LAW. A PUBLICATION ON THE OCCASION OF THE FIFTIETH ANNIVERSARY OF THE UNITED NATIONS AND A CONTRIBUTION TO THE DECADE OF INTERNATIONAL LAW 63 (Nandasiri Jasentuliyana ed., Kluwer, London, 1995)

Ian Brownlie, INTERNATIONAL LAW AND THE USE OF FORCE BY STATES (Clarendon Press, Oxford, 1963)

Ian Brownlie, *Humanitarian Intervention*, *in* LAW AND CIVIL WAR IN THE MODERN WORLD 217 (John N. Moore ed., Johns Hopkins University Press, Baltimore, 1974)

Ian Brownlie, *Remedies in the International Court of Justice*, *in* FIFTY YEARS OF THE INTERNATIONAL COURT OF JUSTICE. ESSAYS IN HONOUR OF SIR ROBERT JENNINGS 389 (Vaughan Lowe & Malgosia A. Fitzmaurice eds., Cambridge University Press, Cambridge, 1996)

Thomas Buergenthal, *The Inter-American Court of Human Rights*, 76 AMERICAN JOURNAL OF INTERNATIONAL LAW 231 (1982)

Thomas Buergenthal, *The Advisory Practice of the Inter American Human Rights Court*, 79 AMERICAN JOURNAL OF INTERNATIONAL LAW 1 (1985)

Thomas Buergenthal, *Self-Executing and Non Self-Executing Treaties in National and International Law*, 235 RECUEIL DES COURS 303 (1992–IV)

Lucius Caflisch, *Is the International Court Entitled to Review Security Council Resolutions Adopted under Chapter VII of the United Nations Charter?*, in INTERNATIONAL LEGAL ISSUES ARISING UNDER THE UNITED NATIONS DECADE OF INTERNATIONAL LAW 633 (Najeeb Al-Nauimi ed., Martinus Nijhoff Publishers, The Hague/London,1995)

Lucius Caflish, *Cent Ans de Règlement Pacifiques de Différends Interétatiques*, 288 RECUEIL DES COURS 285 (2001)

Antônio Augusto Cançado Trindade, *Co-Existence and Co-Ordination of Mechanisms of International Protection of Human Rights (At Global and Regional Levels)*, 202 RECUEIL DES COURS 9 (1987–II)

Antônio Augusto Cançado Trindade, *El Nuevo Reglamento de la Corte Interamericana de Derechos Humanos (2001)*, 30/31 INTER-AMERICAN INSTITUTE OF HUMAN RIGHTS: REVISTA IIDH 45 (2001)

Antônio Augusto Cançado Trindade, *Inter-American Court of Human Rights, Introductory Note, Developments in the Case-Law of the Inter-American Court of Human Rights*, THE GLOBAL COMMUNITY. YEARBOOK OF INTERNATIONAL LAW AND JURISPRUDENCE 1203 (2002–II); *id.*, 1111 (2003–II); *id.*, 1441 (2004–II); *id.*, 1483 (2005–II); *id.*, 1357 (2006–II); *id.*, 1675 (2007–II)

Bruce Carolan, *The Search for Coherence in the Use of Foreign Court Judgments by the Supreme Court of Ireland*, 12 TULSA JOURNAL OF COMPARATIVE & INTERNATIONAL LAW 123 (2004)

David D. Caron, *The Nature of the Iran-US Claims Tribunal and the Evolving Structure of International Dispute Resolution*, 84 AMERICAN JOURNAL OF INTERNATIONAL LAW 104 (1990)

David D. Caron, *The Legitimacy of the Collective Authority of the Security Council*, 87 AMERICAN JOURNAL OF INTERNATIONAL LAW 552 (1993)

Robert Carswell, *Economic Sanctions and the Iran Experience*, 60 FOREIGN AFFAIRS 247 (1981–1982)

Antonio Cassese, *Modern Constitutions and International Law*, 192 RECUEIL DES COURS 331 (1985–III)

Antonio Cassese, TERRORISM, POLITICS AND LAW. THE ACHILLE LAURO AFFAIR (Polity Press, Cambridge 1989) (transl. by S.J.K. Greenleaves of: ANTONIO CASSESE, IL CASO “ACHILLE LAURO”. TERRORISMO, POLITICA E DIRITTO NELLA COMUNITÀ INTERNAZIONALE (Riuniti, Roma,1987))

Antonio Cassese & Prosper Weil eds., CHANGE AND STABILITY IN INTERNATIONAL LAW-MAKING (de Gruyter, Berlin, 1988)

Elizabeth Chadwick, SELF-DETERMINATION, TERRORISM AND THE INTERNATIONAL HUMANITARIAN LAW OF ARMED CONFLICT (Nijhoff, The Hague, 1996)

Kevin Chamberlain, *Collective Suspension of Air Services With States Which Harbour Hijackers*, 32 INTERNATIONAL & COMPARATIVE LAW QUARTERLY 616 (1983)

Jonathan I. Charney, *Disputes Implicating the International Credibility of the Court: Problems of Non-Appearance, Non-Participation, and Non-Performance*, *in* THE INTERNATIONAL COURT OF JUSTICE AT THE CROSSROADS 288 (Lori Fisler Damrosch ed., Transnational Publishers, Dobbs Ferry, New York, 1987)

Jonathan I. Charney, Donald K. Anton & Mary Ellen O'Connell eds., POLITICS, VALUES AND FUNCTIONS. INTERNATIONAL LAW IN THE 21ST CENTURY. ESSAYS IN HONOUR OF PROFESSOR LOUIS HENKIN (Nijhoff, The Hague, 1997)

Jonathan I. Charney, *Is International Law Threatened by Multiple International Tribunals?*, 271 RECUEIL DES COURS 101 (1998–I)

Jonathan I. Charney, *Anticipatory Humanitarian Intervention in Kosovo*, 93 AMERICAN JOURNAL OF INTERNATIONAL LAW 834 (1999)

Jonathan Charney, *The Use of Force Against Terrorism and International Law*, 95 AMERICAN JOURNAL OF INTERNATIONAL LAW 835 (2001)

Steve Charnovitz, TRADE LAW AND GLOBAL GOVERNANCE (Cameron May, London, 2002)

Jean Charpentier, LA RECONNAISSANCE INTERNATIONALE ET L'EVOLUTION DU DROIT DES GENS (Pedone, Paris, 1956)

Ti-Chiang Chen, THE INTERNATIONAL LAW OF RECOGNITION, WITH SPECIAL REFERENCE TO PRACTICE IN GREAT BRITAIN AND THE UNITED STATES (Stevens, London, 1951)

Bin Cheng, *UN Resolutions on Outer Space: "Instant" International Customary Law?*, 5 INDIAN JOURNAL OF INTERNATIONAL LAW 23 (1965)

Bin Cheng, *On the Nature and Sources of International Law*, *in* INTERNATIONAL LAW: TEACHING AND PRACTICE 203 (Bin Cheng ed., Stevens, London, 1982)

Bin Cheng, *Custom: The Future of General State Practice in a Divided World*, *in* THE STRUCTURE AND PROCESS OF INTERNATIONAL LAW: ESSAYS IN LEGAL PHILOSOPHY DOCTRINE AND THEORY 496 (Ronald St. John Macdonald & Douglas M. Johnston eds., Nijhoff, The Hague, 1983)

Christine M. Chinkin, THIRD PARTIES IN INTERNATIONAL LAW (Clarendon Press, Oxford/Sydney, 1993)

Christine M. Chinkin, *Global Summits: Democratising International Law-Making?*, 7 PUBLIC LAW REVIEW 208 (1996)

Christine M. Chinkin, *The Legality of the Imposition by the EU in International Law*, *in* ASPECTS OF STATEHOOD AND INSTITUTIONALISM IN CONTEMPORARY EUROPE 183 (Malcolm D. Evans ed., Dartmouth, Aldershot, 1997)

Christine M. Chinkin, *Kosovo: A "Good" or "Bad" War?*, 93 AMERICAN JOURNAL OF INTERNATIONAL LAW 843 (1999)

Dan Ciobanu, *Litispendence Between the International Court of Justice and the Political Organs of the United Nations*, *in* THE FUTURE OF THE INTERNATIONAL COURT OF JUSTICE 209 (Leo Gross ed., Oceana Publications, Dobbs Ferry, New York, 1976–I)

Brice M. Clagett, *Title III of the Helms-Burton Act Is Consistent with International Law*, 90 AMERICAN JOURNAL OF INTERNATIONAL LAW 434 (1996)

Brice M. Clagett, *The Cuban Liberty and Democratic Solidarity (Libertad) Act, Continued. A Reply to Professor Lowenfeld*, 90 AMERICAN JOURNAL OF INTERNATIONAL LAW 641 (1996)

Richard P. Claude & Burns H. Weston eds., HUMAN RIGHTS IN THE WORLD COMMUNITY: ISSUES AND ACTION (University of Pennsylvania Press, Philadelphia, 1992)

Benjamin J. Cohen, THE FUTURE OF MONEY (Princeton University Press, Princeton, NJ, 2004)

Catherine Collier Fisher, *US Legislation to Prosecute Terrorists: Antiterrorism or Legalized Kidnapping?*, 18 VANDERBILT JOURNAL OF TRANSNATIONAL LAW 915 (1985)

Ninon Colneric, David Edward, Jean-Pierre Puissochet & Dámaso Ruiz-Jarabo Colomer eds., UNE COMMUNAUTÉ DE DROIT. FESTSCHRIFT FÜR GIL CARLOS RODRÍGUEZ IGLESIAS (Berliner Wissenschafts-Verlag, Berlin, 2003)

Luigi Condorelli, *Custom*, *in* INTERNATIONAL LAW: ACHIEVEMENTS AND PROSPECTS 179 (Mohammed Bedjaoui ed., Unesco, Martinus Nijhoff Publishers, Paris, 1991)

Luigi Condorelli, Anne-Marie La Rosa & Sylvie Scherrer eds., LES NATIONS UNIES ET LE DROIT INTERNATIONAL HUMANITAIRE/THE UNITED NATIONS AND INTERNATIONAL HUMANITARIAN LAW (Pedone, Paris, 1996)

Benedetto Conforti, *Cours Général de Droit International Public*, 212 RECUEIL DES COURS 9 (1988–V)

Benedetto Conforti, *Le Pouvoir Discrétionnaire du Conseil de Sécurité en Matière de Constatation d'une Menace Contre la Paix, d'Une Rupture de la Paix ou d'Un Acte d'Agression*, *in* LE DÉVELOPPEMENT DU RÔLE DU CONSEIL DE SÉCURITÉ/THE DEVELOPMENT OF THE ROLE OF THE SECURITY COUNCIL, PEACE-KEEPING AND PEACE-BUILDING, COLLOQUE, LA HAYE, 21–23 JUILLET 1992, 55 (René-Jean Dupuy ed., Nijhoff, Dordrecht, 1993)

Benedetto Conforti, *Notes on the Relationship Between International and National Law*, 3 INTERNATIONAL LAW FORUM 18 (2001)

Benedetto Conforti, LE NAZIONI UNITE (Cedam, Padova, 2005)

Paul Conlon, *Lessons from Iraq: The Functions of the Iraq Sanctions Committee as a Source of Sanctions Implementation Authority and Practice*, 35 VANDERBILT JOURNAL OF INTERNATIONAL LAW 633 (1995)

George R. Constantinople, *Towards a New Definition of Piracy: The Achille Lauro Incident*, 26 VIRGINIA JOURNAL OF INTERNATIONAL LAW 723 (1986)

H.H. Anthony Cooper, *Hostage Rescue Operations: Dénouement at Algeria and Mogadishu Compared*, 26 CHITTY'S LAW JOURNAL 91 (1978)

Robert Cooper, THE POST-MODERN STATE AND THE WORLD ORDER (Demos, London, 1996)

David Cortright & George A. Lopez eds., ECONOMIC SANCTIONS: PANACEA OR PEACEBUILDING IN A POST-COLD WAR WORLD? (Westview Press, Boulder, Colo., 1995)

Michel Cosnard, *Les Lois Helms-Burton & D'Amato-Kennedy, Interdiction de Commercer avec et d'Investir dans Certains Pays*, 62 ANNUAIRE FRANÇAIS DE DROIT INTERNATIONAL 33 (1996)

Michel Cosnard, *Quelques Observations sur les Décisions de la Chambre des Lords du 25 Novembre 1998 et du 24 Mars 1999 dans l'Affaire Pinochet*, 103 REVUE GÉNÉRALE DE DROIT INTERNATIONAL PUBLIC 309 (1999)

Thomas Cottier, STUDIES IN GLOBAL ECONOMIC LAW/STUDIEN ZUM GLOBALEN WIRTSCHAFTSRECHT/ÉTUDES EN DROIT ÉCONOMIQUE MONDIAL (Lang, Bern/Berlin/Frankfurt am Main/Wien, 1999)

Thomas Cottier, *A Theory of Direct Effect in Global Law*, *in* EUROPEAN INTEGRATION AND INTERNATIONAL CO-ORDINATION. STUDIES IN TRANSNATIONAL ECONOMIC LAW IN HONOUR OF CLAUS-DIETER EHLERMANN 99 (Armin von Bogdandy, Petros C. Mavroidis & Yves Meny eds., Kluwer Law International, The Hague, 2002)

Robert W. Cox & Timothy J. Sinclair eds., APPROACHES TO WORLD ORDER (Cambridge University Press, Cambridge, 1996)

Robert W. Cox, *Globalization, Multilateralism and Democracy*, *in* APPROACHES TO WORLD ORDER 530 (Robert W. Cox & Timothy J. Sinclair eds., Cambridge University Press, Cambridge, 1996)

Matthew Craven, *Unity, Diversity and the Fragmentation of International Law*, 14 THE FINNISH YEARBOOK OF INTERNATIONAL LAW 3 (2003)

James Crawford & Susan Marks, *The Global Democracy Deficit: An Essay on International Law and its Limits*, *in* RE-IMAGINING POLITICAL COMMUNITY: STUDIES IN COSMOPOLITAN DEMOCRACY 72 (Daniele Archibugi, David Held & Martin Köhler eds., Polity Press, Cambridge, 1998)

James Crawford, THE INTERNATIONAL LAW COMMISSION'S ARTICLES ON STATE RESPONSIBILITY (Cambridge Univ. Press, Cambridge, 2002)

James Crawford, THE CREATION OF STATES IN INTERNATIONAL LAW (Clarendon Press, Oxford, 2006)

John R. Crook, *The 2000 Judicial Activity of the International Court of Justice*, 95 AMERICAN JOURNAL OF INTERNATIONAL LAW 685 (2001)

John R. Crook, *The 2001 Judicial Activity of the International Court of Justice*, 96 AMERICAN JOURNAL OF INTERNATIONAL LAW 397 (2002)

John R. Crook, *The 2002 Judicial Activity of the International Court of Justice*, 97 AMERICAN JOURNAL OF INTERNATIONAL LAW 352 (2003)

Deirdre Curtin & David O'Keeffe eds., CONSTITUTIONAL ADJUDICATION IN EUROPEAN COMMUNITY AND NATIONAL LAW. ESSAYS FOR THE HON. MR. JUSTICE T. F. O'HIGGINS (Butterworth, Dublin, 1992)

Claire A. Cutler, PRIVATE POWER AND GLOBAL AUTHORITY: TRANSNATIONAL MERCHANT LAW IN THE GLOBAL POLITICAL ECONOMY (Cambridge University Press, Cambridge, 2003)

Wladiyslaw Czaplinsky, *Relationship Between International Law and Polish Municipal Law in the Light of the 1997 Constitution and of the Jurisprudence*, 31 REVUE BELGE DE DROIT INTERNATIONAL 259 (1998)

Anthony D'Amato, *The Invasion of Panama Was a Lawful Response to Tyranny*, 84 AMERICAN JOURNAL OF INTERNATIONAL LAW 516 (1990)

Anthony D'Amato, *The UN Mideast Ceasefire Resolution Paragraph-by-Paragraph*, JURIST'S FORUM (Aug. 13, 2006), *available at* http://jurist.law.pitt.edu/forumy/2006/08/un-mideast-ceasefire-resolution.php.

Jean d'Aspremont Lynden, *Du Dualisme au Monisme*, 4 REVUE BELGE DE DROIT CONSTITUTIONNEL 397 (2003)

Patrick Daillier, *Monisme et Dualisme: Un Débat Depassé?*, *in* DROIT INTERNATIONAL ET DROITS INTERNES, DÉVÉLOPPEMENTS RÉCENTES. COLLOQUE DES 16–17–18 AVRIL 1998 (Rafaâ Ben-Achour & Sadok Belaïd eds., Pedone, Paris, 1999)

Lori Fisler Damrosch ed., THE INTERNATIONAL COURT OF JUSTICE AT THE CROSSROADS (Transnational Publishers, Dobbs Ferry, New York, 1987)

Lori Fisler Damrosch ed., ENFORCING RESTRAINT: COLLECTIVE INTERVENTION IN INTERNAL CONFLICTS (Council on Foreign Relations Press, New York, 1993)

Lori Fisler Damrosch, *The Permanent Five as Enforcers of Controls on Weapons of Mass Destruction. Building on the Iraq "Precedent"?*, 13 EUROPEAN JOURNAL OF INTERNATIONAL LAW 305 (2002)

Lori Fisler Damrosch & Bernard H. Oxman, *Editors' Introduction, Agora: Future Implications of the Iraq Conflict*, 97 AMERICAN JOURNAL OF INTERNATIONAL LAW 553 (2003)

Gennady M. Danilenko, *The New Russian Constitution and International Law*, 88 AMERICAN JOURNAL OF INTERNATIONAL LAW 451 (1994)

Joseph J. Darby, *Self Defense in Public International Law. The Doctrine of Pre-emption and Its Discontents*, INTERNATIONALE GEMEINSCHAFT UND MENSCHENRECHTE – FESTSCHRIFT FÜR GEORG RESS ZUM 70. GEBURTSTAG AM 21 JANUAR 2005, 29 (2005)

Ian Davidson, *U.S., E.C. Disagree on How to Deal With Terrorism: Reaction to U.S. Raid on Libya Underscores Differences Over the Use of Military Force*, EUROPE 16 (1986)

André J.J. De Hoogh, OBLIGATIONS ERGA OMNES AND INTERNATIONAL CRIMES: A THEORETICAL INQUIRY INTO THE IMPLEMENTATION AND ENFORCEMENT OF THE INTERNATIONAL RESPONSIBILITY OF STATES (Kluwer, The Hague, Nijmegen, 1996)

Charles de Martens, NOUVELLES CAUSES CÉLÈBRES DU DROIT DES GENS (Brockhaus, Leipzig, 1843)

Charles De Visscher, THÉORIES ET RÉALITÉS EN DROIT INTERNATIONAL PUBLIC 184 (3rd ed., Pedone, Paris, 1960)

Paul de Visscher, *Les Tendences Internationales des Constitutions Modernes*, 80 RECUEIL DES COURS 511 (1952–I)

Paul de Visscher, *La Constitution Belge et le Droit International*, 19 REVUE BELGE DE DROIT INTERNATIONAL 5 (1986)

Erika De Wet, *Judicial Review as an Emerging General Principle of Law and Its Implications for the International Court of Justice*, 47 NETHERLANDS INTERNATIONAL LAW REVIEW 181 (2000)

Angela Del Vecchio, GIURISDIZIONE INTERNAZIONALE E GLOBALIZZAZIONE. I TRIBUNALI INTERNAZIONALI TRA GLOBALIZZAZIONE E FRAMMENTAZIONE (Giuffrè, Milano, 2003)

Emmanuel Decaux, *Coordination et Suivi dans le Système de Protection des Droits de l'Homme des Nations Unies*, *in* L' EFFECTIVITÉ DES ORGANISATIONS INTERNATIONALES. MÉCANISMES DE SUIVI ET DE CONTRÔLE; JOURNÉES FRANCO-HELLÉNIQUE, 7 – 8 MAI 1999 229 (Hélène Ruiz-Fabri ed., Pedone, Paris, 2000)

Jost Delbrück ed., THE FUTURE OF INTERNATIONAL LAW ENFORCEMENT, NEW SCENARIOS-NEW LAW? PROCEEDINGS OF AN INTERNATIONAL SYMPOSIUM OF THE KIEL INSTITUTE OF INTERNATIONAL LAW, MARCH 25 TO 27, 1992 (Duncker & Humblot, Berlin, 1993)

Jost Delbrück ed., ALLOCATION OF LAW ENFORCEMENT AUTHORITY IN THE INTERNATIONAL SYSTEM. PROCEEDINGS OF AN INTERNATIONAL SYMPOSIUM OF THE KIEL INSTITUTE OF INTERNATIONAL LAW, MARCH 23 TO 25, 1994 (Duncker & Humblot, Berlin, 1995)

Jost Delbrück, *The Impact of the Allocation of International Law Enforcement Authority on the International Legal Order*, *in* ALLOCATION OF LAW ENFORCEMENT AUTHORITY IN THE INTERNATIONAL SYSTEM. PROCEEDINGS OF AN INTERNATIONAL SYMPOSIUM OF THE KIEL INSTITUTE OF INTERNATIONAL LAW, MARCH 23 TO 25, 1994, 135 (Jost Delbrück ed., Duncker & Humblot, Berlin, 1995)

MIREILLE DELMAS-MARTY, TROIS DÉFIS POUR UN DROIT MONDIAL (Seuil, Paris, 1998)

MIREILLE DELMAS-MARTY, GLOBAL LAW. A TRIPLE CHALLENGE (Transnational Publishers, Ardsley, New York, 2003)

Erik Denters ed., REFLECTIONS ON INTERNATIONAL LAW FROM THE LOW COUNTRIES IN HONOUR OF PAUL DE WAART (Nijhoff, The Hague, 1998)

Dermott J. Devine, *Relationship Between International Law and Domestic Law in Domestic Courts*, 24 SOUTH AFRICAN YEARBOOK OF INTERNATIONAL LAW 317 (1999)

Jean-Louis Dewost, *La Communauté, Les Dix, et Les "Sanctions" Économiques: de la Crise Iranienne à la Crise Malouines*, 28 ANNUAIRE FRANÇAIS DE DROIT INTERNATIONAL 217 (1982)

Jean Dhommeaux, *Monismes et Dualismes en Droit International des Droits de l'Homme*, 41 ANNUAIRE FRANÇAIS DE DROIT INTERNATIONAL 447 (1995)

Jean Dhommeaux, *Jurisprudence du Comité des Droits de l'Homme des Nations Unies (novembre 1993–juillet 1996)*, 42 ANNUAIRE FRANÇAIS DE DROIT INTERNATIONAL 679 (1996)

Jean Dhommeaux, *Jurisprudence du Comité des Droits de l'Homme des Nations Unies (novembre 1996–novembre 1998)*, 44 ANNUAIRE FRANÇAIS DE DROIT INTERNATIONAL 613 (1998)

Leticia Diaz & Barry Hart Dubner, *On the Problem of Utilizing Unilateral Action to Prevent Acts of Sea Piracy and Terrorism*, 32 SYRACUSE JOURNAL OF INTERNATIONAL LAW AND COMMERCE 1 (2004)

Yoram Dinstein ed., INTERNATIONAL LAW AT A TIME OF PERPLEXITY. ESSAYS IN HONOUR OF SHABTAI ROSENNE (Nijhoff, Dordrecht, 1989)

Yoram Dinstein, *The Universality Principle and War Crimes*, *in* THE LAW OF ARMED CONFLICT INTO THE NEXT MILLENIUM 17 (Michael N. Schmitt ed., Naval War College, Newport, 1998)

YORAM DINSTEIN, WAR, AGGRESSION AND SELF-DEFENCE (4th ed., Cambridge, Cambridge University Press, 2005)

Christian Dominicé, *Observations sur les Droits de l'État Victime d'un Fait Internationalement Illicite*, Institut des Hautes Études Internationaux, Cours et Travaux, 1981–1982 (1983)

Christian Dominicé, *La Sécurité Collective et la Crise du Golfe*, 2 EUROPEAN JOURNAL OF INTERNATIONAL LAW 85 (1991)

Christian Dominicé, *Le Conseil de Sécurité et le Droit International*, 43 JUGOSLOVENSKA REWVIJA ZA MEDUNARODNO PRAVO 197 (1996)

Jack Donnelly, *Recent Trends in UN Human Rights Activity: Description and Polemic*, 35 INTERNATIONAL ORGANIZATION 633 (1981)

Jack Donnelly, UNIVERSAL HUMAN RIGHTS IN THEORY AND PRACTICE (Cornell University Press, Ithaca, New York, 1989)

Patrick L. Donnelly, *Extraterritorial Jurisdiction over Acts of Terrorism Committed Abroad: Omnibus Diplomatic Security and Antiterrorism Act of 1986*, 72 CORNELL LAW REVIEW 599 (1987)

Agnès Dormenval, PROCÉDURES ONUSIENNES DE MISE EN OEUVRE DES DROITS DE L'HOMME: LIMITES OU DÉFAUTS? (Presses Universitaires de France, Paris, 1991)

Margaret P. Doxey, ECONOMIC SANCTIONS AND INTERNATIONAL ENFORCEMENT (2nd ed., Macmillan, London, 1980)

Margaret P. Doxey, *International Sanctions in Theory and Practice*, 15 CASE WESTERN RESERVE JOURNAL OF INTERNATIONAL LAW 273 (1983)

Margaret P. Doxey, INTERNATIONAL SANCTIONS IN CONTEMPORARY PERSPECTIVE (Macmillan, Basingstoke, 1987)

Louis Dubouis, *Le Juge Administratif Français et les Règles du Droit International*, 17 ANNUAIRE FRANÇAIS DE DROIT INTERNATIONAL 15 (1971)

John H. Dunning, MULTINATIONAL ENTERPRISES AND THE GLOBAL ECONOMY (Addison-Wesley, Wokingham, 1993)

Jeffrey L. Dunoff, *From Green to Global, Toward the Transformation of International Environmental Law*, 19 THE HARVARD ENVIRONMENTAL LAW REVIEW 241 (1995)

Pierre-Marie Dupuy, *Action Publique et Crime International de l'État: A Propos de l'Art. 19 du Projet de la Commission du Droit International sur la Responsabilité des États*, 25 ANNUAIRE FRANÇAIS DE DROIT INTERNATIONAL 539 (1979)

Pierre-Marie Dupuy, *Observations sur le "Crime International de l'État"*, 84 REVUE GÉNÉRALE DE DROIT INTERNATIONAL PUBLIC 449 (1980)

Pierre-Marie Dupuy, *Observations sur la Pratique Récente des "Sanctions" de l'Illicite*, 87 REVUE GÉNÉRALE DE DROIT INTERNATIONAL PUBLIC 523 (1983)

Pierre-Marie Dupuy, *L'Unité de l'Ordre Juridique International*, 297 RECUEIL DES COURS 9 (2002)

René-Jean Dupuy, *Coutume Sage et Coutume Sauvage*, *in* LA COMMUNAUTÉ INTERNATIONALE. MÉLANGES OFFERTS À CHARLES ROUSSEAU 75 (Pedone, Paris, 1974)

René-Jean Dupuy ed., LE DÉVELOPPEMENT DU RÔLE DU CONSEIL DE SÉCURITÉ/THE DEVELOPMENT OF THE ROLE OF THE SECURITY COUNCIL, PEACE-KEEPING AND PEACE-BUILDING, COLLOQUE, LA HAYE, 21–23 JUILLET 1992 (Nijhoff, Dordrecht, 1993)

Réné-Jean Dupuy, *Concept de Démocratie et Action des Nations Unies*, 7–8 BULLETTIN DU CENTRE D'INFORMATION DES NATIONS UNIES 61 (Dec. 1993)

Alison Duxbury, *Saving Lives in the International Court of Justice: The Use of Provisional Measures to Protect Human Life*, 31 CALIFORNIA WESTERN INTERNATIONAL LAW JOURNAL 141 (2000)

Constantin P. Économidès, THE RELATIONSHIP BETWEEN INTERNATIONAL AND DOMESTIC LAW (Council of Europe, Strasbourg, 1994)

Constantin P. Économidès, *La Position du Droit International dans l'Ordre Juridique Interne et l'Application des Règles du Droit International par le Juge National*, 49 REVUE HELLENIQUE DE DROIT INTERNATIONAL 207 (1996)

Pierre M. Eisemann & VINCENT COUSSIRAT-COUSTÈRE, PETIT MANUEL DE LA JURISPRUDENCE DE LA COUR INTERNATIONALE DE JUSTICE (Pedone, Paris, 1984)

Pierre M. Eisemann ed., THE INTEGRATION OF INTERNATIONAL AND EUROPEAN COMMUNITY LAW INTO THE NATIONAL LEGAL ORDER/L'INTÉGRATION DU DROIT INTERNATIONAL ET COMMUNAUTAIRE DANS L'ORDRE JURIDIQUE NATIONAL, ÉTUDE DE LA PRATIQUE EN EUROPE (Kluwer Law International, The Hague, 1996)

Alex G. Oude Elferink & Donald R. Rothwell, OCEANS MANAGEMENT IN THE 21ST CENTURY: INSTITUTIONAL FRAMEWORKS AND RESPONSES (Nijhoff Publishers, Leiden, 2004)

Claude Emanuelli, LES MOYENS DE PRÉVENTION ET DE SANCTION EN CAS D'ACTION ILLICITE CONTRE L'AVIATION CIVILE INTERNATIONALE (Pedone, Paris, 1974)

Atimomo A. Emiko, *The Impact of International Terrorism and Hijacking of Aircraft on State Sovereignty: The Israeli Raid on Entebbe Airport Re-visited*, 23 JOURNAL OF THE INDIAN LAW INSTITUTE 90 (1981)

Chris Engels ed., LABOUR LAW AND INDUSTRIAL RELATIONS AT THE TURN OF THE CENTURY. LIBER AMICORUM IN HONOUR OF ROGER BLANPAIN (Kluwer Law International, The Hague, 1998)

Eric F. Ellen, PIRACY AT SEA (ICC, International Maritime Bureau, Paris, 1989)

Albin Eser, *National Jurisdiction Over Extraterritorial Crimes Within the Framework of International Complementary: A Comparative Survey on Transnational Prosecution of Genocide According to the Principle of Universality*, *in* MAN'S INHUMANITY TO MAN. ESSAYS ON INTERNATIONAL LAW IN HONOUR OF ANTONIO CASSESE 279 (Lal Chand Vohrah ed., Kluwer Law International, The Hague, 2003)

Carlos Darío Espósito, *Male Captus, Bene Detentus: A Propósito de la Sentencia del Tribunal Supremo de Estados Unidos en el Caso Alvarez-Machain*, 62 LECCIONES Y ENSAYOS 17 (1995)

Malcolm D. Evans ed. ASPECTS OF STATEHOOD AND INSTITUTIONALISM IN CONTEMPORARY EUROPE (Dartmouth, Aldershot, 1997)

Richard A. Falk & Cyril E. Black eds., THE FUTURE OF THE INTERNATIONAL LEGAL ORDER. RETROSPECT AND PROSPECT (Center of International Studies, Woodrow Wilson School of Public and International Affairs, Princeton University, Princeton, NJ, 1982)

Richard A. Falk, *The Interplay of Westphalia and Charter Conceptions of the International Legal Order*, *in* THE FUTURE OF THE INTERNATIONAL LEGAL ORDER. RETROSPECT AND PROSPECT 32 (Richard Falk & Cyril E. Black eds., Center of International Studies, Woodrow Wilson School of Public and International Affairs, Princeton University, Princeton, NJ, 1982–I)

Richard A. Falk, *Rethinking Counter-Terrorism*, 6 SCANDINAVIAN JOURNAL OF DEVELOPMENT ALTERNATIVES 19 (1987)

Richard A. Falk, *The Pathways of Global Constitutionalism*, *in* THE CONSTITUTIONAL FOUNDATIONS OF WORLD PEACE 13 (Richard A. Falk, Robert C. Johansen & Samuel S. Kim eds., State University of New York Press, Albany, New York, 1993)

Richard A. Falk, ON HUMANE GOVERNANCE: TOWARD A NEW GLOBAL POLITICS; THE WORLD ORDER MODELS PROJECT REPORT OF THE GLOBAL CIVILIZATION INITIATIVE (Polity Press, Cambridge, 1995)

Richard A. Falk, LAW IN AN EMERGING GLOBAL VILLAGE. A POST-WESTPHALIAN PERSPECTIVE (Transnational Publishers, Ardsley, New York, 1998)

Richard A. Falk, *Kosovo, World Order, and the Future of International Law*, 93 AMERICAN JOURNAL OF INTERNATIONAL LAW 853 (1999)

Richard A. Falk, *What Future for the UN Charter System of War Prevention*, 97 AMERICAN JOURNAL OF INTERNATIONAL LAW 590 (2003)

Richard A. Falk, *World Tribunal on Iraq: Truth, Law, and Justice*, 6 THE GLOBAL COMMUNITY. YEARBOOK OF INTERNATIONAL LAW AND JURISPRUDENCE 15 (2006–I)

Tom J. Farer, *The Regulation of Foreign Intervention in Civil Armed Conflict*, 142 RECUEIL DES COURS 291 (1974–II)

Tom J. Farer, *Beyond the Charter Frame: Unilateralism or Condominium?*, 96 AMERICAN JOURNAL OF INTERNATIONAL LAW 359 (2002)

Tom J. Farer, *The Prospect for International Law and Order in the Wake of Iraq,* 97 AMERICAN JOURNAL OF INTERNATIONAL LAW 621 (2003)

Olu Fasan, *Global Trade Law: Challenges and Options for Africa*, 47 JOURNAL OF AFRICAN LAW 143 (2003)

Bardo Fassbender, *The United Nations Charter as Constitution of the International Community*, 36 COLUMBIA JOURNAL OF TRANSNATIONAL LAW 529 (1998)

Roberta M. Fay, *Citizen's Arrest: International Environmental Law and Global Climate Change*, 14 GLENDALE LAW REVIEW 73 (1995)

David Feldman, *Monism, Dualism and Constitutional Legitimacy*, 20 THE AUSTRALIAN YEARBOOK OF INTERNATIONAL LAW 10 (1999)

Florentino Feliciano & Peter L.H. Van den Bossche, *The Dispute Settlement System of the World Trade Organization: Institutions, Processes and Practice*, *in* PROLIFERATION OF INTERNATIONAL ORGANIZATIONS: LEGAL ISSUES 207 (Niels M. Blokker & Henry G. Schermers eds., Kluwer Law International, The Hague, 2001)

Charles G. Fenwick, *The Recognition*, 38 AMERICAN JOURNAL OF INTERNATIONAL LAW 448 (1944)

Luigi Ferrari Bravo, *Méthodes de Recherche de la Coutume Internationale dans la Pratique des Etats*, 192 RECUEIL DES COURS 233 (1985–III)

David P. Fidler, *International Law and Global Health*, 48 UNIVERSITY OF KANSAS LAW REVIEW 1 (1999)

Dana D. Fisher, *Reporting under the Covenant on Civil and Political Rights: The First Five Years of the Human Rights Committee*, 76 AMERICAN JOURNAL OF INTERNATIONAL LAW 142 (1982)

Pierre Fistié, *Le Japon Face aux Crises Cambodgienne et Afghane*, 3 REVUE FRANÇAISE DE SCIENCE POLITIQUES 451 (1982)

Peter Fitzgerald, *Managing "Smart Sanctions" Against Terrorism Wisely*, 36 NEW ENGLAND LAW REVIEW 957 (2002)

Gerald Fitzmaurice, *The Future of Public International Law and of the International Legal System in the Circumstances of Today*, *in* LIVRE DU CENTENAIRE 1873–1973. EVOLUTION ET PERSPECTIVES DU DROIT INTERNATIONAL. ANNUAIRE DE L'INSTITUT DE DROIT INTERNATIONAL 196 (Karger , Bâle, 1973)

GERALD FITZMAURICE, THE LAW AND PROCEDURE OF THE INTERNATIONAL COURT OF JUSTICE (Grotius Publications, Cambridge, 1986)

Gerald Fitzmaurice, *The General Principles of International Law Considered from Standpoint of the Rule of Law*, 92 RECUEIL DES COURS 5 (1957–II)

Malgosia A. Fitzmaurice, *Liability for Environmental Damage Caused to the Global Commons*, 5 REVIEW OF EUROPEAN COMMUNITY & INTERNATIONAL ENVIRONMENTAL LAW 305 (1996)

Malgosia A. Fitzmaurice & Catherine Redgwell, *Environmental Non-Compliance Procedures and International Law*, 31 NETHERLANDS YEARBOOK OF INTERNATIONAL LAW 35 (2000)

Malgosia A. Fitzmaurice ed., CONTEMPORARY ISSUES IN THE LAW OF TREATIES (Eleven International Publishing, Utrecht, 2005)

Martin S. Flaherty, *History Right?: Historical Scholarship, Original Understanding, and Treaties as "Supreme Law of the Land"*, 99 COLUMBIA LAW REVIEW 2095 (1999)

George P. Fletcher & STEVE SHEPPARD, AMERICAN LAW IN A GLOBAL CONTEXT. THE BASICS (Oxford University Press, Oxford, 2005)

Jean-Pierre L. Fonteyne, *Forcible Self-Help by States to Protect Human Rights: Recent Views from the United Nations*, *in* HUMANITARIAN INTERVENTION AND THE UNITED NATIONS 197 (Richard B. Lillich ed., University Press of Virginia, Charlottesville, 1973)

René Foqué, *Global Governance and the Rule of Law, Human Rights and General Principles of Good Global Governance*, *in* INTERNATIONAL LAW. THEORY AND PRACTICE. ESSAYS IN HONOUR OF ERIC SUY 25 (Karel Wellens ed., Nijhoff, The Hague, 1998)

Gregory H. Fox & Brad R. Roth, *Democracy and International Law*, 27 REVIEW OF INTERNATIONAL STUDIES 327 (2001)

Thomas M. Franck, THE POWER OF LEGITIMACY AMONG NATIONS (Oxford University Press, New York, 1990)

Thomas M. Franck, *The Emerging Right to Democratic Governance*, 86 AMERICAN JOURNAL OF INTERNATIONAL LAW 46 (1992)

Thomas M. Franck, *The Powers of Appreciation: Who Is the Ultimate Guardian of UN Legality?*, 86 AMERICAN JOURNAL OF INTERNATIONAL LAW 519 (1992)

Thomas M. Franck, *Fairness in the International Legal and Institutional System*, 240 RECUEIL DES COURS 13 (1993–III)

Thomas M. Franck, *UN Checks and Balances: The Role of the ICJ and the Security Council*, *in* AMERICAN SOCIETY OF INTERNATIONAL LAW/NEDERLANDSE VERENIGING VOOR INTERNATIONAAL RECHT, CONTEMPORARY INTERNATIONAL LAW ISSUES: OPPORTUNITIES AT A TIME OF MOMENTOUS CHANGE. PROCEEDINGS OF THE 2ND JOINT CONFERENCE HELD IN THE HAGUE, THE NETHERLANDS, JULY 22–24, 1993, 280 (René Lefeber ed., Nijhoff/ Dordrecht, 1994)

Thomas M. Franck, *Legitimacy and the Democratic Entitlement*, *in* DEMOCRATIC GOVERNANCE AND INTERNATIONAL LAW 25 (Gregory H. Fox & Brad R. Roth eds., Cambridge University Press, Cambridge, 2000)

Thomas M. Franck, THE EMPOWERED SELF: LAW AND SOCIETY IN THE AGE OF INDIVIDUALISM (Oxford University Press, Oxford, 2001)

Thomas M. Franck, *Terrorism and the Right of Self-Defence*, 95 AMERICAN JOURNAL OF INTERNATIONAL LAW 839 (2001)

Thomas M. Franck, *The Use of Force in International Law*, 11 TULANE JOURNAL OF INTERNATIONAL & COMPARATIVE LAW 7 (2003)

Thomas M. Franck, *The Power of Legitimacy and the Legitimacy of Power: Law in an Age of Power Disequilibrium*, 100 AMERICAN JOURNAL OF INTERNATIONAL LAW 88 (2006)

Michele Fratianni, PAOLO SAVONA & JOHN J. KIRTON, SUSTAINING GROWTH AND GLOBAL DEVELOPMENT: G7 AND IMF GOVERNANCE (Ashgate, Aldershot, 2003)

Helmut Freudenschuss, *Between Unilateralism and Collective Security: Authorizations of Use of Force by the UN Security Council*, 5 EUROPEAN JOURNAL OF INTERNATIONAL LAW 492 (1994)

Robert A. Friedlander, *Retaliation as an Anti-Terrorist Weapon: The Israeli Lebanon Incursion and International Law*, 8 ISRAEL YEARBOOK OF HUMAN RIGHTS 63 (1978)

Wolfgang Gaston Friedmann, THE CHANGING STRUCTURE OF INTERNATIONAL LAW (Stevens, London, 1964)

Jochen Frowein, *The Federal Republic of Germany*, *in* UNITED KINGDOM NATIONAL COMMITTEE OF COMPARATIVE LAW, THE EFFECT OF TREATIES IN DOMESTIC LAW 96 (Francis G. Jacobs & Shelly Roberts eds., Sweet & Maxwell, London, 1987)

Jochen A. Frowein, *Reactions by Not Directly Affected States to Breaches of Public International Law*, 248 RECUEIL DES COURS 345 (1994–IV)

Jochen A. Frowein & Karin Oellers-Frahm, *L'Application des Traités dans l'Ordre Juridique Interne*, *in* THE INTEGRATION OF INTERNATIONAL AND EUROPEAN COMMUNITY LAW INTO THE NATIONAL LEGAL ORDER/L'INTÉGRATION DU DROIT INTERNATIONAL ET COMMUNAUTAIRE DANS L'ORDRE JURIDIQUE NATIONAL, ÉTUDE DE LA PRATIQUE EN EUROPE 15 (Pierre M. Eisemann ed., Kluwer Law International, The Hague, 1996)

Jochen Frowein, *Ist das Völkerrecht tot?*, 23 FRANKFURTER ALLGEMEINE ZEITUNG NO. 168, 6 (2003)

James D. Fry, *Terrorism as a Crime Against Humanity and Genocide: The Backdoor to Universal Jurisdiction*, 7 UCLA JOURNAL OF INTERNATIONAL LAW AND FOREIGN AFFAIRS 169 (2002)

Giorgio Gaja, *Italy*, *in* UNITED KINGDOM NATIONAL COMMITTEE OF COMPARATIVE LAW, THE EFFECT OF TREATIES IN DOMESTIC LAW 87 (Francis G. Jacobs & Shelly Roberts eds., Sweet & Maxwell, London, 1987)

Reinhold Gallmetzer & Kazuna Inomata, *International Criminal Tribunal for the Former Yugoslavia, Introductory Note*, 1 THE GLOBAL COMMUNITY. YEARBOOK OF INTERNATIONAL LAW AND JURISPRUDENCE 493 (2001)

Johan Galtung, *On the Effects of International Economic Sanctions, With Examples from the Case of Rhodesia*, 19 WORLD POLITICS 378 (1967)

Judith Gardam, *Legal Restraints on Security Council Military Enforcement Action*, 17 MICHIGAN JOURNAL OF INTERNATIONAL LAW 285 (1996)

Judith Gardam, *The Contribution of the International Court of Justice to International Humanitarian Law*, 14 LEIDEN JOURNAL OF INTERNATIONAL LAW 349 (2001)

Judith Gardam, NECESSITY, PROPORTIONALITY AND THE USE OF FORCE BY STATES (Cambridge University Press, Cambridge, 2004)

Richard N. Gardner, *Neither Bush nor the "Jurisprudes"*, 97 AMERICAN JOURNAL OF INTERNATIONAL LAW 585 (2003)

Andrea Giardina, *The International Center for Settlement of Investment Disputes between States and Nationals of Other States*, *in* ESSAYS ON INTERNATIONAL COMMERCIAL ARBITRATION 214 (Petar Šarčević ed., Graham & Trotman, London, 1989)

Geoff Gilbert, *The Criminal Responsibility of States*, 39 INTERNATIONAL & COMPARATIVE LAW QUARTERLY 345 (1990)

Terry D. Gill, *Legal and Some Political Limitations on the Power of the UN Security Council To Exercise Its Enforcement Powers Under Chapter VII of the Charter*, 26 NETHERLANDS YEARBOOK OF INTERNATIONAL LAW 33 (1995)

Michael J. Glennon, *State-Sponsored Abduction: A Comment on United States v. Alvarez Machain*, 86 AMERICAN JOURNAL OF INTERNATIONAL LAW 746 (1992)

Alonso Gómez-Robledo Verduzco, UNITED STATES VS ÁLVAREZ MACHAIN (Universidad Nacional Autonoma, Mexico, 1993)

Vera Gowlland-Debbas, COLLECTIVE RESPONSES TO ILLEGAL ACTS IN INTERNATIONAL LAW: UNITED NATIONS ACTION IN THE QUESTION OF SOUTHERN RHODESIA (Nijhoff, Dordrecht, 1990)

Vera Gowlland-Debbas, *The Relationship Between the International Court of Justice and the Security Council in the Light of the* Lockerbie *Case*, 88 AMERICAN JOURNAL OF INTERNATIONAL LAW 643 (1994)

Vera Gowlland-Debbas, *Security Council Enforcement Action and Issues of State Responsibility*, 43 INTERNATIONAL & COMPARATIVE LAW QUARTERLY 55 (1994)

Vera Gowlland Debbas, *Judicial Insights into Fundamental Values and Interests of the International Community*, *in* THE INTERNATIONAL COURT OF JUSTICE: ITS FUTURE ROLE AFTER FIFTY YEARS (Alexander S. Muller, David Raic, J.M. Thuranzsky eds., Nijhoff, The Hague, 1997)

Vera Gowlland-Debbas, *The Limits of Unilateral Enforcement of Community Objectives in the Framework of UN Peace Maintenance*, 11 EUROPEAN JOURNAL OF INTERNATIONAL LAW 361 (2000)

Bernhard Graefrath, *Leave to the Court What Belongs to the Court. The Libyan Case*, 4 EUROPEAN JOURNAL OF INTERNATIONAL LAW 184 (1993)

Leslie C. Green, *Humanitarian Intervention: 1976 Version*, 24 CHITTY'S LAW JOURNAL 217 (1976)

Leslie C. Green, *Rescue at Entebbe. Legal Aspects*, 6 ISRAEL YEARBOOK ON HUMAN RIGHTS 312 (1976)

Christopher Greenwood, *The Impact of Decisions and Resolutions of the Security Council on the International Court of Justice*, *in* INTERNATIONAL LAW AND THE HAGUE'S 75TH ANNIVERSARY 81 (Wybo P. Heere ed., T.M.C. Asser Press, The Hague, 1999)

Christopher Greenwood, *International Law And The Pre-Emptive Use of Force. Afghanistan, Al-Qaida, and Iraq*, 4 SAN DIEGO INTERNATIONAL LAW JOURNAL 7 (2003)

Donald W. Greig, INTERNATIONAL LAW (2nd ed., Butterworth, London, 1976)

Alicia Morris Groos, *International Trade and Development: Exploring the Impact of Fair Trade Organizations in the Global Economy and the Law*, 34 TEXAS INTERNATIONAL LAW JOURNAL 379 (1999)

Héctor Gros Espiell, *La Convention Américaine et la Convention Européenne des Droits de l'Homme: Analyse Comparative*, 218 RECUEIL DE COURS 167 (1989–IV)

Héctor Gros Espiell, *The Common Heritage of Mankind and the Human Genome*, *in* INTERNATIONAL LAW. THEORY AND PRACTICE. ESSAYS IN HONOUR OF ERIC SUY 519 (Karel Wellens ed., Nijhoff, The Hague, 1998)

Leo Gross, *The International Court of Justice and the United Nations*, 120 RECUEIL DES COURS 313 (1967–I)

Leo Gross ed., THE FUTURE OF THE INTERNATIONAL COURT OF JUSTICE (Oceana Publications, Dobbs Ferry, New York, 1976)

Hugo Grotius, INTERNATIONAL LAW AND THE GROTIAN HERITAGE: A COMMEMORATIVE COLLOQUIUM HELD AT THE HAGUE ON 8 APRIL 1983 ON THE OCCASION OF THE FOURTH CENTENARY OF THE BIRTH OF HUGO GROTIUS (T.M.C. Asser Instituut, The Hague, 1985)

Paul Guggenheim, *Les Deux Eléments de la Coutume en Droit International*, *in* LA TECHNIQUE ET LES PRINCIPES DU DROIT PUBLIC. ÉTUDES EN L'HONNEUR DE GEORGE SCELLE 275 (Librairie Génerale de Droit et de Jurisprudence, Paris, 1950)

Paul Guggenheim, TRAITÉ DE DROIT INTERNATIONAL PUBLIC. AVEC MENTION DE LA PRATIQUE INTERNATIONALE ET SUISSE (2nd ed., Librairie de l'Université, Genève 1967)

Gilbert Guillaume, *L'Echec de l'Assemblée Extraordinaire de l'Oaci et de la Conférence de Droit Aérien de Rome*, 36 REVUE GÉNÉRALE DE L'AIR ET DE L'ESPACE 261 (1973)

Gilbert Guillaume, *The Future of International Judicial Institutions*, 44 INTERNATIONAL & COMPARATIVE LAW QUARTERLY 848 (1995)

Gilbert Guillaume, *La Mondialisation et la Cour Internationale de Justice*, 2 INTERNATIONAL LAW FORUM DU DROIT INTERNATIONAL 242 (2000)

Gilbert Guillaume, LA COUR INTERNATIONALE DE JUSTICE À L'AUBE DU XXIÈME SIÈCLE. LE REGARD D'UN JUGE (Pedone, Paris, 2003)

Isabelle Gunning, *Modernizing Customary International Law: The Challenge of Human Rights*, 31 VANDERBILT JOURNAL OF INTERNATIONAL LAW 211 (1991)

Gerhard Hafner, *Pros and Cons Ensuing from Fragmentation of International Law*, 25 MICHIGAN JOURNAL OF INTERNATIONAL LAW 849 (2004)

Malvina Halberstam, *Terrorism on the High Seas: The Achille Lauro, Piracy and the IMO Convention on Maritime Safety*, 82 AMERICAN JOURNAL OF INTERNATIONAL LAW 269 (1988)

Malvina Halberstam, *In Defense of the Supreme Court Decision in Alvarez-Machain*, 86 AMERICAN JOURNAL OF INTERNATIONAL LAW 736 (1992)

Malvina Halbestram, *The Copenhagen Document: Intervention in Support of Democracy*, 34 HARVARD JOURNAL OF INTERNATIONAL LAW 163 (1993)

Brian F. Havel, *The Constitution in an Era of Supranational Adjudication*, 78 NORTH CAROLINA LAW REVIEW 257 (2000)

Wybo P. Heere ed., INTERNATIONAL LAW AND THE HAGUE'S 750TH ANNIVERSARY (T.M.C. Asser Press, The Hague, 1999)

Eric A. Heinze, *Reconciling Approaches to Enquiry in the Humanitarian Intervention Debate*, 8 INTERNATIONAL JOURNAL OF HUMAN RIGHTS 367 (2004)

David Held, DEMOCRACY AND THE GLOBAL ORDER: FROM THE MODERN STATE TO COSMOPOLITAN GOVERNANCE (Stanford University Press, Stanford, 1995)

David Held & Anthony McGrew, GLOBALIZATION/ANTI-GLOBALIZATION (Polity Press, Cambridge, 2002)

David Held & Anthony G. McGrew, GOVERNING GLOBALIZATION. POWER, AUTHORITY AND GLOBAL GOVERNANCE (Polity Press, Cambridge, 2002)

Louis Henkin, *Kosovo and the Law of "Humanitarian Intervention"*, 93 AMERICAN JOURNAL OF INTERNATIONAL LAW 824 (1999)

Marc Herzelin, *La Compétence Pénale Universelle, Une Question non Résolue par l'Arrêt Yerodia*, 106 REVUE GÉNÉRALE DE DROIT INTERNATIONAL PUBLIC 819 (2002)

Rosalyn Higgins, PROBLEMS AND PROCESS: INTERNATIONAL LAW AND HOW WE USE IT 69 (Clarendon Press, Oxford, 1994)

Rosalyn Higgins, *Interim Measures for the Protection of Human Rights*, *in* POLITICS, VALUES AND FUNCTIONS. INTERNATIONAL LAW IN THE 21ST CENTURY. ESSAYS IN HONOUR OF PROFESSOR LOUIS HENKIN 101 (Jonathan I. Charney, Donald K. Anton & Mary Ellen O'Connell eds., Nijhoff, The Hague, 1997)

Rosalyn Higgins, *The International Court of Justice and Human Rights*, *in* INTERNATIONAL LAW. THEORY AND PRACTICE. ESSAYS IN HONOUR OF ERIC SUY 691 (Karel Wellens ed., Nijhoff, The Hague, 1998)

Rosalin Higgins, *The ICJ, the ECJ, and the Integrity of International Law*, 52 INTERNATIONAL & COMPARATIVE LAW QUARTERLY 1 (2003)

Keith Highet, *The Emperor's New Clothes. Death Row Appeals to the World Court?*, *in* LIBER AMICORUM "IN MEMORIAM" OF JUDGE JOSÉ MARÌA RUDA (Calixto A. Armas Barea ed., Kluwer Law International, The Hague, 2000)

Ernst M. H. Hirsch Ballin, *Beyond the Limits of the Territoriality Principle*, *in* REFLECTIONS ON INTERNATIONAL LAW FROM THE LOW COUNTRIES IN HONOUR OF PAUL DE WAART 278 (Erik Denters ed., Nijhoff, The Hague, 1998)

Stephan Hobe, *Global Challenges to Statehood: The Increasingly Important Role of Nongovernmental Organizations*, 5 INDIANA JOURNAL OF GLOBAL LEGAL STUDIES 191 (1997)

Rainer Hofmann, Juliane Kokott, Karin Oellers-Frahm, Stefan Oeter & Andreas Zimmermann eds., WORLD COURT DIGEST (Springer, Berlin, Vol. I, 1992, Vol. II, 1997)

Rainer Hofmann, NON-STATE ACTORS AS NEW SUBJECTS OF INTERNATIONAL LAW, INTERNATIONAL LAW – FROM THE TRADITIONAL STATE ORDER TOWARDS THE LAW OF THE GLOBAL COMMUNITY. PROCEEDINGS OF AN INTERNATIONAL SYMPOSIUM OF THE KIEL WALTHER-SCHÜCKING-INSTITUTE OF INTERNATIONAL LAW, MARCH 25 TO 28, 1998 (Duncker & Humblot, Berlin, 1999)

Nicholas Howen, *International Human Rights Law-Making-Keeping the Spirit Alive*, 6 EUROPEAN HUMAN RIGHTS LAW REVIEW 566 (1997)

John P. Humphrey, HUMAN RIGHTS AND THE UNITED NATIONS: A GREAT ADVENTURE (Transnational Publishers, Dobbs Ferry, New York, 1984)

Yoshiyuki Iwamoto, *The Protection of Human Life Through Provisional Measures Indicated by the International Court of Justice*, 15 LEIDEN JOURNAL OF INTERNATIONAL LAW 345 (2002)

Yuji Iwasawa, *The Doctrine of Self-Executing Treaties in the United States: A Critical Analysis*, 26 VANDERBILT JOURNAL OF INTERNATIONAL LAW 627 (1986)

John Jackson, Jean-Victor Louis & Mitsuo Matsushita eds., IMPLEMENTING THE TOKYO ROUND: NATIONAL CONSTITUTIONS AND INTERNATIONAL ECONOMIC RULES (University of Michigan Press, Ann Arbor, 1984)

John H. Jackson, *The Perils of Globalization and the World Trading System*, 24 FORDHAM INTERNATIONAL LAW JOURNAL 371 (2000)

Jean Paul Jacqué, *Acte et Norme en Droit International Public*, 227 RECUEIL DES COURS 357 (1991–II)

Francis G. Jacobs & Shelly Roberts eds., UNITED KINGDOM NATIONAL COMMITTEE OF COMPARATIVE LAW, THE EFFECT OF TREATIES IN DOMESTIC LAW (Sweet & Maxwell, London, 1987)

Nandasiri Jasentuliyana ed., PERSPECTIVES ON INTERNATIONAL LAW. A PUBLICATION ON THE OCCASION OF THE FIFTIETH ANNIVERSARY OF THE UNITED NATIONS AND A CONTRIBUTION TO THE DECADE OF INTERNATIONAL LAW (Kluwer, London, 1995)

Kanishka Jayasuriya, *Globalization, Law, and the Transformation of Sovereignty – The Emergence of Global Regulatory Governance*, 6 INDIANA JOURNAL OF GLOBAL LEGAL STUDIES 425 (1999)

Ramon J. Jeffery, THE IMPACT OF STATE SOVEREIGNTY ON GLOBAL TRADE AND INTERNATIONAL TAXATION (Kluwer Law International, London, 1999)

Robert Y. Jennings, *Universal International Law in a Multicultural World, in* INTERNATIONAL LAW AND THE GROTIAN HERITAGE: A COMMEMORATIVE COLLOQUIUM ON THE OCCASION OF THE FOURTH CENTENARY OF THE BIRTH OF HUGO GROTIUS 187 (T.M.C. Asser Instituut, The Hague, 1985)

Robert Y. Jennings, *The Judicial Function and the Rule of Law in International Relations*, INTERNATIONAL LAW AT THE TIME OF ITS CODIFICATION. ESSAYS IN HONOUR OF ROBERTO AGO 139 (Giuffré, Milano, 1987–III)

Robert Y. Jennings, *The Judicial Enforcement of International Obligations*, 47 ZEITSCHRIFT FÜR AUSLÄNDISCHES ÖFFENTLICHES RECHT UND VÖLKERRECHT 3 (1987)

Robert Y. Jennings, *The Proliferation of Adjudicatory Bodies: Dangers and Possible Answers, in* IMPLICATIONS OF THE PROLIFERATION OF INTERNATIONAL ADJUDICATORY BODIES FOR DISPUTE RESOLUTION. PROCEEDINGS OF A FORUM CO-SPONSORED BY THE AMERICAN SOCIETY OF INTERNATIONAL LAW AND THE GRADUATE INSTITUTE OF INTERNATIONAL STUDIES; GENEVA, SWITZERLAND, MAY 13, 1995 AMERICAN SOCIETY OF INTERNATIONAL LAW BULLETIN NO. 9, 2 (Laurence Boisson de Charzournes ed., American Society of International Law Publ., Washington, D. C., 1995)

Robert Y. Jennings, *The Role of the International Court of Justice*, 68 BRITISH YEARBOOK OF INTERNATIONAL LAW 1 (1997)

Robert Y. Jennings, *Contributions of the Court to the Resolution of International Tensions*, *in* INCREASING THE EFFECTIVENESS OF THE INTERNATIONAL COURT OF JUSTICE. PROCEEDINGS OF THE ICJ/UNITAR COLLOQUIUM TO CELEBRATE THE 50TH ANNIVERSARY OF THE COURT 78 (Connie Peck & Roy S. Lee eds., Nijhoff, The Hague, 1997)

Christopher C. Joyner, *The Concept of the Common Heritage of Mankind in International Law*, 13 EMORY INTERNATIONAL LAW REVIEW 615 (1999)

CHRISTOPHER C. JOYNER, INTERNATIONAL LAW IN THE 21ST CENTURY. RULES FOR GLOBAL GOVERNANCE (Rowman & Littlefield, Lanham, 2005)

Stefan Kadelbach, *International Law and the Incorporation of Treaties into Domestic Law*, 42 GERMAN YEARBOOK OF INTERNATIONAL LAW 66 (1999)

Douglas Kash, *Abducting Terrorists Under PDD-39: Much Ado About Nothing New*, 13 AMERICAN UNIVERSITY INTERNATIONAL LAW REVIEW 139 (1997)

Susan Kaufman Purcell, *La Ley Helms-Burton y el Embargo Estadounidense Contra Cuba*, 43 FORO INTERNACIONAL 704 (2003)

Inge Kaul, Isabelle Grunberg & Marc Stern eds., GLOBAL PUBLIC GOODS: INTERNATIONAL COOPERATION IN THE TWENTY-FIRST CENTURY (Oxford University Press, New York, 1999)

Hans Kelsen, *Théorie Générale du Droit International Public*, 4 RECUEIL DES COURS 121 (1932–IV)

Hans Kelsen, *Théorie du Droit International Coutumier*, 1 REVUE INTERNATIONAL DE LA THÉORIE DU DROIT 253 (1939)

Hans Kelsen, *Recognition in International Law. Theorical Observations*, 35 AMERICAN JOURNAL OF INTERNATIONAL LAW 606 (1941)

Hans Kelsen, GENERAL THEORY OF LAW AND STATE (Harvard University Press, Cambridge, 1949)

Hans Kelsen, PRINCIPLES OF INTERNATIONAL LAW (Rinehart, New York, 1952)

Hans Kelsen, DAS PROBLEM DER SOUVERÄNITÄT UND DIE THEORIE DES VÖLKERRECHTS. BEITRAG ZU EINER REINEN RECHTSLEHRE (Scientia Verl., Aalen, 1981)

Hans Kelsen, GENERAL THEORY OF LAW AND STATE (Lawbook Exchange, Union, NJ, 1999)

Paul M. Kennedy, Dirk Messner & Franz Nuscheler eds., GLOBAL TRENDS AND GLOBAL GOVERNANCE (Pluto Press, London, 2002)

Frederic Kirgis, *Some Proportionality Issues Raised by Israel's Use of Armed Force in Lebanon*, ASIL INSIGHT (Aug. 17, 2006), *available at* http://www.asil.org/insights/2006/08/insights060817.html

John J. Kirton, NEW DIRECTIONS IN GLOBAL ECONOMIC GOVERNANCE: MANAGING GLOBALIZATION IN THE TWENTY-FIRST CENTURY (Ashgate, Aldershot, 2001)

John J. Kirton & Junichi Takase eds., NEW DIRECTIONS IN GLOBAL POLITICAL GOVERNANCE: THE G8 AND INTERNATIONAL ORDER IN THE TWENTY-FIRST CENTURY (Ashgate, Aldershot, 2002)

Eckart Klein, *Sanctions by International Organizations and Economic Communities*, 30 ARCHIV DES VÖLKERRECHTS 101 (1992)

M. Knishbacher, *The Entebbe Operation: A Legal Analysis of Israel's Rescue Action,* 12 JOURNAL OF INTERNAL LAW & ECONOMICS 57 (1977)

Harold Hongju Koh, *Paying Decent Respect to International Tribunal Rulings*, 96 AMERICAN SOCIETY OF INTERNATIONAL LAW: PROCEEDINGS OF THE ANNUAL MEETING 45 (2002)

Harold Hongju Koh, *International Law as Part of Our Law*, 98 AMERICAN JOURNAL OF INTERNATIONAL LAW 43 (2004)

Marcelo G. Kohen, *L'Avis Consultatif de la CIJ sur la Liceité de La Menace ou de l'Emploi d'Armes Nucléaires et La Fonction Judiciaire*, 8 EUROPEAN JOURNAL OF INTERNATIONAL LAW 336 (1997)

Marcelo Kohen, *Internationalisme et Mondialisation*, *in* LE DROIT SAISI PAR LA MONDIALISATION 107 (Charles-Albert Morand ed., Bruylant, Bruxelles, 2001)

Robert Kolb, *Universal Criminal Jurisdiction in Matters of International Terrorism: Some Reflections on Status and Trends in Contemporary International Law*, 50 REVUE HELLENIQUE DE DROIT INTERNATIONAL 43 (1997)

Robert Kolb, THÉORIE DU *JUS COGENS* INTERNATIONAL, ESSAI DE RELECTURE DU CONCEPT (Presses Universitaires de France, Paris, 2001)

Robert Kolb, *Aperçus sur la Bonne Foi en Droit International Public*, 54 REVUE HELLÉNIQUE DE DROIT INTERNATIONAL 1 (2001)

Robert Kolb, *Self-Defence and Preventive War at the Beginning of the Millenium*, 59 ZEITSCHRIFT FÜR ÖFFENTLICHES RECHT 111 (2004)

Martti Koskenniemi & Päivi Leino, *Fragmentation of International Law? Postmodern Anxieties*, 15 LEIDEN JOURNAL OF INTERNATIONAL LAW 553 (2002)

Martti Koskenniemi, *Global Governance and Public International Law*, 37 KRITISCHE JUSTIZ 241 (2004)

Michael Krinsky & David Golove eds., UNITED STATES ECONOMIC MEASURES AGAINST CUBA. PROCEEDINGS IN THE UNITED NATIONS AND INTERNATIONAL LAW ISSUES (Aletheia, Northampton, 1993)

Nico Krisch, *The Establishment of an African Court on Human and Peoples' Rights*, 58 ZEITSCHRIFT FÜR AUSLÄNDISCHES ÖFFENTLICHES RECHT UND VÖLKERRECHT 713 (1998)

Vincent Kronenberger, *A New Approach to the Interpretation of the French Constitution in Respect to International Conventions: From Hierarchy of Norms to Conflict of Competence*, 47 NETHERLANDS INTERNATIONAL LAW REVIEW 323 (2000)

Charlotte Ku, *Global Governance and the Changing Face of International Law*, ANNUAL MEETING OF THE ACADEMIC COUNCIL IN THE UNITED NATIONS SYSTEM, 16–18 JUNE, PUEBLA, MEXICO, 2001, ACUNS REPORTS AND PAPERS No. 2 (Cambridge University Press, Cambridge, 2001)

Rajendra Kumar Nayak, GLOBAL HEALTH LAW (Indian Law Institute, New Delhi, 1998)

Barbara Kwiatkowska, DECISIONS OF THE WORLD COURT RELEVANT TO THE UN CONVENTION ON THE LAW OF THE SEA. A REFERENCE GUIDE (Kluwer Law International, The Hague, 2002)

Barbara Kwiatkowska, *The Law of the Sea Related Cases in the International Court of Justice During the Presidency of Judge Stephen M. Schwebel (1997–2000) and Beyond*, 2 THE GLOBAL COMMUNITY. YEARBOOK OF INTERNATIONAL LAW AND JURISPRUDENCE 27 (2002–I)

Barbara Kwiatkowska, *Equitable Maritime Boundary Delimitation, as Exemplified in the Work of the International Court of Justice During the Presidency of Judge Gilbert Guillaume (2000–2003) and Beyond*, 5 THE GLOBAL COMMUNITY. YEARBOOK OF INTERNATIONAL LAW AND JURISPRUDENCE 51 (2005–I)

Antonio La Pergola & Patrick Del Duca, *Community Law and the Italian Constitution*, 79 AMERICAN JOURNAL OF INTERNATIONAL LAW 598 (1985)

Albert de La Pradelle & Nicolas Politis, II RECUEIL DES ARBITRAGES INTERNATIONAUX (1856–72) (Les Editions Internationales, Paris, 1932)

RODRIGO LABARDINI, LA MAGIA DEL INTÉRPRETE: EXTRADICIÓN EN LA SUPREMA CORTE DE JUSTICIA DE ESTADOS UNIDOS: EL CASO ÁLVAREZ MACHÁIN (Editorial Porrúa, Mexico, 2000)

Henri Labayle, *Droit International et Lutte contre le Terrorisme*, 32 ANNUAIRE FRANÇAIS DE DROIT INTERNATIONAL 105 (1986)

Robert Langer, SEIZURE OF TERRITORY. THE STIMSON DOCTRINE AND RELATED PRINCIPLES IN LEGAL THEORY AND DIPLOMATIC PRACTICE (Princeton University Press, Princeton, N.J., 1947)

Mark D. Larsen, *The Achille Lauro Incident and the Permissible Use of Force*, 9 LOYOLA OF LOS ANGELES INTERNATIONAL AND COMPARATIVE LAW JOURNAL 481 (1987)

Elihu Lauterpacht, *The Development of the Law of International Organization by the Decisions of International Tribunals*, 152 RECUEIL DES COURS 377 (1976–IV)

Elihu Lauterpacht, ASPECTS OF THE ADMINISTRATION OF INTERNATIONAL JUSTICE (Grotius Publ., Cambridge, 1991)

Elihu Lauterpacht, *Judicial Review of the Acts of International Organisations*, *in* INTERNATIONAL LAW, THE INTERNATIONAL COURT OF JUSTICE AND NUCLEAR WEAPONS (Laurence Boisson de Chazournes ed., Cambridge University Press, Cambridge, 1999)

Elihu Lauterpacht, Stephen Schwebel, Shabtai Rosenne & Francisco Orrego Vicuña, *Legal Opinion on Guatemala's Territorial Claim to Belize* (2001), *available at* http://www.mfa.gov.bz/library/documents/LegalOpinionon.pdf

Elihu Lauterpacht ed., INTERNATIONAL LAW, COLLECTED PAPERS. VOLUME 5: DISPUTES, WAR AND NEUTRALITY, PARTS IX-XIV (Cambridge University Press, Cambridge, 2003)

Elihu Lauterpacht & Christopher J. Greenwood eds., INTERNATIONAL LAW REPORTS, VOLLS. 1-130, (Cambridge University Press, Cambridge)

Hersch Lauterpacht, RECOGNITION IN INTERNATIONAL LAW (University Press, Cambridge, 1948)

Hersch Lauterpacht, INTERNATIONAL LAW AND HUMAN RIGHTS (Stevens, London, 1950)

Hersch Lauterpacht, THE DEVELOPMENT OF INTERNATIONAL LAW BY THE INTERNATIONAL COURT (Stevens, London, 1958)

Hersh Lauterpacht, *The Legal Effect of Illegal Acts of International Organizations*, *in* CAMBRIDGE ESSAYS IN INTERNATIONAL LAW. ESSAYS IN HONOUR OF LORD MCNAIR 88 (Arnold Duncan McNair ed., Stevens, London, 1965)

Robert M. Lawrence, *The Preventive/Preemptive War Doctrine Cannot Justify the Iraq War*, 33 DENVER JOURNAL OF INTERNATIONAL LAW & POLICY 16 (2004)

Charles Leben, LES SANCTIONS PRIVATIVES DE DROITS OU DE QUALITÉ DANS LES ORGANISATIONS INTERNATIONALES SPECIALISÉES. RECHERCHES SUR LES SANCTIONS INTERNATIONALES ET L'EVOLUTION DU DROIT DES GENS (Bruylant, Bruxelles, 1979)

Charles Leben, *Les Contre-Mesures Inter-Étatiques et les Réactions à l'Illicite dans la Société Internationale*, 28 ANNUAIRE FRANÇAIS DE DROIT INTERNATIONAL 9 (1982)

René Lefeber ed., AMERICAN SOCIETY OF INTERNATIONAL LAW/NEDERLANDSE VERENIGING VOOR INTERNATIONAAL RECHT, CONTEMPORARY INTERNATIONAL LAW ISSUES: OPPORTUNITIES AT A TIME OF MOMENTOUS CHANGE. PROCEEDINGS OF THE 2ND JOINT CONFERENCE HELD IN THE HAGUE, THE NETHERLANDS, JULY 22–24, 1993 (Nijhoff, Dordrecht 1994)

Chia Lehnardt, *European Court Rules on UN and EU Terrorist Suspect Blacklists*, ASIL INSIGHT (Jan. 31, 2007), Vol. 11, Issue 1, *available at* http://www.asil.org/insights/2007/01/insights070131.html

Jeremy Levitt, *Humanitarian Intervention by Regional Actors in International Conflicts, and the Cases of ECOWAS in Liberia and Sierra Leone*, 12 TEMPLE INTERNATIONAL & COMPARATIVE LAW JOURNAL 333 (1998)

David Leyton-Brown ed., THE UTILITY OF INTERNATIONAL ECONOMIC SANCTIONS (Croom Helm, London, 1987)

Zhaojie Li, *Effects of Treaties in Domestic Law: Practice of the People's Republic of China*, 16 DALHOUSIE LAW JOURNAL 62 (1993)

Richard B. Lillich, *Forcible Self-Help by States to Protect Human Rights*, 53 IOWA LAW REVIEW 325 (1967)

Richard B. Lillich ed., HUMANITARIAN INTERVENTION AND THE UNITED NATIONS (University Press of Virginia, Charlottesville, 1973)

Richard B. Lillich ed., ECONOMIC COERCION AND THE NEW INTERNATIONAL ECONOMIC ORDER (Michie, Charlottesville, 1976)

Jules Lobel & Michael Ratner, *Bypassing the Security Council: Ambiguous Authorizations to Use Force, Cease-Fires and the Iraqi Inspection Regime*, 93 AMERICAN JOURNAL OF INTERNATIONAL LAW 124 (1999)

Gerhard Loibl, *The Role of International Organisations in International Law-Making International Environmental Negotiations*, 1 NON-STATE ACTORS AND INTERNATIONAL LAW 41 (2001)

Donald L. Losman, INTERNATIONAL ECONOMIC SANCTIONS: THE CASE OF CUBA, ISRAEL, AND RHODESIA (University of New Mexico Press, Albuquerque, 1978)

Vaughan Lowe & Malgosia A. Fitzmaurice eds., FIFTY YEARS OF THE INTERNATIONAL COURT OF JUSTICE. ESSAYS IN HONOUR OF SIR ROBERT JENNINGS (Cambridge University Press, Cambridge, 1996)

Vaughan Lowe, *US Extraterritorial Jurisdiction. The Helms-Burton and D'Amato Acts*, 46 THE INTERNATIONAL AND COMPARATIVE LAW QUARTERLY 378 (1997)

Vaughan Lowe, *International Legal Issues Arising in the Kosovo Crisis*, 49 THE INTERNATIONAL & COMPARATIVE LAW QUARTERLY 934 (2000)

Andreas F. Lowenfeld, *The Cuban Liberty and Democratic Solidarity (Libertad) Act Congress and Cuba: The Helms-Burton Act*, 90 AMERICAN JOURNAL OF INTERNATIONAL LAW 419 (1996)

Claude-Pierre Lucron, *L'Europe devant la Crise Yugoslave. Mesures Restrictives et Mesures Positives*, 354 REVUE DU MARCHÉ COMMUN ET DE L'UNION EUROPÉENNE 7 (1992)

Ronald St. John Macdonald & Douglas M. Johnston eds., THE STRUCTURE AND PROCESS OF INTERNATIONAL LAW: ESSAYS IN LEGAL PHILOSOPHY DOCTRINE AND THEORY (Nijhoff, The Hague, 1983)

Stephen N. MacFarlane, *On the Front Lines in the Near Abroad: The CIS and the OSCE in Georgia's Civil War*s, *in* BEYOND UN SUBCONTRACTING. TASK-SHARING WITH REGIONAL SECURITY ARRANGEMENTS AND SERVICE-PROVIDING NGOS 115 (Thomas G. Weiss ed., Macmillan, Basingstoke, 1998)

John O. MacGinnis, *The Appropriate Hierarchy of Global Multilateralism and Customary International Law, The Example of the WTO*, 44 VIRGINIA JOURNAL OF INTERNATIONAL LAW 229 (2003)

Richard J. Mac Laughlin, *Sovereignty, Utility, and Fairness: Using U.S. Takings Law to Guide the Evolving Utilitarian Balancing Approach to Global Environmental Disputes in the WTO*, 78 OREGON LAW REVIEW 855 (1999)

Edward MacWhinney, JUDICIAL SETTLEMENT OF INTERNATIONAL DISPUTES. JURISDICTION, JUSTICIABILITY AND JUDICIAL LAW-MAKING ON THE CONTEMPORARY INTERNATIONAL COURT (Nijhoff, Dordrecht, 1991)

Edward MacWhinney, *The International Court as Constitutional Court and the Blurring of the Arbitral/Judicial Processes*, 6 LEIDEN JOURNAL OF INTERNATIONAL LAW 279 (1993)

Edward MacWhinney, *The Role and Mission of the International Court in an Era of Historical Transition*, *in* PERSPECTIVES ON INTERNATIONAL LAW. A PUBLICATION ON THE OCCASION OF THE FIFTIETH ANNIVERSARY OF THE UNITED NATIONS AND A CONTRIBUTION TO THE DECADE OF INTERNATIONAL LAW 217 (Nandasiri Jasentuliyana ed., Kluwer, London, 1995)

Edward MacWhinney, *The International Court and Judicial Law-making. Nuclear Tests Re-visited, in* THEORY OF INTERNATIONAL LAW AT THE THRESHOLD OF THE 21ST CENTURY. ESSAYS IN HONOUR OF KRZYSZTOF SKUBISZEWSKI 509 (Jerzy Makarczyk ed., Kluwer Law International, The Hague, 1996)

Edward MacWhinney, *New International Law and International Law Making*, 16 CHINESE YEARBOOK OF INTERNATIONAL LAW 33 (1997–1998)

Edward MacWhinney, Jeffery Atik & Gregory Shaffer, *Extraterritorial Sanctions and Legality under International and Domestic Law*, 94 AMERICAN SOCIETY OF INTERNATIONAL LAW: PROCEEDINGS OF THE ANNUAL MEETING 82 (2000)

Edward MacWhinney, THE UNITED NATIONS AND THE NEW WORLD ORDER FOR A NEW MILLENIUM. SELF-DETERMINATION, STATE SUCCESSION, AND HUMANITARIAN INTERVENTION (Kluwer Law International, The Hague, 2000)

EDWARD MACWHINNEY, THE SEPTEMBER 11 TERRORIST ATTACKS AND THE INVASION OF IRAQ IN CONTEMPORARY INTERNATIONAL LAW. OPINIONS ON THE EMERGING NEW WORLD ORDER SYSTEM (Nijhoff, Leiden, 2004)

Jean Louis Magdelenat, *La Nouvelle Annexe 17. Le Dernier Apport de l'Aviation Civile Internationale pur la Lutte Contre le Terrorisme*, XI Air & Space Law 87 (1986)

Jerzy Makarczyk ed., ESSAYS IN INTERNATIONAL LAW IN HONOUR OF JUDGE MANFRED LACHS/ÉTUDES DE DROIT INTERNATIONAL EN L'HONNEUR DU JUGE MANFRED LACHS, Institute of State and Law of the Polish Academy of Sciences (Nijhoff, The Hague, 1984)

Jerzy Makarczyk ed., THEORY OF INTERNATIONAL LAW AT THE THRESHOLD OF THE 21ST CENTURY. ESSAYS IN HONOUR OF KRZYSZTOF SKUBISZEWSKI (Kluwer Law International, The Hague, 1996)

Peter Malanczuk, *Reconsidering the Relationship Between the ICJ and the Security Council, in* INTERNATIONAL LAW AND THE HAGUE'S 750TH ANNIVERSARY (Wybo P. Heere ed., T.M.C. Asser Press, The Hague, 1999)

V.S. MANI, *The Friendly Relations Declaration and the International Court of Justice, in* LEGAL VISIONS OF THE 21ST CENTURY. ESSAYS IN HONOUR OF JUDGE CHRISTOPHER WEERAMANTRY 527 (Antony Anghie & Garry Sturgess eds., Kluwer Law International, The Hague, 1998)

Fritz A. Mann, *Reflections on the Prosecution of Persons Abducted in Breach of International Law, in* INTERNATIONAL LAW AT A TIME OF PERPLEXITY. ESSAYS IN HONOUR OF SHABTAI ROSENNE 407 (Yoram Dinstein ed., Nijhoff, Dordrecht, 1989)

Gabrielle Marceau, *A Call for Coherence in International Law, Praises for the Prohibition Against "Clinical Isolation" in WTO Dispute Settlement*, 33 JOURNAL OF WORLD TRADE 87 (1999)

Fernando M. Mariño Menendez ed., EL DERECHO INTERNACIONAL EN LOS ALBORES DEL SIGLO XXI: HOMENAJE AL PROFESSOR JUAN MANUEL CASTRO-RIAL CANOSA (Edit. Trotta, Madrid, 2002)

Michael J. Matheson, *United Nations Governance of Postconflict Societies,* 95 AMERICAN JOURNAL OF INTERNATIONAL LAW 76 (2001)

Nicolas Maziau, *Le Costituzioni Internazionalizzate. Aspetti Teorici e Tentativi di Classificazione*, 4 DIRITTO PUBBLICO COMPARATO ED EUROPEO 1397 (2002)

Robert McCorquodale, *Self-Determination: A Human Rights Approach*, 43 INTERNATIONAL AND COMPARATIVE LAW QUARTERLY 857 (1994)

Jeffrey A. McCredie, *Contemporary Uses of Force Against Terrorism: The United States Response to Achille Lauro. Questions of Jurisdiction and Its Exercis*e, 16 GEORGIA JOURNAL OF INTERNATIONAL AND COMPARATIVE LAW 435 (1986)

Myres S. McDougal & W. Michael Reisman, *Rhodesia and the United Nations: The Lawfulness of International Concern*, 62 AMERICAN JOURNAL OF INTERNATIONAL LAW 1 (1968)

Dominic McGoldrick, THE HUMAN RIGHTS COMMITTEE. ITS ROLE IN THE DEVELOPMENT OF THE INTERNATIONAL COVENANT ON CIVIL AND POLITICAL RIGHTS (Clarendon, Oxford, 1991)

Anthony McGrew, COSMOPOLITANISM AND THE WAR ON TERROR, 6 THE GLOBAL COMMUNITY. YEARBOOK OF INTERNATIONAL LAW AND JURISPRUDENCE 35 (2006–I)

Arnold Duncan McNair ed., CAMBRIDGE ESSAYS IN INTERNATIONAL LAW. ESSAYS IN HONOUR OF LORD MCNAIR (Stevens, London, 1965)

Karl Matthias Meessen, *Unilateral Recourse to Military Force against Terrorist Attacks*, 28 THE YALE JOURNAL OF INTERNATIONAL LAW 341 (2003)

Paolo Mengozzi, *Les Valeurs de l'Intégration Face à la Globalisation des Marchés*, 1 REVUE DU MARCHÉ UNIQUE EUROPÉEN 5 (1998)

Paolo Mengozzi, *La Cour de Justice et l'Applicabilité des Règles de l'OMC en Droit Communautaire à la Lumière de l'Affaire Portugal c. Conseil*, REVUE DU DROIT DE L'UNION EUROPÉENNE 509 (2000)

Paolo Mengozzi, *Private International Law and the WTO Law*, 292 RECUEIL DES COURS 249 (2001)

Paolo Mengozzi, *Court of First Instance and Court of Justice of the European Communities Introductory Note, The European Union Balance of Powers and the Case Law Related to EC External Relations*, 6 THE GLOBAL COMMUNITY. YEARBOOK OF INTERNATIONAL LAW AND JURISPRUDENCE 817 (2006–II)

Martin Mennecke, *Towards the Humanization of the Vienna Convention of Consular Rights. The LaGrand case before the International Court of Justice*, 44 GERMAN YEARBOOK OF INTERNATIONAL LAW 430 (2001)

P.K. MENON, THE LAW OF RECOGNITION IN INTERNATIONAL LAW (Edwin Mellen, Lewiston, New York, 1994)

Theodor Meron, *Norm Making and Supervision in International Human Rights: Reflections on Institutional Order*, 76 AMERICAN JOURNAL OF INTERNATIONAL LAW 754 (1982)

Theodor Meron ed., HUMAN RIGHTS IN INTERNATIONAL LAW: LEGAL AND POLICY ISSUES (Clarendon Press, Oxford, 1984)

Theodor Meron, HUMAN RIGHTS LAW-MAKING IN THE UNITED NATIONS: A CRITIQUE OF INSTRUMENTS AND PROCESS (Clarendon Press, Oxford, 1986)

Theodor Meron, HUMAN RIGHTS AND HUMANITARIAN NORMS AS CUSTOMARY LAW (Clarendon Press, Oxford, 1989)

Theodor Meron, *The Humanization of Humanitarian Law*, 94 AMERICAN JOURNAL OF INTERNATIONAL LAW 239 (2000)

Theodor Meron, THE HUMANIZATION OF INTERNATIONAL LAW (The Hague Academy of International Law Monographs n. 3, Nijhoff, Leiden, 2006)

John Merrills, INTERNATIONAL DISPUTE SETTLEMENT (2nd ed., Grotius Publications, Cambridge, 1991)

John G. Merrills, *The International Court of Justice and the Adjudication of Territorial and Boundary Disputes*, 13 LEIDEN JOURNAL OF INTERNATIONAL LAW 873 (2000)

John G. Merrills, *The Belize-Guatemala Territorial Dispute and the Legal Opinion of January 2002*, 2 THE GLOBAL COMMUNITY. YEARBOOK OF INTERNATIONAL LAW AND JURISPRUDENCE 77 (2002–I)

John G. Merrills, *The International Court of Justice, Introductory Note*, THE GLOBAL COMMUNITY. YEARBOOK OF INTERNATIONAL LAW AND JURISPRUDENCE 277 (2003–I); *id.*, 353 (2005–I)

John G. Merrills, *New Horizons for International Adjudication*, 6 THE GLOBAL COMMUNITY YEARBOOK OF INTERNATIONAL LAW AND JURISPRUDENCE 47 (2006–I)

Roy M. Mersky, CONFERENCE ON TRANSNATIONAL ECONOMIC BOYCOTTS AND COERCION (Oceana Publications, Dobbs Ferry, New York, 1978)

Yves Michaud ed., QU'EST-CE QUE LA SOCIÉTÉ? (Odile Jacob, Paris, 2000)

Luigi Migliorino, *International Terrorism in the United Nations Debates*, 2 ITALIAN YEARBOOK OF INTERNATIONAL LAW 102 (1976)

Paul Mitchell, *English-Speaking Justice: Evolving Responses to Transnational Forcible Abduction after Alvarez-Machain*, 29 CORNELL INTERNATIONAL LAW JOURNAL 383 (1996)

Djamchid Momtaz, *La Délégation par le Conseil de Sécurité de l'Éxecution de ses Actions Coercitives aux Organisations Regionales*, 43 ANNUAIRE FRANÇAIS DE DROIT INTERNATIONAL 105 (1997)

John N. Moore ed., LAW AND CIVIL WAR IN THE MODERN WORLD (Johns Hopkins University Press, Baltimore, 1974)

Charles-Albert Morand ed., LE DROIT SAISI PAR LA MONDIALISATION (Bruylant, Bruxelles, 2001)

Gaetano Morelli, NUOVI STUDI SUL PROCESSO INTERNAZIONALE (Giuffrè, Milano, 1972)

David C. Morrison, *The "Shadow War": The Air Attack on Libya Marks a New Phase in the U.S. Counterterrorism Struggle, An Era in Which the Military Will Likely Play a Much Greater Role*, 18 NATIONAL JOURNAL 1100 (1986)

Costantino Mortati, ISTITUZIONI DI DIRITTO PUBBLICO (9th ed., Cedam, Padova, 1976)

Franco Mosconi, *Ordine di Esecuzione e Mancata Ratifica*, 19 RIVISTA DI DIRITTO INTERNAZIONALE PRIVATO E PROCESSUALE 580 (1983)

Alexander S. Muller, David Raic, J.M. Thuranzsky & Sam Muller eds., THE INTERNATIONAL COURT OF JUSTICE: ITS FUTURE ROLE AFTER FIFTY YEARS (Nijhoff, The Hague, 1997)

Sean D. Murphy, HUMANITARIAN INTERVENTION: THE UNITED NATIONS IN AN EVOLVING WORLD ORDER (University of Pennsylvania Press, Philadelphia, 1996)

Sean D. Murphy, *Developments in Criminal Law. Progress and Jurisprudence of the International Criminal Tribunal for the Former Yugoslavia*, 93 AMERICAN JOURNAL OF INTERNATIONAL LAW 57 (1999)

Sean D. Murphy, *Democratic Legitimacy and the Recognition of States and Governments*, 48 INTERNATIONAL AND COMPARATIVE LAW QUARTERLY 545 (1999)

Sean D. Murphy, *Terrorism and the Concept of "Armed Attack" in Article 51 of the U.N. Charter*, 43 HARVARD INTERNATIONAL LAW JOURNAL 41 (2002)

Sean D. Murphy, *Contemporary Practice of the United States Relating to International Law*, 97 AMERICAN JOURNAL OF INTERNATIONAL LAW 681 (2003)

Roda Mushkat, *Public Participation in Environmental Law Making. A Comment on the International Legal Framework and the Asia-Pacific Perspective*, 1 CHINESE JOURNAL OF INTERNATIONAL LAW 185 (2002)

Eric P.J. Myjer & Nigel D. White, *The Twin Towers Attack: An Unlimited Right to Self-Defence*, 7 JOURNAL OF CONFLICT AND SECURITY LAW 5 (2002)

Ved P. Nanda, LAW IN THE WAR ON INTERNATIONAL TERRORISM (Transnational Publishers, Ardsley, New York, 2005)

Stefania Negri, *Interpreting the European Convention on Human Rights in Harmony with International Law and Jurisprudence: What Lessons from* Öcalan v. Turkey*?*, 4 THE GLOBAL COMMUNITY. YEARBOOK OF INTERNATIONAL LAW AND JURISPRUDENCE 243 (2004–I)

Gerald L. Neuman, *Human Rights and Constitutional Rights, Harmony and Dissonance*, 55 STANFORD LAW REVIEW 1863 (2003)

Gerald L. Neuman, *The Uses of International Law in Constitutional Interpretation*, 98 AMERICAN JOURNAL OF INTERNATIONAL LAW 82 (2004)

Edward Newman & Roland Rich eds., THE UN ROLE IN PROMOTING DEMOCRACY: BETWEEN IDEALS AND REALITY (UN University Press, Tokyo, 2004)

Rafael Nieto-Navia, *International Criminal Tribunal for the Former Yugoslavia, Introductory Note*, THE GLOBAL COMMUNITY. YEARBOOK OF INTERNATIONAL LAW AND JURISPRUDENCE 663 (2002–II); *id.*, 593 (2003–I); *id.*, 623 (2004–I); *id.*, 623 (2005–I); *id.*, 393 (2006–I); *id.*, 367 (2007–I)

Georg Nolte, *Restoring Peace by Regional Action: International Legal Aspects of the Liberian Conflict*, 53 ZEITSCHRIFT FÜR AUSLÄNDISCHES ÖFFENTLICHES RECHT UND VÖLKERRECHT 603 (1993)

Pippa Norris, *Global Governance and Cosmopolitan Citizens*, *in* GOVERNANCE IN A GLOBALIZING WORLD 155 (Joseph S. Nye & John D. Donahue eds., Brookings Institution Press, Washington, 2000)

Manfred Nowak, *Human Rights in EU and EEA Law*, *in* INTERNATIONAL HUMAN RIGHTS MONITORING MECHANISMS: ESSAYS IN HONOUR OF JAKOB TH. MÖLLER (Gudmundur Alfredsson, Jonas Grimheden, Bertram G. Ramcharan & Alfred de Zayas eds., Nijhoff, The Hague, 2001)

Karsten Nowrot & Emily W. Schabacker, *The Use of Force to Restore Democracy: International Legal Implications of the ECOWAS Intervention in Sierra Leone*, 14 AMERICAN UNIVERSITY LAW REVIEW 321 (1998)

Karsten Nowrot, *Legal Consequences of Globalization: The Status of Non-Governmental Organizations Under International Law*, 6 INDIANA JOURNAL OF GLOBAL LEGAL STUDIES 579 (1999)

Joseph S. Nye & John D. Donahue eds., GOVERNANCE IN A GLOBALIZING WORLD (Brookings Institution Press, Washington, 2000)

William V. O'Brien, *Reprisals, Deterrence, and Self-Defense in Counterterror Operations*, 30 VANDERBILT JOURNAL OF TRANSNATIONAL LAW 421 (1990)

Daniel P. O'Connell, INTERNATIONAL LAW (2nd ed., Stevens, London, 1970)

Mary Ellen O'Connell, *Debating the Law of Sanctions*, 13 EUROPEAN JOURNAL OF INTERNATIONAL LAW 63 (2002)

Patrick J. O'Keefe, SHIPWRECKED HERITAGE: A COMMENTARY ON THE UNESCO CONVENTION ON UNDERWATER CULTURAL HERITAGE (Inst. of Art & Law, Leicester, 2002)

Roger O'Keefe, *World Cultural Heritage: Obligations to the International Community as a Whole?*, 53 INTERNATIONAL & COMPARATIVE LAW QUARTERLY 189 (2004)

Shigeru Oda, *The International Court of Justice Viewed from the Bench (1976–1993)*, 244 RECUEIL DES COURS 9 (1993–VII)

Shigeru Oda, *The Compulsory Jurisdiction of the International Court of Justice: A Myth?*, 49 INTERNATIONAL & COMPARATIVE LAW QUARTERLY 251 (2000)

Karin Oellers-Frahm, *Multiplication of International Courts and Tribunals and Conflicting Jurisdiction,* 5 MAX PLANCK YEARBOOK OF UNITED NATIONS LAW 67 (2001)

Kenichi Ohmae, THE END OF THE NATION-STATE: THE RISE OF REGIONAL ECONOMIES (Free Press, New York, 1995)

Richard Stuart Olson, *Economic Coercion in World Politics, With a Focus on North-South Relations*, 31 WORLD POLITICS 471 (1978–1979)

Nicholas Onuf, *In Time of Need: United Nations Reform, Civil Society, and the Late Modern World*, 7 THE GLOBAL COMMUNITY. YEARBOOK OF INTERNATIONAL LAW AND JURISPRUDENCE (2007–I)

Anna Oriolo, *Ratifica e Attuazione in Italia dello Statuto di Roma: Questioni di Compatibilità Costituzionale e Opportunità di un'Armonizzazione Legislativa*, in ATTUAZIONE DEI TRATTATI INTERNAZIONALI E COSTITUZIONE ITALIANA. UNA RIFORMA PRIORITARIA NELL'ERA DELLA COMUNITÀ GLOBALE 265 (Giuliana Ziccardi Capaldo ed., Edizioni Scientifiche Italiane, Napoli, 2003)

Francisco Orrego Viçuna, *The Settlement of Disputes and Conflict Resolution in the Context of a Revitalized Role for the United Nations Security Council*, in LE DÉVELOPPEMENT DU RÔLE DU CONSEIL DE SÉCURITÉ/THE DEVELOPMENT OF THE ROLE OF THE SECURITY COUNCIL, PEACE-KEEPING AND PEACE-BUILDING, COLLOQUE, LA HAYE, 21–23 JUILLET 1992, 41 (René-Jean Dupuy ed., Nijhoff, Dordrecht, 1993)

Francisco Orrego Vicuña, *International Dispute Settlement in an Evolving Global Society, Constitutionalization, Accessibility, Privatisation*, HERSCH LAUTERPACHT MEMORIAL LECTURES 23 (Grotius Publications, Cambridge, 2004)

Ebere Osieke, *The Legal Validity of Ultra Vires Decisions of International Organizations*, 77 AMERICAN JOURNAL OF INTERNATIONAL LAW 239 (1983)

Bernard H. Oxman, *The Rule of Law and the United Nations Convention on the Law of the Sea*, 7 EUROPEAN JOURNAL OF INTERNATIONAL LAW 353 (1996)

Giuseppe Palmisano, *L'Autodeterminazione Interna nel Sistema dei Patti sui Diritti dell'Uomo*, 76 RIVISTA DI DIRITTO INTERNAZIONALE 365 (1996)

Haro F. van Panhuys, THE ROLE OF NATIONALITY IN INTERNATIONAL LAW (Sythoff, Leiden, 1959)

José Antonio Pastor Ridruejo, *Les Procédures Publiques Spéciales de la Commission des Droits de l'Homme des Nations Unies*, 228 RECUEIL DES COURS 182 (1991–III)

Jordan J. Paust, *Entebbe and Self-Help: The Israeli Response to Terrorism*, 2 THE FLETCHER FORUM OF WORLD AFFAIRS 86 (1978)

Jordan J. Paust, *Extradition and United States. Prosecution of the Achille Lauro Hostage-Takers: Navigating the Hazards*, 20 VANDERBILT JOURNAL OF TRANSNATIONAL LAW 235 (1985)

Jordan J. Paust, *Use of Armed Force Against Terrorists in Afghanistan, Iraq, and Beyond*, 35 CORNELL INTERNATIONAL LAW JOURNAL 533 (2002)

Connie Peck & Roy S. Lee eds., INCREASING THE EFFECTIVENESS OF THE INTERNATIONAL COURT OF JUSTICE. PROCEEDINGS OF THE ICJ/UNITAR COLLOQUIUM TO CELEBRATE THE 50TH ANNIVERSARY OF THE COURT (Nijhoff, The Hague, 1997)

Alain Pellet, *Le Tribunal Criminel International pour l'Ex-Yougoslavie. Poudre aux Yeux ou Avancée Décisive?*, 98 REVUE GÉNÉRALE DE DROIT INTERNATIONAL PUBLIC 7 (1994)

Pierre Pescatore, *Monisme, Dualisme et "Effet Utile" dans la Jurisprudence de la Cour de Justice de la Communauté Européenne*, *in* UNE COMMUNAUTÉ DE DROIT. FESTSCHRIFT FÜR GIL CARLOS RODRÍGUEZ IGLESIAS 329 (Ninon Colneric, David Edward, Jean-Pierre Puissochet & Dámaso Ruiz-Jarabo Colomer eds., Berliner Wissenschafts-Verlag, Berlin, 2003)

Ernst-Ulrich Petersmann, THE GATT/WTO DISPUTE SETTLEMENT SYSTEM: INTERNATIONAL LAW, INTERNATIONAL ORGANIZATION AND DISPUTE SETTLEMENT (Kluwer Law International, London, 1997)

Ernest Ulrich Petersmann, *Time for a United Nations "Global Compact" for Integrating Human Rights into the Law of Worldwide Organizations, Lessons from European Integration*, 13 EUROPEAN JOURNAL OF INTERNATIONAL LAW 621 (2002)

Ernst-Ulrich Petersmann, *Justice in International Economic Law? From the "International Law Among States" to "International Integration Law" and "Constitutional Law"*, 6 THE GLOBAL COMMUNITY. YEARBOOK OF INTERNATIONAL LAW AND JURISPRUDENCE, 105 (2006–I)

Mildred J. Peterson, RECOGNITION OF GOVERNMENTS. LEGAL DOCTRINE AND STATE PRACTICE 1815–1995 (Macmillan, Basingstoke, 1997)

Alessandro Pizzorusso, *Percorsi, Contenuti e Aspetti Problematici di una Riforma del Quadro Normativo Relativo all'Attuazione degli Obblighi Comunitari*, L'EUROPA IN ITALIA. VERSO NUOVI STRUMENTI DI ATTUAZIONE DELLE NORMATIVE COMUNITARIE, QUADERNI INTERNAZIONALI DI VITA ITALIANA, PRESIDENZA DEL CONSIGLIO DEI MINISTRI, DIPARTIMENTO PER L'INFORMAZIONE E L'EDITORIA, 61 (Istituto Poligrafico e Zecca dello Stato, Roma, 1999)

Fausto Pocar, *Uso della Forza in Risposta agli Eventi dell'11 Settembre e Legittima Difesa*, DIRITTI DELL'UOMO. CRONACHE E BATTAGLIE 55 (2001)

Fausto Pocar, *Human Rights Under the International Covenant on Civil and Political Rights and Armed Conflicts*, MAN'S INHUMANITY TO MAN. ESSAYS ON INTERNATIONAL LAW IN HONOUR OF ANTONIO CASSESE 729 (Lal Chand Vohrah ed., Kluwer Law International, The Hague, 2003)

John Polakas, *Economic Sanctions: An Effective Alternative to Military Coercion?*, 6 BROOKLYN JOURNAL OF INTERNATIONAL LAW 289 (1980)

Mauro Politi & Giuseppe Nesi eds., THE INTERNATIONAL CRIMINAL COURT AND THE CRIME OF AGGRESSION (Ashgate, Adelrshot, 2004)

Michla Pomerance, THE ADVISORY FUNCTION OF THE INTERNATIONAL COURT IN THE LEAGUE AND UN ERAS (John Hopkins University Press, Baltimore, 1973)

Kenneth L. Port, *The Japanese International Law "Revolution": International Human Rights Law and Its Impact in Japan*, 28 STANFORD JOURNAL OF INTERNATIONAL LAW 139 (1991)

Dharma Pratap, THE ADVISORY JURISDICTION OF THE INTERNATIONAL COURT (Clarendon Press, Oxford, 1972)

Rolando Quadri, LA SUDDITANZA NEL DIRITTO INTERNAZIONALE (Cedam, Padova, 1936)

Rolando Quadri, *Cours Général de Droit International Public*, 113 RECUEIL DES COURS 237 (1964–III)

Rolando Quadri, DIRITTO INTERNAZIONALE PUBBLICO (5th ed., Liguori, Napoli, 1968)

Arnhold Raestad, *La Reconnaissance Internationale des Nouveaux Etats et des Nouveaux Gouvernements*, 27 REVUE DE DROIT INTERNATIONAL ET DE LEGISLATION COMPARÉE 257 (1936)

Bertrand G. Ramcharan ed., HUMAN RIGHTS: THIRTY YEARS AFTER THE UNIVERSAL DECLARATION. COMMEMORATIVE VOLUME ON THE OCCASION OF THE 13TH ANNIVERSARY OF THE UNIVERSAL DECLARATION OF HUMAN RIGHTS (Nijhoff, The Hague, 1979)

Michael D. Ramsey, *International Materials and Domestic Rights. Reflections on Atkins and Lawrence*, 98 AMERICAN JOURNAL OF INTERNATIONAL LAW 69 (2004)

Steven Ratner & Jason Abrams, ACCOUNTABILITY FOR HUMAN RIGHTS ATROCITIES IN INTERNATIONAL LAW (Clarendon Press, Oxford, 1997)

Steven R. Ratner, *International Law: The Trials of Global Norms*, 110 FOREIGN POLICY 65 (1998)

Steven R. Ratner, Jus ad Bellum *and* Jus in Bello *After September 11*, 96 AMERICAN JOURNAL OF INTERNATIONAL LAW 905 (2002)

Serge Regourd, *Raids "Anti-Terroristes" et Développements Récents des Atteintes Illicites au Principe de Non-Intervention*, 32 ANNUAIRE FRANÇAIS DE DROIT INTERNATIONAL 79 (1986)

August Reinisch, *Widening the US Embargo Against Cuba Extraterritorially: A Few Public International Law Comments on the "Cuban Liberty and Democratic Solidarity (Libertad) Act" of 1996*, 7 EUROPEAN JOURNAL OF INTERNATIONAL LAW 545 (1996)

August Reinisch, *Developing Human Rights and Humanitarian Law Accountability of the Security Council for the Imposition of Economic Sanctions* 95 AMERICAN JOURNAL OF INTERNATIONAL LAW 851 (2001)

August Reinisch, *Introductory Note to Court of First Instance of the European Communities: Yassin Abdullah Kadi v. Council of the European Union and Commission of the European Communities*, 45 International Legal Materials 77 (2006)

August Reinisch, *ICSID*, *Introductory Note*, The Global Community. Yearbook of International Law and Jurisprudence 1653 (2005–II); *id.*, 1449 (2006–II): *id.*, 1799 (2007–II)

William Michael Reisman, *Enforcement of International Judgments*, 63 American Journal of International Law 1 (1969)

William Michael Reisman, *Coercion and Self-Determination: Construing Charter Article 2(4)*, 78 American Journal of International Law 642 (1984)

William Michael Reisman, *Sovereignty and Human Rights in Contemporary International Law*, 84 American Journal of International Law 866 (1990)

William Michael Reisman, *The Constitutional Crisis in the United Nations*, *in* Le Développement du Rôle du Conseil de Sécurité/The Development of the Role of the Security Council, Peace-Keeping and Peace-Building, Colloque, La Haye, 21–23 Juillet 1992, 41 (René-Jean Dupuy ed., Nijhoff, Dordrecht, 1993)

William Michael Reisman, *The Supervisory Jurisdiction of the International Court of Justice: International Arbitration and International Adjudication,* 258 Recueil des Cours 13 (1996)

William Micheal Reisman & Douglas L. Stevick, *The Applicability of International Law Standards to United Nations Economic Sanctions Programmes*, 9 European Journal of International Law 86 (1998)

William Michael Reisman, *Unilateral Action and the Transformations of the World Constitutive Process: The Special Problem of Humanitarian Intervention*, 11 European Journal of International Law 3 (2000)

William Michael Reisman, *In Defense of World Public Order*, 95 American Journal of International Law 833 (2001)

Robin Renwick, Economic Sanctions (Center for Internationals Affairs, Harvard University, Cambridge, 1981)

John B. Reynolds, *Export Controls and Economic Sanctions*, 37 The International Lawyer 263 (2003)

Joël Rideau, *Constitution et Droit International dans les États Membres des Communautées Européennes*, 3 Revue Française de Droit Constitutionnel 425 (1990)

Nehamiah Robinson, UNIVERSAL DECLARATION OF HUMAN RIGHTS. ITS ORIGIN, SIGNIFICANCE, APPLICATION AND INTERPRETATION (Institute of Jewish Affairs, New York, 1958)

Cesare Romano, *Mixed Jurisdictions for East Timor, Kosovo, Sierra Leone and Cambodia: The Coming of Age of Internationalized Criminal Bodies?*, 2 THE GLOBAL COMMUNITY. YEARBOOK OF INTERNATIONAL LAW AND JURISPRUDENCE 97 (2002–I)

NATALINO RONZITTI, RESCUING NATIONALS ABROAD THROUGH MILITARY COERCION AND INTERVENTION ON GROUNDS OF HUMANITY (Nijhoff, Dordrecht, 1985)

Shabtai Rosenne, THE WORLD COURT (5th ed., Nijhoff, Dordrecht, 1995)

Shabtai Rosenne, THE LAW AND PRACTICE OF THE INTERNATIONAL COURT, 1920–1996 (3rd ed., Nijhoff, Dordrecht, 1997)

Shabtai Rosenne, *Introductory Note to the Activity of the ICJ in 1999–2001*, 2 THE GLOBAL COMMUNITY. YEARBOOK OF INTERNATIONAL LAW AND JURISPRUDENCE 207 (2002–I)

Shabtai Rosenne, THE PERPLEXITIES OF MODERN INTERNATIONAL LAW (Nijhoff, Leiden, 2004)

Eugene W. Rostow, *"Until What? Enforcement Action or Collective Self-Defence"*, 85 AMERICAN JOURNAL OF INTERNATIONAL LAW 506 (1991)

Brad Roth, GOVERNMENTAL ILLEGITIMACY IN INTERNATIONAL LAW (Clarendon Press, Oxford, 1999)

Charles Rousseau, *Chronique des Faits Internationaux*, REVUE GÉNÉRALE DE DROIT INTERNATIONAL PUBLIC 627 (1978); *id.*, 1004 (1985); *id.*, 646 (1986)

Alfred P. Rubin, *The Law of Piracy*, 15 DENVER JOURNAL OF INTERNATIONAL LAW & POLICY 173 (1987)

Hélène Ruiz-Fabri ed., L' EFFECTIVITÉ DES ORGANISATIONS INTERNATIONALES. MÉCANISMES DE SUIVI ET DE CONTRÔLE; JOURNÉES FRANCO-HELLÉNIQUE, 7 – 8 MAI 1999 (Pedone, Paris, 2000)

Francesco Salerno ed., IL RUOLO DEL GIUDICE INTERNAZIONALE NELL'EVOLUZIONE DEL DIRITTO INTERNAZIONALE E COMUNITARIO, ATTI DEL CONVEGNO DI STUDI IN MEMORIA DI GAETANO MORELLI, CROTONE, 22 – 23 OTTOBRE 1993 (Cedam, Padova, 1995)

Jean J.A. Salmon, LA RECONNAISSANCE D'ETAT (Colin, Paris, 1971)

Philippe Sands ed., GREENING INTERNATIONAL LAW (Earthscan Publications, London, 1993)

Philippe Sands, Ruth Mackenzie & Yuval Shany eds., MANUAL ON INTERNATIONAL COURTS AND TRIBUNALS (Butterworths, London, 1999)

Miriam Sapiro, *Iraq: The Shifting Sands of Preemptive Self-Defense*, 97 AMERICAN JOURNAL OF INTERNATIONAL LAW 599 (2003)

Petar Šarčević ed., ESSAYS ON INTERNATIONAL COMMERCIAL ARBITRATION (Graham & Trotman, London, 1989)

Michel Sastre, *La Conception Américaine de la Garantie Judiciaire de la Supériorité des Traités sur les Lois*, 103 REVUE GÉNÉRALE DE DROIT INTERNATIONAL PUBLIC 149 (1999)

Georges Scelle, *Règles Générales du Droit de la Paix*, 46 RECUEIL DES COURS 331 (1933–IV)

Georges Scelle, *Quelques Réflexions sur une Institution Juridique Primitive: la Reconnaissance Internationale*, INTRODUCTION À L'ETUDE DU DROIT COMPARÉ, RECUEIL D'ETUDES EN L'HONNEUR D'EDOUARD LAMBERT 123 (Recueil Sirey, Paris, 1938–III)

William A. Schabas, GENOCIDE IN INTERNATIONAL LAW (Cambridge University Press, Cambridge, 2000)

William A. Schabas, *International Criminal Tribunal for Rwanda, Introductory Note*, THE GLOBAL COMMUNITY. YEARBOOK OF INTERNATIONAL LAW AND JURISPRUDENCE 591 (2001); *id.*, 1027 (2002–II); *id.*, 705 (2003–I); *id.*, 977 (2004–II); *id.*, 935 (2005–II); *id.*, 641 (2006–II); *id.*, 617 (2007–I)

William A. Schabas, AN INTRODUCTION TO THE INTERNATIONAL CRIMINAL COURT (2nd ed., Cambridge University Press, New York, 2004)

Oscar Schachter, *International Law in Theory and Practice*, 178 RECUEIL DES COURS 9 (1982–V)

Oscar Schachter, *Philip Jessup's Life and Ideas*, 80 AMERICAN JOURNAL OF INTERNATIONAL LAW 878 (1986)

Oscar Schachter, *Is There a Right to Overthrow an Illegitimate Regime*, LE DROIT INTERNATIONAL AU SERVICE DE LA PAIX DE LA JUSTICE ET DU DÉVELOPPEMENT, MÉLANGES VIRALLY 423 (Pedone, Paris, 1991)

Oscar Schachter, *United Nations Law in the Gulf Conflict*, 85 AMERICAN JOURNAL OF INTERNATIONAL LAW 452 (1991)

Oscar Schachter, INTERNATIONAL LAW IN THEORY AND PRACTICE (Nijhoff, Dordrecht 1991)

Henry G. Schermers, *Some Recent Cases Delaying the Direct Effect of International Treaties in Dutch Law*, 10 MICHIGAN JOURNAL OF INTERNATIONAL LAW 266 (1989)

Henry G. Schermers, *The International Court of Justice in Relation to Other Courts*, *in* THE INTERNATIONAL COURT OF JUSTICE: ITS FUTURE ROLE AFTER FIFTY YEARS 261 (Alexander S. Muller, David Raic, J.M. Thuranzsky & Sam Muller eds., Nijhoff, The Hague, 1997)

Michael N. Schmitt ed., THE LAW OF ARMED CONFLICT INTO THE NEXT MILLENIUM (Naval War College, Newport, 1998)

Marc Schreiber, *La Pratique Récente des Nations Unies dans le Domaine de la Protection des Droits de l'Homme*, 145 RECUEIL DES COURS 297 (1975–II)

Stephen M. Schwebel, *Authorizing the Secretary-General of the United Nations to Request Advisory Opinions of the International Court of Justice*, *in* ESSAYS IN INTERNATIONAL LAW IN HONOUR OF JUDGE MANFRED LACHS/ÉTUDES DE DROIT INTERNATIONAL EN L'HONNEUR DU JUGE MANFRED LACHS, INSTITUTE OF STATE AND LAW OF THE POLISH ACADEMY OF SCIENCES 519 (Jerzy Makarczyk ed., Nijhoff, The Hague, 1984)

Stephen M. Schwebel, *The Contribution of the International Court of Justice to the Development of International Law*, *in* INTERNATIONAL LAW AND THE HAGUE'S 750TH ANNIVERSARY 405 (Wybo P. Heere ed., T.M.C. Asser Press, The Hague, 1999)

Egon Schwelb, *Entry into Force of the International Covenants on Human Rights and the Optional Protocol to the International Covenant on Civil and Political Rights*, 70 AMERICAN JOURNAL OF INTERNATIONAL LAW 511 (1976)

Silvana Sciarra, HOW "GLOBAL" IS LABOUR LAW?, THE PERSPECTIVE OF SOCIAL RIGHTS IN THE EUROPEAN UNION (European University Institute, Florence, Department of Law, San Domenico, 1996)

Mohamed Shahabuddeen, *The Evolution of the Global Legal Framework*, *in* 1 BOUTROS BOUTROS-GHALI AMICORUM DISCIPULORUMQUE LIBER 701 (Bruylant, Bruxelles, 1998)

Mohamed Shahabuddeen, *Does the Principle of Legality Stand in the Way of Progressive Development of Law?*, 2 JOURNAL OF INTERNATIONAL CRIMINAL JUSTICE 1007 (2004)

Yuval Shany, THE COMPETING JURISDICTIONS OF INTERNATIONAL COURTS AND TRIBUNALS (Oxford University Press, Oxford, 2003)

Surya S. Sharma, *The American Doctrine of "Pre-emptive Self-defence"*, 43 INDIAN JOURNAL OF INTERNATIONAL LAW 215 (2003)

Roland Hall Sharp, NON-RECOGNITION AS A LEGAL OBLIGATION 1775–1934 (Thone, Liège/Gèneve, 1934)

Jeffrey A. Sheehan, *The Entebbe Raid: The Principle of Self-Help in International Law as Justification for State Use of Armed Force*, 1 THE FLETCHER FORUM OF WORLD AFFAIRS 135 (1977)

Dinah Shelton, *The Environmental Jurisprudence of the European Court of Human Rights, 2003–2004*, 4 THE GLOBAL COMMUNITY. YEARBOOK OF INTERNATIONAL LAW AND JURISPRUDENCE, 293 (2004–I)

George Shultz, *Low-Intensity Warfare: The Challenge of Ambiguity*, 738 DEPARTMENT OF STATE, CURRENT POLICY 4 (January 1986)

Richard H. Shultz (Jr.), *Can Democratic Governments Use Military Force in the War Against Terrorism? The U.S. Confrontation with Libya*, 148 WORLD AFFAIRS 205 (1986)

Bruno Simma & Philip Alston, *The Sources of Human Rights Law: Custom, Ius Cogens, and General Principles*, 12 AUSTRALIAN YEARBOOK OF INTERNATIONAL LAW 82 (1992)

Bruno Simma, *From Bilateralism to Community Interest in International Law*, 250 RECUEIL DES COURS 221 (1994–VI)

Bruno Simma, *International Human Rights and General International Law: A Comparative Analysis*, IV COLLECTED COURSES OF THE ACADEMY OF EUROPEAN LAW 153 (1995–II)

Bruno Simma, *NATO, The UN and the Use of Force: Legal Aspects*, 10 EUROPEAN JOURNAL OF INTERNATIONAL LAW 1 (1999)

Anne Marie Slaughter, *A Global Community of Courts*, 44 HARVARD INTERNATIONAL LAW JOURNAL 191 (2003)

George Slyz, *International Law in National Courts*, 28 NEW YORK UNIVERSITY JOURNAL OF INTERNATIONAL LAW & POLICY 65 (1996)

Rudolf Smend, STAATSRECHTLICHE ABHANDLUNGEN UND ANDERE AUFSATZE (3rd ed., Duncker & Humblot, Berlin, 1994)

Derek C. Smith, *Beyond Indeterminacy and Self-Contradiction in Law: Transnational Abductions and Treaty Interpretation in U.S. v. Alvarez-Machain,* 6 EUROPEAN JOURNAL OF INTERNATIONAL LAW 1 (1995)

Abraham D. Sofaer, *The War Powers Resolution and Antiterrorist Operations*, 86 DEPT. STATE BUL. 68 (August 1986)

Abraham D. Sofaer, *On the Necessity of Pre-emption*, 14 European Journal of International Law 209 (2003)

Louis B. Sohn, *Generally Accepted International Rules*, 61 Washington Law Review 1073 (1986)

Louis B. Sohn, *How New Is the New International Legal Order?*, 20 Denver Journal of International Law & Policy 205 (1992)

Jonathan Somer, *Acts of Non-State Armed Groups and the Law Governing Armed Conflict*, ASIL Insight (Aug. 24, 2006), *available at* http://www.asil.org/insights/2006/08/insights060824.html

Giuseppe Sperduti, *Le Principe de Souveraineté et le Problème des Rapports entre le Droit International et le Droit Interne*, 153 Recueil des Cours 319 (1976–V)

Giuseppe Sperduti, *Dualism and Monism. A Confrontation to Overcome*, 3 Israel Yearbook of International Law 31 (1977)

Peter Spiro, *New Global Communities: Non-Governmental Organizations in International Decision-Making Institutions*, 18 Washington Quarterly 45 (1995)

Carsten Stahn, *Terrorist Acts as "Armed Attack". The Right to Self-Defense, Article 51 (1/2) of the UN Charter and International Terrorism*, 27 The Fletcher Forum of World Affairs 35 (2003)

Vincenzo Starace, *La Responsabilité Résultant de la Violation des Obligations a l'Égard de la Communauté Internationale*, 153 Recueil des Cours 263 (1976–IV)

Vincenzo Starace, *European Court of Human Rights, Introductory Note*, The Global Community. Yearbook of International Law and Jurisprudence 659 (2001); *id.*, 983 (2003–II); *id.*, 1285 (2005–II)

Jopseph G. Starke, An Introduction to International Law (7th ed., Butterworth, London, 1972)

Eric Stein, *External Relations of the European Community: Structure and Process* 1 Collected Courses of the Academy of European Law 115 (1990–I)

Eric Stein, *International Law in Internal Law: Toward Internationalization of Central-Eastern European Constitutions?*, 88 American Journal of International Law 427 (1994)

Eric Stein, *International Law and Internal Law in the New Constitutions of Central-Eastern Europe*, *in* Recht zwischen Umbruch und Bewahrung 865 (Ulrich Beyerlin ed., Springer, Berlin/Heidelberg, 1995)

Eric Stein, *International Integration and Democracy: No Love at First Sight*, 95 AMERICAN JOURNAL OF INTERNATIONAL LAW 489 (2001)

Torsten Stein, *International Measures against Terrorism and Sanctions by and against Third States* 30 ARCHIV DES VÖLKERRECHTS 38 (1992)

Torsten Stein, *Decentralized International Law Enforcement Agent*, ALLOCATION OF LAW ENFORCEMENT AUTHORITY IN THE INTERNATIONAL SYSTEM. PROCEEDINGS OF AN INTERNATIONAL SYMPOSIUM OF THE KIEL INSTITUTE OF INTERNATIONAL LAW, MARCH 23 TO 25, 1994, 107 (Jost Delbrück ed., Duncker & Humblot, Berlin, 1995)

Paul B. Stephan, *The New International Law, Legitimacy, Accountability, Authority, and Freedom in the New Global Order*, 70 UNIVERSITY OF COLORADO LAW REVIEW 1555 (1999)

Paul B. Stephan, *US Constitutionalism and International Law, What the Multilateralist Move Leaves Out*, 2 JOURNAL OF INTERNATIONAL CRIMINAL JUSTICE 11 (2004)

Hugh W. Stephens, *Not Merely the* Achille Lauro: *The Threat of Maritime Terrorism and Piracy*, 9 TERRORISM: AN INTERNATIONAL JOURNAL 285 (1987)

Brigitte Stern, *L'Affaire du Bureau de l'O.L.P. Devant les Juridictions Internes et Internationales*, 34 ANNUAIRE FRANÇAIS DE DROIT INTERNATIONAL 165 (1988)

Brigitte Stern ed., LES ASPECTS JURIDIQUE DE LA CRISE ET DE LA GUERRE DU GOLFE (Montchrestien, Paris, 1991)

Brigitte Stern, *Vers la Mondialisation Juridique? Les Lois Helms-Burton et D'Amato-Kennedy*, 100 REVUE GÉNÉRALE DE DROIT INTERNATIONAL PUBLIC 979 (1996)

Brigitte Stern, *États et Souverainetés: La Souveraineté de l'État Face à la Mondialisation*, *in* QU'EST-CE QUE LA SOCIÉTÉ? 829 (Yves Michaud ed., Odile Jacob, Paris, 2000)

Ethan C. Stiles, *Reforming Current International Law to Combat Modern Sea Piracy*, 27 SUFFOLK TRANSNATIONAL LAW REVIEW 299 (2004).

Christopher D. Stone, THE GNAT IS OLDER THAN MAN: GLOBAL ENVIRONMENT AND HUMAN AGENDA (Princeton University Press, Princeton NJ, 1993)

Helmut Strebel, *Nochmals zur Geiselbefreiung in Entebbe*, 37 ZEITSCHRIFT FÜR AUSLÄNDISCHES ÖFFENTLICHES RECHT UND VÖLKERRECHT 691 (1977)

John Stremlau, SHARPENING INTERNATIONAL SANCTIONS: TOWARD A STRONGER ROLE FOR THE UNITED NATIONS, REPORT TO THE CARNEGIE COMMISSION ON PREVENTING DEADLY CONFLICT (Carnegie Commission on Preventing Deadly Conflict, Washington DC, 1996)

Jane E. Stromseth, *Iraq's Repression of Its Civilian Population: Collective Responses and Continuing Challenges*, *in* ENFORCING RESTRAINT: COLLECTIVE INTERVENTION IN INTERNAL CONFLICTS (Lori F. Damrosch ed., Council on Foreign Relations Press, New York, 1993)

Jane E. Stromseth, *Law and Force After Iraq: A Transitional Moment*, 97 AMERICAN JOURNAL OF INTERNATIONAL LAW 628 (2003)

Alexander M. Stuyt, SURVEY OF INTERNATIONAL ARBITRATIONS 1794–1989 (Nijhoff, Dordrecht, 1990)

Serge Sur, *The State between Fragmentation and Globalization*, 8 EUROPEAN JOURNAL OF INTERNATIONAL LAW 421 (1997)

Paul Szasz, *The Law of Economic Sanctions*, *in* THE LAW OF ARMED CONFLICT INTO THE NEXT MILLENIUM 455 (Michael N. Schmitt ed., Naval War College, Newport, 1998)

William H. Taft IV & Tood F. Buchwald, *Preemption, Iraq, and International Law*, 97 AMERICAN JOURNAL OF INTERNATIONAL LAW 557 (2003)

Stefan Talmon, *The Constitutive Versus the Declaratory Theory of Recognition: Tertium Non Datur?*, 75 THE BRITISH YEARBOOK OF INTERNATIONAL LAW 101 (2004)

Christian J. Tams, *Enforcing Obligations* Erga Omnes *in International Law*, CAMBRIDGE STUDIES IN INTERNATIONAL AND COMPARATIVE LAW No. 43 (2005)

Daniel K. Tarullo, *Law and Governance in a Global Economy*, 93 PROCEEDINGS OF THE ANNUAL MEETING OF THE AMERICAN SOCIETY OF INTERNATIONAL LAW 105 (1999)

Paul Tavernier, NOUVEL ORDRE MONDIAL ET DROITS DE L'HOMME. LA GUERRE DU GOLFE (Publisud, Paris, 1993)

Allyn L. Taylor, *Global Governance, International Health Law and WHO, Looking Towards the Future*, 80 BULLETIN OF THE WORLD HEALTH ORGANIZATION 975 (2002)

Harold Temperley, THE FOREIGN POLICY OF CANNING, 1822–1827 (Bell & Sons, London, 1925)

Giõrgos Ténékides, *L'Action des Nations Unies contre la Discrimination Raciale*, 168 RECUEIL DES COURS 269 (1980–III)

Gunther Teubner ed., GLOBAL LAW WITHOUT A STATE (Dartmouth, Aldershot, 1997)

Dire Thadi, *Reviving the Debate on the Efficacy of the ICJ*, 25 SOUTH AFRICAN YEARBOOK OF INTERNATIONAL LAW 232 (2000)

Ramesh C. Thakur, *Global Norms and International Humanitarian Law, an Asian Perspective*, 83 Revue Internationale de la Croix Rouge 19 (2001)

Hubert Thierry, *Les Résolutions des Organes Internationaux dans la Jurisprudence de la Cour Internationale de Justice*, 167 Recueil des Cours 385 (1980–II)

Hugh Thirlway, *The Law and Procedure of the International Court of Justice 1960–1989, Part Two*, 61 British Yearbook of International Law 1 (1990)

Hugh Thirlway, *Procedural Law and the International Court of Justice*, *in* Fifty Years of the International Court of Justice. Essays in Honour of Sir Robert Jennings 389 (Vaughan Lowe & Malgosia A. Fitzmaurice eds., Cambridge University Press, Cambridge, 1996)

Hugh Thirlway, *The Law and Procedure of the International Court of Justice 1960–1989, Part Ten*, 70 British Yearbook of International Law 1 (1999)

Hugh Thirlway, *The Proliferation of International Judicial Organ: Institutional and Substantive Questions – The International Court of Justice and Other International Courts*, *in* Proliferation of International Organizations: Legal Issues 251 (Niels M. Blokker & Henry G. Schermers eds., Kluwer Law International, The Hague, 2001)

Antonio Tizzano, *La Cour de Justice après Nice: Le Transfert de Compétences au Tribunal de Première Instance*, 4 Revue du Droit de l'Union Europénne 665 (2002)

Antonio Tizzano, *Ancora sui Rapporti tra Corti Europee. Principi Comunitari e c.d. Controlimiti Costituzionali*, Il Diritto dell'Unione Europea 734 (2007)

Christian Tomuschat, *Human Rights in a World-Wide Framework. Some Current Issues*, 45 Zeitschrift für Auslandisches Öffentliches Recht und Völkerrecht 547 (1985)

Christian Tomuschat, *The Lockerbie Case Before the International Court of Justice*, 48 International Commission of Jurists. The Review 38 (1992)

Christian Tomuschat, *Obligations Arising for States Without or Against Their Will*, 241 Recueil des Cours 199 (1993–IV)

Christian Tomuschat, *Case T-306/01, Ahmed Ali Yusuf and Al Barakaat International Foundation v. Council and Commission, Judgment of the Court of First Instance of 21 September 2005; Case T-315/01, Yassin Abdullah Kadi v. Council and Commission, Judgment of the Court of First Instance of 21 September 2005*, 43 Common Market Law Review 537 (2006)

Jean Touscoz, Le Principe d'Effectivité dans l'Ordre International (Pichon et Durand-Auzias, Paris, 1964)

Tullio Treves, LE CONTROVERSIE INTERNAZIONALI. NUOVE TENDENZE, NUOVI TRIBUNALI, Giuffrè, Milano,1999

Cora True-Fros, *The UN Security Council Marks Seventh Anniversary of Resolution 1325 on Women, Peace and Security with Open Debate*, ASIL INSIGHT (Dec. 17, 2007), Volume 11, Issue 29

Grigorij Tunkin I., THEORY OF INTERNATIONAL LAW (Allen Unwin, London, 1974)

David Turns, *The Stimson Doctrine of Non-Recognition, Its Historical Genesis and Influence on Contemporary International Law*, 2 CHINESE JOURNAL OF INTERNATIONAL LAW 105 (2003)

Detlev F. Vagts, *Hegemonic International Law*, 95 AMERICAN JOURNAL OF INTERNATIONAL LAW 843 (2001)

Karel Vasak & Philip Alston eds., THE INTERNATIONAL DIMENSION OF HUMAN RIGHTS (Greenwood Press, Westport, 1982)

Carlos Manuel Vázquez, *Treaty-Based Rights and Remedies of Individuals*, 92 COLUMBIA LAW REVIEW 1082 (1992)

Carlos Manuel Vázquez, *The Four Doctrines of Self-executing Treaties*, 89 AMERICAN JOURNAL OF INTERNATIONAL LAW 695 (1995)

Carlos Manuel Vázquez, *Laughing at Treaties*, 99 COLUMBIA LAW REVIEW 2154 (1999).

Jennifer J. Veloz, *In the Clinton Era, Overturning Alvarez-Machain and Extraterritorial Abduction: How a Unified Western Hemisphere, Through the OAS, Can Win the War on Drugs and Do It Legally*, 12 TEMPLE INTERNATIONAL AND COMPARATIVE LAW JOURNAL 241 (1998)

Jacques Velu, *Les Effets Directs des Instruments Internationaux en Matière de Droits de l'Homme*, 15 REVUE BELGE DE DROIT INTERNATIONAL 293 (1980)

Alfred Verdross, DIE VERFASSUNG DER VÖLKERRECHTSGEMEINSCHAFT (Springer, Wien, 1926)

Alfred Verdross, VÖLKERRECHT (5th ed., Springer, Wien, 1964)

Alfred Verdross & BRUNO SIMMA, UNIVERSELLES VÖLKERRECHT. THEORIE UND PRAXIS (Duncker & Humblot, Berlin, 1984)

Vladlen S. Vereshchetin, *New Constitutions and the Old Problem of the Relationship Between International Law and National Law*, 7 EUROPEAN JOURNAL OF INTERNATIONAL LAW 29 (1996)

Joe Verhoeven, LA RECONNAISSANCE INTERNATIONALE DANS LA PRATIQUE CONTEMPORAINE (Pedone, Paris, 1975)

Joe Verhoeven, *La Notion d' "Applicabilite Directe" du Droit International*, 15 REVUE BELGE DE DROIT INTERNATIONAL 243 (1980)

Ugo Villani, *Legittima difesa e lotta al terrorismo nell'operazione* Enduring Freedom, STUDI DI DIRITTO INTERNAZIONALE IN ONORE DI GAETANO ARANGIO RUIZ 1771 (Editoriale Scientifica, Napoli, 2004–III)

Mark E. Villiger, CUSTOMARY INTERNATIONAL LAW AND TREATIES. A STUDY OF THEIR INTERACTIONS AND INTERRELATIONS WITH SPECIAL CONSIDERATION OF THE 1969 VIENNA CONVENTION ON THE LAW TREATIES (Nijhoff, Dordrecht/Zürich, 1985)

John Vogler, THE GLOBAL COMMONS: ENVIRONMENTAL AND TECHNOLOGICAL GOVERNANCE (2nd ed., John Wiley & Sons, New York, 2000)

Lal Chand Vohrah ed., MAN'S INHUMANITY TO MAN. ESSAYS ON INTERNATIONAL LAW IN HONOUR OF ANTONIO CASSESE (Kluwer Law International, The Hague, 2003)

Claude H. M. Waldock, *Disputed Sovereignty in the Falkland Islands Dependencies*, 25 BRITISH YEARBOOK OF INTERNATIONAL LAW 311 (1948)

Claude H. M. Waldock, *The Regulation of the Use of Force by Individual State in International Law*, 81 RECUEIL DES COURS 455 (1952–II)

Christopher Wall, *Human Rights and Economic Sanctions: The New Imperialisms*, 22 FORDHAM INTERNATIONAL LAW JOURNAL 77 (1998)

Peter Wallensteen, INTERNATIONAL SANCTIONS BETWEEN WORDS AND WARS IN THE GLOBAL SYSTEM (Cass, London, 2005)

Geoffrey R. Watson, *Constitutionalism, Judicial Review, and the World Court*, 34 HARVARD INTERNATIONAL LAW JOURNAL 1 (1993)

Philippe Weckel, *Le Chapitre VII de la Charte et son Application par le Conseil de Sécurité*, 37 ANNUAIRE FRANÇAIS DE DROIT INTERNATIONAL 165 (1991)

Ruth Wedgwood, *NATO's Campaign in Jugoslavia*, 93 AMERICAN JOURNAL OF INTERNATIONAL LAW 828 (1999)

Ruth Wedgwood & Harold K. Jacobson, *Symposium: State Reconstruction after Civil Conflict, Foreword*, 95 AMERICAN JOURNAL OF INTERNATIONAL LAW 1 (2001)

Ruth Wedgwood, *The Fall of Saddam Hussein: Security Council Mandates and Preemptive Self-Defence*, 97 AMERICAN JOURNAL OF INTERNATIONAL LAW 576 (2003)

Prosper Weil, *Towards Relative Normativity in International Law?*, 77 AMERICAN JOURNAL OF INTERNATIONAL LAW 413 (1983)

Joseph H. H. Weiler ed., INTERNATIONAL CRIMES OF STATES: A CRITICAL ANALYSIS OF THE ICL'S DRAFT ARTICLE 19 ON STATE RESPONSIBILITY (de Gruyter, Berlin, 1989)

Thomas G . Weiss ed., BEYOND UN SUBCONTRACTING. TASK-SHARING WITH REGIONAL SECURITY ARRANGEMENTS AND SERVICE-PROVIDING NGOS (Macmillan, Basingstoke, 1998)

David Weissbrodt, *The Contribution of International Nongovernmental Organizations to the Protection of Human Rights*, *in* HUMAN RIGHTS IN INTERNATIONAL LAW: LEGAL AND POLICY ISSUES (Theodor Meron ed., Clarendon Press, Oxford, 1984)

Karel Wellens ed., INTERNATIONAL LAW. THEORY AND PRACTICE. ESSAYS IN HONOUR OF ERIC SUY (Nijhoff, The Hague, 1998)

Karel Wellens, *Fragmentation of International Law and Establishing an Accountability Regime for International Organizations. The Role of the Judiciary in Closing the Gap*, 25 MICHIGAN JOURNAL OF INTERNATIONAL LAW 1159 (2004)

Mark Weller ed., REGIONAL PEACE KEEPING AND INTERNATIONAL ENFORCEMENT. THE LIBERIAN CRISIS (Cambridge University Press, Cambridge, 1994)

Marc Weller, *Undoing the Global Constitution: UN Security Council Action on the International Criminal Court*, 78 INTERNATIONAL AFFAIRS 693 (2002)

Michael Wells, *International Norms in Constitutional Law*, 32 GEORGIA JOURNAL OF INTERNATIONAL & COMPARATIVE LAW 429 (2004)

Wilhelm Wengler, VÖLKERRECHT (Springer, Berlin, 1964)

John Westlake, ETUDES SUR LES PRINCIPES DU DROIT INTERNATIONAL (Castaigne, Bruxelles, 1895)

Burns H. Weston & Stephen P. Marks eds., THE FUTURE OF INTERNATIONAL HUMAN RIGHTS (Transnational Publishers, Ardsley, New York, 1999)

Chanaka Wickremasinghe & Malcolm D. Evans, *Difference Relating to Immunity from Legal Process of a Special Rapporteur of the Commission on Human Rights*, 49 INTERNATIONAL & COMPARATIVE LAW QUARTERLY 724 (2000)

John F. Williams, *La Doctrine de la Reconnaissance en Droit International et Ses Développements Récents*, 44 RECUEIL DES COURS 203 (1933–II)

Barbara Wilson, *L'Efficacité des Mécanismes de Protection des Droits de l'Homme Mis en Place par les Nations Unies*, 13 AKTUELLE JURISTISCHE PRAXIS 1355 (2004)

David Wippman, *Enforcing the Peace: ECOWAS and the Liberian Civil War, in* ENFORCING RESTRAINT: COLLECTIVE INTERVENTION IN INTERNAL CONFLICTS 157 (Lori Fisler Damrosch ed., Council on Foreign Relations Press, New York, 1993)

Steffen Wirth, *Immunity for Core Crimes? The ICJ's Judgment in the Congo v. Belgium Case*, 13 EUROPEAN JOURNAL OF INTERNATIONAL LAW 877 (2002)

Jan Wouters, *The Judgment of International Court of Justice in the Arrest Warrant Case*, 16 LEIDEN JOURNAL OF INTERNATIONAL LAW 253 (2003)

John C. Yoo, *Globalism and the Constitution: Treaties, Non-Self-Execution, and the Original Understanding*, 99 COLUMBIA LAW REVIEW 1955 (1999)

John C. Yoo, *Treaties and Public Lawmaking: A Textual and Structural Defense of Non-Self-Execution*, 99 COLUMBIA LAW REVIEW 2218 (1999)

John C. Yoo, *Kosovo, War Powers, and the Multilateral Future*, 148 UNIVERSITY OF PENNSYLVANIA LAW REVIEW 1673 (2000)

John C. Yoo, *International Law and the War in Iraq*, 97 AMERICAN JOURNAL OF INTERNATIONAL LAW 563 (2003)

Mark S. Zaid, *Military Might Versus Sovereign Right: The Kidnapping of Dr. Humberto Alvarez-Machain and the Resulting Fallout*, 19 HOUSTON JOURNAL OF INTERNATIONAL LAW 829 (1997)

Myint Zan, *US v Alvarez-Machain "Kidnap" Case Revisted*, 70 THE AUSTRALIAN LAW JOURNAL 239 (1996)

Claudio Zanghì, LA PROTEZIONE INTERNAZIONALE DEI DIRITTI DELL'UOMO (Giappichelli, 2006)

Karl Zemanek, *New Trends in the Enforcement of* Erga Omnes *Obligations*, 4 MAX PLANCK YEARBOOK OF UNITED NATIONS LAW 1 (2000)

Karl Zemanek, *Self-Defence Against Terrorism, Reflexions on an Unprecedented Situation in* EL DERECHO INTERNACIONAL EN LOS ALBORES DEL SIGLO XXI: HOMENAJE AL PROFESSOR JUAN MANUEL CASTRO-RIAL CANOSA 695 (Fernando M. Mariño Menendez ed., Edit Trotta, Madrid, 2002)

Piero Ziccardi, LA COSTITUZIONE DELL'ORDINAMENTO INTERNAZIONALE (Giuffré, Milano 1943, reprinted in 2000)

Piero Ziccardi, *L'Intervento Collettivo delle Nazioni Unite e i Nuovi Poteri dell'Assemblea Generale*, 12 LA COMUNITÀ INTERNAZIONALE 221, 415 (1957)

Piero Ziccardi, *Les Caractères de l'Ordre Juridique International*, 95 RECUEIL DES COURS 266 (1958–III)

Piero Ziccardi, *Règles d'Organisation et Règles de Conduite en Droit International. Le Droit Commun et les Ordres Juridiques*, 152 Recueil des Cours 119 (1976–IV)

Giuliana Ziccardi Capaldo, Le Situazioni Territoriali Illegittime nel Diritto Internazionale/Unlawful Territorial Situations in International Law (Editoriale Scientifica, Napoli, 1977)

Giuliana Ziccardi Capaldo, Terrorismo Internazionale e Garanzie Collettive/International Terrorism and Collective Guarantees (Giuffré, Milano, 1990)

Giuliana Ziccardi Capaldo, Repertory of Decisions of the International Court of Justice/Répertoire de la Jurisprudence de la Cour Internationale de Justice (1947–1992) 2 Vols. (Nijhoff, Dordrecht/Boston/London 1995)

Giuliana Ziccardi Capaldo, *Verticalità della Comunità Internazionale e Nazioni Unite. Un Riesame del Caso Lockerbie*, *in* Interventi delle Nazioni Unite e Diritto Internazionale 61 (Paolo Picone ed., Cedam, Padova, 1995)

Giuliana Ziccardi Capaldo ed., Democratizzazione all'Est e Diritto Internazionale, (Edizioni Scientifiche Italiane, Napoli, 1998)

Giuliana Ziccardi Capaldo, *The Law of the Global Community: An Integrated System to Enforce "Public" International Law*, 1 The Global Community. Yearbook of International Law and Jurisprudence 71 (2001)

Giuliana Ziccardi Capaldo, *Treaty Law and National Law in a Globalizing System*, 2 The Global Community. Yearbook of International Law and Jurisprudence 139 (2002–I)

Giuliana Ziccardi Capaldo, *Legality* vs. *Effectivity in the Global Community: The Overthrowing of Saddam Hussein*, 3 The Global Community. Yearbook of International Law and Jurisprudence 107 (2003–I)

Giuliana Ziccardi Capaldo, *Global Trends and Global Court: The Legitimacy of World Governance*, 4 The Global Community. Yearbook of International Law and Jurisprudence 127 (2004–I)

Giuliana Ziccardi Capaldo, *A New Dimension of International Law: The Global Law*, 5 The Global Community. Yearbook of International Law and Jurisprudence xvi (2005–I)

Giuliana Ziccardi Capaldo, *Providing a Right of Self-Defense Against Large-Scale Attacks by Irregular Forces: The Israeli-Hizbollah Conflict*, 48 Harvard International Law Journal Online 101 (2007), http://www.harvardilj.org/online/115

Giuliana Ziccardi Capaldo ed., The Global Community. Yearbook of International Law and Jurisprudence 13 volls (Oceana Publications/Oxford University Press, New York, 2001–2007)

Giuliana Ziccardi Capaldo & Michele Nino, *Globalization of Law Enforcement Mechanisms: Issues of Legality and Legitimacy*, *in* INTERNATIONAL CRIMINAL LAW (3rd ed., M. Cherif Bassiouni ed., *in print*)

Elisabeth Zoller, PEACETIME UNILATERAL REMEDIES: AN ANALYSIS OF COUNTERMEASURES (Transnational Publisher, Dobbs Ferry, New York, 1984)

Elisabeth Zoller, ENFORCING INTERNATIONAL LAW THROUGH U.S. LEGISLATIONS (Transnational Publisher, Dobbs Ferry, New York, 1985)

Index of Case Law

International Courts

Court of First Instance of the European Communities

2002

2003

2004

2005

2006

the European Communities), Judgment of 12 July 2006, 2006 ECR II-52: 285, 294-296

Case T-228/02 (Organisation des Modjahedines du Peuple d'Iran *v.* Council of the European Communities), Judgment of 12 December 2006, 2006 ECR II-4665: 285, 295, 296, 302

Court of Justice of the European Communities

1964

Case 6/64 (Flaminio Costa *v.* E.N.E.L.), Judgment of 15 July 1964, 1964 ECR 585: 180, 195

1970

Case 11/70 (Internationale Handelsgesellschaft mbH *v.* Einfuhr- und Vorratsstelle für Getreide und Futtermittel), Judgment of 17 December 1970, 1970 ECR 1125: 186

1976

Case 87/75 (Conceria Daniele Bresciani *v.* Amministrazione Italiana delle Finanze), Judgment of 5 February 1976, 1976 ECR 129: 181

1978

Case 106/77 (Staatliche Finanzverwaltung *v.* Spa Simmenthal (Simmenthal II)), Judgment of 9 March 1978, 1978 ECR 629: 186

1987

Case 12/86 (Meryem Demirel *v.* Stadt Schwäbisch Gmünd), Judgment of 30 September 1987, 1987 ECR 3719: 180

1989

Case 70/87 (Fédération de l'Industrie de l'Huilerie de la CEE (Fediol) *v.* Commission of the European Communities), Judgment of 22 June 1989, 1989 ECR 1781: 181

1990

Case C-192/89 (S. Z. Sevince *v.* Staatssecretaris van Justitie), Judgment of 20 September 1990, 1990 ECR I-3461: 180

1991

Case C-69/89 (Nakajima All Precision Co. Ltd. *v.* Council of the European Communities), Judgment of 7 May 1991, 1991 ECR I-2069: 181

1994

Case C-432/92 (The Queen *v.* Minister of Agriculture, Fisheries and Food, *ex parte* S.P. Anastasiou (Pissouri) Ltd. and Others), Judgment of 5 July 1994, 1994 ECR I-3087: 180

1995

Case C-162/00 (Land Nordrhein-Westfalen *v*. Beata Pokrzeptowicz-Meyer), Judgment of 29 January 2002, 2002 ECR I-1049: 181

Case C-413/99 (Baumbast, R and Secretary of State for the Home Department), Judgment of 17 September 2002, 2002 ECR I-7091: 180

2003

Case C-76/00 P (Petrotub SA and Republica SA *v*. Council of the European Union), Judgment of 9 January 2003, 2003 ECR I-79: 181

Case C-171/01 (Wählergruppe Gemeinsam Zajedno/Birlikte Alternative und Grüne GewerkschafterInnen/UG and Wählergruppe NBZ - Neue Bewegung für die Zukunft), Judgment of 8 May 2003, 2003 ECR I-4301: 181

Case C-198/01 (Consorzio Industrie Fiammiferi (CIF) and Autorità Garante della Concorrenza e del Mercato), Judgment of 9 September 2003, 2003 ECR I-8055: 186

Case C-93/02 P (Biret International SA *v*. Council of the European Union), Judgment of 30 September 2003, 2003 ECR I-10497: 181

2004

Case C-453/00 (Kühne & Heitz NV and Productschap voor Pluimvee en Eieren), Judgment of 13 January 2004, 2004 ECR I-837: 186

Case C-256/01 (Debra Allonby, and Accrington & Rossendale College, Education Lecturing Services, trading as Protocol Professional, Secretary of State for Education and Employment), Judgment of 13 January 2004, 2004 ECR I-873: 186

Case C-200/02 (Kunqian Catherine Zhu and Man Lavette Chen *v*. Secretary of State for the Home Department), Judgment of 19 October 2004, 2004 ECR I-9925: 180

Case C-245/02 (Anheuser-Busch Inc. *v*. Budějovický Budvar, Národní Podnik), Judgment of 16 November 2004, 2004 ECR I-10989: 182

2005

Case C-377/02 (Léon Van Parys NV *v*. Belgisch Interventie- en Restitutiebureau (BIRB)), Judgment of 1 March 2005, 2005 ECR I-1465: 181

Case C-144/04 (Werner Mangold *v*. Rüdiger Helm), Judgment of 22 November 2005, 2005 ECR I-9981: 186

2006

Case C-341/04 (Eurofood IFSC Ltd.), Judgment of 2 May 2006, 2006 ECR I-3813: 303

2007

Case C-229/05 P (Osman Ocalan, on behalf of the Kurdistan Workers' Party (PKK), Serif Vanly, on behalf of the Kurdistan National Congress (KNK) *v*. Council of the European Union), Judgment of 18 January 2007, 2007 ECR I-439: 285

Case C-354/04 P (Gestoras Pro Amnistía, Juan Mari Olano Olano, Julen Zelarain

Application No. 31253/96 (McElhinney *v.* Ireland), Merits, Judgment of 21 November 2001, 2001-XI Reports of Judgments and Decisions: 290

Application No. 35763/97 (Al-Adsani *v.* The United Kingdom), Merits, Judgment of 21 November 2001, 2001-XI Reports of Judgments and Decisions: 290

Application No. 37112/97 (Fogarty *v.* The United Kingdom), Merits, Judgment of 21 November 2001, 2001-XI Reports of Judgments and Decisions: 290

Application No. 52207/99 (Bankovic, Stojadinovic, Stoimenovski, Joksimovic and Sukovic *v.* Belgium, The Czech Republic, Denmark, France, Germany, Greece, Hungary, Iceland, Italy, Luxembourg, The Netherlands, Norway, Poland, Portugal, Spain, Turkey and The United Kingdom), Decision of 12 December 2001, 2001-XII Reports of Judgments and Decisions: 13, 288, 290

2003

Application No. 46221/99 (Öcalan *v.* Turkey), Merits and Just Satisfaction, Judgment of 12 March 2003: 247, 248, 291

Application No. 36813/97 (Giovanni, Elena, Maria and Giuliana Scordino *v.* Italy), Decision of 27 March 2003, 2003-IV Reports of Judgments and Decisions: 183

2005

Application No. 45036/98 (Bosphorus Hava Yollari Turizm ve Ticaret Anonim Şirketi *v.* Ireland), Merits, Judgment of 30 June 2005, 2005-VI Reports of Judgments and Decisions: 180, 291

Inter-American Court of Human Rights

1998

Velásquez-Rodríguez Case, Merits, Judgment of 29 July 1988, Series C No. 4: 290

International Court of Justice

1948

Corfu Channel (United Kingdom *v.* Albania), Preliminary Objections, Judgment of 25 March 1948, 1947-1948 I.C.J. Reports 15: 99

1949

Corfu Channel (United Kingdom *v.* Albania), Merits, Judgment of 9 April 1949, 1949 I.C.J. Reports 4: 101

Reparation for Injuries Suffered in the Service of the United Nations, Advisory Opinion of 11 April 1949, 1949 I.C.J. Reports 174: 99

1950

Interpretation of Peace Treaties with Bulgaria, Hungary and Romania, 1st Phase, Advisory Opinion of 30 March 1950, 1950 I.C.J. Reports 65: 99, 100, 126

1960

Constitution of the Maritime Safety Committee of the Inter-Governmental Maritime Consultative Organization, Advisory Opinion of 8 June 1960, 1960 I.C.J. Reports 150: 100, 126, 132

Arbitral Award Made by the King of Spain on 23 December 1906 (Honduras *v.* Nicaragua), Judgment 18 November 1960, 1960 I.C.J. Reports 192: 103

1961

Temple of Preah Vihear (Cambodia *v.* Thailand), Preliminary Objections, Judgment of 26 May 1961, 1961 I.C.J. Reports 17: 98, 99

1962

Temple of Preah Vihear (Cambodia *v.* Thailand), Merits, Judgment of 15 June 1962, 1962 I.C.J. Reports 6: 98, 99, 103

Certain Expenses of the United Nations (Article 17, Paragraph 2, of the Charter), Advisory Opinion of 20 July 1962, 1962 I.C.J. Reports 151: 84, 100, 123, 124, 128

1963

Northern Cameroons (Cameroon *v.* United Kingdom), Preliminary Objections, Judgment of 2 December 1963, 1963 I.C.J. Reports 15: 100, 101, 124, 128, 130-132

1964

Barcelona Traction, Light and Power Company Limited (Belgium *v.* Spain), Preliminary Objections, Judgment of 24 July 1964, 1964 I.C.J. Reports 6: 98

1966

South West Africa, 2nd Phase (Ethiopia *v.* South Africa; Liberia *v.* South Africa), Judgment of 18 July 1966, 1966 I.C.J. Reports 6: 1, 49, 130, 243

1969

North Sea Continental Shelf Cases (Federal Republic of Germany *v.* Denmark; Federal Republic of Germany *v.* Netherlands), Merits, Judgment of 20 February 1969, 1969 I.C.J. Reports 3: 110-112, 203

1970

Barcelona Traction, Light and Power Company Limited (New Application: 1962) (Belgium *v.* Spain), Judgment of 5 February 1970, 1970 I.C.J. Reports 3: 49, 111, 234, 243, 270

1971

Legal Consequences for States of the Continued Presence of South Africa in Namibia (South West Africa) Notwithstanding Security Council Resolution 276 (1970), Advisory Opinion of 21 June 1971, 1971 I.C.J. Reports 16: 62, 111, 270, 299

1972

Continental Shelf (Tunisia *v.* Libyan Arab Jamahiriya), Judgment of 24 February 1982, 1982 I.C.J. Reports 18: 101, 103, 111, 112, 203

Application for Review of Judgment No. 273 of the United Nations Administrative Tribunal, Advisory Opinion of 20 July 1982, 1982 I.C.J. Reports 325: 112, 300

Delimitation of the Maritime Boundary in the Gulf of Maine Area (Canada *v.* United States of America), Constitution of Chamber, Order of 8 October 1982, 1982 I.C.J. Reports 3: 105

1984

Continental Shelf (Libyan Arab Jamahiriya *v.* Malta), Application to Intervene, Judgment of 21 March 1984, 1984 I.C.J. Reports 3: 98, 99, 113

Military and Paramilitary Activities in and Against Nicaragua (Nicaragua *v.* United States of America), Provisional Measures, Order of 10 May 1984, 1984 I.C.J. Reports 169: 121

Delimitation of the Maritime Boundary in the Gulf of Maine Area (Canada *v.* United States of America), Judgment of 12 October 1984, 1984 I.C.J. Reports 246: 34, 98, 110, 112, 113, 203

Military and Paramilitary Activities in and Against Nicaragua (Nicaragua *v.* United States of America), Jurisdiction and Admissibility, Judgment of 26 November 1984, 1984 I.C.J. Reports 392: 98, 99, 120, 184, 191

1985

Frontier Dispute (Burkina Faso *v.* Republic of Mali), Constitution of Chamber, Order of 3 April 1985, 1985 I.C.J. Reports 6: 105

Continental Shelf (Libyan Arab Jamahiriya *v.* Malta), Judgment of 3 June 1985, 1985 I.C.J. Reports 13: 103

Application for Revision and Interpretation of the Judgment of 24 February 1982 in the Case Concerning the Continental Shelf (Tunisia *v.* Libyan Arab Jamahiriya), Judgment of 10 December 1985, 1985 I.C.J. Reports 192: 99

1986

Military and Paramilitary Activities in and Against Nicaragua (Nicaragua *v.* United States of America), Merits, Judgment of 27 June 1986, 1986 I.C.J. Reports 14: 45, 73, 98, 99, 101, 110-113, 115, 123, 141, 179, 191, 203, 230, 255

Frontier Dispute (Burkina Faso *v.* Republic of Mali), Judgment of 22 December 1986, 1986 I.C.J. Reports 554: 98, 100, 101, 103, 111, 116, 124, 127

1987

Land, Island and Maritime Frontier Dispute (El Salvador *v.* Honduras; Nicaragua intervening), Constitution of Chamber, Order of 8 May 1987, 1987 I.C.J. Reports 10: 105

Application for Review of Judgement No. 333 of the United Nations Administrative Tribunal, Advisory Opinion of 27 May 1987, 1987 I.C.J. Reports 18: 299

Maritime Delimitation and Territorial Questions Between Qatar and Bahrain (Qatar *v*. Bahrain), Jurisdiction and Admissibility, Judgment of 1 July 1994, 1994 I.C.J. Reports 112: 103

1995

East Timor (Portugal *v*. Australia), Judgment of 30 June 1995, 1995 I.C.J. Reports 90: 111, 113

1996

Land and Maritime Boundary Between Cameroon and Nigeria (Cameroon *v*. Nigeria), Provisional Measures, Order of 15 March 1996, 1996 I.C.J. Reports 13: 103, 116, 127

Legality of the Threat or Use of Nuclear Weapons, Advisory Opinion of 8 July 1996, 1996 I.C.J. Reports 226: 111, 116, 124, 255, 271

1997

Gabcíkovo-Nagymaros Project (Hungary *v*. Slovakia), Judgment of 25 September 1997, I.C.J. Reports 7: 232

1998

Questions of Interpretation and Application of the 1971 Montreal Convention Arising from the Aerial Incident at Lockerbie (Libyan Arab Jamahiriya *v*. United Kingdom), Preliminary Objections, Judgment of 27 February 1998, 1998 I.C.J. Reports 9: 250

Questions of Interpretation and Application of the 1971 Montreal Convention arising from the Aerial Incident at Lockerbie (Libyan Arab Jamahiriya *v*. United States of America), Preliminary Objections, Judgment of 27 February 1998, 1998 I.C.J. Reports 115: 250

Vienna Convention on Consular Relations (Paraguay *v*. United States of America), Provisional Measures, Order of 9 April 1998, 1998 I.C.J. Reports 248: 107, 117

Fisheries Jurisdiction (Spain *v*. Canada), Jurisdiction, Judgment of 4 December 1998, 1998 I.C.J. Reports 432: 105

1999

LaGrand (Germany *v*. United States of America), Provisional Measures, Order of 3 March 1999, 1999 I.C.J. Reports 9: 107, 108, 117, 118, 127

Difference Relating to Immunity from Legal Process of a Special Rapporteur of the Commission on Human Rights, Advisory Opinion of 29 April 1999, 1999 I.C.J. Reports 62: 106, 111, 124

Legality of Use of Force (Yugoslavia (Serbia and Montenegro) *v*. Belgium), Provisional Measures, Order of 2 June 1999, 1999 I.C.J. Reports 124: 105, 110

Legality of Use of Force (Yugoslavia (Serbia and Montenegro) *v*. Spain), Provisional Measures, Order of 2 June 1999, 1999 I.C.J. Reports 761: 120, 121

Legality of Use of Force (Yugoslavia (Serbia and Montenegro) *v*. United States of

of 17 December 2002, 2002 I.C.J. Reports 625: 103

2003

Avena and Other Mexican Nationals (Mexico *v*. United States of America), Provisional Measures, Order of 5 February 2003, 2003 I.C.J. Reports 77: 107, 117, 118

Certain Criminal Proceedings in France (Republic of the Congo *v*. France), Provisional Measures, Order of 17 June 2003, 2003 I.C.J. Reports 102: 127

Application for Revision of the Judgment of 11 September 1992 in the Case Concerning the Land, Island and Maritime Frontier Dispute (El Salvador *v*. Honduras; Nicaragua intervening), Judgment of 18 December 2003, 2003 I.C.J. Reports 392: 103

2004

Avena and Other Mexican Nationals (Mexico *v*. United States of America), Judgment of 31 March 2004, 2004 I.C.J. Reports 12: 118

Legal Consequences of the Construction of a Wall in the Occupied Palestinian Territory, Advisory Opinion of 9 July 2004, 2004 I.C.J. Reports 136: 100, 108, 109, 111, 113, 119, 125, 126, 130, 131, 135, 155, 232, 256, 259, 260, 269-271, 279, 293

2005

Armed Activities on the Territory of the Congo (Democratic Republic of the Congo *v*. Uganda), Judgment of 19 December 2005: 117, 255

2007

Application of the Convention on the Prevention and Punishment of the Crime of Genocide (Bosnia and Herzegovina *v*. Serbia and Montenegro), Judgment of 26 February 2007: 257

International Criminal Tribunal for the Former Yugoslavia

1995

Case No. IT-94-1 (Prosecutor *v*. Duzko Tadic), Decision on the Defence Motion on Jurisdiction of 10 August 1995, Trial Chamber: 128

Case No. IT-94-1 (Prosecutor *v*. Duzko Tadic), Decision on the Defence Motion for Interlocutory Appeal on Jurisdiction of 2 October 1995, Appeals Chamber: 128

1998

Case No. IT-95-17/1 (Prosecutor *v*. Anto Furundzija), Judgment of 10 December 1998, Trial Chamber II: 114

1999

Case No. IT-94-1-A (Prosecutor *v*. Dusko Tadic), Judgment of 15 July 1999, Appeals Chamber: 258

2002

Greco-Bulgarian 'Communities', Advisory Opinion No. 17 of 31 July 1930, 1930 P.C.I.J. Series B, No. 17: 185

1932

Treatment of Polish Nationals and Other Persons of Polish Origin or Speech in the Danzig Territory, Advisory Opinion No. 23 of 4 February 1932, 1932 P.C.I.J. Series A/B, No. 44: 185

Free Zones of Upper Savoy and the District of Gex (France *v.* Switzerland), Judgment No. 17 of 7 June 1932, 1932 P.C.I.J. Series A/B, No. 46: 98, 100

World Trade Organization Dispute Settlement Body

1996

United States-Standards for Reformulated and Conventional Gasoline, Appellate Body Report adopted on 29 April 1996, WT/DS2/AB/R: 13, 289, 290

1998

United States-Import Prohibition of Certain Shrimp and Shrimp Products, Appellate Body Report adopted on 12 October 1998, WT/DS58/AB/R: 289, 290

2000

Korea-Measures Affecting Government Procurement, Panel Report adopted on 1 May 2000, WT/DS163/R: 290

National Courts

Belgium

Court of Cassation

1959

Judgment of 21 September 1959: 183

1971

Judgment of 27 May 1971: 183

1978

Judgment of 26 September 1978: 183

Court of Appeal of Bruxelles

2003

Cour d'Appel de Bruxelles, Chambre des Mises en Accusation, Judgment of 10 June 2003: 107

Costa Rica

Supreme Court of Justice

Documents

Analytical Index

For Product Safety Concerns and Information please contact our EU representative GPSR@taylorandfrancis.com
Taylor & Francis Verlag GmbH, Kaufingerstraße 24, 80331 München, Germany

www.ingramcontent.com/pod-product-compliance
Ingram Content Group UK Ltd.
Pitfield, Milton Keynes, MK11 3LW, UK
UKHW020024200926
475702UK00014B/2044
* 9 7 8 1 1 3 8 3 7 6 4 9 6 *